New Perspectives in Forensic Human Skeletal Identification

New Perspectives in Forensic Human Skeletal Identification

Edited by

Krista E. Latham
Eric J. Bartelink
Michael Finnegan

Academic Press is an imprint of Elsevier
125 London Wall, London EC2Y 5AS, United Kingdom
525 B Street, Suite 1800, San Diego, CA 92101-4495, United States
50 Hampshire Street, 5th Floor, Cambridge, MA 02139, United States
The Boulevard, Langford Lane, Kidlington, Oxford OX5 1GB, United Kingdom

Library of Congress Cataloging-in-Publication Data
A catalog record for this book is available from the Library of Congress

British Library Cataloguing-in-Publication Data
A catalogue record for this book is available from the British Library

ISBN: 978-0-12-805429-1

For information on all Academic Press publications visit our website at
https://www.elsevier.com/books-and-journals

Working together
to grow libraries in
developing countries

www.elsevier.com • www.bookaid.org

Publisher: Sara Tenney
Acquisition Editor: Elizabeth Brown
Editorial Project Manager: Joslyn Chaiprasert-Paguio
Production Project Manager: Lisa Jones
Designer: Victoria Pearson Esser

Cover image: Lukas Darwin Beach

Typeset by TNQ Books and Journals

Dedication

The editors dedicate *New Perspectives in Forensic Human Skeletal Identification* to six pioneers of human skeletal biology and forensic anthropology who we recently lost. Dr. Clyde C. Snow and Dr. George J. Armelagos were instrumental in establishing the Physical Anthropology Section of the American Academy of Forensic Sciences in 1972, which laid the path toward the professionalization of forensic anthropology. Drs. J. Michael Hoffman, Walter Birkby, Jerry Melbye, and Turhon A. Murad were key figures in the Mountain, Desert, and Coastal Forensic Anthropologists Meetings. They were not only engaged with the MD&C Meetings but also brought their students and encouraged them to present papers and meet other professionals in forensic anthropology. All were lifelong mentors and are sorely missed.

Clyde C. Snow, PhD, D-ABFA
(1928–2014)
(Photo credit: Jerry Snow)

J. Michael Hoffman, MD, PhD, D-ABFA
(1944–2012)
(Photo credit: Merla Hoffman)

George J. Armelagos, PhD
(1936–2014)
(Photo credit: Anthropology
Department, Emory University)

Turhon A. Murad, PhD, D-ABFA
(1944–2015)
(Photo credit: Brian Brazeal)

Walter H. Birkby, PhD, D-ABFA
(1931–2015)
(Photo credit: Jacob Chinn)

Jerry Melbye, PhD, D-ABFA
(1936–2017)
(Photo credit: Vicky Melbye)

Contents

List of Contributors

Kanar Alkass
Karolinska Institute,
Stockholm,
Sweden

Bruce E. Anderson
Pima County Office of the Medical Examiner,
Tucson,
AZ,
United States

Janna M. Andronowski
University of Saskatchewan,
Saskatoon,
SK,
Canada

Eric J. Bartelink
California State University, Chico
Chico,
CA,
United States

Melanie M. Beasley
University of Tennessee,
Knoxville,
TN,
United States

Gregory E. Berg
Defense POW/MIA Accounting Agency,
Joint Base Pearl Harbor-Hickam,
HI,
United States

Deona Botha
University of the Witwatersrand,
Johannesburg,
South Africa

Desiré M. Brits
University of the Witwatersrand,
Johannesburg,
South Africa

Bruce A. Buchholz
Lawrence Livermore National Laboratory,
Livermore,
CA,
United States

Jessica N. Byram
Indiana University School of Medicine,
Indianapolis,
IN,
United States

John E. Byrd
Defense POW/MIA Accounting Agency,
Joint Base Pearl Harbor-Hickam,
HI,
United States

Lesley A. Chesson
IsoForensics,
Inc. Salt Lake City,
UT,
United States

Colleen M. Cheverko
The Ohio State University

Angi M. Christensen
Federal Bureau of Investigation Laboratory,
Quantico,
VA,
United States

Steven C. Clark
Occupational Research and Assessment,
Inc.,
Big Rapids,
MI,
United States

Christian M. Crowder
Harris County Institute of Forensic Sciences,
Houston,
TX,
United States

Craig Cunningham
University of Dundee,
Dundee,
Scotland

Susan S. D'Alonzo
Defense POW/MIA Accounting Agency,
Joint Base Pearl Harbor-Hickam,
HI,
United States

Sharon M. Derrick
Harris County Institute of Forensic Sciences,
Houston,
TX,
United States

Victoria M. Dominguez
The Ohio State University,
Columbus,
OH,
United States

Henrik Druid
Karolinska Institute,
Stockholm,
Sweden

Colleen A. Dunn
Office of the Armed Forces Medical Examiner,
Dover,
DE,
United States

Suni M. Edson
Office of the Armed Forces Medical Examiner,
Dover,
DE,
United States,
Flinders University,
Adelaide,
SA,
Australia

Todd W. Fenton
Michigan State University,
East Lansing,
MI,
United States

Benjamin J. Figura
West Tennessee Regional Forensic Center,
Memphis,
TN,
United States

Janet E. Finlayson
University of Florida,
Gainesville,
FL,
United States

Michael Finnegan
Kansas State University,
Manhattan,
KS,
United States

Laura C. Fulginiti
Maricopa County Forensic Science Center,
Phoenix,
AZ,
United States

Nicole Geske
Michigan State University,
East Lansing,
MI,
United States

Priya Goel
Medical Metrics, Inc.,
Houston,
TX,
United States

Thomas Gore
Certified Prosthetist Orthotist (CPO),
Fairfield,
OH,
United States

Pierre Guyomarc'h
Defense POW/MIA Accounting Agency,
Joint Base Pearl Harbor-Hickam,
HI,
United States

Randy L. Hanzlick
Emory School of Medicine and Fulton County Medical
Examiner Office,
Atlanta,
GA,
United States

Michael M. Harmon
Linn County Sheriff's Office,
Albany,
OR,
United States

Kristen Hartnett-McCann
Connecticut Office of the Chief Medical Examiner,
Farmington,
CT,
United States

Gary M. Hatch
University of New Mexico School of Medicine,
Albuquerque,
NM,
United States

Joseph T. Hefner
Michigan State University,
East Lansing,
MI,
United States

John A. Hipp
Medical Metrics, Inc.,
Houston,
TX,
United States

Rachel M. Hoffman
Eli Lilly and Company,
Indianapolis,
IN,
United States

Thomas D. Holland
Strategic Partnerships,
Defense POW/MIA Accounting Agency

Lee Meadows Jantz
University of Tennessee,
Knoxville,
TN,
United States

Melody Josserand
University of North Texas Health Science Center,
Fort Worth,
TX,
United States

Irene L. Kahline
Office of the Armed Forces Medical Examiner,
Dover,
DE,
United States

Michael W. Kenyhercz
Defense POW/MIA Accounting Agency,
Joint Base Pearl Harbor-Hickam,
HI,
United States,
University of Tennessee,
Knoxville,
TN,
United States,
University of Pretoria,
Arcadia,
South Africa

Lyle W. Konigsberg
University of Illinois at Urbana-Champaign,
Urbana,
IL,
United States

Gabriele C. Krüger
University of Pretoria,
Pretoria,
South Africa

Ericka N. L'Abbé
University of Pretoria,
Pretoria,
South Africa

Krista E. Latham
University of Indianapolis,
Indianapolis,
IN,
United States

Leandi Liebenberg
University of Pretoria,
Pretoria,
South Africa

Heather MacInnes
California State University, Chico
Chico,
CA,
United States

Amy T. MacKinnon
California High-Speed Rail Authority,
Sacramento,
CA,
United States

Christopher Maier
University of Nevada,
Reno,
NV,
United States

Justin Maiers
University of Indianapolis,
Indianapolis,
IN,
United States

Timothy McMahon
Armed Forces Medical Examiner System,
Dover Air Force Base,
DE,
United States

Anja Meyer
University of the Witwatersrand,
Johannesburg,
South Africa

Colleen F. Milligan
California State University, Chico
Chico,
CA,
United States

Elizabeth A. Murray
Mount St. Joseph University,
Cincinnati,
OH,
United States

Jolandie Myburgh
University of Pretoria,
Pretoria,
South Africa

Stephen P. Nawrocki
University of Indianapolis,
Indianapolis,
IN,
United States

Jennifer A. O'Rourke
Office of the Armed Forces Medical Examiner,
Dover,
DE,
United States

Anna C. Oettlé
University of Pretoria,
Pretoria,
South Africa,
Sefako Makgatho University,
Pretoria,
South Africa

Anne E. Osborn-Gustavson
Armed Forces Medical Examiner System,
Dover Air Force Base,
DE,
United States

Michael A. O'Brien
Economy Borough Police Department,
Baden,
PA,
United States

Marin A. Pilloud
University of Nevada,
Reno,
NV,
United States

Julia R. Prince-Buitenhuys
University of Notre Dame,
Notre Dame,
IN,
United States

Michelle H. Raxter
Marymount University,
Arlington,
VA,
United States

Kimberly A. Root
Office of the Armed Forces Medical Examiner,
Dover,
DE,
United States

Christopher B. Ruff
Johns Hopkins University School of Medicine,
Baltimore,
MD,
United States

Maureen Schaefer
Michigan State University,
East Lansing,
MI,
United States

G. Richard Scott
University of Nevada,
Reno,
NV,
United States

Andrew C. Seidel
Arizona State University,
Tempe,
AZ,
United States

Kirsty L. Spalding
Karolinska Institute,
Stockholm,
Sweden,
Karolinska Institute,
Huddinge,
Sweden

B.J. Spamer
National Missing & Unidentified Persons System
  (NamUs),
Washington,
DC,
United States

M. Katherine Spradley
Texas State University,
San Marcos,
TX,
United States

Carl N. Stephan
Defense POW/MIA Accounting Agency,
Joint Base Pearl Harbor-Hickam,
HI,
United States

Emily Streetman
Michigan State University,
East Lansing,
MI,
United States

Kyra E. Stull
University of Nevada-Reno,
Reno,
NV,
United States,
University of Pretoria,
Pretoria,
South Africa

Clarisa Sutherland
University of Pretoria,
Pretoria,
South Africa

Brett J. Tipple
IsoForensics, Inc.,
Salt Lake City,
UT,
United States

Bruché E. Trotter
Office of the Armed Forces Medical Examiner,
Dover,
DE,
United States

Douglas H. Ubelaker
Smithsonian Institution,
Washington,
DC,
United States

Mark Viner
Queen Mary University of London,
London,
United Kingdom,
Cranfield University,
Shrivenham,
United Kingdom

Roland Wessling
Cranfield University,
Shrivenham,
United Kingdom

Emily K. Wilson
Defense POW/MIA Accounting Agency,
Joint Base Pearl Harbor-Hickam,
HI,
United States

Lane V. Youmans
Grays Harbor County Coroner's Office, Aberdeen,
WA,
United States

Kristina M. Zarenko
University of South Carolina,
Columbia,
SC,
United States

Foreword

On August 30, 1850, a shockwave rippled through the societal crust of Boston when Dr. John White Webster, a Harvard chemistry professor of some note, was executed for the murder of the wealthy philanthropist and college benefactor, George Parkman. Though the grisly details of Mr. Parkman's dismemberment fixated the general public's attention at the time, it was the fact that the case involved the first recorded use of forensic anthropology in an American courtroom that establishes *Commonwealth v. Webster* as an enduring, albeit little known, footnote in forensic science. Ironically, no forensic anthropologist actually testified at the trial; forensic anthropology had yet to emerge as a discipline in its own right. Instead, the critical testimony in the case was supplied by two well-respected members of the Harvard medical faculty—Jeffries Wyman and Oliver Wendell Holmes Sr.—who opined that the calcined and fragmented human skeletal remains recovered from the furnace in the basement of the Harvard Medical School were consistent with the biological characteristics of the late George Parkman.

In the 160 years since John Webster was hanged by the neck for his crime, forensic anthropology has evolved from somewhat of a boutique scientific interest, generally practiced by nonanthropologists as more hobby than profession, into one of the principal tools in the field of human remains identification, practiced today by professional anthropologists trained in both the rigors of its science and nuance of its art. Despite the mass media ballyhoo of the primacy of DNA analysis, or the seemingly endless spate of crime science television programs that elevate unbelievable technology over believable talent and training, the role of the forensic anthropologist is more important now than ever. The identification problems posed by mass disaster events, or the unfolding diasporic immigration tragedies around the world, or the institutional depravity of genocidal pogroms that result in the commingling and the intentional scattering of victims across the landscape, remain daunting and intractable.

It is tempting to look back to the 1970s as the heyday of forensic anthropology's brief history, at least in the United States. In 1971, the patriarchal Bill Bass arrived in Knoxville. In 1972, the American Academy of Forensic Sciences (AAFS) recognized "physical" anthropology as a separate forensic discipline. Five years later, the American Board of Forensic Anthropology came into existence. And to bookend the decade, in 1979, T.D. Stewart's, *Essentials of Forensic Anthropology*, the first textbook to bear the term "forensic anthropology" in its title, began appearing on store shelves. Heady times to be sure, but to view this period as anything more than a prelude, as anything more than a glimpse behind the curtain, would be to underestimate the potential that characterizes the profession.

Forensic anthropology has proven itself to be quite dynamic and up to the challenge of adapting to the changing societal requirements pressed upon it. Recent progress in systematizing the "best practices" of the profession, such as the work by the Scientific Working Group for Forensic Anthropology (SWGANTH) and the more recent Anthropology Subcommittee of the Organization of Scientific Areas Committee (OSAC), has placed the future of forensic anthropology, as a discipline, on a sound and stable foundation. But more importantly, the science—the nuts and bolts underlying research that is the strength and hallmark of the profession—continues to evolve and improve.

This volume, *New Perspectives in Forensic Human Skeletal Identification*, is a prime example of the breadth and richness of forensic anthropology. The chapters presented here range from the novel use of stable isotopes to source out geographic origins, to the use of bomb-curve radiocarbon analysis to determine the age of hard tissues; from DNA to histology to radiography; from elliptical Fourier analysis to the crafting of multidisciplinary approaches to the identification of human remains. No other forensic science, not fingerprinting (which incidentally was pioneered largely by anthropologists), not ballistics or trace evidence, not odontology or forensic pathology, not even DNA analysis, has such deep and expansive roots in pure academic research. It is from these roots that forensic anthropology continues to draw deep and wide and to flourish.

The profession has come a long way from 1850, when a court had to rely on the testimony of two medical doctors to interpret the fragmentary and calcined skeletal remains of a murder victim. It has come a long way since 1972, when the AAFS recognized the discipline as merely an adjunct of the field of physical anthropology. Today, forensic anthropologists, such as those whose work is represented in this volume, are expanding the scope and capability of the profession in ways that could not have been even imagined even a generation ago.

Happily, the heyday is now.

Thomas D. Holland, J.D., Ph.D.
Director of Strategic Partnerships
Defense POW/MIA Accounting Agency

Preface

In 2013, we were sitting in lawn chairs in the warm air of a Boulder City, NV, evening discussing the presentations we heard for the day at the Mountain, Desert and Coastal (MD&C) Forensic Anthropologists Meeting. The discussion soon moved in a new direction as we started talking about the need for a book incorporating the multitude of identification tools utilized by forensic anthropologists working within the medicolegal system. Advances in previous years and multidisciplinary training allow for a much larger tool kit for personal identification from the skeleton than that found in years past. Eric grabbed a pen and paper and quickly started taking notes as we all mentioned potential chapters and authors to include in such a text. As the list grew to cover the entire page, we recognized the need for having such a comprehensive reference volume. Mike's sage advice helped us all to get organized and to brainstorm ideas and authors.

The MD&C Forensic Anthropologists Meeting officially met for the first time in 1981 in Utah. There were nine forensic anthropologists and their students at this first meeting. In 1986, the MD&C meeting location changed to Boulder City, NV, and has occurred there ever since. The audience continues to be composed of forensic anthropologists (practicing and retired) and forensic anthropology students. By the 1990s, attendance rose to approximately 40 attendees and has stayed steady with an average of 50 attendees per year in the new millennium. While some things have changed over the years, such as replacing the 35-mm projector with a laptop and projector, much has remained the same. The meeting has and will always serve as an arena for practicing, aspiring, and retired forensic anthropologists to come together and discuss important topics and recent advances in the field of forensic anthropology. Informal presentations, workshops, and in-depth discussions allow for a meeting of the minds and an explosion of creativity toward novel research and novel approaches to the field of forensic anthropology.

New Perspectives in Forensic Human Skeletal Identification is distinct from other texts published to date on forensic anthropology because it targets the identification aspect of forensic anthropology practice. It has a very specific focus on identification from the skeleton and is aimed at advanced students and practitioners interested in obtaining a comprehensive understanding of new identification techniques using bones and teeth. It incorporates a variety of different approaches to human identification, including morphological, molecular, and radiographic techniques, and includes an international component focusing on advances in human identification techniques that are being applied to international populations. *New Perspectives in Forensic Human Skeletal Identification* is comprehensive, practical, and relevant to students and current practitioners in the discipline.

We recognize that this text is a snapshot of the current status of identification in anthropology and that the pace of science is always faster than the pace of publishing. However, the techniques included in this volume are relevant and utilized in the process of skeletal identification. The practical applications of each technique are stressed, population-specific criteria are discussed when necessary, and case studies are embedded in many chapters to better illustrate the analytical technique. *New Perspectives in Forensic Human Skeletal Identification* is aimed at forensic anthropology practitioners as well as those who work in closely related disciplines. This badly needed up-to-date text provides a broad spectrum of techniques and enhances the references available to researchers in academic, laboratory, and medicolegal facilities. This book will serve as a valuable reference for all individuals interested in the identification and analysis of human remains including forensic anthropologists, bioarchaeologists, forensic odontologists, medical examiners, coroners, anatomists, and mass disaster specialists at student and professional levels.

The editors would like to thank the contributors for their dedication to crafting informative and scientifically rigorous chapters. It has been a pleasure working with you over the last few years to create this volume. We would like to extend our gratitude to Dr. Timothy Gocha, Dr. Natalie Uhl Nagel, and Dr. James Pokines for reviewing the material and providing feedback on the chapters. We would like to acknowledge Lukas Beach for his contribution to the cover illustration and express our gratitude to Joslyn Chaiprasert-Paguio, Lisa Jones, Elizabeth Brown, and their stellar editorial team at Elsevier for their support and patience throughout this process.

Krista E. Latham
Eric J. Bartelink
Michael Finnegan

CHAPTER 1

Introduction

Krista E. Latham[1] | Eric J. Bartelink[2] | Michael Finnegan[3]

[1]University of Indianapolis, Indianapolis, IN, United States
[2]California State University, Chico, Chico, CA, United States
[3]Kansas State University, Manhattan, KS, United States

Forensic anthropologists apply biological anthropological and archaeological methods and theories, specifically those regarding the recovery and the analysis of skeletal remains, to legal questions. They are often consulted by law enforcement and medical examiners to assist in the recovery of human remains from various contexts, the estimation of time since death, the development of biological profiles (sex, age, ancestry, and stature), the analysis of postmortem alterations to the skeleton, the analysis of antemortem and perimortem trauma, and personal identification of unknown human remains. Recoveries involve the application of archaeological techniques to systematically locate, document, and recover human remains and associated evidence within a medicolegal and/or humanitarian context. Estimations of time since death provide investigators with important information regarding the possible identity of the decedent and the circumstances of their death. Analyses of postmortem alterations to the skeleton provide information regarding the depositional environment and the time since death and are important to consider when trying to differentiate features caused by taphonomic processes versus perimortem trauma. Analysis of skeletal trauma offers insight into the circumstances surrounding the death of an individual and can aid medical examiners in determining cause and manner of death. Finally, identification involves relating a known identity to human remains, referred to as personal identification. Resolving medicolegal and humanitarian cases hinges on accurate identification of the dead. It is this topic that is the primary focus of this book.

Identification carries both legal and moral substance. Legally, matters regarding life insurance (e.g., death benefits), wills, and the like require that the identity of the decedent be established. Morally, identification can provide a sense of closure to grieving relatives. The identification process is based on the results of analytical tests in which antemortem data are compared to features of the unknown decedent to test an identification hypothesis. If the antemortem and postmortem data are inconsistent, the identification hypothesis is rejected. Consistencies between antemortem and postmortem data result in a failure to reject an identification hypothesis. Given enough points of similarity, the data may suggest that the remains belong to a presumed decedent. The specific number and type of forensic tests performed for any given case will vary depending on location and available resources.

Multiple scientific modalities can be employed during the identification process. Some of these fall outside the expertise of the forensic anthropologist, such as fingerprint comparisons; however, identifications involving skeletonized, decomposed, and burned remains often require the consultation of a forensic anthropologist. Various approaches to human skeletal identification can be employed by forensic anthropologists, with best practices being outlined originally by the Scientific Working Group for Forensic Anthropology (SWGANTH) and currently by the Anthropology Subcommittee through the Organization of Scientific Area Committees (OSAC), which is under the auspices of the National Institute of Standards and Technology (NIST). These organizations recommend that medicolegal authorities and law enforcement consult qualified forensic anthropologists, preferably those certified by the American Board of Forensic Anthropology (ABFA) (or similar organization outside the United States) because these practitioners have been vetted by a rigorous evaluation and examination process.

It should be noted that in addition to variation in analytical approaches relating to identification, there is also considerable variation in the terminology utilized by forensic anthropologists. For example, variation is observed in the terms applied to various ancestral groups, such as Black, American Black, African American, or Afroamerican. Additionally, the words "estimate" and "determine" are used interchangeably by some practitioners. However, it should be noted that "estimation" is most appropriate for continuous or ordinal variables, such as age or stature, whereas "determination" is more appropriate when predicting a discontinuous or discrete variable, such as sex or ancestry.

The purpose of this volume is to provide a comprehensive and up-to-date perspective on advanced human identification methods in forensic anthropology. It is designed to serve as an essential resource for researchers, practitioners, and advanced students interested in state-of-the-art methods for human identification. It targets the identification process in forensic anthropology practice and incorporates a variety of different approaches to human identification, including morphological, molecular, and radiographic methods. The contributing authors represent established experts in forensic anthropology and closely related fields from the United States, the United Kingdom, Australia, and South Africa. A volume of this nature that focuses specifically on identification methods from the human skeleton is

New Perspectives in Forensic Human Skeletal Identification. http://dx.doi.org/10.1016/B978-0-12-805429-1.00001-6

timely. The last major volume dedicated specifically to this issue was T. Dale Stewart's edited *Personal Identification in Mass Disasters*, published in 1970.

The volume is divided into four sections: Advances in Biological Profile Construction (Chapters 2–11), Advances in Molecular Methods of Identification (Chapters 12–18), Advances in Radiographic and Superimposition Methods of Identification (Chapters 19–24), and International Studies and Mass Disasters (Chapters 25–29). The first section focuses on understanding biological variation in the human skeleton to reconstruct the decedent's living characteristics and focuses on advanced methods for constructing biological profiles (sex, age, ancestry, and stature) as well as the use of the National Missing and Unidentified Persons System (NamUs). This section focuses on analyses of both adult and juvenile skeletons and includes methods based on analyses of various bones of the skeleton as well as the teeth. The second section focuses on various molecular and microscopic advanced methods that can contribute to identification including DNA profiling, stable isotope analysis, bomb pulse radiocarbon dating, protein radioimmunoassay analysis, and histological analysis. The third section includes various approaches to identification using radiographic and superimposition methods. Advances in comparative medical radiography of various cranial and postcranial features, craniofacial superimposition, elliptical Fourier analysis, and the CADI method of computer-assisted radiographic identification are discussed. The last section focuses on advances in international forensic anthropology and mass disaster identification and includes case studies from South Africa, France, and the United States.

The idea for this volume arose from engaging conversations between the editors at the annual Mountain, Desert & Coastal (MD&C) Forensic Anthropologists meeting. Since its birth in 1981, the MD&C meeting has served as an arena for practicing, aspiring, and retired forensic anthropologists to come together and discuss important topics and recent advances in the field of forensic anthropology. Presentations, workshops, and discussions inspire new collaborations and novel approaches to skeletal analyses. This volume is a celebration of the spirit and intent of the MD&C meeting and its attendees.

ADVANCES IN BIOLOGICAL PROFILE CONSTRUCTION

CHAPTER 2

Human Skeletal Variation and Forensic Anthropology

Stephen P. Nawrocki[1] | Krista E. Latham[1] | Eric J. Bartelink[2]

[1]University of Indianapolis, Indianapolis, IN, United States
[2]California State University, Chico, Chico, CA, United States

Chapter Outline

As human biologists, our analysis of the human skeleton can be broken down into four broad steps. First, we must *describe* the variability in our skeletal samples. This description employs statistical measures of *central tendency* (mean, mode, median) as well as measures of *dispersion* (variance, standard deviation, range, confidence interval, etc.) to characterize each of the variables of interest. Description provides the raw material for the second phase of analysis, *comparison*. During this phase, we search for relationships between skeletal traits within our sample or between different samples. This phase employs statistical procedures designed to *test hypotheses*, for example, to determine whether the means for a variable in subgroups A and B differ, or whether two variables covary. By clarifying the relationships between our variables, then we may be able to *explain* the variability seen in the data set. This third phase may produce powerful causal or interpretive models, such as elucidating how climate and latitude affect head shape or how circulating hormones lead to sex differences in adults. Finally, when explanatory models are well established, we may be able to construct *predictive* models to make inferences about ancient population biology or, in the case of forensic anthropology, to construct hypotheses about the soft tissue features and identity of unknown individuals from their skeletal traits.

Forensic anthropology has traditionally been characterized as an applied branch of biological anthropology (Stewart, 1979) in that its methods and techniques are focused on the goals of (1) individual identification and (2) clarification of the circumstances of death, both of which are central concerns of the medicolegal system when skeletonized remains are encountered. Naturally, then, this applied or practical approach has had a tendency to focus researchers on the prediction phase of skeletal analysis. Most publications in forensic anthropology have been more concerned with creating or testing predictive techniques for determining elements of the biological profile (sex, ancestry, stature, age at death) or the taphonomic profile (time since death, timing and source of fractures) than in describing, comparing, or explaining human skeletal variability. Examples abound of studies that take an isolated skeletal feature and use it to determine, say, the sex of the decedent. While summary statistics (description) and basic statistical tests (comparison) are regularly included in such studies as necessary stepping-stones to prediction, few take a truly comprehensive approach to the analysis of those skeletal features. Statistical models are usually simplistic, incorporating too few variables and relying too heavily on univariate and bivariate (rather than multivariate) statistical techniques. Perhaps more damningly, we rarely acknowledge or attempt to explain the broader patterns of variability we see in the skeleton, instead focusing on smaller subparts that are easily measured and applicable to specific analytical problems. As a result, we tend to present a picture of the skeleton consisting of a jumble of scattered, disjointed features that, individually, may have diagnostic importance but are never really assembled into a holistic image.

We propose that this minimalist, goal-directed approach has hindered the development of a truly comprehensive theoretical paradigm in forensic anthropology. Our near-obsession with prediction has contributed to the somewhat isolated position of forensic anthropology within the broader realm of biological anthropology in general and human biology specifically, painting us as largely atheoretical and unconcerned with the goals of anthropology in its mission to describe and explain human variability at the species level. By couching so much of our research purely in terms of prediction, the data that we do collect become much less useful to other human biologists searching for comprehensive explanations of the roles of hard and soft tissue variability in the larger process of human adaptation and evolution. Perhaps more

New Perspectives in Forensic Human Skeletal Identification. http://dx.doi.org/10.1016/B978-0-12-805429-1.00002-8

importantly, we risk becoming a field of simple technicians working on an assembly line of small, isolated identification problems, in the process losing sight of the very skills that make us most valuable in a medicolegal context in the first place: the ability to scientifically assess the *meaning* and *relevance* of the variability that we do observe.

How, then, are forensic anthropologists to become more relevant to biological anthropology? How are we to inject more rigor and viability into our studies of skeletal variability? This introductory chapter presents three main issues that practitioners should overtly consider when constructing or assessing studies of the skeleton in forensic contexts: (1) the variance equation and the importance of interactions, (2) the use of powerful multivariate statistical procedures to test hypotheses before moving on to predictive models, and (3) the construction of adequate and unbiased study samples.

■ THE VARIANCE EQUATION

Consider the statement "a male cranium is usually longer than a female cranium." Inherent in this supposition is a mathematical relationship between two variables, and we can diagram that relationship in a simple equation:

$$\text{cranial length} = \text{sex} + \text{error}$$

in which cranial length (the *dependent* or response variable) is said to be affected or determined by the sex of the individual (the *independent* or predictor variable). More accurately, the equation is a statement of the relationship between variables in a *sample* or *population* of individuals, and so the more precise statement is that "the variance in cranial length is affected by (*covaries with*) the variance in sex within the sample." At its core, then, the equation is a symbolic or theoretical statement about the sources and determinants of human variability and therefore can be called a *variance equation*. The variance in the dependent variable that cannot be predicted by the independent variable is known as *error*; error is presumably caused by other variables that are not yet controlled for by (included in) the model. The sum of the variance explained by the independent variable (the *explained* or *systematic variance*) and the error (the *unexplained* or *unsystematic variance*) equals the total amount of variance seen (measured) in the dependent variable.

Variance equations can be (and usually are) more complex than the one presented above; we presume that more than just sex affects cranial length, meaning that more independent variables would be needed on the right side of the equation. For example:

$$\text{cranial length} = \text{sex} + \text{ancestry} + \text{age} + \text{climate} + \text{error}$$

The equation given above takes a more comprehensive view of the variables that affect skull form. In other words, as variables are added—presuming that they actually have an effect—more of the variance in the dependent variable can be accounted for. It should be noted that the "+" signs in the equation do not necessarily indicate that the variables must be summed in a strict mathematical sense; instead, they are a simple proxy for the word "and," meaning that "sex *and* ancestry *and* age *and* climate affect length," but the exact relationships remain unspecified until extrapolated through statistical analysis. For example, the effect of being female may be to reduce cranial length in the sample, but the effect of being old may be to increase it.

The variables in the equation can take different forms. Categorical variables are those that vary discretely and have no overlap between types, such as sex, ancestral group, or continent of origin. Continuous variables are those that can take any mathematical value within a specified interval, such as cranial or femur length. In many cases the distinction between categorical and continuous variables can be somewhat arbitrary, depending more on the measurement technique and intent of the researcher than on some hard-wired biological rule. For example, the size of the mastoid process can be scored continuously (vertical length; Moore-Jansen et al., 1994; Langley et al., 2016) or categorically (Buikstra and Ubelaker, 1994); the latter strategy would entail the loss of data and sensitivity by condensing a continuously varying feature down to just a few discrete categories, but at the same time it may capture more information about shape (the "gestalt" of the mastoid) than a single, precisely defined linear measurement.

Dependent and independent variables in the variance equation can be either continuous or categorical, in any combination, and different statistical tests are available for equations taking different resulting forms. Continuous independent variables are known as *covariates*; together with categorical independent variables, they represent the *main effects* of the equation, a reference to the fact that they directly affect the variance in the dependent variable.

Despite the apparent thoroughness of the more detailed equation, many researchers would still overlook an important component of the variance. This omission can be illustrated by the phenomenon of hyperostosis frontalis interna (HFI) (Ortner, 2003, p. 416; Moore, 1955). As many dissection-room anatomists have discovered, the endocranial surfaces of the frontal bones of some individuals display the growth of irregular cortical nodules, usually accompanied by a thickening of the diploe and (in extreme cases) ossifications within the falx cerebri of the dura mater. The senior author has collected data on this condition from US anatomy labs for many years, and an informal summary of its occurrence can be presented in this simple table:

	Male	Female
Younger adult	No HFI	Some HFI
Older adult	Some HFI	Lots of HFI

(For illustrative purposes and simplicity, "age" has been condensed into a categorical trait, <51 vs. >50 years). Although the preponderance of cases of HFI falls in the cell for older females, a few cases of HFI are known to occur in elderly males as well as in younger females; very few if any cases are known for young adult males. One would think that the variance in the occurrence of HFI could be modeled with the following equation.

$$HFI = sex + age\ category + error$$

Indeed, as one scans across the table (along rows), it would seem that HFI is more prevalent in females, and scanning downward (along columns) suggests that HFI increases with age. One could demonstrate these findings statistically by conducting two chi-squared tests, one on sex and one on age category; both tests would likely come back significant. At this point the analyst might be tempted to conclude the analysis, resting on the assumption that both age and sex affect the expression of HFI. She or he may even construct a predictive model for determining sex or age from unknown subjects based on whether HFI is present or absent.

Unfortunately, this approach is incomplete. The format of the equation presumes that sex and age are sufficient to account for the observed variability in HFI, but the presence of such a strong effect in only one of the four cells (elderly females) cannot be predicted from the relatively minor effects of sex and age that occur across the other three cells. Instead, something entirely different is happening that the variance equation is not capturing correctly: it is the *combination* of being female *and* older *simultaneously* that triggers the most significant occurrence of HFI. This phenomenon is known as an *interaction* (Sokal and Rohlf, 2012, p. 325), and it requires the addition of a whole new kind of independent variable to the variance equation:

$$HFI = sex + age\ category + sex^*age + error$$

where "sex*age" is the interaction. The verbal translation of this equation would be "HFI is determined by sex *and* age *and* also by the interaction *between* those two variables." It is useful here to consider the "levels" of each variable: if "sex" has two levels (male and female) and "age category" has two levels (young and old), then "sex*age" has four levels (young male, old male, young female, and old female). The three character traits that would increase the likelihood of HFI occurring in an individual are therefore being "female" (a weak effect), "old" (a weak effect), and "old female" (a strong, entirely separate effect).

The combination of the two main effects (sex and age category) with the interaction (sex*age) should allow one to explain—and more importantly, properly locate the source of—more of the variance in the dependent variable than the two main effects used alone could. Furthermore, it is entirely possible that the influence of the two main effects may not even rise to the level of statistical significance once the (stronger) interaction has been added properly to the model. As a result, the researcher would no longer be able to say that sex or age affects HFI as separate independent variables; she or he would have to say instead that something peculiar about being female *and* elderly triggers the onset of the condition, leading obviously to a possible mechanism based on the unique physiology of menopause.

Interactions are common in the real world: pharmacists must worry about deleterious effects that occur when two relatively safe drugs are combined; an oncologist knows that minor to moderate health risks (asbestos) can be made far more dangerous when the patient falls in a particular health category (smoker); biologists know that the combination of otherwise manageable environmental conditions (drought + disease) can decimate a population. In these situations, the individual additive effects of the independent variables *when considered separately* do not predict the resulting magnified (disproportionate) effect on the dependent variable.

Unfortunately, the possibility of interactions is usually ignored by skeletal researchers. The typical approach is to analyze independent variables singly, sequentially, via isolated tests, for their separate effects on the dependent variable (the skeletal trait in question). When a significant relationship is discovered, it is subsequently used to produce a predictive equation or model that is distinct from any other equation generated for a second significant independent variable. For example, some of the earliest published discriminant formulae for the prediction of ancestry or sex from cranial and postcranial measurements were frequently generated in this fashion (Giles and Elliot, 1962, 1963); one equation is used to determine ancestry, and a second is used to determine sex, without considering the possibility that some of the measurements might have been affected significantly by ancestry*sex interactions.[1] Minimally, this omission could cause problems when the equations are applied to other samples that have different numbers of individuals in the different ancestry*sex groups. If, for example, mastoid size is especially large in Euro-American males (constituting an interaction that is not explained effectively by *either* ancestry *or* sex as separate variables), the original equations' efficacy would have been relatively great if the study included numerous (or even equal numbers of) Euro-American males. When subsequently applied to samples that do not include as many Euro-American males, classification rates for those equations would drop inexplicably, even if the new sample was drawn from the same population for which the *same biological rules of mastoid formation continue to apply*. It is very likely that contradictory results obtained by different researchers for a given skeletal trait, even when their different samples were drawn ostensibly from the same parent population, are attributable at least in part to a combination of the failure to control for significant interactions and poor (uneven) sampling strategies across the studies.

---

[1] FORDISC (Jantz and Ousley, 2005), with its ability to classify unknowns directly into different ancestry*sex groups (such as "black male" or "white female"), is a notable exception.

Ignoring interactions can lead to a phenomenon that we call the "equation multiplication effect." If one examines a typical primer on forensic anthropology (for example, Bass, 2005), one can find many tables and equations for the estimation of stature from long bone length. Multiple permutations are typically provided: using the femur for white males, or the radius for black females, or the tibia for Mexicans, etc.; nearly any combination of bones plus subgroups can be located. The underlying presumption is that all of these subgroups *need* different equations for estimating their stature because their development and proportions differ significantly—and thus stature equations multiply in the literature over time. However, because few of these studies employed even basic hypothesis-testing techniques as a first step, one can never really be sure whether subgroups really differ enough to justify different equations. The appropriate variance equation that models this relationship is:

$$\text{femur length} = \text{sex} + \text{ancestry} + \text{sex*ancestry} + \text{stature} + \text{error}$$

where known stature is a continuous covariate. Most of the explained variance in femur length will be attributable to variance in stature; however, what proportion of explained variance is controlled by sex, ancestry, or the interaction? If only sex is significant, then there is no reason to generate ancestry-specific (black or white) or interaction-specific (black male, black female, white male, white female) equations (general equations that combine those subgroups will suffice). Alternatively, if only the interaction is significant, the current practice of providing a different equation for each subgroup is appropriate.

The problem of equation multiplication leads us to an important point: the omission of interactions from the variance equation can subvert the entire explanation phase of skeletal analysis. Without realizing it, workers have largely presumed a priori that the interactions are the only significant influence besides stature on long bone length, or else they would not have created so many subgroup-specific equations out of the gate. In other words, forensic anthropologists have unwittingly promulgated a (largely untested) theory regarding human variation: the sex*ancestry interaction is more important in determining human long bone length than either variable is acting alone as a main effect. This hidden assumption has subsequently shaped how we generate and use stature-estimation equations within the entire field of skeletal biology—but, for the most part, we do not even know if it is correct!

If interactions are ignored or, as the special case of stature estimation suggests, presumed through ignorance, fundamental principles of biological variation could be missed or misinterpreted. The investigator could then be *misled into constructing predictive equations that are unnecessary* or, worse, *that do not really work the way she or he thinks they do* because they are based on innate variance relationships that differ from the ones the analyst thinks she/he is seeing.

■ ANCOVA AND HYPOTHESIS TESTING

The only way to assess interactions efficiently is to use a procedure that can examine the effects of at least two independent variables simultaneously. The most powerful procedure, and perhaps the one most underused by skeletal biologists, is *analysis of covariance*, or ANCOVA (Sokal and Rohlf, 2012; Lovejoy et al., 1985). The analyst can choose one or more dependent variables, which are usually continuous, and test the effects of a mix of categorical and continuous independents. In a *fully factorial* ANCOVA model, the interactions are generated automatically for all possible combinations of categorical main effects. Variations of ANCOVA exist for categorical dependent variables (ordinal and logistic regression models), although it would appear that the standard version of ANCOVA is generally robust enough as is to handle many of the kinds of categorical dependents that osteologists typically work with, particularly semicontinuous ordinal traits with at least four or five levels (Nawrocki, 1998, 2010).

ANCOVA provides additional benefits over "traditional" approaches. First, it serves as a convenient and comprehensive platform for hypothesis testing. One can explore all or nearly all of the important elements of their data set, and using built-in *posthoc* tests, if interactions are significant, the specific subgroup(s) affected can be identified clearly.

Second, the procedure determines which independents affect your skeletal trait while simultaneously controlling for all of them. In other words, a significant result for one variable is generated while holding all the other variables constant, and so one can consider the effect of one variable on the dependent as truly independent of any other variable in the model. The same cannot be said for sequential tests, such as *t*-tests. Furthermore, the relative importance of each independent variable on the dependent can be ascertained and ranked; if sex is more important than ancestry, the results will point that out, and one can calculate the amount of variance that each independent "controls." This feature is especially important in osteology, where even the most complex variance equations rarely are able to account for even half of the variability observed in any given skeletal trait (Nawrocki, 2010). ANCOVA helps analysts to recognize and acknowledge the huge amount of unexplained skeletal variance in ways that *t*-tests and chi-squared simply cannot, and the results are humbling from a scientific point of view.

Third, ANCOVA helps us to deal with *unbalanced samples*. Most of the data osteologists work with are obtained from skeletal collections assembled not through careful, selective culling but by convenience, through largely random acquisition processes. As a result, the numbers of individuals in each possible category (say, males and females) are not always the same, and when one adds additional independents (ancestry, age at death), it is very unlikely that the sample will be balanced across all subcategories. Even if the number of males and females and old and young are equal, that rarely means that the number of young males, old males, young females, and old females will be equal!

Unbalanced samples can produce spurious and confusing results when using sequentially applied univariate and bivariate statistical procedures, and regression equations are very sensitive to new samples that do not exactly match the structure of the original calibration sample, which has been particularly problematic in studies of age estimation (Nawrocki, 2010). By assessing all independents simultaneously, disparities in subgroup sizes across the sample and any differential effects they *could* have are ameliorated.

■ ADEQUATE SAMPLING

The Detroit, Michigan Public Library Digital Collections website preserves two remarkable photographs (DPA4900 and DPA4901) taken in the late 19th century. Massive piles of American bison skulls, numbering in the hundreds of thousands if not millions, await rendering at a fertilizer factory. The humans standing on and in front of the stacks are dwarfed by comparison. Huge herds of bison were slaughtered in short order as part of western expansion, their remains being harvested and converted unceremoniously for industrial use.

Imagine being a vertebrate osteologist studying bison cranial variation at the time the photos were taken. At hand would be an unprecedented biological sample the likes of which are rarely encountered by any scientist, providing so many specimens at once that the structure of nearly an entire population as it existed at one moment in time might be thoroughly documented! However, the task facing the osteologist is not easily accomplished. Where and how does one attack the pile? Most specimens are, in reality, not accessible; they lay buried deep within the stack. Even those at the surface can only be sampled; collecting data takes time, and even a team of scientists working for weeks might only measure a small percentage of the skulls before they are burned in the kilns. Even those measured are very unlikely to be representative of the entire population; harvesting methods in the field by paid hunters are surely not consistent or homogenous, and shipments coming in by train from all different parts of the plains states are likely to sample different, distinct biological groupings within that greater population of 50–100 million head. As boxcars of skulls and bones are offloaded, the yard boss surely does not take care to randomize the distribution of these already-biased subsamples. The scientist stumbling around the pile, picking skulls here and there as time permits, encounters small pockets of bison that may be closely related in family groupings or stable herds, others that were jumbled together by accident and share nothing in common, and still others that accidentally oversample certain age or sex categories. In short, even in these highly unusual circumstances that would seem to provide for detailed and thorough study, it is extremely difficult to imagine any scenario in which the researcher could obtain an unbiased sample that paints an accurate picture of the original parent population's true characteristics.

We use this rather belabored metaphor to illustrate and underscore an even bigger problem that faces forensic anthropologists. Our human skeletal collections, especially those with good documentation of known identities and even when combined from across the globe, are pitifully small compared to the erstwhile bison sample in Michigan, and they are surely as biased and probably even more so. Established collections each sample only a narrow slice of time and a small wedge of geography; compared to the 3–7 *billion* humans living at any given time since 1950, a few dozen skeletal collections with an average of a few hundred specimens each—while immeasurably valuable to us—represent a literal drop in the bucket of human variability. Furthermore, some of the largest of those collections were assembled in the late 19th and early 20th centuries, at a time when medical practices, environmental stressors, diets, and life ways were very different from those experienced by people living in modern western industrialized centers where most forensic anthropology is conducted today.

Even comprehensive databases, such as the University of Tennessee's Forensic Databank (Jantz and Moore-Jansen, 1988) on which the FORDISC software is based (Jantz and Ousley, 2005), are assembled primarily from the flotsam and jetsam of the forensic caseloads of a fairly small number of research facilities scattered across North America. Considered for a moment as individual assemblages, these locally constructed case files may themselves be subject to considerable biasing forces. For example, during the past three decades, a disproportionate number of anthropology cases in Indiana and the greater Chicagoland area are likely to have originated from a fairly small number of prolific serial killers, whose selection methods and the resulting effects on sample variability are surely nonrandom and unlikely to mimic nonvictim subpopulations. Even the nonserial cases are unlikely to represent the American population at large; certain demographic groups are at higher risk of death than others, and this disparity only increases as one begins to consider homicides, suicides, and accidental deaths separately. Add to this equation a multitude of factors that contribute to some deaths being discovered while others are not: assailant behaviors that are designed to hide bodies in homicides, decedent behaviors that contribute to accidental deaths in remote locales (such as the interaction between hunting and alcohol consumption), and omnipresent taphonomic factors that differentially affect preservation and discovery that cross-cut all of these scenarios.

Autopsies are conducted on fewer than 1% of the total yearly deaths in Indiana, and only a small fraction of those that *are* autopsied or otherwise investigated by the medicolegal system are anthropology cases. Those cases are in turn the result or fallout of many different causative factors and agents in Midwestern society that change and ebb from year to year and decade to decade: drug trafficking, violent crime, socioeconomic downturn, public health policy, criminal justice funding, etc. Some of these factors may be similar to those encountered in other parts of the country, but some are likely to be peculiar to their own locales, and many may not repeat with any regularity because they are, for all intents and purposes, random isolated occurrences.

In this larger context, then, it is difficult to see how our curated skeletal collections plus those skeletons encountered in the course of forensic casework could serve as adequate representatives of the human population at large: they are too small, too unbalanced, and too biased. Furthermore, because of the inconsistency by which individuals find their way into the medicolegal system, the forensic casework cannot be construed as a valid or cohesive sample of its own. In other words, we should not consider our hodgepodge of cases to somehow represent a real, larger "forensic population" of individuals that can be defined by some common thread in biological or social reality. Instead, for the moment, it seems more prudent to view our skeletal data as constructed in much the same way as the bison scientist would have: from bits and pieces torn from the edges of the greater human population, with characteristics that may or may not be particularly revealing of that larger group or *any definable subgroup within it*.

■ CONCLUSIONS

The ultimate goal of skeletal biology is to explain the systematic variation we see in terms of natural and cultural forces. Forensic anthropologists use that systematic variation to make predictions about the characteristics of unknown individuals. However, just because we are primarily end-point consumers of that information in our daily practice does not absolve us of the responsibility to (1) apply it in an informed and cautious fashion, with all cognizance of its limitations and to (2) make sure that the information we generate ourselves is reliable and adheres to best practices from a *scientific* perspective rather than just a *legal* one, so that the information can contribute to the body of knowledge within human biology.

To this end, we make the following recommendations to forensic anthropologists who consume and generate studies of human skeletal variability:

1. Do not just focus on *prediction*, but recognize the broader *descriptive*, *comparative*, and *explanatory* purposes of studies of skeletal variation, which must occur before developing robust predictive methods;
2. Recognize the importance of thorough *hypothesis testing* by using the *variance equation* as a central guide for constructing, articulating, and conducting skeletal studies;
3. Attempt to control for *multiple independent variables* in each study, and do so with statistical procedures (such as fully factorial ANCOVA) that assess those relative effects *simultaneously* rather than employing sequential techniques on separate variables;
4. Do not ignore the potential and actual influence of *interactions* in the data set, and take measures to clearly separate their effects from those of other variables;
5. Do not confuse or substitute statistical procedures that are designed for prediction (such as regression and discriminant analysis) with those that actually test hypotheses (such as ANCOVA);
6. Do not allow measures of *central tendency* to fool you into thinking there is less variability in the sample than there really is, because measures of *dispersion* are usually far more revealing;
7. Increase data sensitivity by using *continuous* rather than *categorical* measuring scales for skeletal traits whenever possible, or increase the number of levels in categorical traits from just two or three to four or more, when valid;
8. Strive to increase sample sizes and sampling diversity whenever possible to improve sample representativeness;
9. Structure studies so that the numbers of individuals in each subgroup are robust and recognize the possible confusion that could result from using unbalanced samples;
10. Independent tests of previously established equations and methods should carefully consider the sample structure of the original study as well as the possible biasing effects of testing with a new sample that has different characteristics;
11. Do not overestimate the reliability of a predictive technique developed on a "forensic" sample when applied other samples, to the population at large, or especially in a medicolegal context, as the inherent biases and transitory characteristics of our "forensic" samples are not well understood and may not allow for generalization across situations;
12. Recognize that few studies of skeletal variability are able to account for all or even most of the variance in the traits in question, and even in comprehensive studies controlling for multiple independent variables, uncontrolled variance (*error*) is usually greater than 50%.

References

Bass, W., 2005. Human Osteology, fifth ed. Missouri Archaeological Society.
Buikstra, J., Ubelaker, D., 1994. Standards for Data Collection from Human Skeletal Remains. Arkansas Archaeological Survey Press, Fayetteville.
Giles, E., Elliot, O., 1962. Race identification from cranial measurements. J. Forensic Sci. 7, 147–156.
Giles, E., Elliot, O., 1963. Sex determination by discriminant function analysis of crania. Am. J. Phys. Anthropol. 21, 53–68.
Jantz, R., Moore-Jansen, P., 1988. A Data Base for Forensic Anthropology. Forensic Anthropology Center, University of Tennessee, Knoxville.
Jantz, R., Ousley, S., 2005. FORDISC 3.0: Computerized Forensic Discriminant Functions. Forensic Anthropology Center, University of Tennessee, Knoxville.
Langley, N., Meadows Jantz, L., Ousley, S., Jantz, R., Milner, G., 2016. Data Collection Procedures for Forensic Skeletal Material 2.0. Forensic Anthropology Center, University of Tennessee, Knoxville.
Lovejoy, O., Meindl, R., Pryzbeck, T., Mensforth, R., 1985. Chronological metamorphosis of the auricular surface of the ilium: a new method for the determination of adult skeletal age at death. Am. J. Phys. Anthropol. 68, 15–28.
Michigan Public Library. https://digitalcollections.detroitpubliclibrary.org/islandora/object/islandora%3A150881).

Moore, C., 1955. Hyperostosis Cranii. CC Thomas, Springfield IL.

Moore-Jansen, P., Ousley, S., Jantz, R., 1994. Data Collection Procedures for Forensic Skeletal Material. Forensic Anthropology Center, University of Tennessee, Knoxville.

Nawrocki, S., 1998. Regression formulae for the estimation of age from cranial suture closure. In: Reichs, K. (Ed.), Forensic Osteology: Advances in the Identification of Human Remains, second ed. C.C. Thomas, Springfield IL, pp. 276–292.

Nawrocki, S., 2010. The nature and sources of error in the estimation of age at death from the skeleton. In: Latham, K., Finnegan, M. (Eds.), Age Estimation from the Human Skeleton. CC Thomas, Springfield, pp. 79–101.

Ortner, D., 2003. Identification of Pathological Conditions in Human Skeletal Remains, second ed. Academic Press.

Sokal, R., Rohlf, J., 2012. Biometry, fourth ed. Freeman, NY.

Stewart, T., 1979. Essentials of Forensic Anthropology. CC Thomas, Springfield IL.

CHAPTER **3**

Advancements in Sex and Ancestry Estimation

M. Katherine Spradley[1] | Kyra E. Stull[2,3]
[1]Texas State University, San Marcos, TX, United States
[2]University of Nevada-Reno, Reno, NV, United States
[3]University of Pretoria, Pretoria, South Africa

Chapter Outline

■ INTRODUCTION

Sex and ancestry are two fundamental pillars of the biological profile that are inherently interconnected. If the ancestry estimation is incorrect, then the identification may be delayed. If the sex is incorrect, the individual may never be identified. While DNA is widely used in forensic cases today and can provide chromosomal information regarding sex, the waiting time for results is lengthy, which necessitates anthropological sex estimation. To date, there has been much new research in sex and ancestry estimation. Methods now exist that can combine metric and nonmetric traits for ancestry estimation (Hefner et al., 2014), and new data types provide more robust estimates of sex and ancestry and glean more information into the underlying biological processes (Spradley and Jantz, 2016). Further, through the collection of large subadult data sets, methodological advancements associated with the subadult biological profile are being sought and it is now possible to confidently estimate sex from subadults (Stull et al., 2017).

While new data and methods have been put forth, there has been even more research concerning the understanding of human sexual dimorphism and human biological variation, factors that inform the techniques utilized by forensic anthropologists. With the advent of computed tomography (CT) machines and surface scanners, i.e., new data types, we are able to learn more about the underlying theory that informs practice. Therefore, the purpose of this chapter is to highlight research that informs practice while highlighting practical applications of sex and ancestry. The following are the two main questions that this chapter will broadly address:

1. What's new in understanding sexual dimorphism as it relates to forensic anthropological practice?
2. What's new in understanding human biological variation and what are the implications to forensic anthropological practice?

■ WHAT IS NEW IN UNDERSTANDING SEXUAL DIMORPHISM AS IT RELATES TO FORENSIC ANTHROPOLOGICAL PRACTICE?

Biological and Environmental Processes and Sexual Dimorphism

Biological and forensic anthropologists quantify the degree of sexual dimorphism, or the size and shape differences between males and females, when estimating biological sex from skeletal remains. Because such a large portion of sexually dimorphic differences can be attributed to overall size differences between the sexes, it is commonly referred to as sexual size dimorphism (SSD). For modern humans the degree of sexual dimorphism across populations is not constant (Eveleth, 1975), but for body size and body mass, males are approximately 10%–15% larger than females (Cabo et al., 2012; Ruff, 2002; Smith and Jungers, 1997). While the expression of many traits is linked to overall body size differences, some skeletal elements, such as the pelvis, reflect functional differences between the sexes (Plavcan, 2012). The forensic anthropologist utilizes skeletal elements that exhibit sexual dimorphism, although the degree of sexual dimorphism varies throughout the skeleton (Gordon et al., 2008).

Adult size variation, and indirectly SSD, is known for varying among populations. Size variation is dependent on influential factors during ontogeny (Hall, 1978; Komlos and Lauderdale, 2007; Valenzuela et al., 1978). While researchers recognize these factors, their impact, magnitude, and interaction throughout the growth and developmental period are complex. While ontogeny is genetically directed, it is environmentally modified (Cameron, 2007; Karlberg, 1989). For example, much of the variation in modern adult stature is due to nutrition and hygiene during infancy and early childhood (Eveleth and Tanner, 1990; Kuzawa, 2007; Victora et al., 2008). The effects of nutritional deficiencies decrease after the infancy period because the individual transitions from an insulin-dependent growth to a hormone-regulated growth (Karlberg, 1989). In contrast, individuals that experience nutritional deficits and adverse environments later in childhood have a slowed pace of maturity, but rarely is the final stature affected (Kuzawa and Bragg, 2012). The environmental modifications experienced during growth contribute to the variation in adult size that exists in contemporary societies, but the impact of those environments vary depending on what stage of growth one is in.

Some argue the degree of SSD within a population is linked to the average adult stature of that population. Males tend to exhibit greater responses, both positive and negative, to changes in environmental and nutritional conditions compared to females (Stinson, 1985). The female buffering hypothesis is founded on the belief that there are sex differences in response to adverse environments during the developmental period (Greulich, 1951). The reason behind the female buffering hypothesis is that, even under poor conditions, females must maintain a reproductively fit body size and retain enough energy for pregnancy and lactation. Therefore, the degree of SSD could be linked to male's allocation of resources during growth. Specifically, SSD is suggested to be due to the lack of resources to allocate to the development of a larger body size in males.

Why Are There Size Differences Between the Sexes?

Prior to interpreting the final size and overall expression of human sexual dimorphism, it is essential to understand processes that guide the expression of sexually dimorphic differences. While sexual dimorphic differences exist in body composition (e.g., muscle mass vs. fat mass) and body weight, linear body size differences that are associated with SSD are largely negligible throughout the growth. Differences in linear measures become quantifiable after the pubertal growth spurt. When discussing the expression of size differences in linear measures, such as stature, the discrepancy in size between the sexes is consequent to the magnitude of the growth spurt (i.e., peak height velocity), later onset of the pubertal growth spurt (i.e., longer childhood growth), and the duration of the growth spurt. It is widely recognized that the age at takeoff, which results in an extended duration in childhood growth, is the most influential factor to the overall sex differences in adult stature (Hauspie et al., 1985, 1980; Hauspie and Roelants, 2012; Koziel et al., 1995).

While SSD, and its relation to stature, has been primarily discussed, different skeletal elements exhibit varying levels of sexual dimorphism. In contrast to stature, which is directly related to the long bone lengths, articular surfaces are up to 20% larger in males than females (Bogin, 1999). Adult sexual dimorphism is generally lower in early growing variables than in later growing variables. During ontogeny, resources are allocated to immediate needs. For example, growth is dedicated to brain growth and mastication first and foremost (e.g., 80% of adult brain weight is reached by 3 years of age). Following brain development, resources are allocated to locomotion (e.g., length of long bones) and reproductive functions; long bone lengths reach 50% of adult size by 7 years of age (Bogin, 1999). Because they are some of the fastest growing elements, they reach their adult size based on efficiency rather than expression. Once these two needs have been met, resources are invested in strength and the development of secondary features associated with sexual dimorphism. In contrast to long bone lengths, the articular breadths are the last skeletal elements to complete growth and therefore have a greater degree of variation in expression (Humphrey, 1998).

■ SUBADULT SEX ESTIMATION

While age estimation is the most common parameter researched in forensic and biological anthropology, there has been a recent research surge dedicated to exploring subadult sexual dimorphism. Because there is a substantial lack of subadult skeletal remains to work with, research is generally conducted on CT images or radiographic images. If advanced imaging techniques are not incorporated into the research, it is likely that the sample originates from a historic population and therefore may not reflect the sexually dimorphic patterns of modern populations. Furthermore, skeletal material from historical specimens tends to result in skewed samples that lack even distribution. Subsequently, age groups are created (i.e., 1- to 5-year olds, 6- to 10-year olds, etc.), and individuals of different body sizes are pooled. Subadult skeletal research is more complex than adult sexual dimorphism research as you have a constant increase in size that is concurrent to the increase in age, let alone the potential size differences between the sexes. Research has included both metric and geometric morphometric approaches and primarily utilizes the long bones and the pelvis.

A large focus for the recent literature has been placed on the subadult pelvis (e.g., Rissech et al., 2003; Rissech and Malgosa, 2005; Wilson et al., 2011, 2008, 2015). Numerous researchers have successfully identified shape differences on the pelvis between the sexes. Using geometric morphometrics, Bilfeld et al. (2013) explored size and shape differences in the pelvis of individuals aged between 1 and 18 years ($n = 188$). While iliac shape differences were evident from 5 to 18 years, the magnitude of differences increased as age increased. Furthermore, shape changes appear to occur prior to size differences (Bilfeld et al., 2013; Wilson et al., 2015). Wilson et al. (2015) note that a female may be 55% shape mature, but only 42% size mature. The authors note that in younger ilia, the shape differences were located in the superior portion. As age increased, the differences in shape transitioned to being more prominent with the width of the bone and the width of the greater sciatic notch. A trend that has been reported by numerous authors is the increase in shape differences that occurs with increased age, specifically around 11 years of age (Bilfeld et al., 2013; Wilson et al., 2011, 2015).

Stull et al. (2017) has recently posited that sex differences are quantifiable in the subadult appendicular skeleton. Differences in the body composition of males and females are evident at a young age, and the varying levels of muscle and fat mass cause differential biomechanical adaptations, which can be quantified and used in subadult sex estimation (Arfai et al., 2002; Garnett et al., 2004; Poissonnet et al., 1984; Prader et al., 1989). Sexual dimorphism and sex estimation using long bone lengths and breadths were explored on a large sample of South African children aged between birth and 12 years. Sympercent (sp) differences in long bone breadth and length measurements between the sexes revealed that there are greater sex differences in the proximal and distal breadths in comparison to the diaphyseal lengths (Stull, 2013) (Fig. 3.1). Birth to 1-year olds and 10- to 12-year olds tend to present different patterns, likely because of size differences at birth as well as the onset of the pubertal growth spurt, respectively. For children between birth to 9 years of age, males have on average 4.2 sp larger proximal breadths, 3.4 sp larger distal breadths, and 3.0 sp larger midshaft breadths than females. In contrast to the sp differences in breadths, long bone lengths show minimal differences between males and females (Stull, 2013).

Following the documentation of sexual dimorphic differences in long bones, attempts were made to use classification statistics and multiple variable subsets to correctly classify sex. Using logistic regression and flexible discriminant analysis, multiple variable models presented with bootstrapped classification accuracies ranging between 70% and 93% (Stull et al., 2017) (Table 3.1). The results are very encouraging, considering the achieved classification accuracies are comparable to morphological and metric analyses of the cranium, pelvis, and long bones of adults. Findings suggest that sex can be estimated independent of age. The exclusion of an age estimate in the model removes any potential compounding of errors in the final estimates, which results in a more reliable estimate. The success of the multiple variable model supports the idea that the more variables collected from numerous anatomical areas and incorporated into the model, the greater the classification accuracy and therefore the likelihood of an accurate sex estimation.

Cranial Sexual Dimorphism

Cranial sexual dimorphism is suggested to be directly related to energetic requirements, body composition differences, and overall muscular robusticity (Bigoni et al., 2010; Franklin et al., 2006; Rosas and Bastir, 2002). Geometric morphometrics have been used to explore both population and sex differences in populations around the world. Traditional linear measurements are not always able to capture the underlying shape differences because that variation may not always be captured with calipers (Spradley and Jantz, 2016). Therefore,

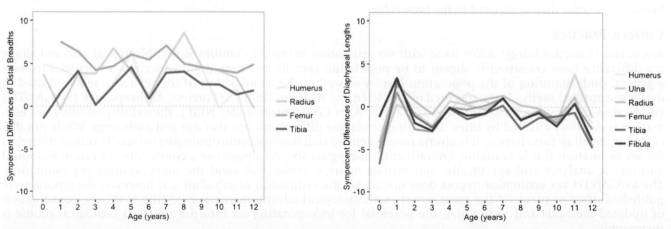

Figure 3.1 Visualizations of sympercent differences of distal breadth measurements (A) and diaphyseal lengths (B) from a contemporary sample of South African children. On average, males present with larger distal breadths while there are negligible sex differences in length.

Table 3.1   Flexible Discriminant Analysis Bootstrapped Classification Accuracies for Exemplar Multiple Variable Subsets

	n	Flexible Discriminant Analysis	
		Bootstrapped Classifications Overall	Bootstrapped 95% Confidence Intervals
All measurement	62	93%	87%–99%
Upper limbs	91	84%	76%–90%
Lower limbs	454	74%	71%–77%
Proximal elements	312	79%	76%–82%
Distal elements	100	78%	70%–86%
Ratios	391	76%	73%–79%

nonstandard landmarks and measurements may provide more insight to the pattern and distribution of human variation, and specifically in quantifying sexual dimorphism. In a modern US sample that included black and white males and females, sex had a significant impact on shape differences, but not size. Specifically, individuals within the same sex and population group were of similar shape, regardless of their overall size (Kimmerle et al., 2008).

Just as skeletal elements throughout the body vary in terms of their degree of sexual dimorphic expression, current research is incorporating geometric morphometrics to explore if specific areas of the cranial complex display varying levels of sexual dimorphism. Whereas the cranial base and neurocranium did not express sexually dimorphic shape differences, the upper face, midsagittal curve, orbital, nasal, and palatal regions did express sexually dimorphic shape differences (Bigoni et al., 2010). Interestingly, these findings substantiate the previously discussed phenomena that later growing elements express greater degrees of sexual dimorphism. Specifically, the neurocranium and cranial base are inextricably linked to the growth of the brain. In contrast, the splanchnocranium develops much later and was the area that Bigoni et al. (2010) discovered to express sexually dimorphic shape differences. Overall, females had a more spherical cranium and shorter vault (i.e., nasion-occipital length), and males had greater projection in the upper facial region (i.e., glabella) and a sloping frontal region.

Sexual dimorphism in cranial morphology has been studied for over a century. Researchers generally recognize that while assessing sex by morphological features is efficient, there is more subjectivity, which impacts the reliability of techniques. Recently, however, geometric morphometrics have been used to clarify and demonstrate supplementary sexually dimorphic features in cranial morphology. On a southern African sample, geometric morphometric research quantified the profile of the frontal bone, form of the supramastoid crest, the projection of glabella, alveolar prognathism, and the size of the posterior airway space (Franklin et al., 2006). Findings suggest the cranial features that are related to muscles or the muscle energetic system, and therefore robusticity/gracility, expressed the highest degrees of sexual dimorphism (Franklin et al., 2006).

Garvin and Ruff (2012) derived metric variables from nonmetric traits, specifically creating values associated with absolute volumes, surface areas, base areas, and relative ratios to explore sexual dimorphism. Volume data were collected from brow and chin regions from the cranium and enabled the quantification of absolute and relative sizes as well as shape analyses (Garvin and Ruff, 2012). When the size differences are accounted for, only the measurements associated with the browridge displayed sexually dimorphic differences. Interestingly, shape differences discerned in the browridge potentially reflect the expression of traits defined in morphological methods. For example, the more inferior projection of the lateral transects for males extends toward the orbits and may contribute to the supraorbital margin that is scored in traditional morphological sexing techniques (e.g., Acsadi and Nemeskeri, 1970; Buikstra and Ubelaker, 1994). Shape variables associated with the chin exhibited sex differences although there was more overlap between the sexes than compared to the browridge.

Current Practice

Regardless of methodology, a key issue with sex estimation using the cranium is that biological size and shape sex difference have consistently shown to be population specific and time period specific. It is crucial to have a general understanding of the population history as well as the composition of the reference material used to derive the applied methods. As specified by the Scientific Working Group in Forensic Anthropology (SWGANTH) (now taken over by the Organization of Scientific Area Committees under NIST), the validity of one's sex estimation is not only affected by inter- and intrapopulation differences, but also age and pathology. While not discussed in detail in this chapter, it is always recommended that forensic anthropologists primarily utilize the pelvis for sex estimation if it is available. Overall, anthropologists should always use a combination of morphological and metric analyses and specifically, multivariate metrics, as this will yield the most accurate sex estimation. The SWGANTH sex estimation report does not advise the estimation of subadult sex; however, the reports were published prior to many of the most recent methodological advancements (e.g., 2010). With the continuation of updated methods and techniques, the potential for incorporating sex into the subadult biological profile is increasing.

■ WHAT IS NEW IN UNDERSTANDING HUMAN BIOLOGICAL VARIATION AND WHAT ARE THE IMPLICATIONS TO FORENSIC ANTHROPOLOGICAL PRACTICE?

Estimation of Ancestry or Geographic Origin

Ancestry estimation using metric data within a statistical framework was first introduced by Karl Pearson in 1926 through the coefficient of racial likeness. As R.A. Fisher (1936) wrote "The purpose of the Coefficient of Racial Likeness is to afford a means of testing whether two groups of skulls, on each of which numerous measurements have been made, could or could not have been drawn at random from the same bulk." In 1962, Giles and Elliot (1962) applied discriminant function analysis (DFA) to three groups, Native American, American Black, and American White and provided an end user application. Later in 1993, FORDISC was introduced, which provided a graphical user interface to apply DFA with reference groups for forensic casework and a separate page for W.W. Howells worldwide data (Howells, 1989, 1973; Ousley and Jantz, 2005). Although recent publications have highlighted novel methods for ancestry classification (Hefner et al., 2014; Maddux et al., 2015; Maier et al., 2015; Sholts and Wärmländer, 2012), DFA still remains the most commonly used method for ancestry estimation to date based on the ease in utility that led to widespread use of FORDISC 3.1. Other methods have been introduced for ancestry estimation using different methodologies with successful classifications; however, at the time of this writing, no method has overcome the practical utility of the DFA and the use of FORDISC.

What has fundamentally changed since the introduction of statistical methods for ancestry estimation using craniometrics are the data. The craniometric data (landmark data, semilandmarks, nontraditional interlandmark distances) have changed over time, and reference data have also seen unparalleled growth. With technological advancements that enable researchers to capture different types of craniometric data, nonstandard interlandmark distances can be computed that capture morphological variables that better differentiate complex groups (i.e., having two or more parental groups) (Spradley and Jantz, 2016). Landmark data can also be analyzed in new ways, which provide further insight to size and shape differences among groups. Understanding morphological variation of recent human groups enhances the forensic anthropologist's ability to estimate ancestry or geographic origin.

At the same time, there has been tremendous growth in genomic data (see the 1000 genomes project) that has allowed researchers to better understand the genetic variation present in our current populations. Time and time again, craniometric data have been shown to parallel genetic data in terms of biological relationships among groups (Relethford, 2004). Cranial morphology is polygenic, influenced by both genes and the environment, and can be used to reconstruct population structure or estimate ancestry. While there is an environmental component that influences the morphological outcome of craniofacial size and shape, the environmental effects do no obscure the underlying genetic variation (Algee-Hewitt, 2016; Carson, 2006; Martinez-Abadias et al., 2009; Relethford, 2004; Roseman et al., 2010). Therefore, the cranium can be used to statistically classify groups or individuals (Hefner et al., 2014; Ousley et al., 2009) and to track environmental noise over time (Relethford, 2004, 2009). Recently, there has been a focus on understanding the biological variation of complex groups in an attempt to better estimate ancestry for these groups (Hughes et al., 2013; Ross et al., 2004; Spradley, 2016, 2014, 2013; Spradley et al., 2008; Spradley and Jantz, 2016).

Studies of the current US population structure help forensic anthropologists better understand the frame of reference for choosing the most appropriate reference data possible when estimating ancestry. The population genetic theory behind ancestry estimation is nothing new, but is less often discussed in forensic anthropology textbooks or journal articles. While it is assumed that the readers may already be familiar with basic theory, this assumption is unwarranted as evidenced by publications that do not understand the fundamentals of population genetic theory and the interpretation of statistical methods of ancestry classification (Armelagos and van Gerven, 2003; Elliot and Collard, 2009; Williams et al., 2005).

How Does Population Genetic Theory Influence the Ability to Estimate Ancestry?

Forensic anthropologists, as anthropologists first, should be aware of the population structure that surrounds them when conducting casework. Population structure refers to factors that affect mate choice and genetic distance between population groups (Mielke et al., 2011). Such factors that maintain population structure include culture, religion, ethnicity, language, and geography, to name a few (Baharian et al., 2016; Ousley et al., 2009; Relethford et al., 1983). Further, population groups living in close geographic proximity are more closely related, therefore more similar, than those that live farther apart, a concept referred to as isolation by distance (Wright, 1943). Ousley et al. (2009) pointed out factors, such as institutional racism and positive assortative mating practices, influence the US population structure to such a degree that a concordance exists between social race categories and biology (Fig. 3.2).

Population structure can be detected through genomic and craniometric data. Recent genetic publications highlight the complexity of population structure for complex populations living in the United States (Bryc et al., 2010a,b). Complex populations refer to population groups that have two or more parental population groups, e.g., American Black or Hispanics. Further, it has been shown that complex populations are more difficult to classify in forensic anthropological casework (Ousley and Jantz, 2005; Spradley et al., 2008).

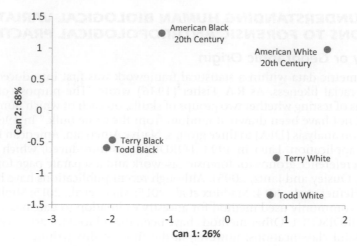

Figure 3.2 Canonical variates plot, using craniometric data, of American Blacks and Whites showing 90% of the total variation. Data come from the Forensic Anthropology Data Bank. Terry and Todd represent individuals born in the late 19th to early 20th century. The American White and Black groups represent individuals born later in the 20th century.

What Has Been Learned Recently About US Populations?

While genetic studies of admixture have shed light within the US population indicating the amount of admixture for complex groups, more recent studies have shown that craniometric data provide similar information. The fact that craniometric data parallel genetic data with reference to admixture is important as it supports the utility of craniometric data for ancestry estimation in forensic anthropological casework. Genetic studies have revealed that the US population displays structure—that is, there is genetic differentiation among perceived racial and ethnic groups residing in the United States. This structure indicates that mating is not random. Many of these studies are a result of widespread data collection to better understand structure in terms of exploring admixture estimates, for application to probability estimates for forensic DNA comparisons, as well as pertaining to health-related fields.

Hispanics have three parental groups, Native American, European, and African (Bryc et al., 2010a; Lisker et al., 1986). It has been found that groups considered Hispanic vary in population structure geographically, by country of origin and also within country of origin (Bryc et al., 2010b). Further, based on the complex population structure, Mexicans exhibit clinal variation in admixture with more European admixture in the North and more Native American admixture in the south. This has also been substantiated with craniometrics (Hughes et al., 2013; Rangel-Villalobos et al., 2008; Rubi-Castellanos et al., 2009). Bryc et al. (2010b) attribute the complex population structure within various Latin American populations to local population size before colonization, the degree that colonizers displaced Native groups, and whether or not slavery was introduced.

Using ancestry informative markers, Seldin et al. (2007) found that higher degrees of European admixture in Argentinians than Mexican-Americans. Martínez-Cruzado et al. (2005) found that Puerto Rican municipalities show higher degrees of Native American ancestry, followed by sub-Saharan Africa. The lack of understanding biological variation of Spanish-speaking populations has, in the past, been a hindrance to ancestry estimation. Today, with technological advances and relatively low-cost genome-wide association studies, we understand more about the genetic variation of Latin American groups. Because these Latin American groups make up the so-called Hispanic population in the United States, forensic anthropologists can now better understand the variation within this particular population group. However, it remains important from an anthropological point of view to recognize migration patterns and population settlement within the United States to use the most appropriate reference groups for classification purposes.

In the past, osteometric data was lacking for Hispanics and although that has changed (Ousley and Jantz, 2005; Slice and Ross, 2009; Spradley, 2013) we are only in the beginning phase of understanding the skeletal biological complexity of all groups that are considered Hispanic. Project identification has provided a data set of contextually identified migrant remains from the Pima County Office of the Medical Examiner available through the Forensic Anthropology Data Bank. This data set continues to be updated as identifications are made; therefore it will be possible to learn more about the variation of the countries where the migrants come from. Further, Tise (2014) has obtained Puerto Rican craniometric data through CT scans of living patients. Because large, documented skeletal collections lack diversity, consisting predominantly of American Black and White donors, nontraditional sources of data such as CT scans from the living should be sought out for research and development. There are large portions of the US population that we know relatively little about including Asian Americans, Indian Americans, and Middle Eastern Americans, to name a few. Even though current skeletal collections lack diversity, there are still less American Blacks than Whites, especially American Black females (Spradley and Jantz, 2011).

In 20 years of data collection efforts of the FDB, the majority of reference data are still predominantly American Blacks and Whites. However, through collection of migrant data, Hispanic males and females are now well represented in the FDB. With these new data for Hispanics and additional data from the FDB, Algee-Hewitt (2016) found, using craniometrics and model-based clustering, similar approximations for both structure and admixture estimations as genetic data.

■ NEW ADVANCES IN APPLICATIONS OF ANCESTRY ESTIMATION

Types of Craniometric Data

In 1983 a committee was appointed through the American Academy of Forensic Sciences Physical Anthropology section to develop metric "standards" for use in forensic anthropology. A total of 24 cranial and 9 mandibular measurements were selected for use based on measurements that were already defined and could be easily taken with sliding or spreading calipers (Spradley and Jantz, 2016). These data standards are still in use today in forensic anthropology practice despite all the technological changes and more ubiquitous use of digitizers that can capture more data in less time (Ousley and McKeown, 2001), provide a better overall archive of size and shape, and from which new metric and geometric morphometric data can be derived for utility in forensic practice. As Spradley and Jantz (2016) have pointed out, interlandmark distances derived from landmark data (obtained from a digitizer) that are not considered "standard" (e.g., the linear distance from left asterion to parietal subtense point) provide better separation among contemporary American groups (especially complex groups) than the "standard" 24 cranial measurements. Programs also exist now, e.g., 3D-ID, that are able to estimate ancestry with landmark data.

Collecting cranial data using a digitizer is also much easier and more efficient than calipers. When teaching students how to measure a cranium, teaching them to hold the calipers properly while putting the endpoints on two different landmarks is more difficult than placing a stylus on one landmark at a time. Often you will find that the endpoints of the calipers slip on one end while the focus is on the other end. Placing the endpoints on the correct landmarks for the one measurement comes with experience. The use of surface scanners has also grown more popular in forensic anthropology and has been used for ancestry estimation. Surface scanners allow the user to focus on particular areas of the cranium if shape is of interest (Garvin and Ruff, 2012). However, surface scans generate a tremendous amount of data; therefore specific areas of interest or semilandmark data are usually extracted for statistical analyses. With the exception of 3D-ID, there is little use of geometric morphometrics or surface scan data for the end user in forensic anthropology practice.

Current Practice

According to best practices outlined by SWGANTH, there is no one-size-fits-all answer to how to estimate ancestry; instead multiple guidelines are given that provide best practices and unacceptable practices. All forensic practitioners should be aware of the most recent best practices. There are several critical concerns for ancestry estimation including reference group selection and statistical methods employed. Further, SWGANTH explicitly states that ancestry estimation is inherently multivariate, there is no single trait that can distinguish among groups, and attempting to do so is an unacceptable practice.

Understanding the population history that has led to the current population structure of the population group at hand is at the utmost importance for ancestry estimation. Additionally, understanding that secular changes, i.e., short-term generational changes, can take place over time and impact reference group selection is equally important. Using data that are considered nonstandard within an appropriate statistical framework may prove better for some complex populations. Our world is currently experiencing mass migrations that will change the demographic and population structure of various geographic areas. Ancestry estimation is not static, what was good for yesterday's population may not work tomorrow. It is up to the forensic anthropologist to think like an anthropologist and be aware of what is going on in her surroundings to provide the best estimate as possible.

■ CONCLUSION

Within forensic anthropology, the emphasis has been placed on population-specific techniques for sex and ancestry. Many countries do not have access to human skeletal collections, and while it is necessary to understand the underlying biological theories that affect the range and pattern of human variation, we also have to produce applicable models. The two greatest contributions anthropologists can make toward estimating sex and ancestry is to (1) understand the underlying biological processes that differentiate groups, either at the sex or population level, and (2) make an effort to capture the true spectrum of variation when designing research. We need continued innovative and transformative research to better understand the biological processes that influence sex and ancestry.

References

Acsadi, G., Nemeskeri, J., 1970. History of Human Life Span and Mortality. Akademiai Kiado, Budapest.

Algee-Hewitt, B.F.B., 2016. Population inference from contemporary American craniometrics: population inference from craniometrics. Am. J. Phys. Anthropol. 160, 604–624. http://dx.doi.org/10.1002/ajpa.22959.

Arfai, K., Pitukcheewanont, P.D., Goran, M.I., Tavare, C.J., Heller, L., Gilsanz, V., 2002. Bone, muscle, and fat: sex-related differences in prepubertal children. Radiology 224, 338–344. http://dx.doi.org/10.1148/radiol.2242011369.

Armelagos, G., van Gerven, D.P., 2003. A century of skeletal biology and paleopathology: contrasts, contradictions, and conflicts. Am. Anthropol. 105, 51–62.

Baharian, S., Barakatt, M., Gignoux, C.R., Shringarpure, S., Errington, J., Blot, W.J., Bustamante, C.D., Kenny, E.E., Williams, S.M., Aldrich, M.C., Gravel, S., 2016. The great migration and African-American genomic diversity. PLoS Genet. 12, e1006059. http://dx.doi.org/10.1371/journal.pgen.1006059.

Bigoni, L., Velemínská, J., Brůzek, J., 2010. Three-dimensional geometric morphometric analysis of cranio-facial sexual dimorphism in a Central European sample of known sex. Homo Int. Z. Für Vgl. Forsch. Am. Menschen 61, 16–32. http://dx.doi.org/10.1016/j.jchb.2009.09.004.

Bilfeld, M.F., Dedouit, F., Sans, N., Rousseau, H., Rougé, D., Telmon, N., 2013. Ontogeny of size and shape sexual dimorphism in the ilium: a multislice computed tomography study by geometric morphometry. J. Forensic Sci. 58, 303–310. http://dx.doi.org/10.1111/1556-4029.12037.

Bogin, B., 1999. Patterns of Human Growth. Cambridge University Press, Cambridge.

Bryc, K., Auton, A., Nelson, M.R., Oksenberg, J.R., Hauser, S.L., Williams, S., Froment, A., Bodo, J.-M., Wambebe, C., Tishkoff, S.A., Bustamante, C.D., 2010a. Genome-wide patterns of population structure and admixture in West Africans and African Americans. Proc. Natl. Acad. Sci. U.S.A. 107, 786–791. http://dx.doi.org/10.1073/pnas.0909559107.

Bryc, K., Velez, C., Karafet, T., Moreno-Estrada, A., Reynolds, A., Auton, A., Hammer, M., Bustamante, C.D., Ostrer, H., 2010b. Genome-wide patterns of population structure and admixture among Hispanic/Latino populations. Proc. Natl. Acad. Sci. U.S.A. 107, 8954–8961. http://dx.doi.org/10.1073/pnas.0914618107.

Buikstra, J.E., Ubelaker, D.H., 1994. Standards for Data Collection from Human Skeletal Remains: Proceedings of a Seminar at the Field Museum of Natural History. Arkansas Archaeological Research Series, Fayetteville.

Cabo, L., Brewster, C., Azpiazu, J., 2012. Sexual dimorphism: interpreting sex markers. In: Dirkmaat, D. (Ed.), A Companian to Forensic Anthropology. John Wiley & Sons, Malden, MA, pp. 248–286.

Cameron, N., 2007. Growth patterns in adverse environments. Am. J. Hum. Biol. Off. J. Hum. Biol. Counc. 19, 615–621. http://dx.doi.org/10.1002/ajhb.20661.

Carson, E.A., 2006. Maximum likelihood estimation of human craniometric heritabilities. Am. J. Phys. Anthropol. 131, 169–180. http://dx.doi.org/10.1002/ajpa.20424.

Elliot, M., Collard, M., 2009. FORDISC and the determination of ancestry from cranial measurements. Biol. Lett. 5, 849–852.

Eveleth, P.B., 1975. Differences between ethnic groups in sex dimorphism of adult height. Ann. Hum. Biol. 2, 35–39.

Eveleth, P., Tanner, J., 1990. Worldwide Variation in Human Growth, second ed. Cambridge University Press, Cambridge.

Fisher, R.A., 1936. "The coefficient of racial likeness" and the future of craniometry. J. R. Anthropol. Inst. G.B. Irel. 66, 57–63. http://dx.doi.org/10.2307/2844116.

Franklin, D., Freedman, L., Milne, N., Oxnard, C.E., 2006. A geometric morphometric study of sexual dimorphism in the crania of indigenous southern Africans. S. Afr. J. Sci. 102, 229–238.

Garnett, S.P., Högler, W., Blades, B., Baur, L.A., Peat, J., Lee, J., Cowell, C.T., 2004. Relation between hormones and body composition, including bone, in prepubertal children. Am. J. Clin. Nutr. 80, 966–972.

Garvin, H.M., Ruff, C.B., 2012. Sexual dimorphism in skeletal browridge and chin morphologies determined using a new quantitative method. Am. J. Phys. Anthropol. 147, 661–670. http://dx.doi.org/10.1002/ajpa.22036.

Giles, E., Elliot, O., 1962. Race identification from cranial measurements. J. Forensic Sci. 7, 147–157.

Gordon, A.D., Green, D.J., Richmond, B.G., 2008. Strong postcranial size dimorphism in *Australopithecus afarensis*: results from two new resampling methods for multivariate data sets with missing data. Am. J. Phys. Anthropol. 135, 311–328. http://dx.doi.org/10.1002/ajpa.20745.

Greulich, W.W., 1951. The growth and developmental status of Guamanian school children in 1947. Am. J. Phys. Anthropol. 9, 55–70. http://dx.doi.org/10.1002/ajpa.1330090105.

Hall, R.L., 1978. Sexual dimorphism for size in seven nineteenth century northwest coast populations. Hum. Biol. 50, 159–171.

Hauspie, R., Das, S., Preece, M., Tanner, J., Susanne, C., 1985. Decomposition of sexual dimorphism in adult size of height, sitting height, shoulder width and hip width in a British and West Bengal sample. In: Ghesquiere, J., Martin, R., Newcombe, F. (Eds.), Human Sexual Dimorphism. Taylor & Francis Ltd., pp. 207–215.

Hauspie, R., Roelants, M., 2012. Adolescent growth. In: Cameron, N., Bogin, B. (Eds.), Human Growth and Development. Elsevier, New York, pp. 57–79.

Hauspie, R.C., Das, S.R., Preece, M.A., Tanner, J.M., 1980. A longitudinal study of the growth in height of boys and girls of West Bengal (India) aged six months to 20 years. Ann. Hum. Biol. 7, 429–440. http://dx.doi.org/10.1080/03014468000004541.

Hefner, J.T., Spradley, M.K., Anderson, B., 2014. Ancestry assessment using random forest modeling. J. Forensic Sci. 1–7. http://dx.doi.org/10.1111/1556-4029.12402.

Howells, W., 1989. Skull Shapes and the Map: Craniometric Analysis in the Dispersion of Modern Homo. Harvard University Press, Cambridge.

Howells, W.W., 1973. Cranial variation in man: a study by multivariate analysis of patterns of difference among recent human populations. In: Papers of the Peabody Museum of Archaeology and Ethnolgy. Harvard University Press.

Hughes, C.E., Tise, M.L., Trammell, L.H., Anderson, B.E., 2013. Cranial morphological variation among contemporary Mexicans: regional trends, ancestral affinities, and genetic comparisons. Am. J. Phys. Anthropol. 151, 506–517. http://dx.doi.org/10.1002/ajpa.22288.

Humphrey, L.T., 1998. Growth patterns in the modern human skeleton. Am. J. Phys. Anthropol. 105, 57–72. http://dx.doi.org/10.1002/(SICI)1096-8644(199801)105:1<57::AID-AJPA6>3.0.CO;2-A.

Karlberg, J., 1989. A biologically-oriented mathematical model (ICP) for human growth. Acta Paediatr. 78, 70–94. http://dx.doi.org/10.1111/j.1651-2227.1989.tb11199.x.

Kimmerle, E.H., Ross, A., Slice, D., 2008. Sexual dimorphism in America: geometric morphometric analysis of the craniofacial region. J. Forensic Sci. 53, 54–57.

Komlos, J., Lauderdale, B.E., 2007. The mysterious trend in American heights in the 20th century. Ann. Hum. Biol. 34, 206–215. http://dx.doi.org/10.1080/03014460601116803.

Koziel, S.K., Hauspie, R.C., Susanne, C., 1995. Sex differences in height and sitting height in the Belgian population. Int. J. Anthropol. 10, 241–247. http://dx.doi.org/10.1007/BF02447882.

Kuzawa, C.W., 2007. Developmental origins of life history: growth, productivity, and reproduction. Am. J. Hum. Biol. 19, 654–661.

Kuzawa, C.W., Bragg, J.M., 2012. Plasticity in human life history strategy: implications for contemporary human variation and the evolution of genus *Homo*. Curr. Anthropol. 53, S369–S382. http://dx.doi.org/10.1086/667410.

Lisker, R., Perez-Briceño, R., Granados, J., Babinsky, V., de Rubens, J., Armendares, S., Buentello, L., 1986. Gene frequencies and admixture estimates in a Mexico City population. Am. J. Phys. Anthropol. 71, 203–207. http://dx.doi.org/10.1002/ajpa.1330710207.

Maddux, S.D., Sporleder, A.N., Burns, C.E., 2015. Geographic variation in zygomaxillary suture morphology and its use in ancestry estimation. J. Forensic Sci. 60, 966–973. http://dx.doi.org/10.1111/1556-4029.12774.

Maier, C.A., Zhang, K., Manhein, M.H., Li, X., 2015. Palate shape and depth: a shape-matching and machine learning method for estimating ancestry from human skeletal remains. J. Forensic Sci. 60, 1129–1134. http://dx.doi.org/10.1111/1556-4029.12812.

Martínez-Abadías, N., Esparza, M., Sjøvold, T., Gonzalez-Jose, R., Santos, M., Hernandez, M., 2009. Heritability of human cranial dimensions: comparing the evolvability of different cranial regions. J. Anat. 214, 19–35. http://dx.doi.org/10.1111/j.1469-7580.2008.01015.x.

Martínez-Cruzado, J.C., Toro-Labrador, G., Viera-Vera, J., Rivera-Vega, M.Y., Startek, J., Latorre-Esteves, M., Román-Colón, A., Rivera-Torres, R., Navarro-Millán, I.Y., Gómez-Sánchez, E., Caro-González, H.Y., Valencia-Rivera, P., 2005. Reconstructing the population history of Puerto Rico by means of mtDNA phylogeographic analysis. Am. J. Phys. Anthropol. 128, 131–155. http://dx.doi.org/10.1002/ajpa.20108.

Mielke, J.H., Konigsberg, L.W., Relethford, J.H., 2011. Human Biological Variation. Oxford University Press, New York.

Ousley, S., Jantz, R., 2005. FORDISC 3.1. The University of Tennessee, Knoxville.

Ousley, S., Jantz, R., Freid, D., 2009. Understanding race and human variation: why forensic anthropologists are good at identifying race. Am. J. Phys. Anthropol. 139, 68–76.

Ousley, S., McKeown, A., 2001. Three dimensional digitizing of human skulls as an archival procedure. BAR Int. Ser. 934, 173–186.

Plavcan, J.M., 2012. Body size, size variation, and sexual size dimorphism in early Homo. Curr. Anthropol. 53, S409–S423. http://dx.doi.org/10.1086/667605.

Poissonnet, C.M., Burdi, A.R., Garn, S.M., 1984. The chronology of adipose tissue appearance and distribution in the human fetus. Early Hum. Dev. 10, 1–11.

Prader, A., Largo, R.H., Molinari, L., Issler, C., 1989. Physical growth of Swiss children from birth to 20 years of age. First Zurich longitudinal study of growth and development. Helv. Paediatr. Acta. Suppl. 52, 1–125.

Rangel-Villalobos, H., Muñoz-Valle, J.F., González-Martín, A., Gorostiza, A., Magaña, M.T., Páez-Riberos, L.A., 2008. Genetic admixture, relatedness, and structure patterns among Mexican populations revealed by the Y-chromosome. Am. J. Phys. Anthropol. 135, 448–461.

Relethford, J., 2004. Boas and beyond: migration and craniometric variation. Am. J. Hum. Biol. 16, 379–386.

Relethford, J.H., 2009. Race and global patterns of phenotypic variation. Am. J. Phys. Anthropol. 139, 16–22. http://dx.doi.org/10.1002/ajpa.20900.

Relethford, J.H., Stern, M.P., Gaskill, S.P., Hazuda, H.P., 1983. Social class, admixture, and skin color variation in Mexican-Americans and Anglo-Americans living in San Antonio. Tex. Am. J. Phys. Anthropol. 61, 97–102.

Rissech, C., Garća, M., Malgosa, A., 2003. Sex and age diagnosis by ischium morphometric analysis. Forensic Sci. Int. 135, 188–196. http://dx.doi.org/10.1016/S0379-0738(03)00215-9.

Rissech, C., Malgosa, A., 2005. Ilium growth study: applicability in sex and age diagnosis. Forensic Sci. Int. Sex Body Size 147, 165–174. http://dx.doi.org/10.1016/j.forsciint.2004.08.007.

Rosas, A., Bastir, M., 2002. Thin-plate spline analysis of allometry and sexual dimorphism in the human craniofacial complex. Am. J. Phys. Anthropol. 117, 236–245. http://dx.doi.org/10.1002/ajpa.10023.

Roseman, C.C., Willmore, K.E., Rogers, J., Hildebolt, C., Sadler, B.E., Richtsmeier, J.T., Cheverud, J.M., 2010. Genetic and environmental contributions to variation in baboon cranial morphology. Am. J. Phys. Anthropol. 143 9999, NA.

Ross, A.H., Slice, D.E., Ubelaker, D.H., Falsetti, A.B., 2004. Population affinities of 19th century Cuban crania: implications for identification criteria in south Florida Cuban Americans. J. Forensic Sci. 49, 1–6.

Rubi-Castellanos, R., Martínez-Cortés, G., Muñoz-Valle, J.F., González-Martín, A., Cerda-Flores, R.M., Anaya-Palafox, M., Rangel-Villalobos, H., 2009. Pre-Hispanic Mesoamerican demography approximates the present-day ancestry of Mestizos throughout the territory of Mexico. Am. J. Phys. Anthropol. 139, 284–294.

Ruff, C., 2002. Variation in human body size and shape. Annu. Rev. Anthropol. 31, 211–232. http://dx.doi.org/10.1146/annurev.anthro.31.040402.085407.

Seldin, M.F., Tian, C., Shigeta, R., Scherbarth, H.R., Silva, G., Belmont, J.W., Kittles, R., Gamron, S., Allevi, A., Palatnik, S.A., Alvarellos, A., Paira, S., Caprarulo, C., Guillerón, C., Catoggio, L.J., Prigione, C., Berbotto, G.A., García, M.A., Perandones, C.E., Pons-Estel, B.A., Alarcon-Riquelme, M.E., 2007. Argentine population genetic structure: large variance in Amerindian contribution. Am. J. Phys. Anthropol. 132, 455–462.

Sholts, S.B., Wärmländer, S.K.T.S., 2012. Zygomaticomaxillary suture shape analyzed with digital morphometrics: reassessing patterns of variation in American Indian and European populations. Forensic Sci. Int. 217. http://dx.doi.org/10.1016/j.forsciint.2011.11.016. 234.e1–6.

Slice, D., Ross, A., 2009. 3D-ID: Geometric Morphometric Classification of Crania for Forensic Scientists.

Smith, R.J., Jungers, W.L., 1997. Body mass in comparative primatology. J. Hum. Evol. 32, 523–559. http://dx.doi.org/10.1006/jhev.1996.0122.

Spradley, M., 2016. Biological distance, migrants, and reference group selection in forensic anthropology. In. Pilloud, M., Hefner, J. (Eds.), Biological Distance Analysis: Forensic and Bioarchaeological Perspectives. Academic Press.

Spradley, M., Jantz, R., 2016. Ancestry estimation in forensic anthropology: geometric morphometric versus standard and nonstandard interlandmark distances. J. Forensic Sci. 61, 892–897. http://dx.doi.org/10.1111/1556-4029.13081.

Spradley, M., Jantz, R., 2011. Sex estimation in forensic anthropology: skull versus postcranial elements. J. Forensic Sci. 56, 289–296.

Spradley, M., Jantz, R., Robinson, A., Peccerelli, F., 2008. Demographic change and forensic identification: problems in metric identification of Hispanic skeletons. J. Forensic Sci. 53, 21–28.

Spradley, M.K., 2014. Toward estimating geographic origin of migrant remains along the United States–Mexico border. Ann. Anthropol. Pract. 38, 101–110. http://dx.doi.org/10.1111/napa.12045.

Spradley, M.K., 2013. Project Identification: Developing Accurate Identification Criteria for Hispanics (NIJ Award No. 2008-DN-BX-K464). National Institute of Justice.

Stinson, S., 1985. Sex differences in environmental sensitivity during growth and development. Am. J. Phys. Anthropol. 28, 123–147. http://dx.doi.org/10.1002/ajpa.1330280507.

Stull, K., 2013. An Osteometric Evaluation of Age and Sex Differences in the Long Bones of South African Children from the Western Cape (Dissertation). University of Pretoria, South Africa.

Stull, K., L'Abbe, E., Ousley, S., 2017. Subadult sex estimation from diaphyseal dimensions. Am. J. Phys. Anthropol. http://dx.doi.org/10.1002/ajpa.23185.

Tise, M., 2014. Craniometric Ancestry Proportions Among Groups Considered Hispanic: Genetic Biological Variation, Sex-Biased Asymmetry, and Forensic Applications. University of South Florida, Tampa, FL.

Valenzuela, C.Y., Rothhammer, F., Chakraborty, R., 1978. Sex dimorphism in adult stature in four Chilean populations. Ann. Hum. Biol. 5, 533–538.

Victora, C.G., Adair, L., Fall, C., Hallal, P.C., Martorell, R., Richter, L., Sachdev, H.S., Maternal and Child Undernutrition Study Group, 2008. Maternal and child undernutrition: consequences for adult health and human capital. Lancet Lond. Engl. 371, 340–357. http://dx.doi.org/10.1016/S0140-6736(07)61692-4.

Williams, F.L., Belcher, R.L., Armelagos, G.J., 2005. Forensic misclassification of Ancient Nubian crania: implications for assumptions about human variation. Curr. Anthropol. 46, 340–346. http://dx.doi.org/10.1086/428792.

Wilson, L., Cardoso, H., Humphrey, L., 2011. On the reliability of a geometric morphometric approach to sex determination: a blind test of six criteria of the juvenile ilium. Forensic Sci. Int. 206, 35–42.

Wilson, L.A., MacLeod, N., Humphrey, L.T., 2008. Morphometric criteria for sexing juvenile human skeletons using the ilium. J. Forensic Sci. 53, 269–278.

Wilson, L.A.B., Ives, R., Cardoso, H.F.V., Humphrey, L.T., 2015. Shape, size, and maturity trajectories of the human ilium. Am. J. Phys. Anthropol. 156, 19–34. http://dx.doi.org/10.1002/ajpa.22625.

Wright, S., 1943. Isolation by distance. Genetics 28, 114–138.

CHAPTER 4

Advances in Cranial Macromorphoscopic Trait and Dental Morphology Analysis for Ancestry Estimation

Marin A. Pilloud[1] | Christopher Maier[1] | G. Richard Scott[1] | Joseph T. Hefner[2]

[1]University of Nevada, Reno, NV, United States,
[2]Michigan State University, East Lansing, MI, United States

Chapter Outline

In forensic anthropology, recovery of the skull is often a critical component for an accurate estimation of ancestry. Cranial dimensions are an important part of this aspect of the biological profile as discussed in Chapter 2 (Spradley, this volume). The focus of this chapter is on the qualitative, or rather, categorical data that are associated with the estimation of ancestry. Forensic anthropologists are relatively familiar, and comfortable, with traits that have been taught in forensic anthropology courses as part of the so-called "trait list" (cf. Rhine, 1990). While this list served as an important first step in ancestry estimation, we focus on how this list evolved, became standardized, and has been subjected to statistical scrutiny. We also focus on a related, but less often used, component of the skull—the teeth. Dental morphology has been regularly used within biological anthropology to establish group affinity and population history; however, it has not been largely adopted within forensic anthropology (e.g., Burns, 1999; Byers, 2002; Christensen et al., 2014; Komar and Buikstra, 2008; Reichs, 1998).

In this chapter, we outline the data sets that are available for both cranial macromorphoscopic traits and dental morphology. We then discuss the current methods available in both areas for the forensic anthropologist, and we explore emerging areas of study. Finally, we conclude with a case study to illustrate the power of these data in the estimation of ancestry.

■ THE DATA

Cranial Macromorphoscopic Traits

Early on in the subfield of forensic anthropology, analysts relied heavily on morphological variation of the cranium to estimate ancestry. This early work was based largely on the contribution of Earnest Hooton, who had compiled and defined morphological data he thought accurately distinguished the various "races" of humans. Although not initially envisioned as a method for estimating group affinity, the work of Hooton resulted in a codified list of traits and their associations with particular "racial" categories that would come to be known as the "Harvard List" (Brues, 1990). That list was passed down, largely unchanged, through Hooton's academic lineage (Brues, 1990; Hefner, 2003). Eventually this list was formalized through the work of Rhine (1990), who outlined various morphological characters as being either associated with "American Caucasoid," "Southwestern Mongoloid," or "American black."

The so-called "trait list" method, represented predominantly by the work of Hooton and Rhine, is inherently descriptive, potentially subjective, and in its current form, lacks a formal method for application. The analyst must rely on experience and a preponderance of the evidence to make an estimation of ancestry. While there are drawbacks to the use of the "trait list," a recent study by Hughes et al. (2011) demonstrated the utility of these traits in the estimation of ancestry. There is little debate over the fact that cranial morphological variation exists and much of this variation is geographically patterned; however, methods in forensic anthropology need standardization, validation, and associated error rates.

As forensic anthropologists move toward a more scientifically rigorous study of ancestry estimation, efforts have been made to standardize the collection of morphological data. Through this work, the cranial morphological traits of interest to forensic anthropologists are now defined as macromorphoscopic traits, which are quasicontinuous variables of the cranium that may reflect soft tissue differences in life. Essentially, these are traits that every individual has, which show variation in expression. This definition is in contrast to nonmetric traits of the cranium, which an individual may or may not have (see Pink et al., 2016 for a detailed description of these traits).

Many macromorphoscopic traits are presented in Hefner (2009) with trait definitions and character states, as well as illustrations. This work helped standardize data collection and provided frequencies of expression for various ancestral groups. Expanding on this work, the software package, *Osteoware*, developed by the Smithsonian Institution Repatriation Laboratory describes and defines 16 macromorphoscopic traits, including the 11 in Hefner (2009). These cranial macromorphoscopic traits are not outlined here; instead, the reader is encouraged to consult these sources for trait descriptions and character state definitions.

Cranial macromorphoscopic traits are recorded on ordinal and binary scales. In the case of ordinal data, scores can be dichotomized such that all data are treated as present or absent. However, this data conversion can pose two potential issues. First, dichotomized data contain inherently less information than nondichotomized data. The full range of expression better represents the individual's place in the global distribution of that trait, which is lost when data are dichotomized. Second, there are no standard procedures for dichotomizing cranial macromorphoscopic data; therefore, data from different researchers may be difficult to compare. In the one published instance of dichotomization (see the description of OSSA later), data are dichotomized based on the relative frequencies of traits between two groups; there is no suggestion for extending that method to include more groups (Hefner and Ousley, 2014).

A final consideration with respect to cranial macromorphoscopic data is that the inheritance of these traits is not well understood. Research has indicated a relationship between some cranial macromorphoscopic traits and environmental variables (e.g., Roseman and Weaver, 2004). While the general consensus is that the environment plays a critical role in the expression of cranial nonmetric traits (e.g., Berry, 1975; Berry and Berry, 1967), the relative effects of environment and genetics on the inheritance of cranial macromorphoscopic traits remain to be thoroughly studied. However, a recent study by Adhikari et al. (2016) found a significant association between variation in midfacial morphology and four genomic regions contained in single-nucleotide polymorphisms (SNPs). These five SNPs (EDAR, DCHS2, RUNX2, GLI3, and PAX1), which seem to govern the expression of ordinal-based nasal morphologies, also bear direct correlations to the expression of macromorphoscopic traits.

Dental Morphology

Forensic anthropologists are most familiar with the six dental morphological traits that Rhine (1990) popularized as part of his seminal publication on "Non-metric skull racing." These traits include shovel-shaped incisors, enamel extensions, incisor rotation, and buccal pits (associated with "Southwestern Mongoloid"); Carabelli's cusp/trait (associated with "American Caucasoid"); and molar crenulations (associated with "American blacks").

With the exception of molar crenulations, these traits were standardized the following year (Turner et al., 1991) in what would become known as the Arizona State University Dental Anthropology System (ASUDAS). The ASUDAS provides trait descriptions of 36 dental morphological variants and 3 nondental oral variables (mandibular and palatine torus, rocker jaw). A set of plaques was developed and distributed worldwide to aid in data collection. These dental traits had been previously described in numerous publications (e.g., Dahlberg, 1951; Hrdlička, 1920, 1921; Owen, 1845; Thompson, 1903) and earlier attempts had even been made at standardization (e.g., Dahlberg, 1956). However, the ASUDAS is currently the method most commonly employed. Again, we will not devote this chapter to describing these traits, as these descriptions and scoring methods can be readily obtained in various sources (e.g., Edgar, 2017; Scott and Irish, 2017; Scott et al., 2015; Scott and Pilloud, 2017; Scott and Turner, 1997; Turner et al., 1991; Van Beek, 1983). Additionally, as with macromorphoscopic data, these traits are outlined in *Osteoware* that uses a subset of traits as defined in Buikstra and Ubelaker (1994).

An advantage to dental morphological data is that there is a large body of research outlining the heritability of these traits (e.g., Harris, 1977; Hughes et al., 2016; Scott, 1973; Townsend et al., 2009). Within this work high heritability rates have been documented for many of these morphological traits, although there is disagreement in the exact levels of inheritance (e.g., Aoyagi, 1967; Biggerstaff, 1973; Scott and Potter, 1984; Škrinjarić et al., 1985). More recently, studies have found an association with the ectodysplasin A receptor gene (EDAR) and shovel-shaped incisors (Kimura et al., 2009), as well as tooth size and the presence of the hypoconulid on the second lower molar (Park et al., 2012).

Much like cranial macromorphoscopic traits, dental morphological traits are scored on a rank scale, such that a trait can be scored anywhere between zero and seven (depending on the trait in question). Therefore, each trait can exhibit a large range of expression, which is often dichotomized into present or absent (0 or 1). This dichotomization is based on predefined "breakpoints," which are thought to represent easily recognizable points on the scale. While Scott and Turner (1997) define breakpoints and focal teeth for the analysis of dental morphological variation in populations, these standards are not universally employed. It is therefore critical to define breakpoints in any study and pay close attention to these definitions when employing a published method. As an example, Rhine (1990) does not discuss in his work at which point incisor shoveling would be considered present. Scott and Turner (1997) define a score of three or higher as present; therefore, in applying Rhine's "trait list," the analyst is not provided with guidance on how to interpret lower-ranked expressions of incisor shoveling. Additionally, one must also pay close attention to the exact tooth under study. For example, is the presence of shoveling included for all maxillary and mandibular incisors and canines, or is the trait considered present if it is only on the central maxillary incisors? Such distinctions make a difference in the application of methods to estimate ancestry.

It is also important to consider asymmetry in the presence of dental morphological traits. While not incredibly common, antimeres can show differences in trait expression. Typically, these are dealt with as defined by the individual count method, such that only one expression of the trait is included in analyses, and this is the side with the higher expression (as defined by the ASUDAS). The assumption is that the higher expression best characterizes the individual's genetic potential for the trait (Scott, 1977). Methods employing dental morphology should expressly state how data were collected and these same protocols should be followed in the application of the method.

■ CURRENT METHODS IN FORENSIC ANTHROPOLOGY

Cranial Macromorphoscopic Traits

Methods for the analysis of cranial macromorphoscopic data are limited, especially under the legal standards outlined in the *Daubert* ruling (Daubert v. Merrell Dow Pharmaceuticals, 1993). The "trait list" approach (e.g., Rhine, 1990), and even trait frequency distributions (e.g., Hefner, 2009), may inform the estimation of ancestry, but the observation of these traits does not qualify as an analytical method that meets strict legal standards of evidence. Therefore, methods are being (and need to be) developed for the analysis of macromorphoscopic data in a statistical framework.

One current option is the optimized summed scored attributes (OSSA) method developed by Hefner and Ousley (2014). The OSSA method relies on the dichotomization of six key macromorphoscopic traits for the estimation of group membership between American white and American black. The traits included in this method are anterior nasal spine, nasal aperture width, inferior nasal aperture, nasal bone contour, interorbital breadth, and postbregmatic depression. Traits are scored on a ranked scale as defined in Hefner (2009) and are then dichotomized. For example, in comparing American black and American white individuals, values for a trait more common in black individuals are converted to "0" and those more common in white individuals are coded as "1." Once all traits are dichotomized, scores are summed and compared to the expected distributions for the reference populations. This method has been used to effectively estimate ancestry in 86% of cases (Hefner and Ousley, 2014). A spreadsheet to assist in the use of OSSA is made available by Stephen Ousley at the website http://math.mercyhurst.edu/~sousley/Software/. However, as this method has only been developed to compare American black and American white individuals, OSSA may have limited applications and should be one of the multiple methods employed in ancestry estimation.

Dental Morphology

As with cranial macromorphoscopic traits, there are various dental morphological traits that are commonly associated with ancestral groups, and a "trait list" approach can be employed. Such an approach could include observations of the six traits outlined by Rhine (1990). Additionally, Scott and Turner (1997) provide a list of 12 traits that have proved effective at identifying geographic patterning. These traits include shoveling, winging, Carabelli's trait, cusp 5, enamel extensions, 2-rooted upper third premolars, odontomes, lower canine root number, 4-cusped lower molars, cusp 6, cusp 7, and 3-rooted lower molars (see their Table E.1, page 316 for group affiliations). However, these approaches do not employ the statistical rigor required in a court of law. Therefore, much like cranial macromorphoscopic traits, approaches are being developed in an attempt to meet these standards.

Edgar (2005) describes a method to distinguish between European Americans and African Americans based on five morphological traits on seven teeth. These traits are *tuberculum dentale* (upper canine), premolar cusp variation (both lower premolars), deflecting wrinkle (lower first molar), trigonid crest (lower first molar), cusp 5 (second and third lower molars), and cusp 7 (lower first molar). This method provides extensive tables that contain probabilities for various combinations of traits. While the method can incorporate missing data and multiple combinations of traits, the tables can be cumbersome to employ and, like OSSA, are only able to discriminate between two groups.

Edgar (2013) later created a method that provides a series of discriminant function equations to estimate ancestry of an unknown individual as European American, African American, or Hispanic. This method employs 13 traits from 20 teeth. These traits include double shoveling (upper first and second incisors and lower first and second incisors), shoveling (upper second incisor and canine), distal accessory ridge (upper and lower canine), *tuberculum dentale* (upper canine), hypocone (upper first molar), metacone (upper first and second molar), metaconule (upper second molar), premolar cusp variation (lower third premolar), anterior fovea (lower first molar), deflecting wrinkle (lower first molar), protostylid (lower first molar), cusp 7 (lower first and second molar), and cusp 5 (lower second molar). These equations are easy to use and provide error rates. One drawback to this method is that very specific teeth are needed for an analysis to proceed. An upper first molar with observable morphology is required to use the first set of discriminant function equations that distinguishes between African American/European Americans and South Florida/New Mexico Hispanics. To use the second equation to distinguish between African- and European Americans, the lower canine and the third premolar are needed. If any of these teeth are missing, the method cannot be used.

Recently, Irish (2015) presented a method for estimating ancestry based on 10 ASUDAS traits. These traits are shoveling (upper first *or* second incisor), double shoveling (upper first *or* second incisor), interruption groove (upper first *or* second incisor), Carabelli's cusp (upper first *or* second molar), enamel extension (upper first molar *or* upper second molar, lower first molar, lower second molar), groove pattern (lower second molar), cusp number (lower first molar), cusp number (lower second molar), deflecting wrinkle (lower first *or* second molar), and cusp 7 (lower first *or* second molar). In his method, traits are recorded according to defined breakpoints and are compared to frequencies for five population groups: East Asian, American Indian, white, Polynesian, and black. The frequencies for each trait and each population are listed; then they are summed. Ancestry is assigned for the unknown individual based on the reference sample with the highest summed score. While this method is intuitive, flexible, and employs a large reference sample with many groups, it does not contain known error rates, which is an important component of forensic anthropological work.

■ STATISTICAL ANALYSES

Traditionally, the analysis of morphology in forensic anthropology depended on a simple majority of traits indicative of a specific ancestry as the basis for estimation. These categorical data (i.e., cranial macromorphoscopic traits and dental morphology) were (and in some cases still are) rarely subjected to statistical analyses. While metric data were recognized early on as a means to identify group affiliation (e.g., Giles and Elliot, 1962), categorical data were much harder to incorporate into statistical analyses, which likely accounts for the lack of methods incorporating these data. However, statistical methods have greatly advanced in the last several decades as has the computing power to process these data.

While we have described various statistical *methods* for the estimation of ancestry using categorical data, we wish to bring attention to emerging analyses within the field as avenues for future exploration. This discussion includes an outline of various nonparametric machine learning methods that are appropriate for categorical data (support vector machines and decision trees). There is also a discussion of the application of canonical analysis of principal coordinates. And, finally we provide a review of the current development of statistical packages to aid in the estimation of ancestry using these data.

Appropriate Reference Samples

Before embarking on a discussion of statistical techniques, it is worth briefly examining the data that are used within these analyses. One important consideration for any classificatory statistic is the use of an appropriate reference sample. The reduced accuracy of craniometric classification when applied to an inappropriate reference sample (Birkby, 1966; Elliott and Collard, 2009; Feldesman, 2002; İşcan and Steyn, 1999; Ramsthaler et al., 2007; Snow et al., 1979; Williams and Rogers, 2006) has been levied as a criticism against the concept of ancestry estimation in general. Therefore, it is especially important in the analysis of cranial macromorphoscopic and dental morphological data that sufficient data from appropriate reference samples are compiled before the estimation of ancestry in an unknown forensic case proceeds.

Traits used in the estimation of ancestry are the products of a population's unique history. The patterns generated by the specific microevolutionary forces to which a population is subject should be accounted for in a reference sample to ensure the most accurate ancestry estimate. While secular change has been well documented in anthropometric studies (e.g., Jantz and Jantz, 1999; Jantz and Meadows Jantz, 2000; Meadows and Jantz, 1995), the effects of more recent time are less understood for cranial macromorphoscopic traits and dental morphology. However, we still argue that for forensic anthropological work, a modern sample representative of the local population is critical in the proper application of classificatory statistical analyses.

Much of the study on dental morphology has focused on archaeological samples, which may not be relevant for forensic anthropological casework. Currently, there is no large reference database on cranial macromorphoscopic traits (although see later for the development of such a reference sample). There is great potential for the development of robust methods once these data are collected and many of the statistical analyses described later could be employed to develop new methods.

Support Vector Machines

Support vector machines are perhaps the most similar of the machine learning methods to the discriminant analyses traditionally employed with metric analysis. Individuals in a training set are arranged in n-dimensional space, and a function, linear or otherwise, that best separates the data by levels of the categorical variable is calculated (Cortes and Vapnik, 1995; Hefner and Ousley, 2014). Trait values for unknown individuals are then assessed relative to this function and classified accordingly (Cortes and Vapnik, 1995). Support vector machines are designed for pairwise comparisons, but recent work has demonstrated that they can effectively estimate ancestry between more than two groups (Hefner et al., 2015). Although support vector machines produce accurate estimates (Hefner and Ousley, 2014; Hefner et al., 2015), they are a nonprobabilistic method, meaning the researcher cannot generate a probability that any given classification is correct (Cortes and Vapnik, 1995).

Decision Trees

Decision trees classify an unknown individual by making "decisions" based on the individual's trait values. Each tree comprises nodes that correspond to traits. An individual passes through those nodes in different directions based on the sectioning point at the node and the value of the trait expressed by the individual (Breiman et al., 1984; Feldesman, 2002; Quinlan, 1987). When an unknown individual reaches a terminal node, it is classified and a value for the accuracy of this classification is generated (Breiman et al., 1984; Feldesman, 2002). Decision trees are robust to nonnormal data and missing values, but can be vulnerable to overfitting (Deng et al., 2011). The random forest model (RFM) is an expansion of the decision tree that helps combat the dangers of overfitting (Breiman, 2001; Breiman and Cutler, 2004; Liaw and Wiener, 2002). In a RFM, a large forest of decision trees is "grown," each with a random arrangement of predictor variables (Breiman, 2001; Breiman and Cutler, 2004). An unknown individual passes through the forest, being classified by each distinctive tree, and the ultimate classification of the individual depends on the majority "vote" of the forest (Breiman, 2001; Breiman and Cutler, 2004). These methods are particularly useful in a forensic context because they are accurate (Hefner and Ousley, 2014; Hefner et al., 2014) and deal well with nonnormally distributed data containing missing values. In a direct comparison to discriminant analyses, RFM was able to use 100% of the reference sample to build a random forest model, whereas discriminant analysis could only use 53% of the data when building the model (Hefner et al., 2014).

Canonical Analysis of Principal Coordinates

Legendre and Legendre (1998) proposed a canonical discriminant analysis performed on the transformed values of the principal coordinates. In short, a canonical analysis of the principal coordinates (CAP) applies a principal coordinate analysis using any one of several distance measures (Anderson and Willis, 2003), transforming categorical variables into continuous, normally distributed variables. In that way, the CAP method is highly effective for dealing with morphoscopic data and enables classification and visualization of the groups in a manner approximating craniometric analyses.

Development of Statistical Packages to Aid in Estimation

rASUDAS

A graphical user interface called rASUDAS has been developed by David Navega and João Coehlo at the University of Coimbra, which allows researchers to apply appropriate statistical methods to the analysis of dental morphology in the estimation of ancestry. The package uses the free program R (R Core Team, 2013) and is based on traits defined in the ASUDAS (Turner et al., 1991). The rASUDAS compares an unknown individual to a large data set of trait frequencies comprising samples from seven major genogeographic groups around the world (East Asia, Southeast Asia and Polynesia, Australo-Melanesia and Micronesia, American Arctic and Northeast Siberia, sub-Saharan Africa, Western Eurasia). The application uses a naïve Bayesian algorithm to estimate group affiliation and provides an associated posterior probability. Still under development, rASUDAS shows promise, returning accurate classifications in 57.3%–91.8% of cases involving two to seven group comparisons. When comparisons are limited to the ancestral groups most commonly used in a forensic context in the United States (i.e., European, Asian, African), accuracy improves to 81%–92% (Scott et al., 2016). The goal is to make rASUDAS freely available to the public and to grow its reference sample to include more modern individuals, making it more applicable to a medicolegal setting. However, there is potential to also include an archaeological reference data set (similar to the Howells data set in ForDisc), which could prove useful in the recovery and analysis of archaeological specimens.

Macromorphoscopic Databank

In an effort to expand the comparable database of cranial macromorphoscopic data, Hefner has recently developed the Macromorphoscopic databank (MaMD) under a grant from the National Institute of Justice (NIJ). Currently, this databank comprises over 2600 individuals from populations around the world. The outcome of the research centered on the MaMD is twofold. A data collection program, Macromorphoscopic Traits 1.6 (MMS 1.6), is currently available in beta form from one of the authors (JTH). This program improves on the user interface in *Osteoware* and is designed specifically for the collection of 17 macromorphoscopic traits (the additional trait is palate shape). The MMS utilizes a relational database for data storage and management. The second aspect of the MaMD project is an analytical program similar in scope and function to ForDisc (Jantz and Ousley, 2005) but utilizes appropriate classification statistics like those mentioned earlier *and* reference data collected from around the world and housed in the MaMD. The analytical program and database will be available for the public at the end of the NIJ-funded project in 2017/2018.

■ CASE STUDY

To illustrate the classificatory power of cranial macromorphoscopic traits and dental morphology in the estimation of ancestry, we present a case study. An individual self-identified as "white" was selected from the donated collection at Michigan State University, Forensic Anthropology Laboratory (Figs. 4.1–4.4). The various methods outlined earlier

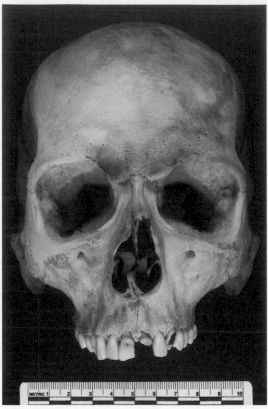

Figure 4.1 Anterior view of case study cranium.

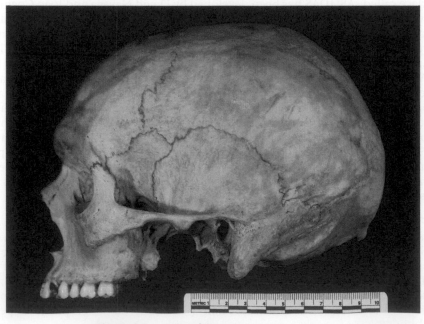

Figure 4.2 Left lateral view of case study cranium.

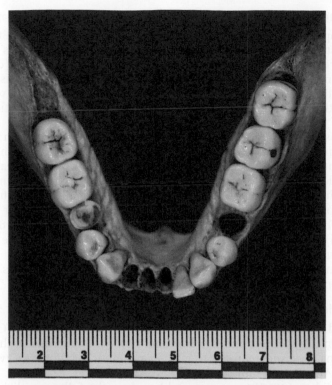

Figure 4.3 Occlusal view of case study mandible.

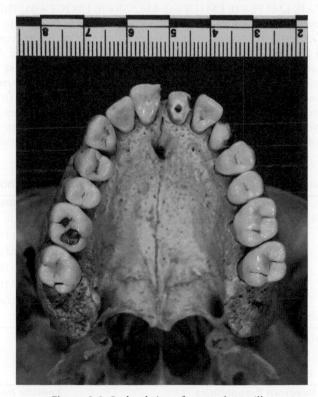

Figure 4.4 Occlusal view of case study maxilla.

were employed to estimate ancestry. These include OSSA and CAP for cranial macromorphoscopic traits. And, for dental morphology the two methods developed by Edgar (2005, 2013), the method of Irish (2015), and the Beta version of rASUDAS (Scott et al., 2016) were employed.

Two of the authors conducted the analyses (MAP and JTH). The cranial macromorphoscopic data were recorded and analyzed by JTH in the Forensic Anthropology Laboratory at Michigan State University. The dental morphological data were recorded and analyzed by MAP using high-quality digital photographs. Both JTH and MAP conducted their analyses in the blind and are independent of each other.

Results: Cranial Macromorphoscopic Traits

Using the macromorphoscopic trait scores (ANS = 2; INA = 1; IOB = 2; NAW = 2; NBC = 4; NO = 0; and PBD = 0), the individual in this case study is most similar to the sample of American whites (note: this sample includes 19th and 20th century Americans of European ancestry). In a five-group canonical (discriminant) analysis of the principal coordinates (CAP method—Hefner and Ousley, 2014) using seven stepwise-selected variables from all 17 variables of the midface, the cranium for this case study classified into American white (Table 4.1). The model correctly classified 51.5% of the individuals in the reference samples (random allocation is 20%) using these same variables. Table 4.1 provides the classification table and supporting statistics.

The D^2 (=9.9) and the posterior probability (=0.383) suggest a moderate strength for the classification. At this time, the typicality probabilities are provided, but because of the nature of macromorphoscopic traits (categorical, nonnormal data distribution) and the calculation of typicality values, these measures should not be used to assess how similar this individual is to any one of the reference samples. When all samples are removed except the American black, American white, and Hispanic populations, this individual still classifies closest to American white.

The OSSA method was also used to assess this cranium. The summed OSSA score for this case study is "5," indicating the ancestry is "white." The associated classification statistics include sensitivity = 85.59; specificity = 85.34; correct classification rate (model) = 86.07; and negative predictive value (NPV) = 81.82. The NPV indicates the likelihood that OSSA is correct when classifying a cranium as "white."

The totality of the macromorphoscopic analysis suggests that the individual in this case study is most similar in trait manifestation to *American whites*.

Results: Dental Morphology

The following dichotomized trait scores (UCTD = 1; LaPCV = 0; LM1DW = 0; LM1TC = 0; LM2C5 = 0; LM3C5 = 0; LM1C7 = 0) were employed in the method outlined by Edgar (2005). The results of the analyses indicated that the majority of trait combinations were most similar to European Americans; however, two sets of trait combinations were most similar to African Americans (Table 4.2).

The method described in Edgar (2013) was employed based on the following dichotomized scores (UI1DS = 0; UI2SS = 0; UI2DS = 0; UCSS = 0; UCTD = 1; UM1HC = 0; UM1MC = 0; UM2MC = 0; UM2C5 = 0; LI2SS = 0; LCDR = 0; LP3LC = 0; LM1AF = 0; LM1DW = 0; LM1PS = 0; LM1C7 = 0; LM2C5 = 0; LM2C7 = 0). This analysis returned two different results depending on the equations employed (Table 4.3). Equations 6–9 indicate the individual is most similar to either African or European Americans. According to this method, if the result from the first set of equations is "Hispanic," there is no need to perform additional analyses. However, if the result is African American or European American, a second set of equations can be employed to differentiate between these two groups. The results from these second set of equations indicated the individual is most similar to European Americans (Table 4.4).

This dentition was also evaluated using the method by Irish (2015). The results from this analysis indicated the individual is most similar to the white sample (Table 4.5 lists the trait scores and results). Finally, dental data were analyzed in the rASUDAS beta version based on 13 observable traits (winging = absent; shoveling UI1 = 0 and 1; interruption groove = 0; hypocone = 4+; Carabelli's trait UM1 = 0 and 1; cusp 5 UM1 = 0; enamel extensions UM1 = 0 and

Table 4.1 Results of Five-Group Classification Table for Case Study Using CAP Method

Group	Classified Into	Distance	Probabilities			
			Posterior	F	Chi	R
American white	X	9.9	0.383	0.213	0.196	0.296
Pacific Island		10.7	0.255	0.190	0.153	0.111
Hispanic		11.6	0.161	0.132	0.114	0.119
American black		11.7	0.155	0.130	0.112	0.148
Southeast Asia		14.1	0.046	0.061	0.049	0.021
Case study 1 is closest to American white using these seven macromorphoscopic traits.						

CAP, canonical analysis of the principal coordinates.

Table 4.2 Case Study Results Based on Edgar (2005)

	Bayesian Probabilities			Logistic Regression Probabilities		
	Total Comparisons	European American*	African American*	Total Comparisons	European American*	African American*
4-Trait	3	2	0	–	–	–
3-Trait	20	12	0	4	1	0
2-Trait	16	5	2	9	4	0
1-Trait	7	1	0	–	–	–

*Probability ≥ .85.

Table 4.3 Case Study Results Based on Edgar (2013) Using the Set of Discriminant Function Equations to Differentiate Between African American/European American and South Florida Hispanics/New Mexico Hispanics

African American (AA)/European American (EA) Versus South Florida Hispanics/New Mexico Hispanics	Result	Std Error	Result
Table 2, Equation 1	Unable to calculate	7.122	NA
Table 2, Equation 2	Unable to calculate	6.064	NA
Table 2, Equation 3	Unable to calculate	4.945	NA
Table 2, Equation 4	Unable to calculate	4.472	NA
Table 2, Equation 5	Unable to calculate	3.558	NA
Table 2, Equation 6	4.912	2.677	AA/EA
Table 2, Equation 7	4.291	1.876	AA/EA
Table 2, Equation 8	3.661	1.429	AA/EA
Table 2, Equation 9	2.686	0.794	AA/EA

Table 4.4 Case Study Results Based on Edgar (2013) Using the Set of Discriminant Function Equations to Differentiate Between African Americans and European Americans

African American Versus European American (EA)	Result	Std Error	Result
Table 3, Equation 1	Unable to calculate	9.564	NA
Table 3, Equation 2	Unable to calculate	8.386	NA
Table 3, Equation 3	Unable to calculate	7.263	NA
Table 3, Equation 4	Unable to calculate	6.272	NA
Table 3, Equation 5	Unable to calculate	4.676	NA
Table 3, Equation 6	Unable to calculate	4.015	NA
Table 3, Equation 7	Unable to calculate	3.121	NA
Table 3, Equation 8	−3.188	2.506	EA
Table 3, Equation 9	−3.81	1.755	EA

1; groove pattern = X and +; 4-cusped LM2 = 4; cusp 6 LM1 = 0; cusp 7 LM1 = 0; protostylid LM1 = 0; deflecting wrinkle = 0–2). In a seven-group analysis, this individual classified most like Western Eurasians (probability = 0.7888).

Based on the totality of the dental morphological data, this individual is most similar to individuals of European ancestry (*American white*).

Results of Case Study

Both the cranial macromorphoscopic traits and the dental morphology indicated an ancestry of American white/European for this individual. While the method outlined in Edgar (2005) indicated African American in a couple trait combinations, the majority of the statistical results indicated an individual of European ancestry. Such findings are not uncommon in forensic anthropology, as we would not expect one individual to perfectly encapsulate a set of morphological traits consistent with a single ancestral group. These results not only highlight the strength of morphological data in the estimation of ancestry but also the need to employ multiple methods to gain a complete picture of the present biological variation.

■ CONCLUSIONS

The estimation of ancestry is often considered one of the most difficult components of the biological profile. As humans are not immune to the forces of evolution, populations will continue to change in ways that are unpredictable. It is therefore critical that forensic anthropologists engage in research on human variation in modern populations. Such research should include metric data of the skull and postcranium, as has been seen broadly in the literature; however, data on morphological variation of the cranium and teeth should not be ignored. These categorical data can now be subject to rigorous statistical analysis and should move beyond the realm of experience-based methods. There is ample room for additional data collection and the development of new and innovative methods for use within forensic anthropology on morphological data. We also encourage the development of new standardizations (e.g., Maier, 2016) and validation studies (e.g., Klales and Kenyhercz, 2015). All of this work is essential to a rich understanding of human variation that can be used in a medicolegal setting.

Table 4.5 Case Study Results Based on Irish (2015)

Trait	Tooth	Score +	Unknown Raw Score	Unknown New Score	East Asian			American Indian			White			Polynesian			Black		
					Score	Present	Absent	Score	Present	Absent	Score	Present	Absent	Score	Present	Absent	Score	Present	Absent
Shovel	UI1 or UI2	4–7	0	0	28	72	28	8.1	91.9	8.1	97.4	2.6	97.4	79.3	20.7	79.3	94.7	5.3	94.7
Double shovel	UI1 or UI2	2–6	0	0	71.2	28.8	71.2	29.5	70.5	29.5	95.8	4.2	95.8	95.5	4.5	95.5	98.9	1.1	98.9
Interruption groove	UI2 or UI1	1+	0	0	57	43	57	49	51	49	61.7	38.3	61.7	64.7	35.3	64.7	86.6	13.4	86.6
Carabelli's cusp	UM1 or UM2	4–7	0	0	83.9	16.1	83.9	94.4	5.6	94.4	76	24	76	78.3	21.7	78.3	83.6	16.4	83.6
Enamel extension	UM1 or UM2	2–3	0	0	46.8	53.2	46.8	56.3	43.7	56.3	96.8	3.2	96.8	79.9	20.1	79.9	99.7	0.3	99.7
Groove pattern	LM2	Y	X	0	92.4	7.6	92.4	90.2	9.8	90.2	76.2	23.8	76.2	81.2	18.8	81.2	47.6	52.4	47.6
Cusp number	LM1	6+	4	0	64.1	35.9	64.1	44.9	55.1	44.9	88.5	11.5	88.5	46.5	53.5	46.5	83.4	16.6	83.4
Cusp number	LM2	4	4	1	20.8	20.8	79.2	8.6	8.6	91.4	77	77	23	33.2	33.2	66.8	24.1	24.1	75.9
Deflecting wrinkle	LM1 or LM2	3	0	0	84.3	15.7	84.3	61.9	38.1	61.9	91.3	8.7	91.3	86	14	86	97.7	2.3	97.7
Cusp 7	LM1 or LM2	1–7	0	0	92.1	7.9	92.1	91.5	8.5	91.5	95.3	4.7	95.3	92.9	7.1	92.9	61.5	38.5	61.5
Totals					641			534			856			738			778		

Acknowledgments

The authors thank the editors of this book, Krista Latham, Eric Bartelink, and Michael Finnegan, for inviting them to participate. This project was supported in part by Award No. 2015-DN-BX-K012 awarded by the National Institute of Justice, Office of Justice Programs, U.S. Department of Justice (JTH). The opinions, findings, and conclusions or recommendations expressed in this publication are those of the authors and do not necessarily reflect those of the Department of Justice.

References

Adhikari, K., Fuentes-Guajardo, M., Quinto-Sanchez, M., Mendoza-Revilla, J., Camilo Chacon-Duque, J., Acuna-Alonzo, V., Jaramillo, C., Arias, W., Lozano, R.B., Perez, G.M., Gomez-Valdes, J., Villamil-Ramirez, H., Hunemeier, T., Ramallo, V., Silva de Cerqueira, C.C., Hurtado, M., Villegas, V., Granja, V., Gallo, C., Poletti, G., Schuler-Faccini, L., Salzano, F.M., Bortolini, M.-C., Canizales-Quinteros, S., Cheeseman, M., Rosique, J., Bedoya, G., Rothhammer, F., Headon, D., Gonzalez-Jose, R., Balding, D., Ruiz-Linares, A., 2016. A genome-wide association scan implicates DCHS2, RUNX2, GLI3, PAX1 and EDAR in human facial variation. Nat. Commun. 7. http://dx.doi.org/10.1038/ncomms11616.

Anderson, M.J., Willis, T.J., 2003. Canonical analysis of principal coordinates: a useful method of constrained ordination for ecology. Ecology 84 (2), 511–525.

Aoyagi, F., 1967. Morpho-genetical studies on similarities in the teeth and dental occlusion of twins. Shikwa Gakuho 67, 606–624.

Berry, A., 1975. Factors affecting the incidence of non-metrical skeletal variants. J. Anat. 120 (Pt 3), 519–535.

Berry, R.J., Berry, A.C., 1967. Epigenetic variation in the human cranium. J. Anat. 101, 361–379.

Biggerstaff, R.H., 1973. Heritability of the Carabelli cusp in twins. J. Dent. Res. 52 (1), 40–44.

Birkby, W.H., 1966. An estimation of race and sex identification from the cranial measurements. Am. J. Phys. Anthropol. 42, 21–27.

Breiman, L., 2001. Random forests. Mach. Learn. 45 (1), 5–32.

Breiman, L., Cutler, A., 2004. Random Forests. Berkeley http://www.stat.berkeley.edu/~breiman/RandomForests/cc_home.htm[stat.berkeley.edu].

Breiman, L., Friedman, J., Stone, C.J., Olshen, R.A., 1984. Classification and Regression Trees. CRC Press, Boca Raton, FL.

Brues, A.M., 1990. The once and future diagnosis of race. In: Gill, G.W., Rhine, S. (Eds.), Skeletal Attribution of Race: Methods for Forensic Anthropology Maxwell Museum of Anthropology, Albuquerque, pp. 1–9.

Buikstra, J.E., Ubelaker, D.H. (Eds.), 1994. Standards for Data Collection from Human Skeletal Remains. Arkansas Archeological Survey Research Series No. 44, Fayetteville, Arkansas.

Burns, K.R., 1999. Forensic Anthropology Training Manual. Prentice-Hall, New Jersey.

Byers, S., 2002. Introduction to Forensic Anthropology: A Textbook. Allyn and Bacon, Boston, MA.

Christensen, A.M., Passalacqua, N.V., Bartelink, E.J., 2014. Forensic Anthropology: Current Methods and Practice. Elsevier, San Diego, CA.

Cortes, C., Vapnik, V., 1995. Support-vector networks. Mach. Learn. 20 (3), 273–297.

Dahlberg, A., 1951. The dentition of the American Indian. In: Laughlin, W.S. (Ed.), The Physical Anthropology of the American Indian. The Viking Fund, New York, pp. 138–176.

Dahlberg, A., 1956. Materials for the Establishment of Standards for Classification of Tooth Characteristics, Attributes, and Techniques in Morphological Studies of the Dentition. Zoller Laboratory of Dental Anthropology, University of Chicago, Chicago.

Daubert v. Merrell Dow Pharmaceuticals, I., 509 U.S. 579, 1993.

Deng, H., Runger, G., Tuv, E., 2011. Bias of importance measures for multi-valued attributes and solutions. Artif. Neural Netw. Mach. Learn. ICANN 2011, 293–300.

Edgar, H.J.H., 2005. Prediction of race using characteristics of dental morphology. J. Forensic Sci. 50 (2), 269–273.

Edgar, H.J.H., 2013. Estimation of ancestry using dental morphological characteristics. J. Forensic Sci. 58 (s1), S3–S8.

Edgar, H.J.H., 2017. Dental Morphology: An Illustrated Manual. Left Coast Press, Walnut Creek, CA (in press).

Elliott, M., Collard, M., 2009. FORDISC and the determination of ancestry from cranial measurements. Biol. Lett. 5 (6), 849–852.

Feldesman, M.R., 2002. Classification trees as an alternative to linear discriminant analysis. Am. J. Phys. Anthropol. 119 (3), 257–275.

Giles, E., Elliot, O., 1962. Race identification from cranial measurements. J. Forensic Sci. 7, 147–157.

Harris, E.F., 1977. Anthropologic and Genetic Aspects of the Dental Morphology of Solomon Islanders, Melanesia. Department of Anthropology. Arizona State University, Tempe, AZ.

Hefner, J.T., 2003. Assessing Nonmetric Cranial Traits Currently Used in the Forensic Determination of Ancestry. Department of Anthropology. University of Florida, Gainesville, FL.

Hefner, J.T., 2009. Cranial nonmetric variation and estimating ancestry. J. Forensic Sci. 54 (5), 985–995.

Hefner, J.T., Ousley, S.D., 2014. Statistical classification methods for estimating ancestry using morphoscopic traits. J. Forensic Sci. 59 (4), 883–890.

Hefner, J.T., Pilloud, M.A., Black, C.J., Anderson, B.E., 2015. Morphoscopic trait expression in "Hispanic" populations. J. Forensic Sci. 60 (5), 1135–1139.

Hefner, J.T., Spradley, M.K., Anderson, B.E., 2014. Ancestry assessment using random forest modeling. J. Forensic Sci. 59 (3), 583–598.

Hrdlička, A., 1920. Shovel shaped teeth. Am. J. Phys. Anthropol. 3, 429–465.

Hrdlička, A., 1921. Further studies of tooth morphology. Am. J. Phys. Anthropol. 4, 141–176.

Hughes, C.E., Juarez, C.A., Hughes, T.L., Galloway, A., Fowler, G., Chacon, S., 2011. A simulation for exploring the effects of the "trait list" method's subjectivity on consistency and accuracy of ancestry estimations. J. Forensic Sci. 56 (5), 1094–1106.

Hughes, T., Townsend, G., Bockmann, M., 2016. An overview of dental genetics. In: Irish, J.D., Scott, G.R. (Eds.), A Companion to Dental Anthropology. Wiley & Sons, Inc., Malden, MA, pp. 124–141.

Irish, J.D., 2015. Dental nonmetric variation around the world: using key traits in populations to estimate ancestry in individuals. In: Berg, G.E., Ta'ala, S.C. (Eds.), Biological Affinity in Forensic Identification of Human Skeletal Remains. CRC Press, Boca Raton, FL, pp. 165–190.

İşcan, Y.M., Steyn, M., 1999. Craniometric determination of population affinity in South Africans. Int. J. Leg. Med. 112 (2), 91–97.

Jantz, L.M., Jantz, R.L., 1999. Secular change in long bone length and proportion in the United States, 1800–1970. Am. J. Phys. Anthropol. 110 (1), 57–67.

Jantz, R., Ousley, S., 2005. FORDISC 3: Computerized Forensic Discriminant Functions. The University of Tennessee, Knoxville.

Jantz, R.L., Meadows Jantz, L., 2000. Secular change in craniofacial morphology. Am. J. Hum. Biol. 12 (3), 327–338.

Kimura, R., Yamaguchi, T., Takeda, Y., Kondo, O., Toma, T., Haneji, K., Hanihara, T., Matsukura, H., kawamura, S., Maki, K., Osawa, M., Ishida, H., Oota, H., 2009. A common variation in EDAR is a genetic determinant of shovel-shaped incisors. Am. J. Hum. Genet. 84 (4), 528–535.

Klales, A.R., Kenyhercz, M.W., 2015. Morphological assessment of ancestry using cranial macromorphoscopics. J. Forensic Sci. 60 (1), 13–20.

Komar, D., Buikstra, J.E., 2008. Forensic Anthropology: Contemporary Theory and Practice. Oxford University Press, Oxford.

Legendre, P., Legendre, L., 1998. Numerical Ecology, second ed. Elsevier, Amsterdam, The Netherlands.

Liaw, A., Wiener, M., 2002. Classification and regression by random forest. R. News 2, 18–22.

Maier, C., 2016. A Novel Method for Recording Palate Shape in the Estimation of Ancestry. American Academy of Forensic Sciences, Las Vegas, NV.

Meadows, L., Jantz, R.L., 1995. Allometric secular change in the long bones from the 1800s to the present. J. Forensic Sci. 40 (5), 762–767.

Owen, R., 1845. Odontography; or, a Treatise on the Comparative Anatomy of the Teeth, Their Physiological Relations, Mode of Development, and Microscopic Structure, in the Vertebrate Animals. Bailliere.

Park, J.-H., Yamaguchi, T., Watanabe, C., Kawaguchi, A., Haneji, K., Takeda, M., Kim, Y.-I., Tomoyasu, Y., Watanabe, M., Oota, H., Hanihara, T., Ishida, H., Maki, K., Park, S.-B., Kimura, R., 2012. Effects of an Asian-specific nonsynonymous EDAR variant on multiple dental traits. J. Hum. Genet. 57 (8), 508–514.

Pink, C.M., Maier, C., Pilloud, M.A., Hefner, J.T., 2016. Cranial nonmetric and morphoscopic data sets. In: Pilloud, M., Hefner, J.T. (Eds.), Biological Distance Analysis: Forensic and Bioarchaeological Perspectives. Academic Press, San Diego, CA, pp. 91–108.

Quinlan, J.R., 1987. Simplifying decision trees. Int. J. Man-Mach. Stud. 27, 221–234.

R Core Team, 2013. R: A Language and Environment for Statistical Computing. R Foundation for Statistical Computing, Vienna, Austria. ISBN:3-900051-07-0 http://www.R-project.org.

Ramsthaler, F., Kreutz, K., Verhoff, M.A., 2007. Accuracy of metric sex analysis of skeletal remains using FORDISC based on a recent skull collection. Int. J. Leg. Med. 121, 477–482.

Reichs, K.J. (Ed.), 1998. Forensic Osteology: Advances in the Identification of Human Remains. Charles C. Thomas Publisher, Ltd., Springfield, Illinois.

Rhine, S., 1990. Non-metric skull racing. In: Gill, G.W., Rhine, S. (Eds.), Skeletal Attribution of Race: Methods for Forensic Anthropology. Maxwell Museum Anthropological, Albuquerque, NM, pp. 9–20. Papers No. 4.

Roseman, C.C., Weaver, T.D., 2004. Multivariate apportionment of global human craniometric diversity. Am. J. Phys. Anthropol. 125 (3), 257–263.

Scott, G.R., 1973. Dental Morphology: A Genetic Study of American White Families and Variation in Living Southwest Indians. Department of Anthropology. Arizona State University, Tempe, AZ.

Scott, G.R., 1977. Classification, sex dimorphism, association, and population variation of the canine distal accessory ridge. Hum. Biol. 49 (3), 453–469.

Scott, G.R., Irish, J.D., 2017. Guidebook to Tooth Crown and Root Morphology: The Arizona State University Dental Anthropology System. Cambridge University Press, Cambridge (in press).

Scott, G.R., Maier, C., Heim, K., 2015. Identifying and recording key morphological (nonmetric) crown and root traits. In: Irish, J.D., Scott, G.R. (Eds.), A Companion to Dental Anthropology. John Wiley & Sons, Inc., Hoboken, NJ, pp. 245–264.

Scott, G.R., Navega, D., Coelho, J., Cunha, E., Irish, J.D., 2016. rASUDAS: a new method for estimating ancestry from tooth crown and root morphology. Am. J. Phys. Anthropol. 159 (S62), 285–286.

Scott, G.R., Pilloud, M.A., 2017. Dental morphology. In: Katzenberg, A., Saunders, S. (Eds.), Biological Anthropology of the Human Skeleton. Wiley-Liss, New York (in press).

Scott, G.R., Potter, R.H.Y., 1984. An analysis of tooth crown morphology in American White twins. Anthropol. Paris 22 (3), 223–231.

Scott, G.R., Turner, C.G., 1997. The Anthropology of Modern Human Teeth. Cambridge University Press, Cambridge.

Škrinjarić, I., Slaj, M., Lapter, V., Muretic, Z., 1985. Heritability of Carabelli's trait in twins. Coll. Antropol. 9 (2), 177–181.

Snow, C.C., Hartman, S., Giles, E., Young, F.A., 1979. Sex and race determination of crania by calipers and computer: a test of the Giles and Elliot discriminant functions in 52 forensic cases. J. Forensic Sci. 24 (2), 448–460.

Thompson, A., 1903. Ethnographic Odontology: The Inca Peruvians. [s. i; s. 1.]. J.

Townsend, G.C., Hughes, T., Luciano, M., Bockmann, M., Brook, A., 2009. Genetic and environmental influences on human dental variation: a critical evaluation of studies involving twins. Arch Oral Biol 54 (Suppl. 1), S45–S51.

Turner, C.G., Nichol, C.R., Scott, G.R., 1991. Scoring procedures for key morphological traits of the permanent dentition: the Arizona State University dental anthropology system. In: Kelley, M.A., Larsen, C.S. (Eds.), Advances in Dental Anthropology. Wiley-Liss, New York, pp. 13–31.

Van Beek, G.C., 1983. Dental Morphology: An Illustrated Guide. Wright, Bristol.

Williams, B.A., Rogers, T.L., 2006. Evaluating the accuracy and precision of cranial morphological traits for sex determination. J. Forensic Sci. 51 (4), 729–735.

CHAPTER 5

Evaluating Mixture Discriminant Analysis to Classify Human Mandibles With (hu)MANid, a Free, R-Based GUI

Michael W. Kenyhercz[1,2] | Gregory E. Berg[1]

[1]Defense POW/MIA Accounting Agency, Joint Base Pearl Harbor-Hickam, HI, United States
[2]University of Pretoria, Arcadia, South Africa

Chapter Outline

■ INTRODUCTION

Anthropologists have long studied the relationship between morphology and group membership (either self-identified or prescribed) to answer research questions or as part of developing a biological profile. Through the years, every imaginable skeletal element has been utilized to examine variation among groups with a variety of employed statistical methods, from the teeth (Irish, 1998; Irish and Hemphill, 2004; Lease and Sciulli, 2005; Lukacs, 1985; Lukacs and Hemphill, 1993; Turner II, 1990) to the cranium (Giles and Elliot, 1963; Howells, 1977, 1989; Jantz and Ousley, 2005; Ross et al., 2004, 2002), the mandible (Berg and Kenyhercz, 2017; Berg, 2008, 2014; Parr et al., 2015), and the postcranium (Dibennardo and Taylor, 1983; Holliday and Falsetti, 1999). While the type of data collected has become more complex—such as morphoscopic traits (Hefner, 2009; Hefner and Ousley, 2014) and geometric morphometrics (Slice and Ross, 2010; Stull et al., 2014)—the primary method used to classify the data, linear discriminant analysis (LDA), has become the field's most popular choice of statistic, with a few notable exceptions (Feldesman, 2002; Hefner et al., 2014; Hefner and Ousley, 2014).

LDA is a data reduction technique similar to principal components analysis (PCA) wherein a linear combination of variables are reduced into discriminant functions that best maximize group separation (Kachigan, 1991). A main distinction between LDA and PCA is that PCA explains the variation within the entire data set, whereas LDA maximizes the variation among groups. Sir Ronald Fisher (1936) first introduced discriminant function analysis using Anderson's *Iris* petal data set. Fisher proposed that a linear combination of variables, in this instance flower petals, could be used to discriminate among groups with a categorical expression (species designation). The discriminant function can be expressed as $L = b_1 x_1 + b_2 x_2 \ldots + b_n x_n$, where x is a particular variable and b is the discriminant function coefficient (unstandardized), or weight, that maximizes group separation. The function is used in tandem with a selected cut-off score that aims to maximize correct classification and minimize misclassification. The number of discriminant functions derived will be one less than the total number of groups in the analysis (k-1). In a discriminant function with more than two comparison groups, the discriminant functions can be plotted in an n dimensional space as a scatterplot; in a two-group case, it can be plotted as a histogram. A centroid, or multivariate average, is calculated for each group from the discriminant functions.

New Perspectives in Forensic Human Skeletal Identification. http://dx.doi.org/10.1016/B978-0-12-805429-1.00005-3

Albrecht (1980) offers an excellent geometric explanation of classification via discriminant function analysis. Essentially, after the discriminant function scores have been calculated, they can be plotted as a scatterplot and then the original axes are rotated until they are parallel to the major and minor axes of variation as observed in the plots (maximizing separation of groups). The next step is to standardize the axes by rescaling the transformed variables (based on the discriminant function coefficients). An individual is classified based on distance to the closest centroid. However, due to the transformations in LDA, Euclidean distance cannot be used; instead, distances are calculated using Mahalanobis generalized distance (D^2). It should be noted that individual data points will be forced into a group given the goal of this operation. This means that even if 10 soccer balls were measured with a group of 100 skulls, the soccer balls would be classified into the skull grouping that had the closest centroid, regardless of the fact that they are not skulls (cf. Fried et al., 2005).

Like any statistical test, LDA analysis carries several assumptions. Klecka (1980) outlines the following six assumptions for LDA: (1) each individual is derived from a mutually exclusive group; (2) the variables are measured at the interval or ratio level; (3) variables within the analysis are not highly correlated; (4) multicollinearity is avoided; (5) the variance covariance matrices among groups are equal; and (6) each group has a multivariate normal distribution.

For the purposes of anthropological classification, LDA is attractive for its ease of implementation, particularly because of widely available computer programs such as FORDISC 3.0 (Jantz and Ousley, 2005). However, it is likely rare that the implementation of LDA is appropriate for classifying humans in forensic contexts given the assumptions listed above. For example, Fisher had no issue meeting the assumption of mutually exclusive group membership (assumption 1) in his use of LDA because flowers can be of only one species. Humans, on the other hand, do not easily fit into prescribed categories, particularly the nebulously defined groups used within the medicolegal community, such as Hispanic, which may violate the assumption. Still, anthropologists are of the mind that the goal of correct classification outweighs the adherence to strict statistical assumptions (Berg, 2008; Hefner, 2009; Walker, 2008) and therefore have discounted this assumption as especially problematic.

Regardless of the above issues, researchers have shown that there is broad geographic patterning to craniometric data (Ousley et al., 2009; Relethford, 2004; Relethford and Harpending, 1994). These patterns tend to be grouped into categories such as Asian, Black, White, or Polynesian. But it is also fair to assume that each "metagroup" will be composed of several, frequently overlapping or admixed, subgroups. For example, when the newly "defined" group Hispanic is examined, it is apparent that the population's individuals are geographically distinct peoples joined together based on shared language. This label does not account for the amount of admixture between the various "metagroups" that have combined to form the regional group [i.e., ultimately, the amount of Native American (Asian), White, and Black genes that have merged to form any one given sector of the "Hispanic" population]. Given the growing complexity within anthropology of how populations are being defined, the types of data being collected, and the conclusions being generated, we feel that it is also time to look for new, updated, or novel approaches to data processing for human classification purposes. In this chapter, we explore the performance of both linear and mixture discriminant analysis (MDA) for group classification. These analytical tools are available in a new, freely distributed classification program called (hu)MANid, which utilizes morphoscopic and metric variables of the human mandible to classify cases.

Mixture Discriminant Analysis

MDA is a classification technique developed by Hastie and Tibshirani (Hastie and Tibshirani, 1996). Very basically, MDA does not assume that there is one multivariate normal (Gaussian) distribution for each group in an analysis, but instead that each group is composed of a mixture of several Gaussian distributions. As such, MDA does not rely on one group centroid, but instead it computes multiple centroids for each group, representing the mixture of the subgroups within each data set.

The MDA procedure makes use of the expectation maximization (EM) algorithm for computing maximum likelihood estimations. Following Hastie et al. (2011), the EM algorithm in MDA works in four steps. The first step is to make an initial guess of the parameters (initialization). For the current purposes, initialization is achieved using a k-means cluster where k is equal to the number of subgroups. A k-means cluster is performed on each group based on multiple random starts to identify the subgroup clusters. The parameters for the initial guess are taken from the k-means cluster analysis of each subgroup. Second, MDA computes the responsibilities, or weights, from each subgroup to the overall group membership (E-step). Third, MDA recalculates the means and covariances to determine the maximum likelihood estimates for each of the subgroups (M-step). Fourth, MDA iteratively alternates between E and M steps until each subgroup cluster maximizes correct assignment (convergence). Simply put, the clusters of subgroups are iteratively recalculated to maximize accurate group assignment and the posterior probabilities are calculated from a mixture of the final subgroup posterior probabilities. Given the use of multiple ground centroids from assumed subgroups, nonlinear decision boundaries can be calculated, thus allowing the analysis to model nonnormal multivariate distributions.

■ MATERIALS AND METHODS

The utility of MDA versus LDA was tested on a subset of mandibular metric and morphoscopic data using the program (hu)MANid (Berg and Kenyhercz, 2017). A brief introduction and tutorial to this program is appropriate here, followed by a detailed description of the analysis. Please note that full reference descriptions for the samples and variables can be found in Berg and Kenyhercz (2017) or in the documentation included within (hu)MANid.

The (hu)MANid Program

(hu)MANid is an R-based graphic user interface (GUI) designed to allow the user to quickly and easily process mandibular metric and morphoscopic data. The GUI provides the user with the ability to classify a mandible into one of the 26 different geographic or time-based reference populations or into one of the several, larger, global groups. Access to (hu)MANid is easy through the Internet, simply navigate to https://www.anthropologyapps.com and click on the (hu)MANid button or directly at https://anthropologyapps.shinyapps.io/humanid/.

When accessing the program, the initial page opens to the (hu)MANid Input tab, which also has four top-line tabs. This is the data input area for the user to begin an analysis (Fig. 5.1). The left side of the screen has drop-down menus for selecting the type of procedure to use, the number of groups (two or more than two), and an option for stepwise analysis. The upper right side of the screen has check buttons for reference population selections, either as individual populations or using composite groups. Below the buttons are the data input fields for each mandibular metric measurement and morphological variable. Several text boxes for inputting the analyst name and case number are also present. Finally, the evaluate button and results tabs follow.

Three other main tabs are present at the top of the opening page, and each is self-explanatory. The Definitions and Diagrams tab contains all of the pertinent information regarding mandibular measurements, morphology, and tools. This should be referred to frequently while undertaking an analysis to make sure the measurements and morphology are being scored/measured correctly. The Print Report tab shows a summary of pertinent results from the analysis (Fig. 5.2). This tab provides a way to easily see and print out the results from an analysis, and it includes headers such as the case number, analyst, and date of the analysis. This print setup is not changeable/customizable at this time, but it does include the typically used output such as the measurements entered into the analysis, classification matrices, the total correct classification of the model, group prediction, posterior and typicality probabilities, group means, and a table showing the difference of the group means from the new data. Finally, the classification plot is shown. The About tab holds three subtabs that include instructions on Using (hu)MANid, the Population Descriptions, and References section. Using (hu)MANid describes the use of the program. The Population Descriptions describes the reference populations, composite groups and provides lists for each of the group codes. The References subtab provides citations for a variety of mandibular studies, statistics, and R packages used in (hu)MANid.

To begin an analysis, the user must tell the program how many groups are to be compared under the drop-down menu labeled "Select Number of Groups to Compare"—two or greater than two. The function used for LDA within R

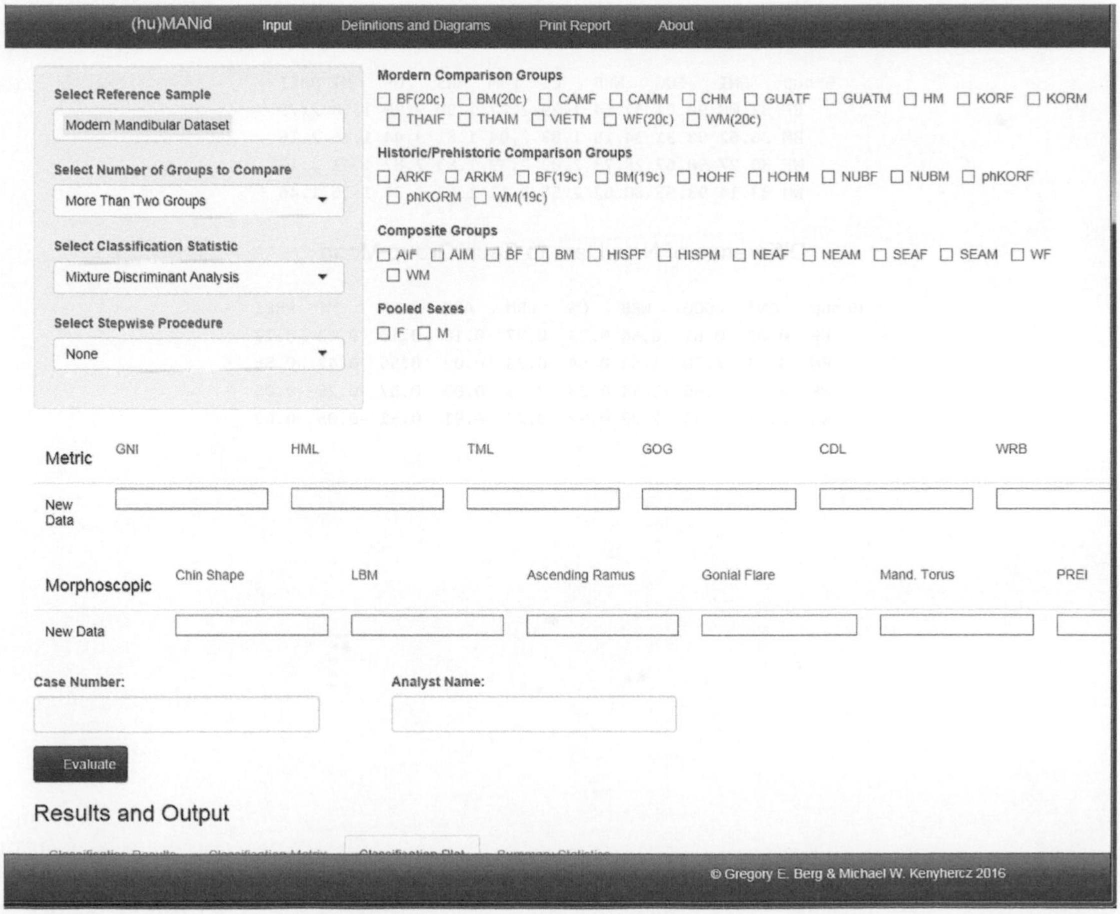

Figure 5.1 Screenshot of (hu)MANid default Input tab.

Sex and Ancestry Estimation Report 2016-11-29

Case Number:

`Test 1`

Analyst:

`A. Hrdlicka`

Measurements Used:

GNI	GOG	WRB	CS	LBM	ARS	GF	MT	PREI
33	90	32	1	2	2	3	2	3

Classification Matrix

	n	BF	BM	WF	WM
BF	78	39	10	19	10
BM	113	8	68	1	36
WF	145	10	2	92	41
WM	296	7	14	21	254

Classification Matrix %

	Predicted			
	BF	BM	WF	WM
BF	50.0	12.8	24.4	12.8
BM	7.1	60.2	0.9	31.9
WF	6.9	1.4	63.4	28.3
WM	2.4	4.7	7.1	85.8

453 out of 632 = 71.7 % Total Correct Classification Cross-validated

Predicted Group = BF

Posterior Probabilities

BF	WF	WM	BM
0.747	0.151	0.064	0.037

Chi-Square Typicalities

BF	WM	WF	BM
0.712	0.527	0.302	0.015

Variable Means by Group

Group	GNI	GOG	WRB	CS	LBM	ARS	GF	MT	PREI
BF	33.08	90.61	32.64	1.29	2.27	1.90	2.90	1.58	2.73
BM	36.62	98.31	34.18	1.83	2.04	1.81	3.44	1.16	2.15
WF	30.27	90.62	28.73	2.03	2.39	1.83	2.87	1.41	2.10
WM	33.14	98.55	30.82	2.55	2.11	1.82	3.38	1.36	1.46

Difference of New Data to Each Group Mean

Group	GNI	GOG	WRB	CS	LBM	ARS	GF	MT	PREI
BF	0.08	0.61	0.64	0.29	0.27	-0.10	-0.10	-0.42	-0.27
BM	3.54	7.70	1.54	0.54	-0.23	-0.09	0.55	-0.42	-0.58
WF	-6.36	-7.69	-5.44	0.20	0.35	0.03	-0.57	0.25	-0.05
WM	2.87	7.93	2.09	0.52	-0.27	-0.01	0.51	-0.05	0.63

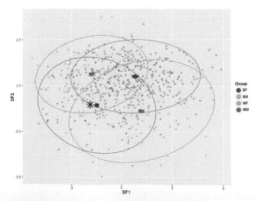

Figure 5.2 An example of the Print Results tab output.

uses different operational procedures for two-group and more than two-group (multigroup) analyses and, as a consequence, the user must select the appropriate option from the drop-down menu for the program to work properly. The statistical procedure is selected (LDA or MDA), and a stepwise procedure can be added at the user's discretion. Next, all reference groups or composite groups should be selected. Composite samples should be used sparingly if individual groups are also part of the analysis. After selecting these items, the analyst simply inputs the data for the variables that are present or are wanted in the analysis—not all data need to be entered as the program will automatically subset the reference data to include only the variables input by the user. The text blocks for case number and analyst are filled out, if so desired, then the analysis is run by pressing the "Evaluate" button.

The analysis results populate the five tabs below the Evaluate button, which include Classification Results, Classification Matrix, Classification Plot, Summary Statistics, and Model Details. The Classification Results tab shows the predicted group membership, posterior probabilities, chi-square typicalities, and the Euclidean distance from the new data's score(s) to each group centroid. The Classification Matrix tab supplies the classification matrix, the total correct classification, the classification matrix converted into percentages, and positive predictive value (PPV) and negative predictive value (NPV). The Classification Plot tab shows a scatterplot of the analysis for cases with more than two groups and a histogram for cases of only two groups. The classified case is shown as a black asterisk in the scatterplot and a black line in the histogram (Fig. 5.3). The Summary Statistics tab shows a wide variety of group and reference population statistics from the analysis. The Model Details tab provides the prior probabilities for each analysis group (these are set to equal), the group means, the discriminant function coefficients, and proportion of trace for each discriminant function. Of note, each and every analysis will overwrite to these tabs, so it is very important to save or print the analysis prior to moving on to a new one.

Mixture Discriminant Analysis and Linear Discriminant Analysis Comparison

We used (hu)MANid to examine MDA versus LDA model performance. Two sets of tests were performed—the first set evaluated the classification model and the second set of tests evaluated correct classification of five mandibles with known demographics. Classification model performance was examined on the basis of total correct classification, individual group correct classification, and PPV and NPV. All metric and morphoscopic variables, both separately and combined, were used to make the following comparisons from the composite groups: pooled females (F) and males (M); American Black females (BF) and males (BM); American White females (WF) and males (WM); and American Black male (BM), Southeast Asian male (SEAM), and American White male (WM). Correct classification was explored based on the correct classification of five mandibles that were not included in the reference sample. All, or nearly all, of the mandibular metric and morphoscopic variables were present for each of the five mandibles. The five mandibles were compared to all males from the composite reference samples using all available variables. For each mandible, correct group classification, posterior probabilities of the three most similar groups, and the total correct classification were recorded for both LDA and MDA analyses.

■ RESULTS

Model Comparison

The total correct and individual group classifications for the pooled female and male references are available in Table 5.1 and the predictive values are shown in Table 5.2. Across the board, MDA outperforms LDA in

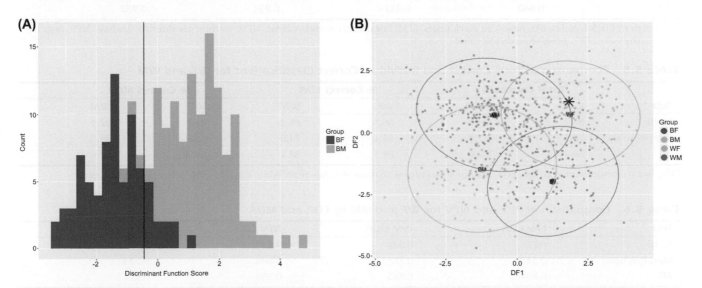

Figure 5.3 An example of the histogram output from two-group analysis (A) and scatterplot from more than two-group analysis (B).

total correct classification, but MDA shows an extremely high bias in correctly classifying males as opposed to females, approaching 50% for morphoscopic variables. While PPVs are higher in MDA across all categories, MDA has lower NPV than LDA, likely reflecting the male bias annotated above. The correct classification results for the BF and BM comparisons are shown in Table 5.3 and the predictive values in Table 5.4. In each comparison, for both classification and predictive values, MDA outperforms LDA. The results of the classifications for WF and WM are available in Table 5.5 and the predictive values in Table 5.6. The use of MDA improves total correct classifications in each comparison, but, as in the pooled sex comparison, with a male bias. Similar to the pooled sex analyses, the PPVs for MDA are greater than those from LDA for each comparison and the NPVs are greater in LDA than MDA in each instance. For the comparison of BM, SEAM, and WM, the correct classifications

Table 5.1   Comparison of Total Correct and Individual Correct Classifications for Males and Females (Pooled)

Test	Total Correct %		% Correct LDA		% Correct MDA	
	LDA	MDA	F	M	F	M
Metric	81.3	84.6	82.1	80.9	67.9	91.9
Morphoscopic	68.6	75.4	65.7	69.9	41.5	90.1
All	83.3	87.1	83.4	83.3	73.4	93.1

LDA, linear discriminant analysis; *MDA*, mixture discriminant analysis.

Table 5.2   Comparison of PPV and NPV for Male and Females (Pooled) by LDA and MDA

Test	PPV LDA	PPV MDA	NPV LDA	NPV MDA
Metric	0.657	0.786	0.913	0.868
Morphoscopic	0.496	0.648	0.828	0.779
All	0.698	0.821	0.922	0.891

LDA, linear discriminant analysis; *MDA*, mixture discriminant analysis; *NPV*, negative predictive value; *PPV*, positive predictive value.

Table 5.3   Comparison of Total Correct and Individual Correct Classifications for BF and BM

Test	Total Correct %		% Correct LDA		% Correct MDA	
	LDA	MDA	BF	BM	BF	BM
Metric	85.9	92.1	85.9	85.8	91.0	92.9
Morphoscopic	75.4	81.2	71.8	77.9	73.1	86.7
All	88.5	95.8	91.0	86.7	96.2	95.6

BF, American Black females; *BM*, American Black males; *LDA*, linear discriminant analysis; *MDA*, mixture discriminant analysis.

Table 5.4   Comparison of PPV and NPV for BF and BM by LDA and MDA

Test	PPV LDA	PPV MDA	NPV LDA	NPV MDA
Metric	0.864	0.899	0.927	0.938
Morphoscopic	0.704	0.792	0.809	0.824
All	0.880	0.927	0.954	0.982

BF, American Black females; *BM*, American Black males; *LDA*, linear discriminant analysis; *MDA*, mixture discriminant analysis; *NPV*, negative predictive value; *PPV*, positive predictive value.

Table 5.5   Comparison of Total Correct and Individual Correct Classifications for WF and WM

Test	Total Correct %		% Correct LDA		% Correct MDA	
	LDA	MDA	WF	WM	WF	WM
Metric	86.2	89.1	86.2	86.1	81.4	92.9
Morphoscopic	70.5	77.3	63.4	74.0	52.4	89.5
All	88.2	91.4	88.3	88.2	84.8	94.6

LDA, linear discriminant analysis; *MDA*, mixture discriminant analysis; *WF*, American White females; *WM*, American White males.

Table 5.6   Comparison of PPV and NPV for WF and MM by LDA and MDA

Test	PPV LDA	PPV MDA	NPV LDA	NPV MDA
Metric	0.778	0.849	0.945	0.911
Morphoscopic	0.547	0.710	0.808	0.793
All	0.804	0.885	0.950	0.927

LDA, linear discriminant analysis; *MDA*, mixture discriminant analysis; *NPV*, negative predictive value; *PPV*, positive predictive value; *WF*, American White females; *WM*, American White males.

are shown in Table 5.7 and the predictive values are shown in Table 5.8. Again, total correct classifications are higher in each of the MDA comparisons than the LDA comparisons. The largest increase in total correct classification is shown in the morphoscopic comparison where there is an increase of 5.8% between LDA (64.2%) and MDA (70.0%). The individual correct classifications each increased when analyzed with MDA as opposed to LDA with the exception of BM. The positive and negative predictive values for MDA are greater than those from LDA. The PPVs for MDA are greater in BM than in the LDA, lesser in SEAM, and greater in the metric and all variable comparisons of WM. Lastly, the NPVs for MDA are greater in SEAM and WM than their comparable LDA values, but slightly less for BM.

Known Mandibles Classification Comparison

The comparison of the classification of five known mandibles is shown in Table 5.9. Each mandible in the analysis had a complete or near compliment of metric and morphological variables used in the analysis. In each case, MDA has greater total correct classifications than LDA. Further, MDA correctly identifies more cases than LDA (four out of five versus three out of five, respectively). Both LDA and MDA misclassify Case 4 (known to be a White male), but only the analysis with MDA includes WM in the top three groups. This fits with the overall accuracy when using the mandible (~70% correct classification using a three-group comparison). When there is an agreement in classification between LDA and MDA, the posterior probabilities for MDA are typically stronger.

Table 5.7 Comparison of Total Correct and Individual Correct Classifications for BM, SEAM, and WM

	Total Correct %		% Correct LDA			% Correct MDA		
Test	LDA	MDA	BM	SEAM	WM	BM	SEAM	WM
Metric	77.8	81.8	81.4	82.9	70.9	77.9	86.7	78.0
Morphoscopic	64.2	70.0	59.3	67.0	63.2	28.3	78.1	77.4
All	84.7	87.8	83.2	87.3	82.4	75.2	91.7	88.2

BM, American Black male; LDA, linear discriminant analysis; MDA, mixture discriminant analysis; SEAM, Southeast Asian male; WM, American White males.

Table 5.8 Comparison of Positive and Negative Predictive Values for BM, SEAM, and WM

	PPV LDA			PPV MDA			NPV LDA			NPV MDA		
Test	BM	SEAM	WM	BM	SEAM	WM	BM	SEAM	WM	BM	SEAM	WM
Metric	0.617	0.831	0.805	0.807	0.817	0.822	0.963	0.868	0.814	0.959	0.892	0.853
Morphoscopic	0.354	0.764	0.722	0.542	0.755	0.676	0.914	0.768	0.766	0.878	0.827	0.826
All	0.701	0.911	0.847	0.846	0.895	0.872	0.968	0.905	0.881	0.960	0.938	0.911

BM, American Black male; LDA, linear discriminant analysis; MDA, mixture discriminant analysis; NPV, negative predictive value; PPV, positive predictive value; SEAM, Southeast Asian male; WM, American White males.

Table 5.9 Results of Five Cases Used to Compare Group Classification, Posterior Probabilities, and Total Correct Classifications Between LDA and MDA

	LDA			MDA		
Case	Group	Posterior Probability	Total Correct Classification	Group	Posterior Probability	Total Correct Classification
Case 1	**WM**	0.949	59.2%	**WM**	0.933	69.3%
	SEAM	0.036		SEAM	0.059	
	NEAM	0.007		HISPM	0.004	
Case 2	**BM**	0.550	62.1%	**BM**	0.700	70.7%
	HISPM	0.296		HISPM	0.177	
	AIM	0.109		AIM	0.060	
Case 3	BM	0.733	62.1%	**WM**	0.422	70.7%
	NEAM	0.126		NEAM	0.405	
	WM	0.071		BM	0.088	
Case 4	SEAM	0.711	59.2%	SEAM	0.853	69.3%
	NEAM	0.234		NEAM	0.120	
	HISPM	0.022		**WM**	0.014	
Case 5	AIM	0.317	59.2%	**WM**	0.569	69.3%
	WM	0.255		AIM	0.159	
	HISPM	0.232		HISPM	0.130	

BM, American Black male; HISPM, Hispanic males; LDA, linear discriminant analysis; MDA, mixture discriminant analysis; NEAM, Northeast Asian males; SEAM, Southeast Asian male; WM, American White males.
Correct group assignment is shown in bold.

■ DISCUSSION

In this chapter, we have explored a "new" data analysis option for anthropologists, MDA, and compare results of multiple analyses using the traditional LDA techniques versus MDA. Multiple discriminant analysis offers practitioners with a flexible classification method that outperforms LDA in virtually all comparisons. Across the board, MDA improved total correct classifications and predictive values and most of the individual group classifications as compared to LDA. Other authors have also found classification improvements using MDA, specifically compared to LDA (Hastie and Tibshirani, 1996; Rausch and Kelley, 2009). However, this comes at some cost; even with greater overall classifications, some analyses included bias, particularly in the pooled sex analyses. This may be a product of smaller sample sizes in pooled females as compared to pooled males (female, n = 470; male, n = 1076). We expect this bias to be less pronounced in analyses that are sex balanced, population specific, or sex specific. For example, the sex bias was greatly reduced in the population-specific comparisons (BF vs. BM and WF vs. WM) as compared to the pooled sex sample. Further, as the reference database grows, inclusion of additional females should mitigate most of the bias.

When using MDA for estimating sex, it is suggested that practitioners utilize the appropriate reference population, if known, given the sex bias observed in the pooled sex analysis. Table 5.10 shows a comparison of pooled versus population specific (American Black) sex biases in classification between MDA and LDA. Using MDA, there is a strong sex bias for males in the pooled analysis. As mentioned above, this is likely due to discrepancies in sample sizes. When a population-specific analysis is conducted, the sex bias approaches zero with the added benefit of increased correct classification. Conversely, there is virtually no sex bias when using LDA with the pooled sex groups, but there is a female bias for BF in the population-specific analysis. In practical terms, we propose that one option is to run a pooled sex analysis using LDA first, followed by a sex-specific ancestry analysis (using either MDA or LDA). Alternatively, when faced with a situation in which both sex and ancestry are unknown, a shotgun approach wherein all reference groups (both males and females) can be tested and refined through the iterative removal of groups that have low posterior and typicality probabilities may be used. If using the shotgun approach, the user should be cognizant of the sex bias in MDA for unbalanced sample sizes between the sexes.

In terms of correctly classifying mandibles, MDA also outperformed LDA. As seen in Table 5.9, MDA produced stronger results, to include posterior probabilities, in each case. The dual misclassified case, number 4, is so morphologically dissimilar from the WM reference group that WMs were not even considered in the top three most similar groups for LDA. However, with the flexibility of MDA using multiple centroids, WMs were at least in the top three most similar groups, albeit the case was still morphologically and metrically unique.

Two of the major assumptions of LDA are that individuals under analysis are from a mutually exclusive group and that all groups follow a multivariate normal distribution. As discussed above, it is likely rare that the types of data used within biological and forensic anthropology do not violate these assumptions. It may be that each human metagroup (e.g., White, Black, Asian, Polynesian, Hispanic, etc.) is composed of latent subgroups; this is likely a more realistic representation of anthropological and forensic data. By allowing for nonlinear decision boundaries within an analysis, we can maximize correct classifications, which is of particular importance especially when considering individuals from admixed populations. Here, MDA does not violate these assumptions and offers an attractive and flexible classification alternative by assuming a mixture of distributions through latent subgroups, multiple group centroids, and nonlinear decision boundaries. In practical terms, MDA violates fewer assumptions than LDA and appears to provide better classification results.

We encourage the reader to become familiar with both LDA and MDA, current and upcoming tools within the anthropological literature. For classifying the human mandible, the program (hu)MANid is now available for individual practitioner, and it contains both MDA and LDA options. When selecting the appropriate tool, the use of MDA over LDA is at the discretion of the end user and their comfort with employing new classification statistics. As is shown here, while MDA violates fewer assumptions in discriminant analysis, it comes with a price as well—increased bias in some types of analyses, particularly pooled sex analyses. Whenever prudent, the user should use ancestry-specific sex comparisons. Bearing that in mind, MDA may be a data exploratory tool for those who are not confident in its application, or for those who are more familiar, a stronger classification method for the complexities of understanding human morphological variation.

Table 5.10 Comparison of Total Percent Correct Classifications and Sex Bias Between Pooled Sex and Population-Specific (American Black) Sex Estimations Using MDA and LDA

Test	Sex	Pooled			Black		Bias	
		F	M	BF	BM	Pooled	Black
MDA	F	73.4	26.6	96.2	3.8	−19.7	0.6
	M	6.9	93.1	4.4	95.6		
LDA	F	83.4	16.6	91.0	86.7	0.1	4.3
	M	16.7	83.3	13.3	86.7		

LDA, linear discriminant analysis; *MDA*, mixture discriminant analysis.

■ CONCLUSIONS

Through the years, the ways in which anthropologists have collected data have become more complex and more information is available, perhaps although the classification statistic of choice, LDA, has remained stagnant. With more powerful analytics at the practitioner's disposal, it is time for anthropologists to start exploring and embracing new techniques. Here, we have shown that MDA outperforms LDA in many analyses when classifying human mandibles. Biases within the analyses are also present, favoring the correct classification of males, particularly within the pooled sex analysis. Both LDA and MDA are available in the free web-based GUI, (hu)MANid, that can be accessed at https://www.anthropologyapps.com and click on the (hu)MANid button, directly at https://anthropologyapps. shinyapps.io/humanid/ or it can be downloaded within R if that program is installed on the host computer (R Development Core Team, 2016). We encourage use of this program; feedback, comments, critiques, or mandibular data can be sent to either of the chapter's authors.

Acknowledgments

The authors appreciate the opportunity to be involved in this complex and up to date new reference work by Dr. Latham, Dr. Bartelink, and Dr. Finnegan. We would like to thank each of the institutions from which the data for this chapter and the (hu)MANid program were collected (all are also acknowledged in the About section of the program). We would like to thank the Oak Ridge Institute for Science and Education for their funding of a fellowship that aided in the creation of this work, as well as participation for Dr. Kenyhercz at DPAA. Thanks also to Dr. John E. Byrd and Dr. Ed Reedy for their support through the development and implementation of the application and evaluation of MDA.

References

Albrecht, G.H., 1980. Multivariate analysis and the study of form, with special reference to canonical variate analysis. Am. Zool. 20, 679–693.
Berg, G., Kenyhercz, M.W., 2017. In review. Introducing huMANid: a free web-based GUI to classify human mandibles. J. Forensic Sci. (in press).
Berg, G.E., 2014. Biological Affinity and Sex from the Mandible Utilizing Multiple World Populations, first ed. CRC Press, Boca Raton.
Berg, G.E., 2008. Biological Affinity and Sex Determination Using Morphometric and Morphoscopic Variables From the Human Mandible (Doctoral dissertation). University of Tennessee, Knoxville.
Dibennardo, R., Taylor, J.V., 1983. Multiple discriminant function analysis of sex and race in the postcranial skeleton. Am. J. Phys. Anthropol. 61, 305–314.
Feldesman, M.R., 2002. Classification trees as an alternative to linear discriminant analysis. Am. J. Phys. Anthropol. 119, 257–275.
Fisher, R.A., 1936. The use of multiple measurements in taxonomic problems. Ann. Eugen. 7, 79–188.
Fried, J.H., Jantz, R.L., Ousley, S.D., 2005. The truth is out there: how NOT to use FORDISC. Am. J. Phys. Anthropol. S40, 103.
Giles, E., Elliot, O., 1963. Sex determination by discriminant function analysis of crania. Am. J. Phys. Anthropol. 21, 53–68.
Hastie, T., Tibshirani, R., 1996. Discriminant analysis by Gaussian mixtures. J. R. Stat. Soc. Ser. B 58, 155–176.
Hastie, T., Tibshirani, R., Friedman, J., 2011. The Elements of Statistical Learning: Data Mining, Inference, and Prediction, second ed. Springer, New York.
Hefner, J.T., 2009. Cranial nonmetric variation and estimating ancestry. J. Forensic Sci. 54, 985–995.
Hefner, J.T., Ousley, S.D., 2014. Statistical classification methods for estimating ancestry using morphoscopic traits. J. Forensic Sci. 59, 883–890.
Hefner, J.T., Spradley, M.K., Anderson, B., 2014. Ancestry assessment using random forest modeling. 59 (3), 583–589.
Holliday, T.W., Falsetti, A.B., 1999. A new method for discriminating African-American from European-American skeletons using postcranial osteometrics reflective of body shape. J. Forensic Sci. 44, 926–930.
Howells, W.W., 1989. Skull Shapes and the Map: Craniometric Analyses in the Dispersion of Modern Homo Papers of the Peabody Museum of Archaeology and Ethnology, vol. 79.
Howells, W.W., 1977. Cranial variation in man. A study by multivariate analysis of patterns of difference among recent human populations. J. Hum. Evol. 6, 513–514.
Irish, J.D., 1998. Ancestral dental traits in recent Sub-Saharan Africans and the origins of modern humans. J. Hum. Evol. 34, 81–98.
Irish, J.D., Hemphill, B.E., 2004. An Odontometric Investigation of Canary Islander Origins, vol. 17, pp. 8–17.
Jantz, R.L., Ousley, S.D., 2005. FORDISC 3: Computerized Forensic Discriminant Functions. University of Tennessee, Knoxville.
Kachigan, S., 1991. Multivariate Statistical Analysis: A Conceptual Introduction, second ed. Radius Press, New York.
Klecka, W.R., 1980. Discriminant Analysis. Analysis. Sage, Beverly Hills.
Lease, L.R., Sciulli, P.W., 2005. Brief communication: discrimination between European-American and African-American children based on deciduous dental metrics and morphology. Am. J. Phys. Anthropol. 126, 56–60.
Lukacs, J.R., 1985. Tooth size variation in prehistoric India. Am. Anthropol. 87, 811–825.
Lukacs, J.R., Hemphill, B.E., 1993. Odontometry and biological affinity in South Asia: analysis of three ethnic groups from Northwest India. Hum. Biol. 65, 279–325.
Ousley, S., Jantz, R., Freid, D., 2009. Understanding race and human variation: why forensic anthropologists are good at identifying race. Am. J. Phys. Anthropol. 139, 68–76.
Parr, N.M., Passalacqua, N.V., Skorpinski, K., 2015. Investigations Into Age-Related Changes in the Human Mandible. Annual Meetings of the American Academy of Forensic Sciences, Orlando.
R Developement Core Team, 2016. R: A Language and Environment for Statistical Computing. R Foundation for Statistical Computing.
Rausch, J.R., Kelley, K., 2009. A comparison of linear and mixture models for discriminant analysis under nonnormality. Behav. Res. Methods 41, 85–98.
Relethford, J.H., 2004. Boas and beyond: migration and craniometric variation. Am. J. Hum. Biol. 16, 379–386.
Relethford, J.H., Harpending, H.C., 1994. Craniometric variation, genetic theory, and modern human origins. Am. J. Phys. Anthropol. 95, 249–270.
Ross, A.H., Slice, D.E., Ubelaker, D.H., Falsetti, A.B., 2004. Population affinities of 19th Century Cuban crania: implications for identification criteria in South Florida Cuban Americans. J. Forensic Sci. 49, 11–16.
Ross, A.H., Ubelaker, D.H., Falsetti, A.B., 2002. Craniometric variation in the Americas. Hum. Biol. 74, 807–818.
Slice, D.E., Ross, A., 2010. 3D-ID: Geometric Morphometric Classification of Crania for Forensic Scientists. NIJ grant 2005-MU-BX-K078.
Stull, K.E., Kenyhercz, M.W., L'Abbé, E.N., 2014. Ancestry estimation in South Africa using craniometrics and geometric morphometrics. Forensic Sci. Int. 245, 206. e1–206.e7.
Turner II, C.G., 1990. Major features of Sundadonty and Sinodonty, including suggestions about East Asian microevolution, population history, and late Pleistocene relationships with Australian Aboriginals. Am. J. Phys. Anthropol. 82, 295–317.
Walker, P.L., 2008. Sexing skulls using discriminant function analysis of visually assessed traits. Am. J. Phys. Anthropol. 136, 39–50.

CHAPTER 6

A Decade of Development in Juvenile Aging

Maureen Schaefer[1] | Nicole Geske[1] | Craig Cunningham[2]

[1]Michigan State University, East Lansing, MI, United States,
[2]University of Dundee, Dundee, Scotland

Chapter Outline

Juvenile age estimation has been a task described within forensic anthropology literature since Krogman first introduced the discipline to the United States. Krogman's seminal paper (1939), "A Guide to the Identification of Human Skeletal Material" identified both the appearance of ossification centers and union of the epiphyses as biological processes that could provide indication of skeletal age. While little has changed since the 1930s in terms of the methods described for providing insight into age prediction, paradigm shifts occurring over the past 80 years have altered the focus of anthropological research. Evolution of the specialty has shifted over time from one that frequently drew upon "normal" or "average" developmental patterns offered within medical literature to a broader mindset that incorporates the importance of human variation in its age prediction.

Modern emphasis is placed not only on documenting the range of normal human variation, but also hones in on observations specific to homogenous groups of people to describe unique growth patterns among different populations. Development of population-specific standards marks one of the current drives within the field of juvenile aging, as well as forensic anthropology as a whole. Such extensive documentation is important in that the timing in which unique populations of people achieve developmental milestones may not occur simultaneously among varying groups of people who do not share a common ancestral, socioeconomic, or geographic background.

In addition to the current drive to create population-specific data, development of standards according to analytic modality is also required. Ages associated with various developmental markers vary depending on whether the skeleton is being assessed via dry bone analysis or technologies, such as conventional radiography, ultrasound, magnetic resonance imaging (MRI), or computed tomography (CT) (Meijerman et al., 2007; Scheuer and Black, 2000). Thus there is a widespread trend to document growth and developmental patterns utilizing some of the newer imaging modalities as they become increasingly popular and more widely accessible.

Much of the focused research dedicated to juvenile age estimation is also sparked by the modern requirement to estimate the age of living individuals. Fluid borders between European countries, international conflict, as well as human trafficking have all increased the rate of immigration in recent years. While many of those immigrants possess official documentation of their birth, others do not. In many instances, the age of an undocumented individual never comes into question. If, however, the individual becomes associated with a criminal investigation, either as the perpetrator of a crime or the victim, chronological age may become vital in determining appropriate punitive measures. While the specific age at which a penalty increases in severity varies by country and state, three common threshold ages exist, those being 16, 18, and 21 years of age. As a result, many of the papers committed to improving the outcome of this endeavor focus on developmental processes that are pertinent to this time period.

New Perspectives in Forensic Human Skeletal Identification. http://dx.doi.org/10.1016/B978-0-12-805429-1.00006-5

The focus of the current chapter is restricted to describing modern work published within the past 10 years. While a 10-year span is hardly considered "modern" to fast-developing disciplines such as genetics, where research quickly becomes outdated within a few years, limiting the chapter's contents to the past decade is considered relatively modern to a slow, but steadily progressing discipline such as forensic anthropology. In appreciation of the significance to which analytic modality contributes to skeletal age estimation, the chapter is segmented according to various examination techniques. As a closing piece, a fictitious case is presented to illustrate how some of the previously discussed research can be implemented into a forensic scenario.

■ DRY BONE SKELETAL ANALYSIS

Dry bone indicators of age vary in their overall utility depending on the overarching developmental time period to which the child belongs. Milestones associated with the union of secondary ossification centers are mostly restricted to the aging of mid to late teenagers, although some of the earlier fusing epiphyses can assist with the aging of adolescents and even pre-adolescents. A limited number of primary ossification centers unite during childhood. The timings of these events are so far and few between, however, that fusion analyses may be useful for grossly categorizing the developmental time period of a child but is unlikely to offer a precise age range prediction.

Bony measurements serve as an additional source from which to base juvenile age estimations when assessing dry bone. This method is most beneficial when estimating the age of young children as stature becomes increasingly variable among children as they grow. In addition to the normal range of variation in the overall height of healthy children, negative environmental factors such as reduced access to nutritional foods or health care can add substantially to variations in stature observed between that of advantaged and disadvantaged populations. For example, poverty has been shown to yield a significantly greater effect on stature than rate of development (Greulich, 1957; Prader et al., 1963). Thus, the socioeconomic status of the child being aged is crucial in the selection of appropriate measurement standards.

While dry bone analysis of skeletal remains frequently represents the primary analytic tool employed by forensic anthropologists, advancements in juvenile aging utilizing this technique are not abundant. One of the largest drawbacks to conducting research in this realm is the fundamental lack of juvenile samples of known skeletal age. While this issue remains a pervasive problem, dry bone studies have historically been derived from four sources: donated anatomical materials, autopsy specimens, documented archaeological collections, and identified victims of war (Scheuer and Black, 2000).

Fusion of Primary and Secondary Ossification Centers

Perhaps the largest dry bone sample examined since McKern and Stewart's (1957) renowned report on epiphyseal union times of American males killed in the Korean War is that of individuals who lost their lives during the Bosnian conflict. Schaefer (2008a) compliments the research of McKern and Stewart by capturing the epiphyseal union profile of younger males not included in the American sample, thus highlighting not only the ages in which many of the later fusing epiphyses complete union but also the ages in which union is observed to initiate in those same centers. Direct comparison between the two studies also revealed that minor population differences between US soldiers in the 1950s and modern Bosnian males exist in the timing of fusion (Schaefer and Black, 2005). This finding supports the current drive to publish and employ population-specific standards that were derived from individuals who are from the same geographic location, socioeconomic status, and time period as the individual(s) who require(s) aging (Langley-Shirley and Jantz, 2010).

Two samples from Portugal have also provided the opportunity for multiple studies on epiphyseal union to be conducted. These studies do not parallel the size of the sample utilized in the Bosnian study for any given age; however, they include individuals from birth to full maturity as well as females, thus furthering our knowledge base of fusion patterns in younger individuals and females (Cardoso, 2008a, 2008b; Coqueugniot and Weaver, 2007). A compilation of the fusing times offered by the two samples as well as those published from the Bosnian sample (Schaefer, 2008a) is provided in Table 6.1.

The Portuguese samples also add significantly to the literature by providing the opportunity to assess bony elements that are frequently ignored due to the complexity of their development, their segmental repetition, or the flake-like nature of their epiphyses, such as those associated with the ribs. This includes recording the union times of both primary and secondary ossification centers of the sacrum as well as the numerous epiphyses of the vertebra, ribs, hands, and feet (Cardoso and Ríos, 2011; Cardoso and Severino, 2010; Cardoso et al., 2014; Ríos and Cardoso, 2009; Ríos et al., 2008). Further research documenting the union times of the vertebral rings was also conducted utilizing the American-based Terry collection housed at the Smithsonian Institute (Albert et al., 2010; Albert and Maier, 2013).

Although described as modern samples, the Portuguese studies were all derived from individuals of mid- to low-socioeconomic status living in the early to mid-1900s. Improvements that have occurred within the past century in regards to health care, working conditions, and increased access to nutritional foods may foster discrepancies in developmental timings between that of their sample and contemporary individuals (Langley-Shirley and Jantz, 2010; Schaefer and Black, 2005). The authors of the Portuguese papers were aware of this potential limitation and thus suggested that their standards be adopted to assist with the aging of archaeological populations and/or forensic cases

Table 6.1   **A Compilation of the Reported Fusing Times Observed in Males and Females From Two Portuguese Samples as Well as a Bosnian Sample**

Bone	Element	Females		Males		
		Cardoso	Coqueugniot	Cardoso	Coqueugniot	Schaefer
Scapula	Coracoid process	11–16	11–17	11–16	15–22	15–18
	Coracoid angle and apex	15–16	/	16–18	/	16–20
	Acromial epiphysis	15–19	17–21	16–18	18–21	17–20
	Glenoid epiphysis	13–16	/	15–18	/	15–18
	Inferior angle	17–20	/	16–18	/	17–22
	Vertebral border	17–20	/	17–19	/	18–22
Clavicle	Sternal epiphysis	17–27	17–29+	19–25	19–29+	17–29
Humerus	Proximal epiphysis	14–19	17–23	16–21	19–21	16–21
	Distal epiphysis	11–14	/	14–16	/	15–18
	Medial epicondyle	11–16	/	16–18	16–20	16–18
Radius	Proximal epiphysis	11–16	12–17	15–18	17–20	15–18
	Distal epiphysis	14–19	17–22	16–21	19–21	16–20
Ulna	Proximal epiphysis	11–14	/	11–15	16–20	15–18
	Distal epiphysis	14–19	17–21	16–20	19–21	17–20
Hand	Metacarpal epiphyses	12–18	/	16–18	/	/
	Phalangeal epiphyses	16–17	/	16–18	/	/
Innominate	Acetabular complex*	11–16	9–17	11–18	15–20	?–18
	Iliac crest epiphysis	15–21	17–26	16–21	16–24	17–21
	Ischial epiphysis	14–19	14–26	15–21	16–24	16–20
	Ramal epiphysis	18–22	/	17–21	/	/
Femur	Proximal epiphysis	14–16	12–22	15–18	16–24	16–20
	Trochanters	13–16	17–19	15–18	16–21	16–20
	Distal epiphysis	14–19	17–19	16–18	16–21	16–20
Tibia	Proximal epiphysis	14–19	12–22	16–19	16–21	16–20
	Distal epiphysis	14–16	14–19	15–18	16–20	16–18
Fibula	Proximal epiphysis	14–17	17–19	16–18	16–21	16–20
	Distal epiphysis	14–16	17–21	15–18	16–21	16–20
Foot	Metatarsal epiphyses	16–17	/	15–18	/	/
	Phalangeal epiphyses	14–17	/	16–18	/	/
	Calcaneal epiphysis	12–17	/	11–17	/	/

* summarizes data gathered from fusion of the three components of the innominate bone: ilium to pubis, pubis to ischium and ischium to ilium; / indicates no observation; ? indicates lower limits unknown.

from developing nations to minimize the possible effects of a positive secular trend. Developmental rates are shown to be less affected by negative environmental factors than that of overall stature. Thus the potential underestimating that may result from application of a historic sample may be minimal. A simple awareness of this possible tendency may be sufficient to appropriately apply the data.

Advancements in statistical reporting of union times have also occurred within the past 10 years. Documentation of fusing activity has traditionally been accomplished by providing summary ages describing, for example, the first and last ages observed to demonstrate each union phase. Statistical analysis tends to be limited to descriptive statistics that provide mean ages and standard deviations associated with the phases. Two recent studies by Cardoso and colleagues (Cardoso and Ríos, 2011; Cardoso et al., 2014) took a more innovative approach by calculating the posterior probabilities of age, given at each stage of fusion, for anatomical elements of the sacrum and vertebrae. Langley-Shirley and Jantz (2010) and Shirley and Jantz (2011) utilized transition analysis to document the average age at which union progresses from one stage into the next in both the spheno–occipital synchondrosis as well as the medial clavicle. Their work on the medial clavicle further utilized Bayesian statistics. They argue that use of transitional analysis and Bayesian statistics helps to address some of the pitfalls associated with developing aging standards utilizing percentile approaches, such as age mimicry and sample size limitations (Konigsberg et al., 2008).

Additional studies have also been published that utilize classical dry bone analysis of epiphyseal union for non-traditional purposes outside of aging juvenile remains. Schaefer (2008b) and Schaefer and Black (2007) consider the sequence in which the various epiphyses of the body unite to aid in the recognition of commingled remains. The underlying premise is that if a fusing sequence that has not been previously documented is observed within a skeleton, then the bony element creating the incongruent pattern may not belong to that individual. The sequences in which the epiphyses initiate union as well as the pattern in which they complete union, including any variation to those configurations, have been recorded. In addition, a supplementary resource has been published that attempts to make the detailed presentation of material more user-friendly (Schaefer, 2014).

Bony Measurements

A plethora of studies correlating bone size with age have flooded the literature in recent years. While long bone measurements have been fully described within the published literature much older than the previous decade, the application of this investigatory technique to age estimation has changed the focus of research in recent years. Much of the previous longitudinal based research focused on documenting normal sequential growth associated with the radiographic length of long bones so that abnormalities to this developmental pattern could be identified and hopefully corrected in living children (Ghantus, 1951; Gindhart, 1973; Maresh, 1970). Modern-day forensic and archaeological research have since diverged from the medical practice of utilizing age to assess size normality by flipping the equation and utilizing measurement data to predict age. A bone measurement is simply "plugged" into a regression formula, and age is calculated via that equation.

Regression analysis for estimating age of juvenile remains has been widely published in both the forensic and archaeological literature. Standards intended for forensic application are more restricted, however, due to the scarcity of juvenile collections of known age. A number of Western European samples have provided documented material to study postnatal growth patterns, including that of the Lisbon and Coimbra collections in Portugal, the Scheuer collection in Scotland, and the London-based collections of St. Bride's and Spitalfields (Cardoso, 2009; Cardoso et al., 2013, 2014; López-Costas et al., 2012; Ríos et al., 2008; Rissech and Black, 2007; Rissech and Malgosa, 2005, 2007; Rissech et al., 2008, 2012, 2013a, 2013b). Regression formulae have been calculated for all major long bones in these samples as well as the scapula and innominate bone. A variety of length and width measurements unique to each bone were analyzed to identify the sectors that deliver the most utility in age estimation.

While the above European samples serve as a great source of documented skeletal material, their utility in forensic application is biased due to the antiquity of the subjects. The children within these samples died between 250 and 50 years ago, thus their measurements may not reflect that of a modern population. Reduced access to health care and nutritional foods may have truncated the overall growth of the historic sample in comparison to that of modern-day advantaged children. To avoid consequential overestimation of age, the authors suggest that their standards may be more appropriately applied to children from developing countries or children from poor communities in developed nations.

New literature describing the relationship between age and size of the basilar portion of the occipital bone has advanced the potential of estimating gestational age in fetal remains (Nagaoka et al., 2012). The pars basilaris serves as an ideal source for gathering metric data in young fragile skeletons due to its relatively thick quadrilateral morphology that is more resistant to decay than the long bones. Aging techniques that utilize the pars basilaris derive their estimates from two lines of evidence including plugging the metric data into a regression formula and considering changes in the shape of the bone. As fetal growth progresses, the pars basilaris alters its length-to-width ratio, originating with a greater anterior posterior dimension and moving to that of a greater bilateral dimension. Nagaoka and colleagues observed that this transition initiated in the first subject within their sample at 6 months gestational age and had occurred in all subjects by 10 months gestational months. While this paper is not the first to consider measurements of the pars basilaris or the flipped ratio as an indicator of age, it spawned an interesting discovery in relation to population-specific standards. Their sample consisted of early to middle 20th-century Japanese individuals who lived during a period of continuous wars and malnutrition. Comparisons between their data and that of other researchers revealed that population differences in terms of length and width measurements of the pars basilaris had already appeared before birth, resulting in smaller dimensions associated with the Japanese sample. The ratio index values, however, proved consistent between the various samples that were compared, implying that the ratio of width to length is an indicator that can be universally applied to temporally, geographically, and economically distinct populations.

Practical Application

Increasing emphasis is being placed on incorporating population-specific standards into analysis and yet few of the dry bone studies mentioned were derived from individuals representing a modern US or even similar population. Clearly this is an idealized but perhaps unrealistic goal as the fundamental dearth of known-aged collections restricts the ability to obtain documentation from a wide range of populations. In practical terms therefore, an anthropologist may simply need to "make-do" with the resources available to him or her.

Awareness as to the limitations of the utilized reference sample can help to adjust the final estimation into one that is more appropriate for the current population. For example, a study that was derived from an antiquated sample has the potential to overestimate age of children within a healthier modern population. Knowledge of this shortcoming may suggest that any estimate derived from this source could be utilized to appropriately represent the higher end of a potential age range but would be inappropriate to define the lower limit. The same rational also applies to standards derived from children of different ancestral backgrounds. If prior knowledge as to the growth pattern of each population is known then comparisons can be made to determine if the development of one population is accelerated or delayed relative to the other. More readily available resources such as radiographic studies may facilitate this comparison and ultimately provide insight as to the potential bias of utilizing the outside standard.

■ SKELETAL ANALYSIS VIA CONVENTIONAL RADIOGRAPHY

Radiographic images serve as an ideal source to visualize skeletal maturity when the presence of soft tissue impedes such investigation. This line of evidence is necessary when estimating the age of living individuals but may also be called upon during investigation of the deceased. Age estimations based on radiographic analysis may take two forms: examination of images that are obtained at the time of need and utilization of preexisting images that were taken at some other time for a medical purpose. According to the latter, the image is aged and then the amount of time that has passed since the image was produced is added to the estimate to derive the individual's current age.

The Study Group on Forensic Age Diagnostics has developed guidelines for the estimation of living age for use within criminal procedures (Schmeling and Black, 2010; Schmeling et al., 2001, 2004a, 2004b, 2006, 2007). They recommend a physical examination as well as dental analysis of an orthopantomogram and radiographic examination of the left hand. If the court requires knowledge as to whether the accused has reached the age of 21, then additional radiographic assessment of the clavicle should be considered. These guidelines have sparked widespread research into dental growth as well as development of the hand, wrist, and clavicle.

Analysis of skeletal maturity via radiographic means is highly beneficial as numerous developmental processes that are useful in the estimation of age may be captured within a single image. Three traditional markers that are commonly used include the appearance of ossification centers, morphological changes that the epiphyses undergo during their postappearance and preunion time periods, and progression of epiphyseal union. Recent literature has focused on advancing documentation in each of the three areas, as well as pioneering new efforts into the investigation of morphometrics, and the extent of mineralization of various bones in relation to age.

Atlas Method

The radiographic atlas technique is a single investigatory method that incorporates the three classic indicators of skeletal maturity into its age prediction. Radiographic atlases include a series of radiographic images (plates) depicting advancing maturity of a specific joint region from birth to complete maturation. Each plate is assigned an age based on "average" developmental rates. The user is instructed to identify the plate that most similarly represents the radiograph under investigation. The age allotted to that plate represents the skeletal age that should be assigned to the individual. While the original intention of the atlases was to identify children whose maturity levels were unnaturally precocious or delayed, their utility in estimating chronological age is clearly apparent. Radiographic atlases were published for many of the joint regions of the upper and lower limb; however, Greulich and Pyle (1959) developed the first and probably most widely utilized atlas on the hand and wrist. The plethora of developmental milestones presented in this multi-bone region, offer a broad time frame from which age estimations can be derived, extending from birth through postadolescence. Based on the vast utility of this bony region, guidelines established by the Study Group on Forensic Age Diagnostics identify the hand/wrist as the joint of choice for age estimation of living subadults via skeletal analysis (Schmeling and Black, 2010; Schmeling et al., 2001, 2004a, 2004b, 2006, 2007).

The popularity of the hand and wrist atlas technique has led to an abundance of publications that test the accuracy of the Greulich and Pyle method when applied to specific populations. Many of the studies conclude that the technique can be applied with sufficient accuracy on groups of people living in different geographic locations or temporal periods than those observed within the original study (Büken et al., 2007; Cantekin et al., 2012; Cunha et al., 2009; Groell et al., 1999; Hackman and Black, 2013; Hsieh et al., 2013; Jimenez-Castellanos et al., 1996; Moradi et al., 2012; Patil et al., 2012; Paxton et al., 2013; Santoro et al., 2012; Santos et al., 2011; Soudack et al., 2012; van Rijn et al., 2001; Zafar et al., 2010). However, other studies warn against or caution its use for certain populations at specific ages (Chiang et al., 2005; Cole et al., 1988; Koc et al., 2001; Mansourvar et al., 2014; Mora et al., 2001; Ontell et al., 1996; Schmidt et al., 2008; Shaikh et al., 1998; Tisè, 2011; Varkkola et al., 2011).

One of the limitations associated with the radiographic atlas technique is that there are a vast number of traits that sometimes provide conflicting information, thus making it difficult to assign a single representative plate. The user must then rely on their own experiences to guide their interpretation as to the features that should be preferentially selected as more robust indicators of age. Dogaroiu et al. (2014) investigated this conundrum by comparing age estimates derived via two plate selection paradigms, one that considered only the number of ossification centers present and the other which more heavily weighted the morphological appearance of the ossification centers. The two estimated ages were then compared to known chronologic age to determine which consideration produced the more accurate estimate. They conclude that morphologic similarity is a better reflection of chronological age than is the total number of centers present.

A second limiting factor associated with the radiographic atlas aging technique is that the prediction comes in the form of a single age rather than that of an age range. Development does not proceed at a uniform rate in all children, thus it is vital that human variation is accounted for to increase the accuracy of the estimate. In response to this issue, Hackman and Black (2013) suggested that two standard deviations be added and subtracted from bone age, as predicted through the Greulich and Pyle method, to transform the rigid estimate into one that is more inclusive and appropriate for forensic use. The standard deviation to apply represents the calculated difference between estimated age and chronological age in a population. Table 6.2 summarizes the standard deviations offered by different researchers for various populations. While much research has been dedicated to testing the accuracy of radiographic atlases on estimating chronological age, only papers that included a standard deviation according to age subgroups rather than every age were included to keep the table size condensed.

In addition to the hand and wrist, radiographic atlases have also been developed in association with the foot and ankle, and elbow and knee (Brodeur et al., 1981; Hoerr et al., 1962; Pyle and Hoerr, 1969). Studies that test the accuracy of these methods on specific populations are less numerous; however, they are still being published. Hackman and Black (2013) investigated the accuracy of the Pyle and Hoerr (1969) radiographic atlas of the knee on a Scottish subadult population. They developed standard deviations associated with the difference between known chronological age and estimated age derived from the atlas and suggested applying their standard deviation (9.9 months for females and 10.8 months for males) when utilizing the Pyle and Hoerr (1969) technique for estimating age (Table 6.2). While their sample size was extensive, infants and young children were underrepresented, leading to a potential inflation of the standard deviation required to represent developmental variations expressed in the very young. Schaefer et al. (2016) exclusively examined knee radiographs from infants, toddlers, and young children and successfully managed to narrow the standard deviation to 2.5 months in females with a skeletal age of under 1 year, 5.2 months in females with a skeletal age between 1 and 3 years, 2.3 months in males with a skeletal age under 1 year and 7.0 months in males with a skeletal age between 1 and 4 years. They conclude that early development is more succinct than that which occurs in older children and adolescents and therefore smaller standard deviations can describe the extent of expected variation.

Additional authors have reported similar results in which smaller differences between skeletal age and chronological age were calculated in association with the hand and wrist of younger children as opposed to older juveniles (Hackman and Black, 2013; Ontell et al., 1996; Patil et al., 2012; Paxton et al., 2013). Schaefer et al. research is unique, however, in that the standard deviations they calculated were grouped according to plate assignment rather than chronological age (Table 6.2). This reporting style more accurately represents a "real" forensic scenario in which chronological age would be the unknown variable. Take for example a male child who was assigned to plate 11 (skeletal age 3 years, 4 months) according to the Greulich and Pyle hand and wrist method, but his "real" chronological age was 4 years and 3 months. The correct standard deviation to apply according to Patil and colleagues would be 6.2 months based on the fact that he is between the ages of 4 and 7 years. Chronological age is unknown, however, and thus it is more likely that the smaller 3.7 standard deviation (for males between the ages of 0–3 years) would be incorrectly applied. Schaefer and colleagues avoid this conundrum by grouping the standard deviations according to plate assignment which is the known variable rather than chronological age.

Table 6.2   *Standard Deviations (SDs) Representing the Differences Between Skeletal Age and Chronological Age According to Different Joint Regions, Populations, Subgroups, and Sex*

Joint Region	Researcher	Population	Male		Female	
			Subgroups	SD	Subgroup	SD
Hand and wrist (Gruelich and Pyle)	Hackman and Black (2013)	Scottish	0–5 years	7.1 months	0–5 years	9.9 months
			6–10 years	17.3 months	6–10 years	13.4 months
			11–15 years	13.0 months	11–15 years	13.5 months
			16–20 years	14.4 months	16–20 years	14.1 months
	Moradi et al. (2012)	Iranian	6–10 years	11.8 months	6–10 years	8.5 months
			10–14 years	11.3 months	10–14 years	10.1 months
			14–18 years	12.0 months	14–18 years	10.1 months
	Patil et al. (2012)	Indian	0–3 years	3.7 months	0–4 years	2.2 months
			4–7 years	6.2 months	4–8 years	6.3 months
			8–12 years	11.7 months	8–13 years	7.8 months
			13–19 years	8.5 months	13–19 years	7.3 months
Knee (Pyle and Hoerr)	Hackman and Black (2013)	Scottish	0–18 years	10.8 months	0–18 years	9.9 months
	Schaefer et al. (2016)	American	Plates 2–6	2.3 months	Plates 2–7	2.5 months
			Plates 7–14	7.0 months	Plates 8–15	5.2 months
Foot and ankle (Hoerr et al.)	Hackman et al. (2013)	Scottish	0–18 years	9.9 months	0–18 years	10.2 months

Reported standard deviations can twice be added and subtracted from skeletal age to transform the single age prediction into an age range estimate that is more appropriate for forensic purposes. Schaefer et al. reported their standard deviations according to subgroups based on plate assignment rather than chronological age to more accurately represent a forensic scenario in which chronological age is the unknown variable.

Underrepresentation of infants and young children is a common problem when assessing radiographic data obtained from a single hospital source. This issue stems from the fact that less mobile children are less likely to injure themselves, and therefore fewer images are available for study. In response to this shortcoming, Mercyhurst University has recently developed and continues to maintain an online juvenile radiographic database that houses images from a variety of joint regions derived from hundreds of children, including large numbers of infants (Ousley et al., 2013). This database is an excellent resource and is currently available for research purposes. To access the database go to http://math.mercyhurst.edu/~sousley/databases/radiographic_database/DBQuery/.

Morphological Changes of the Epiphyses

Aside from the direct visual comparison technique that is applied when utilizing a radiographic atlas, morphological changes that the epiphyses undergo throughout the developmental process have been widely ignored within the literature. O'Connor et al. (2013) have recently added to the sparse literature by defining numerous developmental markers that occur at the knee. Their study examined images obtained from Irish juveniles between the ages of 9 and 19 years. Each indicator was assigned a maturity score reflecting specific criteria associated with graded development of that marker. Summary statistics describing the relationship between age and score for all the indicators were provided in an early version of their work. Recent efforts have led to a more sophisticated approach in which the scores assigned to each criterion are summed, leading to a single composite score that can be inserted into a regression formula (O'Connor et al., 2014).

A new and innovative approach that utilizes dental panorexes and standardized cephalograms to assess both dental and skeletal maturity simultaneously was developed by Lajolo et al. (2013). They advocate use of an Oro-Cervical Radiographic Simplified Score (OCRSS) to assist with age diagnostics in living children. Their method was specifically developed to assign individuals into three different age cohorts (younger than 14 years, between 14 and 18 years, and over 18 years) based on threshold ages specific to Italian law. The OCRSS represents the summation of scores derived from three independent methods, including Demirjian's method for dental age calculation, the cervical vertebral maturation method for skeletal age calculation, and the third molar development for dental age calculation. The two methods for assessing dental age (Demirjian et al., 1973; Kasper et al., 2009) are well established and more specific to the chapter on dental aging, so will not be discussed here. The skeletal maturation method (Baccetti et al., 2005) assesses the morphological shape changes that the C2, C3, and C4 vertebral bodies undergo as they transition from being more trapezoidal in shape to a more rectangular geometry.

Appearance Times and Epiphyseal Union

Research on numerous joint regions has been undertaken to demonstrate appearance and union times occurring in the late teenage years. While analysis of the hand and wrist serves as the recommended method for living age diagnostics, this technique frequently does not provide sufficient evidence to confidently place an individual older than or younger than key threshold ages such as 16, 18, or 21. Thus, research on additional joint areas is required.

A novel approach to determining whether an individual has reached 18 years of age was introduced by Cameriere et al. (2012) in their investigation of the knee in a modern Italian sample. They advocate a multifactorial technique that sums the individual union phases assigned to the distal femoral, proximal fibular, and proximal tibial epiphyses to produce a single composite score. Union phases consisted of open union (score of 0), active union (score of 1), and complete union (score of 3). Conditional probabilities demonstrating the likelihood that an individual who displays X composite scores has attained 18 years of age were calculated and published. The accuracy of this approach when applied to outside populations is an area that requires further testing.

To substantiate the utility of the shoulder in age diagnostics, Schaefer et al. (2015) documented the appearance and union times of the proximal humeral, acromial, and coracoid epiphyses in an American sample. While their main intent was to record the overall timing of these events, they observed a number of milestones that always occurred before the age of 16 or 18 years. This discovery indicates that the shoulder may be of particular value when evaluating the likely direction of an individual's age in relation to either of those two common threshold values. While it is doubtful that any Americans will require living age diagnostics, many of the individuals from their study represent an underprivileged class, and therefore standards derived from this sample may be applicable to an immigrant population.

A number of additional studies have documented the radiographic appearance and fusion times of some of the later developing epiphyses. This includes additional resources on the knee (Dogaroiu and Avramoiu, 2015; O'Connor et al., 2008; Tirpude et al., 2015), as well as the distal radius and ulna (Nemade et al., 2010), iliac crest (Bhise and Nanandkar, 2012; Patel et al., 2011; Singh et al., 2011), distal tibia and fibula (Crowder and Austin, 2005), proximal tibia (Patond et al., 2015), and most uniquely, the proximal epiphysis of the fifth metatarsal (Davies et al., 2013). While some of these studies were derived from populations that are unlikely to require age estimation due to the accuracy in which birth is recorded in their country, many of the papers stem from subjects living within India, a country in which rural births may not be documented to a high degree of accuracy (Aggrawal, 2009). Thus, standards produced within these papers may be utilized to estimate age of individuals representing the same population of people from which they were derived (Bhise and Nanandkar, 2012; Nemade et al., 2010; Patel et al., 2011; Patond et al., 2015; Singh et al., 2011).

While none of the above papers concentrate specifically on differentiating between ages of judiciary importance, any milestone that was observed to always occur before or after a relevant age can help with this endeavor. Table 6.3 displays specific milestones for placing individuals into categories of being older or younger than the key ages of 16, 18, and 21 years of age. Practitioners should keep in mind that each study utilizes distinct criteria in their phasing system, so that what constitutes complete union in one study may not be identical to that of another study. Thus it is important to always reference the original work prior to application to ensure that the specifics of each phasing system are understood.

The late maturation profile of the clavicle serves as a useful diagnostic tool when skeletal maturation has completed elsewhere in the body (Garamendi et al., 2011; Schmelling et al., 2004b). It may also be of utility in situations where some amount of time has passed since requiring the age of an individual. This is particularly true if the perpetrator of a crime is not accused until several years later. If any uncertainty exists as to whether the individual was over the age of 18 years at the time of the crime, the clavicle may assist in answering that question. According to Schmelling et al. (2004b), if complete union of the clavicle with no evidence of an epiphyseal scar is observed, then the individual must have reached the age of 18 years at least 8 years ago. This is based on their observations that the youngest individual (both male and female) to demonstrate complete union was 26 years of age. To illustrate the applicability of this information, if an individual who displays complete union of the clavicle with no evidence of an epiphyseal scar committed a crime 7 years ago, it is likely that the person was at least 19 years old at the time of the incident.

Observation of an epiphyseal scar, or radiopaque line in the location of the previously existing growth plates, is an attribute unique to the radiographic assessment of epiphyseal union. Studies that utilize this trait as part of their scoring criteria consider the radiodense line as a transient developmental phase that disappears within a few years

Table 6.3 Developmental Milestones That Were Always Observed to Occur Prior to or After the Provided Threshold Ages

Sex	Age	Developmental Milestone
Male	<16	Open union in the proximal humerus (Schaefer et al., 2016)
		No acromial epiphysis present (Schaefer et al., 2016)
		Open union of the distal femur (Dogaroiu and Avramoiu, 2015; O'Connor et al., 2008)
		No iliac epiphysis present (Bhise and Nanandkar, 2012)
	≥16	Complete union of the proximal humerus (Schaefer et al., 2016)
		Complete union of the distal radius or ulna (Nemade et al., 2010)
		Recent or complete union of the proximal fibula (O'Connor et al., 2008)
		1/4 union or more of iliac crest (Bhise and Nanandkar, 2012)
	<18	Present but incomplete union of the acromial epiphysis (Schaefer et al., 2016)
		Open union of the proximal fibula (O'Connor et al., 2008)
		No iliac epiphysis present (Singh et al., 2011)
		1/2 or less union of the distal femur (Dogaroiu and Avramoiu, 2015)
		1/4 or less union of the proximal tibia (Dogaroiu and Avramoiu, 2015)
	≥18	Complete union of the iliac crest (Singh et al., 2011)
		Complete union of the distal femur or proximal tibia (Dogaroiu and Avramoiu, 2015)
	<21	3/4 union of iliac crest (Bhise and Nanandkar, 2012)
Female	<16	Open union of the proximal humerus (Schaefer et al., 2016)
		No acromial epiphysis present (Schaefer et al., 2016)
		Present but incomplete union of the acromial epiphysis (Schaefer et al., 2016)
		Open, beginning, or active union of the proximal tibia (O'Connor et al., 2008)
		Open or beginning union of the distal femur or proximal fibula (O'Connor et al., 2008)
		1/4 or less union of the distal femur or proximal tibia (Dogaroiu and Avramoiu, 2015)
	≥16	Complete union of the distal ulna (Nemade et al., 2010)
		1/4 or more union of iliac crest (Bhise and Nanandkar, 2012)
	<18	Present but incomplete union of the acromial epiphysis (Schaefer et al., 2016)
		Active union of the distal femur (O'Connor et al., 2008)
		1/2 or less union of the distal femur (Dogaroiu and Avramoiu, 2015)
		1/4 or less union of the proximal tibia (Dogaroiu and Avramoiu, 2015)
		1/4 union or less of iliac crest (Bhise and Nanandkar, 2012)
	≥18	3/4 union or more of iliac crest (Bhise and Nanandkar, 2012)
		Complete fusion of iliac crest (Patel, 2011)
	<21	NA

Observations from all sources were made via conventional radiographic images.

following complete union. As such, presence of the scar serves as an indication of recent epiphyseal activity that is diagnostic of age. Davies et al. (2013) recently investigated the validity of this finding and found that over 90% of individuals between the ages of 20 and 50 retained some remnant of an epiphyseal scar at the proximal and distal tibiae. Their study refutes Schmelling et al. (2004b) and suggests that presence, or absence, of a radiopaque line has no correlation with age and thus should not be used as an indicator of chronological age.

Metric Analysis

Two innovative approaches that take advantage of computationally derived metric data have recently been introduced into the literature. Cameriere et al. (Cameriere and Ferrante, 2008; Cameriere et al., 2006, 2008, 2012) pioneered a technique that measures the degree of mineralization of the hand and wrist as described by the ratio of bone area over carpal area (Bo/Ca). Their use of a computer-aided drafting program calculated the amount of pixels located within each of the two areas defined by the polygonal lasso function within their software. The polygonal lasso function allows the user to draw straight-sided polygonal shapes around the object or area they want to select. Carpal area was defined by the lasso as a single zone that encompassed all the carpal bones as well as the distal epiphyses of the radius and ulna, whereas bone area (Ba) included a summation of the total number of pixels describing each individual element as defined by multiple lassoed areas. The overarching goal of their paper was to describe the extent of ossification that had taken place, holding size as a constant, and correlate that with age. A regression formula was provided for practical application. Their approach was later adopted by a second team who utilized the technique to describe the relationship between mineralization of the iliac crest epiphysis and age (Wittschieber et al., 2013).

Pujol et al. (2014, 2016) have recently introduced the use of geometric morphometrics applied to radiographic images to describe ontogeny of the femur in a modern female Spanish population. Size and shape variations were quantified using 22 landmarks, and their relationship with age was assessed via principal component analysis. While no practical methods for implementing their findings were offered, the potential of this technique in deriving age estimations is significant.

■ SKELETAL ANALYSIS VIA OTHER IMAGING TECHNIQUES

The use of imaging technology to analyze the patterns of bone growth and development, spanning ossification center appearance to epiphyseal fusion, has been important in the study of skeletal development for decades (Greulich and Pyle, 1959; Maresh, 1943, 1955; Noback, 1944). Indeed, existing radiographic growth data collected on living children from more than half a century ago still contributes to the baseline reference data used for skeletal age analysis today. Fortunately, longitudinal radiographic growth studies of juveniles are no longer carried out, due to the risk that is now known to exist from repeated exposure to ionizing radiation. Therefore, there has been a drive to exploit modern imaging technology for the purposes of developing new methods of skeletal age estimation. This is evidenced by the expanding literature base that has applied a variety of advanced imaging methods to age estimation from both living individuals and human remains (Dedouit et al., 2012; Minier et al., 2014; Schulz et al., 2014). In particular, within the past decade, there has been a focus on applying this imaging technology to enhance our understanding of the relationship between bone development, skeletal age, and chronological age for potential application in forensic age estimation (Brough et al., 2012; Dedouit et al., 2012; Kellinghaus et al., 2010; Minier et al., 2014; Schulz et al., 2014).

Magnetic Resonance Imaging and Ultrasound

There is a current focus on developing methods of age estimation for living children using radiation-free imaging techniques, including MRI (Dedouit et al., 2012; Ebner et al., 2014; Krämer et al., 2014a,b; Laor and Jaramillo, 2009; Saint-Martin et al., 2013, 2014, 2015; Serinelli et al., 2015) and ultrasound (Bilgili et al., 2003; De Sanctis et al., 2014; Mentzel et al., 2005; Schmidt et al., 2013; Schulz et al., 2014; Wagner et al., 1995). MRI studies have tended to focus on the distal radius, knee, and clavicle, whereas those using ultrasound have considered the radius, pelvis, and clavicle. Dedouit et al. (2012) used MRI examinations of the knee in individuals aged 10–30 years to create a staging system based on fusion of the distal femoral and proximal tibial epiphyses, while Saint-Martin et al. (2013, 2014, 2015) examined the distal femur, tibia, and the calcaneus. The authors noted that in cases where patients had both MRI and plain X-rays available, there was some discrepancy in the degree of fusion visible. While fusion appeared to be complete on the X-rays, the higher contrast and definition available on the MRI image revealed persisting edema at the physis indicating incomplete fusion (Dedouit et al., 2012). Furthermore, because MRI is able to view the site of fusion in thin slices without superposition of structures as is seen in radiographs, it is possible to detect much smaller areas of fusion, leading to earlier ages recorded for beginning of the fusion process. As a result, it is difficult to compare results of these studies to earlier radiographic data on the knee and ankle regions (Pyle and Hoerr, 1969; Hoerr et al., 1962). In some cases, however, MRI data has reaffirmed observations first made in radiological studies, for example, that the ossification process at the distal femur occurs earlier in females than in males (Krämer et al., 2014a). This finding also underlines the demand for sex-specific reference data in age estimation practice. Further work supporting the use of MRI data in age estimation includes the verification of the ossification status at the proximal tibial epiphysis as a suitable tool for forensic age estimation (Krämer et al., 2014b). Additionally, age estimation from MRI images of the left hand and wrist has been shown to be a reproducible method demonstrating a good correlation with chronological age (Serinelli et al., 2015). In the area of hand wrist analysis from MRI data, automation of age estimation has been attempted by Ebner et al. (2014) who developed a novel hand bone landmark detection approach.

Schulz et al. (2014) have also created a staging system using radiation-free imaging but have focused on analyzing the developing olecranon using ultrasound, which is a quick, cost-effective, and widely available technology. They found that determining the stage of ossification of the olecranon was possible, but unlike X-ray and MRI, ultrasound cannot access the entire joint surface to assess the stage of ossification (Schulz et al., 2014). Ultrasound is also more subjective and operator dependent than MRI, making it difficult to document findings of an exam and thus posing potential problems for repeatability and interobserver error (Dedouit et al., 2012; Schulz et al., 2014). The ultrasonographic version of the Greulich–Pyle atlas has been shown to be a highly correlated and valid alternative to plain radiography for bone age estimation, enabling estimation of skeletal age without exposing the patient to radiation (Bilgili et al., 2003). Mentzel et al., 2005 also demonstrated the ability of ultrasound to produce an accurate assessment of bone age, again presenting results that were highly correlated with radiographical methods. Furthermore, where there is no legal basis for radiographic examination, ultrasonographic analysis of the distal radius has been shown to be an accurate alternative (Schmidt et al., 2013). However, despite this increasing body of literature, caution over the use of ultrasound has been advised by De Sanctis et al. (2014) in relation to the lack of established population specific data.

Computed Tomography

While plain film radiography and CT are both still widely used to evaluate remains, use of newer technology in the form of multiple detector (also called multislice) CT (MDCT or MSCT) is becoming more widespread (Brough et al., 2012). MDCT has been applied in recent research to develop new standards for estimation of age at death in both fetal and juvenile remains. Additionally, this technology has been used to morphometrically examine the development of different skeletal elements (Brough et al., 2013; Minier et al., 2014). MDCT is superior to standard CT technology by producing both thick and thin slices simultaneously while scanning large anatomical ranges. Thin slices can subsequently be used to create high-quality reconstructions, including off-axis and three-dimensional (3D) images (Goldman, 2008). Skeletal elements can be measured using digitally positioned landmarks in any plane, which can be used in morphometric calculations such as those used for age estimation (Minier et al., 2014). Use of imaging technology to better understand developmental patterns and construct methods of age estimation has great practical value in any situation where skeletal age estimation is required. In forensic settings involving human remains, the noninvasive nature of MDCT means that it can be applied in cases where cleaning and defleshing of bones is undesirable, due to need for evidence protection, issues with feasibility in the field, or religious and cultural concerns (Brough et al., 2013). As age estimation is a critical component of forensic anthropological examination, new technology that facilitates this process is extremely valuable. Of course, it is important that bone measurements made from MDCT images are comparable to osteometric measurements and can therefore be used with similar reliability. Recent studies suggest that in multiple regions of the skeleton, there is no significant difference between measurements taken osteometrically on defleshed bones and measurements taken using MDCT imaging, making this method particularly useful (Brough et al., 2013; Kellinghaus et al., 2010; Minier et al., 2014; Robinson et al., 2008).

Image Analysis of Developing Bone Structure

In recent years, several imaging technologies have also been applied to gain a better understanding of human bone development at a gross structural and histological level (Cunningham and Black, 2009a,b,c, 2010, 2013; Högler et al., 2008). These studies have analyzed how trabeculae ossify and develop the pattern of trabecular bone organization and the relationship between trabecular patterning and cortical structure and thickness. Micro-CT allows for the internal architecture of an intact bone to be viewed with high spatial resolution so that the parameters of trabecular bone structure can be examined and quantified (Cunningham and Black, 2009a; Van Dessel et al., 2013). An understanding of trabecular architecture in juvenile bone can inform how the mechanical properties of bone develop throughout life and in particular how load-bearing properties develop These studies contribute to an understanding of the normal growth of juvenile bone, so that it may be compared to pathological development to evaluate parameters such as low bone density (Bianchi, 2007). Variation in bone mass can have a different level of impact on skeletal fragility depending on how it affects the density of the microarchitecture, as trabecular microarchitecture is a critical factor in overall bone strength (Marcus and Bouxsein, 2008; Van Dessel et al., 2013). By understanding the development of the trabecular pattern in infants and juveniles, it may be possible to better understand the basis for healthy growth throughout development. This may lead to an enhanced understanding of how peak bone mass is obtained in adults, which has an influence on lifetime bone health (Kamel, 2005; Marcus and Bouxsein, 2008; Mehler et al., 2011). Of course, other features of bone geometry, as well as mineral content, are integral to maintaining strength throughout juvenile bone growth, particularly the changing relationship between bone length, diameter, and mass (Högler et al., 2008). MRI and dual-energy X-ray absorptiometry can be used to assess multiple features of bone strength and development, including bone mineral content, cortical mineral density, various measurements of bone area and diameter, and cortical thickness (Högler et al., 2008). Application of this imaging technology using male and female subjects of different ages can also reveal how the mechanical and hormonal influences of puberty will affect the structure of the bone, by providing data on the pattern and rate at which differences in bone geometry develop between sexes (Högler et al., 2008).

As demonstrated, the use of modern imaging equipment has the potential to expand the type of research possible in the field of developmental osteology. The recent literature demonstrates the power of these technologies in facilitating an enhanced understanding of bone growth and development and the bearing that this information has on age estimation in living and deceased individuals.

■ CASE APPLICATION

Sadly, one of the more disturbing tasks that a forensic anthropologist may be asked to perform is to analyze juvenile remains for potential signs of child abuse (Cardoso and Magalhães, 2011; Lambert and Walker, 1997). Neglect is by far the most common form of child mistreatment and results when a caregiver fails to provide the child with the basic necessities of life, such as adequate nutrition, a safe environment in which to live, good hygiene, etc. (Joffe et al., 2005; Ross and Juarez, 2016). Without these basic needs, the child becomes susceptible to negative conditions associated with malnutrition, recurrent infection, and injury. If left untreated, these factors may leave an imprint on the juvenile skeleton in the form of delayed growth and development. Anthropological findings of markedly short stature and delayed skeletal maturity may serve as one line of evidence that can help substantiate claims of chronic neglect and/or severe undernourishment made by the medical examiner or prosecution (Cardoso and Magalhães, 2011; Ross, 2011; Ross and Juarez, 2014, 2016). Of utmost importance in this analysis, however, is the utilization of growth standards specific to the ancestry of the child as certain populations may exhibit markedly reduced stature without having ever been abused. A fictitious case is provided to illustrate the process of how this might be accomplished.

The remains of a 5-year, 2-month-old male child were found at his home in Boondock, United States, where he was living with his mother, who was a known crack addict. The death appeared to be accidental in nature. However, there was concern regarding the amount of supervision provided to the child to ensure safe living conditions. The child also appeared severely undernourished suggesting that chronic neglect was an issue. An anthropologist was consulted to document the stature and skeletal age of the child and determine whether the boy's growth profile was significantly delayed compared to other 5-year-old boys.

In the above scenario, where the body was discovered prior to the onset of marked decomposition, documentation of stature is a relatively straightforward task. Height can be measured directly from the body and then compared to growth charts representing 5-year-old boys from the same or similar ancestry. If circumstances are such that the remains have become skeletonized prior to analysis, or if for whatever reason height cannot be directly measured from the fleshed body, the process is more involved and requires that stature be estimated via long bone measurements. Numerous studies are available that provide regression equations for estimating height using the six major long bones (Telkkä et al., 1962; Feldesman, 1992; Smith, 2007; Ruff, 2007). Practitioners should keep in mind, however, that these studies were derived from living subjects whose long bone lengths were measured radiographically, which may or may not affect stature estimation when utilizing dry bone.

Developmental delays of the skeletal system can also be assessed. Methods utilized for this endeavor will be specific to the overall age category of the child. Assessment of infants and young children may rely heavily on the time in which ossification centers normally appear, as most make their appearance within the first 3 years of life (Schaefer et al., 2009). For those in their teenage years and early twenties, there is likely to be a greater concentration on timing of epiphyseal union. Under normal circumstances, nutritional neglect becomes less of an issue with advancing age, as children become less dependent on their caregivers and have a greater possibility of identifying alternative food sources. In the case of a disabled child, however, independence from their caregiver may not be possible, thus methods that assess maturity levels associated with juveniles nearing adulthood are still relevant.

For children whose age category falls between the timing in which ossification centers appear and fuse, analysis relies on shape changes of the epiphyses. Radiographic atlases that highlight sequential development of various joint regions are an ideal source for this investigatory measure. Once skeletal age is determined via the radiographic atlas, a two standard deviation interval should be applied to determine the normal range of chronological ages observed to demonstrate that developmental profile. The standard deviation should be specific to the joint region being investigated and also reflect the same, or close to the same, population as the child being assessed.

In this example, the standard deviation calculated by Schaefer et al. (2016) and presented in Table 6.2, is utilized as it reflects the variation observed within an American sample specific to young children. Fig. 6.1 represents the radiographic image of the child's knee. The developmental maturity displayed within the radiograph was identified as most closely resembling plate 12 (skeletal age 42 months) within the male section of Pyle and Hoer's radiographic atlas of the knee. A 7.0 months standard deviation was applied to the 42-month skeletal age to produce an expected chronological age range of 28–56 months. The 62-month age of the child in the scenario is older than the maximum expected age of an individual displaying that degree of maturity. While this line of evidence does not prove that the child suffered from maltreatment, it does demonstrate that his development was delayed to that of the norm.

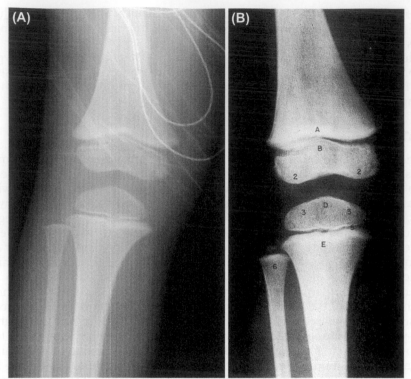

Figure 6.1 Comparison of radiographic images of the knee. Image A represents that of the fictitious 5-year-old boy described in the case scenario and Image B is a replication of Plate 12 within the radiographic atlas of the knee. Note the similarities in shape as well as size relative to the metaphyseal ends of the diaphysis, of the two distal femoral and proximal tibial epiphyses. *Courtesy of Query Patricia, Mercyhurst.*

If soft tissue structures have decomposed to the point at which epiphyses are no longer held in place, the anthropologist is more confined in their analysis of skeletal development. Presence or absence of ossification centers loses its significance, as one is never sure whether the center has yet to appear or whether it simply was not recovered with the remains. In addition, centers first appear as shapeless nodules that are difficult to identify when removed from their original context. Thus, the bone to which the center belongs may not be known. Morphological changes that the epiphyses undergo throughout the developmental process are also difficult to assess, and little research has documented this process on dry bone. Anthropological analysis is therefore confined to fusion assessment. Although most epiphyses are observed to unite throughout the teenage years and early twenties, union of a few primary ossification centers occur early in life and may be of use in this endeavor. Some of these centers include, for example, fusion of the mandibular bodies, vertebral arches (to one another as well as to the vertebral bodies), and sacral bodies.

Assessment of the dentition is generally not considered a good source for supporting evidence of maltreatment, as dental development is less susceptible to environmental stresses. Numerous studies investigating children suffering from growth abnormalities, disease, and/or, malnutrition consistently report dental maturity to be more in sync with chronological age than that of skeletal maturity (Holderbaum et al., 2005; Laor et al., 1982; Ozerovic, 1980; Vallejo-Bolaños and España-López, 1997). That is not to say, however, that dental analysis does not have a role to play in the investigation of child mistreatment cases. In the event that age cannot be proven by birth documents, development of the dentition can instead be used as a predictor of chronological age. A skeletal age that lags significantly behind dental age, or a stature that is considerably shorter than the norm as predicted by dental age, may provide evidence of growth and developmental delays. Practitioners should keep in mind that the difference exhibited between skeletal age and dental age may be less pronounced than between that of skeletal age and chronological age as dental development, although less vulnerable to environmental stresses, can still be affected to some degree by malnutrition (Cardoso, 2007; Conceição and Cardoso, 2011).

■ CONCLUSION

This chapter provides a synthesis of current research regarding juvenile age estimation. It highlights advancements in current methodology and techniques, such as dry bone analysis and the use of new imaging technologies. This chapter also presents developments and trends within the field, including the estimation of age of the living and population-specific standards.

For many practitioners, dry bone analysis has remained the primary tool in juvenile aging. Although research advancing this method has been limited mainly due to the scant number of documented juvenile osteological remains, a number of recent collections located mostly in Western Europe have been curated. These materials have provided an opportunity for researchers to assess new elements, develop statistical methods for timing of epiphyseal union, and create regression equations to correlate bone size with age. Although this research has expanded upon previous knowledge, it should be noted that many of these collections originate from archaeological or historic material or are affected by environmental, socioeconomic, or other extrinsic factors, possibly creating secular differences in the rate of aging.

New technologies, such as conventional radiography, MRI, ultrasound, and CT, are proving to be highly useful for juvenile age estimation. Radiographic techniques are especially important in cases where soft tissue is present and has been used to estimate the age for both the deceased and the living. Radiographic atlases of joints, originally developed for other purposes, have been utilized for juvenile age estimation, especially for living children. The estimation of age of living children is an increasingly necessary task and often used for undocumented immigrants or criminal investigations to determine if the individual has met the legally relevant ages of 16, 18, or 21. This is often completed through technologies that allow for the examination of the appearance of centers of ossification, changes in the epiphyses, and the process of epiphyseal union, as well as new approaches, such as mineralization and geometric morphometrics.

Additional technologies, such as MDCT, have increased in popularity, as MDCT can produce both thick and thin slices in a large body region, as well as create 3D images. Recent studies have also demonstrated that there is no significant difference in osteological measurements taken from MDCT technologies versus dry bone analysis, demonstrating that this method can be useful when soft tissue cannot be removed. Other CT technologies have also examined and documented the trabecular structure of bone to better evaluate the normal growth of bone throughout development.

Radiation-free technologies, such as MRI and ultrasound, offer a safer and often more precise way to assess the age of living children. In comparison to traditional radiography, MRI provides thin slices of the joint at a higher contrast and more detail without the superimposition of structures. The use of ultrasound technologies is also increasing due to its availability and low cost. However, due to the subjectivity in interpretation and lack of legal merit, ultrasound has not been widely accepted.

Within each of these technologies and methods has been a push to develop sex- and population-specific standards. As many techniques were created for use with Western children, studies testing these methods on other populations have resulted in mixed conclusions about their utility in other regions. However, it is clear that a combination of secular and population differences do have an impact on some populations, leading to the need to at least test the utility of methods on groups that do not share similar intrinsic and extrinsic factors.

References

Aggrawal, A., 2009. Estimation of age in the living: in matters civil and criminal. Proceedings of the Anatomical Society of Great Britain and Ireland. J. Anat. 213 (S4), 342–355.

Albert, M.A., Maier, C.A., 2013. Epiphyseal union of the cervical vertebral centra: its relationship to skeletal age and maturation of thoracic vertebral centra. J. Forensic Sci. 58 (6), 1568–1574.

Albert, M., Mulhern, D., Torpey, M.A., Boone, E., 2010. Age estimation using thoracic and first two lumbar vertebral ring epiphyseal union. J. Forensic Sci. 55 (2), 287–294.

Baccetti, T., Franchi, L., McNamara, J.A., 2005. The cervical vertebral maturation (CVM) method for the assessment of optimal treatment timing in dentofacial orthopedics. Semin. Orthod. 11 (3), 119–129.

Bhise, S.S., Nanandkar, S.D., 2012. Age determination from pelvis: a radiological study in Mumbai region. J. Indian Acad. Forensic Med. 34 (2), 104–107.

Bianchi, M.L., 2007. Osteoporosis in children and adolescents. Bone 41 (4), 486–495.

Bilgili, Y., Hizel, S., Kara, S.A., Sanli, C., Erdal, H.H., Altinok, D., 2003. Accuracy of skeletal age assessment in children from birth to 6 years of age with the ultrasonographic version of the Greulich-Pyle atlas. J. Ultrasound Med. 22 (7), 683–690.

Brodeur, A.E., Silberstein, M.J., Graviss, E.R., 1981. Radiology of the Pediatric Elbow. GK Hall Medical Publishers, Boston.

Brough, A.L., Bennett, J., Morgan, B., Black, S., Rutty, G.N., 2013. Anthropological measurement of the juvenile clavicle using multi-detector computed tomography—affirming reliability. J. Forensic Sci. 58 (4), 946–951.

Brough, A.L., Rutty, G.N., Black, S., Morgan, B., 2012. Post-mortem computed tomography and 3D imaging: anthropological applications for juvenile remains. Forensic Sci. Med. Pathol. 8 (3), 270–279.

Büken, B., Şafak, A.A., Yazıcı, B., Büken, E., Mayda, A.S., 2007. Is the assessment of bone age by the Greulich–Pyle method reliable at forensic age estimation for Turkish children? Forensic Sci. Int. 173 (2), 146–153.

Cameriere, R., De Luca, S., De Angelis, D., Merelli, V., Giuliodori, A., Cingolani, M., Cattaneo, C., Ferrante, L., 2012. Reliability of Schmeling's stages of ossification of medial clavicular epiphyses and its validity to assess 18 years of age in living subjects. Int. J. Legal Med. 126 (6), 923–932.

Cameriere, R., Ferrante, L., 2008. Age estimation in children by measurement of carpals and epiphyses of radius and ulna and open apices in teeth: a pilot study. Forensic Sci. Int. 174 (1), 60–63.

Cameriere, R., Ferrante, L., Ermenc, B., Mirtella, D., Štrus, K., 2008. Age estimation using carpals: study of a Slovenian sample to test Cameriere's method. Forensic Sci. Int. 174 (2), 178–181.

Cameriere, R., Ferrante, L., Mirtella, D., Cingolani, M., 2006. Carpals and epiphyses of radius and ulna as age indicators. Int. J. Legal Med. 120 (3), 143–146.

Cantekin, K., Celikoglu, M., Miloglu, O., Dane, A., Erdem, A., 2012. Bone age assessment: the applicability of the Greulich–Pyle method in Eastern Turkish children. J. Forensic Sci. 57 (3), 679–682.

Cardoso, H.F., 2007. Environmental effects on skeletal versus dental development: using a documented subadult skeletal sample to test a basic assumption in human osteological research. Am. J. Phys. Anthropol. 132 (2), 223–233.

Cardoso, H.F., 2008a. Age estimation of adolescent and young adult male and female skeletons II, epiphyseal union at the upper limb and scapular girdle in a modern Portuguese skeletal sample. Am. J. Phys. Anthropol. 137 (1), 97–105.

Cardoso, H.F., 2008b. Epiphyseal union at the innominate and lower limb in a modern Portuguese skeletal sample, and age estimation in adolescent and young adult male and female skeletons. Am. J. Phys. Anthropol. 135 (2), 161–170.

Cardoso, H.F., 2009. A test of three methods for estimating stature from immature skeletal remains using long bone lengths. J. Forensic Sci. 54 (1), 13–19.

Cardoso, H.F.V., Gomes, J., Campanacho, V., Marinho, L., 2013. Age estimation of immature human skeletal remains using the post-natal development of the occipital bone. Int. J. Legal Med. 127 (5), 997–1004.

Cardoso, H.F., Magalhães, T., 2011. Evidence of neglect from immature human skeletal remains: an auxological approach from bones and teeth. In: Abel, S.M., Ross, A.H. (Eds.), The Juvenile Skeleton in Forensic Abuse Investigations. Humana Press, New York, pp. 125–150.

Cardoso, H.F., Pereira, V., Rios, L., 2014. Chronology of fusion of the primary and secondary ossification centers in the human sacrum and age estimation in child and adolescent skeletons. Am. J. Phys. Anthropol. 153 (2), 214–225.

Cardoso, H.F., Ríos, L., 2011. Age estimation from stages of epiphyseal union in the presacral vertebrae. Am. J. Phys. Anthropol. 144 (2), 238–247.

Cardoso, H.F.V., Severino, R.S.S., 2010. The chronology of epiphyseal union in the hand and foot from dry bone observations. Int. J. Osteoarchaeol 20 (6), 737–746.

Chiang, K.H., Chou, A.S.B., Yen, P.S., Ling, C.M., Lin, C.C., Lee, C.C., Chang, P.Y., 2005. The reliability of using Greulich-Pyle method to determine children's bone age in Taiwan. Tzu Chi Med. J. 17 (6), 417–420.

Cole, A.L., Webb, L., Cole, T.J., 1988. Bone age estimation: a comparison of methods. Br. J. Radiol. 61 (728), 683–686.

Conceição, E.L.N., Cardoso, H.F.V., 2011. Environmental effects on skeletal versus dental development II: further testing of a basic assumption in human osteological research. Am. J. Phys. Anthropol. 144 (3), 463–470.

Coqueugniot, H., Weaver, T.D., 2007. Brief communication: infracranial maturation in the skeletal collection from Coimbra, Portugal: new aging standards for epiphyseal union. Am. J. Phys. Anthropol. 134 (3), 424–437.

Crowder, C., Austin, D., 2005. Age ranges of epiphyseal fusion in the distal tibia and fibula of contemporary males and females. J. Forensic Sci. 50 (5), 1001–1007.

Cunha, E., Baccino, E., Martrille, L., Ramsthaler, F., Prieto, J., Schuliar, Y., Cattaneo, C., 2009. The problem of aging human remains and living individuals: a review. Forensic Sci. Int. 193 (1), 1–13.

Cunningham, C.A., Black, S.M., 2009a. Anticipating bipedalism: trabecular organization in the newborn ilium. J. Anat. 214 (6), 817–829.

Cunningham, C.A., Black, S.M., 2009b. Development of the fetal ilium–challenging concepts of bipedality. J. Anat. 214 (1), 91–99.

Cunningham, C.A., Black, S.M., 2009c. Iliac cortical thickness in the neonate–the gradient effect. J. Anat. 215 (3), 364–370.

Cunningham, C.A., Black, S.M., 2010. The neonatal ilium—metaphyseal drivers and vascular passengers. Anat. Rec. 293 (8), 1297–1309.

Cunningham, C.A., Black, S.M., 2013. The vascular collar of the ilium—three-dimensional evaluation of the dominant nutrient foramen. Clin. Anat. 26 (4), 502–508.

Davies, C.M., Hackman, L., Black, S., 2013. The utility of the proximal epiphysis of the fifth metatarsal in age estimation. J. Forensic Sci. 58 (2), 436–442.

De Sanctis, V., Soliman, A.T., Di Maio, S., Bedair, S., 2014. Are the new automated methods for bone age estimation advantageous over the manual approaches? Pediatr. Endocrinol. Rev. 12 (2), 200–205.

Dedouit, F., Auriol, J., Rousseau, H., Rougé, D., Crubézy, E., Telmon, N., 2012. Age assessment by magnetic resonance imaging of the knee: a preliminary study. Forensic Sci. Int. 217 (1), 232.e1–232.e7.

Demirjian, A., Goldstein, H., Tanner, J.M., 1973. A new system of dental age assessment. Hum. Biol. 45 (2), 211–227.

Dogaroiu, C., Avramoiu, M., 2015. Correlation between chronological age and the stage of union of the distal femur and proximal tibia epiphyses in a Romanian sample population. Rom. J. Leg. Med. 23 (3), 171–176.

Dogaroiu, C., Capatina, C.O., Gherghe, E.V., Avramoiu, M., 2014. The importance of the ossification centre morphology in the left hand-wrist bones for age evaluation. Rom. J. Leg. Med. 22 (2), 105–108.

Ebner, T., Stern, D., Donner, R., Bischof, H., Urschler, M., 2014. Towards automatic bone age estimation from MRI: localization of 3D anatomical landmarks. Med. Image Comput. Comput. Assist. Interv. 17 (Pt 2), 421–428.

Feldesman, M.R., 1992. Femur/stature ratio and estimates of stature in children. Am. J. Phys. Anthropol. 87 (4), 447–459.

Garamendi, P.M., Landa, M.I., Botella, M.C., Alemán, I., 2011. Forensic age estimation on digital X-ray images: medial epiphyses of the clavicle and first rib ossification in relation to chronological age. J. Forensic Sci. 56 (s1), S3–S12.

Ghantus, M.K., 1951. Growth of the shaft of the human radius and ulna during the first two years of life. Am. J. Roentgenol. Radium Ther. 65 (5), 784–786.

Gindhart, P.S., 1973. Growth standards for the tibia and radius in children aged one month through eighteen years. Am. J. Phys. Anthropol. 39 (1), 41–48.

Goldman, L.W., 2008. Principles of CT: multislice CT. J. Nucl. Med. Technol. 36 (2), 57–68.

Greulich, W.W., 1957. A comparison of the physical growth and development of American-born and native Japanese children. Am. J. Phys. Anthropol. 15 (4), 489–515.

Greulich, W.W., Pyle, S.I., 1959. Radiographic Atlas of Skeletal Development of the Hand and Wrist, second ed. Stanford University Press, Stanford.

Groell, R., Lindbichler, F., Riepl, T., Gherra, L., Roposch, A., Fotter, R., 1999. The reliability of bone age determination in central European children using the Greulich and Pyle method. Br. J. Radiol. 72 (857), 461–464.

Hackman, L., Black, S., 2013. The reliability of the Greulich and Pyle atlas when applied to a modern Scottish population. J. Forensic Sci. 58 (1), 114–119.

Hoerr, N.L., Pyle, S.I., Francis, C.C., 1962. Radiographic Atlas of Skeletal Development of the Foot and Ankle: A Standard of Reference. Charles C. Thomas, Springfield.

Högler, W., Blimkie, C.J.R., Cowell, C.T., Inglis, D., Rauch, F., Kemp, A.F., Wiebe, P., Duncan, C.S., Farpour-Lambert, N., Woodhead, H.J., 2008. Sex-specific developmental changes in muscle size and bone geometry at the femoral shaft. Bone 42 (5), 982–989.

Holderbaum, R.M., Veeck, E.B., Oliveira, H.W., Silva, C.L., Fernandes, Â., 2005. Comparison among dental, skeletal and chronological development in HIV-positive children: a radiographic study. Braz. Oral Res. 19 (3), 209–215.

Hsieh, C.W., Liu, T.C., Jong, T.L., Tiu, C.M., 2013. Long-term secular trend of skeletal maturation of Taiwanese children between agricultural (1960s) and contemporary (after 2000s) generations using the Tanner-Whitehouse 3 (TW3) method. J. Pediatr. Endocrinol. Metab. 26 (3–4), 231–237.

Jimenez-Castellanos, J., Carmona, A., Catalina-Herrera, C.J., Vinuales, M., 1996. Skeletal maturation of wrist and hand ossification centers in normal Spanish boys and girls: a study using the Greulich-Pyle method. Cells Tissues Organs 155 (3), 206–211.

Joffe, M.D., Giardino, A.P., O'Sullivan, A.L., 2005. Neglect and abandonment. In: Monteleone, J.A., Brodeur, A.E. (Eds.), Child Maltreatment: A Clinical Guide and Reference, third ed. GW Medical Publishing Inc., St Louis, pp. 153–193.

Kamel, H.K., 2005. Male osteoporosis: new trends in diagnosis and therapy. Drugs & Aging 22 (9), 741–748.

Kasper, K.A., Austin, D., Kvanli, A.H., Rios, T.R., Senn, D.R., 2009. Reliability of third molar development for age estimation in a Texas Hispanic population: a comparison study. J. Forensic Sci. 54 (3), 651–657.

Kellinghaus, M., Schulz, R., Vieth, V., Schmidt, S., Schmeling, A., 2010. Forensic age estimation in living subjects based on the ossification status of the medial clavicular epiphysis as revealed by thin-slice multidetector computed tomography. Int. J. Leg. Med. 124 (2), 149–154.

Koc, A., Karaoglanoglu, M., Erdogan, M., Kosecik, M., Cesur, Y., 2001. Assessment of bone ages: is the Greulich-Pyle method sufficient for Turkish boys? Pediatr. Int. 43 (6), 662–665.

Konigsberg, L.W., Herrmann, N.P., Wescott, D.J., Kimmerle, E.H., 2008. Estimation and evidence in forensic anthropology: age-at-death. J. Forensic Sci. 53 (3), 541–557.

Krämer, J.A., Schmidt, S., Jürgens, K.U., Lentschig, M., Schmeling, A., Vieth, V., 2014a. Forensic age estimation in living individuals using 3.0 T MRI of the distal femur. Int. J. Leg. Med. 128 (3), 509–514.

Krämer, J.A., Schmidt, S., Jürgens, K.U., Lentschig, M., Schmeling, A., Vieth, V., 2014b. The use of magnetic resonance imaging to examine ossification of the proximal tibial epiphysis for forensic age estimation in living individuals. Forensic Sci. Med. Pathol. 10 (3), 306–313.

Krogman, W.M., 1939. A guide to the identification of human skeletal material. FBI Law Enforc. Bull. 8 (8), 3–31.

Lajolo, C., Giuliani, M., Cordaro, M., Marigo, L., Marcelli, A., Fiorillo, F., Pascali, V.L., Oliva, A., 2013. Two new oro-cervical radiographic indexes for chronological age estimation: a pilot study on an Italian population. J. Forensic Leg. Med. 20 (7), 861–866.

Lambert, P.M., Walker, P.L., 1997. Skeletal evidence for child abuse: a physical anthropological perspective. J. Forensic Sci. 42 (2), 196–207.

Langley-Shirley, N., Jantz, R.L., 2010. A Bayesian approach to age estimation in modern Americans from the clavicle. J. Forensic Sci. 55 (3), 571–583.

Laor, E., Garfunkel, A., Koyoumdjisky-Kaye, E., 1982. Skeletal and dental retardation in β-thalassemia major. Hum. Biol. 54 (1), 85–92.

Laor, T., Jaramillo, D., 2009. MR imaging insights into skeletal maturation: what is normal? Radiology 250 (1), 28–38.

López-Costas, O., Rissech, C., Trancho, G., Turbón, D., 2012. Postnatal ontogenesis of the tibia. Implications for age and sex estimation. Forensic Sci. Int. 214 (1–3), 207.e1–207.e11.

Mansourvar, M., Ismail, M.A., Raj, R.G., Kareem, S.A., Aik, S., Gunalan, R., Antony, C.D., 2014. The applicability of Greulich and Pyle atlas to assess skeletal age for four ethnic groups. J. Forensic Leg. Med. 22, 26–29.

Marcus, R., Bouxsein, M., 2008. The nature of osteoporosis. In: Marcus, R., Feldman, D., Nelson, D., Rosen, C.J. (Eds.), Osteoporosis, third ed. Elsevier, Inc., Burlington, pp. 27–36.

Maresh, M.M., 1943. Growth of major long bones in healthy children: a preliminary report on successive roentgenograms of the extremities from early infancy to twelve years of age. Am. J. Dis. Child. 66 (3), 227–257.

Maresh, M.M., 1955. Linear growth of long bones of extremities from infancy through adolescence: continuing studies. Am. J. Dis. Child. 89 (6), 725–742.

Maresh, M.M., 1970. Measurements from roentgenograms. In: McCammaon, R.W. (Ed.), Human Growth and Development. CC Thomas, Springfield, pp. 157–200.

Meijerman, L., Maat, G.J., Schulz, R., Schmeling, A., 2007. Variables affecting the probability of complete fusion of the medial clavicular epiphysis. Int. J. Leg. Med. 121 (6), 463–468.

McKern, T.W., Stewart, T.D., 1957. Skeletal Age Changes in Young American Males: Analysed from the Standpoint of Age Identification. Environmental Protection Research Division, Technical Report EP-45. Headquarters Quartermaster Research and Development Command, Natick, MA.

SECTION I

Mehler, P.S., Cleary, B.S., Gaudiani, J.L., 2011. Osteoporosis in anorexia nervosa. Eat. Disord. 19 (2), 194–202.

Mentzel, H.J., Vilser, C., Eulenstein, M., Schwartz, T., Vogt, S., Böttcher, J., Yaniv, I., Tsoref, L., Kauf, E., Kaiser, W.A., 2005. Assessment of skeletal age at the wrist in children with a new ultrasound device. Pediatr. Radiol. 35 (4), 429–433.

Minier, M., Maret, D., Dedouit, F., Vergnault, M., Mokrane, F.Z., Rousseau, H., Adalian, P., Telmon, N., Rougé, D., 2014. Fetal age estimation using MSCT scans of deciduous tooth germs. Int. J. Leg. Med. 128 (1), 177–182.

Mora, S., Boechat, M.I., Pietka, E., Huang, H.K., Gilsanz, V., 2001. Skeletal age determinations in children of European and African descent: applicability of the Greulich and Pyle standards. Pediatr. Res. 50 (5), 624–628.

Moradi, M., Sirous, M., Morovatti, P., 2012. The reliability of skeletal age determination in an Iranian sample using Greulich and Pyle method. Forensic Sci. Int. 223 (1), 372.e1–372.e4.

Nagaoka, S.I., Hassold, T.J., Hunt, P.A., 2012. Human aneuploidy: mechanisms and new insights into an age-old problem. Nat. Rev. Genet. 13 (7), 493–504.

Nemade, K.S., Kamdi, N.Y., Parchand, M.P., 2010. Ages of epiphyseal union around wrist joint–a radiological study. J. Anat. Soc. India 59, 205–210.

Noback, C.R., 1944. The developmental anatomy of the human osseous skeleton during the embryonic, fetal and circumnatal periods. Anat. Rec. 88 (1), 91–125.

O'Connor, J.E., Bogue, C., Spence, L.D., Last, J., 2008. A method to establish the relationship between chronological age and stage of union from radiographic assessment of epiphyseal fusion at the knee: an Irish population study. J. Anat. 212 (2), 198–209.

O'Connor, J.E., Coyle, J., Spence, L.D., Last, J., 2013. Epiphyseal maturity indicators at the knee and their relationship to chronological age: results of an Irish population study. Clin. Anat. 26 (6), 755–767.

O'Connor, J.E., Coyle, J., Bogue, C., Spence, L.D., Last, J., 2014. Age prediction formulae from radiographic assessment of skeletal maturation at the knee in an Irish population. Forensic Sci. Int. 234 (188), e1–8.

Ontell, F.K., Ivanovic, M., Ablin, D.S., Barlow, T.W., 1996. Bone age in children of diverse ethnicity. Am. J. Roentgenol. 167 (6), 1395–1398.

Ousley, S., Daly, S., Frazee, K., Stull, K., 2013. A Radiographic Database for Estimating Biological Parameters in Modern Subadults. Final Technical Report. National Institute of Justice Award.

Ozerovic, B., 1980. Correlation of dental and skeletal age in children with cerebral palsy. Eur. J. Orthod. 2 (3), 193–195.

Patel, G., Shilajiya, D., Govekar, G., Tailor, C., 2011. Radiological study of fusion of iliac crest by digital method. J. Indian Acad. Forensic Med. 33 (4), 301–305.

Patil, S.T., Parchand, M.P., Meshram, M.M., Kamdi, N.Y., 2012. Applicability of Greulich and Pyle skeletal age standards to Indian children. Forensic Sci. Int. 216 (1–3), 200.e1–200.e4.

Patond, S., Tirpude, B., Pande, V., 2015. Age estimation by radiological assessment of proximal tibial epiphysis. J. Med. Sci. 8 (2), 144–149.

Paxton, M.L., Lamont, A.C., Stillwell, A.P., 2013. The reliability of the Greulich-Pyle method in bone age determination among Australian children. J. Med. Imaging Radiat. Oncol. 57 (1), 21–24.

Prader, A., Tanner, J.M., Von Harnack, G.A., 1963. Catch-up growth following illness or starvation: an example of developmental canalization in man. J. Pediatr. 62 (5), 646–659.

Pujol, A., Rissech, C., Ventura, J., Badosa, J., Turbón, D., 2014. Ontogeny of the female femur: geometric morphometric analysis applied on current living individuals of a Spanish population. J. Anat. 225 (3), 346–357.

Pujol, A., Rissech, C., Ventura, J., Turbón, D., 2016. Ontogeny of the male femur: geometric morphometric analysis applied to a contemporary Spanish population. Am. J. Phys. Anthropol. 159 (1), 146–163.

Pyle, S.I., Hoerr, N.L., 1969. A Radiographic Standard of Reference for the Growing Knee, first ed. Charles C. Thomas, Springfield.

Ríos, L., Cardoso, H.F., 2009. Age estimation from stages of union of the vertebral epiphyses of the ribs. Am. J. Phys. Anthropol. 140 (2), 265–274.

Ríos, L., Weisensee, K., Rissech, C., 2008. Sacral fusion as an aid in age estimation. Forensic Sci. Int. 180 (2), 111.e1.

Rissech, C., Black, S., 2007. Scapular development from the neonatal period to skeletal maturity: a preliminary study. Int. J. Osteoarchaeol. 17 (5), 451–464.

Rissech, C., López-Costas, O., Turbón, D., 2013a. Humeral development from neonatal period to skeletal maturity—application in age and sex assessment. Int. J. Leg. Med. 127 (1), 201–212.

Rissech, C., Malgosa, A., 2005. Ilium growth study: applicability in sex and age diagnosis. Forensic Sci. Int. 147 (2), 165–174.

Rissech, C., Malgosa, A., 2007. Pubis growth study: applicability in sexual and age diagnostic. Forensic Sci. Int. 173 (2), 137–145.

Rissech, C., Márquez-Grant, N., Turbón, D., 2013b. A collation of recently published Western European formulae for age estimation of subadult skeletal remains: recommendations for forensic anthropology and osteoarchaeology. J. Forensic Sci. 58 (s1), 163–168.

Rissech, C., Schaefer, M., Malgosa, A., 2008. Development of the femur—implications for age and sex determination. Forensic Sci. Int. 180 (1), 1–9.

Rissech, C., Wilson, J., Winburn, A.P., Turbón, D., Steadman, D., 2012. A comparison of three established age estimation methods on an adult Spanish sample. Int. J. Leg. Med. 126 (1), 145–155.

Robinson, C., Eisma, R., Morgan, B., Jeffery, A., Graham, E.A., Black, S., Rutty, G.N., 2008. Anthropological measurement of lower limb and foot bones using multi-detector computed tomography. J. Forensic Sci. 53 (6), 1289–1295.

Ruff, C., 2007. Body size prediction from juvenile skeletal remains. Am. J. Phys. Anthropol. 133 (1), 698–716.

Ross, A.H., 2011. Fatal starvation/malnutrition: medicolegal investigation from the juvenile skeleton. In: Ross, A.H., Abel, S.M. (Eds.), The Juvenile Skeleton in Forensic Abuse Investigations. Humana Press, New York, pp. 151–165.

Ross, A.H., Juarez, C.A., 2014. A brief history of fatal child maltreatment and neglect. Forensic Sci. Med. Pathol. 10 (3), 413–422.

Ross, A.H., Juarez, C.A., 2016. Skeletal and radiological manifestations of child abuse: Implications for study in past populations. Clin. Anat. http://dx.doi.org/10.1002/ca.22683.

Saint-Martin, P., Rérolle, C., Dedouit, F., Bouilleau, L., Rousseau, H., Rougé, D., Telmon, N., 2013. Age estimation by magnetic resonance imaging of the distal tibial epiphysis and the calcaneum. Int. J. Leg. Med. 127 (5), 1023–1030.

Saint-Martin, P., Rérolle, C., Dedouit, F., Rousseau, H., Rougé, D., Telmon, N., 2014. Evaluation of an automatic method for forensic age estimation by magnetic resonance imaging of the distal tibial epiphysis—a preliminary study focusing on the 18-year threshold. Int. J. Leg. Med 128 (4), 675–683.

Saint-Martin, P., Rérolle, C., Pucheux, J., Dedouit, F., Telmon, N., 2015. Contribution of distal femur MRI to the determination of the 18-year limit in forensic age estimation. Int. J. Leg. Med. 129 (3), 619–620.

Santoro, V., Roca, R., De Donno, A., Fiandaca, C., Pinto, G., Tafuri, S., Introna, F., 2012. Applicability of Greulich and Pyle and Demirijan aging methods to a sample of Italian population. Forensic Sci. Int. 221 (1–3), 153.e1–153.e5.

Santos, C., Ferreira, M., Alves, F.C., Cunha, E., 2011. Comparative study of Greulich and Pyle atlas and Maturos 4.0 program for age estimation in a Portuguese sample. Forensic Sci. Int. 212 (1–3), 276.e1–276.e7.

Schaefer, M.C., 2008a. A summary of epiphyseal union timings in Bosnian males. Int. J. Osteoarchaeol. 18 (5), 536–545.

Schaefer, M.C., 2008b. Patterns of epiphyseal union and their use in the detection and sorting of commingled remains. In: Adams, B.J., Byrd, J.E. (Eds.), Recovery, Analysis, and Identification of Commingled Human Remains. Humana Press, Totowa, pp. 221–240.

Schaefer, M.C., 2014. A practical method for detecting commingled remains using epiphyseal union. In: Adams, B.J., Byrd, J.E. (Eds.), Commingled Human Remains: Methods in Recovery, Analysis, and Identification. Academic Press, San Diego, pp. 123–144.

Schaefer, M.C., Black, S.M., 2005. Comparison of ages of epiphyseal union in North American and Bosnian skeletal material. J. Forensic Sci. 50 (4), 777–784.

Schaefer, M.C., Black, S.M., 2007. Epiphyseal union sequencing: aiding in the recognition and sorting of commingled remains. J. Forensic Sci. 52 (2), 277–285.

Schaefer, M.C., Black, S.M., Scheuer, L., 2009. Juvenile Osteology: A Laboratory and Field Manual. Academic Press, Burlington.

Schaefer, M.C., Aben, G., Vogelsberg, C., 2015. A demonstration of appearance and union times of three shoulder ossification centers in adolescent and post-adolescent children. J. Forensic Radiol. Imaging 3 (1), 49–56.

Schaefer, M.C., Hackman, L., Gallagher, J., 2016. Variability in developmental timings of the knee in young American children as assessed through Pyle and Hoerr's radiographic atlas. Int. J. Leg. Med. 130 (2), 501–509.

Scheuer, L., Black, S.M., 2000. Developmental Juvenile Osteology, first ed. Academic Press, London.

Schmeling, A., Black, S., 2010. An introduction to the history of age estimation in the living. In: Black, S., Aggrawal, A., Payne-James, J. (Eds.), Age Estimation in the Living: The Practitioner's Guide. Wiley-Blackwell, Sussex, pp. 1–18.

Schmeling, A., Geserick, G., Reisinger, W., Olze, A., 2007. Age estimation. Forensic Sci. Int. 165 (2), 178–181.

Schmeling, A., Olze, A., Reisinger, W., Geserick, G., 2001. Age estimation of living people undergoing criminal proceedings. Lancet 358 (9276), 89–90.

Schmeling, A., Olze, A., Reisinger, W., Geserick, G., 2004a. Forensic age diagnostics of living people undergoing criminal proceedings. Forensic Sci. Int. 144 (2), 243–245.

Schmeling, A., Reisinger, W., Geserick, G., Olze, A., 2006. Age estimation of unaccompanied minors: Part I. General considerations. Forensic Sci. Int. 159, S61–S64.

Schmeling, A., Schulz, R., Reisinger, W., Mühler, M., Wernecke, K.D., Geserick, G., 2004b. Studies on the time frame for ossification of the medial clavicular epiphyseal cartilage in conventional radiography. Int. J. Leg. Med. 118 (1), 5–8.

Schmidt, S., Koch, B., Schulz, R., Reisinger, W., Schmeling, A., 2008. Studies in use of the Greulich–Pyle skeletal age method to assess criminal liability. Leg. Med. 10 (4), 190–195.

Schmidt, S., Schiborr, M., Pfeiffer, H., Schmeling, A., Schulz, R., 2013. Sonographic examination of the apophysis of the iliac crest for forensic age estimation in living persons. Sci. Justice 53 (4), 395–401.

Schulz, R., Schiborr, M., Pfeiffer, H., Schmidt, S., Schmeling, A., 2014. Forensic age estimation in living subjects based on ultrasound examination of the ossification of the olecranon. J. Forensic Leg. Med. 22, 68–72.

Serinelli, S., Panebianco, V., Martino, M., Battisti, S., Rodacki, K., Marinelli, E., Zaccagna, F., Semelka, R.C., Tomei, E., 2015. Accuracy of MRI skeletal age estimation for subjects 12–19. Potential use for subjects of unknown age. Int. J. Leg. Med. 129 (3), 609–617.

Shaikh, A.H., Rikhasor, R.M., Qureshi, A.M., 1998. Determination of skeletal age in children aged 8–18 years. J. Pak. Med. Assoc. 48 (4), 104–105.

Shirley, N.R., Jantz, R.L., 2011. Spheno-occipital synchondrosis fusion in modern Americans. J. Forensic Sci. 56 (3), 580–585.

Singh, J., Chavali, K.H., 2011. Age estimation from clavicular epiphyseal union sequencing in a Northwest Indian population of the Chandigarh region. J. Forensic Leg. Med. 18 (2), 82–87.

Smith, S.L., 2007. Stature estimation of 3–10-year-old children from long bone lengths. J. Forensic Sci. 52 (3), 538–546.

Soudack, M., Ben-Shlush, A., Jacobson, J., Raviv-Zilka, L., Eshed, I., Hamiel, O., 2012. Bone age in the 21st century: is Greulich and Pyle's atlas accurate for Israeli children? Pediatr. Radiol. 42 (3), 343–348.

Telkkä, A., Palkama, A., Virtama, P., 1962. Prediction of stature from radiographs of long bones in children. J. Forensic Sci. 7, 474–479.

Tirpude, B., Patond, S., Murkey, P., Nagrale, N., 2015. A radiological study of age estimation from epiphyseal fusion of distal end of femur in the Central India population. J. Indian Acad. Forensic Med. 37 (1), 8–11.

Tisè, M., Mazzarini, L., Fabrizzi, G., Ferrante, L., Giorgetti, R., Tagliabracci, A., 2011. Applicability of Greulich and Pyle method for age assessment in forensic practice on an Italian sample. Int. J. Leg. Med. 125 (3), 411–416.

Vallejo-Bolaños, E., España-López, A.J., 1997. The relationship between dental age, bone age and chronological age in 54 children with short familial stature. Int. J. Paediat. Dent. 7 (1), 15–17.

Varkkola, O., Ranta, H., Metsäniitty, M., Sajantila, A., 2011. Age assessment by the Greulich and Pyle method compared to other skeletal X-ray and dental methods in data from Finnish child victims of the Southeast Asian Tsunami. Forensic Sci. Med. Pathol. 7 (4), 311–316.

Van Dessel, J., Huang, Y., Depypere, M., Rubira-Bullen, I., Maes, F., Jacobs, R., 2013. A comparative evaluation of cone beam CT and micro-CT on trabecular bone structures in the human mandible. Dentomaxillofac. Radiol. 42 (8), 20130145.

van Rijn, R.R., Lequin, M.H., Robben, S.G., Hop, W.C., van Kuijk, C., 2001. Is the Greulich and Pyle atlas still valid for Dutch Caucasian children today? Pediatr. Radiol. 31 (10), 748–752.

Wagner, U.A., Diedrich, V., Schmitt, O., 1995. Determination of skeletal maturity by ultrasound: a preliminary report. Skelet. Radiol. 24 (6), 417–420.

Wittschieber, D., Vieth, V., Domnick, C., Pfeiffer, H., Schmeling, A., 2013. The iliac crest in forensic age diagnostics: evaluation of the apophyseal ossification in conventional radiography. Int. J. Leg. Med. 127 (2), 473–479.

Zafar, A.M., Nadeem, N., Husen, Y., Ahmad, M.N., 2010. An appraisal of Greulich-Pyle Atlas for skeletal age assessment in Pakistan. J. Pak. Med. Assoc. 60 (7), 552.

CHAPTER 7

Estimation of Immature Age From the Dentition

Douglas H. Ubelaker
Smithsonian Institution, Washington, DC, United States

The estimation of age of immature individuals represents a common and important aspect of the practice of modern forensic anthropology. Such age estimation is needed to assess issues with living individuals, especially related to problems of adoption, immigration, and legal applications (Black et al., 2010). In the analysis of skeletal remains, age estimation of immature individuals represents a key component of the biological profile that can lead to identification. When teeth are present, they offer the most accurate and reliable information for age estimation among the young.

Although this chapter focuses specifically on age estimation from the immature dentition, it is important to point out that valuable age information can be gleaned from other sources (Ubelaker, 2010). The extent of bone size and development plays a key role in age assessment of the very young, especially fetal remains (Fazekas and Kósa, 1978). During fetal development, the deciduous dentition is in early formation. In the recovery of skeletonized fetal remains, the tiny developing tooth components may be overlooked and left behind at the scene. Even if the forming teeth are recovered, they can be difficult to identify as to tooth type and thus of limited use in age estimation.

For older children and adolescents, the extent of bone union and epiphyseal development and union can prove useful as well. The timing of epiphyseal union presents marked sexual dimorphism with females preceding males by many months. In addition, the process of epiphyseal union is gradual ranging from initial points of union to complete union and obliteration of the epiphyseal line. Differences also exist in definitions of "union" within various publications, influencing use of their data in casework (e.g., Greulich and Pyle, 1950; McKern and Stewart, 1957; Pyle and Hoerr, 1955; Todd and D'Errico, 1928).

Although data from different aging systems should be incorporated into an overall assessment, teeth provide key information and are of primary importance. However, anyone attempting age assessment from the dentition should be trained and experienced in dental development and morphology. Errors in judging if recovered teeth are deciduous or permanent can lead to huge errors in age estimation. Similarly, if teeth are improperly assessed regarding tooth type, serious errors can result.

The 20 deciduous teeth commence formation during fetal development and are usually completely formed by about the age of 3 years. They consist of two incisors, one canine, and two molars on both the left and right sides of the maxilla and mandible. Formation, as in the permanent dentition, begins with the occlusal surface of the crown and terminates at the tip of the roots. Deciduous teeth can be distinguished from their permanent counterparts by being smaller, with different patterns of coloration.

The 32 permanent teeth begin to form at about 6 months and may continue development until the late teens to early 20s. The permanent teeth also consist of two incisors and one canine like their deciduous counterparts. However, the permanent teeth include two premolars and three molars. Note, however, this normal pattern can display variants, especially in the congenital absence of the third molars.

Crown morphology is very similar between deciduous and permanent teeth in the incisors and canines. However, the form of the deciduous first molar is similar to that of the permanent premolars. Morphology of the deciduous second molar relates more closely to that displayed by the permanent molars. With experience, practitioners should be able to recognize tooth groups of both the deciduous and permanent dentition and perhaps be able to distinguish individual teeth. As mentioned earlier, no one should attempt age assessment from the dentition if they are not able to recognize the tooth groups and distinguish deciduous and permanent teeth.

Tooth attributes useful for age estimation in the immature skeleton include the extent of formation, emergence and eruption, antemortem loss of the deciduous teeth, and the root resorption of deciduous teeth prior to loss. Of all of these, formation provides the most reliable data for age assessment; however, the other attributes deserve some discussion.

Eruption refers to the process in which a tooth travels from its site of formation to the functional occlusal plane. The related term "emergence" can indicate when eruption has penetrated the bony alveolus or the gingival mucosa or the occlusal plane (Harris et al., 2010). Due to the confusing use of these terms in the published literature, it is important to ascertain the particular definition when using data from a specific study. The timing of eruption/emergence displays some population variation that can introduce error into estimation (Anderson et al., 1976, Banerjee and Mukherjee, 1967; Christensen and Kraus, 1965, Coughlin and Christensen, 1966; Dahlberg and Menegaz-Bock, 1958; Demisch and Wartmann, 1956; Glister et al., 1964; Hurme, 1948; Kraus, 1959; Lunt and Law, 1974, Meredith, 1946, Moorrees, 1965, Moorrees et al., 1963a, 1963b; Nolla, 1960, Robinow et al., 1942; Steggerda and Hill, 1942). In addition, some teeth are more predictable than others with the permanent third molar presenting extensive variation.

Antemortem loss of the deciduous dentition also offers some age-related information with caveats. In normal development, all of the fully formed deciduous teeth are lost antemortem to make way for the eruption of the permanent teeth. While a normal timing pattern can be defined for each deciduous tooth, the exceptions are considerable. Of course, deciduous teeth can be lost prematurely through trauma. At the other extreme, many adults retain deciduous teeth, even well into adult life.

The normal loss of deciduous teeth is preceded by their root resorption. Reduction in root size and volume facilitates their expulsion and represents a normal and necessary aspect of tooth development. If root resorption can be properly recognized, it can assist in age assessment. More importantly, it is imperative that advanced root resorption of deciduous teeth not be confused with incomplete root formation. Such confusion could introduce a multiyear error into the age assessment.

Assessment of the extent of dental formation represents the singular most accurate approach to age assessment of immature individuals, if teeth are present and recognizable. Although the timing of dental formation displays some population variation, it is not of the magnitude seen with other immature age indicators. For these reasons, assessment of dental formation should represent a high priority for those attempting to estimate age of immature individuals (Rogers, 2009; Scheuer and Black, 2000, 2004; Ubelaker, 1999).

The published literature offers distinct approaches and data in age assessment of dental formation. Data also are now available from different regions of the world facilitating analysis if the origin of the individual examined is known. Information formats include popular charts depicting the timing of dental formation, as well as more detailed tooth-specific information. In general, the dental charts offer an easy visual overview of the status of dental formation and a general assessment of age. However, each tooth presents particular information that cannot be captured adequately in a general chart. For these reasons, published data on individual teeth should be consulted for the most accurate estimates.

Of the dental charts, a historically popular version was authored by Schour and Massler (1941) and published by the American Dental Association in 1944. This chart was used by generations of clinical dentists and also by many working with forensic issues. The original chart has been criticized (Garn et al., 1959; Miles, 1963; Sundick, 1972) since it was based upon a small nondiverse sample and groups formation and eruption data into age estimates.

In 1978, Ubelaker published a modification of the Schour and Massler chart based on worldwide published information regarding dental formation (e.g., Anderson et al., 1976; Banerjee and Mukherjee, 1967; Christensen and Kraus, 1965; Coughlin and Christensen, 1966; Dahlberg and Menegaz-Bock, 1958; Demisch and Wartmann, 1956; Glister et al., 1964; Hurme, 1948; Kraus, 1959; Lunt and Law, 1974; Meredith, 1946; Moorrees, 1965; Moorrees et al., 1963a, 1963b; Nolla, 1960; Robinow et al., 1942; Steggarda and Hill, 1942). The timing information presented in this chart thus is based on an extremely large and diverse sample size. It also presents greater age ranges than suggested by Schour and Massler. The Ubelaker chart (Fig. 7.1) has been reproduced in many publications and is especially useful for age assessment in worldwide populations. However, like all such charts, it does not present separate formation and eruption data on individual teeth.

To obtain the most accurate age assessment from the immature dentition, population-specific data on individual teeth should be consulted. Moorrees et al. (1963a, 1963b) present a useful approach. In their system, sequential stages of development are defined and visually presented for individual teeth. These stages range from initial formation of the occlusal cusps to complete apical closure. Variations within this sequence reflect different tooth morphology. Stages for deciduous teeth include sequential root resorption. Data are also presented on the mean values and variation around the mean for each stage of formation for each tooth, derived from large sample sizes of individuals from Ohio. Separate data are presented for males and females as well. This system allows for an objective determination of the stage of formation of a particular tooth. The statistical presentation allows for an age estimate accompanied by an expression of the related range of variation.

In 1973, Demirjian et al. published a new system of dental age assessment. Their approach involves evaluation of the stage of formation of seven teeth on the left side of the mandible. These permanent teeth consist of the central incisor, lateral incisor, canine, first premolar, second premolar, first molar, and second molar. The stage of formation of each tooth was scored using an eight-stage system (A–H). Using panoramic radiographs, data were collected from 1446 boys and 1482 girls of French Canadian ancestry. In their aging system, scores of the seven teeth are summed to produce a dental maturity age that can then be converted to age. Like the Moorrees et al. system, the Demirjian et al. approach offers objective scoring of the stage of formation of the teeth examined. In addition, it offers a method that combines data from different teeth.

In 1976, Anderson et al. offered a significant improvement to the Moorrees et al. (1963a,b) system. Anderson et al. (1976) employed the Moorrees et al. classification system in a longitudinal study of 121 boys and 111 girls using annual cephalograms at the Burlington Growth Centre in Toronto, Canada. Their study produced data for all permanent teeth of both the maxilla and mandible for males and females. This more comprehensive study greatly enhanced the application of the Moorrees et al. (1963a, 1963b) system.

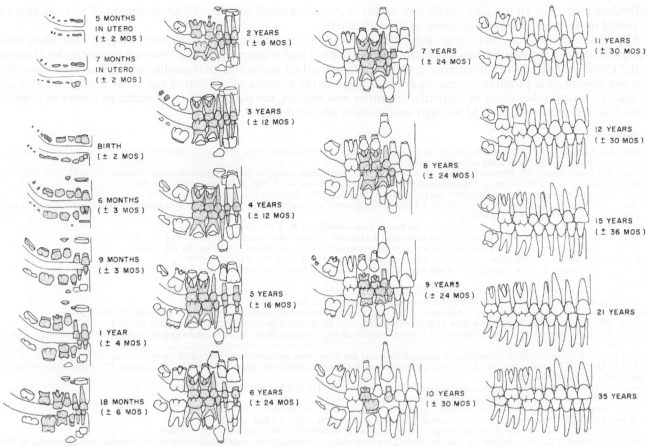

Figure 7.1 Timing of dental formation and eruption in global populations. *From Ubelaker, D.H., 1999. Human Skeletal Remains: Excavation, Analysis, Interpretation, third ed. Taraxacum, Washington, DC.*

The Demirjian system also has been augmented with data from different populations and methodological modifications. Willems et al. (2001) applied the system to 1265 boys and 1258 girls from Belgium. They found that the original Demirjian technique overestimated age in the Belgian sample. They offered a modified scoring system that produced greater accuracy in their sample. Similar tests and modifications were published by Chaillet et al. (2004) for Finnish children.

Numerous studies in addition to those discussed earlier have documented aspects of population variation in tooth formation. These include Harris and McKee (1990) from the middle southern United States; Haavikko (1970), Mornstad et al. (1995), Nystrom and Ranta (2003), Liversidge (2000), and Nystrom et al. (1977) from Western Europe; and Alimskii et al. (1999) from Eastern Europe, among others. See also the Queen Mary of London Atlas of Tooth Development and Eruption and its web application (https://atlas.dentistry.qmul.ac.uk/). These studies generally have documented population variation in the timing of dental formation and the value of utilizing data from populations relating as closely as possible to the individual being examined.

Data on the formation of the primary dentition are available in studies published by Lunt and Law (1974), Kraus and Jordon (1965), and Ubelaker (1999).

Conclusion: Estimation of the age of immature individuals should always utilize a comprehensive approach. Specific methods utilized depend to a large extent upon the available tissues and the general age of the individual within the immature range. While a variety of aging methods may be available, priority should focus on dental formation since of all the developmental systems, it has the strongest correlation with chronological age. Anthropologists and odontologists share interest and expertise in assessing age from dental development; however, the former offers more experience in the interpretation of the postcranial skeleton. Population variation of the timing of dental formation exists but much less than that in other processes of skeletal development.

Of the different age-related processes of dental development, dental formation exhibits the highest correlation with chronological age and thus the smallest error in age estimation. Dental eruption/emergence, root resorption of deciduous teeth, and antemortem loss of deciduous teeth offer some age information but are less valuable in estimation than formation data.

Chronological charts depicting the general timing of dental development are very useful for a rapid and easy assessment of the approximate age of the individual but do not offer the accuracy and precision of formation data of individual teeth. The charts also can be very useful to provide a visual overview of development of all teeth that can be useful in the sorting and recognition of individual teeth.

Numerous studies have been published offering population-specific data on the formation of individual teeth. The most utilized systems for tooth formation classification and assessment were pioneered in studies by Moorrees et al. (1963a, 1963b) and Demirjian et al. (1973). These seminal works and their modifications provide comprehensive, sex-specific, and population-specific methodology for the accurate estimation of age in the immature. Although forensic casework takes place in particular countries and regions, the individuals represented in cases can originate from different parts of the world through immigration and world travel.

References

Alimskii, A.V., Shalabaeva, K.Z., Dolgoarshinnykh, A., 1999. The time periods for the formation of the permanent occlusion in children born and permanently living in a region close to a former nuclear test range. Stomatolog 78, 53–56.

Anderson, D.L., Thompson, G.W., Popovich, F., 1976. Age of attainment of mineralization stages of the permanent dentition. J. Forensic Sci. 21 (1), 191–200.

Banerjee, P., Mukherjee, S., 1967. Eruption of deciduous teeth among Bengalee children. Am. J. Phys. Anthropol. 26 (3), 357–358.

Black, S., Aggrawal, A., Payne-James, J. (Eds.), 2010. Age Estimation in the Living. Wiley-Blackwell, Chichester, West Sussex, UK.

Chaillet, N., Nyström, M., Kataja, M., Demirjian, A., 2004. Dental maturity curves in Finnish children: Demirjian's method revisited and polynomial functions for age estimation. J. Forensic Sci. 49 (6), 1324–1331.

Christensen, G.J., Kraus, B.S., 1965. Initial calcification of the human permanent first molar. J. Dent. Res. 44 (6), 1338–1342.

Coughlin, J.W., Christensen, G.J., 1966. Growth and calcification in the prenatal human primary molars. J. Dent. Res. 45 (5), 1541–1547.

Dahlberg, A., Menegaz-Bock, R.M., 1958. Emergence of the permanent teeth in Pima Indian children. J. Dent. Res. 37, 1123–1140.

Demirjian, A., Goldstein, H., Tanner, J.M., 1973. A new system of dental age assessment. Hum. Biol. 45 (2), 211–227.

Demisch, A., Wartmann, P., 1956. Calcification of the mandibular third molar and its relation to skeletal and chronological age in children. Child Dev. 27 (4), 459–473.

Fazekas, I.G., Kósa, F., 1978. Forensic Fetal Osteology. Akadémiai Kaidó, Budapest.

Garn, S.M., Lewis, A.B., Polacheck, D.L., 1959. Variability of tooth formation. J. Dent. Res. 38, 135.

Glister, J.E., Smith, F.H., Wallace, G.K., 1964. Calcification of mandibular second primary molars in relation to age. J. Dent. Child. 31, 284–288.

Greulich, W.W., Pyle, S.I., 1950. Radiographic Atlas of Skeletal Development of the Hand and Wrist. Stanford University Press, Stanford.

Haavikko, K., 1970. The formation and the alveolar and clinical eruption of the permanent teeth: an orthopantomographic study. Suom. Hammaslaak. Toim. 66, 103–170.

Harris, E.F., McKee, J.H., 1990. Tooth mineralization standards for blacks and whites from the middle southern United States. J. Forensic Sci. 35, 859–872.

Harris, E.F., Mincer, H.H., Anderson, K.M., Senn, D.R., 2010. Age estimation from oral and dental structures. In: Senn, D.R., Stimson, P.G. (Eds.), Forensic Dentistry, second ed. CRC Press, New York.

Hurme, V.O., 1948. Standards of variation in the eruption of the first six permanent teeth. Child Dev. 19 (1–2), 213–231.

Kraus, B.S., 1959. Calcification of the human deciduous teeth. J. Am. Dent. Assoc. 59 (5), 1128–1136.

Kraus, B.S., Jordon, R.E., 1965. The Human Dentition Before Birth. Lea and Febiger, Philadelphia.

Liversidge, H.M., 2000. Crown formation times of human permanent anterior teeth. Arch. Oral Biol. 45, 713–721.

Lunt, R.C., Law, D.B., 1974. A review of the chronology of calcification of deciduous teeth. J. Am. Dent. Assoc. 89, 599–606.

McKern, T.W., Stewart, T.D., 1957. Skeletal age changes in young American males. In: Headquarters, Quartermaster Research and Development Command, Technical Report EP-45. Natick, Mass.

Meredith, H.V., 1946. Order and age of eruption for the deciduous dentition. J. Dent. Res. 25 (1), 43–66.

Miles, A.E.W., 1963. The dentition in the assessment of individual age. In: Brothwell, D.R. (Ed.), Dental Anthropology. Pergamon, Oxford.

Moorrees, C.F.A., 1965. Normal variation in dental development determined with reference to tooth eruption status. J. Dent. Res. 44 (1), 161–173.

Moorrees, C.F.A., Fanning, E.A., Hunt Jr., E.E., 1963a. Formation and resorption of three deciduous teeth in children. Am. J. Phys. Anthropol. 21, 205–213.

Moorrees, C.F.A., Fanning, E.A., Hunt Jr., E.E., 1963b. Age variation of formation stages for ten permanent teeth. J. Dent. Res. 42 (6), 1490–1502.

Mornstad, H., Reventlid, M., Teivens, A., 1995. The validity of four methods for age determination by teeth in Swedish children: a multicentre study. Swed. Dent. J. 19, 121–130.

Nolla, C.M., 1960. The development of the permanent teeth. J. Dent. Child. 27, 254–266.

Nystrom, M., Kilpinen, E., Kleemola-Kujala, E., 1977. A radiographic study of the formation of some teeth from 0.5 to 3.0 years of age. Proc. Finn. Dent. Soc. 73, 167–172.

Nystrom, M., Ranta, H., 2003. Tooth formation and the mandibular symphysis during the first five postnatal months. J. Forensic Sci. 48, 373–378.

Pyle, S.I., Hoerr, N.L., 1955. Radiographic Atlas of Skeletal Development of the Knee. Charles C. Thomas, Springfield.

Robinow, M., Richards, T.W., Anderson, M., 1942. The eruption of deciduous teeth. Growth 6, 127–133.

Rogers, T.L., 2009. Skeletal age estimation (Chapter 18). In: Blau, S., Ubelaker, D.H. (Eds.), Handbook of Forensic Archaeology and Anthropology. Left Coast Press, Walnut Creek, California, pp. 2018–2221.

Scheuer, L., Black, S., 2000. Developmental Juvenile Osteology. Academic Press, New York.

Scheuer, L., Black, S., 2004. The Juvenile Skeleton. Elsevier, London.

Schour, I., Massler, M., 1941. The development of the human dentition. J. Am. Dent. Assoc. 28, 1153–1160.

Steggarda, M., Hill, T.J., 1942. Eruption time of teeth among whites, negroes, and Indians. Am. J. Orthod. Oral Surg. 28 (1), 361–370.

Sundick, R.I., 1972. A new method for assigning ages to immature skeletons. Am. J. Phys. Anthropol. 37 (3), 42.

Todd, T.W., D'Errico Jr., J., 1928. The clavicular epiphyses. Am. J. Anat. 41, 25–50.

Ubelaker, D.H., 1999. Human Skeletal Remains: Excavation, Analysis, Interpretation, third ed. Taraxacum, Washington, DC.

Ubelaker, D.H., 2010. Recent advances in the estimation of age at death from the assessment of immature bone. In: Latham, K.E., Finnegan, M. (Eds.), Age Estimation of the Human Skeleton. Charles C. Thomas, Springfield, IL, pp. 177–189.

Willems, G., Olmen, A.V., Spiessens, B., Carels, C., 2001. Dental age estimation in Belgian children: Demirjian's technique revisited. J. Forensic Sci. 46 (4), 893–895.

CHAPTER 8

Adult Age-at-Death Estimation in Unknown Decedents: New Perspectives on an Old Problem

Kristen Hartnett-McCann[1] | Laura C. Fulginiti[2] |
Andrew C. Seidel[3]

[1]Connecticut Office of the Chief Medical Examiner, Farmington, CT, United States,
[2]Maricopa County Forensic Science Center, Phoenix, AZ, United States,
[3]Arizona State University, Tempe, AZ, United States

Chapter Outline

■ INTRODUCTION

The process of aging begins at the time of conception. Even in the very young, new cells are constantly being regenerated to replace dead ones in both soft and hard tissues. Bone, like soft tissue, is a living and dynamic tissue subject to renewal, repair, and remodeling in response to numerous stimuli and, because of this, it exhibits age-related changes. Aging is continuous, happens to all humans, and manifests as three general states in all bodily tissues: growth, maintenance, and atrophy (Angel et al., 1986).

Age can be divided into two types: chronological and biological. Chronological age is the number of years lived since birth, while biological age is determined by key physiological factors such as the rate which a body's organs and systems are developing or degenerating. Chronological and biological ages are correlated but do not always coincide. Chronological age is independent of any social and natural factors, including sex, since the number of years lived

New Perspectives in Forensic Human Skeletal Identification. http://dx.doi.org/10.1016/B978-0-12-805429-1.00008-9

always increases from birth to death. Biological age can be affected by social and natural factors, such as environment and health conditions (Acsádi and Nemeskéri, 1970; Angel et al., 1986). When anthropologists estimate age, they are attempting to determine chronological age based on physiological changes reflective of either developmental or degenerative processes in the skeleton (Cox, 2000).

■ MACROSCOPIC AGE ESTIMATION FROM THE ADULT SKELETON

In subadults, age estimation is based on the progression of growth and development, which follows similar and predictable sequences across populations. In the adult, the pattern of aging is not so obvious and recognizable. Once growth has ended and adulthood is reached, age determination becomes more difficult because less distinct stages are produced by the processes of remodeling and deterioration, and different external environmental factors act upon each individual. Therefore, error ranges for age estimates tend to increase with increasing age. This increase is referred to as the "trajectory effect" (Nawrocki, 2010).

One of the main responsibilities of a forensic anthropologist is the creation of a biological profile (estimated age, sex, ancestry, and living stature) for unknown decedents. The forensic approach to determining age-at-death from the skeleton usually involves one individual at a time. Because the anthropologist is required to estimate age for that one individual using standards that were created based on population data, and because variation exists in the aging process, broad age estimates are often created. While simple methods for age estimation in adults are preferred, multifactorial estimates can provide more reliable results.

Aging methods in adults are based on four main criteria: (1) the final stages of skeletal maturation taking place into the twenties; (2) the morphological changes to joints such as the pubic symphysis, sternal rib ends, auricular surface, and acetabulum; (3) general age indicators such as cranial sutures, osteoarthritis, and ossification of carti-laginous structures in the body; and (4) histological changes in bone structure (Cox, 2000). This chapter focuses on the macroscopic methods for estimating age-at-death in adult skeletons, the need for population-specific standards and provides recommendations for current methods to use in forensic settings. A quick reference guide containing method descriptions and results is included as an Appendix.

Pubic Symphysis

Todd (1920) was the first to systematically chart the changes in the symphyseal face on the pubic bone and develop an aging standard for this anatomical feature (Fig. 8.1). Using 306 white males from the Western Reserve collection aged 18 years and older, he created 10 phases with corresponding age ranges into which pubic bones could be placed. In 1921, Todd defined 10 age phases of pubic symphysis metamorphosis for black males, black females, and white females from the Western Reserve collection using his method from 1920. Therefore one set of standards, using 10 phases that could be used to estimate age for an individual of any ancestry group or sex was formulated (Todd, 1921). Todd's 10 phases served as the basis for future aging studies of symphyseal joints, especially of the pubic symphysis.

Todd's technique remained unchallenged until Brooks (1955) tested the method in comparison to the cranial suture method. Brooks' (1955) study included comparisons between ages derived from pubic symphysis and cranial suture closure, males and females, and prehistoric and modern skeletons. The most important part of her study was

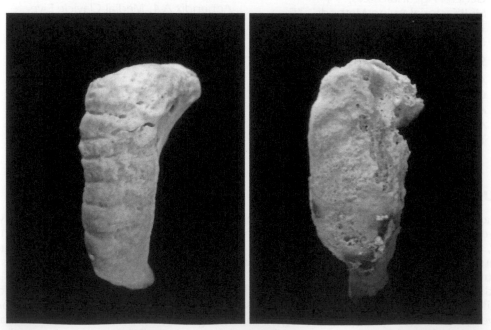

Figure 8.1 Pubic symphyseal face of a young individual (left) and an older, Phase 7 individual (right).

the work on modifying Todd's pubic symphysis phases. The first major alternative to Todd's method appeared in a report by McKern and Stewart (1957) based on an in-depth study of skeletal aging in 450 Americans war dead from the Korean War. The authors reduced the number of features to examine from nine in Todd's study to three: dorsal plateau, ventral rampart, and symphyseal rim. Each of the three components was subdivided into six stages (0–5) and the results were expressed in a formula consisting of three numbers. Once each component was scored, the total score was compared to a table of mean age, standard deviation, and age ranges obtained from the symphyseal formulae (McKern and Stewart, 1957).

The McKern and Stewart (1957) standards were innovative but problematic because they could not be applied to females. To rectify this problem, Gilbert and McKern (1973) provided descriptions of morphological components of the female *os pubis*, their developmental stages, and age relationships in a sample of 180 females aged 17–55 years. They found that females were different in the rate and locality of age-related metamorphic changes in the pubic bone, likely due to hormonal influences, childbirth, and pregnancy. The components and stages were structured very similarly to the original component system defined for males in McKern and Stewart (1957). Gilbert (1973) compared ages estimated in females using McKern and Stewart's (1957) male method and Gilbert and McKern's (1973) new female method. Gilbert's (1973) research reinforced the fact that males and females require different standards for pubic symphysis age estimation.

Six years later, Suchey (1979) reexamined the problems in the aging of females using the Gilbert and McKern (1973) method for the *os pubis*. Before the next major revamping of the pubic symphysis method by Suchey et al. (1984, 1986), several other studies attempted to improve on the work of Todd (1920), McKern and Stewart (1957), and Gilbert and McKern (1973) including Acsádi and Nemeskéri (1970), Hanihara and Suzuki (1978), Jackes (1985), Meindl et al. (1985), Pfeiffer (1985), and Snow (1983). The landmark study in modern pubic symphysis research was published in 1986 by Suchey et al. Pubic bones from 739 males aged 14–92 were collected from autopsies performed at the Department of the Chief Medical Examiner-Coroner in Los Angeles County between 1977 and 1979. Each of the 739 pubic symphysis pairs was aged by Suchey using Todd's (1920, 1921) and McKern and Stewart's (1957) methods. The authors recommended collapsing some of Todd's categories, as Brooks (1955) and Meindl et al. (1985) had earlier suggested, into a total of six phases (Katz and Suchey, 1986; Suchey, 1986, 1987; Suchey et al., 1986).

Brooks and Suchey (1990) developed the six-phase unisex method for pubic symphysis age estimation. Their study sample consisted of the original male pubic symphysis sample of 739 individuals but, in addition, 273 females were included for a total sample size of 1013 individuals. A single set of phase descriptions were generated that could be used for both sexes and all ancestry groups. While the written descriptions can be applied to both males and females, separate drawings and cast sets made by France Casting are available to enhance the information presented in the descriptions. Today, most forensic anthropologists rely on these casts to age specimens (Garvin and Passalacqua, 2012), largely due to a study by Klepinger et al. (1992). More recent reevaluations of the Suchey–Brooks method, however, have proposed refinements to the phases, descriptions, and statistical methods, as well as population-specific recommendations, and should be considered when choosing an appropriate aging method (Berg, 2008; Berg et al., 2004; Chen et al., 2008; Djuric et al., 2007; Fleischman, 2013; Hartnett, 2007, 2010a; Hens et al., 2008; Kimmerle et al., 2008a,b; Konigsberg et al., 2008; Shirley and Ramirez Montes, 2015). For instance, Djuric et al. (2007) evaluated the Suchey–Brooks method on skeletons from the Balkans and made recommendations for the application of the method to Serbian populations. Hens et al. (2008) tested the Suchey–Brooks method on an Italian population and concluded that although the method could be used for this population, bias and inaccuracy increased with age and actual age was often underestimated in older individuals.

Berg (2008) defined and tested a new phase (7) in females and redefined the later phases using a sample from the Balkans and Eastern Tennessee. Kimmerle et al. (2008a) also used the Balkan sample to test the Todd (1920) and Suchey–Brooks methods and developed population-specific estimates using Bayesian analysis. Interobserver error in age estimation from the pubic symphysis was quantified by Kimmerle et al. (2008b) on the Balkan sample. Chen et al. (2008) developed a method for estimating age from the pubic symphysis in Chinese Han males using nine morphological features of the face and rim. The nine features were divided into categories, and four equations for age estimation were created. The authors produced improved accuracy and reliability of age estimation from the pubic symphysis by using the formulae and in their publication claim accuracy within 1 year. Fleischman (2013) later tested the authors' high success rate on the known sample from the Forensic Science Center (FSC) in Phoenix, Arizona, and found that the method was accurate for aging middle-aged adults (error c. 6 years), but that there were limitations with population specificity, subjectivity, and the intricate scoring system.

Hartnett and Fulginiti (H–F) amassed a large, modern, and diverse sample of over 600 pubic bones obtained from autopsies at the FSC in Phoenix, Arizona, to address some of the criticisms of the Suchey–Brooks method (Hartnett, 2007, 2010a). In this study, Hartnett and Fulginiti tested the accuracy of the Suchey–Brooks method using three observers and found significant differences in the observed versus actual ages. Significant interobserver differences were also noted, while intraobserver error was negligible. The FSC pubic bones were then sorted and seriated without knowing age, which formed the basis for revised phase descriptions and age ranges. Minor modifications were made in the original Suchey–Brooks phase descriptions, and the accompanying age ranges and means were adjusted. In addition, a phase 7 was described for both males and females and is comprised mainly of males and females over 70 years of age-at-death. The H–F study emphasized the role of bone quality in age estimation, which had been previously underutilized. In younger individuals, the bone is heavier and feels smooth and dense to the touch, while in older individuals, the bone loses mass and feels roughened and porous to the touch. While the seven overall phases are not specific to sex, there are several characteristics specific to sex that are embedded within the descriptions. Separate age statistics for males and females are associated with each phase. Merritt (2014) tested the Hartnett (2010a) revised phase descriptions and statistics on a modern sample from the William Bass collection. The results indicated that accuracy and bias scores were significantly better with the H–F method than the Suchey–Brooks method, suggesting that the revised mean ages-at-death for the H–F method better reflect the study population. Merritt (2014) also concluded that overall, the H–F method is reliable and has improved on accuracy, especially for older individuals (see also Seidel, 2013).

Technological advances in the medical field have led some researchers to explore new avenues instead of traditional morphological visual approaches to aging (Hutchinson and Russell, 2001). As early as 1999, Pasquier et al. developed an age prediction system using a pubic symphysis numerical database obtained from CT and X-ray data through quantification of age-linked parameters. Age estimates created using the Suchey–Brooks method on this sample provided standard deviations of 10.18 years ($R^2 = 0.49$), but their estimates using CT and X-ray data produced standard deviations of only 7.3 years ($R^2 = 0.74$). Telmon et al. (2005) also demonstrated excellent agreement between the Suchey–Brooks results of the analysis of the three-dimensional (3D) images of the bones in soft tissue and the actual bony morphology once the soft tissue was removed. More recently, Wink (2014) used pelvic CT scans to estimate age from the pubic symphysis using the Suchey–Brooks method. Intraobserver reliability was good and correlation results indicated that clinical CT scans are adequate for creating 3D images for age-estimation purposes. Villa et al. (2015) incorporated a mathematical approach to analyze the curvature variation in 3D scans and laser scans of pelvic bones and casts and concluded that their new procedure achieved similar correlations to the classic methods.

In response to increased medicolegal expectations for method reliability and replicability, Slice and Algee-Hewitt (2015) created a fully quantitative method for estimating age from the pubic symphysis using a variance-based score of surface complexity computed from vertices obtained from 3D scans of the joint surface. Criticisms regarding method and observer error in the visual phase–based systems for aging are well known, therefore the authors combat these issues with their more objective and quantitative method that produces results significantly associated with known age-at-death. Future methods for age estimation in all indicators must take into consideration the need to satisfy stringent evidentiary standards (Daubert v. Merrell Dow Pharmaceuticals, Inc. 509 US. 579, 1993).

Sternal Rib Ends

Although the sternal end of the rib was noted to undergo age-related metamorphosis by earlier researchers (e.g., Kerley, 1970), it was the work of İşcan et al. (1984a,b) that first sought to utilize these changes as a means of estimating age-at-death (Fig. 8.2). Initially introduced as a component system describing six sequential stages of development pertaining to the depth of the sternal pit, its shape, and the configuration of the pit's rim and walls (İşcan et al., 1984a), this system was promptly reworked into a series of nine morphological phases (0 through 8) as this was deemed easier to both learn and apply (İşcan et al., 1984b). This phase system has become one of the standard techniques for the estimation of age-at-death within forensic anthropology (Garvin and Passalacqua, 2012).

Basing their observations on an autopsy sample of 118 white males, İşcan et al. (1984b) described a series of morphological changes undergone by the sternal end of the right fourth rib. A separate phase system, based on an autopsy sample of 86 individuals, was later developed for use with white females (İşcan et al., 1985). These two phase systems are hereafter referred to collectively as the I–L method of age estimation. The development of the I–L method was based on the sternal fourth rib, primarily due to the ease with which it can be accessed during autopsy procedures. The fourth rib, however, may not always be easy to identify or may be damaged or otherwise unavailable. As a result, several researchers have investigated the degree to which intercostal morphological variability affects the application of the I–L method. Dudar (1990, 1993) found that ribs II through IX fell within one morphological phase of the fourth rib 87.6% of the time and concluded that the I–L method can be used with caution when the fourth rib is unobservable. This result is confirmed by Yoder et al. (2001), who found no significant differences between the phase scores of ribs III and V through IX and the phase score of their fourth rib counterpart. These researchers suggest using the average phase score of available ribs in place of a phase score from a single rib when estimating age-at-death. In contrast, İşcan et al. suggest that only ribs III and V should be substituted for the fourth rib, finding that these three ribs fell into the same morphological phase in more than 79% of their sample and were within one morphological phase 98% of the time (İşcan and Loth, 1989; Loth et al., 1994). A recent, 3D morphometric study of the sternal fourth rib found that significant differences in the shape of the sternal pit exist between the fourth rib and all other ribs except the third (Nikita, 2013). Although not discussed here, it should be noted that separate standards have been developed for the estimation of age-at-death using morphological changes of the first rib (e.g., DiGangi et al., 2009; Kunos et al., 1999).

As with any age-estimation technique, methods must undergo validation using independent skeletal samples. The I–L method has been rigorously assessed by a number of researchers (e.g., Baccino et al., 1999; Dudar et al., 1993; Fanton et al., 2010; Hartnett, 2007, 2010b; Kimmerle et al., 2008b; Martrille et al., 2007), often with somewhat conflicting results. Discrepancies in the findings of these researchers, however, likely derive from differences in the

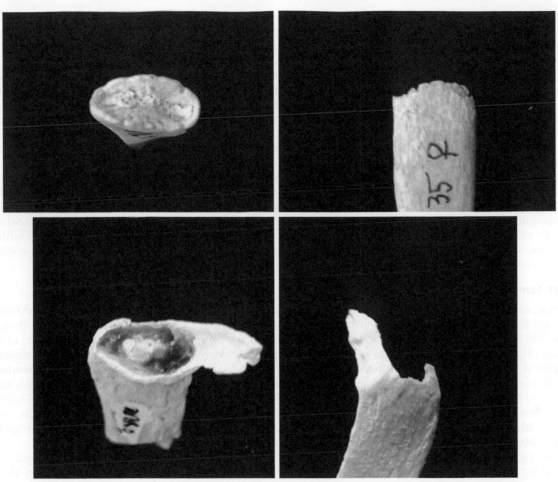

Figure 8.2 Sternal end of the fourth rib of a young individual (top) and an older individual (bottom).

skeletal samples used as well as the relative levels of experience of the investigators. Readers are encouraged to refer to these publications for further details of their findings.

The effects of population specificity on the efficacy of the I–L method have also been addressed. İşcan et al. (1987), in applying their phase system to a sample of 73 African-Americans, noted a tendency for the standards developed on individuals of European ancestry to overage African-American individuals who died past the age of 30. This result was contradicted by the findings of Russell et al. (1993), who, working with a sample of 80 individuals from the Hamann–Todd collection, concluded that the I–L method had a slightly increased level of accuracy when applied to African-American individuals as well as a nonsignificant tendency to underage them. Oettlé and Steyn (2000), testing the I–L method on a sample of 339 South Africans of African ancestry, found that the I–L method tended to simultaneously underage younger individuals and overage older individuals. A similar pattern was found for Bosnian males (Sarajlić, 2006) and the opposite pattern appears to apply to a sample of Hungarian males (Wolff et al., 2012). The I–L method is reported to underestimate age-at-death in a sample of 71 Mexican males (Cerezo-Román and Hernández Espinosa, 2014) as well as in a sample of 88 Thai individuals (Gocha et al., 2015). In contrast, the I–L method performed admirably without any modification when applied to a Turkish sample of 294 individuals (Yavuz et al., 1998). The combined results of these studies indicate that the age-progressive morphological changes identified and utilized by the I–L method appear to be a universal pattern but that the ages encompassed by each phase are population specific.

Observations of the effects of population specificity as well as research suggesting that the I–L method suffers from relatively high interobserver variability (e.g., Fanton et al., 2010; Hartnett, 2007, 2010b; Kimmerle et al., 2008b) have led to the introduction of alternative techniques to estimate age from the sternal rib. Oettlé and Steyn (2000) published revised descriptions for each of the nine phases initially described by İşcan et al. for use with individuals of African descent, although this method has been found to perform relatively poorly when compared to the I–L method as applied to African-Americans (Geske, 2013). The H–F method, developed using a modern autopsy sample of 630 individuals, revises the phase descriptions set forth by İşcan et al., decreases the total number of phases utilized to seven, and, importantly, emphasizes the role of bone texture and density in assigning a phase number to a specimen (Hartnett, 2007, 2010b). In a test of these revisions, Merritt (2014) concluded that the H–F method performs comparably to the I–L method. While the H–F method did not place as many individuals into the correct age phase as the I–L method, Merritt suggested this to be an artifact of the smaller standard deviations reported for the H–F method. This suggestion would seem to be confirmed by the fact that, in a sample of 182 individuals from the Hamann–Todd collection, the H–F method placed an individual within one phase of their correct age phase 90.7% of the time (Seidel, 2013). The H–F method also demonstrated decreased bias and increased accuracy when applied to females, individuals of European ancestry, and individuals over the age of 60 (Merritt, 2014).

In a departure from the qualitative, phase-based systems for age estimation, Nikita (2013) attempted to develop a fully quantitative method for age estimation using 3D morphometrics of the sternal rib. Perhaps due to an inability to accurately capture the morphological changes taken into account in phase-based systems, correct classification rates using this morphometric approach rarely exceeded 50% and, therefore, this method has limited utility to forensic anthropologists as currently formulated.

Recent work has suggested that the I–L method can be used to assess age-at-death on multislice computed tomography reconstructions of the sternal rib with comparable accuracy to using dry bone (Dedouit et al., 2008), a result which also extends to first rib aging techniques (Moskovitch et al., 2010). Oldrini et al. (2016) evaluated the sternal plastron and lower chest with a volume rendering technique which ultimately allowed them to make a quick, in vivo age estimate with results similar to the traditional methods. These results are important in that they potentially allow for examination of sternal rib morphology in living individuals. In turn, this could allow for longitudinal studies of changing rib morphology as well as the construction of large, virtual, known-age collections, both of which would be of immense value to our understanding of interindividual variation in sternal rib morphology and, consequently, our ability to estimate age-at-death from the sternal rib.

Auricular Surface

Developed upon a large sample composed of 250 archaeological specimens from the Libben Site, 500 individuals of known age from the Hamann–Todd collection, and 14 contemporary forensic cases from the Cuyahoga County Coroner's Office, the Lovejoy et al. (1985b) method combines age-progressive morphological changes of the auricular surface (Fig. 8.3) into eight distinct phases. Applying the Lovejoy et al. (1985b) method to a mixed skeletal sample derived from the Terry collection, Murray and Murray (1991) concluded that the method performs equally well regardless of sex or ancestry, an observation supported by the work of Osborne et al. (2004). This conclusion would seem to be contradicted by the work of Schmitt (2004), who finds that the Lovejoy et al. (1985b) method consistently underages individuals from a Thai sample. Schmitt's findings, however, may result from the tendency of individuals with smaller body size to be underaged by osteological methods, including those that employ the auricular surface (Merritt, 2015), rather than that indicate population specificity.

Several researchers have noted that the Lovejoy et al. (1985b) method tends to overage younger individuals and underage older ones (Bedford et al., 1993; Hens et al., 2008; Murray and Murray, 1991; Saunders et al., 1992) as

Figure 8.3 Auricular surface on the right *os coxa*.

well as a trend toward increased inaccuracy when estimating the age of older individuals (Martrille et al., 2007; Schmitt, 2004). In an effort to correct for these shortcomings, a number of alternative methods for estimating age-at-death from the auricular surface have been introduced. Buckberry and Chamberlain (2002) converted the Lovejoy et al. (1985b) phase method into a component-based system. Eliminating retroauricular activity from consideration, the method presented by Buckberry and Chamberlain (2002) focuses on transverse organization, surface texture, microporosity, macroporosity, and apical changes. Osborne et al. (2004) present a six-stage modification of Lovejoy et al.'s (1985b) phase system, expanding the age intervals for each phase to take into account the wide range of variation in auricular surface morphology for a given age. A more recent approach to the estimation of age from the auricular surface utilizes multiple regression analysis and dummy variables to create what is essentially a component system for the estimation of age-at-death relying upon the presence or absence of either nine (for males) or seven (for females) traits relating to both the texture and the relief of the auricular surface and the surrounding area (Igarashi et al., 2005).

While the method presented by Igarashi et al. (2005) has not been evaluated and the efficacy of the method presented by Osborne et al. (2004) has only been minimally addressed, several studies have assessed the utility of the method presented by Buckberry and Chamberlain (2002). Mulhern and Jones (2005) tested both the Lovejoy et al. (1985b) method and the Buckberry and Chamberlain (2002) method on a sample of 309 individuals from the Terry and Huntington collections. They conclude that Lovejoy et al. (1985b) method is more accurate for individuals under the age of 50 while the Buckberry and Chamberlain (2002) method is more accurate for older individuals. A similar result was obtained by Gocha et al. (2015), who concluded that, on a sample of Thai individuals, the method of Buckberry and Chamberlain (2002) is more effective for individuals over the age of 50 while that of Osborne et al. (2004) exhibits higher accuracy for younger individuals. These observations are likely due in some part to age mimicry as Buckberry and Chamberlain's (2002) reference sample contains a larger proportion of older individuals than that of Osborne et al. (2004). Other researchers have emphasized the wide range of morphological variation of the auricular surface for a given age, resulting in substantial inaccuracy (Moraitis et al., 2014), and suggested that the Buckberry and Chamberlain method (2002) be revised through the creation of fewer phases with larger age ranges (Falys et al., 2006; Hens and Belcastro, 2012).

Recent work involving the use of computed tomography suggests that some aspects of auricular surface morphology utilized in age-estimation techniques can be readily assessed through medical imaging (Barrier et al., 2009; Ferrant et al., 2009). The lack of fine detail currently available from 3D reconstructions of the auricular surface, however, suggests the need to modify auricular surface aging techniques for use with such visualizations (Villa et al., 2013). Villa et al. (2015) suggest that quantifying the degree of curvature present within 3D scans of the auricular surface may serve as an adequate, objective substitute for the morphological characteristics tracked within phase systems.

As a component of one of the primary weight-bearing joints in the body, the morphology of the auricular surface is affected by body size. Obesity has been shown to be associated with overestimation of age as well as decreased accuracy when using the Buckberry and Chamberlain (2002) method (Wescott and Drew, 2015), whereas smaller body sizes tend to result in the underaging of skeletal remains using the auricular surface (Merritt, 2015). Age estimates derived from auricular surface methods are not significantly affected by parity (Bongiovanni, 2016). The morphology of the auricular surface, however, appears to be largely unaffected by sex or ancestry (Lovejoy et al., 1985a,b; Murray and Murray, 1991; Osborne et al., 2004). As a result, auricular surface methods retain some utility and remain a standard for the estimation of age-at-death within forensic anthropology (Garvin and Passalacqua, 2012).

Cranial Sutures

Most forensic anthropologists will assess the degree of fusion in cranial vault sutures during their preliminary examination of a cranium. As early as the 1500s, anatomists observed that sutures in the adult vault began fusing, eventually becoming obliterated (Fig. 8.4) in some individuals (White et al., 2012). In the 1920s, Todd and Lyon evaluated over 500 skulls and determined that sutures begin to fuse first in the endocranium and that the rate of fusion is independent of sex and ancestry (1924; 1925a,b,c). McKern and Stewart (1957) built on this research by examining 450 North American male crania. Both sets of scientists found a rough correlation between the degree of closure in the sutures of the cranial vault and age-at-death and both cautioned that individual variability precluded dependence on this method for an accurate estimation (McKern and Stewart, 1957; Todd and Lyon, 1924, 1925a,b,c). Acsádi and Nemeskéri (1970) developed a scoring system that was used widely in Europe and, according to Galera et al. (1998), performed reasonably well across populations in the Terry collection.

Meindl and Lovejoy (1985) utilized the Hamann–Todd collection to create a system of evaluating the degree of cranial suture closure that was divided by the area of the vault. The total or composite score was correlated to an age range with a standard deviation. In 1986, Krogman and İşcan published data on the basilar synchondrosis that allowed forensic anthropologists to determine a minimum age of 20–25 with a mean of 23 when that suture is fused. Mann et al. (1991) contributed standards for the closure of maxillary sutures. Buikstra and Ubelaker (1994) combined several methods in a volume of standards for forensic anthropology. They recommend the evaluation of 17 cranial suture segments using a numerical score and provide exemplar photographs (1994). Using linear regression analyses on scores from multiple areas of the cranial vault, Nawrocki (1998) suggests that the method is effective for estimating age, especially when inaccuracy and bias are considered. Aiello et al. (2004) used the Spitalfields skeletal collection to evaluate cranial suture closure and concluded that ancestry confounded the results.

Figure 8.4 Superior view of a cranium with open sutures (left) and obliterated sutures (right).

Gorea et al. (2004) used CT scan technology to evaluate older Indian individuals (40–70 years) to determine the order of closure in vault sutures and established a five score system. Most recently, Boyd et al. (2015) examined 231 individuals ranging in age from 19 to 89 and concluded that (1) CT scan technology was a useful tool for scoring suture closure and (2) individuals could be reliably placed into three age categories: young, middle, and older adult.

Cranial suture closure has been recognized for centuries as an age indicator and has been studied extensively with regard to its correlation with age-at-death. There is disagreement about the precision of the method but consensus is that it is a useful tool for distinguishing among general age categories in adult skulls (Galera et al., 1998; Ley et al., 1994).

Late Fusing Epiphyses

Epiphyseal fusion rates have been studied extensively and are covered in detail in a separate chapter in this volume (see Chapter 4). There is a fairly uniform progression of epiphyseal union in all humans, and it follows a broader primate model (Schultz, 1944). Although the majority of epiphyses fuse during adolescence, a few persist into early adulthood, such as the medial end of the clavicle, iliac crest, sacrum, sternum, and vertebral ring epiphyses (McKern, 1970). Most osteology textbooks and manuals include tables and charts that illustrate age stages and timetables for fusion rates of the major epiphyses from childhood until complete fusion in adolescence or early adulthood (Baker et al., 2005; Bass, 1995; Bennett, 1987; Buikstra and Ubelaker, 1994; Burns, 1999; Krogman and Iscan, 1986; Steele and Bramblett, 1988; Ubelaker, 1989; White et al., 2012).

The medial clavicle is the first fetal bone to begin ossification and the last to complete epiphyseal union, therefore displaying the longest period of growth-related activity (Loth and İşcan, 1989). Research on the medial clavicle epiphysis began in 1924 with Stevenson's study, followed by Todd and D'Errico's (1928) study on the Western Reserve Collection, and McKern and Stewart's (1957) analysis of a sample of Male Korean War dead. Based on McKern and Stewart's (1957) five-phase findings, there is general acceptance that the medial epiphysis begins to unite between 18 and 25 and becomes completely united by the early 30s (Fig. 8.5). Webb and Suchey (1985) examined over 800 individuals from 1970's autopsies and developed a four-phase system with different ranges for males and females. Black and Scheuer (1996) evaluated individuals derived from English and Portuguese collections, developing a similar system to Webb and Suchey (1985) and providing age ranges that did not distinguish between males and females.

Most recently, Langley-Shirley and Jantz (2010) scored clavicles from 1289 individuals from the 20th century, including males and females of different population groups. The expressed goal of the research was to control for population differences and to examine secular trends in the American population. Bayesian analyses indicate that in modern populations the medial clavicle epiphyses commence fusion approximately 4 years earlier than in individuals from earlier in the century. Improved nutrition and socioeconomic status as well as increases in obesity are among the factors affecting this change. Females appear to commence fusion a year earlier than males but no significant differences among population groups are discerned.

The iliac crest is the first of the late fusing epiphyses to reach maturity. Some disagreement exists over the timing of the fusion of this epiphysis (see also Krogman and Iscan, 1986; McKern and Stewart, 1957). Cox (2000) concluded that the onset of menses always preceded the appearance of the iliac crest epiphysis by a few months and suggests that complete fusion of the iliac crest occurs in females at 18 years, 1 month, and in males at 18 years, 6 months. According to Suchey et al. (1984) and Webb and Suchey (1985), complete fusion is achieved a little later.

The epiphyses of the vertebral column are often good predictors of age because the vertebral ring epiphyses are among the last to unite. Stewart (1979) states that the first seven thoracic vertebral rings, especially T4 and T5, are

Figure 8.5 Medial clavicle epiphysis with flake that is beginning union (Phase 2 of Langley-Shirley and Jantz (2010) five-phase system).

the last epiphyses to fuse in the vertebral column and can often persist into the 23rd year. According to more recent research, the vertebral ring epiphyses form and begin to unite around at an age of 14 years in females and 16 years in males, completely uniting by about 26–27 in both sexes (Albert, 1998; Albert and Maples, 1995; Albert and McCallister, 2004).

The sternum is the most morphologically variable bone in the body. Normally, the body of the sternum fuses to the manubrium by 22–23 years of age, but can remain unfused as late as 27 years. The epiphyseal plate for the surface of the clavicular notch unites between 18 and 22, with the greatest activity occurring around 19 years (Stewart, 1970). Jit and Bakshi (1984) assessed the time of union of the mesosternum with the manubrium and xiphoid process in over 1000 Indian males and females aged 5–85 years. They concluded that sternal data could not produce reliable age estimates after age 20.

The several elements that comprise the sacrum begin to fuse from the bottom, proceeding upward and along the sides (Scheuer and Black, 2000). By age 23 years, ossification is complete except between the first and second sacral elements, which may not fuse until as late as 32 years (Stewart, 1970). McKern and Stewart (1957) included the sacrum in their study of male Korean War dead and concluded that if the junction between S1 and S2 is visible the individual is younger than 27 years old. A modern study by Passalacqua (2009) assessed seven traits of the sacrum, including the auricular surface of the sacrum and fusion of sacral elements, to develop a six-phase component system for evaluating age which was not affected by sex and ancestry. Colarusso (2015) tested Passalacqua's (2009) method and concluded that although there were high levels of accuracy and low intraobserver error, it was not practical to use in forensic contexts due to the broad age ranges it produced.

Scheuer and Black (2000) published *Developmental Juvenile Osteology*, a comprehensive review of growth and development in humans. Each of the epiphyses is described in detail and age ranges are provided for each. This volume has become *de rigueur* for most physical and forensic anthropology libraries. Future comprehensive studies will likely take advantage of modern advances in digital imaging, with improved clarity and visualization of these surfaces (see Garamendi et al., 2011; Zhang et al., 2015).

Acetabulum

Age-at-death methods for the adult acetabulum (Fig. 8.6) are relatively new. Rouge-Maillart et al. (2007) were the earliest proponents of the acetabulum as an adult age indicator. The authors used seriation in their sample to identify four features that changed with advancing age; rim appearance, fossa appearance, lunate surface porosity, and apical activity. Rissech et al. (2006, 2007) developed and refined a method for the adult acetabulum as a stand-alone age indicator using the Coimbra, Lisbon, Barcelona, and St. Bride's skeletal collections. With the statistical program (IDADE2) created for this method, the authors claimed that an accuracy of 89% could be achieved using 10-year intervals.

Calce and Rogers (2011) tested Rissech et al.'s (2006, 2007) method on a Canadian collection and ultimately suggested revising the trait descriptions and reducing the number of variables per trait. Calce and Rogers (2011) also confirmed that the method works best when the reference population is geographically close to the individual specimen in question. Calce (2012) recently published a revision of the Rissech et al. (2006) method in which the method's application was expanded to females. Calce's (2012) acetabulum method reduces the variables scored to three and utilizes only three broad age ranges that correspond to young, middle, and old adults. This new method reports 81% accuracy, reduces inter- and intraobserver error, and provides a rapid method to determine general age.

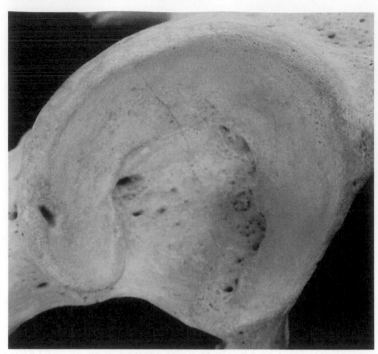

Figure 8.6 Acetabulum.

To date, Mays (2014) published the only test of Calce's (2012) technique which produced results that were only 45% accurate. He attributed the lower accuracy to population differences in the reference sample and the study sample. Clearly, more research and population-specific standards are needed before the acetabulum could be considered a mainstream skeletal age indicator. Until then, the Calce (2012) method for aging the acetabulum may still prove to be useful in cases of fragmentary or poorly preserved remains, with the caution that population differences from the reference sample might skew results.

General Age Indicators

While anthropologists generally use specific features or traits that are correlated with age, there are several indicators on the skeleton that are not directly correlated to an age, but rather a stage (i.e., young adult or old adult). These indicators are often used to corroborate the age-estimation results from the more traditional indicators, or when those indicators are absent or damaged. These general indicators may include osteoarthritis, osteoporosis, bone density changes, the ossification of cartilaginous structures, entheseal changes, and other age-related skeletal pathologies.

Costal and laryngeal cartilage ossification has historically been used to provide information about general age-at-death. Early research on costal cartilage ossification produced scoring systems and age ranges (McCormick and Stewart, 1988; Michelson, 1934). Recently, Oldrini et al. (2016) evaluated the sternal plastron using CT images for 456 living individuals and achieved high rates of correlation with age. Garvin (2008) tested Cerny's (1983) method for age estimation based on the ossification of laryngeal structures for accuracy and concluded that although a consistent sequence of ossification exists, large amounts of variation in timing does not allow for the accurate application of the method for age estimation. Dang-Tran et al. (2010) further evaluated the ossification patterns of the thyroid cartilage using CT scans and determined that correlations between age and ossification changes were found, however, the methods based on ossification rates in the larynx were not accurate enough for assessing individual age. In a poster presented at the 2016 American Academy of Forensic Sciences Annual Meeting in Las Vegas, NV, Bolhofner and Fulginiti (2016) reaffirmed that the ossification process of the thyroid cartilage is not correlated with age and should not be used as an age indicator.

Osteoarthritis and osteoporosis are more common in, although not limited to, individuals of advanced age (Stewart, 1979). Listi and Manhein (2012) examined the relationship between osteoarthritis and osteophytosis and age on the vertebrae of 104 individuals. The authors determined that although both conditions are correlated with age, they can only be used for establishing a general estimate of age. Osteoporosis in the form of decreased bone density is typically more common in older individuals, especially females, resulting from an imbalance between bone loss and bone formation (Agarwal, 2008).

Listi (2016) evaluated entheseal changes in the femur and *os coxa* in 200 white individuals over 40 years of age. Results indicated that significant relationships exist between age and entheseal changes, but that the relationship is not strong enough to formulate age predictions. Nevertheless, Listi (2016) concludes that the data may be still useful for suggesting an age of over 60 or over 70 years of age-at-death.

Multifactorial Aging Methods

No single age indicator is 100% accurate, nor is a group of age indicators used together. However, using more than one indicator at a time increases the accuracy of the age estimation. The multiregional, or multifactorial, approach relies on the concept that diverse areas such as cranial sutures, pubic symphyses, and dentition are influenced by different types of stress, so their combination should yield a more balanced reflection of aging (İşcan, 1989b). McKern and Stewart (1957) combined maturational scores assigned to age-related changes in epiphyseal union, third molar eruption, suture closure, and vertebral osteophytosis from their Korean War sample into a regression equation to calculate an age-at-death. Acsádi and Nemeskéri (1970) were the first to develop a "complex method" in aging adults using the age changes observed in the humerus and femur, Todd's (1920, 1921) 10-phase pubic symphysis method, and cranial suture closure based on a Hungarian autopsy and cemetery sample. Lovejoy et al. (1985a) presented a multifactorial method that used principal components weighing five indicators: pubic symphysis, auricular surface, proximal femur radiographs, dental wear, and cranial suture closure.

Later, Meindl and Lovejoy (1989) compared the inaccuracy and bias in the multifactorial, pubic symphysis, and auricular surface methods. Age was estimated for a small sample from the Todd collection (n=96). The authors concluded that there was substantial bias in current pubic symphysis methods and that the auricular surface method deserved a more major role in age estimation, but that the summary age method was more accurate than any single pelvic age indicator. The positive and negative qualifications of the multiple indicator methods of Acsádi and Nemeskéri (1970) and Lovejoy et al. (1985a) were compared by Maat (1987). While both produced better estimates than single indicators alone, and both had acceptable degrees of confidence, Maat (1987) found that Acsádi and Nemeskéri's (1970) method was preferable because it was simpler to apply (see also Baccino et al., 1999; Bedford et al., 1993; Saunders et al., 1992).

More recent advances and a better understanding of statistics in anthropology resulted in several studies revisiting the utility of multifactorial methods. In 2002, Boldsen et al. developed a multifactorial technique using Bayesian statistics. The authors used new scoring methods to evaluate the pubic symphysis, auricular surface, and cranial sutures, and combined them in a computer program called ADBOU. Samworth and Gowland (2007) combined the Suchey–Brooks' pubic symphysis and Lovejoy et al.'s auricular surface methods in a multifactorial approach using "lookup" tables. These "lookup" tables were compiled from updated skeletal samples and are more accurate than using the Suchey–Brooks or Lovejoy methods alone. Moreover, Passalacqua (2010) tested the lookup tables and concluded that the method was statistically robust, it should be immediately used for age estimation in the United States, and that further testing is needed to make it applicable to other populations. Uhl and Nawrocki (2010) formulated a regression-based multifactorial approach that appears to generate more accurate and precise results compared to other multifactorial methods.

Transition Analysis

Transition analysis was devised in response to the Rostock Manifesto (Hoppa and Vaupel, 2002) and out of a need to compromise between a mathematically sound methodology for the estimation of age-at-death and the ability to apply it to small samples or even single skeletons. Developed for use with the vagaries of osteological data, this methodology can be used with any trait that can be arranged into an invariant sequence of age-related changes. Because this method allows researchers to make inferences regarding the timing of the shift from one age stage to another it has become known as "transition analysis" (Boldsen et al., 2002).

In the majority of age-estimation methods used by forensic anthropologists, the morphological state of an age indicator is used to infer age-at-death. Such inferences are usually based upon known-age reference samples in which a given age indicator has been arranged into a unidirectional series of age-progressive stages and a mean age, standard deviation, and range (or some other suite of descriptive statistics) are calculated for each stage. Broadly speaking, such methods are effectively treating age-at-death as the dependent variable in a regression analysis.

This is a process that, in the calibration literature, is referred to as inverse calibration. Inverse calibration, while generating (although unrealistically) small estimates of the variance in age-at-death, also produces biased estimates of mean age-at-death since it is heavily influenced by the composition of the reference sample (Boldsen et al., 2002; Konigsberg et al., 1994; Masset, 1989). For example, if the reference sample is heavily biased toward older individuals, then, strictly as a matter of sampling error, a trait will appear to be more common in older individuals, even if the trait is in actuality more common in younger individuals. This bias underlies the phenomenon noted by Bocquet-Appel and Masset (1982) whereby age estimates produced by a given method tend to take on the age distribution of the reference sample upon which the method was developed. This has come to be referred to as "age mimicry" (Boldsen et al., 2002) and often leads to inaccurate results from the unconsidered application of standard age-estimation techniques. On the other hand, regressing morphological states on age, while less sensitive to the age composition of the reference sample, does not provide a useful estimate of age-at-death (Boldsen et al., 2002; Bocquet-Appel and Masset, 1982; Hoppa, 2000; Konigsberg et al., 1994; Masset, 1989).

Transition analysis circumvents this dilemma through the use of Bayesian statistics. Using Bayes' theorem, researchers can estimate the entire probability density function for age-at-death given a particular suite of morphological attributes by using the relatively easily obtainable probability that an individual will exhibit those attributes at a given age (Boldsen et al., 2002). This requires an estimate of the age-at-death distribution of the sample from which an individual is drawn. To this purpose, Boldsen et al. (2002) recommend the use of an uniform prior distribution or, when such information is available, an informative prior based on information that is independent of the skeletal sample. The selection of such an informed prior, however, can be a complicated and, at times, impossible process (Steadman et al., 2006). Readers are referred to Boldsen et al. (2002) for an in-depth discussion of the mathematics underlying transition analysis and to Steadman et al. (2006) and Konigsberg et al. (2008) for informative examples of how such analyses are performed. More information and a tutorial on how to perform transition analysis using the R statistical package is available from Dr. Lyle Konigsberg's website (link available at http://www.anthro.illinois.edu/people/lylek), and the ADBOU program developed by Boldsen et al. (2002) is available from http://math.mercyhurst.edu/~sousley/Software/.

An advantage to using transition analysis is that, being based in Bayesian statistics, it allows for the calculation of a likelihood ratio—a summary statistic effectively expressing the strength of an estimate of age-at-death. This is especially pertinent to forensic anthropologists as it allows for an evaluation of the evidentiary value of a biological profile (Steadman et al., 2006; Konigsberg et al., 2008). Although likelihood ratios calculated for single age indicators are often low, likelihood ratios from multiple age indicators can be multiplied together, potentially increasing the strength of a given age estimate (Steadman et al., 2006; Konigsberg et al., 2008). Readers are referred to Steadman et al. (2006) for an especially cogent discussion of the applicability of likelihood ratios within a forensic setting.

Further, if an appropriate prior age-at-death distribution is employed, the age intervals that transition analysis produces provide adequate "coverage." For example, if a particular sternal rib method is stated to have 95% coverage, then 95% of the individuals within a specific sternal rib phase should have ages that lie within the stated age limits for that phase. An additional 2.5% of individuals should have ages falling below that range and the remaining 2.5% of individuals with that morphology should be older than the stated range. Having adequate coverage, a quality frequently absent in standard age-estimation techniques, tends to reduce bias in age estimation (Konigsberg et al., 2008).

Transition analysis has successfully been used to increase the accuracy and decrease the bias of a number of age-estimation methods, including those employing the pubic symphysis (e.g., Berg, 2008; Dudzik and Langley, 2015; Godde and Hens, 2012, 2015; Hartnett, 2007; Kimmerle et al., 2008a,b; Lottering et al., 2013), clavicle (e.g., Langley-Shirley and Jantz, 2010), dental attrition (e.g., Boldsen, 2005; Prince et al., 2008), sacral fusion (Ríos et al., 2008), and third molar development (Tangmose et al., 2015). To date, however, transition analysis has primarily been used as a calibration technique to adapt established methods of age estimation to different populations. While differing populations may have significantly different mean ages-at-transition, the absolute limits for a given level of coverage remain relatively unaffected. This suggests that the construction of global samples for the evaluation of age changes may be of more utility than the continued evaluation of population specificity (Konigsberg et al., 2008). Although transition analysis is extremely promising, a recent validation study indicates that it does not perform as well as experience-based assessments of age-at-death, concluding that further work is required, preferably incorporating age indicators from several different anatomical regions (Milner and Boldsen, 2012).

Case Study

In April 2014, two hikers discovered a plastic tub concealed under a grove of trees along a trail. After dragging it out onto the trail, they tipped it over and discovered human skeletal remains with clothing (Fig. 8.7). Law enforcement personnel responded to the scene and brought the remains to the Office of the Medical Examiner for further study and identification.

A complete skeleton was present. The skeletal elements exhibited morphological and metric features consistent with a European (white) female between 16 and 26 years of age-at-death who stood approximately 5 ft 2 in. The estimated age interval was based on cranial sutures, late fusing epiphyses, the pubic symphysis, and sternal ends of the fourth ribs. The cranial sutures were patent with no bony bridges, except for the sagittal suture which was completely stenosed. The epiphyses along the ischial tuberosities were nearly fused but the line of fusion was still visible and palpable (age 19–23) (Scheuer and Black, 2000). The medial ends of the clavicles (Fig. 8.8) exhibited an epiphyseal flake in the active fusion stage (phase 3 of the five-phase system), consistent with an individual between 16.7 and 25.7 years at a 95% confidence interval (Langley-Shirley and Jantz, 2010). The pubic symphysis (Fig. 8.8) exhibited characteristics of Hartnett (2010a) Phase I (18–22 years, mean = 19.8 years). The ridge and furrow system was well defined with extension onto the pubic tubercle and the quality of bone was very good. The sternal ends of the fourth ribs exhibited characteristics of Hartnett (2010b) Phase I (18–22 years, mean = 19.57 years). The pit was shallow with billowing in the floor. The bone was very firm with thick edges and the beginnings of scalloping. The junction between S1 and S2 was patent. S1–S2 is usually completely fused by the age of 25 years (Scheuer and Black, 2000).

After the examination was complete, the biological profile and the description of the clothing were released to the public via law enforcement and the media. The family of a young woman who had been missing approximately 5 years came forward and stated that they thought the remains were of their daughter. Dental comparison confirmed the identification. The skeletal remains were identified as a young white woman, aged 20 years 4 months when she disappeared, who stood approximately 5 ft 1 in. tall in life. All of the age markers, with the exception of the stenosed sagittal suture were consistent with her chronological age.

Figure 8.7 Scene photograph of the unknown individual in the plastic bin.

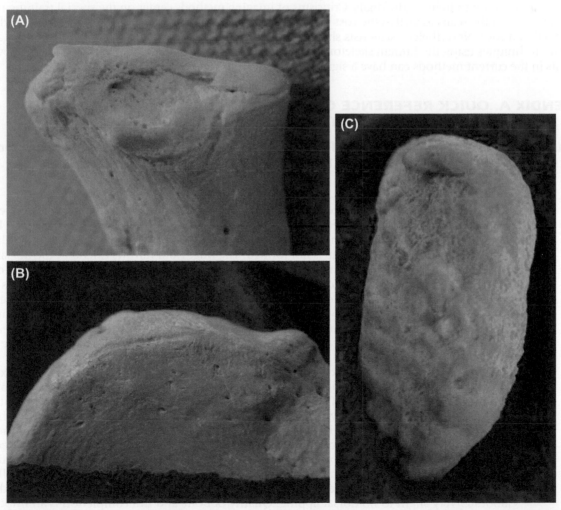

Figure 8.8 Age indicators for the young individual from the plastic bin. (A) Medial clavicle, (B) ischial tuberosity, and (C) pubic symphysis.

Table 8.1 Recommended Current Methods for Use in Macroscopic Age-at-Death Estimation From the Adult Skeleton

Skeletal Age Indicator	Recommended Method(s)
Pubic symphysis	Hartnett (2010a) and Brooks and Suchey (1990)
Sternal rib ends	Hartnett (2010b), İşcan et al. (1984b), and İşcan et al. (1985)
Auricular surface	Osborne et al. (2004)
Cranial sutures	Only as a general age indicator (e.g., young, middle, old adult)
Medial clavicle	Langley-Shirley and Jantz (2010)
Acetabulum	Calce (2012)
General indicators	■ Sternal plastron/costal cartilage via CT analysis: Oldrini et al. (2016) ■ Laryngeal cartilage: not recommended for use, see Bolhofner and Fulginiti (2016) ■ Osteoarthritis: Listi and Manhein (2012) ■ Entheseal changes: Listi (2016)

■ SUMMARY

Individual age-at-death estimation in forensic situations can be assessed using many different indicators in the adult human. Estimation of age-at-death involves comparing the morphological features observed in skeletal remains to changes recorded for recent populations with known individual ages. Criticisms of many of the adult age-estimation techniques center on the large error ranges that are ultimately provided in the biological profile. Large ranges are practical for forensic casework because, due to the complexity of aging, the interval must be large enough to encompass normal human biological variation. Table 8.1 provides recommended current methods to use for practical application. Phase descriptions, stage descriptions, and associated age statistics for the recommended methods can be found in Appendix A.

Since the early 1900s, anthropologists have consistently revised and reformulated aging methods for the major and minor indicators. Modern medical technology incorporating the use of 2D and 3D X-ray and scan analyses in forensic anthropology offers advantages over bone removal and preparation, preventing damage to the bone, and allows for the possibility of application to living individuals. Criticisms of imaging methods center on the special training needed to conduct and interpret the scans as well as the cost-prohibitive nature and/or availability of the equipment and software for smaller laboratories. Nevertheless, scientists should develop an appreciation of these new technological advances. Age-at-death techniques using the human skeleton requires constant improvement and continual study, as even small refinements in the current methods can have a significant impact in forensic applications.

■ APPENDIX A. QUICK REFERENCE GUIDE FOR PRACTICAL APPLICATIONS OF ADULT AGE-AT-DEATH ESTIMATION TECHNIQUES

Appendix A-1. Hartnett–Fulginiti (H–F) Revised Pubic Symphysis Phase Descriptions and Statistics (Hartnett, 2010a, pp. 1147, 1148, 1151)

Phase 1	A clear ridge and furrow system extends from the pubic tubercle onto the inferior ramus. Ridges and furrows are deep and well defined, and do not look worn down. There is no dorsal lipping. Bone is of excellent quality and is firm, heavy, dense, and smooth on the ventral and dorsal body. There is no rim formation. The dorsal plateau is not formed. The ridges and furrows extend to the dorsal edge.
Phase 2	The rim is in the process of forming, but mainly consists of a flattening of the ridges on the dorsal aspect of the face and ossific nodules present along the ventral border. Ridges and furrows are still present. The ridges and furrows may appear worn down or flattened, especially on the dorsal aspect of the face. The furrows are becoming shallow. The upper and lower rim edges are not formed. There is no dorsal lipping. The bone quality is very good and the bone is firm, heavy, dense, and smooth on the ventral and dorsal body, with little porosity. The pubic tubercle may appear separate from the face.
Phase 3	The lower rim is complete on the dorsal side of the face and is complete until it ends approximately halfway up the ventral face leaving a medium to fairly large gap between the lower and upper extremities on the ventral face. This enlarged "V" is longer on the dorsal side than the ventral side. Some ridges and shallow furrows are still visible, but appear worn down. In some cases, the face is becoming slightly porous. The rim is forming both on the dorsal aspect of the face and the upper and lower extremities. In some cases, there is a rounded buildup of bone in the gap between the upper and lower extremities above the enlarged "V." Bone quality is good; the bone is firm, heavy, dense, and has little porosity. The dorsal surface of the body is smooth and there are small bony projections near the medial aspect of the obturator foramen. The ventral aspect of the body is not elaborate. Very slight to no dorsal lipping. Quality of bone and rim completion is an important deciding factor. Variant: In some cases, a deep line or epiphysis is visible on the ventral aspect parallel to and adjacent to the face (males only).

Phase 4   In most cases, the rim is complete at this stage, but may have a small ventral hiatus on the superior and ventral aspect of the rim. The face is flattened and not depressed. Remnants of ridges and furrows may be visible on the face, especially on the lower half. The quality of bone is good, but the face is beginning to appear more porous. The dorsal and ventral surfaces of the body are roughened and becoming coarse. There is slight dorsal lipping. In females with parturition pits, dorsal lipping can be more pronounced. The ventral arc may be large and elaborate in females.

Phase 5   The face is becoming more porous and is depressed, but maintains an oval shape. The face is not irregularly-shaped or erratic. The rim is complete at this stage. In general, the rim is not irregular. Ridges and furrows are absent on the face. There may be some breakdown of the rim on the ventral border, which appears as irregular bone (not rounded/solid). The ventral surface of the body is roughened and irregular, with some bony excrescences. The dorsal surface of the body is coarse and irregular. Projections are present on the medial aspect of the obturator foramen. Bone quality is good to fair; it is losing density and is not smooth. The bone is moderately light in weight. In females the ventral arc is prominent.

Phase 6   The face is losing its oval shape and is becoming irregular. The rim is complete, but breaking down, especially on the ventral border. The rim and face are irregular, porous, and macroporous. Bone quality is fair and the bone is lighter and more porous, even with bony buildup on the ventral body surface. The rim is eroding. The dorsal surface of the bone is rough and coarse. There are no ridges and furrows. Dorsal lipping is present. Projections are present at the medial aspect of the obturator foramen. Bone weight is a major deciding factor between phases 6 and 7.

Phase 7   The face and rim are very irregular in shape and are losing integrity. The rim is complete but is eroding and breaking down, especially on the ventral border. There are no ridges and furrows. The face is porous and macroporous. Dorsal lipping is pronounced. Bone quality is poor, and the bone is very light and brittle. Bone weight is an important deciding factor. The dorsal surface of the bone is roughened. The ventral surface of the body is roughened and elaborate. Projections are present at the medial wall of the obturator foramen. The pubic tubercle is elaborate and proliferative. Bone weight is a major deciding factor between phases 6 and 7.

Variant   The rim is complete except for a lytic/sclerotic appearing hiatus at the superior ventral margin that extends toward the pubic tubercle and sometimes underneath the ventral rim, which should not be confused with a hiatus.

| Phase | H–F Females | | | | H–F Males | | | |
	n	Mean	SD	Range[a]	n	Mean	SD	Range[a]
1	5	19.8	1.33	18–22	14	19.29	1.93	18–22
2	5	23.2	2.38	20–25	14	22.14	1.86	20–26
3	25	31.44	5.12	24–44	36	29.53	6.63	21–44
4	35	43.26	6.12	33–58	69	42.54	8.8	27–61
5	32	51.47	3.94	44–60	90	53.87	8.42	37–72
6	35	72.34	7.36	56–86	34	63.76	8.06	51–83
7	56	82.54	7.41	62–99	96	77	9.33	58–97

[a]100% of individuals.

Appendix A-2. Hartnett–Fulginiti (H–F) Revised Fourth Sternal Rib End Phase Descriptions and Statistics (Hartnett, 2010b, pp. 1154, 1156)

Phase 1   The pit is shallow and flat and there are billows in the pit. The pit is shallow U-shaped in cross section. The bone is very firm and solid, smooth to the touch, dense, and of good quality. The walls of the rim are thick. The rim may show the beginnings of scalloping.

Phase 2   There is an indentation to the pit. The pit is V-shaped in cross section, and the rim is well defined with round edges. The rim is regular with some scalloping. The bone is firm and solid, smooth to the touch, dense, and of good quality. There is no flare to the rim edges; they are parallel to each other. The pit is still smooth inside, with little to no porosity. In females, the central arc, which manifests on the anterior and posterior walls as a semicircular curve, is visible.

Phase 3   The pit is V-shaped and there is a slight flare to the rim edges. The rim edges are becoming undulating and slightly irregular and there may be remnants of scallops, but they look worn down. There are no bony projections from the rim. There is porosity inside the pit. The bone quality is good; it is firm, solid, and smooth to the touch. The rim edges are rounded, but sharp. In many females, there is a buildup of bony plaque, either in the bottom of the pit, or lining the interior of the pit, creating the appearance of a two-layer rim. An irregular central arc may be apparent.

Phase 4   The pit is deep and U-shaped. The edges of the pit flare outwards, expanding the oval area inside the pit. The rim edges are not undulating or scalloped, but are irregular. There are no long bony projections from the rim and the rim edges are thin, but firm. The bone quality is good, but does not feel dense or heavy. There is porosity inside the pit. In some males, two distinct depressions are visible in the pit. In females, the central arc may be present and irregular; however, the superior and inferior edges of the rim have developed, decreasing the prominence of the central arc.

Phase 5   There are frequently small bony projections along the rim edges, especially at the superior and inferior edges of the rim. The pit is deep and U-shaped. The rim edges are irregular, flared, sharp, and thin. There is porosity inside the pit. The bone quality is fair; the bone is coarse to the touch and feels lighter than it looks.

Phase 6   The bone quality is fair to poor, light in weight, and the surfaces of the bone feel coarse and brittle. There are bony projections along the rim edges, especially at the superior and inferior edges, some of which may be over 1 cm long. The pit is deep and U-shaped. The rim is very irregular, thin, and fragile. There is porosity inside the pit. In some cases, there may be small bony extrusions inside the pit. In females, the central arc is not prominent.

Phase 7   The bone is in very poor quality, and in many cases, translucent. The bone is very light, sometimes feeling like paper, and feels coarse and brittle to the touch. The pit is deep and U-shaped. There may be long bony growths inside the pit. The rim is very irregular with long bony projections. In some cases, much of the cartilage has ossified and window formation occurs. In some females, much of the cartilage in the interior of the pit has ossified into a bony projection extending more than 1 cm in length.

Variant   In some males, the cartilage has completely or almost completely ossified. The ossification tends to be a solid extension of bone, rather than a thin projection. All of the bone is of very good quality, including the ossification. It is dense, heavy, and smooth. In these instances, bone quality should be the determining factor. There are probably other factors, such as disease, trauma, or substance abuse, that caused premature ossification of the cartilage. When the individual is truly very old, the bone quality will be very poor. Be aware of these instances where a rib end may appear very old due to ossification of the cartilage, but is really actually a young individual, which can be ascertained by bone quality. In these cases, consult other age indicators in conjunction with the rib end.

Phase	Females				Males			
	n	Mean	SD	Range[a]	n	Mean	SD	Range[a]
1	7	19.57	1.67	18–22	20	20.00	1.45	18–22
2	7	25.14	1.17	24–27	27	24.63	2.00	21–28
3	22	32.95	3.17	27–38	27	32.27	3.69	27–37
4	21	43.52	3.08	39–49	47	42.43	2.98	36–48
5	32	51.69	3.31	47–58	76	52.05	3.50	45–59
6	18	67.17	3.41	60–73	61	63.13	3.53	57–70
7	71	81.20	6.95	65–99	75	80.91	6.60	70–97

[a]100% of individuals.

Appendix A-3. Osborne et al. (2004, p. 909) Combined Sex Phase Descriptions and Statistics for Adult Age Estimation for the Auricular Surface

Phase 1   Billowing with possible striae; mostly fine granularity with some coarse granularity possible

Phase 2   Striae; coarse granularity with residual fine granularity; retroauricular activity may be present

Phase 3   Decreased striae with transverse organization; coarse granularity; retroauricular activity present; beginnings of apical change

Phase 4   Remnants of transverse organization; coarse granularity becoming replaced by densifications; retroauricular activity present; apical change; macroporosity is present

Phase 5   Surface becomes irregular; surface texture is largely dense; moderate retroauricular activity; moderate apical change; macroporosity

Phase 6   Irregular surface; densification accompanied by subchondral destruction; severe retroauricular activity; severe apical change; macroporosity

Phase	n	Mean	SD	Range
1	11	21.1	2.98	≤27
2	13	29.5	8.20	≤46
3	37	42.0	13.74	≤69
4	82	47.8	13.95	20–75
5	17	53.1	14.14	24–82
6	102	58.9	15.24	29–89

Appendix A-4. Langley-Shirley and Jantz (2010, pp. 573,581) Medial Clavicle Five-Phase Descriptions and Statistics. In the Three-Phase System, Phases 2–4 Are Lumped Into One "Fusing" Stage

Phase 1   No union. No remnant of the flake is fused to the shaft. The medial articular surface has a coral-like appearance.

Phase 2   Beginning union. The epiphyseal flake has commenced fusion to the medial articular surface, but less than 50% of the surface was covered by the flake.

Phase 3   Active union. 50% or more of the surface is covered by epiphyseal flake, and fuse is actively occurring. The epiphysis is considered actively fusing if the flake clearly appears as a separate entity with some space between the edges of the flake and the bone surface.

Phase 4   Recent union. The flake is completely fused to the shaft but a trace of the fusion event remains in the form of a fusion scar and/or as small bony nodules on the outer rim of the medial surface.

Phase 5   Complete union. No trace of the fusion event remains, and the articular surface is quiescent.

Males	Highest Posterior Density	50% CI	75% CI	90% CI	95% CI
Five-Phase System					
1	12.7	≤13.7	≤15.2	≤16.6	≤17.4
2	18.2	16.8–19.8	15.9–21.0	15.0–22.2	14.4–23.0
3	22.2	20.6–23.9	19.5–25.2	18.5–26.6	17.0–27.5
4	25.1	23.4–26.9	22.3–28.2	21.2–29.6	20.5–30.6
5	34.7	≥29.1	≥26.9	≥25.1	≥24.1
Three-Phase System					
1	12.6	≤13.7	≤15.2	≤16.6	≤17.4
2	20.9	18.3–23.5	16.8–25.4	15.6–27.3	14.9–28.5
3	34.8	≥29.1	≥26.9	≥25.0	≥24.0

Females	Highest Posterior Density	50% CI	75% CI	90% CI	95% CI
Five-Phase System					
1	–	≤13.1	≤14.3	≤15.5	≤16.2
2	16.8	15.6–18.2	14.8–19.2	14.0–20.3	13.5–21.0
3	20.7	19.2–22.4	18.2–23.6	17.3–24.9	16.7–25.7
4	24.1	22.6–25.8	21.5–27.0	20.5–28.4	19.9–29.3
5	30.1	≥25.9	≥24.3	≥23.2	≥22.5
Three-Phase System					
1	–	≤13.2	≤14.6	≤15.8	≤16.5
2	18.8	16.8–21.9	15.7–24.0	14.6–25.9	14.1–27.1
3	30.1	≥25.7	≥24.1	≥22.9	≥22.1

Appendix A-5. Calce (2012, pp. 15–17) Descriptions for Acetabular Age Estimation

Descriptions of variables 1 (acetabular groove), 2 (osteophyte development), and 3 (apex growth) for the young adult, 17–39.

A. No groove. No anatomical interruption between lunate surface and rim; lunate surface appears smooth and dense; rim appears rounded.

B. Slight groove may surround 25% or less of the surface area of acetabular rim. Slight groove is visible and palpable by running thumb from superior portion of lunate surface over acetabular rim which may appear slightly sharpened as a result. Fossa appears shallow.

C. Bone appears smooth or dense in the superior area of the lunate surface, below the anterior inferior iliac spine. Normal bone density is observed in this area. Architecture of the rim where it meets the lunate surface is generally dense and exhibits little to no osteophytic development. Microporosities (<1 mm) on the ilio-pubis and/or ilio-ischial surfaces may be found adjacent to the rim.

D. At posterior lunate surface: apex is blunted, rounded, and smooth to the touch; no spicule has formed.

E. In cases of slight activity, apex is still somewhat rounded but a sharp point at the apex is palpable. Apex has become longer or a small spicule less than 1 mm can be felt.

Descriptions of variables 1 (acetabular groove), 2 (osteophyte development), and 3 (apex growth) for the middle adult, 40–64.

A. Pronounced groove is visible between lunate surface and rim; surrounds 25%–75% surface area below the acetabular rim. Clear anatomical interruption is observed between lunate surface and rim; groove is deepened: (1) making the rim appear sharp and (2) forming a noticeable crest along most of the rim. As a result, fossa appears at a lower position relative to the rim extending inward from the lunate surface.

B. Osteophyte development on the superior area of the lunate surface below the anterior inferior iliac spine results in either: (1) a slight raise of the acetabular rim which is roughened to the touch, although no spicules are present or (2) a rough acetabular rim where bone is spiculed and sharp. Bone is not rounded or smooth in this area. As a result of spiculed bone, slight crest formation is visible, but bone still appears dense. Micro- and macroporosity (>1 mm) may be observed.

C. Moderate activity at apex; a conspicuous osteophyte develops larger than 1 m, which can be seen with the naked eye and may surround the entire horn of the posterior lunate surface.

Descriptions of variables 1 (acetabular groove), 2 (osteophyte development), and 3 (apex growth) for the old adult, 65+.

A. Very pronounced groove is visible between lunate surface and rim; surrounds more than 75% surface area below the acetabular rim. Very pronounced groove is extremely deep. There is obvious discontinuity between this area and the lunate surface. As a result, rim appears sharp and crest is heightened so that fossa appears at a lower position relative to the rim extending inward from the lunate surface.

B. Groove may be obliterated by extreme osteophyte development on the rim; bone remodeling at the rim eliminates a once present groove, replacing it with an irregular surface of spiculed bone or porous crest. Tissue discontinuity between the lunate surface and the rim is faint or nonexistent.

C. A destructured rim is found below the anterior inferior iliac spine. Bone growth encroaches on the superior area of the lunate surface forming a raised rim or very high crest. Bone may be porous in this area but micro- and macroporosity is depending on degree of osteophytic development. Alternatively, bone may appear dense with large bony spicules to form an irregular, bumpy surface that is roughened to the touch.

D. Extreme activity at apex; a prominent osteophyte develops larger than 3 mm and may surround the entire horn of the posterior lunate surface. Osteophyte may cross acetabular notch to meet with the anterior horn of lunate surface and may be larger than 5 mm.

References

Acsádi, G.Y., Nemeskéri, J., 1970. History of Human Lifespan and Mortality. Akademiai Kiado, Budapest.

Aiello, L.C., Key, C.A., Molleson, T., 2004. Cranial suture closure and its implications for age estimation. Int. J. Osteoarchaeol. 4, 193–207.

Agarwal, S.C., 2008. Light and broken bones: examining and interpreting bone loss and osteoporosis in past populations. In: Katzenberg, A.M., Saunders, S.R. (Eds.), Biological Anthropology of the Human Skeleton, second ed. Wiley-Liss, New York, pp. 387–410.

Albert, A.M., 1998. The use of vertebral ring epiphyseal union for age estimation in two cases of unknown identity. Forensic Sci. Int. 97, 11–20.

Albert, A.M., Maples, W.R., 1995. Stages of epiphyseal union for thoracic and lumbar vertebral centra as a method of age determination for teenage and young adult skeletons. J. Forensic Sci. 40, 623–633.

Albert, A.M., McCallister, 2004. Estimating age at death in teenagers and young adults from thoracic and lumbar vertebral ring epiphyseal union data. In: Poster Presented at the American Association of Physical Anthropologists Annual Meeting, Tampa, FL.

Angel, J.L., Suchey, J.M., İşcan, M.Y., Zimmerman, M.R., 1986. Age at death estimated from the skeleton and viscera. In: Zimmerman, M.R., Angel, J.L. (Eds.), Dating and Age Determination of Biological Materials. Croom Helm, London, pp. 179–220.

Baccino, E., Ubelaker, D.H., Hayek, L.C., Zerilli, A., 1999. Evaluation of seven methods of estimating age at death from mature human skeletal remains. J. Forensic Sci. 44, 931–936.

Baker, S.J., Dupras, T.L., Tocheri, M.W., 2005. The Osteology of Infants and Children. A&M University Press, College Station, TX.

Barrier, P., Dedouit, F., Braga, J., Joffre, F., Rouge, D., Rousseau, H., Telmon, N., 2009. Age at death estimation using multislice computed tomography reconstructions of the posterior pelvis. J. Forensic Sci. 54, 773–778.

Bass, W.M., 1995. Human Osteology: A Laboratory and Field Manual, fourth ed. Missouri Archaeological Society, Columbia, MO.

Bedford, M.E., Russell, K.F., Lovejoy, C.O., Meindl, R.S., Simpson, S.W., Stuart-Macadam, P.L., 1993. Test of the multifactorial aging method using skeletons with known ages-at-death from the Grant Collection. Am. J. Phys. Anthropol. 91, 287–297.

Bennett, K.A., 1987. A Field Guide for Human Skeletal Identification. Charles C. Thomas, Springfield, IL.

Berg, G.E., Kimmerle, E., Konigsberg, L., 2004. Aging the elderly: a new look at an old method. In: Paper Presented at the Annual Meeting of the American Academy of Forensic Sciences, Dallas, TX.

Berg, G.E., 2008. Pubic bone age estimation in adult women. J. Forensic Sci. 53, 569–577.

Black, S.M., Scheuer, J.L., 1996. Age changes in the clavicle: from the early neonatal period to skeletal maturity. Int. J. Osteoarchaeol. 7, 2–10.

Bocquet-Appel, J.P., Masset, C., 1982. Farewell to paleodemography. J. Hum. Evol. 11, 321–333.

Boldsen, J.L., 2005. Analysis of dental attrition and mortality in the medieval village of Tirup, Denmark. Am. J. Phys. Anthropol. 126, 169–176.

Boldsen, J.L., Milner, G.R., Konigsberg, L.W., Wood, J.W., 2002. Transition analysis: a new method for estimating age from skeletons. In: Hoppa, R.D., Vaupel, J.W. (Eds.), Paleodemography: Age Distributions from Skeletal Samples. Cambridge University Press United Kingdom, pp. 73–106.

Bolhofner, K.L., Fulginiti, L.C., 2016. Patterns of ossification in macerated thyroid cartilages: implications for age and sex determination. In: Poster Presented at the Annual Meeting of the American Academy of Forensic Sciences, Las Vegas, NV.

Bongiovanni, R., 2016. Effects of parturition on pelvic age indicators. J. Forensic Sci. 61, 1034–1040.

Boyd, K.L., Villa, C., Lynnerup, N., 2015. The use of CT scans in estimating age at death by examining the extent of ectocranial suture closure. J. Forensic Sci. 60, 363–369.

Brooks, S.T., 1955. Skeletal age at death: the reliability of cranial and pubic indicators. Am. J. Phys. Anthropol. 13, 567–597.

Brooks, S.T., Suchey, J.M., 1990. Skeletal age determination based on the os pubis: a comparison of the Acsádi-Nemeskéri and Suchey–Brooks methods. J. Hum. Evol. 5, 227–238.

Buckberry, J.L., Chamberlain, A.T., 2002. Age estimation from the auricular surface of the ilium: a revised method. Am. J. Phys. Anthropol. 119, 231–239.

Buikstra, J.E., Ubelaker, D.H., 1994. Standards for Data Collection from Human Skeletal Remains (Report Number 44). Arkansas Archaeological Survey, Fayetteville, AR.

Burns, K.R., 1999. Forensic Anthropology Training Manual. Prentice Hall, Upper Saddle River, NJ.

Calce, S.E., 2012. A new method to estimate adult age-at-death using the acetabulum. Am. J. Phys. Anthropol. 148, 11–23.

Calce, S.E., Rogers, T.L., 2011. Evaluation of age estimation technique: testing traits of the acetabulum to estimate age at death in adult males. J. Forensic Sci. 56, 302–311.

Cerezo-Román, J.I., Hernández Espinosa, P.O., 2014. Estimating age at death using the sternal end of the fourth ribs from Mexican males. Forensic Sci. Int. 236, 196. e1–196.e6.

Cerny, M., 1983. Our experience with estimation of an individual's age from skeletal remains of the degree of thyroid cartilage ossification. Acta Univ. Palacki. Olomuc. Fac. Med. 3, 121–144.

Chen, X., Zhang, Z., Tao, L., 2008. Determination of male age at death in Chinese Han population: using quantitative variables statistical analysis from pubic bones. Forensic Sci. Int. 175, 36–43.

Colarusso, T., 2015. A test of the Passalacqua age at death estimation method using the sacrum. J. Forensic Sci. 61, S22–S29.

Cox, M., 2000. Assessment of parturition. In: Cox, M., Mays, S. (Eds.), Human Osteology in Archaeology and Forensic Science. Greenwich Medical Media Ltd., London, pp. 131–142.

Dang-Tran, K., Dedouit, F., Joffre, F., Rouge, D., Rousseau, H., Telmon, N., 2010. Thyroid cartilage ossification and multislice computed tomography examination: a useful tool for age assessment? J. Forensic Sci. 55, 677–683.

Daubert v. Merrell Dow Pharmaceuticals, Inc. 509 US 579, 1993.

Dedouit, F., Bindel, S., Gainza, D., Blanc, A., Joffre, F., Rouge, G., Telmon, N., 2008. Application of the İşcan method to two- and three-dimensional imaging of the sternal end of the right fourth rib. J. Forensic Sci. 53, 288–295.

DiGangi, E.A., Bethard, J.D., Kimmerle, E.H., Konigsberg, L.W., 2009. A new method for estimating age-at-death from the first rib. Am. J. Phys. Anthropol. 138, 164–176.

Djuric, M., Djonic, D., Nikolic, S., Popovic, D., Marinkovic, J., 2007. Evaluation of the Suchey–Brooks method for aging skeletons in the Balkans. J. Forensic Sci. 52, 21–23.

Dudar, J.C., 1990. An investigation of intercostal variation in adult sternal rib ends. Can. Soc. Forensic Sci. J. 23, 139.

Dudar, J.C., 1993. Identification of rib number and assessment of intercostal variation at the sternal rib end. J. Forensic Sci. 38, 788–797.

Dudar, J.C., Pfeiffer, S., Saunders, S.R., 1993. Evaluation of morphological and histological adult skeletal age-at-death estimation techniques using ribs. J. Forensic Sci. 38, 677–685.

Dudzik, B., Langley, N.R., 2015. Estimating age from the pubic symphysis: a new component-based system. Forensic Sci. Int. 257, 98–105.

Falys, C.G., Schutkowski, H., Weston, D.A., 2006. Auricular surface aging: worse than expected? A test of the revised method on a documented historic skeletal assemblage. Am. J. Phys. Anthropol. 130, 508–513.

Fanton, L., Gustin, M.P., Paultre, U., Schrag, B., Malicier, D., 2010. Critical study of observation of the sternal end of the right 4th rib. J. Forensic Sci. 55, 467–472.

Ferrant, O., Rougé-Maillart, C., Guittet, L., Papin, F., Clin, B., Fau, G., Telmon, N., 2009. Age at death estimation of adult males using coxal bone and CT scan: a preliminary study. Forensic Sci. Int. 186, 14–21.

Fleischman, J.M., 2013. A comparative assessment of the Chen et al. and Suchey–Brooks pubic aging methods on a North American sample. J. Forensic Sci. 58, 311–323.

Galera, V., Ubelaker, D.H., Hayek, L.C., 1998. Comparison of macroscopic cranial methods of age estimation applied to skeletons of the Terry Collection. J. Forensic Sci. 43, 933–939.

Garamendi, P.M., Landa, M.I., Botella, M.C., Aleman, I., 2011. Forensic age estimation on digital X-ray images: medial epiphyses of the clavicle and first rib ossification in relation to chronological age. J. Forensic Sci. 56, S3–S12.

Garvin, H.M., 2008. Ossification of laryngeal structures as indicators of age. J. Forensic Sci. 53, 1023–1027.

Garvin, H.M., Passalacqua, N.V., 2012. Current practices by forensic anthropologists in adult skeletal age estimation. J. Forensic Sci. 57, 427–433.

Geske, N.L., 2013. Evaluation of the Oettlé and Steyn sternal rib end aging method on an American sample. In: Poster Presented at the Annual Meeting of the American Academy of Forensic Sciences, Washington DC.

Gilbert, B.M., 1973. Misapplication to females of the standard for aging the male os pubis. Am. J. Phys. Anthropol. 38, 39–40.

Gilbert, B.M., McKern, T.W., 1973. A method for aging the female os pubis. Am. J. Phys. Anthropol. 38, 31–38.

Gocha, T.P., Ingvoldstad, M.E., Kolatorowicz, A., Cosgriff-Hernandez, M.T.J., Sciulli, P.W., 2015. Testing the applicability of six macroscopic skeletal aging techniques on a modern Southeast Asian sample. Forensic Sci. Int. 249, 318.e1–318.e7.

Godde, K., Hens, S.M., 2012. Age-at-death estimation in an Italian historical sample: a test of the Suchey–Brooks and transition analysis methods. Am. J. Phys. Anthropol. 149, 259–265.

Godde, K., Hens, S.M., 2015. Modeling senescence changes of the pubic symphysis in historic Italian populations: a comparison of the Rostock and forensic approaches to aging using transition analysis. Am. J. Phys. Anthropol. 156, 466–473.

Gorea, R.K., Kapila, A.K., Oberoi, S.S., Singh, P., 2004. Age estimation in old individuals by CT scan of skull. J. Ind. Acad. Forensic Med. 26 (1), 10–13.

Hanihara, K., Suzuki, T., 1978. Estimation of age from the pubic symphysis by means of multiple regression analysis. Am. J. Phys. Anthropol. 48, 233–240.

Hartnett, K.M., 2007. A Re-evaluation and Revision of Pubic Symphysis and Fourth Rib Aging Techniques (Ph.D. dissertation). School of Human Evolution and Social Change. Arizona State University, Tempe.

Hartnett, K.M., 2010a. Analysis of age-at-death estimation using data from a new, modern autopsy sample – part I: pubic bone. J. Forensic Sci. 55, 1145–1151.

Hartnett, K.M., 2010b. Analysis of age-at-death estimation using data from a new, modern autopsy sample – part II: sternal end of the fourth rib. J. Forensic Sci. 55, 1152–1156.

Hens, S.M., Belcastro, M.G., 2012. Auricular surface aging: a blind test of the revised method on historic Italians from Sardinia. Forensic Sci. Int. 214, 209.e1–209.e5.

Hens, S.M., Rastelli, E., Belcastro, M.G., 2008. Age estimation from the human os coxa: a test on a documented Italian Collection. J. Forensic Sci. 53, 1040–1043.

Hoppa, R.D., 2000. Population variation in osteological aging criteria: an example from the pubic symphysis. Am. J. Phys. Anthropol. 111, 185–191.

Hoppa, R.D., Vaupel, J.W., 2002. The Rostock Manifesto for paleodemography: the way from stage to age. In: Hoppa, R.D., Vaupel, J.W. (Eds.), Paleodemography: Age Distributions from Skeletal Samples. Cambridge University Press, Cambridge, United Kingdom, pp. 1–8.

Hutchinson, D.L., Russell, K.F., 2001. Pelvic age estimation using actual specimens and remote images. J. Forensic Sci. 46, 1224–1227.

Igarashi, Y., Uesu, K., Wakebe, T., Kanazawa, E., 2005. New method for estimation of adult skeletal age at death from the morphology of the auricular surface of the ilium. Am. J. Phys. Anthropol. 128, 324–339.

İşcan, M.Y., 1989b. Research strategies in age estimation: the multiregional approach. In: İşcan, M.Y. (Ed.), Age Markers in the Human Skeleton. Charles C. Thomas, Springfield, IL, pp. 325–339.

İşcan, M.Y., Loth, S.R., 1989. Assessment of intercostal variation on the estimation of age from the sternal end of the rib. Am. J. Phys. Anthropol. 78, 245.

İşcan, M.Y., Loth, S.R., Wright, R.K., 1984a. Metamorphosis at the sternal rib end: a new method to estimate age at death in white males. Am. J. Phys. Anthropol. 65, 147–156.

İşcan, M.Y., Loth, S.R., Wright, R.K., 1984b. Age estimation from the rib by phase analysis: white males. J. Forensic Sci. 29, 1094–1104.

İşcan, M.Y., Loth, S.R., Wright, R.K., 1985. Age estimation from the rib by phase analysis: white females. J. Forensic Sci. 30, 853–863.

İşcan, M.Y., Loth, S.R., Wright, R.K., 1987. Racial variation in the sternal extremity of the rib and its effect on age determination. J. Forensic Sci. 32, 452–466.

Jackes, M., 1985. Pubic symphysis age distributions. Am. J. Phys. Anthropol. 68, 281–299.

Jit, I., Bakshi, V., 1984. Incidence of foramina in North Indian sterna. J. Anat. Soc. India 33, 77–84.

Katz, D., Suchey, J.M., 1986. Age determination of the male os pubis. Am. J. Phys. Anthropol. 69, 427–435.

Kerley, E.R., 1970. Estimation of skeletal age: after about 30 years. In: Stewart, T.D. (Ed.), Personal Identification in Mass Disasters. National Museum of Natural History, Washington, DC, pp. 57–70.

Kimmerle, E.H., Konigsberg, L.W., Jantz, R.L., Baraybar, J.P., 2008a. Analysis of age-at-death estimation through the use of pubic symphyseal data. J. Forensic Sci. 53, 558–568.

Kimmerle, E.H., Prince, D.A., Berg, G.E., 2008b. Inter-observer variation in methodologies involving the pubic symphysis, sternal ribs, and teeth. J. Forensic Sci. 53, 594–600.

Klepinger, L.L., Katz, D., Micozzi, M.S., Carroll, L., 1992. Evaluation of cast methods for estimating age from the os pubis. J. Forensic Sci. 37, 763–770.

Konigsberg, L.W., Frankenberg, S.R., Walker, R.B., 1994. Regress what on what? Paleodemographic age estimation as a calibration problem. In: Paine, R.R. (Ed.), Integrating Archaeological Demography: Multidisciplinary Approaches to Prehistoric Population. Center for Archaeological Investigations Occasional Paper No. 24. Southern Illinois University, Carbondale, IL, pp. 64–88.

Konigsberg, L.W., Herrmann, N.P., Wescott, D.J., Kimmerle, E.H., 2008. Estimation and evidence in forensic anthropology: age-at-death. J. Forensic Sci. 53, 541–557.

Krogman, W.M., Iscan, M.Y., 1986. The Human Skeleton in Forensic Medicine, second ed. Charles C. Thomas, Springfield, Illinois.

Kunos, C.A., Simpson, S.W., Russell, K.F., Hershkovitz, I., 1999. First rib metamorphosis: its possible utility for age-at-death estimation. Am. J. Phys. Anthropol. 110, 303–323.

Langley-Shirley, N., Jantz, R.L., 2010. A Bayesian approach to age estimation in modern Americans from the clavicle. J. Forensic Sci. 55, 571–583.

Ley, C.A., Aiello, L.C., Molleson, T., 1994. Cranial suture closure and its implications for age estimation. Int. J. Osteoarchaeol. 4, 193–207.

Listi, G.A., 2016. The use of entheseal changes in the femur and os coxa for age assessment. J. Forensic Sci. 61, 12–18.

Listi, G.A., Manhein, M.H., 2012. The use of vertebral osteoarthritis and osteophytosis in age estimation. J. Forensic Sci. 57, 1537–1540.

Loth, S.R., İşcan, M.Y., 1989. Morphological assessment of age in the adult: the thoracic region. In: Iscan, M.Y. (Ed.), Age Markers in the Human Skeleton. Charles C. Thomas, Springfield, IL, pp. 105–135.

Loth, S.R., İşcan, M.Y., Scheuerman, E.H., 1994. Intercostal variation at the sternal end of the rib. Forensic Sci. Int. 65, 135–143.

Lottering, N., MacGregor, D.M., Meredith, M., Alston, C.L., Gregory, L.S., 2013. Evaluation of the Suchey–Brooks method of age estimation in an Australian subpopulation using computed tomography of the pubic symphyseal surface. Am. J. Phys. Anthropol. 150, 386–399.

Lovejoy, C.O., Meindl, R.S., Mensforth, R., Barton, T.J., 1985a. Multifactorial determination of skeletal age at death: a method and blind tests of its accuracy. Am. J. Phys. Anthropol. 68, 1–14.

Lovejoy, C.O., Meindl, R.S., Pryzbeck, T.R., Mensforth, R.P., 1985b. Chronological metamorphosis of the auricular surface of the ilium: a new method for the determination of adult skeletal age at death. Am. J. Phys. Anthropol. 68, 15–28.

Maat, G.J.R., 1987. Practising methods of age determination. Comments on methods combining multiple age indicators. Int. J. Anthropol. 2, 293–299.

Mann, R.W., Jantz, R.L., Bass, W.M., Willey, P., 1991. Maxillary suture obliteration: a visual method for estimating skeletal age. J. Forensic Sci. 36, 781–791.

Martrille, L., Ubelaker, D.H., Cattaneo, C., Seguret, F., Tremblay, M., Baccino, E., 2007. Comparison of four skeletal methods for the estimation of age at death on white and black adults. J. Forensic Sci. 52, 302–307.

Masset, C., 1989. Age estimation based on cranial sutures. In: İşcan, M.Y. (Ed.), Age Markers in the Human Skeleton. Charles C. Thomas, Springfield, IL, pp. 71–104.

Mays, S., 2014. A test of a recently devised method of estimating skeletal age at death using features of the adult acetabulum. J. Forensic Sci. 59, 184–187.

McCormick, W.F., Stewart, J.H., 1988. Age related changes in the human plastron: a roentgenographic and morphologic study. J. Forensic Sci. 33, 100–120.

McKern, T.W., Stewart, T.D., 1957. Skeletal age changes in young American males. In: Headquarters Quartermaster Research and Development and Command Technical Report EP-45. Natick, Massachusetts.

McKern, T.W., 1970. Estimation of skeletal age: from puberty to about 30 years of age. In: Personal Identification in Mass Disasters. National Museum of Natural History, Washington, DC.

Meindl, R.S., Lovejoy, C.O., 1989. Age changes in the pelvis: implications for paleodemography. In: İşcan, M.Y. (Ed.), Age Markers in the Human Skeleton. Charles C. Thomas, Springfield, IL, pp. 137–168.

Meindl, R.S., Lovejoy, C.O., Mensforth, R.P., Walker, R.A., 1985. A revised method of age determination using the os pubis, with a review and tests of accuracy of other current methods of pubic symphyseal aging. Am. J. Phys. Anthropol. 68, 29–45.

Merritt, C.E., 2014. A test of Hartnett's revisions to the pubic symphysis and fourth rib methods on a modern sample. J. Forensic Sci. 59, 703–711.

Merritt, C.E., 2015. The influence of body size on adult skeletal age estimation methods. Am. J. Phys. Anthropol. 156, 35–57.

Michelson, N., 1934. The calcification of the first costal cartilage among Whites and Negroes. Hum. Biol. 6, 543–557.

Milner, G.R., Boldsen, J.L., 2012. Transition analysis: a validation study with known-age modern American skeletons. Am. J. Phys. Anthropol. 148, 98–110.

Moraitis, K., Zorba, E., Eliopoulos, C., Fox, S.C., 2014. A test of the revised auricular surface aging method on a modern European population. J. Forensic. Sci. 59, 188–194.

Moskovitch, G., Dedouit, F., Braga, J., Rouge, D., Rousseau, H., Telmon, N., 2010. Multislice computed tomography of the first rib: a useful technique for bone age assessment. J. Forensic Sci. 55, 865–870.

Mulhern, D.W., Jones, E.B., 2005. Test of revised method of age estimation from the auricular surface of the ilium. Am. J. Phys. Anthropol. 126, 61–65.

Murray, K.A., Murray, T., 1991. A test of the auricular surface aging technique. J. Forensic Sci. 36, 1162–1169.

Nawrocki, S.P., 1998. Regression formulae for estimating age at death from cranial suture closure. In: Reichs, K.J. (Ed.), Forensic Osteology: Advances in the Identification of Human Remains. Charles C. Thomas, Springfield, IL, pp. 276–292.

Nawrocki, S.P., 2010. The nature and sources of error in the estimation of age at death from the skeleton. In: Latham, K.E., Finnegan, M. (Eds.), Age Estimation of the Human Skeleton. Charles C. Thomas, Springfield, IL, pp. 79–101.

Nikita, E., 2013. Quantitative assessment of the sternal rib end morphology and implications for its application in aging human remains. J. Forensic Sci. 58, 324–329.

Oettlé, A.C., Steyn, M., 2000. Age estimation from sternal ends of ribs by phase analysis in South African blacks. J. Forensic Sci. 45, 1071–1079.

Oldrini, G., Harter, V., Witte, Y., Martrille, L., Blum, A., 2016. Age estimation in living adults using 3D volume rendered CT images of the sternal plastron and lower chest. J. Forensic Sci. 61, 127–133.

Osborne, D.L., Simmons, T.L., Nawrocki, S.P., 2004. Reconsidering the auricular surface as an indicator of age at death. J. Forensic Sci. 49, 905–911.

Pasquier, E., De Saint Martin Pernot, L., Burdin, V., Mounayer, C., Le Rest, C., Colin, D., Mottier, D., Roux, C., Baccino, E., 1999. Determination of age at death: assessment of an algorithm of age prediction using numerical three-dimensional CT data from pubic bones. Am. J. Phys. Anthropol. 108, 261–268.

Passalacqua, N.V., 2009. Forensic age-at-death estimation from the human sacrum. J. Forensic Sci. 54, 255–262.

Passalacqua, N.V., 2010. The utility of the Samworth and Gowland age-at-death "look-up" tables in forensic anthropology. J. Forensic Sci. 55, 482–487.

Pfeiffer, S., 1985. Comparison of adult age estimation techniques, using an ossuary sample. Can. J. Anthropol. 4, 13–17.

Prince, D.A., Kimmerle, E.H., Konigsberg, L.W., 2008. A Bayesian approach to estimate skeletal age-at-death utilizing dental wear. J. Forensic Sci. 53, 588–593.

Ríos, L., Weisensee, K., Rissech, C., 2008. Sacral fusion as an aid in age estimation. Forensic Sci. Int. 180, 111.e1–111.e7.

Rissech, C., Estabrook, G.F., Cunha, E., Malgosa, A., 2006. Using the acetabulum to estimate age-at-death of adult males. J. Forensic Sci. 51, 213–229.

Rissech, C., Estabrook, G.F., Cunha, E., Malgosa, A., 2007. Estimation of age-at-death for adult males using the acetabulum, applied to four Western European populations. J. Forensic Sci. 52, 774–778.

Rouge-Maillart, C., Jousset, N., Vielle, B., Gaudin, A., Telmon, N., 2007. Contribution of the study of acetabulum for the estimation of adult subjects. Forensic Sci. Int. 171, 103–110.

Russell, K.F., Simpson, S.W., Genovese, J., Kinkel, M.D., Meindl, R.S., Lovejoy, C.O., 1993. Independent test of the fourth rib aging technique. Am. J. Phys. Anthropol. 92, 53–62.

Samworth, R., Gowland, R., 2007. Estimation of adult skeletal age-at-death: statistical assumptions and applications. Int. J. Osteoarchaeol. 17, 174–188.

Sarajlić, N., 2006. Age estimation based on sternal rib ends changes in Bosnian male population. Med. Arch. 60, 343–346.

Saunders, S.R., Fitzgerald, C.M., Rogers, T.L., Dudar, C., McKillop, H., 1992. A test of several methods of skeletal age estimation using a documented archaeological sample. Can. Soc. Forensic Sci. 25, 97–118.

Scheuer, L., Black, S., 2000. Juvenile Developmental Osteology. Academic Press, San Diego.

Schmitt, A., 2004. Age-at-death assessment using the os pubis and the auricular surface of the ilium: a test on an identified Asian sample. Int. J. Osteoarchaeol 14, 1–6.

Schultz, A.H., 1944. Age change and variability in gibbons: a morphological study on a population sample of a man-like ape. Am. J. Phys. Anthropol. 2, 1–29.

Seidel, A.C., 2013. An evaluation of the Hartnett–Fulginiti method for age-estimation on an independent skeletal sample. In: Poster Presented at the Annual Meeting of the American Academy of Forensic Sciences, Washington DC.

Shirley, N.R., Ramirez Montes, P.A., 2015. Age estimation in forensic anthropology: quantification of observer error in phase versus component-based methods. J. Forensic Sci. 60, 107–111.

Slice, D.E., Algee-Hewitt, B.F.B., 2015. Modeling bone surface morphology: a fully quantitative method for age-at-death estimation using the pubic symphysis. J. Forensic Sci. 60, 835–843.

Snow, C.E., 1983. Equations for estimating age at death from the pubic symphysis: a modification of the McKern–Stewart method. J. Forensic Sci. 28, 864–870.

Steadman, D.W., Adams, B.J., Konigsberg, L.W., 2006. Statistical basis for positive identification in forensic anthropology. Am. J. Phys. Anthropol. 131, 15–26.

Steele, D.G., Bramblett, C.A., 1988. The Anatomy and Biology of the Human Skeleton. A & M University Press, College Station, TX.

Stewart, T.D. (Ed.), 1970. Personal Identification in Mass Disasters. National Museum of Natural History, Washington, DC.

Stewart, T.D., 1979. Essentials of Forensic Anthropology Especially as Developed in the United States. Charles C. Thomas, Springfield, IL.

Suchey, J.M., 1979. Problems in the aging of females using the os pubis. Am. J. Phys. Anthropol. 51, 467–470.

Suchey, J.M., 1986. Skeletal age standards derived from an extensive multiracial sample of modern Americans. Am. J. Phys. Anthropol. 69, 269.

Suchey, J.M., 1987. Use of the Suchey–Brooks system for aging the male os pubis. Am. J. Phys. Anthropol. 72, 259.

Suchey, J.M., Owings, P.A., Wisely, D.V., Noguchi, T.T., 1984. Skeletal aging of unidentified persons. In: Rathbun, T.A., Buikstra, J.E. (Eds.), Human Identification: Case Studies in Forensic Anthropology. Charles C. Thomas, Springfield, IL, pp. 278–298.

Suchey, J.M., Wisely, D.V., Katz, D., 1986. Evaluation of the Todd and McKern–Stewart methods for aging the male os pubis. In: Reichs, K.J. (Ed.), Forensic Osteology: Advances in the Identification of Human Remains. Charles C. Thomas, Springfield, IL, pp. 33–67.

Tangmose, S., Thevissen, P., Lynnerup, N., Willems, G., Boldsen, J., 2015. Age estimation in the living: transition analysis on developing third molars. Forensic Sci. Int. 257, 512.e1–512.e7.

Telmon, N., Gaston, A., Chemla, P., Blanc, A., Joffre, F., Rouge, D., 2005. Application of the Suchey–Brooks method to three-dimensional imaging of the pubic symphysis. J. Forensic Sci. 50, 507–512.

Todd, T.W., 1920. Age changes in the pubic bone: I. The male white pubis. Am. J. Phys. Anthropol. 3, 285–339.

Todd, T.W., 1921. Age changes in the pubic bone. Am. J. Phys. Anthropol. 4, 1–77.

Todd, T.W., D'Errico Jr., J., 1928. The clavicular epiphyses. Am. J. Anat. 41, 25–50.

Todd, T.W., Lyon, D.W., 1924. Endocranial suture closure: its progress and age relationship. Part 1–adult males of white stock. Am. J. Phys. Anthropol. 7, 325–383.

Todd, T.W., Lyon, D.W., 1925a. Cranial suture closure: its progress and relationship. Part 2–ectocranial closure in adult males of white stock. Am. J. Phys. Anthropol. 3, 23–45.

Todd, T.W., Lyon, D.W., 1925b. Cranial suture closure: its progress and age relationship. Part 3.–endocranial closure in adult males of negro stock. Am. J. Phys. Anthropol. 8, 47–71.

Todd, T.W., Lyon, D.W., 1925c. Cranial suture closure: its progress and age relationship. Part 4–ectocranial closure in adult males of negro stock. Am. J. Phys. Anthropol. 8, 149–168.

Ubelaker, D.H., 1989. Human Skeletal Remains: Excavation, Analysis, Interpretation. Taraxacum, Washington, DC.

Uhl, N.M., Nawrocki, S.P., 2010. Multifactorial estimation of age at death from the human skeleton. In: Latham, K.E., Finnegan, M. (Eds.), Age Estimation of the Human Skeleton. Charles C. Thomas, Springfield, IL, pp. 243–261.

Villa, C., Buckberry, J., Cattaneo, C., Lynnerup, N., 2013. Technical note: reliability of Suchey–Brooks and Buckberry–Chamberlain methods on 3D visualizations from CT and laser scans. Am. J. Phys. Anthropol. 151, 158–163.

Villa, C., Buckberry, J., Cattaneo, C., Frohlich, B., Lynnerup, N., 2015. Quantitative analysis of the morphological changes of the pubic symphyseal face and the auricular surface and implications for age at death estimation. J. Forensic Sci. 60, 556–565.

Webb, P.A., Suchey, J.M., 1985. Epiphyseal union of the anterior iliac crest and medial clavicle in a modern multiracial sample of American males and females. Am. J. Phys. Anthropol. 68, 457–466.

Wescott, D.J., Drew, J.L., 2015. Effect of obesity on the reliability of age-at-death indicators of the pelvis. Am. J. Phys. Anthropol. 156, 595–605.

White, T.D., Black, M.T., Folkens, P.A., 2012. Human Osteology, third ed. Elsevier, Burlington, MA.

Wink, A.E., 2014. Pubic symphyseal age estimation from three-dimensional reconstructions of pelvic CT scans of live individuals. J. Forensic Sci. 59, 696–702.

Wolff, K., Vas, Z., Sótonyi, P., Magyar, L.G., 2012. Skeletal age estimation in Hungarian population of known age and sex. Forensic Sci. Int. 223, 374.e1–374.e8.

Yavuz, M.F., İşcan, M.Y., Çöloğlu, A.S., 1998. Age assessment by rib phase analysis in Turks. Forensic Sci. Int. 98, 47–54.

Yoder, C., Ubelaker, D.H., Powell, J.F., 2001. Examination of variation in sternal rib end morphology relevant to age assessment. J. Forensic. Sci. 46, 223–227.

Zhang, K., Chen, X., Zhao, H., Dong, X., Deng, Z., 2015. Forensic age estimation using thin-slice multidetector CT of the clavicular epiphyses among adolescent Western Chinese. J. Forensic Sci. 60, 675–678.

CHAPTER 9

Multivariate Regression Methods for the Analysis of Stature

Lyle W. Konigsberg[1] | Lee Meadows Jantz[2]
[1]University of Illinois at Urbana-Champaign, Urbana, IL, United States,
[2]University of Tennessee, Knoxville, TN, United States

Chapter Outline

■ INTRODUCTION

There is a long history of using linear regression to estimate stature from long bone lengths (Dupertuis and Hadden, 1951; Genovés, 1967; Houghton et al., 1975; Pearson, 1899; Trotter and Gleser, 1952). This approach, which Stewart (1979) referred to as "mathematical," can be contrasted with what Stewart referred to as an "anatomical" approach. The anatomical approach was first codified by Fully (1956) and has seen revision and careful description in Raxter et al. (2006, 2007) as further described in Raxter and Ruff's chapter from this volume. As Raxter and Ruff do provide a chapter in this volume on the "Fully technique," it is unnecessary to further discuss this method at length. As originally given by Fully, his method used a sum of the following heights to obtain a total skeletal height: basion–bregma, second cervical body height through fifth lumbar height, first sacral height, bicondylar femoral length, tibial length (without spines), and articulated talus/calcaneal height. To this skeletal height Fully suggested a constant of 10.0, 10.5, or 11 cm (depending on the measured skeletal height) be added to account for the soft tissue contribution to stature. In the revision as given by Raxter et al. there is a smidgen of the mathematical (regression) approach in that they regressed living stature onto skeletal height. As the correlation between skeletal height and stature is greater than that between long bones and stature, the anatomical method is the preferred method. But given problems with missing boney elements from individual cases, one often must fall back on the "mathematical" approaches for estimating stature. This is the subject matter for this chapter, though we close with a brief comparison between the two methods.

Before examining methods for stature estimation, we should acknowledge that there are various uses of the term "stature." Ousley (1995) makes the broad distinction between "forensic stature" and "measured stature." We would relabel "forensic stature" (by which Ousley is primarily referring to driver's license–listed statures) as "reported statures." Reported statures may be biased because of "rounding up" or because of exaggerations in reference to "dwarfs" or "giants." For example, Charles Byrne, who is used as an extensive example in this chapter, had reported statures as tall as 8'4" in advertisements for some of his appearances as the "Irish Giant" (of which there were at least two other individuals, being Patrick Cotter and Cornelius McGrath, who used this billing). This stated stature is much taller than the stature measured from the articulated skeleton from this individual. In contrast to reported stature, measured statures are taken by someone with experience in the process of taking the measurement. The measured stature may be a living height as would be taken during a routine physical, it may be a cadaver length which typically will exceed the living height by about 2.5 cm (Trotter and Gleser, 1952), or it may be of skeleton length in the grave (Boldsen, 1984). Our use of the term "stature" in this chapter will refer to measured statures rather than reported statures.

■ OF RAW DATA AND SUMMARY MULTIVARIATE STATISTICS

We will make the argument here that summary multivariate statistics are extremely useful in making inferences about stature for individual forensic cases. But to make this argument we will first need access to a raw data set. For this we use the stature and maximum lengths for the humerus, ulna, radius, femur, tibia, and fibula for 2015 individuals from the second author's dissertation (Jantz, 1996). Given the large number of individuals, one would expect that there would be data errors. Five errors were readily identified by inspection (see Table 9.1) and were corrected before proceeding any further with the analysis. The two cases where the tibia and fibula lengths appear to have been transposed could be identified by looking at the difference between the maximum lengths of these two bones. The tibia is typically longer than the fibula, though exclusion of the medial malleolus from the tibial measurement (Jantz et al., 1995) can reverse this. Fig. 9.1 shows the distribution of differences between the tibia and fibula for the sample of 2015 individuals after swapping the tibia and fibula measurements within FDB 1248 and 1329. Also shown are the differences for these two individuals if the bones were not swapped. In the case of Terry 1237, this individual originally had an ulna length of 297 and a radial length of 320, which is a clear transposition. For WW2 1156 and WW2 1333 prediction of a questioned value from the other long bones suggested that the recorded values were miswritten.

Table 9.1 Errors Corrected in the Reference Sample of 2015 Individuals

Collection	Case #	Error	Solution
FDB	1248	Tibia and fibula values transposed	Values swapped
FDB	1329	Tibia and fibula values transposed	Values swapped
Terry	1237	Radius and ulna values transposed	Values swapped
WW2	1156	Recorded radius = 236, predicted = 257	Value of 256 entered
WW2	1333	Recorded humerus = 307, predicted = 354	Value of 357 entered

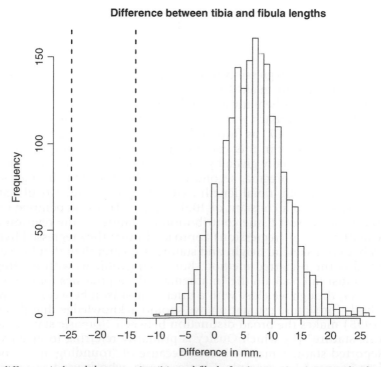

Figure 9.1 Histogram of the difference in length between the tibia and fibula for the sample of 2015 individuals after correcting two apparent transpositions of the measurements for these two bones. The *dashed lines* show the differences without swapping the apparent transpositions.

■ TO LOG OR NOT TO LOG?

As mentioned earlier, we will make extensive use of multivariate summary statistics in this chapter. As a consequence, we must first decide whether these statistics can be calculated from untransformed data or whether the data must first be converted to a logarithmic scale. Previous analyses of long bone lengths have varied in their perspective on whether the data should be log transformed prior to analysis. Those analyses that focus primarily on limb allometry in humans have often used log-transformed data (Auerbach and Sylvester, 2011; Holliday and Ruff, 2001; Meadows and Jantz, 1995; Temple and Matsumura, 2011; Weinstein, 2005). Smith (1980, p. 98) argued that the use of log transformation should not be viewed as a necessity in allometric studies, writing that:

> In 1942, D'Arcy Thompson reevaluated some of Huxley's (1932) data and demonstrated that untransformed linear equations fit several data sets just as well as power functions. In addition, he pointed out that linear data, when transformed to logs, will remain linear.

Smith's reference to D'Arcy Thompson's (1942) examples of "untransformed linear equations" refers to Thompson's analyses of mandible and body lengths in Stag beetles and Reindeer beetles and of facial and cranial lengths in Sheepdogs. Thompson provided linear–linear plots for Reindeer beetles (his Figure 55) and Sheepdogs (his Figure 56), in contrast to Huxley's (1932) log–log plots for three species of Stag beetles (his Figure 58) and Sheepdogs (his Figure 9).

Smith (1980) found that only in 12 of his 60 empirical examples was log transformation necessary, and all 12 of these examples were at the interspecific level. As we are dealing here with a single species, the use of log transformation seems unnecessary. We show this in an analysis of maximum femur length and stature from the 2015 individuals. Fig. 9.2 shows what is known as a "convex hull peel" (Green, 2006) for the 2015 individuals where the successive convex hulls from outer to inner contain 100%, 95%, 80%, 50%, 25%, and 10% of the bivariate (femur and stature) data. The scale here is intentionally drawn well beyond the limits of any of the data, with stature on a scale of from 0 to 3500 mm and maximum femur length on a scale of from 0 to 1000 mm. Also drawn in Fig. 9.2 is the linear regression of femur length regressed onto stature, as would be the case in allometric studies where "organ" size is regressed onto body size. Also shown are two nonlinear regression curves. The two-parameter power function is $y = ax^b$, while the three-parameter function is $y = c + ax^b$ (Packard et al., 2011) where x is stature and y is femur length. The two-parameter power function is similar to the least squares regression of log femur length on log stature, save that the former minimizes sums of squares in the straight scale for femur length while the latter minimizes sums of squares in the log scale. As a consequence, the two-parameter power function error terms are additive, while the log scale regression error terms are multiplicative. Fig. 9.2 also shows the line that passes through the origin (0,0) for the graph and the bivariate mean. In linear regression the y-intercept must be at the origin if the bone is isometric with stature, or in other words if there is a constant of proportionality.

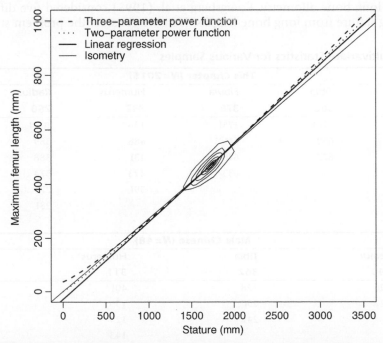

Figure 9.2 Convex hull "peel" for the femur and stature from 2015 individuals. The convex hulls are shown for that include 100%, 95%, 80%, 50%, 25%, and 10% of the data. The various *lines* and *curves* are described in the text.

Fig. 9.2 shows, first of all, that there is slight positive allometry in the linear scale, as shorter individuals have relatively shorter femora, while taller individuals have relatively longer femora. This result was also found by Meadows Jantz and Jantz (1999), though the deviation from isometry is quite slight. For example, in our analysis an individual who was 1400 mm tall would have a predicted maximum femur length that was 26.9% that of the individual's stature versus 27.5% in an individual who was 2000 mm tall. Sylvester et al. (2008) have found that in general human limb long bones are nearly isometric, though their analysis used internally defined size rather than stature or body mass as an overall measure of body size. In any event, the near isometry for the femur against stature means that there is essentially no difference in predicted femur length whether one uses linear regression in the straight scale, in the log scale, or nonlinear regression with two or three parameters. It is only at extremely unreasonable statures, such as 500 mm (about 20 inches) and 3000 mm (about 9 feet and 10 inches), that the various lines/curves depart. Within the range of the actual data, linear regression and the two and three parameter power curves are indistinguishable. Given this fact, we use the long bone and stature data in their original scale without subjecting them to log transformation, and we will work from summary multivariate statistics based on the untransformed data.

■ SUMMARY STATISTICS

The necessary summary statistics for a multivariate analysis of stature based on p measurements (including stature as one of the variables) is of size $(p^2 + 3p + 2)/2$, where p is the number of means (means for all measurements as well as stature), $p(p + 1)/2$ is the number of unique elements in the variance–covariance matrix among the measurements and stature, and there is one additional statistic which is the sample size. Some authors, such as Trotter and Gleser (1952), have chosen to present the standard deviations and one triangle of the correlation matrix, from which the full variance–covariance matrix can be obtained. This is just an alternate parameterization, so it also requires $(p^2 + 3p + 2)/2$ parameters. As an example, Trotter and Gleser's (1952) Table 3, which summarizes the data on 16 long bone measurements and stature, has $(17^2 + 3 \times 17 + 2)/2 = 171$ values in it if one counts the sample size listed in the heading. Our Table 9.2 lists the sample sizes and summary multivariate statistics for our sample, for a male Chinese sample (Stevenson, 1929), for male and female French samples (Rollet, 1888), for male and female Mesoamerican samples (Genovés, 1967), and for a pygmy sample (Jungers, 1988). The term "pygmy" is not used here in any pejorative sense, but rather as a reference to equatorial peoples with statures under 5 feet tall (Jungers et al., 2016). The Mesoamerican samples included only those individuals designated as "indigenous" for the males and as "indigenous" or "mestizo" for the females. The pygmy sample includes both sexes and is lacking one individual reported in Jungers (1988) as that individual lacked upper limb long bones. The statures for all samples were cadaver or living statures save for the pygmy sample, which had "Fully statures" made prior to recent methodological revisions (Raxter et al., 2006).

■ WHICH OF THE FIVE REGRESSION LINES TO USE IN ALLOMETRIC ANALYSIS?

Before turning to the multivariate analysis, we must answer the question of which linear function is the most useful for studying human long bone allometry. Konigsberg et al. (1998) considered five different such lines within the context of estimating stature from long bone lengths. Here we consider the problem strictly as one of studying

Table 9.2 Summary Multivariate Statistics for Various Samples

This Chapter (N = 2015)						
Stature	**Femur**	**Tibia**	**Fibula**	**Humerus**	**Radius**	**Ulna**
1710	**466**	**386**	**378**	**332**	**250**	**269**
7141	2071	1761	1751	1368	1034	1042
	799	659	641	488	389	389
		677	640	431	388	391
			633	423	374	379
				391	277	277
					281	280
						295

Male Chinese (N = 48)				
Stature	**Femur**	**Tibia**	**Humerus**	**Radius**
1689	**440**	**362**	**311**	**238**
3005	796	728	401	372
	327	250	159	121
		241	129	118
			143	80
				99

Table 9.2   *Summary Multivariate Statistics for Various Samples*—Cont'd

Male French (N = 50)

Stature	Femur	Tibia	Humerus	Radius
1663	**452**	**368**	**330**	**244**
3089	1079	785	699	457
	574	351	313	211
		330	243	168
			241	155
				140

Male Mesoamericans (N = 22)

Stature	Femur	Tibia	Fibula	Humerus	Radius	Ulna
1640	**432**	**359**	**351**	**311**	**237**	**255**
2611	877	1043	963	535	412	428
	445	382	413	277	251	210
		590	394	307	220	278
			502	284	217	227
				213	179	155
					154	131
						164

Female French (N = 50)

Stature	Femur	Tibia	Humerus	Radius
1540	**416**	**334**	**298**	**215**
3031	1009	825	653	410
	519	382	306	197
		354	237	168
			237	145
				123

Female Mesoamericans (N = 15)

Stature	Femur	Tibia	Fibula	Humerus	Radius	Ulna
1523	**396**	**325**	**319**	**282**	**228**	**211**
4502	1212	1233	1102	685	761	697
	467	412	362	250	312	257
		454	356	233	287	252
			369	223	262	226
				164	185	160
					219	184
						174

Pygmy (N = 18)

Stature	Femur	Tibia	Humerus	Radius
1405	**377**	**320**	**276**	**217**
6567	1590	1723	1141	1079
	476	466	300	314
		504	312	324
			230	206
				236

The top row gives sample means while the subsequent rows give the unique part of the variance–covariance matrix.

allometry itself. Later we will show how the stature estimation problem is related to the study of allometry. The five linear functions Konigsberg et al. considered can be rephrased within allometric study. The simplest linear function is one that passes through the origin (stature and long bone lengths both equal to zero) and the bivariate mean. This linear function assumes isometry so that the predicted long bone length is in a constant proportion to stature. The other linear functions are related to "isodensity" ellipses as Sjøvold (1990) has shown.

Fig. 9.3 shows an example using the summary statistics for maximum femur length and stature from our reference sample. The drawn "isodensity" ellipse (Tatsuoka and Lohnes, 1988) is the 95% ellipse. Also shown is a rectangle that is tangent to four points on the ellipse. We refer to these four tangent points as the "bottom,"

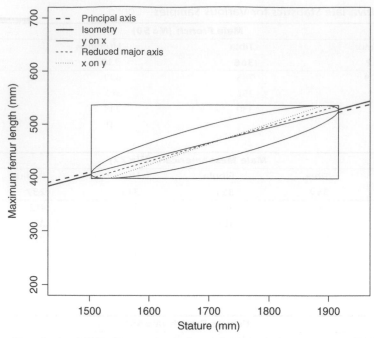

Figure 9.3 The 95% isodensity ellipse for the sample of 2015 individuals and the *rectangle* that is tangent to four points on the *ellipse*. The regression of *y* on *x*, *x* on *y*, and the reduced major axis relates to these tangent points as described in the text. The principal axis and isometry lines do not relate to the tangent points, but both are similar to the regression of *y* on *x* in this example.

"left," "top," and "right" points. The line for the regression of "*y*" (femur length) on "*x*" (stature) is the one that traditionally is used in allometry studies. This line passes through the "left" and "right" points. The regression of "*x*" on "*y*," which is never used in allometry studies, passes through the "bottom" and "top" points. The reduced major axis line is an "average" of the *y* on *x* and *x* on *y* regression lines, and as a consequence it is a diagonal line that passes through the lower left and upper right vertices of the rectangle. Finally, the principal axis is the line that passes through the maximal extent of the ellipse. Of these five lines, the regression of *y* on *x* is routinely used when the *x* variable is a measure of body size. This follows from the idea that organ size is dependent on body size. Reduced major axis regression is routinely used when allometry is studied for two organs in the absence of a direct measure of body size. This follows from the idea that the size of neither organ is dependent on the other, but rather that they both depend on the unmeasured body size. For all of our analyses we exclusively use linear regressions of long bone lengths onto stature. Again, the justification for doing so follows directly from the literature on allometry.

■ A LENGTHY DIGRESSION ON REGRESSION

Having dispatched with reduced major axis and principal axis analysis, and realizing that isometry is a special case of regression, we are left with the problem of estimating regression coefficients for long bone lengths onto stature. A central theme of this chapter is the ability to do all the analyses starting from summary multivariate statistics. To find the regression coefficients of one or more long bones on stature we assume that the variance–covariance matrix among stature and the bones (**V**) is available as is the mean stature ($\bar{x}$) and the vector of long bone means ($\bar{y}$) or the scalar ($\bar{y}$) if only a single long bone is being used. From the variance–covariance matrix we have the variance of stature, v_x, the column vector of covariances of stature with long bones, $\mathbf{v}_{xy}$, and the variance–covariance matrix among long bones, $\mathbf{V}_{yy}$. These latter two items are scalars in the event that only a single long bone is being studied. Some studies give the vector of standard deviations, which we write as **s**, and the correlation matrix **R** instead of the variance–covariance matrix. Letting $S = \text{diag}(\mathbf{s})$ where $\text{diag}(\cdot)$ places the vector into a diagonal matrix, the variance–covariance matrix is $\mathbf{V} = \mathbf{SRS}$. The regression coefficients (slopes, **b**) and intercepts (**a**) for long bones regressed on stature are then:

$$\mathbf{b} = \mathbf{v}_{xy}/\mathbf{v}_x$$
$$\mathbf{a} = \bar{\mathbf{y}} - \mathbf{b}\bar{\mathbf{x}}.$$

(9.1)

The residual variance–covariance matrix among long bones (after "regressing out" stature) is then:

$$\mathbf{C} = \left(\mathbf{V}_{yy} - \mathbf{v}_{xy} v_x^{-1} \mathbf{v'}_{xy}\right) \times (N-1)/(N-2)$$

(9.2)

To find the variance–covariance matrix among the estimated parameters in Eq. (9.1) we need to find an additional matrix as follows:

$$\mathbf{G} = \begin{bmatrix} v_x \times (N-1) + N \times (\overline{x})^2 & -N \times \overline{x} \\ -N \times \overline{x} & N \end{bmatrix} \Big/ \left(v_x \times (N-1) \times N \right), \tag{9.3}$$

where v_x is the (sample) variance of stature. The $\mathbf{G}$ matrix is the $(\mathbf{X'X})^{-1}$ matrix that figures so prominently in multivariate analyses. The variance–covariance matrix among the estimated parameters is then $V(\theta) = \mathbf{G} \otimes \mathbf{C}$ where $\otimes$ is a Kronecker product. The square roots of the diagonal elements of $\mathbf{V}(\theta)$ are then the standard errors for the regression parameters where the standard errors are listed first for intercepts (within bones) and then for slopes (within bones).

Although we council against the practice of routinely regressing stature onto one or more long bones, we should note that the equations given earlier are general enough that they can be used in multiple regression. Multiple regression is warranted when the case in hand can reasonably be assumed to have been drawn from a population that is well represented by the reference sample. The regression coefficients from multiple regression are as follows:

$$\mathbf{b} = \mathbf{v}_{xy} \mathbf{V}_{yy}^{-1}$$
$$a = \overline{y} - \mathbf{b}' \overline{\mathbf{x}}, \tag{9.4}$$

and the residual variance (square of the standard error of estimate) in stature is as follows:

$$c = \left(v_x - \mathbf{v}_{xy} \mathbf{V}_{yy}^{-1} \mathbf{v}_{xy}' \right) \times (N-1)/(N-1-p), \tag{9.5}$$

where p is the number of long bones. We will need the symmetric matrix $\mathbf{Y'Y}$, the upper triangular elements of which are as follows:

$$\mathbf{Y'Y}_{1,1} = N$$
$$\mathbf{Y'Y}_{i=1, \, j=2\ldots p+1} = N \times \overline{y}_j$$
$$\mathbf{Y'Y}_{i=j=2\ldots p+1} = v_{y_i} (N-1) + N \times \overline{y}_i^2 \tag{9.6}$$
$$\mathbf{Y'Y}_{i=2\ldots p+1, j>i} = v_{y_i} v_{y_j} \times (N-1) + N \overline{y}_i \overline{y}_j,$$

where i indexes the rows, j indexes the columns, and there are p long bones. For a new case we write the vector of long bone measurements appended to 1.0 as the first element of a column vector $\mathbf{y}_n$. The estimated value of stature is then $\hat{x}_n = \mathbf{y}_n' (a \| \mathbf{b})$ where $(a \| \mathbf{b})$ appends the vector of "slope" coefficients $\mathbf{b}$ to the intercept a. The prediction interval for this estimate is as follows:

$$\pm \, t(1 - \alpha/2, N-1-p) \sqrt{c \left(1 + \mathbf{y}_n' (\mathbf{Y'Y})^{-1} \mathbf{y}_n \right)}, \tag{9.7}$$

where t is Student's t-distribution. Eq. (9.7) is the multiple regression generalization of the simple linear regression prediction interval given in Giles and Klepinger (1988).

■ DO HUMAN POPULATIONS HAVE THE SAME ALLOMETRIES?

Much has been written in the forensic anthropology literature about the need for "population specific" stature estimation equations (Ahmed, 2013; Athwale, 1963; Dayal et al., 2008; Didia et al., 2009; Duyar and Pelin, 2010; Jantz et al., 2008; Mahakkanukrauh et al., 2011) and is a point raised in Raxter and Ruff's chapter in this volume. Krishan et al. (2012, pp. 47–48) have written that: "Different formulae…need to be derived for different population groups, owing to inherent population differences in various dimensions that are attributed to genetic and environmental factors…" The call for population-specific stature estimation equations primarily arises from the problem that most analyses, rather than taking an allometric approach and regressing long bone lengths onto stature, have instead regressed stature onto long bone lengths. Konigsberg et al. (1998) showed that the allometric approach followed by solving the regression equation for stature is equivalent to a Bayesian analysis taking an uninformative (uniform) prior for stature. Conversely, regressing stature on long bone length is equivalent to a Bayesian analysis but using an informative prior, where this prior is a normal distribution with the mean and standard deviation of stature taken from the reference distribution. Using the proper allometric approach removes the bias induced by the reference sample stature distribution. Alternatively, one can use the allometric approach but with a prior stature distribution that is appropriate for the application at hand (Konigsberg et al., 2006; Ross and Konigsberg, 2002; Ross and Manneschi, 2011).

Approaching stature estimation from the standpoint of an allometric analysis can remove the bias induced by a reference sample that is on average taller or shorter than the case under consideration. But this does not address the problem of attempting to estimate stature for a case that departs from the reference sample allometry. We consider this problem in greater detail in a later section, but for the moment it will be useful to look at the femur, tibia, humerus, and radius allometry information contained in the summary statistics from Table 9.2. Fig. 9.4 shows a plot of the 95% isodensity ellipses for these bones across the seven samples from Table 9.2. In

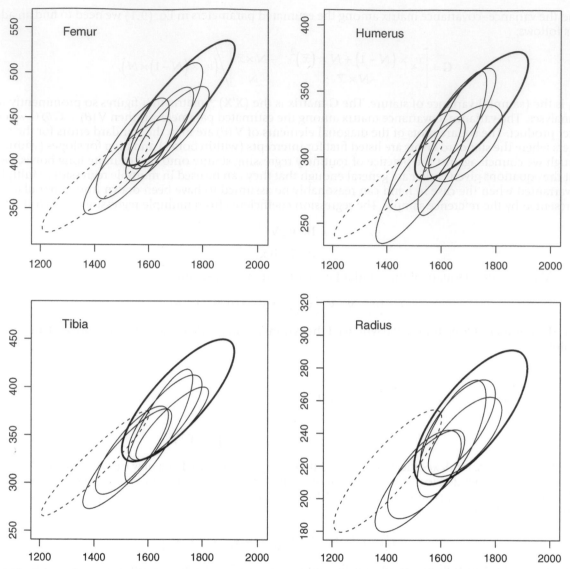

Figure 9.4 The 95% isodensity *ellipses* for four long bone lengths against stature from the seven samples summarized in Table 9.2. The *ellipses* drawn with *thicker lines* are from the sample (*N* = 2015) in this chapter, while the *dashed lines* are for the Pygmy sample (*N* = 18).

general, the figure demonstrates common allometric patterns across the seven samples, but the figure provides no information on the level of uncertainty attached to the intercepts and slopes. Figs. 9.5 and 9.6 plot the 95% confidence intervals for these parameters across the seven samples. With the exception of the tibia y-intercept from male Mesoamericans and the slopes for the humerus from Chinese males and tibia from Mesoamerican males, all confidence intervals intersect with the narrow confidence interval from our sample. There is consequently virtually no support from these figures for the idea that there are different allometric patterns across the human samples represented here.

■ CALCULATED EXAMPLE FROM A 7′7″ TALL INDIVIDUAL

Konigsberg et al. (2006) previously examined data from pygmies as an example of estimating stature from long bone lengths when there is extrapolation away from the reference sample stature distribution. In this chapter we again look at extrapolation, but this time using long bone data from a "giant." Gigantism is difficult to define, as it perforce must be defined as far exceeding the "norm" of stature for a given population. In the medical literature the threshold for classifying someone as a giant is above 7′4″ (Sotos, 1996) or 7′6″ (Hayles, 1980). We will use long bone data from Charles Byrne's skeleton as an example of estimating stature for a very tall individual. Previous authors have used regression analysis to estimate stature for very tall individuals, most notably Musgrave's work in Frankcom and Musgrave (1976). Musgrave found using Trotter and Gleser's regression equations on the bones from Patrick Cotter that his stature was underestimated. Musgrave (Frankcom and Musgrave, 1976, p. 104) went on to write that "The most likely explanation for these results is that these regression tables were not intended to accommodate individuals whose stature lay so far outside the range of normal variation." It is within the context of this previous failing

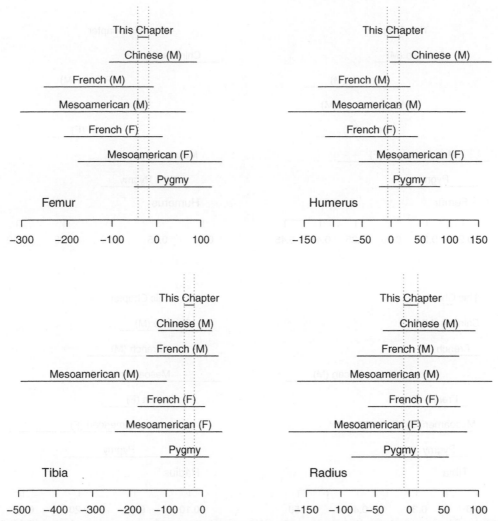

Figure 9.5 The 95% confidence intervals for y-intercepts in regressions of bones against stature for the seven samples from Table 9.2. The *vertical dotted lines* enclose the confidence intervals for the sample used in this chapter.

that we apply our methods to the long bone measurements from Charles Byrne as it is unlikely that there will ever be regression equations derived from a reference sample of giants.

Charles Byrne was born in what is now Northern Ireland in 1761 and died in London in 1783. His obituary listed on June 1, 1783, in *The Gentleman's Magazine and Historical Chronicle* (Urban, 1783, p. 541) provided the following information regarding his stature:

> *Our philosophical readers may not be displeased to know, on the credit of an ingenious correspondent who had opportunity of informing himself, that Mr. Byrne in August 1780 measured exactly 8 feet; that in 1782 he had gained 2 inches; and after he was dead he measured 8 feet 4 inches.*

The "ingenious correspondent" appears to have drawn these figures from advertisements for Byrne's public appearances and as a consequence there is almost certainly hyperbole in the stated statures. Byrne's mounted skeleton at the Hunterian Museum of the Royal College of Surgeons has a reported stature of 2310 mm (7′7″). Fleetwood (1959, p. 310) commented on Byrne's stature that: "His height was stated to be 8 feet 4 inches, but as the skeleton is only 7 feet 7 inches his real height was probably no more than 7 feet 10 inches." We will take 2310 mm as his actual stature, as Cunningham (1887, p. 568) noted that "the articulator has been very liberal with his supply of intervertebral substance." Consequently, Fleetwood's addition of 3 inches seems unwarranted. Cunningham ultimately considered Byrne's stature to be 7′6″, but this was based on estimation from femoral length.

Our Table 9.3 gives the long bone measurements reported in Cunningham's Tables 11, 12, 18, and 19. Applying Eqs. (9.4)–(9.7) to the average of left and right bones using the summary statistics from our reference data on 2015 individuals, the multiple regression estimate of Byrne's stature is 2159 mm with a 95% prediction interval of from 2079 to 2238 mm. Note that this interval, with a maximum of 2238 mm (7′4″), does not include the measured

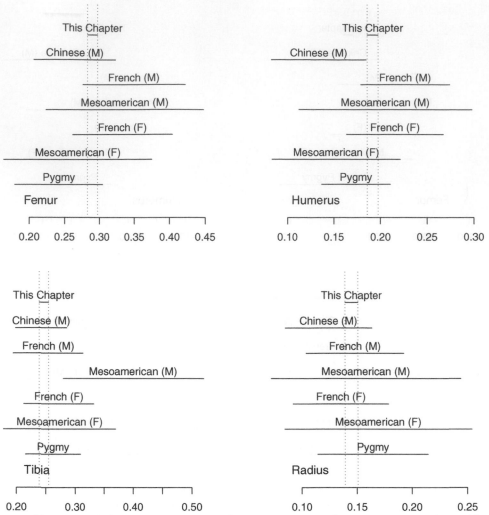

Figure 9.6 The 95% confidence intervals for slopes in regressions of bones against stature for the seven samples from Table 9.2. The *vertical dotted lines* enclose the confidence intervals for the sample used in this chapter.

Table 9.3   Long Bone Maximum Lengths From Charles Byrne's Skeleton

Bone	Right	Left	Average
Humerus	450	430	440
Radius	334	324	329
Femur	625	642	633.5
Tibia	541	537	539

Data from Cunningham, D.J., 1887. The skeleton of the Irish giant, Cornelius Magrath. Trans. Roy. Ir. Acad. 29, 553–612.

skeletal height of 7′7″. This underestimation of Byrne's stature is a direct result of using an informative prior (from the reference sample) that is a normal distribution with a mean of 1710 mm (5′7″) and a standard deviation of 84.5 mm (3.3″). As a contrast, we can use a maximum likelihood method (profile likelihood) of estimating stature that takes a uniform prior for stature. This method can also be applied starting directly from summary statistics, but it requires solving an equality for two roots (Uhl, 2014) and is too complicated to describe here. In the next section we will show how the simple use of a freely available program can replace the complicated math necessary in the profile likelihood method. For comparison in the next section, the profile likelihood estimate of Byrne's stature was 2292 mm with a 95% prediction interval of from 2201 to 2384 mm. Note that the profile likelihood estimate of Byrne's stature (equivalent to 7′6″) is just an inch less than Byrne's 7′7″ skeletal height and that the skeletal height is well within the prediction interval of from 7′3″ to 7′10″.

■ A MARKOV CHAIN MONTE CARLO EXAMPLE FROM A 7'7' TALL INDIVIDUAL

Konigsberg and Frankenberg (2013) have extensively reviewed applications of Bayesian methods within biological anthropology (including forensic anthropology) and in particular have focused on the application of Markov Chain Monte Carlo (MCMC) methods. These methods are well-suited to the stature estimation problem and can be used to find maximum likelihood estimates if one assumes a uniform prior for stature. They can also be used with an informative prior from the reference sample, which is identical to applying multiple regression of stature onto long bones. Finally, the method can be used quite generally so that the likelihood function (the relationship of long bone lengths to stature in the reference sample) can be combined with an informative prior for stature that is appropriate to the case in hand (Konigsberg et al., 2006). The Appendix contains the MCMC code that reproduces our analysis from the previous section. This code can be run in either OpenBUGS (http://www.openbugs.net/w/FrontPage) or WinBUGS (http://www.mrc-bsu.cam.ac.uk/software/bugs/). Our preference is to use OpenBUGS.

Looking at the "data" statement in the code in the Appendix, the vector "theta" is from Eq. (9.1) and the matrix "tau" is the matrix inverse of Eq. (9.2). Using this script with a "burn-in" of 1000 iterations and then running 10,000 subsequent iterations, the 2.5%, 50%, and 97.5% values of stature when using an uninformative prior are 2202, 2292, and 2383 mm. This is in comparison to the calculated values from the previous section of 2201, 2292, and 2384. Similarly, using an informative prior (a normal distribution with a mean of 1710 mm and standard deviation of 84.5 mm from the reference data) the percentile values are 2077, 2158, and 2238 from MCMC and 2079, 2158, and 2238 from direct calculations. Fig. 9.7 shows kernel density plots from the MCMC to once again demonstrate that taking an informative prior for Byrne's stature results in a prediction interval which excludes Byrne's actual stature of 7'7". Note that the standard deviation for the MCMC, which is the equivalent of the standard error of estimate from calculation, is lower when we take an informative prior. As a consequence, the prediction interval is smaller when using an informative prior. Following the "best practices" suggested in the Scientific Working Group for Forensic Anthropology's draft statement on stature estimation (retrieved from http://www.swganth.org/products--drafts.html) "the best formula is the one with the smallest prediction interval." This is clearly a misguided directive as the greater statistical efficiency using an informative prior comes at the expense of producing biased estimations when we extrapolate.

A useful check on our procedure is to look at what are known as "posterior predictive distributions." In the MCMC code these are the "Y.pred" values, and they are the distributions of predicted long bone lengths conditional on the posterior density of stature. Fig. 9.8 shows the posterior predictive distributions as empirical cumulative density functions for the four long bone lengths under a uniform prior for stature. For each bone the shaded gray region represents the central 95% of the cumulative density, so the left boundary is at the 2.5% value and the right boundary is at the 97.5% value. Note that the observed bone lengths are well within the 95% central part of the posterior predictive distributions. This is in contrast to Fig. 9.9 drawn using an informative prior for stature from the reference sample. Note that the bones are all longer than the 97.5% values indicating that the observed lengths are in the upper 2.5% tails of the predictive distributions. This is a clear sign that the multiple regression approach underestimates stature because it takes an inappropriate prior.

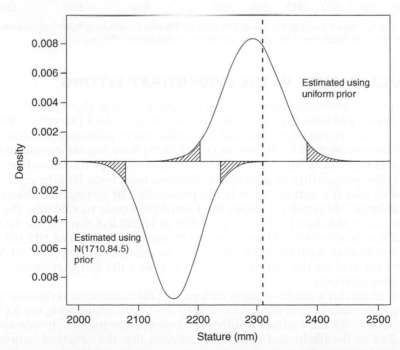

Figure 9.7 Posterior distributions of stature for Charles Byrne using the femur, tibia, humerus, and radius lengths. The *hatched areas* are the bottom and top 2.5% tails. The *heavy dashed vertical line* is at a stature of 2310 mm, the skeletal height for Charles Byrne.

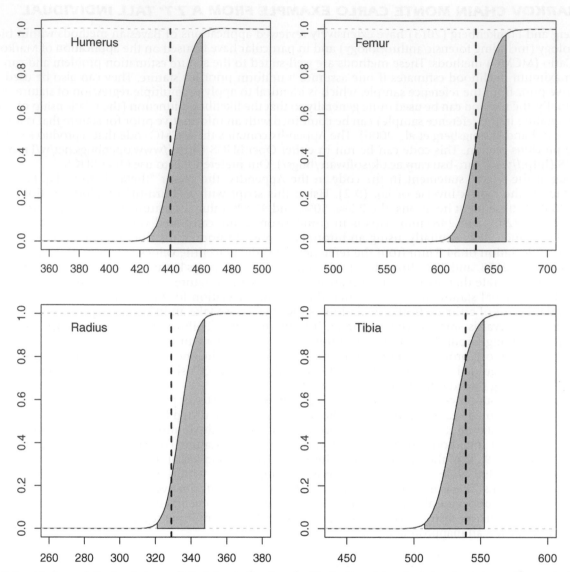

Figure 9.8 Empirical cumulative (posterior predictive) density functions for Charles Byrne's long bone lengths given a uniform prior for stature. The *dashed vertical lines* are the observed lengths and the *gray shaded regions* are the central 95% regions.

■ LONG BONES AND STATURE IN THE EVIDENTIARY SETTING

Long bone measurements are sometimes used in an evidentiary setting to show that the bone lengths produce a stature estimate that is consistent with the known stature for an individual (Teixeira, 1985) or within the identification process for a "closed population" (Ríos et al., 2010) where estimated statures can be compared to a list of statures from the known decedents. Steadman et al. (2006) have argued instead that such data should be treated in the same context that one would treat DNA data by calculating a likelihood ratio. Here the numerator in the likelihood ratio is the probability of getting the observed long bone lengths given the known stature for a presumed identification, and the denominator is the probability of getting the observed long bone lengths from the "population-at-large." Appendix II shows the OpenBUGS code to calculate the log-likelihoods using the "deviance" function (note: this function is not available in WinBUGS though the deviance for the model is available). The log-likelihoods are evaluated for a normal stature distribution of $N(2310, 25)$ mm as versus the "population-at-large" distribution represented by the reference sample with $N(1710, 84.5)$ mm. The normal of $N(2310, 25)$ gives a 95% interval on the prior of 7'5"–7'9" to reflect the fact that the articulated skeletal height of 7'7" has been called into question.

The code only needs to be run for a single iteration with each of the conditions as there are no stochastic elements. Using the $N(2310, 25)$ stature distribution the log-likelihood is −14.38, while using the $N(1710, 84.5)$ stature distribution the log-likelihood is −33.22. Taking the difference between the log-likelihoods and exponentiating gives $\exp(18.84) = 152{,}092{,}584$ as the likelihood ratio. This indicates that the observed long bone lengths are about 152 million times more likely to have been obtained from someone with a 95% chance of having a stature between

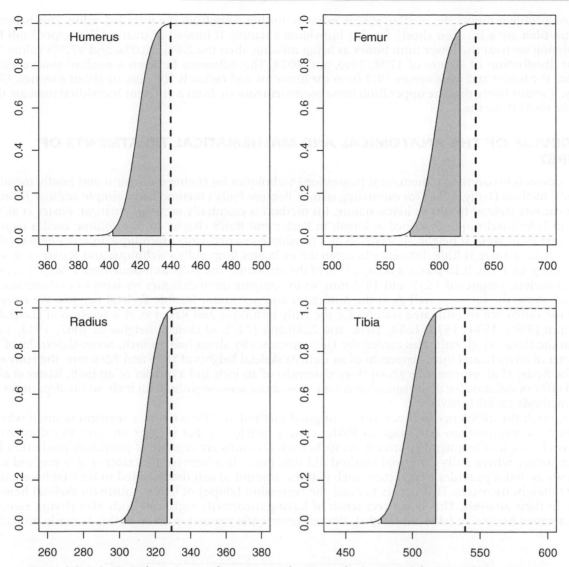

Figure 9.9 As in Fig.9 8 but using an informative prior for stature of $N (1710, 84.5)$ from the reference sample.

7′5″ and 7′9″ than from the population-at-large. This shows the power of using stature information and long bone lengths when the individual in question is an outlier in the stature distribution. In contrast, Konigsberg and Jantz calculated a likelihood ratio of only 1.6 for the identification of the remains of Joseph Mengele from long bone lengths and stature because Mengele's recorded stature was only one millimeter different from the mean for the population-at-large.

■ DEPARTURES FROM ALLOMETRY

In an earlier section on "Do Human Populations Have the Same Allometries?" we raised the question of what is to be done if a case in hand differs in its allometry from the reference sample. As an example of this problem, we examined all 2015 individuals in the reference sample to find the one with the greatest allometric departure. To identify this individual we used a regression diagnostic that Brown (1993, p. 110) has referred to as R and which is given as Eq. (16) in Konigsberg et al. (1998), Eq. (1) in Uhl et al. (2013), and the first equation in Grabowski et al. (2015). The individual with the greatest allometric departure from the reference sample was Terry 999, who had a recorded stature of 1728 mm and humerus, radius, femur, and tibia lengths of 367, 292, 464, and 388 mm, respectively. Using the MCMC script with an uninformative prior (uniform from 0 to 10,000 mm.) and these bone lengths, the 2.5%, 50.0%, and 97.5% values from the posterior distribution of stature were 1641, 1732, and 1825. The median of 1732 agrees well with the recorded stature of 1728. The posterior predictive distribution for the four long bones shows that the upper limb bones are "too long." The most expedient way to remove the upper limb bones from the analysis is to replace the measurements with missing data values (in OpenBUGS and WinBUGS this is "NA" for "not available."). Doing so produces 2.5%, 50.0%, and 97.5% values from the posterior distribution of stature of 1610, 1705, and 1801. Ironically, removing the upper limb bones from the stature estimation problem moves the median stature estimate further away from the recorded value. This is because the femur and tibia are a bit "too short" for this individual's stature. If instead of treating the upper limb bones as being missing we treat the lower limb bones as being missing, then the 2.5%, 50.0%, and 97.5% values from the posterior distribution of stature of 1794, 1910, and 2024. The difference between a median stature estimate of 1705 from the femur and tibia versus 1910 from the humerus and radius is 205 mm, or about 8 inches. Given this disparity, it seems likely that the upper limb bone measurements are from a different individual than are the lower limb bone measurements.

■ MARRIAGE OF THE ANATOMICAL AND MATHEMATICAL TREATMENTS OF STATURE?

We have extensively covered mathematical (regression) techniques for stature estimation and briefly mentioned an anatomical method (Fully, 1956) for estimating stature. Because Fully's method had a simple additive factor for soft tissue to convert skeletal height to living stature, his method is essentially nonmathematical. Raxter et al.'s (2006) revision to Fully's technique described at length in Raxter and Ruff's chapter in this volume used a regression of living stature onto skeletal height, so Raxter et al.'s revision converted Fully's technique to a mathematical one. As a practical matter, there is little difference between the estimates from Fully's technique and Raxter et al.'s revision (not including age). Fig. 9.10 shows a comparison of the estimates. The Fully technique uses a "step function" with "knots" at skeletal heights of 1535 and 1655 mm, so to compare the techniques we have to evaluate statures just below and above the knots as well as at the minimum and maximum feasible skeletal heights. We consequently evaluate the difference in estimated statures for the Fully technique and Raxter et al.'s revision at skeletal heights of 1067 mm (3'6"), 1534, 1536, 1654, 1656, and 2286 mm (7'6"). At skeletal heights of 1067, 1534, 1536, and 1654 mm the Raxter et al. estimates exceed the Fully estimates by about half an inch, seven-sixteenths of an inch, one-quarter of an inch, and three-sixteenths of an inch. At skeletal heights of 1656 and 2286 mm, the Fully estimates exceed the Raxter et al. estimates by about three-sixteenths of an inch and a quarter of an inch. Raxter et al. list the standard error of estimate for their regression equation as about seven-eighths of an inch, so the departures between the two methods are fairly trivial.

Even though the difference between Fully's original method and Raxter et al.'s revision is small where point estimates are concerned, an advantage of Raxter et al.'s revision is that it takes an anatomical approach and generalizes it to a mathematical approach. As such, their revisions are capable of providing prediction intervals for living stature where Fully's original method did not. But a disadvantage of Raxter et al.'s method when age is unknown is that it provides a correction such that the amount of soft tissue added to skeletal height decreases as skeletal height increases. This occurs because the regression (slope) of living stature on skeletal height is less than 1.0 in their analysis. This is a direct result of having incorrectly regressed body size (living stature) onto a component of body size (skeletal height). We can reverse the regression, though this is made difficult by the

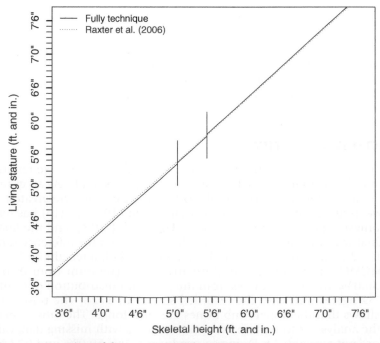

Figure 9.10 Comparison of living stature estimated from skeletal height using the Fully technique and Raxter et al.'s (2006) revision without age. The *two vertical lines* show the locations for the "knots" in the Fully step function.

fact that Raxter et al.'s publication does not provide the summary statistics for their bivariate data. From the provided correlation, slope of living stature on skeletal height, and standard error of estimate, we can calculate the variance of living height in their sample of 119 individuals as 56.46857, the variance of skeletal height as 51.58958, and the covariance of the two variables as 51.38322. The mean living stature and skeletal height cannot be calculated from statistics in Raxter et al.'s publication nor are they provided there, but their Fig. 2 suggests a mean living stature of about 165 cm, which would lead to a calculated value (from Raxter et al.'s regression equation) for average skeletal height of 153.9 cm. From these summary statistics we can calculate the regression equation for skeletal height (SH) on living stature (LS) as:

$$SH = 0.910 \times LS + 3.76, \tag{9.8}$$

where the slope is 51.38322/56.46857 = 0.910 and the intercept is 153.9 − 0.910 × 165. Solving Eq. (9.8) for living stature gives:

$$LH = 1.099 \times SH - 4.13. \tag{9.9}$$

To convert Eq. (9.9) back to a format more like Fully's, where there is an additive factor for soft tissue, we can rewrite the equation as:

$$LS = SH + (0.099 \times SH - 4.13), \tag{9.10}$$

where the parenthetical term is the increment to be added for soft tissue. Raxter et al.'s equation in comparable form is as follows:

$$LS = SH + (-0.004 \times SH + 11.7), \tag{9.11}$$

equivalent to Raxter and Ruff's (this volume) Eq. (10.2). The positive multiplier for skeletal height in Eq. (9.10) shows that the soft tissue correction we propose increases with increasing skeletal height. For example, at a skeletal height of 100 cm the soft tissue correction from Eq. (9.10) is 5.8 cm and at 200 cm it is 15.7 cm. This is as one would expect to see given the anatomical relationships between bone and soft tissue. Conversely, the negative multiplier in Eq. (9.11) shows that the soft tissue correction from Raxter et al. decreases with increasing skeletal height. At skeletal heights of 100 and 200 cm the corrections from Eq. (9.11) are 11.3 and 10.9 cm, respectively.

As stated earlier, an advantage of taking a mathematical approach to the Fully technique is that we can provide prediction intervals on stature estimates. Fig. 9.11 shows an example using a skeletal height of 200 cm. From Eq. (9.9) and rounding to the nearest millimeter the estimated living stature for an individual with a skeletal height of 200 cm is 215.7. Solving for the intersections of a skeletal height of 200 cm with the 95% prediction bounds for skeletal height given living stature (as shown in Fig. 9.11) gives the prediction interval for living stature as 210.2–221.5 cm.

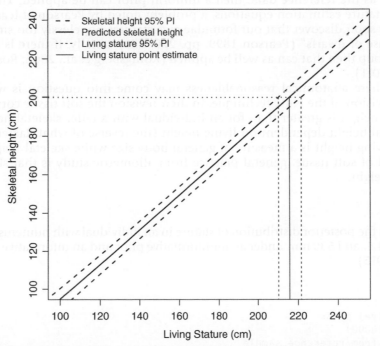

Figure 9.11 Example of estimating living stature and the 95% prediction interval for an individual with a skeletal height of 200 cm. The *heavy lines* are from the regression of skeletal height on living stature based on summary statistics from Raxter et al. (2006). The *"dropped" vertical lines* show how the regression can be "inverted" so that living stature is estimated from skeletal height.

Using Eq. (9.12.3) from Snedecor and Cochran (1989) the 95% prediction intervals for living stature given skeletal height are as follows:

$$165 + 1.0035 \times \left(\hat{l} \pm 1.98 \times 2.426 \times \sqrt{1.005 + \left(\hat{l}\right)^2 \big/ 6663} \right)$$

$$\hat{l} = \left(SH - 153.9\right) \big/ 0.9099,$$

(9.12)

where $\hat{l}$ is the estimate of living stature relative to the mean living stature and 1.98 is the "critical" t-value for the upper 0.025 tail area with 117 degrees of freedom.

■ CONCLUSION

This chapter has taken a decidedly mathematical approach to estimating stature, but we argue that this approach should never be at the expense of anatomical reasonableness. For example, treating body size (stature) as a "dependent" variable and organ size (e.g., humerus length) as the "independent" variable is not reasonable. This is because there is a causal direction such that one would never expect to see analyses of, say, brain size and body size where body size was treated as (partially) "caused" by brain size. For example, in Pearl's (1905) classic study he always showed brain weight as being regressed on stature, never the reverse. Similarly, it is not anatomically reasonable to consider stature (body size) as being "caused" or "explained" by humerus, ulna, or radius lengths (organ size). This approach of questioning anatomical reasonableness becomes more difficult when considering the regression of stature onto lower limb elements such as the femur and tibia. The issue often raised here is that the lower limb long bones provide an additive component to stature and so they are viewed as in part "causing" or "explaining" stature. One could likewise make the statement that heart mass is an additive component to body mass, yet in allometric studies one never finds body mass regressed onto heart mass. Similarly, one should never find femur length regressed onto stature.

The regression of long bones onto stature may seem counterintuitive given the long history in forensic anthropology of regressing stature onto long bones. With that said, it is the case that provided with the complete summary statistics one can form the multivariate regression of long bones onto stature or the multiple regression of stature onto long bones. Further, if the multivariate regression of long bones onto stature is used for the likelihood and the reference sample stature distribution is used for the prior, then the posterior distribution of predicted stature is the same as that obtained from traditional multiple regression of stature onto long bones. Consequently, the multivariate regression of long bone lengths onto stature provides for more flexible-predicted values. If the case in question can truly be thought of as deriving from the reference sample, then one can use the reference sample as an informative prior. In other words, one could apply the traditional multiple regression. If it is unknown whether the case in question can reasonably be thought of as deriving from the same sample as the reference data, then a uniform prior can be applied. This obviates the need for "population specific" stature estimation equations, a problem noted by Pearson at least as early as 1899 when he wrote that: "we very soon discover that our formulae give statures hopelessly too small in the case of giants, and too large in the case of dwarfs" (Pearson 1899, pp. 220–221). Finally, if there is an informative prior for stature from a living group then that can as well be applied (Konigsberg et al., 2006; Ross and Konigsberg, 2002; Ross and Manneschi, 2011).

Another example where anatomical reasonableness may come into question is when considering Raxter et al.'s (2006, 2007) revision of the Fully technique. In their revision the soft tissue correction for an individual with a shorter skeletal height is greater than for an individual with a taller skeletal height. As we have shown here, by making skeletal height dependent on living height (the reverse of what Raxter et al. did) the problem vanishes. Given that living height is a measure of general body size while skeletal height is a measure of skeletal system size devoid of soft tissue, general practice from allometric study is that skeletal height should be regressed onto living height.

■ APPENDIX I

OpenBUGS code to find the posterior distribution of stature in an individual with humerus, radius, femur, and tibial lengths of 440, 329, 633.5, and 539 mm under an uninformative prior and an informative prior for stature from the reference sample (N = 2015):

```
model
{
# Uniform (uninformative) prior
   stat[1] ~ dunif(0,10000)
# N(1710, 84.5) prior from reference sample
   stat[2] ~ dnorm(1710, 0.00014)

   for(j in 1:4){
```

```
        for(i in 1:2) {Y.pred[i,j]<-theta[j] + theta[4+j] * stat[i]}}
        for(i in 1:2) {Y[i,1:4] ~ dmnorm(Y.pred[i,], tau[,])}

}

#data
list(Y=structure(.Data=c(440,329,633.5,539,440,329,633.5,539),
.Dim=c(2,4)),theta=c(4.4156, 2.396, -29.9263, -35.693,
0.1915698, 0.1447976, 0.2900154, 0.2466041), tau =
structure(.Data= c(0.01405, -0.006103, -0.003993, 0.000363,
-0.006103, 0.019939, 0.000473, -0.00886, -0.003993, 0.000473,
0.010499, -0.005133, 0.000363, -0.00886, -0.005133,
0.011968),.Dim=c(4,4)))
```

■ APPENDIX II

OpenBUGS code for calculation of the log-likelihoods assuming the long bones are from individuals drawn from a stature distribution of $N(2310, 25)$ versus individuals with a stature distribution of $N(1710, 84.5)$.

```
model
{
  bones[1:4] ~ dmnorm(bones.pred[], tau[,])
  Log.like<- -deviance(bones[1:4],bones[1:4])/2
}

#data - for N(1710, 84.5)
list(bones=c(440,329,633.5,539),bones.pred=c(332, 250, 466,
386),tau = structure(.Data= c(0.0131532986, -0.00570302,
-0.0053065435, 6.0402E-05, -0.00570302, 0.0197598473,
0.0010589323, -0.0087248683, -0.0053065435, 0.0010589323,
0.0085757009, -0.0055758772, 6.0402E-05, -0.0087248683,
-0.0055758772, 0.0118660013),.Dim=c(4,4)))

#data - for N(2310, 25)
list(bones=c(440,329,633.5,539),bones.pred=c(446.9419, 336.8786,
640.0092, 533.9625),tau = structure(.Data= c(0.0137861427,
-0.0059854557, -0.0043798194, 0.0002739931, -0.0059854557,
0.0198858971, 0.0006453392, -0.0088201931, -0.0043798194,
0.0006453392, 0.0099327771, -0.0052630986, 0.0002739931,
-0.0088201931, -0.0052630986, 0.0119380905),.Dim=c(4,4)))
```

"tau" is the inverse of the variance–covariance matrix of predicted bone lengths, where the variance–covariance matrix is as follows:

$$V = bb' \times var(stature) + C,$$

where bb' is the outer product of the regression slopes from Eq. (9.1) and C is from Eq.(9.2). "bones.pred" are predicted bone lengths given (mean) statures of 1710 and 2310 mm.

References

Ahmed, A.A., 2013. Estimation of stature using lower limb measurements in Sudanese Arabs. J. Forensic Legal. Med. 20 (5), 483–488.

Athwale, M., 1963. Anthropological study of height from length of forearm bones. A study of one hundred Maharastrian male adults of ages between twenty five and thirty years. Am. J. Phys. Anthropol. 21, 105–112.

Auerbach, B.M., Sylvester, A.D., 2011. Allometry and apparent paradoxes in human limb proportions: implications for scaling factors. Am. J. Phys. Anthropol. 144 (3), 382–391.

Boldsen, J., 1984. A statistical evaluation of the basis for predicting stature from lengths of long bones in European populations. Am. J. Phys. Anthropol. 65 (3), 305–311.

Brown, P.J., 1993. Measurement, Regression, and Calibration. Oxford University Press, New York.

Cunningham, D.J., 1887. The skeleton of the Irish giant, Cornelius Magrath. Trans. R. Ir. Acad. 29, 553–612.

Dayal, M.R., Steyn, M., Kuykendall, K.L., 2008. Stature estimation from bones of South African whites. S. Afr. J. Sci. 104 (3–4), 124–128.

Didia, B.C., Nduka, E.C., Adele, O., 2009. Stature estimation formulae for Nigerians. J. Forensic Sci. 54 (1), 20–21.

Dupertuis, C., Hadden, J.A., 1951. On the reconstruction of stature from long bones. Am. J. Phys. Anthropol. 9 (1), 15–54.

Duyar, I., Pelin, C., 2010. Estimating body height from ulna length: need of a population-specific formula. Eurasian J. Anthropol. 1 (1), 11–17.

Fleetwood, J.F., 1959. The Irish resurrectionists. Ir. J. Med. Sci. 34 (7), 309–321.

Frankcom, G., Musgrave, J.H., 1976. The Irish Giant. Duckworth.

Fully, G., 1956. Une nouvelle méthode de détermination de la taille. Ann. Med. Leg. 35, 266–273.

Genovés, S., 1967. Proportionality of the long bones and their relation to stature among Mesoamericans. Am. J. Phys. Anthropol. 26 (1), 67–77.

Giles, E., Klepinger, L.L., 1988. Confidence intervals for estimates based on linear regression in forensic anthropology. J. Forensic Sci. 33 (5), 1218–1222.

Grabowski, M., Hatala, K.G., Jungers, W.L., Richmond, B.G., 2015. Body mass estimates of hominin fossils and the evolution of human body size. J. Hum. Evol. 85, 75–93.

Green, P.J., 2006. Peeling data. In: Kotz, S., Read, C.B., Balakrishnan, N., Vidakovic, B. (Eds.), Encyclopedia of Statistical Sciences, second ed. Wiley-Interscience, Hoboken, NJ (e-book version).

Hayles, A.B., 1980. Gigantism. Pediatr. Ann. 9 (4), 54–62.

Holliday, T.W., Ruff, C.B., 2001. Relative variation in human proximal and distal limb segment lengths. Am. J. Phys. Anthropol. 116 (1), 26–33.

Houghton, P., Leach, B.F., Sutton, D.G., 1975. The estimation of stature of prehistoric Polynesians in New Zealand. J. Polynesian Soc. 84 (3), 325–336.

Huxley, J.S., 1932. Problems of Relative Growth. L. MacVeagh: The Dial Press, New York, NY.

Jantz, L.M., 1996. Secular Change and Allometry in the Long Limb Bones of Americans from the Mid 1700's Through the 1900's, Anthropology. University of Tennessee, Knoxville, TN.

Jantz, R.L., Hunt, D.R., Meadows, L., 1995. The measure and mismeasure of the tibia: implications for stature estimation. J. Forensic Sci. 40 (5), 758–761.

Jantz, R.L., Kimmerle, E.H., Baraybar, J.P., 2008. Sexing and stature estimation criteria for Balkan populations. J. Forensic Sci. 53 (3), 601–605.

Jungers, W.L., 1988. Lucy's length: stature reconstruction in *Australopithecus afarensis* (A.L. 288-1) with implications for other small-bodied hominids. Am. J. Phys. Anthropol. 76, 227–231.

Jungers, W.L., Grabowski, M., Hatala, K.G., Richmond, B.G., 2016. The evolution of body size and shape in the human career. Philos. Trans. R. Soc. B 371 (1698), 20150247.

Konigsberg, L.W., Frankenberg, S.R., 2013. Bayes in biological anthropology. Yb. Phys. Anthropol. 57, 153–184.

Konigsberg, L.W., Hens, S.M., Jantz, L.M., Jungers, W.L., 1998. Stature estimation and calibration: Bayesian and maximum likelihood perspectives in physical anthropology. Yb. Phys. Anthropol. 41, 65–92.

Konigsberg, L.W., Jantz, L.M. The probabilistic basis for identifying individuals in biohistorical research. In: Stojanowski, C., Duncan, W. (Eds.), Studies in Forensic Biohistory: Anthropological Perspectives, Cambridge University Press, New York, NY.

Konigsberg, L.W., Ross, A.H., Jungers, W.L., 2006. Estimation and evidence in forensic anthropology: stature. In: Schmitt, A., Cunha, E., Pinheiro, J. (Eds.), Forensic Anthropology and Medicine: Complementary Sciences from Recovery to Cause of Death. Humana Press, Totowa, NJ, pp. 317–331.

Krishan, K., Kanchan, T., Menezes, R.G., Ghosh, A., 2012. Forensic anthropology casework—essential methodological considerations in stature estimation. J. Forensic Nurs. 8 (1), 45–50.

Mahakkanukrauh, P., Khanpetch, P., Prasitwattanseree, S., Vichairat, K., Troy Case, D., 2011. Stature estimation from long bone lengths in a Thai population. Forensic Sci. Int. 210 (1) 279. e1–279. e7.

Meadows Jantz, L., Jantz, R.L., 1999. Secular change in long bone length and proportion in the United State 1800–1970. Am. J. Phys. Anthropol. 110, 57–67.

Meadows, L., Jantz, R.L., 1995. Allometric secular change in the long bones from the 1800s to the present. J. Forensic Sci. 40 (5), 762–767.

Ousley, S., 1995. Should we estimate biological or forensic stature? J. Forensic Sci. 40 (5), 768–773.

Packard, G.C., Birchard, G.F., Boardman, T.J., 2011. Fitting statistical models in bivariate allometry. Biol. Rev. 86 (3), 549–563.

Pearl, R., 1905. Biometrical studies on man: I. Variation and correlation in brain-weight. Biometrika 4 (1/2), 13–104.

Pearson, K., 1899. Mathematical contributions to the theory of evolution. V. On the reconstruction of the stature of prehistoric races. Philos. Trans. R. Soc. Lond. 192, 169–244.

Raxter, M.H., Auerbach, B.M., Ruff, C.B., 2006. Revision of the fully technique for estimating statures. Am. J. Phys. Anthropol. 130 (3), 374–384.

Raxter, M.H., Ruff, C.B., Auerbach, B.M., 2007. Technical note: revised fully stature estimation. Am. J. Phys. Anthropol. 133, 817–818.

Ríos, L., Ovejero, J.I.C., Prieto, J.P., 2010. Identification process in mass graves from the Spanish Civil War I. Forensic Sci. Int. 199 (1), e27–e36.

Rollet, E., 1888. De la mensuration des os longs des membres. Theses pour le doctorat en medicine, 1st series 43, 1–128.

Ross, A.H., Konigsberg, L.W., 2002. New formulae for estimating stature in the Balkans. J. Forensic Sci. 47, 165–167.

Ross, A.H., Manneschi, M.J., 2011. New identification criteria for the Chilean population: estimation of sex and stature. Forensic Sci. Int. 204 (1) 206. e1–206. e3.

Sjøvold, T., 1990. Estimation of stature from long bones utilizing the line of organic correlation. Hum. Evol. 5, 431–447.

Smith, R.J., 1980. Rethinking allometry. J. Theor. Biol. 87, 97–111.

Snedecor, G., Cochran, W., 1989. Statistical Methods. Iowa State University Press, Ames, IA.

Sotos, J.F., 1996. Overgrowth. Clin. Pediatr. 35 (11), 577–590.

Steadman, D.W., Adams, B.J., Konigsberg, L.W., 2006. Statistical basis for positive identification in forensic anthropology. Am. J. Phys. Anthropol. 131, 15–26.

Stevenson, P.H., 1929. On racial differences in stature long bone regression formulae, with special reference to stature reconstruction formulae for the Chinese. Biometrika 21, 303–321.

Stewart, T.D., 1979. Essentials of Forensic Anthropology. Charles C. Thomas, Springfield, IL.

Sylvester, A.D., Kramer, P.A., Jungers, W.L., 2008. Modern humans are not (quite) isometric. Am. J. Phys. Anthropol. 137 (4), 371–383.

Tatsuoka, M.M., Lohnes, P.R., 1988. Multivariate Analysis: Techniques for Educational and Psychological Research, second ed. Macmillan Publishing Co, Inc., New York, NY.

Teixeira, W.R.G., 1985. The Mengele report. Am. J. Forensic. Sci. Pathol. 6 (4), 279–283.

Temple, D.H., Matsumura, H., 2011. Do body proportions among Jomon foragers from Hokkaido conform to ecogeographic expectations? Evolutionary implications of body size and shape among northerly hunter-gatherers. Int. J. Osteoarchaeol. 21 (3), 268–282.

Thompson, D.A.W., 1942. On Growth and Form. Cambridge University Press, New York, NY.

Trotter, M., Gleser, G.C., 1952. Estimation of stature from long bones of American Whites and Negroes. Am. J. Phys. Anthropol. 10 (4), 463–514.

Uhl, N.M., 2014. Using Multivariate Calibration to Evaluate Hominin Brain/Body Size Relationships, Anthropology. University of Illinois at Urbana-Champaign.

Uhl, N.M., Rainwater, C.W., Konigsberg, L.W., 2013. Testing for size and allometric differences in fossil hominin body mass estimation. Am. J. Phys. Anthropol. 151 (2), 215–229.

Urban, S., 1783. Gentleman's Magazine and Historical Chronicle, vol. LIII. J. Nichols, London.

Weinstein, K.J., 2005. Body proportions in ancient Andeans from high and low altitudes. Am. J. Phys. Anthropol. 128 (3), 569–585.

CHAPTER 10

Full Skeleton Stature Estimation

Michelle H. Raxter[1] | Christopher B. Ruff[2]
[1]Marymount University, Arlington, VA, United States,
[2]Johns Hopkins University School of Medicine, Baltimore, MD, United States

Chapter Outline

Stature is an important component of the biological profile that forensic anthropologists use to help identify decedents with unknown or tentative identification. There are two main types of techniques available for adult stature estimation: "mathematical" and "anatomical" (Dwight, 1894; Lundy, 1985). The mathematical method uses regression formulae based on the correlation of individual skeletal elements to living stature. The anatomical method involves the reconstruction of adult stature by the measurement and addition of the lengths or heights of a series of skeletal elements from the cranium through the foot, plus factors to account for the soft tissue components. Dwight (1894) described an early anatomical method that rearticulates the necessary elements in anatomical orientation to estimate stature. The spinal elements were rearticulated using clay. The calculated proportions of spinal regions to total spinal length in cadavers were used to aid in the estimation of intervertebral tissue in anatomical stature reconstruction using disarticulated remains. The vertebrae were to be arranged so that each spinal region corresponded to the calculated proportions. Instructions are given on how to position the pelvis as well as the femur within the acetabulum to give proper allowances for soft tissues. He then directed the addition of the following to account for soft parts: scalp (6 mm), the joint between the skull and the spine (3 mm), the knee (6 mm), ankle (6 mm), and the sole of the foot (12 mm).

Fully's (1956) anatomical method was developed using a sample of adult European males who died in a World War II German concentration camp. The method called for the measurement of individual skeletal elements and included soft tissue correction factors that were to be added to calculated skeletal height to obtain a final estimation of living stature. The measurements to be taken were as follows:

- basion–bregma height (BBH) of the cranium (Fig. 10.1),
- maximum height of the corpus of the C2–L5 vertebra measured separately,
- anterior height of the first sacral segment,
- oblique (physiological) length of the femur,
- maximum length of the tibia without the spine and including the malleolus,
- articulated height of the talus and calcaneus.

Fully's (1956) correction factors are then added to calculated skeletal height to obtain a final estimate of adult living stature, as follows:

- Skeletal height equal to or below 153.5 cm, add 10 cm.
- Skeletal height between 153.6 and 165.4 cm, add 10.5 cm.
- Skeletal height equal to or above 165.5 cm, add 11.5 cm.

Since it is a greater challenge to rearticulate the skeleton as described by Dwight (1894), Fully's (1956) technique has subsequently been more readily used by anthropologists (Snow and Williams, 1971; Marquer, 1972; Feldesman and Lundy, 1988; Jungers, 1988; Sciulli et al., 1990; Formicola, 1993; Formicola and Franceschi, 1996).

New Perspectives in Forensic Human Skeletal Identification. http://dx.doi.org/10.1016/B978-0-12-805429-1.00010-7

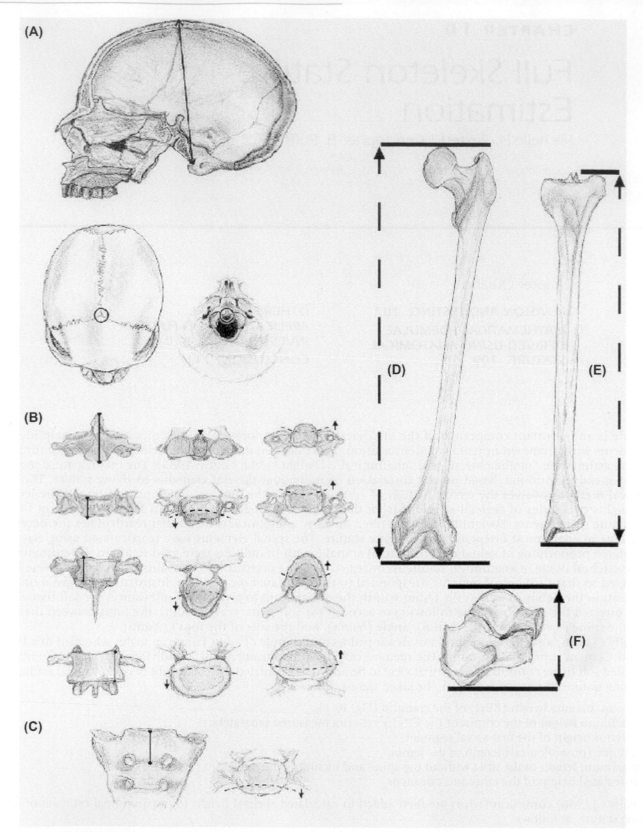

Figure 10.1 (A) Basion–bregma height of the cranium. (B) Vertebral body heights: C2 (top): odontoid process to inferior anterior rim; C3–L5: maximum anterior to pedicles. (C) Height of first sacral segment. (D) Physiological length of the femur. (E) Tibial length: lateral condyle to medial malleolus. (F) Articulated talocalcaneal height. *Reproduced with permission from Raxter, M.H., Auerbach, B.M., Ruff, C.B., Revision of the Fully technique for estimating statures. Am. J. Phys. Anthropol. 2006. © John Wiley and Sons.*

■ REVISION AND TESTING

While Fully's (1956) method was increasingly used to estimate stature in the years since it was proposed, few studies had systematically tested it (see later). In addition, some of the dimensions in Fully's directions were not explicitly described, leaving uncertainty regarding the exact measurement technique that should be employed when applying the method. Raxter et al. (2006) carried out a study that provided new guidelines regarding the implementation of Fully's (1956) original method. They tested the accuracy and applicability of Fully's technique on a new ethnically diverse sample, devised a revision of the original method by offering more detailed descriptions of measurements, and developed new formulae to estimate living stature from skeletal height. Their skeletal sample consisted of adult American black and white males and females of known age, ancestry, sex, and cadaveric stature from the Smithsonian Institution's Terry Collection (Hunt and Albanese, 2005). Cadaveric statures were adjusted to living statures by subtracting 2.5 cm from cadaveric stature, following Trotter and Gleser's (1952) recommendation. Raxter et al. found that while statures derived using the original Fully technique were strongly correlated with living statures in this sample, they underestimated living stature by an average of about 2.4 cm.

The study particularly clarified the measurement of vertebral body heights, tibial length, and the articulated height of the talus and calcaneus with the following instructions:

- Vertebral bodies (sliding calipers): Measure maximum anterior height of the vertebrae. For thoracic and lumbar vertebrae, measurement should be anterior to the rib articular facets and pedicles (Raxter et al., 2006).
- Length of the tibia (osteometric board): The medial malleolus is placed on the stationary end and the lateral condyle against the mobile end. Use a trackless osteometric board to permit freedom to move the mobile end of the board (Martin and Saller, 1957).
- Articulated talocalcaneal height (osteometric board): Articulate the talus and calcaneus. The trochlea of the talus is positioned on the stable end of the board so that the board forms a tangent to the midpoint of the trochlear surface, i.e., the calcaneus and talus are held in anatomical position. The most inferior point of the calcaneal tuber is placed on the mobile end of the osteometric board (Raxter et al., 2006).

After summing the dimensions to obtain skeletal height, one of two equations is applied to estimate living stature (dimensions in centimeters, age in years):

$$\text{Living stature} = 1.009 \times \text{Skeletal height} - 0.0426 \times \text{age} + 12.1. \tag{10.1}$$

$$\text{Living stature} = 0.996 \times \text{Skeletal height} + 11.7. \tag{10.2}$$

There was no effect of sex or ancestry on stature prediction and resulting stature estimates were accurate to within 4.5 cm in 95% of the individuals in the sample, with no directional bias. The equations are applicable to individuals who differ ancestrally and temporally from the study's samples.

Because stature changes with age, adjustment for this factor is often made when estimating stature (Lundy, 1983; Lundy and Feldesman, 1987; Sciulli et al., 1990; Sciulli and Giesen, 1993; Bidmos, 2005; Petersen, 2005); thus, the preferred formula for converting skeletal height to living stature is the one that incorporates an age term (Eq. 10.1). Since age is sometimes unknown, a second equation without an age term was also provided (Eq. 10.2). However, the applicability of the second equation to populations or individuals who vary systematically in age from the Terry reference sample is questionable (also see later). For example, archaeological samples commonly include mainly younger and middle-aged adults, while the Terry sample used in the sample had a mean age of 54 years. In a subsequent technical note, Raxter et al. (2007) tested a subsample of individuals from the original Terry sample composed only of individuals under 50 years of age, with a mean age of 38 years. In addition, ages were binned into mid-values of decadal age ranges for each known age, simulating archaeological or forensic contexts where age can only be more broadly approximated. They found no significant difference between true living stature and stature estimated using the mid-value age; however, estimated stature calculated without the age term significantly underestimated living stature, by an average of almost 1 cm. It is thus recommended that, when possible, the equation with the age term be employed even if decadal or other broad range age estimates must be used (Raxter et al., 2007).

Konigsberg and Jantz (this volume) criticize the use of ordinary least squares regression to derive the equations given earlier, pointing out that this results in a (slight) reduction in the soft tissue correction factor with an increase in skeletal height, when using Eq. (10.2) (without the age term). However, as noted earlier, Eq. (10.1) (with the age term) is strongly recommended, and this equation does include a positive regression coefficient (i.e., 1.009, greater than 1.0), resulting in an increase in soft tissue correction with an increase in skeletal height. In their hypothetical example, Konigsberg and Jantz suggested that alternative equation results in an almost threefold increase in the soft tissue correction factor (from 5.8 to 15.7 cm) with a doubling of skeletal height (from 100 to 200 cm), which seems disproportionately high from an anatomical standpoint. A similar "overcompensation" problem using this approach was noted earlier in comparisons of different regression techniques for estimating body mass in juveniles (Ruff, 2007). Eq. (10.1) from Raxter et al. (2006) results in a relatively small increase of about a centimeter over this size range. It may be that the most anatomically reasonable correction factor lies somewhere between these two estimates, and this deserves further study. In any event, we agree with these authors that problems resulting from the use of different regression techniques are greatly exacerbated when they are applied well outside of the size range of the reference sample. The range of skeletal heights in the sample used by Raxter et al. (2006) was 136.6–172.8 cm, which is much narrower than that used in the hypothetical example given earlier. The difference in estimated stature at the extremes of this distribution, using Eq. (10.1) from Raxter et al. (2006) and assuming an age of 60 years and using Eq. (9.9) from Konigsberg and Jantz (this volume), is 1.4 cm at the low end and 1.9 cm at the high end, both of which are well within 1 standard error of estimate (SEE) of the Raxter et al. (2006) equation. Thus, the choice of soft tissue correction equation makes relatively little difference.

The typical human spine is composed of 7 cervical, 12 thoracic, and 5 lumbar vertebrae, for a total of 24 presacral vertebrae, as well as 5 fused sacral vertebrae. Numerical variation from this standard occurs and Fully (1956) did not address its potential effect on stature estimation. In a technical note (Raxter and Ruff, 2010), we examined a sample from the Terry Collection with varying vertebral formulae and found no statistically significant effect of ancestry or sex on directional and absolute errors, corresponding with previous results (Raxter et al., 2006) for individuals possessing standard counts of vertebrae. Lundy (1988a) noted that the relative position of the first and second sacral segments in individuals with six sacral vertebrae might affect decisions on whether to include one or both in stature estimates. In our sample, individuals who possessed a normal number of presacral vertebrae along with six sacral segments were found to generally have taller pelves compared to individuals with standard spinal column region counts. In concordance with Lundy (1988b), we recommend the application of the standard anatomical technique to reconstruct stature (including measurement of only S1 height), regardless of vertebral pattern. However, when an individual possesses six sacral vertebrae together with a normal number of presacral segments (including five lumbars), we advise the addition of a correction factor of 1.3 cm or 0.8% of estimated stature (Raxter and Ruff, 2010).

One of the limitations of the anatomical method is that it requires the measurement of a large number of intact skeletal elements. The necessary dimensions may be unavailable for measurement due to damage, disease, or the particular element not being present. The archaeological, forensic, and fossil contexts anthropologists typically work in frequently return incomplete or poorly preserved skeletons due to taphonomic factors. Fully and Pineau (1960) developed regression equations that permitted the estimation of stature when the cranium and some vertebrae are absent. The formulae included five lumbar vertebrae and femur and tibia lengths, respectively, as well as skeletal height (C2–L5). The downside to this method is that it was based on the remains of European males only, so its applicability may be limited to this group.

Lundy (1985) presented a technique for estimating individual vertebral heights as a percentage of total vertebral column length. The disadvantage is that it relies on almost complete vertebral columns, which is not common in archaeological or forensic contexts. Auerbach (2011) presented more comprehensive recommendations for estimating the dimensions of missing vertebrae and talocalcaneal height that can expand the potential sample to which the revised Fully method (Raxter et al., 2006) may be applied. The study examined over 2000 Holocene adult male and female indigenous North and South American skeletons. Missing elements were simulated using skeletons that possessed all the elements for the particular dimension under study, e.g., only skeletons with complete vertebral columns were used when estimating missing vertebrae. Auerbach (2011) directed the following:

- Vertebral body heights may be estimated by calculating the average heights of adjacent vertebrae except for the following vertebrae: C2, C3, C6, T2, T11, L1, and L5. For these vertebrae, the best method is to calculate a percentage of the height of one of the adjacent vertebrae or use one of the new multiple regression equations presented in the paper.
- When multiple cervical and thoracic vertebrae are unavailable for measurement, it is recommended that the entire length of the vertebral column be estimated, again using new regression formulae presented.
- The physiological lengths of the tibia and femur may be accurately estimated from measured maximum lengths of these elements.
- Talocalcaneal height may be estimated from femur and tibia length using new regression formulae presented.

General estimation formulae were not developed for BBH of the cranium because of significant group differences in the relative contribution of BBH to skeletal stature. Similarly, general estimation equations for femur and tibia length were not developed due to group differences in crural and cormic indices.

Maijanen (2009) investigated several permutations of the anatomical method on 34 white males from the W.M. Bass Donated Skeletal Collection. Techniques tested included different methods for measuring the heights of C3–L5 and different soft tissue correction factors. The stature estimates were compared to corrected self-reported stature using equations from Rowland (1990) that evaluated measured and self-reported statures. Comparisons were also made to corrected cadaver stature, derived by subtracting 2.5 cm from cadaveric stature following Trotter and Gleser's (1952) recommendation, as Raxter et al. (2006) had done, and to "corrected living stature," which was an average corrected reported and corrected cadaver stature. Corrected living stature was considered to more closely approximate the living statures of her sample, citing an expectation of somewhat inflated self-reported statures. Maijanen found that Fully's (1956) method using anterior midline vertebral height tends to underestimate living stature, and it was recommended that this technique for measuring the vertebrae not be employed. The methods with the smallest errors between estimates and corrected living statures were Raxter et al.'s (2006) method, Eq. (10.1), followed by, Fully's (1956) original technique but using maximum midline and posterior midline vertebral heights.

Most recently, Hayashi et al. (2016) examined 38 American males of European ancestry from the W.M. Bass Donated Skeletal Collection, proposed amendments to the anatomical method, and offered new stature regression formulae. In calculating skeletal height, the authors suggested the measurement of only the portions of the elements that directly contribute to standing height. They reported that posterior vertebral heights yielded the most accurate stature estimates for their sample. They also incorporated a measurement of the vertical space between sacral prom- ontory and the superior margins of the acetabulae as an alternative to the usual measurement of just S1 height. Physiological length of the tibia was employed, also referred to as condylar–astragal length, described as being taken from mid-medial condyle to the articular surface of the distal tibia, excluding the malleolus. The authors then added 15 mm to this tibia length to account for the distal projection of the tibial malleolus, citing Raxter et al. (2006). Stature regression equations were then computed based on their method for measuring total skeletal height. Niskanen et al. (2013) presented new stature regression formulae that addressed age-related changes in height (further discussed later). Hayashi et al. compared stature estimates from their new equations to estimates from Fully (1956), Raxter et al. (2006), and Niskanen et al. (2013) and analyzed them with respect to adjusted cadaver statures using Trotter and Gleser's (1952) 2.5 cm downward correction. They found that the estimates from their new equations were on average accurate to within 20 mm of the adjusted cadaver stature and had the highest pro- portions of test individuals within one or two standard error of estimates of their predicted value. By incorporating a true vertical distance between the proximal end of the sacrum and the proximal edge of the hip joint, the authors reduced uncertainty in estimation of this dimension (part of the correction factor incorporated into the traditional method—see Raxter et al., 2006, Table 4). However, the method for acquiring this dimension was complex, involv- ing replication of soft tissue structures, rearticulation of the complete pelvis in anatomical position, measurement of 3D landmarks using a digitizer, and geometrical derivations from these data. Despite the authors' claim that all of their measurements could also be acquired using traditional osteometric instruments, this would appear to be difficult. This measurement also requires a complete or nearly complete pelvis, further limiting its application to more fragmentary skeletal material. Finally, the method should be tested on other population samples with varying body (including pelvic) proportions.

■ MATHEMATICAL FORMULAE DERIVED USING ANATOMICAL STATURE

The anatomical method involves the direct reconstruction of stature by measuring and adding together skeletal mea- sures from the cranium through the foot. Thus, differences in body proportions are inherently incorporated into the technique. The anatomical method is practical in both forensic and archaeological cases wherein sufficient material is preserved. The common reasons it is not used are related to the speed of an investigation or incomplete remains, and it is in these situations that the mathematical method for estimating stature is often utilized.

The mathematical method employs regression equations based on the correlation of individual skeletal ele- ments to living stature. Long bones have the highest correlation to total stature and produce the most accurate estimations. However, because of possible differences in body proportions, a number of authors have cautioned against using stature regression equations derived from one population for other populations (Pearson, 1899; Stevenson, 1929; Dupertuis and Hadden, 1951; Trotter and Gleser, 1952, 1958). One demonstration of this found that Trotter and Gleser's equations for American black males overestimated South African males' statures, with differences ranging from 2 to 8 cm (Lundy and Feldesman, 1987). Another study reported that Trotter and Gleser's (1958) "Mongoloid" formulae consistently overestimated the statures of Ohio River Valley Native American skel- etons (Sciulli et al., 1990).

Human proportions vary systematically between populations, in part in response to climatic factors (Eveleth and Tanner, 1976; Ruff, 1994; Holliday, 1997; Holliday and Ruff, 1997); therefore, the most accurate mathematical estimates of stature are produced when the population under study is as similar as possible in proportions to the population used to create the equations (Holliday and Ruff, 1997). Following this rationale, several authors have used the anatomical method to derive population-specific regression equations for estimating adult stature from long bones. Statures are first estimated using the anatomical technique on specimens with preservation of sufficient skeletal material. These statures are then used to develop mathematical equations that can be applied to less com- plete remains.

Earlier work used the original Fully (1956) technique to derive formulae. Formicola and Franceschi (1996) devel- oped sex-specific stature regression equations for Neolithic Europeans. They reported that the resulting formulae showed high correlations and low standard errors of estimate, with an average deviation from anatomical stature of about 1.3 cm and few cases exceeding 2 cm.

Lundy and Feldesman (1987) developed regression formulae for both sexes of a South African sample from the Raymond Dart Collection. Standard errors of estimate did not exceed 3.8 cm for the long bones.

More recent studies have employed Raxter et al.'s (2006) revision. Raxter et al. (2008) developed new stature regression formulae for adult ancient Egyptians based on anatomical reconstruction of stature. Results indicated that the estimates from the new formulae produced more consistently accurate stature estimates compared to estimates from previously employed regression equations, including those by Trotter and Gleser (1952, 1958) and modifica- tions thereof (Robins and Shute, 1986). The Egyptian sample consisted of individuals from varying provenances; however, results indicated no significant effect of time period or social class on proportions so all skeletons for each sex were subsequently pooled in the remaining analyses to maximize the sample. The resulting formulae thus may also be broadly applicable to Egyptian archaeological samples.

Auerbach and Ruff (2010) offered three new sets of stature estimation regression equations derived from anatomically reconstructed stature for male and female Arctic, temperate, and Great Plains indigenous North Americans. Some previous studies had used Trotter and Gleser's (1958) "Mongoloid" formulae in this context; however, their use is problematic as the "Mongoloid" sample was composed of a mixture of Japanese, Chinese, "American Indian," Melanesian, Micronesian, and Polynesian individuals, a number of whom additionally had European ancestry. As previously mentioned, these formulae were also found to have overestimated the statures of Ohio River Valley samples (Sciulli et al., 1990). Auerbach and Ruff (2010) found their new formulae to perform better than other commonly used equations, although Genovés' (1967) equations are a useful alternative for Southwestern regions. They caution applying the new equations in modern, forensic contexts, and they are not recommended for South American samples, as South American populations were not included in their study.

Trotter and Gleser's (1952, 1958) formulae based on modern Americans have also been used to estimate the statures of early European skeletons. However, a number of studies have noted problems with the estimates (Wells, 1963; Hanson, 1992; Formicola, 1993; Maijanen and Niskanen, 2006; Vercellotti et al., 2009). Ruff et al. (2012a) applied the revised anatomical method to 501 European skeletons of both sexes. The regions represented in the sample were the British Isles, Scandinavia, North Central Europe, France, Italy, the Iberian Peninsula, and the Balkans. The time periods represented spanned the Mesolithic to very recent (>1900 AD). Percent errors were smaller using the new equations compared to the prior mathematical methods used. Based on the patterning of the percent errors, the authors report that the new equations appear to be broadly applicable to skeletons from different European regions and temporal periods.

Several other studies developed more regionally applicable stature regression formulae for various populations based on anatomically reconstructed statures, including indigenous South Africans (Lundy and Feldesman, 1987), medieval Scandinavians (Vercelotti et al., 2009), early medieval Polish (Maijanen and Niskanen, 2010), late Holocene central Pantagonian (Béguelin, 2011), Andean (Pomeroy and Stock, 2012), 19th to 20th century northeast Thai (Gocha et al., 2013), early medieval Czech (Sladék et al., 2015), and 14th to 20th century Korean (Jeong and Jantz, 2016).

■ OTHER PRACTICAL APPLICATIONS AND FURTHER INVESTIGATIONS

Published reports that have examined the anatomical method in a forensic context are limited. Snow and Williams (1971) investigated the skeletal remains of a 45-year-old male who had 19 antemortem statures available from police and hospital records. The authors compared stature estimates between the anatomical method (Fully, 1956) and the long bone regression equations of Trotter and Gleser (1958). They reported that the overall mean of the antemortem measurements of the individual's height was in close agreement to the stature estimate derived from Fully's method. It was recommended that Fully's technique be employed to help corroborate estimates yielded using Trotter and Gleser (1958). Lundy (1988c) applied Fully's (1956) method to the skeletons of three white male US Navy aviators with antemortem statures recorded under the supervision of a physician during naval training. The anatomical estimates were compared with those obtained from Trotter and Gleser's (1958) regression equations. He found the Fully technique (1956) to be as accurate as the regression equations, and in one case to be more accurate.

Petersen (2005, 2011) proposed that skeletal length in the grave could provide an accurate estimate of living stature by comparing it to anatomical estimates. Boldsen's (1984) definition of skeletal length in the grave was used, defined as in situ vertex to talus length with the decedent buried in an extended supine position. Twenty adult medieval Dane skeletons comprised of 10 males and 10 females were examined. Differences were calculated as anatomical method minus skeletal length in the grave. Results using Raxter et al.'s (2006) Eq. (10.1) showed that skeletal length in the grave underestimated living stature by 2.58 cm on average. The author proposed further testing the measurement of skeletal length in the grave to the most distal point of the calcaneus rather than the talus, with the former technique utilizing the calcaneus having already been previously suggested by Kurth (1950). Until further testing could be made, Petersen (2011) recommended that skeletal length in the grave continue to be measured to the most distal point on the talus and 2.5 cm be added to the dimension to obtain an estimate of living stature.

Bidmos and Manger (2012) attempted to test the Fully method by applying it to full body MRI scans of 28 indigenous South African male volunteers whose living standing heights were taken with a stadiometer. They found that previous anatomical methods (Fully, 1956; Raxter et al., 2006) underestimated the living statures of their subjects and thus introduced new larger "soft tissue" correction factors. However, it was subsequently noted that challenges in identifying boundaries between bone and soft tissue in MRI images due to shading artifacts, as well as out-of-plane effects, may have led to mismeasurement of elements, specifically vertebral and talocalcaneal height (Ruff et al., 2012b); problems in measuring the latter were noted by the original authors (Bidmos and Manger, 2012). Tibial length was also not measured in the same way as that typically used for the anatomical technique, with the authors measuring from the medial condyle, rather than from the lateral condyle. The above issues likely accounted for the larger differences between skeletal height and living stature found in this study (Ruff et al., 2012b).

Age-related stature decline appears primarily to be due to decrease in intervertebral disk height, vertebral body compression, and changes in posture (Freidlaender et al., 1977). An adjustment for age is thus necessary when estimating living statures from skeletal remains. Forensically, especially for older adults, it can be important to have an estimate of both maximum adult stature and stature at age of death (Niskanen et al., 2013), as many individuals continue to report their stature from an earlier age before stature decline (Galloway, 1988).

The age adjustment most often used is Trotter and Gleser's (1952) equation: [loss = 0.06 × (age – 30)], with the assumption that stature loss begins after 30 years of age. Their correction, however, does not account for sex differences or the quadratic pattern of stature decline with age (Niskanen et al., 2013). Niskanen et al.'s results indicated that an age-related decline in stature starts before any skeletal height reduction, likely due to intervertebral disk thickness reduction and postural changes (Friedlaender et al., 1977). The authors also offered three new equations, two of which they recommend to correct for age in stature estimates based on a sample from the Smithsonian's Terry Collection. Their anatomical measures are identical to Raxter et al.'s (2006) except for their vertebral heights, which were measured in the anterior midline. The new formulae use cadaver stature rather than adjusted living stature and follow previous work (Cline et al., 1989) indicating age decline commencement at 40 years. The measurements the authors used to compute skeletal height were identical to those in Raxter et al. (2006) save for vertebral body heights, which were measured in the anterior midline. Eq. (10.3) is a continuous and linear age correction, resulting in curvilinear stature estimation error, and is consequently not recommended by the authors for estimating cadaveric statures at death. They found sex-specific regression slopes to be similar and subsequently pooled the sexes to compute Eqs. (10.4) and (10.5). Eq. (10.4) is recommended when age at death older than 40 years is known or can be reasonably estimated. Eq. (10.5) is to be applied to obtain maximum cadaveric statures in individuals under 40 years of age and those of unknown or uncertain ages. A new correction factor to convert cadaver stature to living stature was based on 34 volunteers of both sexes to account for the difference between living wall height (stature measured with the subject standing against a wall) and living free-standing height (stature measured with the subject standing free). Cadaver statures in the Terry Collection were taken in a supine, standing position on an upright table (cadaveric wall height) and can be converted to living wall height by multiplying cadaver stature by the authors' proposed correction factor of 0.9851.

Niskanen et al. (2013) equations

$$\text{Cadaver Stature} = 1.039 \times \text{Skeletal height} - 0.075 \times \text{age} + 13.127. \tag{10.3}$$

$$\text{Cadaver Stature} = 1.043 \times \text{Skeletal height} - 0.103 \times \text{age} + 14.586. \tag{10.4}$$

$$\text{Cadaver Stature} = 1.051 \times \text{Skeletal height} - 8.136. \tag{10.5}$$

Very recently, Cardoso et al. (2016) have questioned Trotter and Gleser's (1952) 2.5-cm reduction from cadaveric stature to obtain living stature, a correction commonly employed by a number of researchers (Genovés, 1967; Byers et al., 1989; Raxter et al., 2006; Maijanen, 2009; Hayashi et al., 2016). The authors contended that Trotter and Gleser's correction was based on an indirect assessment since cadaveric stature was not compared to living stature for the same individuals but rather to similar living samples. In their study, cadaveric statures, measured in a supine position, were on average 4.3 cm greater than living statures, a mean difference that is larger than most previously reported corrections (in addition to Trotter and Gleser, 1952; also see Manouvrier, 1892; Pearson, 1899; Correa, 1932; Bidmos, 2005). Cardoso and colleagues still considered the cadaveric statures of individuals from the Terry Collection to closely resemble living stature, citing their measurement in an upright, "standing" position via a specially constructed board developed by Terry (1940), which allowed a standing posture to be reproduced. However, Cardoso et al. did not directly investigate Terry's "standing" technique for measuring cadaver stature as the cadaver statures in their sample were measured lying in the supine position; therefore, no evidence was provided to indicate that the original 2.5 cm correction is incorrect. Additionally, an analysis by Terry (1940) showed little difference between supine and "standing" statures in his cadaver sample. This suggests that Cardoso et al.'s downward correction to supine statures applies in some manner to statures measured in a standing position, indicating that the cadaver statures in the Terry Collection are not equivalent to living statures.

■ CONCLUSION

Mathematical methods are useful for estimating adult stature when the skeleton is incomplete, which is often the case in archeological and forensic contexts. The mathematical method can also be applied faster than the anatomical method. However, proclivity for speed may be at the expense of obtaining a more accurate estimate in employing the anatomical method. The anatomical method takes longer to apply and requires the availability of several skeletal elements; however, when most of the skeleton is present, the anatomical method is the preferred technique because differences in body proportions, e.g., trunk length to lower limb length, are naturally incorporated into the method. A comparison of anatomical statures with statures measured using Trotter and Gleser's (1952) equations showed less error in estimating individual statures, as each estimate is "customized" to each individual (Raxter et al., 2006).

When most of the necessary elements are available to apply the anatomical method, the use of Raxter et al. (2006) Eq. (10.1) (with age term) or Niskanen et al. (2013) equations is recommended.

References

Auerbach, B.M., 2011. Methods for estimating missing human skeletal element osteometric dimensions employed in the revised Fully technique for estimating stature. Am. J. Phys. Anthropol. 145, 67–80.

Auerbach, B.M., Ruff, C.B., 2010. Stature estimation formulae for indigenous North American populations. Am. J. Phys. Anthropol. 141, 190–207.

Béguelin, M., 2011. Stature estimation in a central Patagonian Prehispanic population: development of new models considering specific body proportions. Int. J. Osteoarchaeol. 21, 150–158.

Bidmos, M.A., 2005. On the non-equivalence of documented cadaver lengths to living stature estimates based on Fully's method on bones in the Raymond A. Dart Collection. J. Forensic Sci. 50, 1–6.

Bidmos, M.A., Manger, P.R., 2012. New soft tissue correction factors for stature estimation: results from magnetic resonance imaging. Forensic Sci. Int. 214, 212.e1–212.e7.

Boldsen, J.L., 1984. A statistical evaluation of the basis for predicting stature from lengths of long bones in European populations. Am. J. Phys. Anthropol. 65, 305–311.

Byers, S., Akoshima, K., Curran, B., 1989. Determination of adult stature from metatarsal length. Am. J. Phys. Anthropol. 79, 275–279.

Cardoso, H.F.V., Marinho, L., Alabanese, J., 2016. The relationship between cadaver, living and forensic stature: a review of current knowledge and a test using a sample of adult Portuguese males. Forensic Sci. Int. 258, 55–63.

Cline, M.G., Meredith, K.E., Boyer, J.T., Burrows, B., 1989. Decline of height with age in adults in a general population sample: estimating maximum height and distinguishing birth cohort effects from actual loss of stature with aging. Hum. Biol. 61, 415–425.

Correa, A.A., 1932. La taille des Portuguais d'apre's les os longs. Anthropologie 10, 268–272.

Dupertuis, C.W., Hadden, J.A., 1951. On the reconstruction of stature from long bones. Am. J. Phys. Anthropol. 9, 15–54.

Dwight, T., 1894. Methods of estimating the height from parts of the skeleton. Med. Rec. N.Y. 46, 293–296.

Eveleth, P.B., Tanner, J.M., 1976. Worldwide Variation in Human Growth. Cambridge University Press, New York.

Feldesman, M.R., Lundy, J.K., 1988. Stature estimates for some African Plio-Pleistocene fossil hominids. J. Hum. Evol. 17, 583–596.

Formicola, V., 1993. Stature reconstruction from long bones in ancient population samples: an approach to the problem of its reliability. Am. J. Phys. Anthropol. 90, 351–358.

Formicola, V., Franceschi, M., 1996. Regression equations for estimating stature from long bones of early Holocene European samples. Am. J. Phys. Anthropol. 100, 83–88.

Friedlaender, J.S., Costa Jr., P.T., Bosse, R., Ellis, E., Rhoads, J.G., Stoudt, H.W., 1977. Longitudinal physique changes among healthy white veterans at Boston. Hum. Biol. 49, 541–558.

Fully, G., 1956. Une nouvelle methode de determination de la taille. Ann. Med. Leg. 35, 266–273.

Fully, G., Pineau, H., 1960. Determination de la stature au moyen du squelette. Ann. Med. Leg. 40, 145–154.

Galloway, A., 1988. Estimating actual height in the older individual. J. Forensic Sci. 33, 126–136.

Genovés, S., 1967. Proportionality of the long bones and their relation to stature among Mesoamericans. Am. J. Phys. Anthropol. 26, 67–78.

Gocha, T.P., Vercellotti, G., McCormick, L.E., Van Deest, T.L., 2013. Formulae for estimating skeletal height in modern South-East Asians. J. Forensic Sci. 58 (5), 1279–1283.

Hanson, C.L., 1992. Population-specific stature reconstruction for medieval Trondheim, Norway. Int. J. Osteoarchaeol. 2, 289–295.

Hayashi, A., Emanovsky, P.D., Pietrusewsky, M., Holland, T.D., 2016. A procedure for calculating the vertical space height of the sacrum when determining skeletal height for use in the anatomical method of adult stature estimation. J. Forensic Sci. 61 (2), 415–423.

Holliday, T.W., 1997. Body proportions in Late Pleistocene Europe and modern human origins. J. Hum. Evol. 32, 423–447.

Holliday, T.W., Ruff, C.B., 1997. Ecogeographic patterning and stature prediction in fossil hominids: comment on Feldesman and Fountain. Am. J. Phys. Anthropol. 103, 137–140.

Hunt, D.H., Albanese, J., 2005. History and demographic composition of the Robert J. Terry anatomical collection. Am. J. Phys. Anthropol. 127, 406–417.

Jeong, Y., Jantz, L.M., 2016. Developing Korean-specific equations of stature estimation. Forensic Sci. Int. 105.e1–105.e11.

Jungers, W.L., 1988. Lucy's length: stature reconstruction in Australopithecus afarensis (AL288-1) with implications for other small-bodied hominids. Am. J. Phys. Anthropol. 76, 227–231.

Kurth, G., 1950. Uber die Verwendbarkeit der Grablange vorund fruhgeschichtlicher Reihengraberserien zur Bestimmung einer genauen Korperhohe. Z Morphol. Anthropol. 42, 293–306.

Lundy, J.K., 1983. Living stature from long limb bones in the South African Negro. S. Afr. J. Sci. 79, 337–338.

Lundy, J.K., 1985. The mathematical versus anatomical methods of stature estimate from long bones. Am. J. Forensic Med. Pathol. 6, 73–75.

Lundy, J.K., 1988a. Sacralization of a sixth lumbar vertebra and its effect upon the estimation of living stature. J. Forensic Sci. 33, 1045–1049.

Lundy, J.K., 1988b. Possible effects of numerical variation in presacral vertebrae on stature. S. Afr. J. Sci. 84, 65–66.

Lundy, J.K., 1988c. A report on the use of Fully's anatomical method to estimate stature in military skeletal remains. J. Forensic Sci. 33, 534–539.

Lundy, J.K., Feldesman, M.R., 1987. Revised equations for estimating living stature from the long bones of the South African Negro. S. Afr. J. Sci. 83, 54–55.

Maijanen, H., 2009. Testing anatomical methods for stature estimation on individuals from the W.M. Bass donated skeletal collection. J. Forensic Sci. 54, 746–752.

Maijanen, H., Niskanen, M., 2006. Comparing stature-estimation methods on Medieval inhabitants of Westerhus, Sweden. Fennosc. Archaeol. 23, 37–46.

Maijanen, H., Niskanen, M., 2010. New regression equations for stature estimation for Medieval Scandinavians. Int. J. Osteoarchaeol. 20, 472–480.

Manouvrier, L., 1892. Determination de la taille d'apres les grands os des membres. Rev. Ecole Anthopol. 2, 227–233.

Marquer, P., 1972. Nouvelle contribution a l'etude du squelette des Pygmees occidentaux. Mem. Mus. Nat. Hist. Nat. Ser. A Zool. 72, 1–122.

Martin, R., Saller, K., 1957. Lehrbuch der Anthropologie in systematischer Darstellung mit besonderer Berucksichtigung der anthropologischen Methoden. Zweiter Band: Kraniologie, Osteologie, third ed. Verlag Von Gustav Fischer, Stuttgart.

Niskanen, M., Maijanen, H., McCarthy, D., Junno, J.-A., 2013. Application of the anatomical method to estimate the maximum adult stature and the age-at-death stature. Am. J. Phys. Anthropol. 152, 96–106.

Pearson, K., 1899. Mathematical contribution to the theory of evolution: on the reconstruction of the stature of prehistoric races. Philos. Trans. R. Soc. Lond. Biol. 192, 169–244.

Petersen, H.C., 2005. On the accuracy of estimating living stature from skeletal length in the grave and by linear regression. Int. J. Osteoarchaeol. 15, 106–114.

Petersen, H.C., 2011. A Re-evaluation of stature estimation from skeletal length in the grave. Am. J. Phys. Anthropol. 144, 327–330.

Pomeroy, E., Stock, J.T., 2012. Estimation of stature and body mass from the skeleton among coastal and mid-altitude Andean populations. Am. J. Phys. Anthropol. 147, 264–279.

Raxter, M.H., Auerbach, B.M., Ruff, C.B., 2006. Revision of the Fully technique for estimating statures. Am. J. Phys. Anthropol. 130, 374–384.

Raxter, M.H., Ruff, C.B., 2010. The effects of vertebral numerical variation on anatomical stature estimation. J. Forensic Sci. 55, 464–466.

Raxter, M.H., Ruff, C.B., Auerbach, B.M., 2007. Technical note: revised Fully stature estimation technique. Am. J. Phys. Anthropol. 133, 817–818.

Raxter, M.H., Ruff, C.B., Azab, A., Erfan, M., Soliman, M., El-Sawaf, A., 2008. Stature estimation in ancient Egyptians: a new technique based on anatomical reconstruction of stature. Am. J. Phys. Anthropol. 136, 147–155.

Robins, G., Shute, C.C.D., 1986. Predynastic Egyptian stature and physical proportions. Hum. Evol. 1, 313–324.

Rowland, M.L., 1990. Self-reported weight and height. Am. J. Clin. Nutr. 52, 1125–1133.

Ruff, C.B., 1994. Morphological adaptation to climate in modern and fossil hominids. Yearb. Phys. Anthropol. 37, 65–107.

Ruff, C.B., 2007. Body size prediction from juvenile skeletal remains. Am. J. Phys. Anthropol. 133 (1), 698–716.

Ruff, C.B., Holt, B.M., Niskanen, M., Sladék, V., Berner, M., Garofalo, E., Garvin, H.M., Hora, M., Maijanen, H., Niinimäki, S., Salo, K., Schuplerová, E., Tompkins, D., 2012a. Stature and body mass estimation from skeletal remains in the European Holocene. Am. J. Phys. Anthropol. 148, 601–617.

Ruff, C., Raxter, M., Auerbach, B., 2012b. Comment on Bidmos and Manger, "New soft tissue correction factors for stature estimation: results from magnetic resonance imaging". Forensic Sci. Int. 222, e42–e43.

Sciulli, P.W., Giesen, M.J., 1993. Brief communication: an update on stature estimation in prehistoric Native Americans of Ohio. Am. J. Phys. Anthropol. 92, 395–399.

Sciulli, P.W., Schneider, K.N., Mahaney, M.C., 1990. Stature estimation in prehistoric native Americans of Ohio. Am. J. Phys. Anthropol. 83, 275–280.

Sladék, V., Machacek, J., Ruff, C.B., Schuplerová, E., Prichystalova, R., Hora, M., 2015. Population-specific stature estimation from long bones in the early medieval Pohansko (Czech Republic). Am. J. Phys. Anthropol. 158, 312–324.

Snow, C.C., Williams, J., 1971. Variation in premortem statural measurements compared to statural estimates of skeletal remains. J. Forensic Sci. 16, 455–464.

Stevenson, P.H., 1929. On racial differences in stature long bone regression formulae for the Chinese. Biometrika 21, 303–318.

Terry, R.J., 1940. On measuring and photographing the cadaver. Am. J. Phys. Anthropol. 26 (1), 433–447.

Trotter, M., Gleser, G., 1952. Estimation of stature from long bones of American whites and Negroes. Am. J. Phys. Anthropol. 10, 469–514.

Trotter, M., Gleser, G., 1958. A re-evaluation of estimation of stature based on measurements taken during life and the long bones after death. Am. J. Phys. Anthropol. 16, 79–123.

Vercellotti, G., Agnew, A.M., Justus, H.M., Sciulli, P.W., 2009. Stature estimation in an Early Medieval (XI-XII c.) Polish Population: testing the accuracy of regression equations in a bioarcheological sample. Am. J. Phys. Anthropol. 140, 135–142.

Wells, L.H., 1963. Stature in earlier races of mankind. In: Brothwell, D., Higgs, E. (Eds.), Science in Archaeology. Basic Books, New York, pp. 365–378.

CHAPTER 11

The History and Use of the National Missing and Unidentified Persons System (NamUs) in the Identification of Unknown Persons

Elizabeth A. Murray[1] | Bruce E. Anderson[2] | Steven C. Clark[3] | Randy L. Hanzlick[4]

[1]Mount St. Joseph University, Cincinnati, OH, United States
[2]Pima County Office of the Medical Examiner, Tucson, AZ, United States
[3]Occupational Research and Assessment, Inc., Big Rapids, MI, United States
[4]Emory School of Medicine and Fulton County Medical Examiner Office, Atlanta, GA, United States

Chapter Outline

■ INTRODUCTION

In October 2009, Stephanie Beverly Clack and her sister, Alice Beverly, learned of a television public service announcement promoting a new US government–sponsored website, the National Missing and Unidentified Persons System (NamUs, pronounced "name us"), which was open to the public. They had not seen their older sister, Paula Beverly Davis, since August 1987. Clack went to her computer, found NamUs.gov and clicked to enter the unidentified persons database. There in a quick search, she entered her sister's age as 21 years when last seen and that she was a white female. In the new database, only 10 unknown white female cases emerged as possible matches based on the search criteria. Stephanie and Alice reviewed each of the cases, looking for features that might be unique to their missing sister. Within 30 min, they came to the 10th and final case in the list—that of an unidentified woman with a pair of tattoos representing a rose and a unicorn (Fig. 11.1), just like those of their sister. Using the contact information provided, Clack reached out to the Montgomery

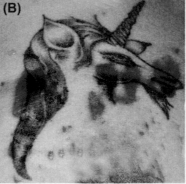

Figure 11.1 Photographs of a rose tattoo (A) and a unicorn tattoo (B) from the unidentified persons case.

New Perspectives in Forensic Human Skeletal Identification. http://dx.doi.org/10.1016/B978-0-12-805429-1.00011-9

County Coroner's Office in Dayton, Ohio, where the unidentified body had been found in August 1987, the day after her sister's disappearance. A DNA family reference sample (FRS), provided by the missing woman's father in early December of 2009, confirmed the remains were those of Paula Beverly Davis (Fisher, 2010; NamUs, 2011; Pettem, 2012).

It may be difficult to imagine how a connection was not made sooner between Paula Beverly Davis's missing persons case (filed by her mother, Esther Beverly, the morning after she was last seen) and the discovery of an unknown decedent fitting her description a mere 14 h after the report was filed (Fisher, 2010; NamUs, 2011). This is especially true considering Davis was last seen at a truck stop on Interstate 70 in Missouri, and the very next day the seminude body of an unknown strangulation victim, matching her description, was found about 560 miles away along an entrance ramp to Interstate 70 in Ohio (driving time of approximately 8 h). However, that distance crosses many jurisdictional boundaries and the use of the internet and other law enforcement networking media were not nearly as well developed in 1987 as they are today. In addition, Davis was an adult who could have left of her own accord, as police had pointed out to her family (Pettem, 2012). Given no obvious signs of foul play, an adult's disappearance would not have been treated with the same intensity by law enforcement as that of a missing child or a case in which any person's disappearance was obviously the result of criminal activity.

For years, Stephanie Beverly Clack and Alice Beverly had searched for their older sister, including on a variety of other websites. It was not until 22 years after she disappeared that they finally learned their sister's fate through NamUs. This connection was only possible because the Montgomery County authorities had not given up on their unidentified person's case either. Their 1987 Jane Doe was one of the first persons Ken Betz, Director of the Montgomery County Coroner's Office, had entered into NamUs in April 2008 (Pettem, 2012). The decedent's profile was assigned the number 985, meaning when it was entered there were fewer than 1000 unidentified persons cases in the system. Betz, and then Coroner James H. Davis, had learned of the new technology through colleagues at the National Association of Medical Examiners (NAME) and entered their several unknown persons cases into NamUs (Pettem, 2012). Though the unknown female had been buried for two decades, the Montgomery County Coroner's Office had the foresight to retain biological samples from her remains, so the identification was quickly confirmed through DNA testing; Davis's body did not need to be exhumed until her family wanted to move her remains closer to home (Pettem, 2012). Today, she is interred in Missouri near her mother, who died in 2005 without knowing what had happened to Paula. Davis's killer has not been found (Fisher, 2010).

NamUs primarily consists of two sister databases; one contains the profiles of missing persons (both US and foreign nationals) and the other holds profiles of unidentified decedents found within US borders. Algorithms compare information between the two databases. By its nature, there are no "happy endings" when matches occur within NamUs, since an association means the missing person is deceased. The importance of such a national identification network, however, cannot be overstated. On any given day in the United States, there are approximately 100,000 active missing persons cases, and there are estimated to be 40,000 cases in the US involving unknown persons (Ritter, 2007). NamUs provides answers for families searching for missing loved ones, as well as case resolution for those working in law enforcement and coroner/medical examiner settings.

Although there are other databases containing information about missing and/or unidentified individuals, NamUs is unique. NamUs was the first 100% web-based data system sponsored by the US Federal Government that allowed direct data input from medicolegal offices (Medical Examiner, Coroner, and Justice of the Peace) whose morgues housed the unidentified bodies as well as input from the public who had direct knowledge of the missing person. While public users can only see limited data within NamUs, they can easily participate in searches and look for potential matches. This helps empower the families and friends of missing persons and the broader general public to assist law enforcement and medicolegal investigators in their quest to resolve open—and often cold—cases.

The two databases were connected into one system in the summer of 2009, and as of mid-2016 of the nearly 14,000 unknown persons cases entered into NamUs, over 2300 have been identified (NamUs, 2016). NamUs has been credited with aiding in 33% of those identifications (NamUs, 2016). On the missing persons side, of the nearly 23,500 cases entered into the system, nearly half are now marked as closed (for a variety of reasons), and NamUs has been credited with assisting in 12% of those case closures (NamUs, 2016). The system has seen positive growth over its years of service, yet there are challenges to be overcome to improve its success rates.

■ A BRIEF HISTORY OF NAMUS

NamUs has its roots in a pair of pilot projects that were known as the Unidentified Decedent Reporting System (UDRS) and the Endangered Missing Persons Reporting System (EMPRS) designed by coauthors Randy Hanzlick and Steven Clark beginning in 2005. At that time the National Crime Information Center (NCIC) contained information about unknown and missing persons, however, access to NCIC is limited mainly to law enforcement. Unless coroner and medical examiner offices obtain their own originating agency identifier (commonly called an ORI), they have to rely on law enforcement for NCIC data input and searching. Additionally, NCIC was not proving to be a very successful source of matches between the missing and unidentified. The International Homicide Investigators Association had already been discussing the problems with NCIC and the need to have a single repository for data related to missing and unknown persons that would be available to law enforcement, the medicolegal community, and the general public. As early as 2003, the Office for Victims of Crime, US Department of Justice (DOJ), had been funding "working group" meetings with the goal of developing some version of a stand-alone national registry of missing and unidentified persons. The DOJ was also holding regional conferences directed at missing and unidentified persons issues, and these continued to raise awareness about the topic. In 2007, the DOJ's research and development arm, the National Institute of Justice (NIJ), provided funding to the National Center for Forensic Science (NCFS) at the University of Central Florida; this funding was partly directed toward technologies that could improve the investigation of missing and unknown individuals.

Several internet websites containing information about unknown and missing persons were already open to the public. The Doe Network, the National Center for Missing Adults, and the National Center for Missing and Exploited Children (NCMEC) had organizational websites that included information on open cases, but none of these sites were connected with each other. Nevada's Clark County Coroner's Office had a website that featured their unknown persons cases, as did the office of coauthor Randy Hanzlick, who was then the chief medical examiner for Fulton County, Atlanta, Georgia. With knowledge of the overarching issues surrounding identification of the unknown dead, in 2004, Hanzlick approached coauthor Steven Clark, of Occupational Research and Assessment, Inc. (ORA), to see if he would consider designing a pilot database that could network unknown persons cases from a variety of agencies. ORA already had a successful history of federally funded grant projects involving death investigation, including NIJ-funded work with the University of Central Florida's NCFS to develop a "best practices" document for identification of unknown persons in coroner and medical examiner settings (NCFS, 2009). By the summer of 2005, Hanzlick and Clark launched their original version of UDRS out of ORA in Big Rapids, Michigan. Although they had been assisted and encouraged by NAME, the International Association of Coroners and Medical Examiners (IACME), and many other groups, at that point UDRS was unfunded by any governmental agency.

Following a limited launch to NAME members in 2006, Hanzlick demonstrated the UDRS database for NCFS (1 of over 20 such presentations by Hanzlick and/or Clark between 2005 and 2008). This preview was part of a regularly scheduled focus group meeting, convened to develop "best practices" for using technology to assist in identifying human remains and resulted in ORA receiving technological upgrade funding through the NIJ for 2007–08 to enhance the pilot system and further awareness of this project within the medicolegal community. The relationship between Hanzlick/Clark and the NAME membership provided an avenue to register additional users into UDRS. As the number of unknown persons cases in the system grew, individuals at the NIJ, the NCFS, and the National Forensic Science Technology Center (NFSTC) began discussions of making UDRS an independently funded project, separate from other ongoing work at the University of Central Florida. Simultaneously, those at the DOJ were discussing a sister database for missing persons (on which ORA had been doing proof-of-concept work since early 2006), and the title "National Missing and Unidentified Persons System" was already being used to describe what many hoped would soon become a reality. The working title of ORA's missing persons pilot database was EMPRS, and it was to mirror UDRS in functionality. By mid-2007, both sites were functional, but separate, and ORA began working on how the two sister databases would ultimately interact. Ahead of its still-in-progress missing persons counterpart, the NamUs unidentified persons database (NamUs-UP) was officially announced and demonstrated on September 12, 2007, at the National Press Club in Washington, DC (USDOJ/OJP, 2007).

By this time, NFSTC had been awarded a 3-year NIJ contract, spanning 2008–11, to develop the missing persons side of the system (NamUs-MP) and then merge the two databases. NFSTC hired and trained individuals as Regional System Administrators (RSAs) to assist the missing persons project. Many of these RSAs were prior members of earlier NIJ working groups, persons with experience in missing and unidentified case investigations, and/or forensic specialists in related areas, such as DNA and fingerprints. Todd Matthews of the Doe Network was enlisted to recruit people to enter missing persons cases into a beta system called "Operation Passageway" to test the interactions between the two databases. Ultimately, NFSTC also began to employ part-time consultants in odontology and anthropology (including coauthors Bruce Anderson and Elizabeth Murray in 2009). Meanwhile, NCFS continued to focus on developing "best practice" standards for missing and unidentified persons cases, which now included promoting the evolving NamUs system. Approximately 100 missing persons cases were entered by hand into the beta Operation Passageway system in the first half of 2008; some were actual cases found on missing persons websites, some from state-based missing persons clearinghouse records, and a few were from law enforcement agency missing persons case files, while others were fabricated to test the matching algorithms running between the two systems. By the summer of 2008, the missing persons beta system was interacting with NamUs-UP and finding potential matches. To improve the likelihood of real identifications, however, more cases—both missing and unidentified—had to be brought into NamUs. Realizing there was no standardized electronic case management system nor a national standardized format for case data, ORA devised a software solution in which exported unidentified case files could be opened, reviewed manually, parsed (through syntactic analysis), and converted electronically for importing into NamUs; this intermediate web-based system became known as "Crosswalk." In addition, cases could be hand entered from paper records into Crosswalk for data review and eventual importing. The Crosswalk system allowed ORA staff and Doe Network volunteers to enter missing persons cases into the system, which significantly increased the number of cases in the system, while also performing a quality review of case data. Recognizing the variety of syntax patterns used by existing missing and/or unidentified persons data systems, as well as standardizing data formats, were both essential for importing existing records into NamUs, including from NCIC, state databases, and institution/agency databases.

On January 1, 2009, the missing persons database (NamUs-MP) was operational and open for data input, even by the general public. That feature was the long-awaited hallmark of the NamUs system; its ability to "harness the power of the public" has been fundamental to its success (as illustrated by the Paula Beverly Davis case). In July 2009, algorithms were deployed to generate automated system-suggested matches between the NamUs-MP and NamUs-UP databases and to allow NamUs Case Managers to enter exclusions for cases that do not match. The power of the NamUs system as a technology to improve missing and unidentified case investigations was quickly recognized. NamUs received the 2009 International Association of Chiefs of Police iXP Excellence in Technology Award and a Computerworld Honors Program 2010 Laureate Medal for software that serves society. (The system later received the 2011 Samuel J. Heyman Service to America Medal, the 2011 August Vollher Award for Excellence in Forensic Science, and the 2012 Paul H. Chapman Award from the Foundation for Improvement of Justice.)

In 2010, NCMEC partnered with NamUs to play a significant role in case review and follow-up for NamUs cases involving children. Their staff was given RSA status for both NamUs-MP and NamUs-UP, and NCMEC Project Alert volunteers traveled to selected medical examiner and coroner offices around the United States, including the Pima County Office of the Medical Examiner (PCOME), where coauthor Anderson is employed, to review medical examiner/coroner and law enforcement records. Numerous cases entered into NamUs, including many at the PCOME, were improved through the efforts of the Project Alert volunteers. These collaborations were critical in illustrating the value of NamUs to policymakers in Washington, DC, given NCMEC's long history of involvement with the cases of missing children (dating back to 1984). Also in 2010, select DNA labs were given access to edit information on DNA testing within NamUs case profiles, including the Federal Bureau of Investigation and University of North Texas (there are currently several others). In addition, NamUs forensic odontologists covering Arizona were given permission to review and edit the dental pages for the NamUs-UP cases of the PCOME, which became a model for other jurisdictions to follow.

National organizations endorsed the NamUs system, including the American Board of Medicolegal Death Investigators (ABMDI), IACME, and NAME. By the close of 2010, NamUs was quickly becoming a standard online investigative tool for medicolegal death investigators across the United States. Users were attesting that NamUs had been instrumental in some resolutions of both missing and unidentified persons cases across multiple state and local jurisdictions. Continued support from the NIJ was secured and a more formal infrastructure of technical assistance and support was created within NamUs. In addition, the NIJ funded ORA to develop and conduct five National NamUs Training Academies during 2010–11 to create a multidisciplinary community of "expert" users who would hopefully go forth and not only use the system, but also train others on the system. All four of the chapter coauthors participated in the NamUs Training Academies, which were held in Albuquerque, Atlanta, Baltimore, Los Angeles, and St. Louis. The resulting increased awareness and use by investigative agencies was followed by an increase in NamUs-"assisted" case resolutions—progress was being made nationally to clear current and cold missing and unidentified persons cases. In 2011, the first journal article about NamUs and its development was published by Hanzlick et al. (2011), to help promote the system, especially among forensic pathologists. Further recognition came in 2011, when Charles Heurich (NamUs NIJ Program Manager, along with Danielle Weiss) and the NamUs Team were awarded the Justice and Law Enforcement Service to America Medal.

In the fall of 2011, administration of the NIJ grant for NamUs moved from NFSTC to the University of North Texas (UNT) through its Center for Human Identification for a 5-year period extending through September of 2016, at which point the grant was renewed until 2021. Since 2004, this organization was already the home of an NIJ-funded laboratory and continues to direct and improve the NamUs system. NamUs 2.0 is slated for release in 2017 and will include several changes.

■ SYSTEM OVERVIEW

To use NamUs or to submit a case for inclusion in the database, individuals first visit the NamUs website (www.namus.gov) and choose the area of interest. Selecting the unidentified persons icon will transfer to the unidentified persons database for user registration and/or data entry; choosing the missing persons option will take the user to the missing persons database for registration and/or data entry. When an individual registers with either NamUs database and is approved by NamUs personnel, the resulting permissions level is primarily based on the registrant's role (i.e., law enforcement, coroner/medical examiner, public user, etc.). The permissions level dictates what types of information can be seen, and potentially edited, by a NamUs user in a given database. Some data are automatically blocked from view for some user categories, such as members of the general public, and other data can be selected to be publicly viewable or not.

NamUs case profiles in the two sister databases contain much in common; however, there are necessary differences between information included for unidentified persons as compared with missing persons and vice versa. Table 11.1 highlights the main data pages in NamUs and key differences between the unidentified persons (UP) database and the missing persons (MP) database (as of midyear 2016). Cases entered are automatically assigned a unique, sequential/chronological UP or MP case number at the time a registered user employs the "New Case" data entry tab on either the NamUs-UP or NamUs-MP website. On the unidentified side, the data entrant becomes the "Case Manager" unless and until case management is later changed; on the missing persons side, NamUs staff will verify the case with the investigating law enforcement agency, which then may elect to manage the case (or it may remain with NamUs staff for case management). Some information (albeit minimal data) is required to be input before a case can be submitted to NamUs personnel, and—for MP cases—verified, before being published. All MP cases are cross-checked with authorities; UP cases are assumed valid, since only coroners, medical examiners, or

Table 11.1 NamUs Website Data Pages and Sample Content on Each (NamUs.gov, 2008; NamUs.gov, 2010)

Data Entry Pages		Explanation/Examples of Page Subfields (Abbreviations Explained Below)
Case information	UP	Coroner/ME case number; NCIC/ViCAP/NCMEC numbers[a]; date found; current disposition/location of remains[a]; local contact; case manager; list of excluded MPs
	MP	Name (including nicknames/aliases); DOB[a]; NCIC/ViCAP/NCMEC numbers[a]; date last seen; age last seen; current age; race; ethnicity; sex; height; weight; blood type[a]
Demographics	UP	Age range; race; ethnicity; sex; weight; height range; condition (recognizable, skeletal, etc.); estimated PMI; inventory (complete, partial, etc.)
	MP	N/A—This page is not included in the missing persons database (such information is on the "Case Information" page in the MP database)
Circumstances	UP	Location discovered (GPS, address, city, county, state); autopsy facility (if not same county)[a]; cause/manner of death[a]; public circumstances; nonpublic circumstances[a]
	MP	Location from where missing (address[a], city, county, state); public circumstances (last seen leaving work, etc.); nonpublic circumstances[a]; financial transactions[a]
Physical/medical	UP	Hair color and description (including facial/body hair); eye color; distinctive features (scars/marks, tattoos, piercings, amputations, medical implants, prior surgery, etc.)
	MP	Hair color and description (including facial/body hair); eye color; distinctive features (scars/marks, tattoos, prior surgery[a], medications[a], drugs of abuse[a], illnesses[a], etc.)
Clothing and accessories	UP	Clothing on body; clothing found with body; footwear; jewelry; eyewear; other potentially associated items
	MP	Clothing last seen wearing; footwear; jewelry; eyewear; other potentially associated items
Dental	UP	Status of availability of records (not available, charted in NamUs, etc.); availability of radiographs[a]; treatments[a] (dentures, restorations, braces, root canals, etc.); coding[a]
	MP	Status of availability of records (not available, charted in NamUs, etc.); availability of radiographs[a]; treatments[a]; coding[a]; dentist information[a]
DNA	UP	Sample(s) status (not available, submitted but testing not complete, complete, etc.); type (mtDNA, nucDNA, Y-STR)[a]; laboratory[a]; lab reference number[a]
	MP	Sample(s) status (not available, complete, etc.); sample relationship (mother, brother, etc.)[a]; type (mtDNA, nucDNA, Y-STR)[a]; laboratory[a]; lab reference number[a]
Fingerprints	UP	Status of availability of records (not available, coded in NamUs, etc.); fingerprint coding[a]
	MP	Status of availability of records (not available, coded in NamUs, etc.); fingerprint coding[a]
Images	UP	Uploaded as jpg files and designated as publicly viewable or not; images can be captioned and categorized (print card, dental radiograph, tattoo, clothing, etc.)
	MP	Uploaded as jpg files and designated as publicly viewable or not; images can be captioned and categorized (print card, dental radiograph, tattoo, clothing, etc.)
Documents	UP	Other file types can be uploaded (pdf, docx, etc.) and designated as publicly viewable or not; documents can be titled and categorized (skeletal findings, dental chart, etc.)
	MP	Other file types can be uploaded (pdf, docx, etc.) and designated as publicly viewable or not; documents can be titled and categorized (skeletal findings, dental chart, etc.)
Investigating agency	UP	Name(s), jurisdiction(s), and contact for investigators; law enforcement circumstances (details not intended for public) (this page is not visible to the public in the UP database)
	MP	Name(s), jurisdiction(s), and contact information for personnel involved in investigation; law enforcement circumstances (details not intended for public)[a]
Exclusions	UP	Missing persons excluded as the UP; reason for exclusion, date exclusion was made; NamUs MP number (if MP is in NamUs) (this page is not visible to the public)
	MP	Unknown persons excluded as being the missing person; reason for exclusion; date exclusion was made; NamUs UP number (this page is not visible to the public)
Possible matches	UP	List of same-state system-suggested MP matches; means to alter search for other possibilities (other state, DNA status, etc.) (this page is not visible to the public)
	MP	List of same-state system-suggested UP matches; means to alter search for other possibilities (other state, DNA status, etc.) (this page is not visible to the public)
Reports	UP	Case report (HTML case profile, minus nonpublic items); case report without exclusions[a]; case chronology report (HTML of all NamUs profile activity)[a]; case activities log report[a]
	MP	Case report (HTML case profile, minus nonpublic items); case chronology report (HTML of all NamUs profile activity)[a]; case activities log report[a]; printable pdf MP poster
Contacts	UP	Local contact (coroner/ME); case manager(s); regional system administrator (NamUs personnel)
	MP	Local contact[a]; case manager(s); regional system administrator (NamUs personnel)
Electronic communications	UP	N/A—This page is not included in the unidentified persons database
	MP	Cell phone activity; pager information; internet access history (social media sites, etc.) (this page is not visible to the public)
Transportation methods	UP	N/A—This page is not included in the unidentified persons database
	MP	Make, model, year, color of any associated vehicle; VIN[a]; information on license plate/tag; relevant airline and/or bus information
Secondary parties	UP	N/A—This page is not included in the unidentified persons database
	MP	Name, relationship, address, phone number of any associated party (whether potentially involved in disappearance or otherwise) (this page is not visible to the public)

DOB, date of birth; *GPS*, global positioning system; *mtDNA*, mitochondrial DNA; *NCIC*, National Crime Information Center; *NCMEC*, National Center for Missing and Exploited Children; *nucDNA*, nuclear DNA; *PMI*, postmortem interval; *ViCAP*, Violent Criminal Apprehension Program; *VIN*, vehicle identification number; *Y-STR*, short tandem repeat on Y chromosome.
[a]Not visible to the public.

their registered designees can enter them. Publishing means that an RSA makes the case visible to other users of the system. However, as previously noted, not all information is available to all categories of NamUs users. For example, in NamUs-UP, the decedent's cause and manner of death are blocked from public view and any images the Case Manager or RSA deem unsuitable for the general public can be excluded from public users. In NamUs-MP, the medical conditions of missing persons are not viewable by the public due to the privacy imposed by the US Health Insurance Portability and Accountability Act of 1996 (HIPAA). Birthdates of missing persons are also withheld from public users to help prevent identity theft, and contact information for relatives is typically blocked from view to thwart unwanted solicitations from the media or others.

Data entry is accomplished using a combination of drop-down menus with preset options, radio buttons (only one option can be chosen), check boxes (multiple options can be chosen), and free-text fields. Some information is automatically provided for selection once another choice is made (e.g., when the state is chosen from a drop-down menu, the system automatically provides a drop-down listing of all counties in that state for selection). Each case profile includes an "Activities Log" in which all persons involved can contribute to an indelible and ongoing record of comments related to the case; each entry can be made publicly viewable or not. Users can choose to "Track" a case of interest; for example, a UP Case Manager may choose to track one or more missing persons cases, to be automatically notified whenever any addition or other change is made to those MP cases (e.g., when DNA testing is complete, when dental records have been uploaded, when any Activities Log entry is made, etc.). Users of either database can generate a variety of HTML and pdf reports on their or other cases, and missing persons flyers can be generated for NamUs-MP cases with the click of a button.

Computer algorithms interface the NamUs-UP and NamUs-MP databases and generate lists of system-suggested possible matches for each case. There are a limited number of automatic comparison parameters, which are sex, ancestry, and height for both UP and MP cases, as well as US state and date of body discovery for unknown persons cases, and US state and date where last seen for missing persons cases. However, any of these parameters can be manually adjusted or turned on/off and many other search criteria—both general and specific—can be easily added. Users can build and run their own independently designed searches to capture any data field or data option they choose, including free-text fields in which specific terminology may have been entered (e.g., tattoo designs, types/brands of clothing or jewelry, or other specifics). System users can save those searches and run them at any future time or share searches and their results with other NamUs users.

When a Case Manager has compared two NamUs profiles (a UP and MP) and is satisfied that they do not represent the same individual, the pair can be marked as an exclusion. An exclusion made in one database is automatically populated to the other (i.e., if a UP Case Manager excludes a missing person, that UP case will appear as an exclusion in the counterpart MP case profile and vice versa). Users must realize, though, that NamUs does not run its own automated searches and contact Case Managers with results. Interested parties must conduct their own searches and review each of the resulting system-suggested matches for its value as a possible association or exclusion. Too often, however, there are insufficient data to reach a firm conclusion and Case Managers or RSAs must seek out additional case information or biometrics for comparison. Especially in cold cases that are decades old, supplementary data are frequently unavailable, for example, in situations where antemortem dental radiographs were never obtained from a missing person's dentist who has long-since closed his practice or cases in which unidentified remains were cremated without retaining biological samples for DNA testing.

Additionally, cases involving missing persons whose families are unwilling to reach out to authorities or who have given up their search, and cases that law enforcement officials do not enter into the MP database, cannot be resolved by NamUs, even if their corresponding unidentified persons case is in the system. Likewise, until a decedent's remains are discovered (which can neither be controlled nor predicted) and—if not readily identified—have their case information put into the NamUs-UP database by a coroner, medical examiner, or their designee, any missing person in NamUs to which those remains belong will never be matched to that decedent by the system. It is only through a combination of awareness of missing and unknown persons cases, sufficient and accurate demographic and biometric data, quality data entry, and dedication to using NamUs that any two cases be associated within the system.

■ ADVANCED TOOLS, RESOURCES, AND CHALLENGES

Since its origin, the use of NamUs in case investigations has grown steadily (Figs. 11.2 and 11.3). Among the reasons for this growth are that NamUs provides system users with a variety of resources, including investigative assistance and forensic analyses. RSAs often serve as consultants and intermediaries between NamUs-UP and NamUs-MP Case Managers and can make the necessary contacts during attempts to obtain additional information or biometric data. They can facilitate document transfers between agencies or investigators, such as dental records, radiographs, and fingerprint cards. NamUs RSAs can also arrange for DNA collection and analysis (both nuclear and mitochondrial), for cases entered into either NamUs database conducted at the University of North Texas Center for Human Identification (UNTCHI). NamUs employs forensic odontologists, who will generate dental charting and/or make radiographic comparisons at no charge. Free forensic fingerprint comparisons are also available to NamUs users. Forensic anthropology services can be obtained through the UNTCHI Department of Forensic Anthropology.

In addition to these invaluable resources, NamUs can be used by Case Managers as a single repository in which to consolidate data, documents, images, and communications about a case and—perhaps most importantly—make that information available (on a selective basis) to other users of the system in their NamUs searches. Above and beyond all the free resources NamUs provides, it is the willingness of agencies to enter their cases and share their information that makes case resolution possible within the system. At present, the use of NamUs by law enforcement, state clearinghouses, and coroner/medical examiner offices is largely voluntary and some groups utilize the technology more than others. However, in June 2016, the State of New York became the first state to mandate the use of NamUs for the entry of unidentified decedents by its county coroners and medical examiners (USDOJ/OJP, 2016). Legislation such as this will undoubtedly enhance the number of unidentified persons cases into the system—at least in New York—but the New York statute does not address the missing persons side of the NamUs database. Nevertheless, growth of the system has been slow but sure.

Attesting to the increasing use of NamUs by missing persons investigators, Fig. 11.2 illustrates the cumulative number of NamUs-MP entries from 2009 to mid-2016, including columns for open (still missing) and resolved cases (whether found, or closed for some other reason). As of mid-2016 there were 11,789 unresolved MP cases in NamUs and 9952 former NamUs-MP cases that were resolved/closed; thus, of 21,741 total MP cases entered, 45.8% were resolved. When a case is closed, a Case Manager can designate whether NamUs aided with the case resolution (although this is optional), and at the time of this writing, just over 12% of resolved NamUs-MP cases were indicated as "NamUs-Aided" in their disposition (NamUs, 2016).

Fig. 11.3 depicts the accumulated UP cases from year 2009 to mid-2016, including columns for those who remain unknown and those in which the decedents have been identified (or removed from NamUs for some other reason, such as inadvertent case duplication). By mid-2016 there were 10,601 open UP cases in NamUs and 1995 identified/closed UP cases; therefore, of 12,596 total UP cases entered, 15.8% were closed. Though far fewer UP cases have been resolved, Case Managers have indicated that 33% (about one-third) of those were identified with assistance from NamUs (NamUs, 2016).

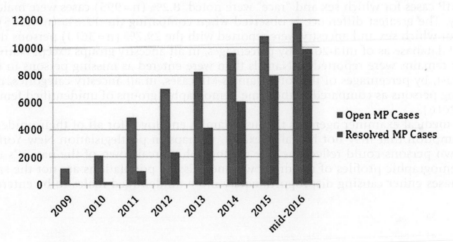

Figure 11.2 Cumulative number of NamUs missing persons (MP) cases by year.

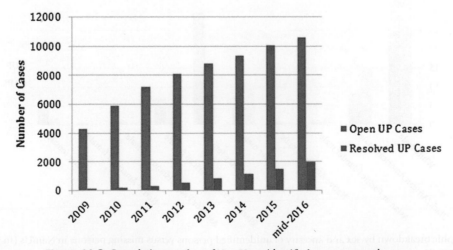

Figure 11.3 Cumulative number of NamUs unidentified persons cases by year.

By mid-2016 there were nearly twice as many total MP cases (n = 21,741) that had been entered into the NamUs system compared with UP cases (n = 12,596); and almost half of those MP cases had been resolved, while just over 15% of UP cases had been closed (NamUs, 2016). Some reasons for these differences are obvious: missing persons are an open and fluid population; individuals may voluntarily disappear, and—if still living—may eventually choose to reconnect with relatives and/or friends. When missing persons contact or return to their families, and the authorities are notified, their cases are closed. Further, each family typically has a single "case" to actively search and therefore, may be able to devote a great deal of time, effort, and resources in their attempts to locate a missing relative, which includes putting the case into the NamUs-MP database or requesting that law enforcement or a NamUs RSA do so on their behalf.

An unknowable fraction of all missing persons cases actually reflect individuals who have died; not all the dead are found, and not all of those discovered will receive a competent medicolegal investigation. Although unknown persons theoretically represent a closed/fixed population at any given time, unidentified cases cannot enter the NamUs-UP system until the remains of decedents are discovered; the physical remains of any given decedent who represents a missing person may never be found, leaving some MP cases open indefinitely. Likewise, unidentified remains that are discovered may reflect people for whom no one is searching; this is especially true of those who are homeless, transient, or those without a permanent address. Often, these are individuals who have few close relatives, or who are otherwise estranged from their families. Medicolegal offices also are typically not actively seeking out the remains of unidentified persons; they are simply dealing with those that come through their morgues. Some agencies have several—if not many—unidentified cases to handle at any given time and do their best to juggle them simultaneously, despite limited time and resources.

When NamUs cases are broken down by demographics, patterns emerge between the UP and MP databases (Fig. 11.4). Cases entered into NamUs through mid-2016 for which sex and ancestry (i.e., "race" in NamUs) were known or estimated reflect different demographic profiles. Of the 8623 total NamUs-UP cases for which both sex and "race" were designated, 50.7% (n = 4370) were reported as white males, while of the 12,147 NamUs-MP cases for which both sex and "race" were designated, 39.5% (n = 4792) were reported as white males. Of those same 8623 total NamUs-UP cases, 15.2% (n = 1308) were designated as black/African American males, while of the 12,147 total MP cases for which sex and "race" were noted, 8.2% (n = 995) cases were males of black/African American ancestry. The greatest difference is observed when comparing the 12.6% (n = 1085) white females in the UP database for which sex and ancestry were reported with the 29.7% (n = 3613) persons designated as white females in the MP database as of mid-2016. By percentages, in all ancestry groups except Native American, more unidentified male remains were reported to NamUs than were entered as missing persons in those same demographics. In contrast, by percentages of the total NamUs-MP cases, in all ancestry categories, more females were recorded as missing persons as compared to the same demographic groups of unidentified female remains in the system (NamUs, 2016).

If coroner and medical examiner agencies that use NamUs employ it for all of their unidentified cases without bias (an assumption that may not be valid, except, perhaps in postlegislation New York State), then this sample of unknown persons could reflect the true demographic breakdown of the nation's unidentified dead. Regardless, the demographic profiles of the unknown and missing populations are not the same. There appear to be reporting biases either causing disproportionately more unidentified males to be entered into NamUs as

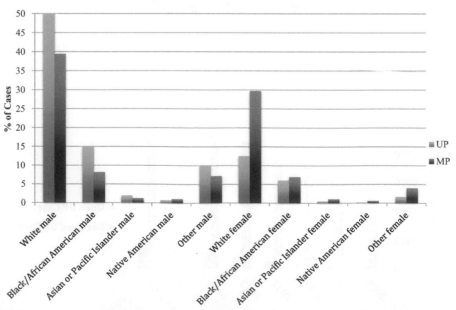

Figure 11.4 Demographic breakdown by sex and ancestry of unidentified persons versus missing persons in NamUs (in %). *UP*, unidentified persons; *MP*, missing persons.

compared with missing males in nearly all demographic categories, or a disproportionately higher number of missing females reported to the system than are entered into the UP database in all demographic groups. The disparate percentages between the two databases could reflect underlying sociological or criminological issues, including perhaps domestic violence and stalking (which may cause disproportionately more females to voluntarily disappear), perpetrator behavior (whether in abductions or homicides in which bodies are concealed or deliberate attempts made to thwart identification), reporting biases on the part of law enforcement or medicolegal authorities, and/or the willingness of family members of missing persons to come forward to authorities in some cases over others.

It should also be considered, however, that ancestry (i.e., "race" in NamUs) is "reported" by family members and others who describe missing persons, whereas in unknown persons cases it is "assessed" or "estimated" by coroners/medical examiners, pathologists, and/or their forensic anthropology consultants. [This is also the reason that of the 12,596 NamUs unknown persons cases as of mid-2016, only 8623 had been assigned both sex and "race" (NamUs, 2016), since it is strongly encouraged that agencies not assign demographics in NamUs case profiles if there are not confident indicators.] Assumptions regarding the sex and ancestry of unknown persons may increase in complexity and decrease in accuracy, depending on the body condition and the completeness of the remains. Three-fourths (n = 9139) of all unknown persons cases entered into NamUs since its inception (both open and resolved) in which a body condition was selected (n = 12,202) were designated as being unrecognizable for a variety of reasons (Fig. 11.5) (NamUs, 2016). Of those 9139 UP cases designated as unrecognizable, 52.1% (n = 4760) are cases in which the decedent was represented by a partial, complete, or near complete skeleton (NamUs, 2016). Thus, the discrepancies observed between the percentages of various demographic groups in the NamUs-UP and NamUs-MP databases could also reflect potential inherent inaccuracies in the methods used to assess sex and/or "race" from skeletal remains. The demographic discrepancies between the UP and MP databases may also illustrate why there have thus far been a limited number of matches between cases in the system.

Relevant to discussions of body condition, 25.1% of the unidentified persons who have been entered into the NamUs system with a designated body condition (n = 12,202) had a recognizable face (n = 3063) (NamUs, 2016). In fact, some UP cases seem to have virtually no reason they should remain unidentified except, perhaps, that no one is searching for them (at least not in the United States and/or not by using NamUs). One such case is NamUs UP 4790, a white female whose body was discovered on April 24, 1981, along the side of the road in Newton, Ohio, in Miami County. She was fully clothed and had been dead for only hours. Her age is estimated at between 18 and 26 years (using visual and dental clues), and she was 5 ft 6 in. tall and weighed 130 pounds. Her case was originally input to the NamUs-UP database as an NCIC data transfer (in December 2008), and in 2010, her NamUs record was enhanced (by coauthor Elizabeth Murray) using autopsy and police records. These included morgue photos that showed she had freckles and dark hair braided into two pigtails (Fig. 11.6A). In 2016, artists from NCMEC enhanced the morgue photo, and since then, their image has been used as the primary case profile photo for NamUs UP 4790 (Fig. 11.6B).

The autopsy report utilized to enhance the UP case profile indicated the victim's eyes were light brown, and it contained detailed descriptions of scars, birthmarks, and moles on her skin, as well as her injuries. Also uploaded to NamUs in 2010 were images of the unique clothing worn by the victim. At the time her body was found, the victim was wearing blue jeans (Wrangler brand, size 30L), a white bra (size 32D), and a patterned brown and orange pullover turtleneck sweater (size L) beneath a unique, fringed, tan leather poncho-type jacket (Fig. 11.7). Yet, despite

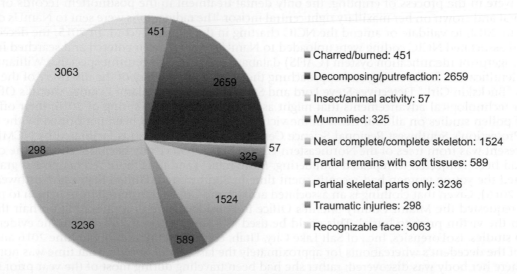

Charred/burned: 451
Decomposing/putrefaction: 2659
Insect/animal activity: 57
Mummified: 325
Near complete/complete skeleton: 1524
Partial remains with soft tissues: 589
Partial skeletal parts only: 3236
Traumatic injuries: 298
Recognizable face: 3063

Figure 11.5 NamUs UP cases by reported body condition. (In all categories above other than "Recognizable face" the phrase "Not recognizable" precedes the body condition designation in NamUs, i.e., "Not recognizable—Charred/burned," etc.)

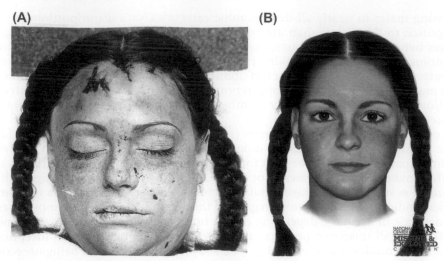

Figure 11.6 (A) Morgue photo of NamUs 4790. (B) National Center for Missing and Exploited Children reconstruction 2016.

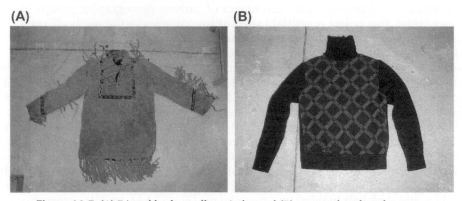

Figure 11.7 (A) Fringed leather pullover jacket and (B) patterned turtleneck sweater.

much of this information having been released to the media shortly after her discovery in 1981, her long-standing entry in NCIC, and a NamUs case profile available to the public since 2008, she had not been identified.

Regarding biometric data, the victim's DNA had been previously tested by the Miami Valley Regional Crime Lab in 2001, resulting in a nuclear DNA profile, and in 2009, soon after the case entry into NamUs, a full short tandem repeat (STR) and mitochondrial profile had been obtained by the DNA lab at the University of North Texas and was uploaded and searching at national CODIS. The victim's teeth had neither caries nor dental restorations and her third molars were in the process of erupting; the only dental treatment in the postmortem records or radiographs was a root canal and crown on her maxillary right central incisor. The radiographs were sent to NamUs odontologist, John Filippi, in 2012, to validate or amend the NCIC charting in the NamUs record. In 2015, the decedent's fingerprint card and associated NCIC coding were uploaded to NamUs and had been entered and searched in the Cogent Automated Fingerprint Identification System (CAFIS) database by NamUs fingerprint specialist William Bailey.

With no identification forthcoming and approaching the 35-year anniversary of the discovery of the victim often referred to as "Buckskin Girl," Detectives Steve Lord and Steve Hickey of the Miami County Sheriff's Office began to look to other technological advancements that might assist identification. In spring of 2016, their office obtained the results of pollen studies on all four items of the victim's clothing that had been performed by the US Customs and Border Protection's Southwest Regional Science Center in Houston, Texas (as facilitated by NCMEC). Most of the pollen present was from trees of the Northeastern United States, had clearly been on some of the clothing for a while, and had been subjected to repeated laundering. More intact (and thus more recent) pollen grains from the jacket indicated the young woman had recently spent time in Southwestern United States or Northwestern Mexico (Augenstein, 2016). Given that clothing is an associated artifact and can be transferred from person to person, coauthor Murray requested the Miami County Sheriff's Office to consider stable isotope testing on hair that had been retained from the victim prior to burial. This could be used as a comparison to the geographic evidence provided by the pollen studies. IsoForensics, Inc., of Salt Lake City, Utah, completed their testing in June 2016 and provided a chronology of the decedent's whereabouts for approximately the last year of her life. That time was not spent in the Ohio area where her body was discovered; rather she had been traveling during most of the year prior to her death, but on at least two different occasions for as long as 2 months or more, she had spent time in northern Texas and/or southern Oklahoma (Hollenhorst, 2016).

If so-called "Buckskin Girl" was fairly transient in at least the last year of her life and showed no evidence of residing for any length of time in the mid-Ohio region where her remains were discovered, it is not surprising that she was not identified back in 1981, particularly if press releases about the case did not reach far beyond the Midwest. The Automated Fingerprint Identification System (AFIS) was in its infancy, forensic DNA analysis was still on the horizon, and there was no internet. Despite all the advances in forensic science and technology to come—including NamUs—and all the information, images, and biometric evidence in her case and its database profile, UP 4790 remains unidentified as of this writing.

The "Buckskin Girl" case illustrates the frustrations typical when local authorities are responsible for identifying the remains of persons that clearly are not from the local area, and the unlikelihood that some such cases will ever be resolved, despite a wealth of data. When an unknown individual is missing from the same local area in which his or her remains are found, it is much more likely there will be a quick identification, particularly if there was already an existing missing persons investigation. As illustrated by the Paula Beverly Davis case that opened this chapter, many chronic missing and unidentified persons cases are probably the result of situations in which the locations from which persons go missing are far from the places where their remains are ultimately found. This can result from a perpetrator transporting a victim across numerous jurisdictional boundary lines, even in a single day as in the Davis case; but missing persons can also travel on their own accord, die, and wind up in a location far from where they went missing, which may have been the case with the "Buckskin Girl."

■ SUCCESS ACROSS NATIONAL BOUNDARIES

The PCOME in Tucson, Arizona, handles many cases involving non-US nationals who cross the southern US border and perish, typically in the Sonoran desert. In November 2012, three forensic anthropologists at the PCOME analyzed incomplete skeletal remains and associated clothing found a month earlier in a remote location in Arizona. There were no leads as to the identity, so a description of this unknown individual was entered into NamUs as UP 10822. The identification process nearly always involves someone—a forensic scientist, a law enforcement official, or next of kin—connecting several dots that will hopefully lead to a better understanding of at least some of the events that occurred between the time a person went missing and the time a decedent was found. However, in November 2012, no such dots had been connected for case UP 10822. The mother of a young man missing from Mexico would soon begin making those connections.

During the final week of December 2012, Carolina Chan Almeida, the mother of Mexican national Marco Antonio Chaparro Chan, was dutifully looking for her missing 19-year-old son, as she had been doing since the previous summer when she last saw him. The young man had clandestinely crossed the international border, entering the US somewhere in the Sonoran desert near the official US port of entry at Lukeville in southwest Arizona. A week earlier, at Christmas, Carolina had found the NamUs website and was utilizing the newly launched Spanish language version as she painfully looked at descriptions of decedent after decedent within the NamUs-UP database. When she finally happened upon case UP 10822, she recognized a pair of shoes from their written description as being the type Marco had been wearing when he left his home in Obregon, Sonora, in July 2012.

Through an Arizona friend, Carolina immediately contacted the NamUs RSA assigned to case UP 10822, who, in turn, contacted the PCOME. Marco's mother additionally sought assistance from the Tucson-based humanitarian organization *Derechos de Humanos*, which also contacted the PCOME. The exchange of antemortem and postmortem information had officially begun. The additional inquiries made by Marco's mother prompted the PCOME to augment the descriptions already published in NamUs and add photographs of the recovered personal effects, including the shoes and a pair of camouflage pants (Fig. 11.8), neither of which appeared to be overtly distinctive.

A few days later, University of Arizona doctoral student Robin Reineke, who was then heading the PCOME Missing Migrant Project, was on the telephone with Carolina collecting a physical description of her son and helping her navigate the pages in the NamUs case profile (today, Dr. Reineke heads the nonprofit organization, The Colibri Center for Human Rights, the de facto family assistance center for foreign national cases being investigated by the PCOME). After the pair looked at newly entered photographs of the shoes and other personal effects, Carolina gave Robin an additional piece of information that supported a circumstantial identification: Carolina was certain that the pants

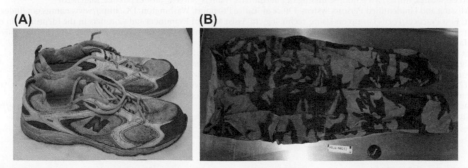

Figure 11.8 (A) Shoes worn by decedent UP 10822. (B) Camouflage pants worn by decedent UP 10822.

belonged to her son because she saw that the original location of the button on the waistband of the pants had been altered to accommodate a different size waist. That size difference was between Marco and his father, who was the original owner of the pants, and Carolina had been the one who moved the button.

Because clothing should never be the basis of a positive identification, the PCOME forensic anthropologists examined a comparison sheet of the physical description of the decedent and physical description of Marco that Robin had created as an identification hypothesis. Age, stature, ancestry, and dental condition were in general agreement, as were the estimated postmortem interval of several months and the recovery location north of Lukeville. Given the consistencies in both personal effects and physical description, a positive identification was sought through DNA testing. The PCOME and Carolina both made contact with the Tucson Office of the Mexican Consulate for assistance with the costs and logistics of DNA testing. Under contract with the Mexican Consulate, Bode Technologies (now Bode Cellmark) has developed DNA profiles for nearly 1000 currently unidentified suspected migrants from the PCOME and is the DNA lab of choice for comparisons to foreign national FRS profiles. Bode compared the STR profile derived from a bone sample from case UP 10822 with FRS STR profiles derived from buccal swabs taken from Carolina and her daughter. The results showed only a weak statistical relationship, due to a common STR profile between the postmortem profile and the FRS profiles, necessitating an additional DNA analysis from another blood relative. A few months later, Marco's father provided a sample. In December 2013, the sum of the DNA analyses confirmed NamUs case UP 10822 was Marco Antonio Chaparro Chan; the final dots between UP and MP had been connected.

The exchange between Marco's family and the governmental agencies charged with trying to identify him took nearly 1 year and would not have occurred if not for NamUs.

■ CONCLUSION

The opening and closing case studies included in this chapter attest to the power of the NamUs system. A relative or concerned friend of a missing person now has the opportunity, 24 h a day, to search through descriptions and photographs—in either Spanish or English—of unidentified decedents and their personal effects. By doing so, they may find a singular piece of information that can be used to marshal the strength to contact authorities and begin the process of antemortem and postmortem data exchange. NamUs is the publicly accessible tool that makes this possible in ways that were not available to families in the past. Those individuals who have the professional responsibility of finding missing persons and identifying unknown human remains have likened NamUs to a "one-stop shop" for missing and unidentified persons case management, as well as for information storage and data exchange. The system also allows ready comparison of records for potential case resolution and provides necessary resources and services. In order for missing and unidentified persons to be resolved with the use of NamUs, however, there needs to be more widespread use of the system by authorities. It is hoped that NamUs will become a commonplace tool in case management, which will allow the system to reach its full potential.

Acknowledgments

The authors would like to thank Todd Matthews, NamUs Director of Case Management and Communications, and Amy Dobbs, NamUs Regional System Administrator, for reviewing the draft manuscript. We gratefully acknowledge the assistance of the staff at Occupational Research and Assessment. Thanks are due to Robin Reineke of the Colibri Center for Human Rights and Ashley Rodriguez of NCMEC. We would also like to recognize the many individuals who work tirelessly to resolve missing and unknown persons cases, as well as the families waiting for answers.

References

Augenstein, S., 2016. http://www.forensicmag.com/article/2016/05/forensic-palynologist-tracks-near-invisible-national-security-cold-cases.

Fisher, M.S., 2010. Body Found in 1987 Near Dayton Identified. The Columbus Dispatch. http://www.dispatch.com/content/stories/national_world/2010/02/07/missing_mystery.ART_ART_02-07-10_A10_FCGH844.html#.

Hanzlick, R., Clark, S., Lothridge, K., November 2011. History of the national missing and unidentified persons system (NamUs). Acad. Forensic Pathol. 4, 310–321.

Hollenhorst, J., July 6, 2016. KSL Broadcasting Salt Lake City Utah. KSL.com. https://www.ksl.com/?sid=40545046&nid=148&title=utah-firm-makes-breakthrough-in-1981-ohio-murder-case.

NamUsgov, 2008. National Missing and Unidentified Persons System/NamUs Missing Persons Database. National Institute of Justice, Office of Justice Programs, U.S. Department of Justice. https://www.findthemissing.org/en.

NamUsgov, 2010. National Missing and Unidentified Persons System/NamUs Unidentified Persons Database. National Institute of Justice, Office of Justice Programs, U.S. Department of Justice. https://identifyus.org/en.

NamUs, 2011. NamUs Success Stories. https://www.findthemissing.org/documents/NamUs_Success_Stories.pdf Rev. March 2011.

NamUs, 2016. National Missing and Unidentified Persons System. Office of Justice Programs, Washington, DC. http://www.namus.gov/index.htm.

NCFS, 2009. Final Report: Best Practices/Focus Group on Using Technology to Assist Medical Examiners and Coroners in the Identification of Human Remains (i.e., NamUs/UDRS). Prepared by Katherine Sullivan NCFS Project/Technical Manager, National Center for Forensic Science (NCFS) The University of Central Florida (UCF), Orlando, Florida. https://identifyus.org/help/Best_Practices.pdf.

Pettem, S., July 27, 2012. Cold Case Research Resources for Unidentified, Missing, and Cold Homicide Cases, first ed. CRC Press. 2012.

Ritter, N., 2007. Missing persons and unidentified remains: the Nation's Silent Mass Disaster. NIJ J. (256). (Office of Justice Programs) https://www.findthemissing.org/documents/Missing_Persons_and_Unidentified_Remains_Nations_Silent_Mass_Disaster.pdf.

USDOJ/OJP, September 12, 2007. US Department of Justice, Office of Justice Programs, News Center (2007) Regina B. Schofield, Assistant Attorney General. Missing and Unidentified Persons National Press Club Event, Washington, DC. http://ojp.gov/newsroom/speeches/2007/07_0912schofield.htm.

USDOJ/OJP, 2016. US Department of Justice, Office of Justice Programs Identifying Missing Persons Through Legislation (2016). http://www.nij.gov/topics/law-enforcement/investigations/missing-persons/Pages/identifying-missing-persons-through-legislation.aspx.

ADVANCES IN MOLECULAR AND MICROSCOPIC METHODS OF IDENTIFICATION

CHAPTER **12**

The Utilization of Databases for the Identification of Human Remains

Anne E. Osborn-Gustavson[1] | Timothy McMahon[1] | Melody Josserand[2] | B.J. Spamer[3]

[1]Armed Forces Medical Examiner System, Dover Air Force Base, DE, United States
[2]University of North Texas Health Science Center, Fort Worth, TX, United States
[3]National Missing & Unidentified Persons System (NamUs), Washington, DC, United States

Chapter Outline

■ INTRODUCTION

The development of modern forensic DNA analyses arose due to six main scientific advancements over the last 156 years. These advancements include defining nuclear DNA as the genetic material (Watson and Crick, 1953); the identification of mitochondrial DNA (Nass and Nass, 1963); the ability to sequence DNA (Maxam and Gilbert, 1977; Sanger et al., 1977); the identification of short tandem-repetitive regions and hypervariable regions in human DNA (Jeffreys et al., 1985a,b); the ability to amplify DNA (Mullis and Faloona, 1987); and the publication of a full human mitochondrial genome sequence (Anderson et al., 1981). These advancements paved the way for the need to develop DNA databases for use in the identification of human remains as well as perpetrators of crimes.

Deoxyribonucleic acid (DNA) was first described in the late 1860s by Friedrich Miescher. While Miescher was studying various types of proteins that made up human leukocytes, he discovered a material that precipitated in acid and dissolved with the addition of alkali. Miescher believed that based on the histochemical properties the precipitate had to have come from the nuclei, and thus called this compound "nuclein" (Miescher, 1869; Dahm, 2005). Through additional experiments, Miescher was able to show that the substance was not a protein, but was made up largely of phosphorous, carbon, hydrogen, and nitrogen. Moreover, he determined that the substance was not a random mixture of chemicals, but rather a mixture of closely related chemicals (Miescher, 1869; Dahm, 2005). It was Miescher's work with leukocytes and salmon sperm that set the stage for extended research into the material known as nuclein.

Between 1885 and 1901, Albrecht Kossel worked to explain the chemical structure of "nucleic acid" (nuclein from acid precipitation) and was able to identify building blocks that had a special concentration of nitrogen. His research defined the five integral components of DNA and RNA, known now as adenine, guanine, cytosine, thymine, and uracil. He also discovered that yeast nucleic acid contained a pentose sugar (Magner, 1994). In 1901, Kossel won the Noble Prize in physiology and medicine for his research into the chemical composition of the cell nucleus (www.nobleprize.org). However, it was not until 1909 that Phoebus Levene correctly identified the pentose sugar in yeast nucleic acid as ribose, which redefined it as ribonucleic acid (RNA). It took Levene and his colleagues until 1929 to identify the pentose sugar in thymonucleic acid as 2-deoxribose and was thus redefined as DNA (Levene and London, 1929).

As early as 1928, it was hypothesized that DNA was the carrier of genetic information. At this time, Frederick Giffith showed that mice coinjected with heat-killed virulent (smooth coat) and nonvirulent (rough coat) pneumococci died. Moreover, he discovered that the infected mice contained living virulent pneumococci and postulated that some transforming material allowed this to occur. Avery, Macleod, and McCarty, in 1944, published that the active transforming material was DNA. This publication led to two and a half decades of explosive research into the structure and function of DNA. There are several notable publications during this time, one of which includes Chargaff's rule. This rule led to the conclusion that DNA has a 1:1 ratio of pyrimidines and purine bases (Chargaff et al., 1952). Hershey and Chase published their radiolabeled bacteriophage experiment in 1952, which conclusively demonstrated that DNA was a genetic material (Hershey and Chase, 1952). In 1953, Watson and Crick published the structure of DNA, which was only possible with the use of the existing data published by Chargaff and the X-ray diffraction data compiled by Rosalind Franklin. Nuclear DNA had been researched for over a century before mitochondrial DNA (mtDNA) was even described in 1963. It was at this time that Nass published electron micrograph images of DNA from chicken liver mitochondria (Nass and Nass, 1963) and Schatz isolated mtDNA from yeast (Schatz, 1963).

Once nuclear and mitochondrial DNA were defined the ensuing two decades saw the development of many new DNA testing methods that would lead to modern DNA forensic testing methods. Most notably was the publication by Smith and colleagues, who showed that double-stranded breaks could be introduced into human DNA by incubating it with purified restriction endonucleases that cut at specific sites (Smith and Wilcox, 1970; Kelly and Smith, 1970). Digestion of DNA with multiple restriction endonucleases allowed scientist to identify polymorphic regions within DNA and allowed for linkage maps as well as inheritance patterns to be determined. Coupled with this was the development of the Southern hybridization technique, which involves the separation of DNA strands, the transfer of it to a nylon membrane, and the visualization of specific targets by the hybridization of a complimentary probe to the membrane (Southern, 1975). The utilization of restriction enzymes and the Southern hybridization technique allowed scientists to study nuclear and mitochondrial DNA in more detail but only at a macro level, in that the inheritance and genetic diversity of mtDNA could be explored. As a cytoplasmic DNA molecule, it was assumed that the inheritance pattern of mtDNA was not governed by typical Mendelian genetics. The inheritance of human mtDNA was established by Giles and colleagues (Giles et al., 1980), by utilizing the research of Hutchison et al. (1974) and Brown (1980). Hutchinson, using restriction mapping demonstrated that mtDNA is maternally inherited in mammals, while Brown was able to identify restriction polymorphisms in human mtDNA molecules from racially and geographically diverse individuals. Combining restriction digestion and Southern analysis of human mtDNA from three generations of maternal and paternal family members, Giles established that mtDNA is only maternally inherited.

The use of restriction fragments to probe for DNA targets and restriction polymorphisms were essential developments for modern DNA forensics, but it was the ability to determine the individual base sequences of specific DNA molecules that allowed for the identification of repetitive sequence elements (Sanger et al., 1977; Maxam and Gilbert, 1977). Allan Maxam published the Maxam and Gilbert chemical method for sequencing DNA (Maxam and Gilbert, 1977), and Fredrick Sanger published the Sanger chain-terminating methods (Sanger et al., 1977). The Maxam and Gilbert sequencing method relies on terminally labeling DNA with a radioactive ATP, typically gamma-^{32}P ATP, followed by a chemical treatment which is broken up into four distinct and separate reactions. The chemical treatments applied cleave DNA at one or two of the four nucleotides, either guanine (G), adenine and guanine (A+G), cytosine (C), or cytosine and thymine (C+T). To determine the purine bases, the G and A+G reactions are chemically treated such that the conditions promote the release of the guanine bases. The A+G reactions are further treated to also allow the release of adenine molecules. Similar principles are applied to the C and C+T reactions. This process creates a series of radiolabeled DNA fragments that range in size, as determined, where the cleavage site occurred. The four reactions are then run in parallel on a gel. After exposure to X-ray film, the fragments appear as series of bands, the analysis of which can be used to ascertain the DNA sequences when read from bottom to top (Fig. 12.1). Conversely, the Sanger sequencing method or dye-terminating method is an enzyme-based sequencing method that relies on the use of a combination of dNTPs and radiolabeled ddNTPs. The ddNTPs are missing the 3′OH group, which after incorporation into the growing DNA strand terminates the ability to add additional dNTPs. Four independent reactions are set up where the same single-stranded DNA template is added to all four tubes, each tube contains a different radiolabeled ddNTP. The samples are run in parallel on a gel, and the pattern of bands allows for the DNA sequence to be read from the bottom of the gel to the top. Due to its simplicity and ease of use, the Sanger sequencing method has become the gold standard for sequencing of unknown DNA and has evolved into a single-tube reaction due to the ability to label ddNTPs with a different color fluorophore. Utilizing Sanger sequencing in 1981, Anderson et al. published the "Sequence and organization of the human mitochondrial genome". This sequence is known as the Cambridge Reference Sequence (CRS). The CRS was revised in 1999 to include 18 corrected or confirmed nucleotides and is referred to as the Revised Cambridge Reference Sequence (rCRS) (Andrews et al., 1999). The rCRS is the consensus sequence currently used for mtDNA forensic testing.

For nuclear DNA to be considered for use in forensics and identity testing, probes specific to hypervariable regions that were multiallelic and had a high degree of heterozygosity would be needed. In 1980, Wyman and White defined the first minisatellite, restriction fragment length polymorphism (RFLP), or tandem repetitive DNA sequence, that was not associated with a gene (Wyman and White, 1980). Over the next few years, many more repetitive DNA sequences were identified. However, for the first time, in July 1985, Jeffreys et al. published that these repetitive DNA elements were somatically stable and could be used as a DNA fingerprint to identify individuals as well as establish paternity (Jeffreys et al., 1985a). Later that year, Gill and his partners published on the "forensic application of DNA fingerprints" (Gill et al., 1985). In 1987, not long after this, Tommy Lee Andrews became the first man in the United States

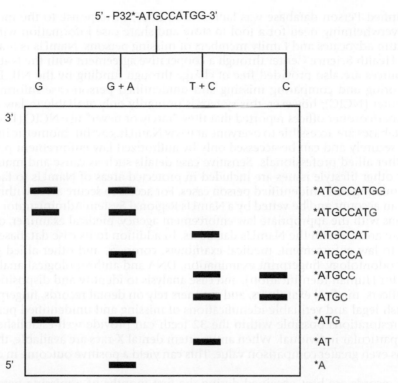

Figure 12.1 An example of Maxam and Gilbert sequencing. Cleaved and labeled DNA fragments are run in parallel on a gel. The sequence can be determined by reading the X-rayed gel from bottom to top.

to be convicted as a result of accepted DNA evidence. Although RFLPs became the first accepted forensic DNA testing method in the United States, it had several drawbacks such as it required restriction enzymes to cut the DNA and a large amount of DNA was needed to accomplish testing. This posed problematic considering many DNA samples from crime scenes are degraded and of low quantity.

The publication of a polymerase-catalyzed chain reaction (PCR) by Kerry Mullis in 1987 described a method that allowed scientists to make billions of DNA fragments, 1000–2000 base pairs in size, (Mullis and Faloona, 1987) in vitro using a DNA polymerase enzyme. Unfortunately, this method had one drawback, RFLP fragments used at this time were larger than could be amplified utilizing the PCR method. However, this drawback was resolved in 1991, when Thomas Caskey and Albert Edwards filed for a patent. They described short tandem repeat (STR) sequences between two and seven base pairs. Caskey and Edwards developed the first STR kit, which contained oligonucleotide primer pairs that flanked the regions of the defined repetitive sequences of interest. These STRs could be multiplexed and separated by size. Moreover, they are unique enough to generate good statistical relevance (Application number EP20050020832). These two advances marshalled in the age of modern DNA forensics.

In 1991, the US Government began utilizing mtDNA sequencing to assist with the identification of US service member remains from the Vietnam War and STR testing of causalities from the first Gulf War. The success of using DNA testing methods to assist with the identification of human remains prompted the US Government to establish a DNA specimen repository for all active duty and reserve military as well as a family reference database to assist with identification of service members from World War II, Korea, and Vietnam. Due to the success of RFLPs and the development of faster PCR-based STR assays, the FBI started a pilot program that consisted of 14 laboratories and the CODIS software to assist with storing DNA references and matching DNA crime samples to these references (Niezgoda, 1998). By 1997, over 47 states had passed a legislation that all convicted individuals had to submit a DNA sample for databasing purposes, and CODIS had been installed in over 80 laboratories to assist with criminal DNA forensics.

The strength of databases is measured by their ability to identify a missing individual or the perpetrator of a crime. The different types of databases that arose out of the definition of DNA and development of the novel assays discussed above will be described in this chapter. The processing of reference samples for the generation of databases can be accomplished through the utilization of blood or buccal samples collected on a variety of sample types and then processed either manually or through the utilization of robotic platforms and expert analysis systems. However, discussions on what a laboratory should consider when building a DNA database will not be discussed in this chapter.

■ THE USE OF NONGENETIC DATABASES FOR IDENTIFICATION

The National Missing and Unidentified Persons System (NamUs) is a national resource center and central repository for information related to missing persons, unidentified decedents, and unclaimed persons (individuals who have been identified by name, but next of kin has not been located to make death notification and dispose the remains). The Unidentified Person database was launched in 2007, in response to the medicolegal death investigation community's overwhelming need for a tool to store and share case information with other criminal justice agencies, as well as victim advocates and family members of missing persons. NamUs is managed by the University of North Texas (UNT) Health Science Center through a cooperative agreement with the National Institute of Justice (NIJ). All NamUs resources are also provided free of charge through funding by the NIJ. Before NamUs, the only national system for storing and comparing missing and unidentified person case information was the National Crime Information Center (NCIC); however, this system is primarily only available to law enforcement. Moreover, 80% of medical examiner/coroner offices reported that they "rarely or never" use NCIC (Hickman et al., 2004).

The NamUs case databases are accessible to everyone at www.NamUs.gov, but biometric information and sensitive case details are stored securely and can be accessed only by authorized law enforcement personnel, medical examiners, coroners, and other allied professionals. Sensitive case details such as cause and manner of death, substance abuse, prostitution, or other lifestyle issues are included in protected areas of NamUs to facilitate more productive comparisons between missing and unidentified person cases. For access to secure areas within the NamUs databases, users must register for an account and be vetted by a NamUs Regional System Administrator (RSA). NamUs RSAs vet all new user registrations with the appropriate law enforcement agency, medical examiner, or coroner office prior to granting access to secure areas within the NamUs databases. In addition to its case databases, NamUs also provides the following services to law enforcement, medical examiners, coroners, and other allied professionals across the United States: forensic odontology, fingerprint examination, DNA and anthropological analyses (through an affiliation with UNT Center for Human Identification), and case analysis to identify and disposition tips and leads.

Law enforcement officers, medical examiners, and coroners rely on dental records, fingerprints, and DNA, among other things, to establish legal and verifiable identifications of missing and unidentified persons. The human tooth and the multitude of restorations possible within the 32 teeth can provide well-established postmortem forensic odontology data for a particular individual. When antimortem dental X-rays are available, the accuracy of the forensic odontology data has even greater comparison value. This can yield a positive outcome in one day if dental records are available.

Antimortem dental records are best obtained during the first months of a missing person investigation. Many investigators delay in obtaining dental records until a body is found and a positive identification is needed; however, records may be destroyed or lost if not obtained quickly. A complete dental record for a missing person should include all written treatment records, all dental radiographs, all dental photographs, dental models of teeth, and referrals to specialists who may have additional dental records. Investigators who require dental records for a missing person may use the standard NCIC medical/dental release form. However, NamUs also uses a dental record request form that will indicate what a dental office should release to provide the most comprehensive dental record. Utilizing NamUs and its in-house forensic odontologists, dental information can be coded and uploaded to the secure databases and professionally compared around the clock.

Fingerprints are a reliable means of comparison between missing and unidentified persons. When readily available, fingerprints can provide a rapid positive identification or exclusion of potentially matching cases. Fingerprint cards submitted to NamUs are uploaded to a secure area within the NamUs case file and are then entered into the NamUs Cogent Automated Fingerprint Identification System (CAFIS) for continual, proactive comparison against other NamUs cases. For best results, all fingerprint images submitted to NamUs should be scanned at 500 dots per inch or photographed in a 1:1 scale. Ten-print cards will produce the most effective search results; however, all fingerprint images of sufficient resolution will be proactively stored and compared in the NamUs CAFIS database.

The NamUs CAFIS system, implemented in 2014, is the only system which proactively compares missing and unidentified person fingerprints against one another. In the first months of its implementation, the NamUs CAFIS database produced its first cold hit between a man missing since 1992 and an unidentified decedent found in the same year, approximately 200 miles from the location where the young man had gone missing. While both of these cases occurred in the same state, and there were fingerprint cards available for both the missing and the unidentified case, neither fingerprint card had ever been searched through a state or federal fingerprint database. Other systems, including AFIS, allow for local storage or one-time searching of missing and unidentified fingerprints, but typically do not serve as a permanent repository for this type of biometric record unless an agency requests the fingerprint record be stored in the Unsolved Latent section of a local, state, or federal AFIS database.

The NamUs Analytical Unit conducts complex case analysis and searching to develop potential matches and other leads in missing and unidentified person cases. In the case of unidentified decedents, NamUs analysts have assisted in the resolution of cases by locating matches to unidentified decedents through NCIC offline searches, including searches of canceled NCIC records; locating matches between missing and unidentified person entries in NamUs based on comparisons of physical descriptors, geography, or circumstantial information; and locating family members for DNA collections and/or next of kin death notifications.

The NamUs Unidentified Person database is the most comprehensive and complete database of unidentified decedents in the country. There are currently almost 11,000 active unidentified decedent cases entered into NamUs, and over 2100 unidentified decedent cases in NamUs have been resolved since 2007. Vetted criminal justice users of the system can search literally every field in the NamUs database to locate correlations between cases. In addition to the ability to manually search the NamUs databases, the system will automatically perform comparisons based on a subset of metadata, which includes age, sex, race, height, geographic location, and date missing or located deceased.

The NamUs "Possible Match" screen will list these potentially matching cases for further review and allows for cases to be marked as "exclusions" for a permanent record of all comparisons that have taken place.

Associations between missing and unidentified person cases are often made through unique physical characteristics, such as medical implants, tattoos, prior surgeries, skeletal fractures, or other unique skeletal features such as scoliosis. Potential associations have also been made between missing and unidentified persons based on anecdotal or circumstantial case information, including items as seemingly insignificant as an article of clothing or jewelry. In one case, the fact that a missing case and unidentified person case both had a duffel bag noted in the NamUs file prompted a tip which eventually led to a positive identification of the decedent.

After a regional training event, the NamUs Analytical Unit was asked to assist with a long-term unidentified decedent case that involved a young man who died in an automobile accident. In the young man's personal affects, a handwritten identification card was found; however, all investigative efforts to locate a missing male matching that name and the young man's description met with negative results. Operating under the theory that the young man may have been a runaway, a NamUs analyst obtained a list of all canceled NCIC missing person entries matching the young man's description, on the chance that a prior runaway incident might be located. Analyzing the list of approximately 15,000 results, the analyst located three young men with a name similar to the name on the identification card. One of those cases involved a young man with a tattoo in a similar location to the decedent being investigated. Based on information found in the missing person report for that young man, the NamUs analyst located current contact information for family. Investigators made contact with a family member who made a visual identification of the decedent, followed by a positive identification via DNA comparison.

■ THE USE OF CUSTOM DNA DATABASES FOR IDENTIFICATION: LABORATORY INFORMATION SYSTEMS APPLICATIONS

The Armed Forces Medical Examiner System's Armed Forces DNA Identification Laboratory (AFDIL) is charged under Title 10 USC with the identification of American service members lost in both current and past conflicts. Current active duty military personnel and reservists are required to submit a DNA blood specimen card to the Armed Forces Repository of Specimen Samples for the Identification of Remains (AFRSSIR), to hopefully never be needed. However, in the event of a current day loss, the stored DNA specimen card under chain of custody is given to the AFDIL for processing and comparison to an unknown specimen. The practice of collecting DNA references before a loss occurs was put in place in the early 1990s when the move to utilize DNA as a method of identification was made.

Due to DNA forensics not being option prior to 1987, AFRSSIR cannot be utilized in the identifications of the 82,600 service members missing from past conflicts, such as World War II, Southeast Asia, Korea, and Cold Wars. Instead, references must be collected from located family members of the missing. These family reference samples, or FRSs, are processed and used to build a database—not a small undertaking.

Past accounting of missing service members began in the early 1990s when remains were repatriated from Southeast Asia. Due to the limitations of the available forensic technologies at this time, only mitochondrial DNA (mtDNA) testing was successfully performed on bone specimens taken from the osseous material thought to be associated with missing service members. Although mtDNA is not unique to an individual, it does have certain advantages when considering the condition of the skeletal samples received, as well as the needs of building a reference database. First, the portion of the mitochondrial genome, called the control region, which is being sequenced for identification purposes, has evolved rapidly over time. The hypervariable regions within the control region have an increased rate of mutation as compared to the nuclear genome. Moreover, this area is a noncoding region in that it contains no genes, which is favorable as no ethical issues should arise from the analysis performed. Second, each cell contains hundreds to thousands of copies of the mitochondrial genome whereas each cell contains only one copy of the nuclear genome, which is comprised of two copies of each chromosome, one of each pair inherited from each parent. These additional copies increase the likelihood of recovering mtDNA from a skeletal specimen, especially when quantities of DNA are limited or degraded due to environmental conditions, such as exposure to acidic soil as is found in Vietnam. Lastly, mtDNA is maternally inherited; it is passed from mother to child. Thus, anyone sharing a consanguineous maternal relationship with a missing service member could be used as mtDNA reference (Hutchison et al., 1974; Saccone et al., 2000). This greatly increases the pool of potential donors as sometimes it is necessary to seek out second and third cousins or even maternal great-grandnieces to find viable references (Fig. 12 2).

Although at one time the AFDIL was only able to successfully target mtDNA in skeletal specimens, with advances in technology, this is no longer the case. Chromosomal DNA found within the nucleus of the cell can now be targeted. Everyone receives a unique combination of chromosomes from their parents, one pair of them from their mother and the other pair from their father. Areas of these chromosomes contain STRs, which can be analyzed. Autosomal chromosomes are all of the 22 pairs of chromosomes except the two sex-determining chromosomes, X and Y. STRs located on these chromosomes are called auSTRs and can easily be compared to a missing service member's parents, children, or siblings. Advanced statistical software can be used to calculate relationship likelihoods from family members with more distant relationships who might not otherwise be suitable donors, such as aunts, uncles, nieces, and nephews. STRs located on the Y chromosome, called Y-STRs can also be used for identification.

Only males have a Y chromosome, and as such they are paternally inherited, passed from father to son. Thus, any male sharing a paternal relationship with a missing service member could be used as a Y-STR reference, which opens up another large pool of potential donors (Gusmão et al., 1999; Jobling and Tyler-Smith, 2003).

Service Casualty Officers (SCOs) from each military branch are responsible for identifying and locating potential family members who can be used as DNA references. To accomplish this enormous and ongoing task, the SCOs utilize genealogists to research family lines and attempt to find potential donors to collect from. The United States has made every attempt to provide fallen service members' families with the fullest possible accounting. When the DNA began to support the past accounting mission, family members were asked to provide a blood sample, which was drawn by a medical professional, which usually required a donor to go to a special facility. Once received by the AFDIL, the vial of blood was spotted and preserved on a Whatman Filter paper bloodstain card, much like the samples stored by AFRSSIR for our current active duty military members. However, this too has changed over time. Instead, oral swabs are used for sample collection, which is a far easier and virtually painless process. By using oral swabs instead of a blood sample, donors are able to self-collect using a collection kit that is sent to their home. The donor can then directly send the oral swabs, usually taken in triplicate, to the AFDIL for DNA processing.

Once the swabs are received at the laboratory, they are assigned a unique FRS case number. Each FRS is then sorted by the FRS databasing team into groups based on what testing is needed. For example, if the donor is a biological full brother of the missing service member, then the FRS case will be placed in a group that will be processed concurrently with mtDNA, Y-STRs, and auSTRs testing. Currently, the AFDIL has the flexibility to process anywhere from one FRS case manually to up to ninety FRS cases in one group using a combination of manual and automated methods. This is due in large part not only to the instrumentation used for processing, but also due to the Laboratory Information Systems Applications (LISA), an in-house developed laboratory information management system (LIMS), that allows AFDIL to electronically manage a DNA sample from receipt to report.

The LISA was custom designed and developed by Future Technologies, Inc. (FTI) specifically for the unique needs of the AFDIL. LISA is an integrated sample management system which is used at all times during the processing of specimens, from receipt to profile comparisons. All specimens received, regardless of whether it is an FRS or a sample, which is believed to be the remains of a missing service member (also referred to as an unknown specimen), are

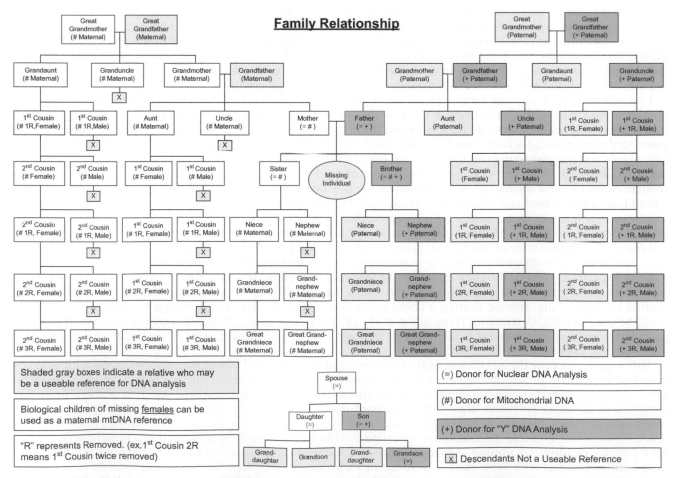

Figure 12.2 The family tree guide that was developed and is used by the AFDIL to determine the viability of a prospective FRS donor.

accessioned in LISA and assigned the appropriate case type and number. Once logged into LISA, the case can then be tracked as it goes through laboratory processing.

For example, after an FRS is received and the databasing team has grouped it according to what testing is required, the FRS, along with the group it is in, is placed on a worklist in LISA for laboratory processing. This worklist can then be tracked in LISA through all stages of processing. Furthermore, LISA is also able to automatically generate all laboratory work forms required for processing. This not only greatly increases efficiency but also eliminates the possibility of human transcriptional errors, which could be made when using worksheets filled in by hand. Through continual support from FTI, LISA has evolved with the AFDIL to meet the changing needs of the laboratory when new processes and technologies are brought online for casework use.

Case tracking and processing is just one subsystem of the AFDIL's LISA, it also has the ability to store all of the profiles (mtDNA, Y-STR, and auSTR, as applicable) generated for a specimen, as well as perform searches, comparisons, and statistical calculations. When a sample is first accessioned into LISA and given a case number, it is also assigned to a specific conflict, such as World War II, Southeast Asia, or Korea. All of the FRSs received are also linked to their associated missing service member when they are received. This becomes important because once the data have been uploaded into LISA, all unknown specimens need to be searched against all of the FRSs associated with their specific conflict, or against the CPD. If after a comparison is performed and reference and unknown are found to be consistent, then LISA can also be utilized to perform statistical calculations to determine the significance of the match.

■ THE USE OF DNA DATABASES FOR IDENTIFICATION: CODIS

One software package used by many laboratories to organize and compare DNA profiles is the Combined DNA Index System (CODIS) (www.fbi.gov). This database software is used by over 190 public crime laboratories in the United States and in over 50 countries worldwide. In the United States, crime labs using the CODIS system are interconnected. However, no international country has connectivity to the US network. The Federal Bureau of Investigation is authorized by law (DNA Identification Act of 1994) to manage the CODIS system and distribute the CODIS software to assist law enforcement agencies.

DNA profiles from different types of biological specimens are entered into separate compartments (indexes) in the CODIS software. These indexes are described in Table 12.1. By law, no personally identifying information (name, date of birth, social security number, etc.) for any specimen is stored in the CODIS database. This ensures the privacy of the relatives voluntarily donating samples to the database as well as the privacy of any person whose sample may be housed in CODIS. The DNA profiles in each index are then compared to profiles contained within the other indexes in an attempt to identify direct matches or potential relationships (genetic associations indicated not by exact profile matches, but by shared genetic data). Searches that attempt to identify potential family relationships are only performed for missing persons and unidentified remains casework samples. This is very different than criminal familial searching. The Unidentified Human (Remains) index contains DNA profiles from human remains. Samples from the remains such as blood, bone, teeth, tissue, etc. can be tested and the resulting profiles are entered into this index. The Relatives of Missing Person (RMP) index contains DNA profiles from samples voluntarily collected from biological relatives of a missing individual. Usually these specimens are buccal swabs, but they may also be blood or other biological samples. The Pedigree Tree index is an index in which the individual relatives' specimens are organized into family groups to allow for better searching of the database. By organizing several relatives into a single pedigree tree the group will be searched as a unit, allowing for more informative searches to occur. Family reference samples and the pedigree trees containing them are only compared to the Unidentified Human Remains index in CODIS. Missing persons' samples, those collected directly from the missing person or a personal effect belonging to the missing person, are stored in the Missing Person index. Personal effects can include toothbrushes, hairbrushes, baby teeth, etc. The Convicted Offender index contains DNA profiles from individuals convicted of qualifying criminal offenses. These specimens may be in the form of blood or buccal swabs, depending on state statutes regarding the sample collection. Arrestee samples (samples from persons arrested on suspicion of committing a qualifying offense) are also collected in some states. Detainee specimens are samples collected from non-US persons detained under the authority of the United States and required by law to

Table 12.1 The Different Indexes of the CODIS Software

CODIS Index	Description
Unidentified Human (Remains)	DNA profiles obtained from unidentified human remains
Missing Person	DNA reference profiles from a missing person
Relatives of Missing Person	DNA profiles contributed voluntarily by biological relatives of a missing person
Offender	DNA profiles obtained from persons convicted of qualifying offenses
Arrestee	DNA profiles obtained from arrested persons (if allowed by state law)
Detainee	DNA profiles obtained from persons being detained under legal authority
Forensic	DNA profiles obtained from crime scene evidence

provide a DNA sample. Another index that may be helpful in some instances for the identification of remains is the Forensic index. This index contains DNA profiles from biological crime scene evidence. The profiles may be from blood stains, semen stains, etc. If the source of a Forensic DNA profile is known (attributed to a putative perpetrator who has been identified) then the direct match of a Forensic DNA profile to that from unidentified remains can assist in identification.

To detect matches and associations in the CODIS database, each index of DNA profiles is searched against other relevant indexes. These searches are configured based on the target and candidate indexes being compared, and on the result being sought (an association or a direct match). DNA profiles in the Unidentified Human (Remains) index are compared to all other indexes in CODIS. Direct matches can be found by comparing the remains DNA profiles to Convicted Offenders, Arrestees, Detainees, Missing Persons, and Forensic specimens, as well as to other remains profiles. Comparing the Unidentified Human (Remains) index to itself can result in the reassociation of scattered remains. This can be particularly helpful in disaster scenarios such as explosive events, airplane crashes, etc. As well as performing direct comparisons, the CODIS software can be configured to identify potential genetic associations. For example, the Relatives of Missing Person and the Pedigree Tree indexes are compared to the Unidentified Human (Remains) index in an attempt to find DNA profiles consistent with known patterns of inheritance (genetic associations) instead of direct matches. If a father and mother were seeking a missing child, the CODIS search would be configured to return candidates that share genetic information consistent with a parent–child relationship. The Relatives of Missing Person index is only searched against the Unidentified Human (Remains) index. No other comparisons are made to RMP specimens because the sole purpose of their inclusion in CODIS is to attempt to identify the remains of their missing family member. Comparison to other indexes does not fulfill this purpose and is prohibited.

In the United States, the CODIS network is organized in a hierarchical manner to allow for each state to adhere to its own unique DNA database legislation. There are three levels to this organization. They are the local (LDIS), state (SDIS), and national (NDIS) DNA index systems (Fig. 12.3). Each LDIS or SDIS laboratory may enter profiles into the standard indexes supported by the software and may also create specialized indexes for use locally. An LDIS or SDIS laboratory may also customize the software to store additional DNA data obtained by the laboratory that is not eligible for upload to the national level of CODIS. However, each LDIS and SDIS laboratory, while having some flexibility in the type of DNA profiles that they can house in the database, is still constrained by state and federal law. LDIS databases are those located at each NDIS participating laboratory throughout the country and contain DNA profiles developed and owned by the individual laboratory. Any eligible DNA profiles are uploaded from the LDIS level to the SDIS level. This allows the data from LDIS laboratories within a state to be collected into a state database and compared to data from the other LDIS laboratories within that state. From the SDIS level, eligible profiles are then uploaded to NDIS, the national level of CODIS, and the highest level in the hierarchy. Data from all SDIS laboratories are housed in a single national database, and it is there that DNA profiles from each state are compared to data from the other states in the country.

To compare the DNA profiles entered into CODIS by different laboratories around the country, there must be standardization of the type DNA data that is obtained and submitted to CODIS. To this end the FBI has chosen a core set of STRs that each profile should contain to be comparable across the country. This core set originally consisted of 13 genetic loci commonly called the CODIS Core 13. However, as the size of the NDIS database has grown, additional genetic markers are required to prevent random, spurious associations within the database. The additional required STR markers bring the number of required genetic loci to 20 (Table 12.2). Manufacturers of genetic testing kits have created many kits to include these core STRs. While different testing kits may be used at different laboratories, the set of genetic markers being tested is standardized and therefore the data are comparable across the CODIS system.

Laboratories must demonstrate that all data entered into CODIS are generated according to standard, validated protocols that follow a robust quality assurance system. The quality program at each CODIS participating laboratory must meet a minimum set of standards when performing forensic analysis. To demonstrate compliance of quality

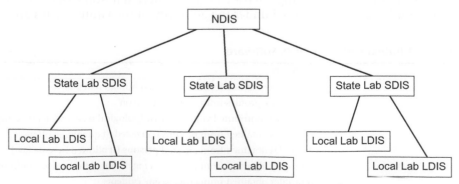

Figure 12.3 The hierarchy of the CODIS network.

Table 12.2 The Core CODIS Loci

CODIS Core 13 Loci	CODIS Core 20 Loci
CSF1PO	CSF1PO
FGA	FGA
THO1	THO1
TPOX	TPOX
vWA	vWA
D3S1358	D3S1358
D5S818	D5S818
D7S820	D7S820
D8S1179	D8S1179
D13S317	D13S317
D16S539	D16S539
D18S51	D18S51
D21S11	D21S11
	D1S1656
	D2S441
	D2S1338
	D10S1248
	D12S391
	D19S433
	D22S1045

assurance standards, laboratories must undergo an external audit every 2 years. In addition, laboratories must be accredited by an outside agency for the performance of forensic analysis.

■ EMERGING DNA TECHNOLOGIES AND THEIR APPLICATION TO FORENSIC GENETICS

Continual advancement in the technologies used by the forensic DNA community is essential to the creation, building, and maintenance of DNA databases. Advancements which look to lower DNA detection limits for evidence samples could allow for better results from even less or results from samples which were previously unsuccessful. Other desirable advances include obtaining results faster and increasing processing throughput, and all for a lower cost. One other consideration while thinking of advancements in the field is the move toward the global compatibility of results. Over the years, many technological advances have been made to meet these growing needs and demands of the forensic DNA community.

One approach to advancing the technologies utilized by the forensic community is to improve upon the various steps and methods used in processing, from extraction and quantification to amplification and detection. For example, DNA extraction methods can be improved upon to make them more efficient and to use fewer hazardous chemicals. Another example is the creation of new amplification kits such as AmpF/STR GlobalFiler and PowerPlex Fusion, which greatly increases the number of STR markers obtained in one reaction. These kits also allow for better international compatibility as markers overlap, thus allowing for more productive searches and comparisons. Recent updates in technology have led to the development of direct amplification kits. These kits allow for a sample to be extracted and amplified in the same tube and are also thus not dependent on a quantification step. Direct amplification kits use familiar chemistries and equipment which aid in adoption by the laboratory. Moreover, these kits allow for faster results in addition to less analyst manipulation.

Another approach is to take technologies developed for and readily used in other fields and adapt them to meet the needs of DNA forensics. The forensic DNA community has begun to adopt one such technology, next-generation sequencing (NGS), also called massive parallel sequencing (MPS), to investigate the potential to utilize sequence variation within STR's; the use of ancestry, identity, and phenotypic single nucleotide polymorphisms (SNPs) to assist in cold cases; and its ability to assist with human remains identification. However, this technology is already readily used in other fields including genetic screening and cancer research. NGS is commonly referred to as "sequencing on steroids." This is because NGS provides a greater throughput by producing an enormous amount of data, with the added benefit of being at a reduced cost.

There are two general methods for using NGS technologies. One method, which is known as shotgun sequencing, does not target any specific region of DNA, but rather aims to sequence every double-stranded DNA molecule in a sample. While this might sound great for forensic DNA analysts, shotgun sequencing is not actually ideal. This method not only requires a large amount of starting DNA, which many forensic samples do not have, but would also generate large amounts of data which would be laborious to analyze. One other problem with this method is reproducibility. Since no specific targets are being used, two shotgun sequencing runs using the same sample could give different results (Børsting and Morling, 2015). This is obviously not ideal if comparisons are being made between references and unknown evidence specimens.

Targeted sequencing is an alternative to shotgun sequencing. This method uses an enrichment step that amplifies selected regions using PCR, or uses probes to capture the region, or uses a combination (Børsting and Morling, 2015). Recently, the AFDIL developed the NGS mitoGenome Capture protocol which uses this technology. The protocol presently uses in-solution hybridization capture, which recovers very small DNA fragments that are then enriched using limited cycle PCR (AFDIL, 2016). The new protocol is an improvement over Sanger sequencing strategies (Børsting and Morling, 2015). Sanger sequencing as well as the other standard forensic genotyping technologies have limitations when low amounts of DNA are available and when the available DNA is heavily degraded. These are both concerns of the AFDIL, particularly when processing a specific subset of specimens from the Korean War which were embalmed prior to burial. Such chemical treatment resulted in severely damaged and fragmented DNA. However, this new protocol has helped to overcome these issues and has proved to have deep sequence coverage and increased sensitivity as compared to Sanger sequencing strategies, which previously failed to produce results for these challenging samples (AFDIL, 2016). Moreover, the protocol developed by the AFDIL yields data for the whole mitochondrial genome, rather than just the control region. Analyzing the full genome allows increased discrimination between samples, particularly for those that have common haplotypes.

Although NGS is a sequencing technology, it can go beyond this and can also be used for STR analysis. The core loci used in forensic DNA databasing are processed using traditional PCR and capillary electrophoresis methods. While results can be obtained in as little time as a day using these methods, there are certain limitations, such as the number of STR loci that can be multiplexed. However, NGS is not constrained by dye channels and size separation and thus STR loci fragments can be designed to be as short as possible. This will not only allow for processing of more loci at once, but also significantly improve results from degraded samples. Also, since NGS is ultimately also sequencing, more STR variations can be observed. Standard capillary electrophoresis–based analysis only provides the size or the number of repeats for a given allele, but provides no information about the actual repeats. But this is not the case with NGS methods as alleles with the same length can have different sequence compositions. For example, in one study, standard PCR and capillary electrophoresis methods were able to detect 15 different alleles for D12S391, whereas 53 were detected using NGS (Børsting and Morling, 2015). Having the ability to further differentiate alleles of the same size by looking also at the sequence would aid in deconvoluting mixtures of more than one contributor, a problem frequently encountered by forensic DNA analysts.

In order for NGS technologies to be a viable option for the forensic community, assays must contain the CODIS core loci. Otherwise, there would be no compatibility with historic case samples and current DNA databases. Some commercial NGS kits have already been developed for the forensic DNA community. One example is the ForenSeq DNA Signature Prep kit by Illumina. This kit amplifies 27 auSTRs, 7 X chromosome STRs, 24 Y-STRs, and 94 autosomal human identification single nucleotide polymorphisms (SNPs), all in one reaction. There is even the option to add 56 ancestry informative markers as well as 22 autosomal SNPs associated with phenotypic traits to this single reaction (Børsting and Morling, 2015).

The advantages of using this NGS over traditional PCR and capillary electrophoresis methods are enormous, and although the forensic DNA community is beginning to embrace NGS technologies, there are still some hurdles that need to be addressed before adoption is widespread. However, there is very little doubt that NGS technology will be implemented in more DNA forensic laboratories in the not so distant future.

■ CONCLUSION

Over 150 years of scientific discoveries and advancements led to the application of DNA analysis to the field of forensic science. With the ability to use DNA to aid in the identification of human remains as well as aid in the ability to identify perpetrators of crimes, came the need to create databases for such investigations. Since their implementation, both nongenetic-based and DNA-based databases have proven vital to the forensic community, which is unlikely to change in the foreseeable future. Thus, continued adoption of available advancements is necessary for maintaining the high-standard expectations of these databases.

References

AFDIL Validation Folder, Validation of Next-Generation Sequencing of Degraded Specimens Using Hybridizaton Capture Enrichment of the Mitochondrial Genome and Massively Parallel Sequencing on the Illumina MiSeq Platform and CLC Genomics Workbench 2016.

Anderson, S., Bankier, A.T., Barrell, B.G., de Bruijn, M.H., Coulson, A.R., Drouin, J., Eperon, I.C., Nierlich, D.P., Roe, B.A., Sanger, F., Schreier, P.H., Smith, A.J., Staden, R., Young, I.G., 1981. Sequence and organization of the human mitochondrial genome. Nature 290, 457–465.

Andrews, R.M., Kubacka, I., Chinnery, P.F., Lightowlers, R.N., Turnbull, D.M., Howell, N., 1999. Reanalysis and revision of the Cambridge reference sequence for human mitochondrial DNA. Nat. Genet. 23, 147.

Avery, O.T., Macleod, C.M., McCarty, M., 1944. The studies on the chemical nature of the substance inducing transformation of pneumococcal types: induction of transformation by a deoxyribonucleic acid fraction isolated from pneumococcus Type III. J. Exp. Med. 79 (2), 137–158.

Børsting, C., Morling, N., 2015. Next generation sequencing and its applications in forensic genetics. Forensic Sci. Int. Genet. 18, 78–89.

Brown, W.M., 1980. Polymorphism in mitochondrial DNA of humans as revealed by restriction endonuclease analysis. Proc. Natl. Acad. Sci. U.S.A. 77 (6), 3605–3609.

Chargaff, E., Lipshitz, R., Green, C., 1952. Composition of the deoxypentose nucleic acids of four genera of sea-urchin. J. Biol. Chem. 195 (1), 155–160.

Dahm, R., 2005. Friedrich Miescher and the discovery of DNA. Dev. Biol. 278 (2), 274–288.

DNA Identification Act of 1994, codified at 42 U.S.C. §14132, and amendments.

Giles, R.E., Blanc, H., Cann, H.M., Wallace, D.C., 1980. Maternal inheritance of human mitochondrial DNA. Proc. Natl. Acad. Sci. U.S.A. 77 (11), 6715–6719.

Gill, P., Jeffreys, A.J., Werrett, D.J., 1985. Forensic applications of DNA fingerprints. Nature 318, 577–579.

Gusmão, L., Brion, M., González-Neira, A., Lareu, M., Carracedo, A., 1999. Y chromosome specific polymorphisms in forensic analysis. Leg. Med. 1 (2), 55–60.

Hershey, A., Chase, M., 1952. Independent functions of viral protein and nucleic acid in growth of bacteriophage. J. Gen. Physiol. 36 (1), 39–56.

Hickman, Matthew, Hughes, Strom, Ropero-Miller, 2004. Bureau of Justice Statistics Special Report. Medical Examiners and Coroners' Offices. Web http://www.bjs.gov/content/pub/pdf/meco04.pdf.

Hutchison III, C., Newbold, J., Potter, S., Edgell, M., 1974. Maternal inheritance of mammalian mitochondrial DNA. Nature. 251, 536–538. https://www.fbi.gov/about-us/lab/biometric-analysis/codis.

Jeffreys, A.J., Wilson, V., Thein, S.L., 1985a. Individual-specific fingerprints of human DNA. Nature 316, 76–79.

Jeffreys, A., Wilson, V., Thein, S., 1985b. Hypervariable "minisatellite" regions in human DNA. Nature 314, 67–73.

Jobling, M.A., Tyler-Smith, C., 2003. The human Y chromosome: an evolutionary marker comes of age. Nat. Rev. Genet. 4 (8), 598–612.

Kelly Jr., T.J., Smith, H.O., 1970. A restriction enzyme from *Hemophilus influenzae*: II. Base sequence of the recognition site. J. Mol. Biol. 51 (2), 393–409.

Levene, P.A., London, E.S., 1929. The structure of thymonucleic acid. J. Biol. Chem. 83, 806–816.

Magner, L.N., 1994. A History of the Life Sciences. Dekker, New York.

Maxam, A.M., Gilbert, W., 1977. A new method for sequencing DNA. Proc. Natl. Acad. Sci. U.S.A. 74 (2), 560–564.

Miescher, F., February 26, 1869. Letter I; to Wilhelm his; Tqbingen. In: His, W., et al. (Ed.), Die Histochemischen und Physiologischen Arbeiten von Friedrich Miescher—Aus dem wissenschaftlichen Briefwechsel von F. Miescher, vol. 1. F.C.W. Vogel, Leipzig, pp. 33–38.

Mullis, K.B., Faloona, F.A., 1987. Specific synthesis of DNA in vitro by a polymerase-catalyzed chain reaction. Methods Enzym. 155, 335–350.

Nass, M.M., Nass, S., 1963. Intramitochondrial fibers with DNA characteristics. I. Fixation and electron staining reactions. J. Cell Biol. 19, 593–611.

Niezgoda, S., 1998. CODIS Program Overview, GenePrint Profiles in DNA Typing.

Saccone, C., Gissi, C., Lanave, C., Larizza, A., Pesole, G., Aurelio Reyes, A., 2000. Evolution of the mitochondrial genetic system: an overview. Gene 261 (1), 153–159.

Sanger, F., Nicklen, S., Coulson, A.R., 1977. DNA sequencing with chain-terminating inhibitors. Proc. Natl. Acad. Sci. U. S. A. 74 (12), 5463–5467.

Schatz, G., 1963. The isolation of possible mitochondrial precursor structures from aerobically grown baker's yeast. Biochem. Biophys. Res. Commun. 12, 448–451.

Smith, H.O., Wilcox, K., 1970. A restriction enzyme from *Hemophilus influenza*. I. Purification and general properties. J. Mol. Biol. 51 (2), 379–391.

Southern, E.M., 1975. Detection of specific sequences among DNA fragments separated by gel electrophoresis. J. Mol. Biol. 98 (3), 503–517.

Watson, J.D., Crick, F.H., 1953. Molecular structure of nucleic acids; a structure for deoxyribose nucleic acid. Nature 171, 737–738.

Wyman, A., White, R., 1980. A highly polymorphic locus in human DNA. Proc. Natl. Acad. Sci. U. S. A. 77 (11), 6754–6758.

Further Reading

Griffith, F., 1928. The significance of pneumococcal types. J. Hyg. 27 (2), 113–159.

CHAPTER 13

Flexibility in Testing Skeletonized Remains for DNA Analysis Can Lead to Increased Success: Suggestions and Case Studies

Suni M. Edson[1,2] | Kimberly A. Root[1] | Irene L. Kahline[1] | Colleen A. Dunn[1] | Bruché E. Trotter[1] | Jennifer A. O'Rourke[1]

[1]Office of the Armed Forces Medical Examiner, Dover, DE, United States,
[2]Flinders University, Adelaide, SA, Australia

Chapter Outline

■ INTRODUCTION

Constant adaptation to new methods and new techniques is a hallmark of science. In the last few decades, there have been enormous advancements in the area of DNA science and human identification. It was almost 100 years from the theories of inheritance developed by Gregor Mendel to the description of the physical structure of DNA by Watson and Crick in the 1950s (Watson and Crick, 1953). It was another 32 years before Sir Alec Jeffreys, Peter Gill, and associates released two seminal papers that revolutionized human identification (Jeffreys et al., 1985; Gill et al., 1985). From there, techniques and technologies available have changed rapidly: Kary Mullis and polymerase chain reaction (Mullis and Faloona, 1987); the descriptions of various minisatellites in nuclear DNA for human identification (Hammond et al., 1994; Urquhart et al., 1994); and the standardization of nomenclature of short tandem repeat (STR) analysis (Bar et al., 1994). Not to be ignored is Sanger sequencing of mitochondrial DNA (mtDNA) (Anderson et al., 1981; Holland et al., 1993; Holland and Parsons, 1999; Sanger et al., 1977) and STR analysis of the Y-chromosome (Butler, 2003).

As a field, forensic DNA analysis for human identification has continued to grow and expand and is largely unrecognizable from the early years of manual manipulation of samples during PCR analysis. No longer are tubes

New Perspectives in Forensic Human Skeletal Identification. http://dx.doi.org/10.1016/B978-0-12-805429-1.00013-2

manually transferred from water baths or hot blocks of specific temperatures to amplify DNA. Thermal cyclers do it with little human input other than to push a button. Southern blot analysis of hypervariable regions is mostly a thing of the past, and indeed, most college students in forensic DNA analysis or biochemistry courses today would be puzzled to realize that such analysis took days rather than 8h or less. With the advent of rapid DNA analysis equipment (among many: Bienvenue et al., 2010; Hopwood et al., 2010; Tan et al., 2013), the "instant science" of CSI has become a reality.

While the new technologies are exciting and will continue to change the "face" of human identification, it is important for the practitioner to remember that many of these new technologies are rooted in the original fundamentals of the science. STRs would probably not have been discovered so rapidly without the initial work of Jeffreys. New techniques exist because of the history of the field. It is beneficial to keep an eye on the past to continue to move forward. This chapter will serve as an examination of some of the testing protocols used for DNA analysis of skeletonized remains and a reminder that flexibility in protocols can lead to more successful results.

■ EXTRACTION OF DNA FROM SKELETONIZED REMAINS

Dried skeletal specimens and teeth are the typical sample types that the Past Accounting Section at the Armed Forces DNA Identification Laboratory (AFDIL) receives from the Defense POW/MIA Accounting Agency (DPAA) Laboratory, formerly Joint POW/MIA Accounting Command—Central Identification Laboratory (also known as JPAC-CIL or also CILHI). AFDIL assists the DPAA Scientific Analysis Division (more commonly called DPAA-Lab) in identifying service members from past military conflicts, such as World War II, Korean War, Southeast Asia conflict, the Cold War, and other incidents, by processing the DNA analysis from the remains. From its inception in 1992, AFDIL used an organic extraction method in the extraction of total genomic DNA from skeletonized remains. This protocol, described in Edson et al. (2004), typically used 2.5 g of pulverized osseous material dissolved overnight at 56°C in an extraction buffer (10 mM Tris, pH 8.0; 100 mM NaCl; 50 mM EDTA, pH 8.0; 0.5% SDS) and proteinase K, followed by purification with 25:24:1 phenol:chloroform:isoamyl alcohol and, the now obsolete, Centricon-100 centrifugal filters (Millipore). At the time, the only DNA platform testing used was Sanger sequencing of mtDNA. In a survey of skeletal samples tested from 1992 to 2003, success was found to be somewhat predictable: Femora were the most successful element for mtDNA testing and should be sampled preferentially.

In 2006, AFDIL validated a new demineralization technique ("Demin1:" Loreille et al., 2007; Edson and McMahon, 2016) that reduced the input of skeletal material from 2.5 to 0.25 g. The extraction buffer itself was modified to be primarily EDTA (0.5 M EDTA, pH 8.0; 1% N-Lauroylsarcosine), but otherwise the protocol did not change significantly. Purification of the extract still occurred using PCIA and a purification filter, now Amicon Ultra-4 Centrifugal Filter Units (EMD Millipore, Germany). The fundamentals of the procedure itself remained largely unchanged, even with the reduction in input of the sample. However, the success rates for mtDNA testing increased markedly. Gone was the preferential selection of the femur or other compact bones. Any skeletal sample selected would tend to give a reportable mtDNA sequence (Edson et al., 2011).

At the same time, AFDIL was expanding testing to include STR analysis. Modified PowerPlex 16 (Promega Corporation, Madison, WI) or AmpFLSTR Yfiler (Thermo Fisher Scientific, Waltham, MA) protocols were successfully used to identify the remains of soldiers from the Vietnam War, Korean War, and World War II (Irwin et al., 2007a,b). While useful, these modified protocols were not broadly incorporated into casework use at the time. It took another change in the extraction protocol for STR analysis to be fully implemented for use on a daily basis.

In 2011, the Past Accounting Section of AFDIL adopted a modification of the inorganic purification protocol (Edson and McMahon, 2016) that was already in use by the Current Accounting Section for use on fresh skeletal remains and other agencies and laboratories, such as the International Commission on Missing Persons (ICMP), on aged remains (Amory et al., 2012; Davoren et al., 2007; Lee et al., 2010; Rohland and Hofreiter, 2007). The AFDIL protocol remains the same as the demineralization technique adopted in 2006, with the introduction of silica column purification step using the QIAquick PCR Purification Kit (QIAGEN, Valencia, CA) and the elimination of any PCIA purification step. In theory, this protocol would be faster, more efficient, more successful, and less harmful to the staff. While the last is certainly true, the remaining did not necessarily turn out as expected.

Examination of the mtDNA success rates for all samples showed that the inorganic purification technique, known as "Demin2" in-house, gave an 80% success rate across all skeletal samples tested. This is understandably disappointing after the almost 90% success for Demin1. In addition, the overall quality of the data being reported was decreased. The target for reporting in the control region of mtDNA is 611–705 bases. Demin2 generated an average of 543 bases reported. While not as low as the average for the original extraction method (459 bases), it is still rather disappointing. What was markedly more successful was STR testing. Demin2 proved to provide a marked improvement in almost all STR platforms tested over either Demin1 or the original extraction protocol (Table 13.1).

As with many labs, AFDIL is increasing the output of degraded skeletal remains tested with STR kits. Demin2 would seem to be a relatively decent fit to the workflow of the laboratory: success with STR analysis is needed; and mtDNA analysis is becoming less dominant, despite the makeup of the family reference database. However, some samples have been exposed to environmental conditions immediately antemortem, perimortem, or postmortem that may inhibit PCR processing should the materials coextract with the DNA.

Table 13.1 Summary of Testing Done at AFDIL From 1992 Until the Spring of 2016

	Original Extraction	Demin1	Demin2
MtDNA Sanger Sequencing			
Number of samples tested	5809	6256	1805
% successfully reported	75%	89%	80%
Avg.# bases reported	459	611	543
MiniFiler Testing			
Number of samples tested	103	839	411
% successfully reported	32%	29%	48%
Avg.# loci reported	3	2.4	3.9
Yfiler Testing			
Number of samples tested	173	988	634
% successfully reported	40%	31%	57%
Avg.# loci reported	4	2.8	6.7
Identifiler Testing			
Number of samples tested	7	24	37
% successfully reported	86%	50%	73%
Avg.# loci reported	10	5.9	7.3
Fusion Testing			
Number of samples tested	0	81	50
% successfully reported	n/a	77%	96%
Avg.# loci reported	n/a	8.9	15.8

MtDNA Sanger Sequencing testing is of the hypervariable regions I and II of the control region. The target to be considered successful is 100 bp or more of DNA amplified in duplicate and confirmed to be consistent by two independent analyses. Identifiler (AmpFLSTR Identifiler: Thermo Fisher Scientific), MiniFiler (AmpFLSTR MiniFiler PCR Amplification Kit: Thermo Fisher Scientific), and PowerPlex Fusion (Promega Corporation, Madison, WI) reactions are unmodified from the manufacturers' recommendations. Yfiler (AmpFLSTR Yfiler: Thermo Fisher Scientific) is a combination of low copy number testing and unmodified. All short tandem repeat testing platforms are considered "successful" with the reporting of four or more loci that are confirmed through duplicate amplifications. Not all kits and protocols used at Armed Forces DNA Identification Laboratory are included in this table.

In 2015, the DPAA disinterred 45 graves from the National Memorial Cemetery of the Pacific containing the highly commingled remains of sailors and marines who died on the USS *Oklahoma* December 7, 1941. Since 1941, the remains had undergone a series of burials and disinterments, including an extended period within the hull of the breached ship. During this time, the fuel from the ship had leaked into the water and the hull and extensively contaminated the remains. Even with time and cleaning, skeletal samples sent to AFDIL for DNA testing retain the scent of fuel.

The first set of skeletal samples sent to AFDIL was extracted twice according to our standard operating procedure (SOP); however, Demin1 was used for the first extraction and Demin2 for the second. The goal was to determine which of the extraction protocols would work consistently better for mtDNA and STR testing on this particular set of samples. Given the presence of fuel, it should not be surprising that the Demin2 extraction protocol did not work as well as could be expected for this specific set of samples. The fuel could bind to the silica column and prevent the DNA from binding during the wash steps, thus increasing the amount of DNA lost. Previous work on other cases that have been exposed to inhibitory materials, as will be discussed later in this chapter, has shown that Demin1 tends to work better overall when the remains are chemically compromised. As with those cases, the samples from the USS *Oklahoma* tended to work better overall with an organic purification.

GC/MS analysis of bone powder removed from the remains during the cleaning process indicates that there is fuel oil still present on the remains along with some by-products of decay (Fig. 13.1). The fuel itself cannot be characterized, as the US Navy does not have on file mass spectrometry data on the fuels used in the 1940s; however, components of the fuel, including anthracene and its derivatives, can be identified. GC/MS analysis of the DNA extracted from the same sample indicates that the fuel is not completely removed during the extraction procedure and a small amount is coextracted with the DNA. It does not appear to have a deleterious effect on the process of PCR.

Demin1 is now commonly used at AFDIL when working on chemically compromised skeletal samples such as those from the USS *Oklahoma*. Demin2 is used on all other sets of skeletal samples. This particular incident is a good example of how it is useful to laboratories to keep "older" methods as active SOPs. Flexibility in thought and activity served to save time and increase the chance of identifying the sailors and marines involved in this incident and others. As this chapter continues, additional possible alternatives to the "common wisdom" will be discussed.

■ SMALL SAMPLES AND THE POSSIBILITY OF NONHUMAN REMAINS

Extracting DNA from extremely small osseous samples can be extremely challenging. The focus here is on samples that are submitted for DNA extraction that are under 0.30 g in gross weight. Due to the size, the standard cleaning methods used have to be altered to accommodate the samples. Typically, samples received from DPAA are sanded

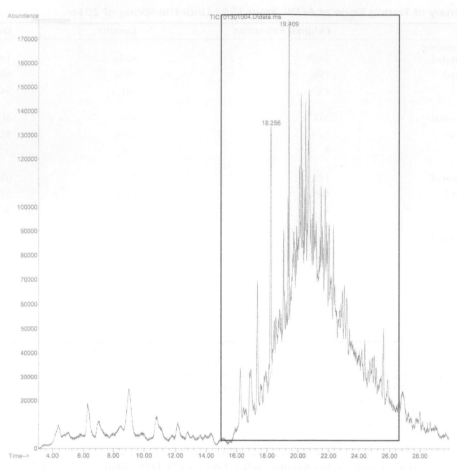

Figure 13.1 A GC/MS trace of bone powder removed from the exterior of a skeletal sample from the USS *Oklahoma*. The area marked with the box is an accelerant trace that would be able to be associated with the specific fuel used on the USS *Oklahoma*. However, GC/MS analysis of that specific fuel was not done at the time. Components of the fuel, such as anthracene, can be identified in the trace itself.

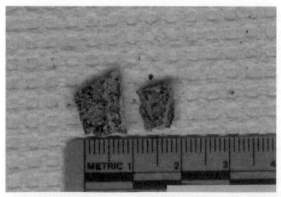

Figure 13.2 Scapula, 0.23 g. Sample was cleaned by light sanding and sonicating. A full control region mitochondrial DNA sequence (565 bp) was obtained for this sample.

using a small sanding bit attached to a Dremel tool (Bosch, Mt. Prospect, IL). Because of the small size, one way in which these samples are cleaned is by just lightly sanding them, instead of a vigorous sanding, to remove any modern contaminates on the outer layer. However, this method may not be enough in some circumstances. Sonication of the sample, usually in a 50 mL conical tube containing either sterile water or a 10% bleach solution, for a period of time between 30 s and 5 min has been used at AFDIL. Sonication can be for a single or multiple sessions, depending on the amount of debris perceived to be present (Fig. 13.2). This method is well suited for small samples with a large amount of trabecular bone that may contain pockets of dirt or other exogenous materials.

Another challenge of small samples comes with the lower quality that is generally associated with these types of samples. In most instances, these samples are small due to severe fragmentation of the bones, which often goes hand in hand with lower quality DNA. This severe fragmentation may be due to disintegration at time of death (e.g., loss of personnel in high speed plane crashes), long periods of time, or environmental factors, such as the acidity of soil or high temperatures, which may cause the bone to be brittle and break resulting in the small fragments (Fig. 13.3).

Samples of this size are typically consumed within a single extraction. After cleaning, the fragments are usually less than 0.15 g. At AFDIL, it is preferred to have to duplicate extractions of an osseous sample to confirm the mtDNA sequence or STR profile obtained; however, with a standard target powder weight of 0.20–0.25 g per extraction it is not possible to obtain a second extraction. Most samples submitted by JPAC-CIL have additional intact bone associated: either there is remaining bone to sample from or material could be taken from a bone that can be articulated to the initial sample. The first sample sent for testing is often the best available, and any subsequent submissions are not expected to give any better quality data. In some instances, bone that is submitted is all that is available. These samples are deemed "critical" (Fig. 13.4). The critical designation is a simple manner for the submitting agency to inform the testing laboratory that no additional materials remain for analysis.

If it cannot be determined to which skeletal element the fragment belongs, samples will be submitted as "bone fragment" or "long bone." With these bones, the possibility of a nonhuman origin exists. While there are other methods for species identification of biological materials (melt curve analysis: Kitpipit et al., 2016; cytochrome b: Ciavaglia et al., 2015; Linacre and Lee, 2016; Tobe and Linacre, 2010), AFDIL uses a rapid screen of samples with in-house designed primers to amplify a section of the 12S region of mtDNA. The region is approximately 100 bp in size, which is small enough to amplify most highly degraded human samples, and is not human specific. After Sanger sequencing, the data are compared to a human reference sequence. If the sequence is 100% consistent with the reference, the sample is believed to be of human origin. If the sequence is not 100% consistent with the reference, the sequence is searched against the nucleotide Basic Local Alignment Search Tool (BLAST) on the National Center for Biotechnology Information website (http://blast.ncbi.nlm.nih.gov/Blast.cgi). The BLAST is not peer reviewed and

Figure 13.3 Fragment, 0.18 g. Sample was cleaned by light sanding and washing. Osseous material was very brittle. Inconclusive mitochondrial DNA testing results were obtained.

Figure 13.4 Bone fragment, 0.14 g. Submitted to AFDIL from DPAA as a critical sample. Testing using 12S primers indicated that the sample originated from *Sus scrofa*.

individuals can upload the sequences they have into the tool; therefore, results may be skewed or incorrect, although this is rare.

Melton and Holland (2007) determined that the BLAST can supply a high degree of confidence when determining an animal species based on the sequence obtained from a 12S analysis. They also found that primate species can be up to 98% homologous (as with *Pan troglodytes*, the chimpanzee); however, that 2% difference is enough to be able to differentiate between the chimpanzees and humans.

Cryptids may be found when searching the BLAST tool. The kting voar (*Pseudonovibos spiralis*), also known as the snake-eating cow or spiral-horned ox, is one such cryptid. Some believe that the kting voar is a cowlike animal with twisting horns and spotted fur that has a primary distribution range in Cambodia. This designation is the source of some controversy (summarized in Olson and Hassanin, 2003). Most supposed specimens have been determined to be cow horns, artificially shaped by locals for ritualistic or medicinal purposes (Brandt et al., 2001). DNA studies that have been done on historical samples concur that the remains are closely related to or are domestic cows (Hassanin et al., 2001) or water buffalo (Kuznetsov et al., 2001). What is unfortunate is that some 12S sequence data for the "kting voar" have made their way into GenBank (e.g., GenBank Accession No. AF231029) and may occasionally match results from DPAA samples.

AFDIL uses the 12S testing for primarily two situations: the first being when a sample is submitted specifically for the 12S testing to be performed because the anthropologist is unsure of the species origin. For these samples, 12S is the first amplification that is attempted on the sample. If the sample is shown to be nonhuman, the sample is ream-plified for verification and the case is completed. If the sample is consistent with the human reference, then routine mtDNA testing is continued. It is sufficient for the purposes of the lab to simply identify a sample as human or non-human, although it is interesting to determine the specific species sampled. Since implementation of this protocol, 384 samples have been analyzed using 12S. Only 68 were determined to be human.

The second use of 12S testing is when a sample fails to amplify using the normal processing methods. In these cases, 12S amplification is used as an investigative tool to determine if the sample is failing due to being nonhuman or due to severe degradation or inhibition. Most of the samples that are determined to be nonhuman are bone frag-ments or long bones. Nevertheless, there have been occasions in which a bone is submitted as a human bone but is later determined to be nonhuman in origin (see Figs. 13.5 and 13.6). During normal processing, if a sample does not amplify, the analyst has the option to attempt a 12S amplification. There are three different outcomes an analyst would expect to see. The first is that the sample data are consistent with *Homo sapiens* (human). In this scenario, the sample is believed to be human; however, caution is exercised due to the possibility of exogenous contamination by scientists or locals. The second is that the sample data are determined to be nonhuman in origin (after a BLAST search is performed). The third is that the 12S amplification does not produce a positive amplification and the ana-lyst is unable to determine species. However, this outcome does provide some insight, as the quality of the sample is also likely very poor if the 12S region does not amplify.

Case Study #1

A sample was submitted to the AFDIL listed as a "fragment" with a gross weight of 0.30 g (Fig. 13.7). The sample was noted as being very spongy and brittle, dirty and partially blue–green in color. After sanding, the sample was soni-cated in water three times. The resulting 12S sequence data appeared to be a mixture of *H. sapiens* and a species within the family Bovidae. A resampling of the fragment was obtained with a gross weight of 0.05 g (Fig. 13.8). The sample was not sanded due to the size, but rather cleaned by a 2 min sonication in each of the following solutions: twice in a bleach dilution, twice with sterile water, and twice with ethanol. The 12S data obtained from the resampling were a clean sequence consistent with a species of the family Bovidae. The human data observed were believed to be from handling of the bone sample at some point prior to examination and the sample was reported as nonhuman.

Case Study #2

A set of 13 samples from the same site was submitted to the AFDIL. The letter from the client stated that the samples were sent specifically for 12S testing and subsequent mtDNA testing if the 12S results were positive for human. Of the

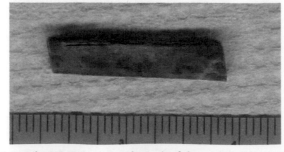

Figure 13.5 Sample submitted as a rib. 12S rRNA testing determined the sample to have originated from a cow (*Bos taurus*).

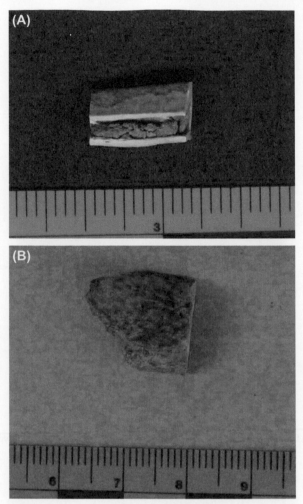

Figure 13.6 Samples submitted as a rib (A) and a humerus (B) from two different cases. 12S rRNA testing determined the samples to have originated from a pig (*Sus scrofa*).

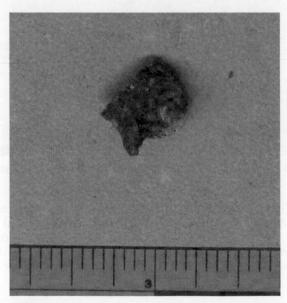

Figure 13.7 Sample submitted a fragment weighing 0.3 g. 12S testing produced a mixture of sequences: *Homo sapiens* and a species in the family Bovidae.

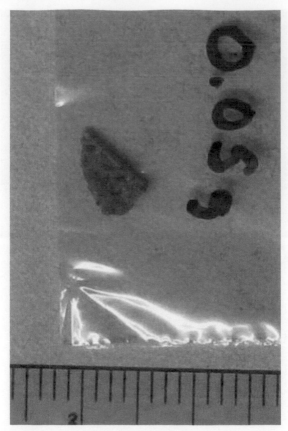

Figure 13.8 A resampling of the bone fragment in Fig. 13.7. 12S testing determined the fragment to have originated from a species in the family Bovidae.

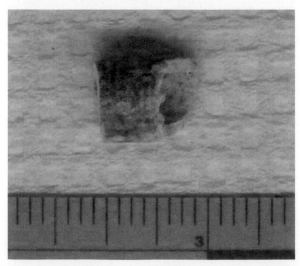

Figure 13.9 Sample submitted as a 0.53 g metacarpal. 12S testing determined the sample to have originated from *Canis lupus* (dog).

13 samples, 8 were submitted as "Long Bone" and 5 submitted with specific bone designations. Four of the long bones were inconclusive, in both mtDNA and 12S testing, three were human and reported with mtDNA sequences, and one was determined to be nonhuman. Two of the samples with human bone designations were inconclusive, and two were human and reported. The fifth sample was sent in as a metacarpal (Fig. 13.9). After 12S testing, the sample was determined to have originated from *Canis lupus* or part of the same genus as the domestic dog and wolf.

■ SAMPLING OF TEETH

Since AFDIL started processing samples from DPAA-Lab, 12% of the samples submitted have been teeth. When working with skeletonized human remains, teeth are often ideal due to the success of the sample type in recovering DNA. The success of teeth is due in part to their structure. A whole tooth is surrounded by enamel and cementum, which helps protect the DNA of the tooth from environmental and modern contaminants (Adler et al., 2011). Prior to 2008, the DPAA Laboratory would prepare the tooth sample by drilling the tooth and sending the tooth powder to the AFDIL. Contamination issues were consistently observed in the powdered tooth and the AFDIL decided to validate and implement their own protocol of preparing teeth for extraction of DNA.

The DPAA-Lab has numerous factors they consider when choosing a tooth to send to the AFDIL for any type of DNA testing. Teeth will not typically be sampled if identification can be made based on antemortem dental X-rays. Intact, whole teeth are preferred, whereas teeth with cavities, fractures, or are otherwise structurally compromised are generally avoided due to possible contamination of the interior of the tooth. If several teeth are attached to a jaw fragment, only one tooth needs to be sampled. The remaining teeth are available for testing in case inconclusive DNA results are obtained or if the sample becomes contaminated, as it is presumed that all teeth articulated in the same jaw belong to the same individual.

Loose teeth that cannot be associated with a mandible or maxillary bone may be submitted for DNA testing. Previously, a tooth would be chosen for sampling and the DPAA-Lab odontologist would drill the interior of the tooth structure to obtain as much dentin as possible. The powder was collected in a 15 mL conical tube that was packaged and sent to AFDIL for DNA testing. All of the tooth powder removed by the odontologists would be needed for the original extraction protocol, leaving AFDIL only one opportunity to extract the DNA successfully. Over time, AFDIL began to note that a certain percentage of samples received showed either gross or low-level contamination. AFDIL believed that the contamination was potentially being introduced when the odontologists were drilling the teeth. In some cases, the profile that was produced from the sample was consistent with the odontologist that drilled the tooth. Due to the manner in which the powdered tooth was sent to AFDIL, there was the potential for additional contamination. Tooth powder frequently was found in the threads of the 15 mL tube used for shipping, allowing for the possibility of other materials entering the tube. There was also some tooth powder loss and the potential for contamination by the DNA analyst. To eliminate these issues, AFDIL decided to validate and implement an SOP for the preparation of teeth prior to DNA extraction.

The teeth received by AFDIL from DPAA-Lab have been exposed to varying environmental conditions. They can be covered in dirt, debris, and as with many of the samples from the USS *Oklahoma*, in fuel (Fig. 13.10A and B). The

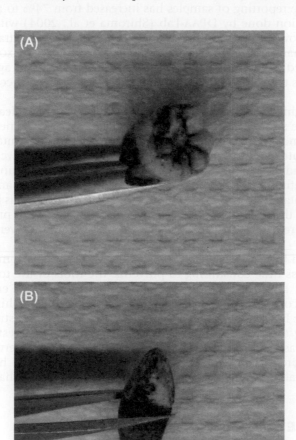

Figure 13.10 A molar (A) and a premolar (B) submitted from remains recovered from the USS *Oklahoma*.

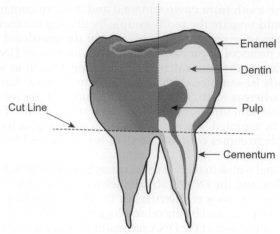

Figure 13.11 Diagram of the structure of a human tooth.

exterior condition of the samples is not always optimal, but due to the enamel and cementum that surrounds the interior of the tooth, the DNA rich dentin (Fig. 13.11) is preserved and ideal for yielding DNA results. The exterior of the tooth simply needs to be thoroughly cleaned to prevent transfer any of the exterior contaminants to the interior portion of the tooth. By 2008, AFDIL developed a method for the preparation of teeth samples in-house and had applied the procedure to casework for the extraction of DNA.

The tooth preparation and extraction process became more fluid by incorporating tooth preparation as the Day 1 of the extraction procedure followed by Day 2 the organic extraction of DNA. Since the implementation of this protocol, the success rate for the reporting of samples has increased from 74% to approximately 90%. The AFDIL SOP mirrors the tooth preparation done by DPAA-Lab (Shiroma et al., 2004) with some slight modifications to accommodate the AFDIL workflow. The portion of the tooth targeted for DNA extraction is the dentin (Fig. 13.11). The dentin is protected by the hard enamel and cementum, which makes it an excellent source of DNA. The pulp is typically completely desiccated in the samples that the AFDIL receives due to age and extended environmental exposure. In fresh tooth samples the pulp is the recommended source for DNA because that is the source of blood flow to the tooth.

The preparation of teeth begins by cleaning the tooth with an 8.5% (v/v) bleach solution. If the tooth has a detached root or fractures in the structure, it is cleaned with a gauze pad moistened with the bleach solution and wiped down with a gauze pad moistened with absolute ethanol. If the tooth is intact, it is sonicated in the bleach solution and rinsed with absolute ethanol. In both cases, the tooth is then allowed to air dry for 15 min under a UV light. A horizontal cut around the base of the crown at the cemento-enamel junction is made with a dental bur allowing for the eventual separation of the crown from the root (Fig. 13.11). Separating the tooth structure in this manner allows for better reorientation of the crown to the root after the dentin has been drilled out of the root and crown. Following the drilling of the tooth, the tooth powder that is collected can proceed to the extraction of DNA and the remaining tooth structure is returned to DPAA-Lab for reassembly and eventual return to the family members on identification.

The choice to drill the dentin from the interior of the tooth can be seen as somewhat counter to the common wisdom, as it is simpler and less time consuming to pulverize the roots of the tooth, or the entire tooth. Some publications (Adler et al., 2011; Baker et al., 2001) espouse the crushing of the entire tooth out of ease and the reduction of the possibility of contamination of the sample. However, the crushing of the crown will introduce higher levels of enamel into the DNA extract, leading to inhibition of the downstream PCR testing. Higgins et al. (2015) recommended selecting tooth tissue depending on the type of DNA testing to be done. Cementum is preferred for STR testing; whereas, its testing found that mtDNA was better preserved in the dentin and the roots. Pulverization of the root may provide sufficient DNA for both types of testing; however, retention of the entire tooth is often seen to be preferable in human identification casework so as to have some biological material to return to a family member.

■ SKELETAL SAMPLES RETRIEVED FROM WATER

The advances in technologies for DNA extraction and analysis have allowed for testing on a variety of specimens previously considered unviable. This has increased the opportunity to successfully identify missing individuals, victims of mass disasters, and victims of crime. Postmortem interval (PMI), or time passed since death, is one of the factors used to assist in the identification. Pursuant to this, numerous studies have been conducted on tissue decomposition of remains that have been buried, exposed to the open air, scattered by scavengers, and defleshed by insects and microorganisms. Fewer studies have made aquatic environments their focus, thereby creating a gap in the information necessary to efficiently collect, examine, and process specimens found in wet locations. Of the few, most are dedicated to determining PMI with very little data on DNA recoverability. Given that other bodily tissues would be compromised or missing, bone is likely the best candidate for DNA testing of samples found in water.

Bone is composed of collagen (protein), hydroxyapatite (mineral), and organic compounds. The collagen and hydroxyapatite are strongly bound together, which is why bone persists long after the soft tissue is gone. Degradation of bone, or diagenesis, will begin when collagenases (enzymes) attack collagen, reduce it to amino acids, and weaken the protein–mineral bond. The minerals are vulnerable to leaching into the environment, a process exacerbated by water and microorganisms. This continues until the bone eventually disintegrates.

For diagenesis to occur, the enzymes and microorganisms that break down bone must obtain access to it, thus the decomposition of the rest of the body must also be understood. Some factors affecting aquatic decomposition include bacterial content of the water, temperature, salinity, presence or absence of scavengers, and water movement. The literature for decomposition in water does little to distinguish between the possible environments—some freshwater data are from bodies found in pools and bath tubs, which could have a drastically different bacterial content than a lentic water source (such as a pond), which could be drastically different from seawater. Due to the lack of diverse experimentation and conclusions, the probity of bone samples recovered from these sites is not well understood.

Soft Tissue Decomposition in Water

In an attempt to test generalizations made regarding bodies found in water, a project by Ayers (2010) at Texas State University—San Marcos used pig carcasses to observe decomposition in different environments, including freshwater and saltwater. The major differences observed between them were that freshwater bodies had abdominal protrusions, which attracted insects/scavengers and released bacteria. This was attributed to an osmotic effect that would differ between the fresh and salt waters. The saltwater bodies had no insect activity and suffered mainly from skin slippage, which allowed the bones to sink without observation or documentation. In neither case was adipocere present.

Adipocere, also known as grave wax, is formed by saponification or the hydrolysis of fatty acids. Hydrolysis is the chemical breakdown of a compound due to a reaction with water. Certain conditions must be met for its creation: presence of adipose, anaerobic/warm/wet environment, and putrefactive bacteria. The hydrolysis is aided by anaerobic bacteria, which generate ammonia-rich waste, thereby creating an alkaline environment. The alkalinity prevents further bacterial activity and stops putrefaction (O'Brien and Kuehner, 2007). Soft tissue becomes waxy and pale; the body is preserved and stable due to the increased melting temperature of the adipocere. When it dries, the adipocere does not further decay but rather becomes brittle, making PMI approximation exceptionally difficult. The presence of adipocere preserves the bone as well as internal organs, which will desiccate over time. Due to the ideal circumstances required for its formation, O'Brien and Kuehner (2007) use the term "Goldilocks Phenomenon": If too dry or too cold the tissue will desiccate, if too wet or too hot it will soften and liquefy, but when it's "just right," adipocere forms and soft tissue does not decompose. This can occur within a few weeks or up to a few years. The first individual to investigate adipocere was a French chemist named Antoine Fourcroy. In 1789 he exhumed bodies from the *Cimitiere des Innocents* in Paris and noticed a fatty and waxy tissue formation most noticeable in the cheeks and breasts. Fourcroy named it *"adipocire"* using the Latin terms for fat and wax, *"adeps"* and *"cera,"* respectively.

Case Study #3

A body was found in a dam on the Seine River outside of Paris, France, with a document in the clothing suggesting it was a man who had been missing for 3 years. Since the head and limbs were missing, DNA testing was necessary for identification. Saponified muscle and a clavicle were tested for nuclear DNA. The saponified tissue did not yield results but the clavicle produced a partial autosomal STR (auSTR) profile that was sufficient for identification (Crainic et al., 2002). The presence of saponified tissue gives some clues to the water environment the body was left in and the successful DNA testing indicates that those aquatic conditions may be favorable to bone preservation.

Wet Tissue Is an Issue, What About Bone?

An important question for researchers has been: what is the relationship of DNA in bone with other components of the bone tissue and how might that affect its survivability? DNA has a high affinity to water; however, DNA has been recovered from bone samples in aquatic environments, in higher quantity and quality than other tissues in the same conditions. This indicates that there is something affecting DNA in bone that increases its survivability, even after years of bones being submerged in water.

There have been several studies focusing on the binding of DNA to hydroxyapatite. Götherström et al. (2002) used modern bovid samples, artificially degraded in a laboratory, and ancient horse samples. The ancient samples showed that collagen preservation was linked to hydroxyapatite and that with an increase in crystallinity of hydroxyapatite, there was a decrease in amplifiable DNA. Bone dissolution, or the dissolving of bone minerals, renders DNA susceptible to degradation, supporting their theory that the complex to preserve DNA includes collagen, and DNA is adsorbed and stabilized by apatite.

Despite Götherström et al. (2002) linking increased crystallinity to decreased DNA yield, Salamon et al. (2005) found intergrown crystal aggregates that are resistant to separation may create a barrier and thus protect DNA from environmental degradation—basically DNA becomes trapped within an impenetrable ring of crystals. Environmental and biotic degraders would be thwarted, but the DNA extraction techniques used in laboratories include demineralization steps that release the trapped DNA. Salamon et al. (2005) found that while the quality of the DNA extracted from such samples was better, there were fewer DNA molecules recovered. The benefit is greatest for fossil bones or other remains for which modern contamination is a concern, but could limit forensic testing, which requires reproducibility.

Another experiment testing the relationship of DNA and hydroxyapatite was conducted by Brundin et al. (2013) in which extracted bacterial DNA was added to ceramic hydroxyapatite, then incubated for 3 months in water, sera, and DNase I—an enzyme that nonspecifically cleaves DNA. At intervals during the 3 months, they tested for the presence of DNA. It was detectable in all samples after 3 months. Extracted DNA without hydroxyapatite was used as a control and also added to water, sera, and DNase I. With the exception of sera, which had a faint positive result, none had detectable DNA after 3 weeks. These data demonstrate that DNA does have a binding affinity for hydroxyapatite, which appears to stabilize and prevent the DNA from binding to the water, otherwise a significant loss of DNA in water would have been true for both the experimental and control samples. Sera gave a weak result for detectable DNA, but it demonstrates protein may also play a role in DNA preservation. The collagen protein and hydroxyapatite mineral complex in bone likely serve as a strong stabilizer for DNA, aiding in its preservation in water.

Given the strength of the protein–mineral bond, what leads to its breakdown and is there a way to screen for viability prior to testing? While the type of bone sampled has been shown to correlate to the quality and quantity of DNA (Edson et al., 2004; Misner et al., 2009; Johnston and Stephenson, 2016), visible skeletal weathering has not. The appearance of the bone has not been shown to be predictive of DNA viability, since damage to the bone would not necessarily affect DNA, and damage to DNA does not necessarily result in visible deterioration of the bone (Misner et al., 2009). Whether this translates to bones damaged in water remains to be seen. A study conducted at the University of New Haven examined the changes of morphology of sharp force trauma when abraded by sand and diatomaceous earth in a moving water environment (Appleton, 2014). Diatomaceous earth was more abrasive, resulting in more bone tissue loss, but the effects on DNA recoverability were not examined.

As remains decay, a danger to bone tissue is bioerosion. Bioerosion of the microstructure of bone has been observed in ancient bone samples, and there is some debate as to whether the bacteria responsible are endogenous or exogenous. An experiment conducted by White and Booth (2014) used stillborn and juvenile pig carcasses (buried and above ground) to investigate which of the two is the culprit. Their findings support endogenous bacteria and also suggest that since the bacteria are aggressive, with prolonged putrefaction there would be little to no well-preserved bone. The extensive bioerosion of the microstructure would expose DNA to enzymes, bacterial attack, and total degradation. Given that there is a high incidence of well-preserved bone, rapid skeletonization likely occurred to prevent putrefaction, which aids in DNA yield. The freshwater bodies of Ayers (2010) did release bacteria due to the abdominal protrusions while the saltwater bodies did not. DNA testing was not performed for that study, so the question remains of whether the presence of endogenous bacteria from a putrefying corpse may have an effect on the DNA yield of freshwater bones once the body has skeletonized.

Thus far, the research regarding DNA in bones submerged in water mimics the advice for compromised bone samples on land:

■ Cortical bone is denser and a better option for DNA testing than cancellous since the microstructure in cancellous bones makes them more susceptible to degradation (Misner et al., 2009).
■ Femur, teeth, tibia, fibula, and the petrous portion of temporal bones are the best to sample given they are dense cortical bone or well protected from the surrounding environment (Edson et al., 2004, 2009; Johnston and Stephenson, 2016), although this can be highly dependent on extraction procedures.
■ High heat during bone sampling (i.e., prolonged high speed drilling) and high stress during DNA extraction should be avoided since they may further degrade fragile DNA (Courts and Madea, 2011).
■ Increased bone powder in extraction and an added concentration step can increase DNA yield (Mameli et al., 2014).

Further research is necessary for specific data and suggestions to clarify the reasons for possible loss in yield, to distinguish challenges of freshwater versus saltwater specimens and to truly optimize protocols for DNA extraction of samples in various aquatic environments.

Case Study #4

December 15, 1942: A group of the US Army Air Force B-26 Marauders, a twin-engine medium bomber used in World War II, were sent to bomb an Axis-controlled airport in Tunis. After their attack, one plane was witnessed crashing into the water near Tunis. Since they were lost over water, the crewmen were not recovered.

The crash site was located in Lac Sud in 1948 by the US Army Graves Registration Service; however, only large pieces of the aircraft were able to be retrieved since methods for underwater recovery were decades away from being developed. The crew of the crashed aircraft was deemed "nonrecoverable."

November 2000: The US Embassy in Tunis contacted the US Army Central Identification Laboratory-Hawaii (CILHI: currently known as the Defense POW/MIA Accounting Agency Laboratory), informing them that an American aircraft and some human remains had been found in Lac Sud during a dredging project. CILHI sent a team to evaluate the site, and subsequent collaborations among CILHI, US Navy divers, and Tunisian Navy divers through February 7, 2001, lead to the recovery of material evidence and human remains.

Lac Sud is a portion of Lake Tunis that is separated from the rest of the lake by a causeway. The water at the excavation site was described as brackish, muddy, and shallow. The state of the recovered remains was documented as being excellent with attribution to the anaerobic state of the soil on the lake floor and the presence of fuel. Both of these factors slowed decomposition, thus the remains were well preserved. Twenty-eight bone (cranial, humerus, and os coxa) and tooth samples were sent to AFDIL for mtDNA testing. The testing was successful on all but one tooth and compared to the mtDNA references obtained from the missing aircrew's families. The mtDNA results, along with anthropological and odontological evidence, resulted in the identification of the entire crew in 2002.

Almost 60 years had passed since the crewmen were lost and viable mtDNA was still recoverable and reportable. In the 14 years since those identifications, DNA methods have improved significantly, further advancing the argument that bone is a strong candidate for DNA testing of samples in water and worthy of a more thorough look in the forensic community.

■ COMMINGLING OF REMAINS: INTENTIONAL AND COINCIDENTAL

As is known, human identification efforts cannot be done based on one method alone. It may be necessary to partner with different agencies, personnel and even countries to obtain the correct information. Such partnership has developed between the DPAA and AFDIL over many years to incorporate anthropological, archaeological, DNA, and other identification methods. Though many cases can provide quick answers, others are not as straight forward.

The tedious task of skeletal reassociation is further hindered when sites unexpectedly contain the remains of more than one individual. Commingling of remains can either be accidental or intentional. Elements belonging to one individual may be spread across multiple sites, which may not be collected at the same time and may introduce the risk of failing to identify all elements belonging to that individual. In these cases, this issue moves beyond the field and into the laboratory. Sample selection, the number of specimens to process, and the possibility of sample-to-sample contamination are all confounding factors that can cause delays in generating DNA results. The importance of communication between the different agencies, a sharing of the history of the site and recovery, and the availability of different scientific methods is crucial in such scenarios. While initial DNA testing can be done in the blind, sharing of site conditions and incident circumstances will aid the DNA analysts in making choices about the methods to be used. As demonstrated at the beginning of the chapter, extraction protocols may vary depending on what the skeletal remains may have been exposed to. Examples of such situations and strength of partnership are seen in the identification process of service members from World War II and Korean War.

Unintentional Commingling During World War II—Cabanatuan

Following the attack on Pearl Harbor, the Japanese military attacked the United States and Filipino forces in the Philippines, overrunning their positions by April 9, 1942. Survivors were taken prisoner and marched northward from the Bataan Peninsula to prison camps in central Luzon in the 65-mile "Bataan Death March," followed by a 25-mile train car journey to Capas, and a 9-mile march to prisoner of war (POW) Camp O'Donnell. As result of overcrowding and an excessively high death rate at Camp O'Donnell, the Japanese Army began transferring POWs to Camp Cabanatuan, 60 miles north of Manila, a few months later.

On entrance into the camp, the personal property of the prisoners, including dog tags, was confiscated. Those individuals who were able to keep their identification tags often gave them to friends in the hopes of getting the tags home to their families. As a result many individuals died without identification while others were found with multiple tags on their person. Attempts were made by other soldiers to identify decedents by placing slips of paper bearing the name of the person in his/her hand or mouth before burial. Unfortunately, most of these slips of papers had disintegrated by the time American Graves Registration Service (AGRS) began disinterring graves at the camp following the war. As a result, most individuals passed away with no individually identifiable information on their body.

At Camp Cabanatuan burials were conducted daily. All individuals who died in a given 24 h period were buried together in a mass grave. However, due to a great deal of disorder at the camp and the high death rate, many graves went undocumented and record keeping was incomplete at best. Following the war, AGRS created *The Cabanatuan Death Report*. This was a list of dates, times, causes of death, and some basic biographical information for those who died at the camp. Information on the grave number in which individuals were buried was not indicated and the report was limited in other information.

Between December 1945 and March 1946, AGRS exhumed interments at Camp Cabanatuan, a process hampered by overgrowth of vegetation as well as a high water table. Remains were reinterred 12 miles north of Manila at a temporary collection facility before being moved to the Manila Mausoleum for analysis and storage.

One particular grave from Camp Cabanatuan had records indicating that 14 bodies had been interred within it. Of these, 1 was identified with dog tags and 3 others were identified in the 1940s, leaving 10 unknown individuals. The 10 unidentified remains were reinterred briefly at the temporary collection facility before being moved to the Manila Mausoleum. Skeletal and dental charts of the remains were compiled, but the reassociation of the remains with the 10 individuals believed to be in the grave was unsuccessful. The remains were individually buried as unknowns in the Manila American Cemetery and Memorial in February 1950 and 1952.

In August 2014, the caskets of these 10 individuals were disinterred for identification purposes. Identification by anthropological means was hampered due to circumstances of the original burial and the previous disinterments and analyses, increasing the likelihood that the remains had been extensively commingled. In addition, dental comparisons were complicated by the fact that postmortem dental records could appear significantly different from the last available official chart as malnutrition and violence at the camp could have contributed to tooth loss and work could have been performed during captivity. Thus, DNA analysis was considered highly useful for the sorting of the remains and possible identification.

Cabanatuan Sample Processing

Small cuttings of skeletal elements were submitted for testing. Initially extractions of the bone samples were performed using the Demin2 inorganic extraction protocol. However, after the first round of extractions and subsequent mtDNA amplifications the success rate of obtaining data was very low. Further investigation uncovered that the samples buried in the Manila American Cemetery had been treated with a preservative powder believed to contain magnesium sulfate ($MgSO_4 \cdot 7H_2O$), ammonia alum [$NH_4Al(SO_4)_2 \cdot 12H_2O$], plaster of Paris, and other compounds that were inhibiting the release of DNA during the extraction process. Rather than continue to work with Demin2, AFDIL changed to using Demin1 to improve the quantity and quality of the DNA obtained from the samples.

Resulting data from the DNA analysis using mtDNA and modified Y-STR testing indicate the presence of at least 16 different individuals present among the bone samples submitted. Given the historical documents, the remains of only 10 individuals were thought to be present after the identification of burial of 4 of the original 14 persons buried in the grave. This discrepancy from the historical record further illustrates the fact that unintentional commingling of the remains occurred both at the time the grave was initiated and later during the numerous handlings of the remains in the 1940s and 1950s.

The treatment of the samples also underpins the importance of maintaining a variety of processing tools available for use. By maintaining numerous validated testing methods, the laboratory was able to quickly and smoothly transition from one testing method to another with minimal loss of time, reagents, and sample extract. This case also demonstrates how important it is for laboratories doing testing of unknown remains to have as much information as possible about any previous processing or storage of submitted samples so the best method of extraction can be utilized to maximize the success rate for the requested samples.

■ SUSPECTED INTENTIONAL COMMINGLING DURING THE KOREAN WAR

According to the DPAA, over 7800 US service members remain missing from the Korean War. Though there is still much to do to identify the missing, this number is relatively small due in large part to the efforts of soldiers and anthropologists of the Army Central Identification Unit, AGRS, Quartermaster, and 108th Graves Registration Platoon during the war. Throughout the Korean War, causalities were being recovered, transported, or buried in temporary cemeteries. It was one of the first attempts by the United States to return and possibly identify war dead while battle was ongoing. In the beginning, lack of resources hindered appropriate recordkeeping; however, as the recovery effort continued the necessity to maintain detailed information on each individual became critical for proper processing of the casualties. A mortuary was established at Camp Kokura in Japan, which allowed for a uniform method of processing remains prior to shipment back to the United States. The availability of personal effects, eye witness accounts, available service, medical and dental records, along with accessioning with a new Information Business Management system, made identifications faster than before.

A historic battle of the Korean War occurred at the Chosin Reservoir in what is now North Korea, or the Democratic People's Republic of Korea (DPRK). This area was known for its tundralike conditions during late fall and early winter. At times, it was referred to as the "Frozen Chosin" or "Frozen Hell" and those who survived the conditions were known as the "Chosin Few." In late 1950, soldiers from the US Army were positioned along the eastern side of the Chosin, providing assistance and relief to the first marines. In an effort to move south out of the region, the units came under attack by Chinese forces and an intense battle occurred for several days. The commander of the first Battalion, 32nd Infantry distinguished himself in combat, but was mortally wounded during the battle. While some soldiers and marines were able to retreat to safety, thousands of others were captured or left for dead.

In particular to this battle, casualties who were unable to be recovered at the time were removed or buried on site by the opposing forces. After the war ended in 1953, the UN and Communist coalitions developed three repatriation pacts; the first two, Operation Little Switch and Operation Big Switch, were for the return of POWs immediately after war. The final pact, Operation Glory, was to return war dead of the opposing side. Commencing September 1954, the exchanges occurred in demilitarized zones and continued through the end of October 1954. A total of 4219 UN remains were returned, of which, 2944 were considered American.

Korean War Sample Analysis

After the completion of Operation Glory, questions lingered about whether more unrecovered remains were still in the combat area. Beginning in 1990 and continuing through 1994, 208 boxes were repatriated to the United States by North Korea, each believed to contain the remains of a single US service member. It was reported that the remains were excavated from 21 different locations, including former POW camps and battlegrounds. As anthropologists began the task of identifying the remains, the supposed single individuals were found to be highly commingled. Initial observations estimated there were 200–400 individuals distributed between all containers; however, the current MNI is around 600 (Jin et al., 2014).

The advancement of scientific technology provided an opportunity to utilize, what was then a new and novel, mtDNA technique in the identification process. Working together, DPAA and AFDIL partnered to process this large set of remains. DPAA would undertake the task of separating and associating remains, based on anthropological techniques. A cutting would be sent to AFDIL, where scientists would conduct the DNA analysis and provide testing on the evidence and any available family reference samples. The first set of bones and teeth was received by AFDIL in the mid-1990s. Current work continues on this set of remains, with nearly 50 identifications being made from the K208 this year (FY2016).

Almost 50 years after the Battle of the Chosin Reservoir, DPAA was able to perform recoveries from that region. Between 1994 and 2005, the United States conducted joint field activities with the DPRK to visit suspected areas of unrecovered US service members. In 2004, the recovery team traveled to a location close to the initial retreat point during the 1950 battle of the Chosin Reservoir. A primary site of burial was reportedly disturbed during a construction project and remains were moved by a construction worker to a different location. The secondary burial site was excavated and remains were recovered, with an estimated MNI of 5–6. Along with the skeletal elements, personal effects were recovered and accessioned for further evaluation. The purported primary burial was examined by the recovery team, and no additional objects were recovered. Due to the conditions of recovery, there was some suspicion by the team that the recovered remains might be highly commingled.

On receipt of the samples at DPAA, the specimens were sampled and sent to AFDIL for DNA analysis. A total of 103 specimens in six submissions were submitted from 2005 to 2012. Results showed 32 different mtDNA sequences from the initial set of remains. The advancement of DNA technology has grown tremendously throughout the years, giving even greater testing sensitivity for environmentally challenged and degraded specimens. However, DNA testing alone is not enough. If family references are not available for comparison, samples will remain unidentified. By using available dental records, anthropological estimations, and available family references, only 10 identifications have been made from the potential 32 individuals. As protocols continue to improve and advance, and as more family references are received, it is hoped that the others will be identified in the future.

■ CONCLUSIONS

The challenges presented in identifying individuals from war or from other large- or long-scale disasters are unique. What may appear to be obvious at first glance may not be true after analysis is undertaken. Records may be poor. Methods once thought to be sound, such as the treatment of samples with a preservation compound, can, unfortunately, hamper future attempts at identification.

What is hopefully apparent through the course of this chapter is that DNA testing of skeletonized remains does not always take a straight course. As scientists we need to fully consider the circumstances of death and postmortem conditions before making a decision on how to proceed and not accept that the standard technique is the best. Techniques that we use now are rooted firmly in the past techniques and the future may be lateral moves in thought or a return to an older technique. Demin1 proving to be of better use in some cases for DNA extraction from skeletonized remains is an excellent example of the latter. By keeping this as an active SOP in the laboratory, AFDIL was able to return to the procedure and improve the testing results of compromised samples.

The former, lateral moves in protocols are fast on the forensic identification community. Next Generation Sequencing (NGS), or Massively Parallel Sequencing, has the possibility of completely changing the approach of HID using DNA. AFDIL recently incorporated NGS into the normal workflow for compromised samples. In 6 months of regular usage, 78 DPAA samples have been reported. While the success rate (28%) may seem to be low, consider that many of the samples tested had been unsuccessfully processed multiple times with standard protocols. Other techniques, such as mass spec analysis of the materials contained within the bone samples themselves (Edson and Roberts, *in progress*), may lead to increased efficiencies in DNA extraction and provide additional information on the postmortem conditions of the remains.

It is the task of scientists to communicate with their partners in the identification process and to provide the best science possible in their efforts. Identification of a missing person, be they a soldier or a civilian, is crucial to family members. Not only do we do a disservice to ourselves in not fully thinking about the scientific choices we can make, but also to the families as well.

Disclaimer

The opinions or assertions presented in this document are the private views of the authors and should not be construed as official or as reflecting the views of the Department of Defense, its branches, the Defense POW/MIA Accounting Agency, the US Army Medical Research and Material Command, the Armed Forces Medical Examiner System, the Armed Forces DNA Identification Laboratory, or the American Registry of Pathology. Commercial equipment, instruments, and materials are identified to specify experimental procedures as completely as possible and does not imply that any of the commercial products identified are necessarily the best available for the purpose.

References

Adler, C.J., Haak, W., Donlon, D., Cooper, A., The Geographic Consortium, 2011. Survival and recovery of DNA from ancient teeth and bones. J. Archaeol. Sci. 38 (5), 956–964.

Anderson, S., Bankier, A.T., Barrell, B.G., de Bruijn, M.H., Coulson, A.R., Drouin, J., Eperon, I.C., Nierlich, D.P., Roe, B.A., Sanger, F., Schreier, P.H., Smith, A.J., Staden, R., Young, I.G., 1981. Sequence and organization of the human mitochondrial genome. Nature 290, 457–465.

Amory, S., Huel, R., Bilić, A., Loreille, O., Parsons, T.J., 2012. Automatable full demineralization DNA extraction procedure from degraded skeletal remains. Forensic Sci. Int. Genet. 6 (3), 398–406.

Appleton, A., 2014. The Effects of Particulate-laden Water on Skeletal Trauma. Honors thesis. University of New Haven, New Haven, Connecticut.

Ayers, L.E., 2010. Differential Decomposition in Terrestrial, Freshwater, and Saltwater Environments: A Pilot Study. Master of Arts thesis. Texas State University, San Marcos.

Baker, L.E., McCormick, W.F., Matteson, K.J., 2001. A silica-based mitochondrial DNA extraction method applied to forensic hair shafts and teeth. J. Forensic Sci. 46 (1), 126–130.

Bar, W., Brinkmann, B., Lincoln, P., Mayr, W.R., Rossi, U., 1994. DNA recommendations – 1994 report concerning further recommendation for the DNA Commission of the ISFH regarding PCR-based polymorphisms in STR (short tandem repeat) systems. Int. J. Leg. Med. 107, 159–160.

Bienvenue, J.M., Legendre, L.A., Ferrance, J.P., Landers, J.P., 2010. An integrated microfluidic device for DNA purification and PCR amplification of STR fragments. Forensic Sci. Int. Genet. 4, 178–186.

Brandt, J.H., Maurizio, D., Hassanin, A., Melville, R.A., Olson, L.E., Seveau, A., Timm, R.M., 2001. Debate on the authenticity of *Pseudonovibos spiralis* as a new species of wild bovid from Vietnam and Cambodia. J. Zool. Lond. 255, 437–444.

Brundin, M., Figdor, D., Sundqvist, G., Sjögren, U., 2013. DNA binding to hydroxyapatite: a potential mechanism for preservation of microbial DNA. J. Endod. 39 (2), 211–216.

Butler, J., 2003. Recent developments in Y-short tandem repeat and Y-single nucleotide polymorphism analysis. Forensic Sci. Rev. 15 (2), 91–111.

Ciavaglia, S.A., Tobe, S.S., Donnellan, S.C., Henry, J.M., Linacre, A., 2015. Molecular identification of python species: development and validation of a novel assay for forensic investigations. Forensic Sci. Int. Genet. 16, 64–70.

Courts, C., Madea, B., 2011. Full STR profile of a 67-year-old bone found in a fresh water lake. J. Forensic Sci. 56 (S1), S172–S175.

Crainic, K., Paraire, F., Lettereux, M., Durigon, M., de Mazancourt, P., 2002. Skeletal remains presumed submerged in water for three years identified using PCR-STR analysis. J. Forensic Sci. 47 (5), 1025–1027.

Davoren, J., Vanek, D., Konjhodzić, R., Crews, J., Huffine, E., Parsons, T.J., 2007. Highly effective DNA extraction method for nuclear short tandem repeat testing of skeletal remains from mass graves. Croat. Med. J. 48, 478–485.

Edson, S.M., Christensen, A.F., Barritt, S.M., Meehan, A., Leney, M.D., Finelli, L.N., 2009. Sampling of the cranium for mitochondrial DNA analysis of human skeletal remains. Supplemental Series Forensic Sci. Int. Genet. 2, 269–270.

Edson, S.M., Christensen, A.F., Meehan, A., Barritt-Ross, S.M., 2011. Increased efficiency of mitochondrial DNA extraction from human skeletal remains: a protocol change leads to reduced sample size requirements. Abstract. In: International Association of Forensic Sciences 19th World Meeting. Funchal, Madeira, Portugal.

Edson, S.M., McMahon, T.P., 2016. Extraction of DNA from skeletal remains. In: Goodwin, W. (Ed.), Forensic DNA Typing Protocols, second ed. Springer Science and Business Media, LLC, New York, pp. 69–87.

Edson, S.M., Ross, J.P., Coble, M.D., Parsons, T.J., Barritt, S.M., 2004. Naming the dead – confronting realities of rapid identification of degraded skeletal remains. Forensic Sci. Rev. 16, 63–90.

Gill, P., Jeffreys, A.J., Werrett, D.J., 1985. Forensic application of DNA 'fingerprints'. Nature 318, 577–579.

Götherström, A., Angerbjörn, A., Collins, M.J., Lidén, K., 2002. Bone preservation and DNA amplification. Archaeometry 44 (3), 395–404.

Hammond, H.A., Jin, L., Zhong, Y., Caskey, C.T., Chakraborty, R., 1994. Evaluation of 13 short tandem repeat loci for use in personal identification applications. Am. J. Hum. Genet. 55, 175–189.

Hassanin, A., Seveau, A., Thomas, H., Bocherens, H., Billiou, D., Nguyen, B.X., 2001. Evidence from DNA that the mysterious 'linh duong' (*Pseudonovibos spiralis*) is not a new bovid. Comptes Rendus de L'Academie des Sciences. Life Sci. 324, 71–80.

Higgins, D., Rohrlach, A.B., Kaidonis, J., Townsend, G., Austin, J.J., 2015. Differential nuclear and mitochondrial DNA preservation in post-mortem teeth with implications for forensic and ancient DNA studies. PLoS One 10 (5), e0126935. http://dx.doi.org/10.1371/journal.pone.0126935.

Holland, M.M., Fisher, D.L., Mitchell, L.G., Rodriguez, W.C., Canik, J.J., Merrill, C.R., Weedn, V.W., 1993. Mitochondrial DNA sequnce analysis of human skeletal remains: identification of remains from the Vietnam War. J. Forensic Sci. 38 (3), 542–553.

Holland, M.M., Parsons, T.J., 1999. Mitochondrial DNA sequence analysis – validation and use for forensic casework. Forensic Sci. Rev. 11 (1), 21–50.

Hopwood, A.J., Hurth, C., Yang, J., Cai, Z., Moran, N., Lee-Edghill, J.G., Nordquist, A., Lenigk, R., Estes, M.D., Haley, J.P., 2010. Integrated microfluidic system for rapid forensic DNA analysis: sample collection to DNA profile. Anal. Chem. 82, 6991–6999.

Irwin, J.A., Edson, S.M., Loreille, O., Just, R.J., Barritt, S.M., Lee, D.A., Holland, T.D., Parsons, T.J., Leney, M.D., 2007a. DNA identification of "Earthquake McGoon" 50 years postmortem. J. Forensic Sci. 52 (5), 1115–1118.

Irwin, J.A., Leney, M.D., Loreille, O., Barritt, S.M., Christensen, A.F., Holland, T.D., Smith, B.C., Parsons, T.J., 2007b. Application of Low Copy number STR typing to the identification of aged, degraded skeletal remains. J. Forensic Sci. 52 (6), 1322–1327.

Jeffreys, A.J., Wilson, V., Thein, S.L., 1985. Hypervariable 'minisatellite' regions in human DNA. Nature 314, 67–73.

Jin, J., Burch, A.L., LeGarde, C., Okrutny, E., 2014. The Korea 208: a large commingling case of American remains from the Korean War. In: Adams, B.J., Byrd, J.E. (Eds.), Commingled Human Remains: Methods in Recovery, Analysis, and Identification. Elsevier Academic Press, San Diego, CA, pp. 407–423.

Johnston, E., Stephenson, M., 2016. DNA profiling success rates from degraded skeletal remains in Guatemala. J. Forensic Sci. 61 (4), 898–902.

Kitpipit, T., Penchart, K., Ouithavon, K., Satasook, C., Linacre, A., Thanakiatkrai, P., 2016. A novel real time PCR assay using melt curve analysis for ivory identification. Forensic Sci. Int. 12 (267), 210–217.

Kuznetsov, G.V., Kulikov, E.E., Petrov, N.B., Ivanova, N.V., Lomov, A.A., Kholodova, M.V., Poltaraus, A.B., 2001. The "linh duong" *Pseudonovibos spiralis* (Mammalia, Artiodactyla) is a new buffalo. Naturwissenschaften 88, 123–125.

Lee, H.W., Park, M.J., Kim, N.Y., Sim, J.E., Yang, W.I., Shin, K., 2010. Simple and highly effective DNA extraction methods from old skeletal remains using silica columns. Forensic Sci. Int. Genet. 4 (5), 275–280.

Linacre, A., Lee, J.C., 2016. Species determination: the role and use of cytochrome b gene. Methods Mol. Biol. 1420, 287–296.

Loreille, O.M., Diegoli, T.M., Irwin, J.A., Coble, M.D., Parsons, T.J., 2007. High efficiency DNA extraction from bone by total demineralization. Forensic Sci. Int. Genet. 1 (2), 191–195.

Mameli, A., Piras, G., Delogu, G., 2014. The successful recovery of low copy number and degraded DNA from bones exposed to seawater suitable for generating a DNA STR profile. J. Forensic Sci. 59 (2), 470–473.

Melton, T., Holland, C., 2007. Routine forensic use of the mitochondrial 12S ribosomal RNA gene for species identification. J. Forensic Sci. 52 (6), 1305–1307.

Misner, L.M., Halvorson, A.C., Dreier, J.L., Ubelaker, D.H., Foran, D.R., 2009. The correlation between skeletal weathering and DNA quality and quantity. J. Forensic Sci. 54 (4), 822–828.

Mullis, K.B., Faloona, F.A., 1987. Specific synthesis of DNA *in vitro* via a polymerase-catalyzed chain reaction. Methods Enzym. 155, 335–350.

O'Brien, T.G., Kuehner, A.C., 2007. Waxing grave about adipocere: soft tissue change in an aquatic context. J. Forensic Sci. 52 (2), 294–301.

Olson, L.E., Hassanin, A., 2003. Contamination and chimerism are perpetuating the legend of the snake-eating cow with twisted horns (*Pseudonovibos spiralis*). A case study of the pitfalls of ancient DNA. Mol. Phylogenetics Evol. 27, 545–548.

Rohland, N., Hofreiter, M., 2007. Ancient DNA extraction from bones and teeth. Nat. Protoc. 2, 1756–1762.

Salamon, M., Tuross, N., Arensburg, B., Weiner, S., 2005. Relatively well preserved DNA is present in the crystal aggregates of fossil bones. Proc. Natl. Acad. Sci. U.S.A. 102 (39), 13783–13788.

Sanger, F., Ncklen, S., Coulson, A.R., 1977. DNA sequencing with chain-terminating inhibitors. Proc. Natl. Acad. Sci. U.S.A. 74 (12), 5463–5467.

Shiroma, C.Y., Fielding, C.G., Lewis, J.A., Gleisner, M.R., Dunn, K.N., 2004. A minimally destructive technique for sampling dentin powder for mitochondrial DNA testing. J. Forensic Sci. 49, 1–5.

Tobe, S.S., Linacre, A., 2010. DNA typing in wildlife crime: recent developments in species identification. Forensic Sci. Med. Pathol. 6 (3), 195–206.

Tan, E., Turingan, R.S., Hogan, C., Vasantgadkar, S., Palombo, L., Schumm, J.W., Selden, R.F., 2013. Fully integrated, fully automated generation of short tandem repeat profiles. Investig. Genet. 4, 16.

Urquhart, A., Kimpton, C.P., Downes, T.J., Gill, P., 1994. Variation in short tandem repeat sequences – a survey of twelve microsatellite loci for use as forensic identification markers. Int. J. Leg. Med. 107, 13–20.

Watson, J.D., Crick, F.H.C., 1953. Molecular structure of nucleic acids. Nature 171, 737–738.

White, L., Booth, T.J., 2014. The origin of bacteria responsible for bioerosion to the internal bone microstructure: results from experimentally-deposited pig carcasses. Forensic Sci. Int. 239, 92–102.

CHAPTER **14**

Forensic Identification of Human Skeletal Remains Using Isotopes: A Brief History of Applications From Archaeological Dig Sites to Modern Crime Scenes

Lesley A. Chesson[1] | Brett J. Tipple[1] | Lane V. Youmans[2] |
Michael A. O'Brien[3] | Michael M. Harmon[4]

[1]IsoForensics, Inc., Salt Lake City, UT, United States,
[2]Grays Harbor County Coroner's Office, Aberdeen, WA, United States,
[3]Economy Borough Police Department, Baden, PA, United States,
[4]Linn County Sheriff's Office, Albany, OR, United States

Chapter Outline

■ INTRODUCTION

While walking through the woods of Beaver County, Pennsylvania, on December 12, 2014, a teenager discovered the severed head of a female. The woman appeared to be in her 60s, with gray, curled hair (Fig. 14.1). She had been professionally embalmed and small red rubber balls had been fitted into her eye sockets, potentially following organ donation. Investigators suspected that—while she likely died of natural causes—someone illegally intervened as her body was in transit for final disposition (Miller, 2015).

The Economy Borough Police Department tried a variety of methods for identifying the woman, including:

Forensic facial reconstruction (2D and 3D, with age regression)
Dental records
DNA profiling
Reviews of recent organ/body donations

None of these investigative techniques or tools provided the evidence needed to give the decedent her name. Other commonly used human identification methods—examinations of personal effects, fingerprints, and birthmarks or surgical scars—were not applicable to the case. What other methods could the police try?

New Perspectives in Forensic Human Skeletal Identification. http://dx.doi.org/10.1016/B978-0-12-805429-1.00014-4

ORIGINAL   ALTERNATIVE   AGE-REGRESSED (30s)

Figure 14.1 Artist renderings of an unidentified woman, whose severed, embalmed head was found in the woods of western Pennsylvania on December 12, 2014.

In this chapter we describe a relatively new investigative technique, forensic isotope analysis, for the identification of human skeletal remains. The technique capitalizes on information recorded by an individual about his or her dietary and water inputs through the transfer of elements into tissues. The "snapshot" of time represented by different tissues varies, providing information on an individual's past (via tooth enamel and/or bone) and more recent history (via hair and/or nails). Forensic isotope analysis of human remains can reveal features of an unidentified decedent's geographic life history and dietary lifestyle by examining the elemental—and associated isotopic—record stored in tissues. While these features cannot pinpoint exact provenance, measurement of isotopes in tissues can help exclude many potential search areas and provide focus to continuing investigations.

Not All Atoms of an Element Are Alike

Most elements of biological interest exist in multiple forms, distinguished by different numbers of neutrons within the nucleus (Hoefs, 2009). The addition of neutrons gives rise to isotopes, atoms of an element with slightly different masses. While isotopes of an element have the same chemical properties, the kinetic and thermodynamic properties of different isotopes of an element will vary; the magnitude of these variations typically decreases as atomic weight increases (Urey, 1947). Some isotopes (e.g., ^{14}C or "radiocarbon") are radioactive, and their known rate of decay can be used for dating human remains (Alkass et al., 2011). Of arguably more importance to forensic human identification, however, are the stable isotopes that do not undergo radioactive decay.

The shorthand used to describe isotopes is derived from the total number of protons and neutrons within the nucleus. For example, an atom of the element oxygen (O) with eight protons and eight neutrons is known as the stable isotope ^{16}O, while the addition of two neutrons gives rise to another stable isotope of oxygen, ^{18}O. The natural abundances of these stable isotopes differ, with ^{16}O at about 99.8% and ^{18}O at about 0.2% (Schwarcz and Schoeninger, 1991).

Abundances of stable isotopes of an element are described as the ratio (R) of the rare or heavy form to the common or light form (e.g., $R = {}^{18}O/{}^{16}O$). Since these ratios are small, it is routine practice in stable isotope research to express results in δ-notation as parts per thousand (‰) difference from an accepted reference point, where:

$$\delta = \left(R_{sample} / R_{standard} - 1 \right)$$

In the case of the oxygen stable isotope ratio ($\delta^{18}O$), the equation becomes:

$$\delta^{18}O = \left[\left({}^{18}O/{}^{16}O_{sample} \right) / \left({}^{18}O/{}^{16}O_{standard} \right) - 1 \right]$$

Negative δ-values indicate the sample had a lower ratio (R) than the standard, while positive δ-values indicate the sample had a higher R than the standard. This δ-notation is also used for expressing the stable isotope ratios of hydrogen (H), carbon (C), nitrogen (N), and sulfur (S), collectively described as the bio-elements. In contrast, isotope abundances of more massive elements and radiogenic isotopes, such as strontium (Sr) and lead (Pb), are typically expressed as simple ratios (e.g., $^{87}Sr/{}^{86}Sr$, $^{204}Pb/{}^{206}Pb$, $^{207}Pb/{}^{206}Pb$, $^{208}Pb/{}^{206}Pb$).

The standards used to express isotope abundances in δ-notation are primary (calibration) materials, which have absolute isotopic compositions accepted internationally (Table 14.1). Many of these calibration materials no longer exist, or never physically existed at all. Instead available to analysts are a variety of secondary (reference) materials

Table 14.1   A List of Primary (Calibration) Materials Used to Express the Stable Isotope Abundances of Bio-Elements in the Traditional δ-Notation

Abbreviation	Isotopes	R	Full Name
VSMOW	$^{2}H/^{1}H$	0.00015576	Vienna Standard Mean Ocean Water
VSMOW	$^{18}O/^{16}O$	0.0020052	Vienna Standard Mean Ocean Water
VPDB	$^{13}C/^{12}C$	0.0112372	Vienna Pee Dee Belemnite
VPDB	$^{18}O/^{16}O$	0.0020671	Vienna Pee Dee Belemnite
Air	$^{15}N/^{14}N$	0.0036765	Atmospheric Air
VCDT	$^{34}S/^{32}S$	0.0450045	Vienna Canyon Diablo Troilite

(Table 14.2), which have been calibrated to the primary materials and can be purchased, albeit under carefully controlled conditions to prevent exhaustion.

Analytical laboratories use secondary reference materials to calibrate in-house (laboratory) reference materials (Carter and Barwick, 2011). These laboratory reference materials can be made in quantity and chemically matched to the materials a laboratory analyzes regularly. These laboratory reference materials are used in day-to-day operation both for expressing results of an individual analysis on international isotope scales and for collecting quality assurance data over the long term.

A Specialized Form of Mass Spectrometry Measures Isotope Abundances

Isotope ratio mass spectrometry (IRMS) is the most common method used to analyze stable isotope abundances (Muccio, 2010; Muccio and Jackson, 2009). In this technique, materials are converted to simple gases for measurement. Gases are separated via gas chromatography and then ionized before moving through a magnetic field where molecular ions containing various combinations of light and heavy isotopes are separated into ion streams based on differences in mass-to-charge ratio. Ion streams containing gas molecules with lighter isotopes bend at smaller radii than streams with heavier isotopes. Finally, a collection of Faraday cups is used to measure the current of each ion stream.

The first IRMS systems used variable-volume dual inlets to alternately introduce sample gas and a reference gas of known isotopic composition into the mass spectrometer; the origin of δ-notation comes from the observation of a difference, or delta, between the sample and reference gases. The technique is generally considered to be the most precise method of measuring the isotope ratios of bio-elements. However, dual inlet–IRMS requires significant investment of effort as a single measurement can take several minutes, not including the time needed for sample gas preparation, which is produced "off-line."

Since the 1990s, most stable isotope analyses are made using continuous flow–IRMS (Muccio and Jackson, 2009). As the name suggests, the continuous flow technique requires a constant stream of gases into the IRMS, and thus a carrier gas, typically helium, is used. Sample gas preparation occurs immediately before introduction to the mass spectrometer ("in-line") using one of a variety of peripherals. The sample gas is measured just once; reference gas may be measured before or after sample gas. While the precision of continuous flow–IRMS is somewhat less than that of dual inlet–IRMS, the technique dramatically increases throughput.

Commonly used peripherals for the forensic isotope analysis of human tissues include the following:

- Elemental analyzers (EAs), for the measurement of C, N, and S stable isotope ratios as CO_2, N_2, and SO_2 gases, respectively, from the combustion of samples (e.g., bone collagen, muscle proteins, and keratin); the EAs can also be used to measure N_2 generated from the "thermal decomposition" of samples (Gentile et al., 2013; Lott et al., 2015).
- High-temperature thermal conversion EAs, for the measurement of H and O stable isotope ratios as H_2 and CO gases, respectively, from the pyrolysis of samples (e.g., urine, keratin, etc.).
- Acid digestion accessories, for the measurement of C and O stable isotope ratios as CO_2, from the reaction of bio-minerals (e.g., bioapatite and carbonate in tooth enamel or bone).

SELECTION AND PREPARATION OF REMAINS FOR ISOTOPE ANALYSIS

Any human tissue could be measured via IRMS, but most casework has focused on isotope analyses of hair, nail, teeth, and bone. Hair and nail can be considered "recent" recorders—because these tissues are continuously growing throughout the life of an individual, the isotopes within hair strands and finger- or toe-nails carry a record of the recent past (Lehn et al., 2015a; Meier-Augenstein and Kemp, 2012; Thompson et al., 2014). Hair grows approximately 1 cm per month, while nail grows approximately 1.5–3 mm per month (Lehn et al., 2011); the longer the hair strands or nails, the more time recorded prior to death. On the other hand, teeth and bone can be considered "historic" recorders. Depending on the individual's age and dentition, tooth enamel is either formed when an individual is perinatal or a juvenile. The isotopes in tooth enamel thus carry a record of the individual's past, particularly the years of early childhood or adolescence (Posey, 2011; Regan, 2006). Bone is continuously remodeled during an individual's lifetime, with approximately 10% of the skeleton replaced each year (Stenhouse and Baxter, 1979). Bone thus provides a "double exposed" or "smeared" snapshot of time about 10 years before death.

The different growth periods and rates of human tissues allow investigators to build a chronology of an individual's history through analysis of the isotopes contained within. Measurements may be made on inorganic material,

Table 14.2 A Nonexhaustive List of Secondary (Reference) Materials Commercially Available for Purchase; These Materials Have Been Certified and Can be Used to Calibrate In-House (Laboratory) Reference Materials

Reference Material	Material	δ^2H_{VSMOW}	$\delta^{18}O_{VSMOW}$	$\delta^{18}O_{VPDB}$[a]	$\delta^{13}C_{VPDB}$	$\delta^{15}N_{Air}$	$\delta^{34}S_{VCDT}$
GISP	Water	−189.7	−24.78				
SLAP	Water	−427.5[b]	−55.5[b]				
IAEA-CH-7	Polyethylene foil	−100.3			−32.15		
NBS18	Carbonatite			−23.01	−5.01		
NBS19	Limestone			−2.2[b]	+1.95[b]		
LSVEC	Lithium carbonate				−46.6[b]		
IAEA-600	Caffeine		−3.48				
IAEA-601	Benzoic acid		+23.14				
IAEA-602	Benzoic acid		+71.28				
NBS22	Oil	−116.9			−30.03		
USGS-32	Potassium nitrate		+25.4			+180[b]	
USGS-40	L-glutamic acid				−26.39	−4.52	
USGS-41	L-glutamic acid				+37.63	+47.57	
IAEA-S-1	Silver sulfide						−0.3[b]
IAEA-S-2	Silver sulfide						+22.62
IAEA-S-3	Silver sulfide						−32.49

[a]The VPDB scale (as opposed to the VSMOW scale) is used for reporting $\delta^{18}O$ values of carbonates. The recommended conversion between scales is as follows: $\delta^{18}O_{VSMOW} = 1.0391 \times \delta^{18}O_{VPDB} + 30.91$ (Coplen et al., 1983).

[b]These δ-values have *no* associated uncertainty and are the *exact* values defining the relevant isotope scale along with the primary (calibration) materials (Brand et al., 2014).

VCDT, Vienna Canyon Diablo Troilite; *VPDB*, Vienna Pee Dee Belemnite; *VSMOW*, Vienna Standard Mean Ocean Water.

such as the bioapatite component of tooth enamel or bone, or organic material, such as keratin of hair/nail or collagen extracted from bone. It should be noted that some tissues, such as bone, contain both an inorganic and organic (protein) fraction, which may record isotopes of different inputs. For example, research has shown that the bioapatite fraction of bone reflects whole diet, while bone collagen records the isotopic composition of dietary protein in particular (Ambrose and Norr, 1993; Tieszen and Fagre, 1993).

Material condition and sample integrity are important concerns prior to isotope analysis. In some cases, human tissue samples may be fresh, collected from a recently deceased individual. In other cases, remains may have been buried or exposed at the surface for some period of time. With time and exposure comes an opportunity for chemical alteration of tissues, a process called diagenesis. Useful metrics for assessing sample condition include element concentrations and material yields, as described in detail elsewhere (Bartelink et al., 2014b; Hedges, 2002; Lee-Thorp, 2002; Tuross, 2002). For investigations of most modern decedents, diagenesis is not typically a concern; this is not true, however, for investigations of remains from archaeological sites and under particular environmental conditions, where time and exposure may alter the original chemical and isotopic signature.

It is also important that all exogenous material is removed from the tissue sample prior to analysis, since this material represents environmental contamination and not the intrinsic or endogenous record indicative of the individual's geographic life history and dietary lifestyle. A variety of methods have been published to clean and prepare human tissues for isotope analysis, including:

- solvent washes for hair and nails (O'Connell et al., 2001; Tipple et al., 2013),
- enamel powder collections for teeth (Kusaka and Nakano, 2014; Passey et al., 2007),
- extraction to collect bone collagen (Ambrose, 1990; DeNiro, 1985), and
- isolation of bioapatite from bones (Koch et al., 1997; Snoeck and Pellegrini, 2015; Yoder and Bartelink, 2010).

These methods have been reviewed in details elsewhere (Bartelink et al., 2014b; Katzenberg, 2008; Schwarcz and Schoeninger, 1991) and will not be covered here.

■ INTERPRETATION OF ISOTOPE DATA FROM HUMAN REMAINS

While individuals do record information about their inputs in tissues, the isotopic composition of a tissue will not exactly match that of the food they ate or water they drank. This is due to natural processes that lead to isotopic fractionation, whereby a mixture (of isotopes in this case) is separated into fractions that vary in composition. The differing kinetic and thermodynamic properties of isotopes are largely responsible for changes in isotopic composition following biological, chemical, and metabolic reactions, with greater effects seen in the bio-elements (elements with lower atomic weights) than biological trace elements, such as strontium or lead.

Carbon and Nitrogen Isotopes

Carbon isotope ratios of human tissues primarily provide dietary information, specifically about the photosynthetic pathway of plant material–fixing carbon at the base of the food chain. There are two main photosynthetic pathways important for human nutrition, characterized by distinctive isotope fractionations of carbon from CO_2 in the atmosphere to starch. The C_3 pathway, used by temperate grasses, trees, and domesticates such as wheat, typically results in lower values for plant tissues (e.g., $\delta^{13}C \approx -26‰$), while the C_4 pathway, used by tropical grasses and domesticates such as maize and sugar cane, typically results in more positive values (e.g., $\delta^{13}C \approx -12‰$) (Cerling et al., 1997; Tipple and Pagani, 2007). Plants using Crassulacean acid metabolism (CAM) photosynthesis have carbon isotopic compositions between C_3 and C_4 plants (O'Leary, 1988), but very few CAM plants (e.g., agave, pineapple) are regularly ingested by humans or meat animals.

Carbon may either be ingested by humans directly as plant material or indirectly as animal products, such as dairy or meat. The carbon isotopic composition of tissues—such as human hair or bone collagen—should reflect the composition of the diet with a slight offset of 1‰–3‰ (Schoeninger, 1985; Schoeninger and DeNiro, 1984). Carbon isotope ratio analyses in human remains are often used to determine whether or not an individual fits a known population or has had dietary shifts over time, either reflecting geographical movements or significant changes in eating habits.

Nitrogen isotope ratios of animal tissues have been shown to reflect the quality and quantity of protein consumed (Robbins et al., 2010, 2005). This is due to fractionation as nitrogen moves through trophic levels, resulting in progressively higher $\delta^{15}N$ values in animals relative to plants or animals lower on the food chain (Post, 2002). This signal is propagated into the tissues of the consumer with an increase of approximately 3‰ per trophic level. Similar to carbon, nitrogen isotope ratio analyses are often used in determining whether or not an individual has changed dietary habits.

Hydrogen and Oxygen Isotopes

Hydrogen and oxygen isotope ratios in water covary with geographic location in a predictable and well-defined manner across the globe. Factors such as latitude, longitude, altitude, the distance from large bodies of water, and season lead to fractionation of hydrogen and oxygen isotopes within the water cycle, affecting isotopic composition (Craig, 1961; Dansgaard, 1964, 1954; Gat, 1996). Warmer climates generally have higher δ^2H and $\delta^{18}O$ values of precipitation, while colder, higher latitude locations have lower values. These spatial variations can be displayed graphically as isotope landscapes, or isoscapes (West et al., 2006).

The local signals resulting from this predictable water isotope fractionation are propagated through plants and animals and can be recovered from tissues such as hair, tooth enamel, or bone, providing geolocation information. The recovered signals will be characteristic of a range of isotopically similar locations (Bowen et al., 2007; Bowen and Revenaugh, 2003), or iso-regions. If an individual moves across an isotopic gradient, and hence to a new iso-region, differences in the isotopic values of drinking water will influence the isotopic composition of body water and will ultimately be recorded in an individual's body tissues. Geographic movements can therefore potentially be reconstructed by analyzing segments along the length of hair to provide a record of the last month or from tissues representing different periods of an individual's life (e.g., tooth vs. bone vs. hair).

How Human Tissues Record Water Isotopes

The proteins in hair and nail can be derived from amino acids in the diet, amino acids synthesized de novo from dietary inputs, and amino acids recycled from muscle degradation. During protein digestion in the human gut, the oxygen isotopes in the amino acids exchange with and reflect the isotopic composition of gut water; its isotopic composition, in turn, is related to that of drinking water. While the same process occurs with hydrogen atoms at the C-terminus of amino acids during protein degradation, the hydrogen atoms associated with R-groups of amino acids retain their original isotope values. Thus, there is not a full exchange of H isotopes in amino acids with body water as is the case with oxygen isotopes. In unidentified decedent investigations, oxygen isotope ratios can be considered indicative of iso-region, while a combined dietary and iso-region signal is attributed to the measured hydrogen isotope ratio values (Ehleringer et al., 2008; Thompson et al., 2014).

The carbonate and phosphate minerals that form tooth enamel or bone bioapatite reflect the isotopic composition of water imbibed by an animal as a liquid or contained within food (Kohn, 1996). For large animals—such as humans—the impact of food on tooth and bone bioapatite oxygen isotope ratios is much less than the impact of drinking water. Thus, there is a strong relationship between the oxygen isotope ratios of bioapatite minerals (carbonate and phosphate) and water imbibed by an individual. It is easier and faster to measure the oxygen isotope ratios of carbonate than it is to measure phosphate. As such, most analytical facilities measure the $\delta^{18}O_{VSMOW}$ value of carbonate (converted from $\delta^{18}O_{VPDB}$) and estimate the $\delta^{18}O_{VSMOW}$ value of phosphate following measurement. A common method for estimating phosphate oxygen isotopic composition from carbonate (Iacumin et al., 1996) assumes no diagenesis has occurred in the tooth or bone during burial/environmental exposure. The $\delta^{18}O_{VSMOW}$ value of drinking water can then be predicted from the estimated $\delta^{18}O_{VSMOW}$ of phosphate (Daux et al., 2008).

Strontium Isotopes

Strontium isotope ratios in the local environment vary spatially due to variations in the local geology. One isotope of strontium—^{87}Sr—is the product of radioactive decay of rubidium (^{87}Rb), and the abundance of ^{87}Sr in a material is thus dependent on the initial concentration of ^{87}Rb and the age of the material. Young materials with low Rb concentrations, such as modern volcanic basalts, typically have low $^{87}Sr/^{86}Sr$ ratios (i.e., 0.702–0.706), whereas old and Rb-rich materials, such as granites, have higher $^{87}Sr/^{86}Sr$ ratios (i.e., 0.710 and greater). Different geographic regions are characterized by variations in the geologic age of bedrock, which is the principal determinant of $^{87}Sr/^{86}Sr$ ratios seen throughout the local environment in soil, water, plants, and animals (Bataille and Bowen, 2012; Beard and Johnson, 2000).

Due to similarities in charge and atomic radius, Sr readily substitutes for calcium (Ca) in tooth enamel or bone. It's generally assumed that there is little or no isotopic fractionation with Sr incorporation. Therefore, both primary producers and higher-level consumers reflect local geology in the $^{87}Sr/^{86}Sr$ ratios of their skeletal tissues (Beard and Johnson, 2000). In hair, Sr is incorporated from bathing water; analysis of $^{87}Sr/^{86}Sr$ ratios of hair keratin thus provides information on the exogenous Sr signal recorded by an individual as his or her hair is exposed to water (Tipple et al., 2013).

■ HISTORY OF APPLICATION OF ISOTOPE ANALYSIS IN FORENSIC CASEWORK

The use of isotope analysis in modern casework would not be possible without decades of pioneering work in the fields of archaeology, anthropology, geology, nutritional ecology, and plant physiology. To acknowledge that foundation, we next briefly review the timeline of isotope analysis of human remains. We note that more exhaustive reviews have been published previously (Ambrose and Krigbaum, 2003; Katzenberg, 2008; Schwarcz et al., 2010; Schwarcz and Schoeninger, 1991, 2012).

The first reports of variations in the $\delta^{13}C$ values of plants—now known to relate to differences in the C_3, C_4, and CAM photosynthetic pathways—were published in the 1960s and 1970s (Bender, 1971; Bender et al., 1973; Osmond et al., 1973; Park and Epstein, 1961, 1960; Smith and Epstein, 1971). Application of this phenomenon to archaeological settings came shortly thereafter, when the $\delta^{13}C$ values of human bone collagen were used to quantify the importance of maize cultivation at prehistoric sites in New York state (Vogel and van der Merwe, 1977). This was followed a year later by a study on the diets of prehistoric humans living in North American woodlands (van der Merwe and Vogel, 1978).

In 1978, carbon isotope analyses of liver tissues collected during autopsies in New York state, Norway, Scotland, and Switzerland were published to generate "baseline data" for comparing $\delta^{13}C$ values among different human populations (Gaffney et al., 1978). The authors used the data to quantify nutritional differences between US Americans and Europeans, estimating the diets of individuals from New York were approximately 75% C_4 plant-based, while those of the European populations were approximately 70% C_3 plant-based. Capitalizing on isotopic variation of diet in different geographic locations, $\delta^{13}C$ values of beard hair were used to investigate travel by individuals between German, Japan, and the United States (Nakamura et al., 1982). Interestingly, the dietary differences first observed almost 40 years ago for individuals living in the United States and Europe are still observed today in studies of modern human hair carbon isotopes ratios (Hülsemann et al., 2015; Valenzuela et al., 2012).

Also in 1978, researchers studying carbon isotope variation in multiple tissues from a single individual noted that "isotope ratios of component biochemical fractions such as fats and proteins may be less variable than those of whole tissues of variable composition" (Lyon and Baxter, 1978), arguably setting the precedent for tissue-specific isotope analyses. A 1981 publication documented the relationship between $\delta^{13}C$ values of bone bioapatite and bone "gelatin" (Sullivan and Krueger, 1981), demonstrating that—while the carbon isotopic compositions of the bone fractions were different—both reflected the isotopic composition of diet. Relationships between the isotopic composition of the inorganic and organic fractions of bone have been reviewed in detail fairly recently (Hedges, 2003).

The first review of carbon isotope analysis and archaeology was published in 1982 (van der Merwe, 1982), with slightly later reviews incorporating the use of nitrogen isotope analysis (DeNiro, 1987; Klepinger, 1984). Studies on nitrogen isotope ratios of human tissues generally lagged those on carbon isotopes by a few years. A 1981 publication presented the $\delta^{15}N$ values of bone collagen from humans living in the Tehuacan Valley (Mexico) over a period of 7000 years (DeNiro and Epstein, 1981). Nitrogen isotope ratios decreased through time, suggesting that less animal protein and more legumes were found in the diets of individuals occupying the site more recently—or that diagenesis had affected bone collagen $\delta^{15}N$ values of older remains. Nitrogen isotopes later proved useful to investigate the contribution of marine resources to prehistoric human diet (Schoeninger et al., 1983; Schoeninger and DeNiro, 1984) and also the relative "trophic" position of humans in food webs (Katzenberg, 2008).

The first study highlighting isotope analysis as a possible tool for human identification was published in 1989 by Katzenberg and Krouse. After discussing the use of carbon (and sulfur) isotopes to relate humans with dietary inputs, the authors presented δ^2H and $\delta^{18}O$ values of urine collected from a traveler who visited Brisbane, Australia, from Calgary, Canada, documenting the relatively rapid turnover of body water as the individual changed location. The authors then described the case of a deceased male found in Banff National Park in 1986 who was not identified for almost a year, and noted:

If hair and bone collagen had been analysed for isotope composition the possibilities for long-term residence could have been narrowed down. Isotopic differences among hair, collagen, and other tissues may have provided an estimate of the time spent in the Calgary/Banff area.

Katzenberg and Krouse (1989)

The 1990s and 2000s saw the first applications of oxygen isotope ratios to investigate (prehistoric) human origin and movement (Dupras and Schwarcz, 2001; Schwarcz and Schoeninger, 1991; White et al., 2004, 1998). About that same time, researchers were beginning to measure strontium—as well as lead (Gulson et al., 1997)—isotope ratios of human tissues to address questions of migration. The use of strontium isotopes as "tracers" of human behavior was suggested initially in 1985 (Ericson, 1985). By the 2000s, several studies had been published using $^{87}Sr/^{86}Sr$ to investigate prehistoric populations living in North America (Beard and Johnson, 2000; Ezzo et al., 1997; Price et al., 1994b), South America (Hodell et al., 2004; Knudson et al., 2004), Africa (Sealy et al., 1991), and Europe (Bentley and Knipper, 2005; Grupe et al., 1997; Price et al., 1994a).

Despite the long history of stable isotope analyses of human remains in archaeological, anthropological, and biomedical/nutritional settings, use of the technique in modern forensic settings is not widespread. Laura Regan's dissertation research in 2006 generated a data set of carbon, oxygen, strontium, and lead isotope ratios of tooth enamel from more than 280 (modern) Asians and US Americans to aid in the identification of fallen service members from the Vietnam War. As noted by the committee chair, the study was "the first of its kind to compile a reference sample of isotopic values associated with known natal regions to be utilized in forensic work" (Regan, 2006). Relatively few reference data sets of human remains have been published in the intervening years, including strontium isotope analysis results for 19 teeth donated by Mexican-born individuals (Juarez, 2008); $^{87}Sr/^{86}Sr$ ratios along with $\delta^{18}O$ values of teeth from 62 subjects living in the Middle East (Posey, 2011); and a compilation of about 4000 $\delta^{13}C$ and $\delta^{15}N$ values of human hair and nail from the literature to generate a global database (Hülsemann et al., 2015). More limited reference data sets on hair have been published for other isotopes (e.g., H, O, S) as well (Fraser et al., 2006; Fraser and Meier-Augenstein, 2007; Lehn et al., 2015b). A recently published final report on work funded by the National Institute of Justice presented carbon, oxygen, nitrogen, and strontium isotope ratios of modern human bone, teeth, and hair from three skeletal collections located in the United States, a total of 290 individuals (Herrmann et al., 2015). In 2016, Regan's initial data set of modern US American teeth was revisited to generate isoscapes of $\delta^{13}C$, $\delta^{18}O$, $^{87}Sr/^{86}Sr$, and $^{206}Pb/^{207}Pb$ for provenancing human remains (Keller et al., 2016).

Similar to the work by Regan (2006), there are published studies applying forensic isotope analysis to war dead. The $\delta^{13}C$ values of tooth bioapatite from a Vietnam War plane crash were used in 2012 to identify a fallen serviceman as a Westerner, rather than a local to Southeast Asia (Holland et al., 2012). Two years later, carbon and nitrogen isotope ratios of bone collagen and carbon isotope ratios of bone bioapatite were used to screen remains recovered from Asia as more likely to be from a US service member or an indigenous local (Bartelink et al., 2014a). Oxygen and strontium isotopes were used in 2015 to determine that two sets of remains found at the site of World War II battle in the Netherlands were likely from the United Kingdom (Font et al., 2015a). A recent study utilized Regan's (2006) data set to build a model for discriminating US and Japanese soldiers using $\delta^{13}C$ and $\delta^{18}O$ values of tooth enamel (Someda et al., 2016).

Along with application to war dead, forensic isotope analysis has also been used in criminal investigations of human remains. The first published study came from Germany, where a male was found buried near an expressway in 2002 (Rauch et al., 2007). A combination of strontium and lead isotopes of teeth and bone was used to assign him to Romania; he was later identified. A year later, Meier-Augenstein and Fraser published details on the case of the "Scissor Sisters," which involved a dismembered male body found in Dublin, Ireland, in 2005 (Meier-Augenstein, 2014; Meier-Augenstein and Fraser, 2008). Analysis of oxygen isotopes of bone revealed the decedent had migrated to Ireland from the Horn of Africa. Following identification, investigators learned he fathered a child with one of the sisters.

The $\delta^{18}O$ values of hair were used in two cases from the United States to reconstruct the travel history of Nikole Bakoles (known originally as "Saltair Sally") and Mary Alice Willey (known originally as "Jane Doe") in the months before their death, providing investigators new search areas for missing persons that matched other characteristics of the decedents (Chesson et al., 2014; Ehleringer et al., 2010; Kennedy et al., 2011; Remien et al., 2014). Hair—along with bone collagen—was measured in the investigation of three unidentified decedents from Germany (Lehn et al., 2015b). Results helped to constrain potential provenance, and all three individuals were eventually identified.

In 2014, isotope analyses of carbon, oxygen, strontium, and lead in tooth enamel, bone, and hair were used to determine that "Little Miss Lake Panasoffkee," found in Florida in 1971, was most likely a foreigner, hailing from southeastern Europe, possibly Greece (Kamenov et al., 2014). She remains unidentified to this day. A recent publication from the Netherlands used carbon, nitrogen, oxygen, strontium, and lead isotope analyses of tooth enamel and bone from a drowned male to indicate areas near the Carpathian Mountains as his probable region of origin; this assignment was confirmed when he was identified as moving from south-west Poland (Font et al., 2015b).

■ RECENT CASE STUDY EXAMPLES

While published examples of forensic isotope analysis in human identification have—not surprisingly—focused largely on success stories, there are thousands of unidentified decedent cases in the United States alone (Ritter, 2007) where the technique may be useful. We next present results from some of our recent casework. All results were previously provided to investigators and are presented here, with permission, in the hopes of bringing additional attention to the cases.

"Lyle Stevik"

On Saturday, September 15, 2001, a man checked himself into a motel in the Lake Quinault area of the Olympic Peninsula, Washington under the name of "Lyle Stevik" from Meridian, Idaho, perhaps inspired by a character from the Joyce Carol Oates' novel *You Must Remember This* (although the family name was "Stevick" in the novel). The only possessions he carried were a toothbrush and toothpaste. The address he gave for Meridian lead to a motel, where no one remembered him. On Sunday morning he was found hanging, lifeless, with a note reading "suicide" and $120 in crisp $20 bills—with another note reading "for the room"—providing little context to his death (Patterson, 2006).

Estimated to be between 20 and 30 years old, "Lyle" was possibly Caucasian/African or Caucasian/Native American and 6'1" tall. He wore jeans, a blue plaid shirt over a gray t-shirt, Timberland boots (size 10), and a black leather belt. His jeans were too large for his frame, indicating he had perhaps lost 30 or 40 pounds before death. There was surgical scar on his abdomen, possibly due to the removal of his appendix, and evidence of prior orthodontic work. Fingerprints, dental records, and a DNA profile lead to no matches.[1] We completed analyses of oxygen isotope ratios in hair and a molar for "Lyle" in 2015.

A total of 54 hair segments were collected; however, 18 hair segments (every third segment) were analyzed for oxygen isotope ratios. The $\delta^{18}O$ values of analyzed hair segments ranged from 11.6‰ to 12.5‰. The measured oxygen isotope ratios of sequential hair segments exhibited variation throughout the 12 months preceding death, suggesting he had likely moved or traveled multiple times within that period. Two distinct isotope ranges in the hair-segment time sequence—in which the measured oxygen stable isotope ratios of the hair segments are relatively constant—have been identified in Fig. 14.2.

---

1. This case is currently open: NamUS UP # 11,100, https://identifyus.org/cases/11100. Anyone with information is encouraged to contact Coroner Lane Youmans with the Grays Harbor County Coroner's Office.

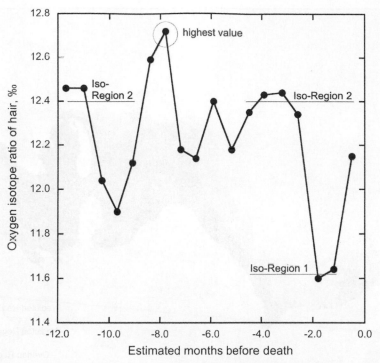

Figure 14.2 Measured oxygen isotope ratios of individual hair segments from "Lyle Stevik." Assuming an average hair growth rate of 0.39 mm per day and 30.5 days per month, segment lengths were converted to months preceding the death of the individual. Two distinct isotope ranges have been identified. The maximum oxygen isotope ratio value measured for analyzed hair segments is also identified.

The identified isotope ranges were used to predict regions within the continental USA where the individual might have resided in the months preceding his death (Fig. 14.3A). In addition, predictions were extended through North America (Fig. 14.3B), since "Lyle" may have spoken with a Canadian accent during check-in. We note the resolution of predictions for North Americans is coarser than that of predictions for the United States, since predictions presented in Fig. 14.3B are based on a precipitation isoscape and not a tap water isoscape, as they are in Fig. 14.3A.

At the time of death, the oxygen isotope data for the decedent's hair were not consistent with values expected for a resident of the Olympic Peninsula, Washington. The isotopic evidence supports the position that he was a traveler through the area at the time of death, coming from a region characterized by a warmer climate. However, the isotope record observed in the hair 1–2 months before death was consistent with a resident of the Olympic Peninsula, Washington, but not Idaho.

The decedent's location of discovery—the Olympic Peninsula, Washington—was not among the broad-predicted geographical regions for the tooth enamel (Fig. 14.4). Neither was Idaho. Based on the oxygen isotope ratios of the enamel, no areas of the Pacific Northwest were included in predicted regions. We note that this map was extended through North America by using a precipitation isoscape, as done previously for hair (Fig. 14.3B).

The Embalmed Head

We opened this chapter with details of the case of the embalmed head, found December 2014 in Beaver County, Pennsylvania.[2] Analyses of oxygen isotope ratios in hair and oxygen plus strontium isotope ratios in tooth enamel were completed for the unidentified female decedent in 2015.

A total of 33 hair segments were collected and analyzed. Measured oxygen stable isotope ratios of sequential hair segments exhibited variation throughout the 7.5 months preceding death (Fig. 14.5), suggesting that she had likely moved or traveled multiple times within that period. The $\delta^{18}O$ values of analyzed hair segments ranged from 11.1‰ to 12.6‰; in Fig. 14.5 we have highlighted two distinct isotope ranges in the time sequence during which the measured oxygen isotope ratios of the hair segments are relatively constant. We identify these regions as "Iso-Region 1" (nearest in time to death) and "Iso-Region 2" (furthest in time to death). In addition, we have identified the lowest measured oxygen isotope ratios for the analyzed hair segments, observed at approximately 4.5 months and also 6 months prior to death.

One interpretation of the data is that the individual resided in "Iso-Region 2" until approximately 7 months before death and then moved to a region characterized by a cooler climate. Her residency in this cooler climate region was episodic and likely included at least one travel movement to a region with a warmer climate, as seen in the changes in

---

2. This case is currently open: NamUS UP # 13,338, https://identifyus.org/cases/13338. Anyone with information is encouraged to contact Chief Michael O'Brien with the Economy Borough Police Department.

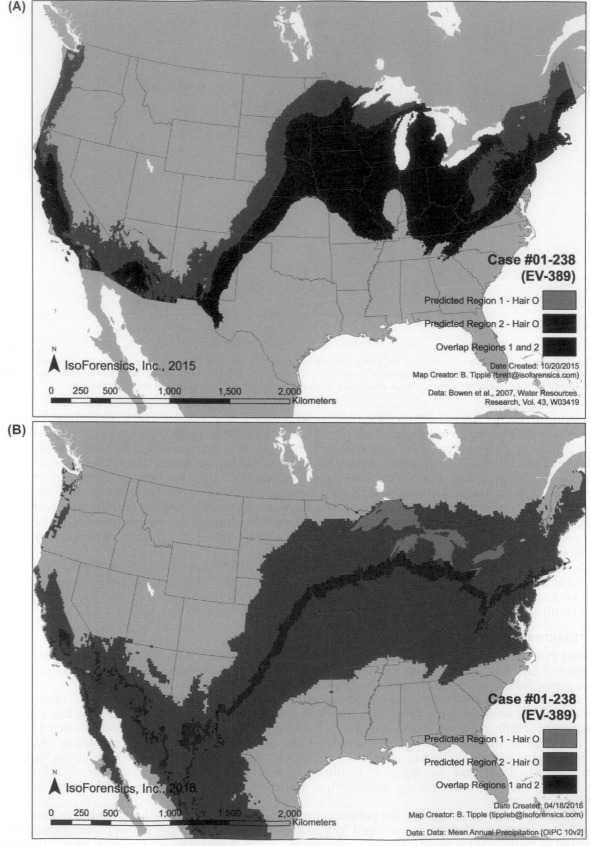

Figure 14.3 A Geographic Information System representation of both "Iso-Region 1" and "Iso-Region 2," the geographic locations that are consistent with the observed oxygen isotope ratio data indicated in Fig. 14.2 for hair collected from "Lyle Stevik." For these predictions, we used a range of $\delta^{18}O$ values that spans ±0.5‰ of the predicted average observed $\delta^{18}O$ values in Fig. 14.2. Predictions in Panel (A) are based on tap water as the drinking water input; to extend predictions outside the continental USA, predictions in Panel (B) are based on precipitation.

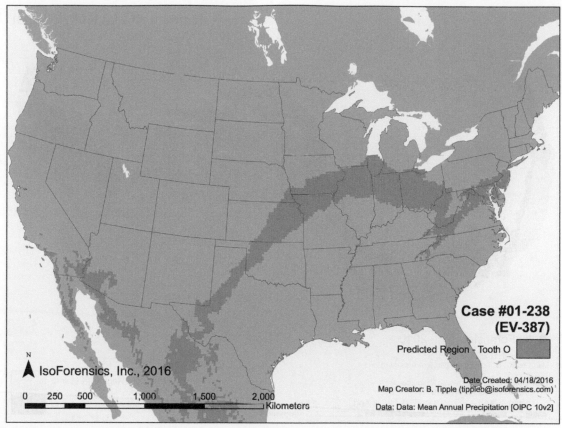

Figure 14.4 A Geographic Information System map representing the geographic locations that are consistent with the measured oxygen isotope ratio data for tooth enamel from "Lyle Stevik." Predictions are based on precipitation.

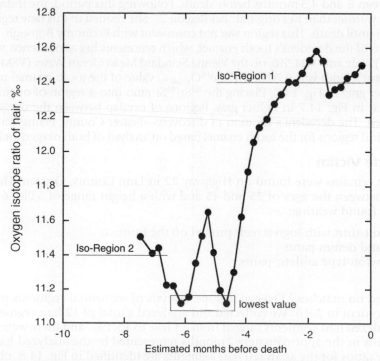

Figure 14.5 Measured oxygen isotope ratios of hair segments from an embalmed head found in Pennsylvania in 2014. Segments lengths were converted to months preceding death by assuming an average hair growth rate of 0.39 mm per day and 30.5 days per month. Two distinct isotope ranges have been identified. The minimum oxygen isotope ratio values measured for analyzed hair segments are also identified.

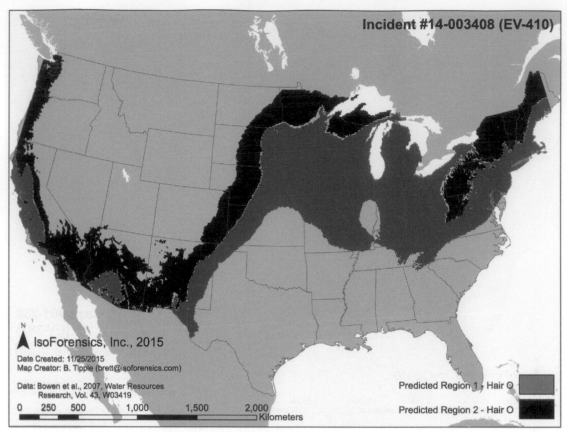

Figure 14.6 A Geographic Information System representation of "Iso-Region 1" and "Iso-Region 2," the geographic locations that are consistent with the observed oxygen isotope ratio data indicated in Fig. 14.5 for hair collected from an embalmed head. For these predictions, we used a range of $\delta^{18}O$ values that spans ±0.5‰ of the predicted average observed $\delta^{18}O$ values in Fig. 14.5.

her hair $\delta^{18}O$ values between 6 and 4.5 months before death. Following this period, the individual moved to a region characterized by a climate warmer than her original "Iso-Region 2." She resided in this new region, "Iso-Region 1," from 3 months before her death until death. This region was not consistent with Economy Borough, Pennsylvania (Fig. 14.6).

The oxygen isotope ratio of the decedent's tooth enamel, which represents her adolescence, was −6.2‰ on the Vienna Pee Dee Belemnite (VPDB) scale and +24.5‰ on the Vienna Standard Mean Ocean Water (VSMOW) scale. The strontium isotope ratio of the decedent's tooth was 0.70967. The $\delta^{18}O_{VSMOW}$ value of the tooth enamel predicted the geographical regions presented in darker gray in Fig. 14.7. Placing the $^{87}Sr/^{86}Sr$ ratio into a region-of-origin model predicts the geographical regions presented in Fig. 14.7 in lighter gray. Regions of overlap between the oxygen and strontium predictions are highlighted in red. The decedent's location of discovery—Beaver County, Pennsylvania—was not among the broad-predicted geographical regions for the tooth enamel based on analysis of both oxygen and strontium isotope ratios.

Linn County Homicide Victim

In October 2006, human remains were found on Highway 22 in Linn County, Oregon. The remains were believed to be a Caucasian male between the ages of 25 and 45 and with a height range of 5′08″–6′01″. The decedent was a homicide victim. He was found wearing:

A gray "Sideout" brand t-shirt with logo screen-printed on the front
Black "Dungarees" brand denim pants
Blue with black trim nylon-type athletic pants
K-Air shoes

DNA profiling provided no matches.[3] Oxygen isotope analysis of sequential segments of hair was completed for the unidentified male decedent in 2016. We collected and analyzed a total of 12 hair segments.

The $\delta^{18}O$ values of analyzed hair segments ranged from 13.6‰ to 15.1‰, and there were clear differences in measured oxygen isotope ratios in the approximately 2 months represented by the analyzed hair segments. The highest measured oxygen isotope ratios for the analyzed hair segments are identified in Fig. 14.8, observed at approximately

---

3. This case is currently open: NamUS UP # 7309, https://identifyus.org/cases/7309. Anyone with information is encouraged to contact Detective Mike Harmon with the Linn County Sheriff's Office.

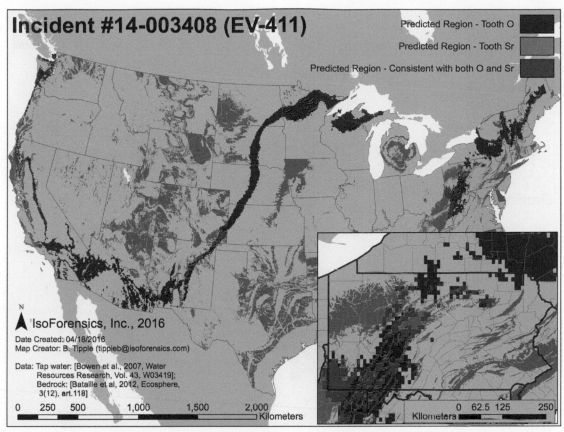

Figure 14.7 A Geographic Information System map representing the geographic locations that are consistent with both the measured oxygen and strontium isotope ratio data for tooth enamel from the embalmed head discovered in Pennsylvania in 2014.

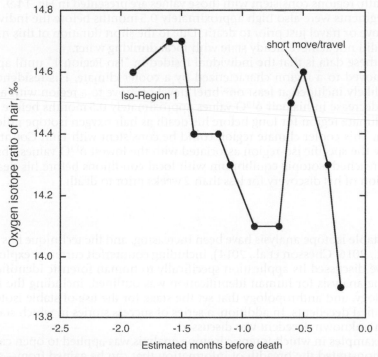

Figure 14.8 Measured oxygen isotope ratios of hair segments from a young man found dead in Linn County, Oregon in 2006. Segments lengths have been converted to months preceding death using an average hair growth rate of 0.39 mm per day and assuming 30.5 days per month. The highest oxygen isotope ratios have been identified. The relative constancy of values identified as "Iso-Region 1" suggest that the individual resided in this region for a sufficient period of time that his hair was in isotopic equilibrium with local drinking water. Another high oxygen isotope ratio value measured for analyzed hair segments is also identified as a travel of short duration.

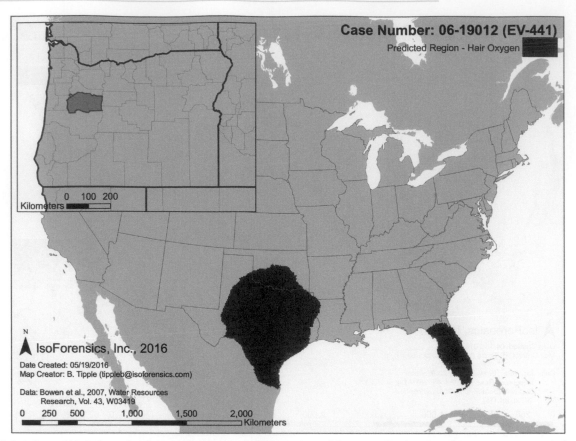

Figure 14.9 A Geographic Information System representation of "Iso-Region 1," the geographic locations that are consistent with the observed oxygen isotope ratio data indicated in Fig. 14.8 for unidentified male decedent found in Linn County, Oregon in 2006. For these predictions, we used a range of $\delta^{18}O$ values that spans $\pm0.5‰$ of the predicted average observed $\delta^{18}O$ values in Fig. 14.8.

1.5–2 months prior to death; regions consistent with those values are presented in Fig. 14.9. We note that oxygen isotope ratios for the hair segments were also high approximately 0.5 months before the individual's death, indicating he made another brief move or travel just prior to death. Due to the short duration of this move or travel, the oxygen isotope ratios of his hair did not achieve steady state with local drinking water.

One interpretation of these data is that the individual resided in "Iso-Region 1" until approximately 1.5 months before death and then moved to a region characterized by a cooler climate. His residency in this cooler climate region was episodic and likely included at least one brief travel or move to a region with a warmer climate, as seen in the increase and then decrease in his hair $\delta^{18}O$ values approximately 0.5 months before death. The decedent did not reside in the cooler climate region for long before his death as hair oxygen isotope ratios did not reach a steady state value prior to death. This cooler climate region could be consistent with Linn County, Oregon; however, it is not possible to determine the specific iso-region associated with the lowest $\delta^{18}O$ values observed for the decedent's hair because he had not reached isotopic equilibrium with local conditions before his death. The data suggest the individual was in the region of his discovery for less than 2 weeks prior to death.

■ CONCLUSION

Forensic applications of stable isotope analysis have been increasing, and the technique has been applied to a variety of materials (Cerling et al., 2016; Chesson et al., 2014), including counterfeit currency, explosives, food, illegal drugs, wildlife, etc. Here we have discussed its application specifically to human forensic identification. A brief history of the use of forensic isotope analysis for human identification was outlined, including the foundational research in the fields of ecology, geology, and anthropology that set the stage for the use of stable isotopes in modern forensic investigations of unidentified decedents. In addition, a series of success stories in which stable isotopes helped lead to the identification of an unknown decedent was discussed.

We closed with three examples in which forensic isotope analysis was applied to open cases of unnamed individuals. These examples demonstrated the breadth of information that can be gained from—as well as the limitations of—analyses of the isotope ratios of human tissues. Further, these examples illustrated how an investigator can build a chronology, and thus investigative leads, from the personal history encoded in the isotope ratios of an unknown decedent's tissues.

Isotope analysis has proven useful in multiple cases of forensic human identification. However, the technique is underutilized in modern casework, likely due to its novelty in forensic application, ongoing research, and additional expense. Most applications of forensic isotope analysis for human identification are based on very old, "cold" cases, ones in which all other investigative avenues have been exhausted and where making an identification is very difficult due to the passage of time. Nonetheless, recent interest from numerous local, state, and federal investigative and scientific agencies indicates a growing recognition of the utility of forensic isotope analysis in cases where human identification is needed. Stable isotope analysis is still a developing technology, but one that is well suited for forensic investigations, as it is grounded in the foundations of chemistry and physics, in addition to decades of peer-reviewed basic and applied research. The identification of unknown decedents will remain a fundamental challenge for forensic investigators, and stable isotope analysis of human tissues is an additional tool to provide a name to a face.

References

Alkass, K., Buchholz, B.A., Druid, H., Spalding, K.L., 2011. Analysis of ^{14}C and ^{13}C in teeth provides birth dating and clues to geographical origin. Forensic Sci. Int. 209, 34–41.

Ambrose, S.H., 1990. Preparation and characterization of bone and tooth collagen for isotopic analysis. J. Archaeol. Sci. 17, 431–451. http://dx.doi.org/10.1016/0305-4403(90)90007-R.

Ambrose, S.H., Krigbaum, J., 2003. Bone chemistry and bioarchaeology. J. Anthropol. Archaeol. 22, 191–192. http://dx.doi.org/10.1016/S0278-4165(03)00032-1.

Ambrose, S.H., Norr, L., 1993. Experimental evidence for the relationship of the carbon isotopes ratios of whole diet and dietary protein to those of bone collagen and carbonate. In: Lambert, J.B., Grupe, G. (Eds.), Prehistoric Human Bone: Archaeology at the Molecular Level. Springer-Verlag, Berlin, pp. 1–37.

Bartelink, E.J., Berg, G.E., Beasley, M.M., Chesson, L.A., 2014a. Application of stable isotope forensics for predicting region of origin of human remains from past wars and conflicts. Ann. Anthropol. Pract. 38, 124–136. http://dx.doi.org/10.1111/napa.12047.

Bartelink, E.J., Berry, R., Chesson, L.A., 2014b. Stable isotopes and human provenancing. In: Mallett, X., Blythe, T., Berry, R. (Eds.), Advances in Forensic Human Identification. CRC Press, Taylor & Francis Group, Boca Raton, Florida, USA, pp. 165–192.

Bataille, C.P., Bowen, G.J., 2012. Mapping ^{87}Sr/^{86}Sr variations in bedrock and water for large scale provenance studies. Chem. Geol. 304–305, 39–52.

Beard, B.L., Johnson, C.M., 2000. Strontium isotope composition of skeletal material can determine the birth place and geographic mobility of humans and animals. J. Forensic Sci. 45, 1049–1061.

Bender, M.M., 1971. Variations in the ^{13}C/^{12}C ratios of plants in relation to the pathway of photosynthetic carbon dioxide fixation. Phytochemistry 10, 1239–1244.

Bender, M.M., Rouhani, I., Vines, H.M., Black, C.C., 1973. ^{13}C/^{12}C ratio changes in Crassulacean Acid Metabolism plants. Plant Physiol. 52, 421–430.

Bentley, R.A., Knipper, C., 2005. Geographical patterns in biologically available strontium, carbon and oxygen isotope signatures in prehistoric SW Germany. Archaeometry 47, 629–644.

Bowen, G.J., Ehleringer, J.R., Chesson, L.A., Stange, E., Cerling, T.E., 2007. Stable isotope ratios of tap water in the contiguous United States. Water Resour. Res. 43, W03419. http://dx.doi.org/10.1029/2006WR005186.

Bowen, G.J., Revenaugh, J., 2003. Interpolating the isotopic composition of modern meteoric precipitation. Water Resour. Res. 39, 1299–1311.

Brand, W.A., Coplen, T.B., Vogl, J., Rosner, M., Prohaska, T., 2014. Assessment of International reference materials for isotope-ratio analysis (IUPAC Technical Report). Pure Appl. Chem. 86, 425–467.

Carter, J.F., Barwick, V. (Eds.), 2011. Good Practice Guide for Isotope Ratio Mass Spectrometry.

Cerling, T.E., Barnette, J.E., Bowen, G.J., Chesson, L.A., Ehleringer, J.R., Remien, C.H., Shea, P., Tipple, B.J., West, J.B., 2016. Forensic stable isotope biogeochemistry. Annu. Rev. Earth Planet. Sci. 44. http://dx.doi.org/10.1146/annurev-earth-060115-012303.

Cerling, T.E., Harris, J.M., MacFadden, B.J., Leakey, M.G., Quade, J., Eisenmann, V., Ehleringer, J.R., 1997. Global vegetation change through the Miocene/Pliocene boundary. Nature 389, 153–158.

Chesson, L.A., Tipple, B.J., Howa, J.D., Bowen, G.J., Barnette, J.E., Cerling, T.E., Ehleringer, J.R., 2014. Stable isotopes in forensics applications. In: Treatise on Geochemistry. Elsevier, pp. 285–317.

Coplen, T.B., Kendall, C., Hopple, J., 1983. Comparison of stable isotope reference samples. Nature 302, 236–238. http://dx.doi.org/10.1038/302236a0.

Craig, H., 1961. Isotopic variations in meteoric waters. Science 133, 1702–1703.

Dansgaard, W., 1964. Stable isotopes in precipitation. Tellus 16, 436–468.

Dansgaard, W., 1954. The O^{18}-abundance in fresh water. Geochim. Cosmochim. Acta 6, 241–260.

Daux, V., Lécuyer, C., Héran, M.-A., Amiot, R., Simon, L., Fourel, F., Martineau, F., Lynnerup, N., Reychler, H., Escarguel, G., 2008. Oxygen isotope fractionation between human phosphate and water revisited. J. Hum. Evol. 55, 1138–1147.

DeNiro, M.J., 1987. Stable isotopy and archaeology. Am. Sci. 75, 182–191.

DeNiro, M.J., 1985. Postmortem preservation and alteration of in vivo bone collagen isotope ratios in relation to paleodietary reconstruction. Nature 317, 806–809.

DeNiro, M.J., Epstein, S., 1981. Influence of diet on the distribution of nitrogen isotopes in animals. Geochim. Cosmochim. Acta 45, 341–352.

Dupras, T.L., Schwarcz, H.P., 2001. Strangers in a strange land: stable isotope evidence for human migration in the Dakhleh Oasis, Egypt. J. Archaeol. Sci. 28, 1199–1208. http://dx.doi.org/10.1006/jasc.2001.0640.

Ehleringer, J.R., Bowen, G.J., Chesson, L.A., West, A.G., Podlesak, D.W., Cerling, T.E., 2008. Hydrogen and oxygen isotope ratios in human hair are related to geography. Proc. Natl. Acad. Sci. U.S.A. 105, 2788–2793. http://dx.doi.org/10.1073/pnas.0712228105.

Ehleringer, J.R., Thompson, A.H., Podlesak, D., Bowen, G.J., Chesson, L.A., Cerling, T.E., Park, T., Dostie, P., Schwarcz, H.P., 2010. A framework for the incorporation of isotopes and isoscapes in geospatial forensic investigations. In: West, J.B., Bowen, G.J., Dawson, T.E., Tu, K.P. (Eds.), Isoscapes: Understanding Movement, Pattern, and Process on Earth through Isotope Mapping. Springer, Dordrecht, The Netherlands, pp. 357–387.

Ericson, J.E., 1985. Strontium isotope characterization in the study of prehistoric human ecology. J. Hum. Evol. 14, 503–514. http://dx.doi.org/10.1016/S0047-2484(85)80029-4.

Ezzo, J.A., Johnson, C.M., Price, T.D., 1997. Analytical perspectives on prehistoric migration: a case study from East-Central Arizona. J. Archaeol. Sci. 24, 447–466. http://dx.doi.org/10.1006/jasc.1996.0129.

Font, L., Jonker, G., van Aalderen, P.A., Schiltmans, E.F., Davies, G.R., 2015a. Provenancing of unidentified World War II casualties: application of strontium and oxygen isotope analysis in tooth enamel. Sci. Justice 55, 10–17. http://dx.doi.org/10.1016/j.scijus.2014.02.005.

Font, L., van der Peijl, G., van Leuwen, C., van Wetten, I., Davies, G.R., 2015b. Identification of the geographical place of origin of an unidentified individual by multi-isotope analysis. Sci. Justice 55, 34–42. http://dx.doi.org/10.1016/j.scijus.2014.06.011.

Fraser, I., Meier-Augenstein, W., 2007. Stable ^{2}H isotope analysis of modern-day human hair and nails can aid forensic human identification. Rapid Commun. Mass Spectrom. 21, 3279–3285.

Fraser, I., Meier-Augenstein, W., Kalin, R.M., 2006. The role of stable isotopes in human identification: a longitudinal study into the variability of isotopic signals in human hair and nails. Rapid Commun. Mass Spectrom. 20, 1109–1116.

Gaffney, J.S., Irsa, A.P., Friedman, L., Slatkin, D.N., 1978. Natural ^{13}C/^{12}C ratio variations in human populations. Biol. Mass Spectrom. 5, 495–497. http://dx.doi.org/10.1002/bms.1200050807.

Gat, J.R., 1996. Oxygen and hydrogen isotopes in the hydrological cycle. Annu. Rev. Earth Planet. Sci. 24, 225–262.

Gentile, N., Rossi, M.J., Delémont, O., Siegwolf, R.T.W., 2013. δ^{15}N measurement of organic and inorganic substances by EA-IRMS: a speciation-dependent procedure. Anal. Bioanal. Chem. http://dx.doi.org/10.1007/s00216-012-6471-z.

Grupe, G., Price, T.D., Schröter, P., Söllner, F., Johnson, C.M., Beard, B.L., 1997. Mobility of Bell Beaker people revealed by strontium isotope ratios of tooth and bone: a study of southern Bavarian skeletal remains. Appl. Geochem. 12, 517–525.

Gulson, B.L., Jameson, C.W., Gillings, B.R., 1997. Stable lead isotopes in teeth as indicators of past domicile – a potential new tool in forensic science? J. Forensic Sci. 42, 787–791.

Hedges, R.E.M., 2003. On bone collagen – apatite-carbonate isotopic relationships. Int. J. Osteoarchaeol. 13, 66–79. http://dx.doi.org/10.1002/oa.660.

Hedges, R.E.M., 2002. Bone diagenesis: an overview of processes. Archaeometry 44, 319–328. http://dx.doi.org/10.1111/1475-4754.00064.

Herrmann, N., Li, Z.-H., Warner, M., 2015. Isotopic and Elemental Analysis of the William Bass Donated Skeletal Collection and Other Modern Donated Collections (Final Report No. 248669). NCJRS Library.

Hodell, D.A., Quinn, R.L., Brenner, M., Kamenov, G., 2004. Spatial variation of strontium isotopes ($^{87}Sr/^{86}Sr$) in the Maya region: a tool for tracking ancient human migration. J. Archaeol. Sci. 31, 585–601.

Hoefs, J., 2009. Stable Isotope Geochemistry, sixth ed. Springer, Berlin.

Holland, T.D., Berg, G.E., Regan, L.A., 2012. Identification of a United States airman using stable isotopes. Proc. Am. Acad. Forensic Sci. 18, 420–421.

Hülsemann, F., Lehn, C., Schneider, S., Jackson, G., Hill, S., Rossmann, A., Scheid, N., Dunn, P.J.H., Flenker, U., Schänzer, W., 2015. Global spatial distributions of nitrogen and carbon stable isotope ratios of modern human hair. Rapid Commun. Mass Spectrom. 29, 2111–2121. http://dx.doi.org/10.1002/rcm.7370.

Iacumin, P., Bocherens, H., Mariotti, A., Longinelli, A., 1996. Oxygen isotope analyses of co-existing carbonate and phosphate in biogenic apatite: a way to monitor diagenetic alteration of bone phosphate? Earth Planet. Sci. Lett. 142, 1–6.

Juarez, C.A., 2008. Strontium and geolocation, the pathway to identification for deceased undocumented Mexican border-crossers: a preliminary report. J. Forensic Sci. 53, 46–49.

Kamenov, G.D., Kimmerle, E.H., Curtis, J.H., Norris, D., 2014. Georeferencing a cold case victim with lead, strontium, carbon, and oxygen isotopes. Ann. Anthropol. Pract. 38, 137–154. http://dx.doi.org/10.1111/napa.12048.

Katzenberg, M.A., 2008. Stable isotope analysis: a tool for studying past diet, demography, and life history. In: Katzenberg, M.A., Saunders, S.R. (Eds.), Biological Anthropology of the Human Skeleton. John Wiley & Sons, Inc., Hoboken, NJ, USA, pp. 411–441.

Katzenberg, M.A., Krouse, H.R., 1989. Application of stable isotope variation in human tissues to problems in identification. Can. Soc. Forensic Sci. J. 22, 7–19.

Keller, A.T., Regan, L.A., Lundstrom, C.C., Bower, N.W., 2016. Evaluation of the efficacy of spatiotemporal Pb isoscapes for provenancing of human remains. Forensic Sci. Int. 261, 83–92. http://dx.doi.org/10.1016/j.forsciint.2016.02.006.

Kennedy, C.D., Bowen, G.J., Ehleringer, J.R., 2011. Temporal variation of oxygen isotope ratios ($\delta^{18}O$) in drinking water: implications for specifying location of origin with human scalp hair. Forensic Sci. Int. 208, 156–166.

Klepinger, L.L., 1984. Nutritional assessment from bone. Annu. Rev. Anthropol. 13, 75–96. http://dx.doi.org/10.1146/annurev.an.13.100184.000451.

Knudson, K.J., Price, T.D., Buikstra, J.E., Blom, D.E., 2004. The use of strontium isotope analysis to investigate Tiwanaku migration and mortuary ritual in Bolivia and Peru. Archaeometry 46, 5–18. http://dx.doi.org/10.1111/j.1475-4754.2004.00140.x.

Koch, P.L., Tuross, N., Fogel, M.L., 1997. The effects of sample treatment and diagenesis on the isotopic integrity of carbonate in biogenic hydroxylapatite. J. Archaeol. Sci. 24, 417–429. http://dx.doi.org/10.1006/jasc.1996.0126.

Kohn, M.J., 1996. Predicting animal $\delta^{18}O$: accounting for diet and physiological adaptation. Geochim. Cosmochim. Acta 60, 4811–4829.

Kusaka, S., Nakano, T., 2014. Carbon and oxygen isotope ratios and their temperature dependence in carbonate and tooth enamel using a GasBench II preparation device. Rapid Commun. Mass Spectrom. 28, 563–567.

Lee-Thorp, J.A., 2002. Two decades of progress towards understanding fossilization processes and isotopic signals in calcified tissue minerals. Archaeometry 44, 435–446. http://dx.doi.org/10.1111/1475-4754.t01-1-00076.

Lehn, C., Lihl, C., Roßmann, A., 2015a. Change of geographical location from Germany (Bavaria) to USA (Arizona) and its effect on H–C–N–S stable isotopes in human hair. Isotopes Environ. Health Stud. 1–12. http://dx.doi.org/10.1080/10256016.2014.995645.

Lehn, C., Mutzel, E., Rossmann, A., 2011. Mult-element stable isotope analysis of H, C, N, and S in hair and nails of contemporary human remains. Int. J. Legal Med. 125, 695–706.

Lehn, C., Rossmann, A., Graw, M., 2015b. Provenancing of unidentified corpses by stable isotope techniques – presentation of case studies. Sci. Justice 55, 72–88. http://dx.doi.org/10.1016/j.scijus.2014.10.006.

Lott, M.J., Howa, J.D., Chesson, L.A., Ehleringer, J.R., 2015. Improved accuracy and precision in $\delta^{15}N_{AIR}$ measurements of explosives, urea, and inorganic nitrates by elemental analyzer/isotope ratio mass spectrometry using thermal decomposition. Rapid Commun. Mass Spectrom. 29, 1381–1388. http://dx.doi.org/10.1002/rcm.7229.

Lyon, T.D.B., Baxter, M.S., 1978. Stable carbon isotopes in human tissues. Nature 273, 750–751. http://dx.doi.org/10.1038/273750a0.

Meier-Augenstein, W., 2014. Forensic isotope analysis. In: McGraw-Hill Yearbook of Science & Technology 2014. McGraw-Hill Professional, pp. 120–124.

Meier-Augenstein, W., Fraser, I., 2008. Forensic isotope analysis leads to identification of a mutilated murder victim. Sci. Justice 48, 153–159.

Meier-Augenstein, W., Kemp, H.F., 2012. Stable isotope analysis: hair and nails. In: Jamieson, A., Moenssens, A. (Eds.), Wiley Encyclopaedia of Forensic Science, second ed. Wiley-Blackwell.

Miller, M.E., December 15, 2015. The strange, sad quest to match a severed, embalmed head with its story. Wash. Post. (Web. August 16, 2016).

Muccio, Z., 2010. Isotope Ratio Mass Spectrometry – a Rapidly Developing Tool for Forensic Samples (Ph.D.). Ohio University.

Muccio, Z., Jackson, G.P., 2009. Isotope ratio mass spectrometry. Analyst 134, 213–222.

Nakamura, K., Schoeller, D.A., Winkler, F.J., Schmidt, H.-L., 1982. Geographical variations in the carbon isotope composition of the diet and hair in contemporary man. Biol. Mass Spectrom. 9, 390–394. http://dx.doi.org/10.1002/bms.1200090906.

O'Connell, T.C., Hedges, R.E.M., Healey, M.A., Simpson, A.H.R., 2001. Isotopic comparison of hair, nail and bone: modern analyses. J. Archaeol. Sci. 28, 1247–1255.

O'Leary, M.H., 1988. Carbon isotopes in photosynthesis. Bioscience 38, 328–336.

Osmond, C.B., Allaway, W.G., Sutton, B.G., Troughton, J.H., Queiroz, O., Lüttge, U., Winter, K., 1973. Carbon isotope discrimination in photosynthesis of CAM plants. Nature 246, 41–42. http://dx.doi.org/10.1038/246041a0.

Park, R., Epstein, S., 1961. Metabolic fractionation of C^{13} & C^{12} in plants. Plant Physiol. 36, 133–138. http://dx.doi.org/10.1104/pp.36.2.133.

Park, R., Epstein, S., 1960. Carbon isotope fractionation during photosynthesis. Geochim. Cosmochim. Acta 21, 110–126. http://dx.doi.org/10.1016/S0016-7037(60)80006-3.

Passey, B.H., Cerling, T.E., Levin, N.E., 2007. Temperature dependence of oxygen isotope acid fractionation for modern and fossil tooth enamels. Rapid Commun. Mass Spectrom. 21, 2853–2859. http://dx.doi.org/10.1002/rcm.3149.

Patterson, L., 2006. Cold Cases Haunt Detective. Wenatchee World, p. B04.

Posey, R.G., 2011. Development and Validation of a Spatial Prediction Model for Forensic Geographical Provenancing of Human Remains (Ph.D.). University of East Anglia, School of Chemistry.

Post, D.M., 2002. Using stable isotopes to estimate trophic position: models, methods and assumptions. Ecology 83, 702–718.

Price, T.D., Grupe, G., Schröter, P., 1994a. Reconstruction of migration patterns in the Bell Beaker period by stable strontium isotope analysis. Appl. Geochem. 9, 413–417. http://dx.doi.org/10.1016/0883-2927(94)90063-9.

Price, T.D., Johnson, C.M., Ezzo, J.A., Ericson, J., Burton, J.H., 1994b. Residential mobility in the prehistoric southwest United States: a preliminary study using strontium isotope analysis. J. Archaeol. Sci. 21, 315–330. http://dx.doi.org/10.1006/jasc.1994.1031.

Rauch, E., Rummel, S., Lehn, C., Büttner, A., 2007. Origin assignment of unidentified corpses by use of stable isotope ratios of light (bio-) and heavy (geo-) elements – a case report. Forensic Sci. Int. 168, 215–218.

Regan, L.A., 2006. Isotopic Determination of Region of Origin in Modern Peoples: Applications for Identification of U.S. War-dead from the Vietnam Conflict (Ph.D.). University of Florida, Gainesville, FL.

Remien, C.H., Adler, F.R., Chesson, L.A., Valenzuela, L.O., Ehleringer, J.R., Cerling, T.E., 2014. Deconvolution of isotope signals from bundles of multiple hairs. Oecologia 175, 781–789. http://dx.doi.org/10.1007/s00442-014-2945-3.

Ritter, N., 2007. Missing persons and unidentified remains: the nation's silent mass disaster. NIJ J. 256, 2–7.

Robbins, C.T., Felicetti, L.A., Florin, S.T., 2010. The impact of protein quality on stable nitrogen isotope ratio discrimination and assimilated diet estimation. Oecologia 162, 571–579.

Robbins, C.T., Felicetti, L.A., Sponheimer, M., 2005. The effect of dietary protein quality on nitrogen isotope discrimination in mammals and birds. Oecologia 144, 534–540.

Schoeninger, M., DeNiro, M., Tauber, H., 1983. Stable nitrogen isotope ratios of bone collagen reflect marine and terrestrial components of prehistoric human diet. Science 220, 1381–1383. http://dx.doi.org/10.1126/science.6344217.

Schoeninger, M.J., 1985. Trophic level effects on $^{15}N/^{14}N$ and $^{13}C/^{12}C$ ratios in bone collagen and strontium levels in bone mineral. J. Hum. Evol. 14, 515–525.

Schoeninger, M.J., DeNiro, M.J., 1984. Nitrogen and carbon isotopic composition on bone collagen from marine and terrestrial animals. Geochim. Cosmochim. Acta 48, 624–639.

Schwarcz, H.P., Schoeninger, M.J., 2012. Stable isotopes of carbon and nitrogen as tracers for paleo-diet reconstruction. In: Baskaran, M. (Ed.), Handbook of Environmental Isotope Geochemistry. Springer Berlin Heidelberg, Berlin, Heidelberg, pp. 725–742.

Schwarcz, H.P., Schoeninger, M.J., 1991. Stable isotope analyses in human nutritional ecology. Am. J. Phys. Anthropol. 34, 283–321. http://dx.doi.org/10.1002/ajpa.1330340613.

Schwarcz, H.P., White, C.D., Longstaffe, F.J., 2010. Stable and radiogenic isotopes in biological archaeology: some applications. In: West, J.B., Bowen, G.J., Dawson, T.E., Tu, K.P. (Eds.), Isoscapes: Understanding Movement, Pattern, and Process on Earth Through Isotope Mapping. Springer, Dordrecht, The Netherlands, pp. 335–356.

Sealy, J.C., van der Merwe, N.J., Sillen, A., Kruger, F.J., Krueger, H.W., 1991. $^{87}Sr/^{86}Sr$ as a dietary indicator in modern and archaeological bone. J. Archaeol. Sci. 18, 399–416. http://dx.doi.org/10.1016/0305-4403(91)90074-Y.

Smith, B.N., Epstein, S., 1971. Two categories of $^{13}C/^{12}C$ ratios for higher plants. Plant Physiol. 47, 380–384. http://dx.doi.org/10.1104/pp.47.3.380.

Snoeck, C., Pellegrini, M., 2015. Comparing bioapatite carbonate pre-treatments for isotopic measurements: part 1—impact on structure and chemical composition. Chem. Geol. 417, 394–403. http://dx.doi.org/10.1016/j.chemgeo.2015.10.004.

Someda, H., Gakuhari, T., Akai, J., Araki, Y., Kodera, T., Tsumatori, G., Kobayashi, Y., Matsunaga, S., Abe, S., Hashimoto, M., Saito, M., Yoneda, M., Ishida, H., 2016. Trial application of oxygen and carbon isotope analysis in tooth enamel for identification of past-war victims for discriminating between Japanese and US soldiers. Forensic Sci. Int. 261, 166.e1–166.e5. http://dx.doi.org/10.1016/j.forsciint.2016.02.010.

Stenhouse, M.J., Baxter, M.S., 1979. The uptake of bomb ^{14}C in humans. In: Radiocarbon Dating: Proceedings of the Ninth International Conference, Los Angeles and La Jolla, 1976. University of California Press, Berkeley, pp. 324–341.

Sullivan, C.H., Krueger, H.W., 1981. Carbon isotope analysis of separate chemical phases in modern and fossil bone. Nature 292, 333–335. http://dx.doi.org/10.1038/292333a0.

Thompson, A.H., Wilson, A.S., Ehleringer, J.R., 2014. Hair as a geochemical recorder. In: Treatise on Geochemistry. Elsevier, pp. 371–393.

Tieszen, L.L., Fagre, T., 1993. Effect of diet quality and composition on the isotopic composition of respiratory CO_2, bone collagen, bioapatite, and soft tissues. In: Lambert, J.B., Grupe, G. (Eds.), Prehistoric Human Bone. Springer Berlin Heidelberg, Berlin, Heidelberg, pp. 121–155.

Tipple, B.J., Chau, T., Chesson, L.A., Fernandez, D.P., Ehleringer, J.R., 2013. Isolation of strontium pools and isotope ratios in modern human hair. Anal. Chim. Acta 798, 64–73.

Tipple, B.J., Pagani, M., 2007. The early origins of terrestrial C_4 photosynthesis. Annu. Rev. Earth Planet. Sci. 35, 435–461. http://dx.doi.org/10.1146/annurev.earth.35.031306.140150.

Tuross, N., 2002. Alterations in fossil collagen. Archaeometry 44, 427–434. http://dx.doi.org/10.1111/1475-4754.00075.

Urey, H.C., 1947. The thermodynamic properties of isotopic substances. J. Chem. Soc. Resumed 562. http://dx.doi.org/10.1039/jr9470000562.

Valenzuela, L.O., Chesson, L.A., Bowen, G.J., Cerling, T.E., Ehleringer, J.R., 2012. Dietary heterogeneity among Western industrialized countries reflected in the stable isotope ratios of human hair. PLoS One 7, e34234. http://dx.doi.org/10.1371/journal.pone.0034234.

van der Merwe, N.J., 1982. Carbon Isotopes, Photosynthesis, and Archaeology: different pathways of photosynthesis cause characteristic changes in carbon isotope ratios that make possible the study of prehistoric human diets. Am. Sci. 70, 596–606.

van der Merwe, N.J., Vogel, J.C., 1978. ^{13}C content of human collagen as a measure of prehistoric diet in woodland North America. Nature 276, 815–816. http://dx.doi.org/10.1038/276815a0.

Vogel, J.C., van der Merwe, N.J., 1977. Isotopic evidence for early maize cultivation in New York State. Am. Antiq. 42, 238. http://dx.doi.org/10.2307/278984.

West, J.B., Bowen, G.J., Cerling, T.E., Ehleringer, J.R., 2006. Stable isotopes as one of nature's ecological recorders. Trends Ecol. Evol. 21, 408–414.

White, C.D., Longstaffe, F.J., Law, K.R., 2004. Exploring the effects of environment, physiology and diet on oxygen isotope ratios in ancient Nubian bones and teeth. J. Archaeol. Sci. 31, 233–250. http://dx.doi.org/10.1016/j.jas.2003.08.007.

White, C.D., Spence, M.W., Stuart-Williams, H.L.Q., Schwarcz, H.P., 1998. Oxygen isotopes and the identification of geographical origins: the Valley of Oaxaca versus the Valley of Mexico. J. Archaeol. Sci. 25, 643–655. http://dx.doi.org/10.1006/jasc.1997.0259.

Yoder, C.J., Bartelink, E.J., 2010. Effects of different sample preparation methods on stable carbon and oxygen isotope values of bone apatite: a comparison of two treatment protocols. Archaeometry 52, 115–130. http://dx.doi.org/10.1111/j.1475-4754.2009.00473.x.

CHAPTER 15

Applications of Stable Isotope Forensics for Geolocating Unidentified Human Remains From Past Conflict Situations and Large-Scale Humanitarian Efforts

Eric J. Bartelink[1] | Gregory E. Berg[2] | Lesley A. Chesson[3] | Brett J. Tipple[4] | Melanie M. Beasley[5] | Julia R. Prince-Buitenhuys[6] | Heather MacInnes[1] | Amy T. MacKinnon[7] | Krista E. Latham[8]

[1]California State University, Chico, Chico, CA, United States
[2]Defense POW/MIA Accounting Agency, Joint Base Pearl Harbor-Hickam, HI, United States
[3]IsoForensics, Inc., Salt Lake City, UT, United States
[4]University of Utah, Salt Lake City, UT, United States
[5]University of Tennessee, Knoxville, TN, United States
[6]University of Notre Dame, Notre Dame, IN, United States
[7]California High-Speed Rail Authority, Sacramento, CA, United States
[8]University of Indianapolis, Indianapolis, IN, United States

Chapter Outline

■ INTRODUCTION

The application of stable isotope analysis (SIA) to aid in the identification of human remains has become increasingly common over the past decade (see Chesson et al., 2017). Stable isotope ratios measured in human tissues serve as chemical tracers that record inputs from water and foods consumed during life. Using a specialized form of mass spectrometry, stable isotope ratios measured in different tissues of the body that form over different time intervals (e.g., hair, nails, bone, and teeth) can reveal information about an individual's dietary history, region(s) of origin, and antemortem travel history. Most commonly, SIA in the investigation of human remains has focused on bioelements such as hydrogen (H), carbon (C), nitrogen (N), oxygen (O), and sulfur (S) as well as the geo-elements of strontium (Sr) and lead (Pb). This chapter focuses on recent applications of SIA as an investigative tool for unknown human remains from the Vietnam War recovered by the Defense POW/MIA Accounting Agency (DPAA) and from deceased undocumented border crossers (UBCs) recovered from South Texas. For more in-depth coverage of the basis of forensic applications of SIA for provenancing human remains in prior casework, the interested reader should also refer to recent published reviews (see Bartelink et al., 2014a,b, 2016; Cerling et al., 2016; Chesson et al., 2014, 2017; Ehleringer et al., 2007, 2010; Meier-Augenstein, 2007, 2010).

■ BRIEF BACKGROUND ON THE APPLICATION OF STABLE ISOTOPE ANALYSIS TO UNIDENTIFIED HUMAN REMAINS

As demonstrated previously, SIA is a useful tool for provenancing unidentified decedents from various contexts, including "Jane Does" and "John Does" investigated by local jurisdictions (Chesson et al., 2014; Ehleringer et al., 2010; Kennedy et al., 2011; Meier-Augenstein, 2007, 2010; Meier-Augenstein and Fraser, 2008; Rauch et al., 2007), remains recovered from the sites of past wars and conflicts (Bartelink et al., 2014a; Beard and Johnson, 2000; Holland et al., 2012; Regan, 2006), and UBCs found along the United States–Mexico border (Bartelink, 2017; Bartelink et al., 2016; Juarez, 2008). The use of SIA as a provenancing tool for human remains is based on the premise that the isotope ratios recorded in body tissues reflect the sources of consumed foods and imbibed water. A variety of biological, chemical, environmental, and geological processes account for the variation observed in the isotope ratios of these inputs and the associated biological body tissues.

Carbon and nitrogen isotope ratios measured in human tissue (e.g., hair, nails, bone, and teeth) act as dietary tracers (Chesson et al., 2014; Ehleringer et al., 2007, 2010; Meier-Augenstein, 2007, 2010; Valenzuela et al., 2011). Carbon isotope ratios (reported as $\delta^{13}C$ values) measured in human tissues reflect the relative consumption of plants (as well as the animals that consume those plants) that utilize one of the three photosynthetic pathways (i.e., C_3, C_4, CAM), as well as dietary inputs from marine resources (e.g., fish, shellfish) (Fry, 2006). More than 95% of the earth's vegetation comprises C_3 plants, which include fruits and vegetables, beans and sprouts, nuts and seeds, and many types of grains, as well as processed foods derived from these resources. Plants that utilize the C_4 photosynthetic pathway comprise less than 5% of plants found on the globe, but include numerous cultigens that are extremely important food resources, such as corn (maize), sugar, millet, sorghum, and amaranth. Crassulacean acid metabolism (CAM) plants include cacti and succulents from desert environments and are rarely economically important food resources for modern humans. C_3 plants discriminate against ^{13}C in favor of ^{12}C when fixing CO_2 during photosynthesis, resulting in relatively negative carbon isotope values ($\delta^{13}C \approx -26.0‰$) (Cerling et al., 1997). In contrast, C_4 plants (as well as CAM plants) have less discrimination between ^{13}C and ^{12}C when fixing CO_2 during photosynthesis, resulting in relatively positive carbon isotope values ($\delta^{13}C \approx -12.5‰$). Marine protein resources ultimately derive most of their carbon from dissolved bicarbonate in the ocean, resulting in more positive $\delta^{13}C$ values that can overlap with C_4 plant resources. Due to differences in the relative consumption of C_3, C_4/CAM, and marine resources between populations, carbon SIA is informative regarding cultural and regional dietary practices of modern humans (Bartelink et al., 2014a; Hülsemann et al., 2015; Kellner and Schoeninger, 2007; Mützel Rauch et al., 2009; Nardoto et al., 2006; Thompson et al., 2010; Valenzuela et al., 2011). Controlled feeding studies on rodents fed on pure C_3, C_4, or mixed diets found that the carbon derived from dietary protein are preferentially routed to collagen, whereas the carbon atoms in bioapatite are derived from blood bicarbonate and track whole diet (e.g., carbohydrates, fats, and proteins) of an organism (Ambrose and Norr, 1993; Tieszen and Fagre, 1993). Thus, using carbon isotoperatios of collagen in conjunction with bioapatite permits greater discrimination of the contributions of different macronutrients to the diet (Kellner and Schoeninger, 2007; Froehle et al., 2010).

Nitrogen isotope ratios (reported as $\delta^{15}N$ values) provide information on trophic level and demonstrate a 2‰–4‰ stepwise increase for each level of the food chain (Minagawa and Wada, 1984; Petzke et al., 2005; Schoeninger et al., 1983). Thus, the tissues of meat consumers will be characterized by higher $\delta^{15}N$ values as compared to vegetarians and vegans. Carbon and nitrogen isotope ratios measured in unidentified human remains are most effective at identifying an individual who consumed a diet that differed isotopically from the local population.

Oxygen isotope ratios (reported as $\delta^{18}O$ values) measured in human tissues reflect the sources of imbibed drinking water. Oxygen isotope ratios vary in the hydrological cycle, with $\delta^{18}O$ values of both cloud vapor and precipitation decreasing as water moves inland from the ocean, over the landscape (Craig, 1961; Dansgaard, 1964). The $\delta^{18}O$ values of water are impacted by factors such as distance from large bodies of water (i.e., the "continentality effect"), aridity, altitude, and temperature. Oxygen isotope ratios of serial sections of hair and nails can provide information regarding recent travel history of an unidentified individual, indicated by changes in drinking water $\delta^{18}O$ values, whereas the carbonate in tooth enamel and bone bioapatite reflects childhood region of origin and more long-term region of residence, respectively.

Strontium is weathered from the local bedrock and soils and can be incorporated into human tissues through the consumption of plant and animal resources as well as drinking water from the local environment. Thus, strontium isotope ratios (reported as $^{87}Sr/^{86}Sr$) of bone and teeth reflect the geological signature of the source(s) of food and water (Beard and Johnson, 2000; Bentley, 2006). Strontium substitutes for calcium in the skeleton, and trace amounts in bone and teeth can be measured using mass spectrometry. Used together, oxygen and strontium isotope ratios can be spatially projected using geographical information systems to generate isotope landscapes, or "isoscapes" (Bowen et al., 2009). These isoscapes can serve as geolocation tools to predict possible regions of origin with environmental conditions fitting the isotope signatures measured in the tissues.

Provenancing Human Remains From the Vietnam War

The mission of the DPAA is to account for the approximately 83,000 missing US military service members from past wars and conflict situations (DPAA, 2017). The DPAA operates under the US Department of Defense, and laboratory personnel include a forensic pathologist, forensic anthropologists, archaeologists, odontologists, historians, and military specialists. DPAA recovery teams work to recover human remains worldwide and consist of both civilian and military personnel (Holland et al., 2008). Recovery missions involve the excavation of aircraft crash sites (e.g., planes and helicopters) as well as individual and mass burials of fallen service members. Remains have also been turned over to the DPAA from foreign governments, frequently lacking provenience information. In these instances, it is often difficult to assess whether the remains are those of US service personnel versus the remains of an indigenous person. Significant monetary and scientific investment is regularly undertaken (e.g., anthropological, odontological, and/or mitochondrial DNA analyses) on remains that are later determined not to be US service members. For these cases, applications of SIA can serve as a useful analytical tool for distinguishing fallen US service personnel (Bartelink et al., 2014a; Berg et al., 2016; Regan, 2006; Someda et al., 2016). SIA can not only assist in determining whether remains are of US versus non-US origin, it can also provide additional information regarding possible region(s) of origin for an unidentified individual. SIA studies of samples of US and Asian origin (e.g., Southeast Asia, Korea, and Japan) have successfully differentiated these different regions based on carbon isotopic variation resulting from dietary preference (Bartelink et al., 2014a; Berg et al., 2016; Holland et al., 2012; Regan, 2006; Someda et al., 2016). For example, US Americans have a significantly higher contribution of C_4-based resources in their diets—resulting in higher $\delta^{13}C$ values of their tissues—due to the consumption of corn products, cane sugar, and animal products derived from animals that consumed corn as feed, compared to the more C_3-based diets (e.g., rice, wheat, etc.) of most East Asian populations. These dietary differences can be identified by analyzing carbon isotope ratios of bone collagen as well as bone or tooth bioapatite, providing an effective screening tool for many identification efforts handled by the DPAA. Once carbon isotope ratios have been used as a screening tool for a general region of origin (e.g., United States vs. Southeast Asia), anthropological, odontological, and/or mitochondrial DNA analyses can be performed. In addition, the analysis of oxygen and/or strontium isotope ratios can then be used in conjunction with these more traditional forensic anthropological tools to further predict a narrower region of origin within a specific region (e.g., Southwestern United States, Pacific Northwest, etc.).

Provenancing Human Remains of Undocumented Border Crossers

Over the past three decades, the increasing militarization of the United States–Mexico border has resulted in a dramatic increase in the number of UBCs found deceased within the United States. Border security policies that promote prevention through deterrence, such as *Operation Hold the Line* in El Paso, Texas (1993); *Operation Gatekeeper* in San Diego, California (1994); *Operation Safeguard* in southern Arizona (1995); and *Operation Rio Grande* in southern Texas (1997), have resulted in UBCs attempting to cross the border through more clandestine and dangerous routes, resulting in an increased risk of death (Martínez et al., 2014; Reineke and Martínez, 2014; Rose, 2012). This increase in migrant deaths has occurred despite the fact that US Border Patrol apprehensions have steadily declined over the past decade (Baker, 2014; De León, 2015). While most migrant deaths have historically occurred in southern Arizona, annual UBC deaths in South Texas surpassed Arizona as of 2012 (Kovic, 2013). Estimates of UBC deaths along the United States–Mexico border from 1998 to 2015, vary from 5000 to 7500 (Jimenez, 2009), and many of these remains are still unidentified. Causes of death are often difficult to determine, although deaths often appear to be due to the prolonged effects of environmental exposure as migrants become ill, injured, or dehydrated during their journey to the United States (De León, 2015; Martínez et al., 2014).

In South Texas, a large number of UBC deaths occur approximately 70 miles north of the United States–Mexico border near the Falfurrias Border Patrol Checkpoint in Brooks County (Kovic, 2013). UBCs attempt to bypass the checkpoint on foot through privately owned ranch land and often become lost and disoriented resulting in death due to dehydration or heat-related illness. Due to limited resources available within Brooks County, deceased UBCs were often buried within the local Sacred Heart Cemetery in Falfurrias with little effort undertaken toward identification and repatriation (Kovic, 2013). Many barriers exist to identification of deceased UBCs, including a lack of fingerprint, dental, and medical records; DNA family reference samples; and identification cards. Beginning in 2013, an effort was made to identify these UBC remains, initially undertaken by faculty and students from the University of Indianapolis (beyondborders.uindy.edu) and Baylor University, and more recently by the involvement of faculty and students from Texas State University (http://www.txstate.edu/anthropology/facts/outreach/opid.html). This humanitarian effort (named *Operation Identification*) includes exhumation, analysis, identification, and repatriation of remains through the collaborative efforts of several universities, law enforcement agencies, nongovernmental organizations (e.g., Colíbri Center for Human Rights, South Texas Human Rights Center, Argentine Forensic Anthropology Team), the National Missing and Unidentified Persons System or NamUs, the University of North Texas Center for Human Identification, and Bode Cellmark Forensics. All UBC remains from Falfurrias are presently curated at Texas State University.

■ SAMPLES

Defense POW/MIA Accounting Agency Samples

The DPAA bone samples included in this study derive from a variety of sites associated with 20th-century US military losses in East Asia and the Pacific. Thirty samples were analyzed, representing 24 different individuals from active casework (a few individuals were represented by more than one skeletal element). These samples represent individuals of known geographic origin, including positively identified individuals as well as individuals with haplogroup information derived from mtDNA analysis. In the latter case, geographic origin was inferred through DNA haplogroups, which strongly correlate with genetic variations found in different populations. The majority of the US American samples derive from Vietnam, although a few samples derive from Cambodia and the Korean Peninsula, representing US service personnel from both the Vietnam and Korean wars. The remaining samples represent individuals native to Vietnam. Thus, these remains include both US soldiers and Vietnamese individuals who were sampled as part of mtDNA identification effort by DPAA and submitted to the California State University, Chico (CSU, Chico) Human Identification Laboratory for SIA sample preparation in 2013.

Undocumented Border Crosser Samples

The UBC samples from South Texas derive from burials exhumed from the Sacred Heart Cemetery in Falfurrias, Texas, during the 2013 field season. In 2014, the University of Indianapolis Archeology and Forensics Laboratory submitted samples from 12 unidentified UBCs (bone and tooth samples when possible) to the CSU, Chico Human Identification Laboratory. These skeletonized remains were discovered on privately owned ranches and were recovered by the Brooks County Sheriff's Office prior to their interment at the Sacred Heart Cemetery.

■ SAMPLE PREPARATION AND ANALYSIS

Stable isotope ratios were measured through isotope ratio mass spectrometry (IRMS), and values are reported relative to international standards using the delta (δ) notation: $\delta = (R_{sample}/R_{standard}) - 1$, where R is the ratio of the heavy-to-light stable isotope (e.g., $^{13}C/^{12}C$). In δ-notation, values are expressed in "permil" (‰), meaning "parts per thousand" (Fry, 2006). The $\delta^{13}C$ and $\delta^{15}N$ values of bone collagen were measured by continuous-flow IRMS at the Stable Isotope Facility at the University of California, Davis, using an elemental analyzer (PDZ Europa ANCA-GSL) interfaced with an isotope ratio mass spectrometer (PDZ Europa 20-20). The $\delta^{13}C$ and $\delta^{18}O$ values of bone and tooth bioapatite were measured by continuous-flow IRMS at IsoForensics, Inc. in Salt Lake City, Utah, using a GasBench II (Thermo Scientific) interfaced to an isotope ratio mass spectrometer (Thermo Electron Corporation, Finnigan MAT 253). Oxygen isotope ratios of bioapatite were normalized to the VPDB standard scale. For the UBC samples, strontium isotope ratios ($^{87}Sr/^{86}Sr$) were measured at the Department of Geology and Geophysics at the University of Utah via high-resolution multi-collector inductively coupled plasma-mass spectrometry (Thermo Scientific Neptune Plus). Sample preparation procedures for carbon, nitrogen, and oxygen isotope ratio analyses are reported in Bartelink et al. (2014a).

■ RESULTS AND INTERPRETATION

Defense POW/MIA Accounting Agency Sample Results

For the 30 DPAA bone collagen samples, $\delta^{13}C$ values vary from −20.5‰ to −14.7‰ (mean and SD = −17.4 ± 2.1‰) and $\delta^{15}N$ values vary from +9.2‰ to +14.2‰ (mean and SD = +11.9 ± 1.1‰) (Table 15.1). For bioapatite samples,

Table 15.1 Descriptive Statistics of the Carbon and Nitrogen Isotope Data Collected for the Defense POW/MIA Accounting Agency Samples

	$\delta^{13}C_{collagen}$ (‰)	$\delta^{15}N_{collagen}$ (‰)	$\delta^{13}C_{apatite}$ (‰)	$\delta^{18}O_{apatite}$ (‰)
United States ($n = 18$)				
Mean	−16.0	+11.8	−11.4	−7.5
SD	1.2	1.1	1.3	1.2
Southeast Asia ($n = 12$)				
Mean	−19.5	+11.9	−15.7	−7.3
SD	0.5	1.1	1.0	0.5
Total				
Mean	−17.4	+11.8	−13.1	−7.4
SD	2.0	1.1	2.5	1.0

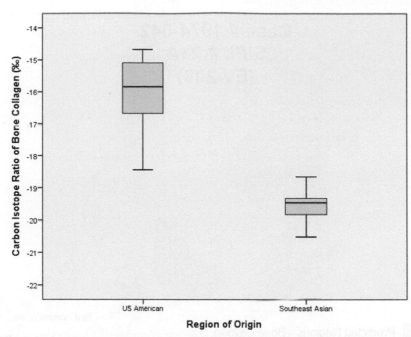

Figure 15.1 Box-and-whisker plot comparing collagen $\delta^{13}C$ values between the Defense POW/MIA Accounting Agency samples of US origin and Southeast Asian origin.

$\delta^{13}C$ values vary from $-17.1‰$ to $-8.9‰$ (mean and SD $= -13.2 \pm 2.6‰$). The $\delta^{13}C$ data show a bimodal distribution, separating the US individuals (higher $\delta^{13}C$ values) from the Southeast Asian individuals (lower $\delta^{13}C$ values), reflecting the impact of differing amount of C_4 and C_3 plants in diets (Fig. 15.1). As expected, samples from individuals of US origin had $\delta^{13}C$ values significantly higher than samples from Southeast Asia, reflecting greater contribution of C_4 resources in the diets of US Americans as compared to Southeast Asians. Very little overlap was identified between the US origin and Southeast Asian samples, with collagen and bioapatite $\delta^{13}C$ values showing statistically significant differences between regions (collagen $\delta^{13}C$, $t = 11.4$, df $= 24.5$, $P < .001$; bioapatite $\delta^{13}C$, $t = 9.9$, df $= 28$, $P < .001$). In prior research on these samples, linear discriminant function analysis (LDA) with leave-one-out cross-validation was used to determine how well samples of known origin classify into their respective groups (Bartelink et al., 2014a). The LDA showed a 96.7% correct classification rate (cross-validated) using collagen and bioapatite $\delta^{13}C$ values, indicating that LDA is a powerful tool for determining origin between these groups based on SIA data. The $\delta^{15}N$ values of bone collagen, in contrast, are nearly identical between US American and Southeast Asian groups and are not considered further.

Two case studies from the DPAA data set are presented below to demonstrate how SIA can be used initially as a screening tool for a general region of origin followed by a more specific provenancing tool. Case 1974-02 is a sample from Vietnam that was determined to be that of a local individual based on mtDNA results. The $\delta^{13}C$ values of bone collagen and bioapatite are $-19.4‰$ and $-15.3‰$, respectively, consistent with a diet primarily composed of C_3-based resources. These values, as predicted by the LDA, classify the samples as Southeast Asian in origin. When mapped using an isoscape for this region (Fig. 15.2), the bioapatite $\delta^{18}O$ value of $-6.9‰$ is consistent with several regions within Southeast Asia, including Vietnam and Cambodia.

Case 2013-003-I-01 is a sample from an individual found in Vietnam that was determined to be from a US service person based on mtDNA results. The bone collagen and bioapatite $\delta^{13}C$ values are $-16.0‰$ and $-10.5‰$, respectively, which are consistent with a diet heavily emphasizing C_4 plant–based resources. These values, as predicted by the LDA, classify the samples as United States in origin, consistent with belonging to a US service member. When mapped using an isoscape for this region (Fig. 15.3), the bioapatite $\delta^{18}O$ value of $-8.8‰$ is consistent with several regions within the United States, including areas along the West Coast and in the Southwest, Midwest, and Northeast.

Undocumented Border Crosser Sample Results

For the 12 UBC bone collagen samples, $\delta^{13}C$ values vary from $-17.9‰$ to $-11.4‰$ (mean and SD $= -14.2 \pm 2.0‰$) and $\delta^{15}N$ values vary from $+8.0‰$ to $+12.2‰$ (mean and SD $= +10.4 \pm 1.1 ‰$) (Table 15.2). For bioapatite samples, $\delta^{13}C$ values vary from $-11.1‰$ to $-3.4‰$ (mean and SD $= -6.7 \pm 2.6‰$). The $\delta^{13}C$ data are consistent with a diet that heavily emphasized C_4 resources such as corn. The upper end of these carbon values are consistent with those previously observed in the United States and Mexico (Bartelink et al., 2014a; Hülsemann et al., 2015). The majority of these data, however, are different than currently published data for the United States and are more consistent with values observed in countries south of the Mexican border (Hülsemann et al., 2015). The $\delta^{15}N$ values of bone collagen are characterized by low variation within the sample set. However, this is not unexpected given the relatively low amount of variation in $\delta^{15}N$ values generally observed between nations across the globe (Hülsemann et al., 2015).

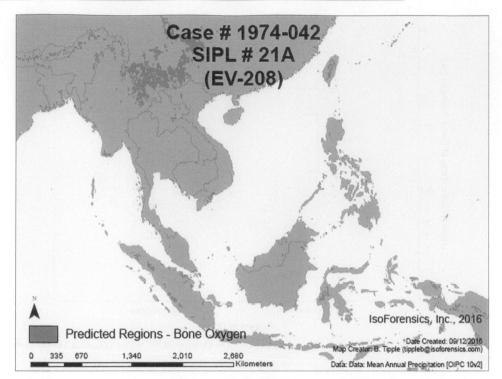

Figure 15.2 Region of origin predictive map for Case 1974-02 using the oxygen isotope ratio of bone bioapatite to estimate drinking water. The geographic extent of drinking water $\delta^{18}O$ values is predicted from mean annual precipitation reference data.

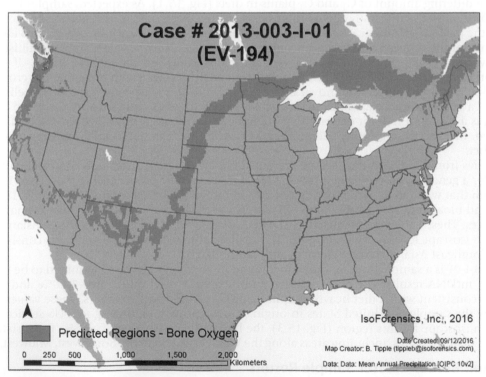

Figure 15.3 Region of origin predictive map for Case 2013-003-I-01 using the oxygen isotope ratio of bone bioapatite to estimate drinking water. The geographic extent of drinking water $\delta^{18}O$ values is predicted from mean annual precipitation reference data.

Two case studies from the UBC data set are presented to demonstrate how SIA can be used to provenance remains of suspected border crossers. Case UI-65-13:4 is a 20- to 50-year-old Hispanic female who was found deceased near Falfurrias, Texas, in 2013. The $\delta^{13}C$ values of bone collagen and bioapatite are −11.7‰ and −4.0‰, respectively, consistent with a diet primarily incorporating C_4 plant–based resources. The tooth bioapatite $\delta^{18}O$ value of −4.2‰ is consistent with several regions within Latin America (Fig. 15.4). Prediction of possible region of origin using $\delta^{18}O$ values alone includes a range of regions of similar climate and not a specific location. This individual has since been

Table 15.2 Descriptive Statistics of the Isotope Data Collected for the Falfurrias, Texas, Undocumented Border Crosser (UBC) Samples

	$\delta^{13}C_{collagen}$ (‰)	$\delta^{15}N_{collagen}$ (‰)	$\delta^{13}C_{apatite}$ (‰)	$\delta^{18}O_{apatite}$ (‰)	$^{87}Sr/^{86}Sr_{whole\ bone}$
UBC					
Mean	−14.2	+10.4	−6.7	−4.7	0.70736
SD	2.0	1.1	2.6	1.6	0.0001

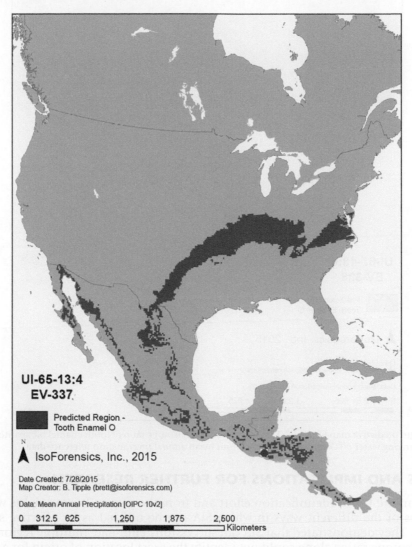

Figure 15.4 Region of origin predictive map for UI-65-13:4 using the oxygen isotope ratio of tooth enamel bioapatite to estimate drinking water. The geographic extent of drinking water $\delta^{18}O$ values is predicted from mean annual precipitation reference data. The *red dot* highlights El Salvador, the (now) known origin for the individual.

identified, and predicted region of origin based on $\delta^{18}O$ value of tooth bioapatite is consistent with her known region of origin of El Salvador. While detailed base maps of $^{87}Sr/^{86}Sr$ ratios in the local environment do not exist for Central America, the $^{87}Sr/^{86}Sr$ ratio (0.70675) is consistent with values reported in bioarchaeological skeletons from the Maya lowland regions (see Hodell et al., 2004; Laffoon et al., 2017; Wright, 2005), suggesting the addition of Sr isotope analysis would help to further constrain predicted region of origin in UBC casework.

Case UI-67-13:6 is a Hispanic female who was found deceased near Falfurrias, Texas, in 2013. The $\delta^{13}C$ values of bone collagen and bioapatite are −17.3‰ and −11.1‰, respectively, consistent with a diet that emphasized C3-based resources. These $\delta^{13}C$ values are clear outliers relative to the rest of the data set of UBC samples and are similar to the $\delta^{13}C$ values of US samples from the DPAA casework discussed above. The tooth bioapatite $\delta^{18}O$ value of −7.5‰ is not consistent with any region south of the United States–Mexico border and is only consistent with areas within the United States and Canada, including areas in the western United States and US states in the Southwest, Midwest, and Northeast (Fig. 15.5). Given the disparity of UI-67-13:6 when compared to the other UBC samples, the isotope data suggest it is very possible that this individual is either not a foreign national from Central or South America or that she was a UBC who spent her childhood in the United States and not in Central or South America.

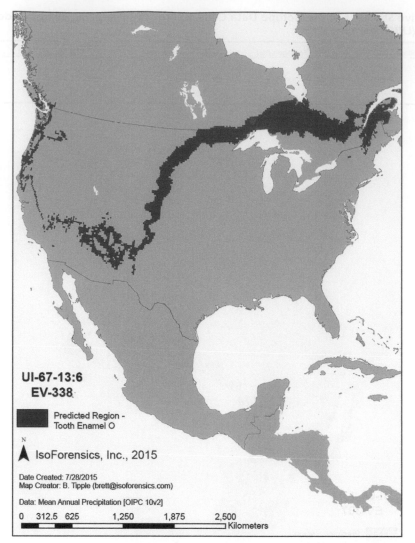

Figure 15.5 Region of origin predictive map for UI-67-13:6 using the oxygen isotope ratio of tooth enamel bioapatite to estimate drinking water. The geographic extent of drinking water $\delta^{18}O$ values is predicted from mean annual precipitation reference data.

■ CONCLUSIONS AND IMPLICATIONS FOR FURTHER RESEARCH

These case studies from the DPAA identification effort and from the current human rights work to identify UBCs are excellent examples of the different ways in which SIA can be utilized as an effective screening tool for the identification process. They demonstrated that SIA can successfully eliminate multiple regions from consideration even if the measured isotope ratios alone could not identify the exact location of origin for a decedent without the contribution of other contextual evidence. However, by eliminating region of origin possibilities, SIA can contribute toward the identification process, especially when working within a globalized world with human populations of high mobility.

Of great importance, also, is the potential for SIA casework to further contribute to future identifications. The DPAA data set, for example, helped provide a method for differentiating individuals of Southeast Asian origin from those of US origin (as have been sampled thus far). The US data from this pilot study were able to then contribute to US reference data in the UBC casework. Without this additional US data, it would have been more difficult to say with confidence that the UBC remains are unlikely to be from the United States. This reference data was integral in assessing whether the UBC remains found in Falfurrias, Texas, were most likely from Latin America versus the United States.

There are clear limitations to this work, many discussed in Chesson et al. (2017) and in other sources (Hülsemann et al., 2015). While carbon isotope ratios can be useful for differentiating individuals from the United States versus some East Asian countries, there is the potential for overlap in isotope signatures due to the ongoing globalization of food resources. Additional factors, such as migration and temporal differences in diet, are important factors to consider as well when using measured isotope ratios as dietary tracers. Consider, for example, the overlap of carbon isotope values of human tissues from the United States and Mexico that has been published to date (Bartelink et al., 2014a; Hülsemann et al., 2015; Valenzuela et al., 2012). In the context of the United States–Mexico border, it is potentially misleading to look at carbon isotope data alone; it cannot exclude the United States as a potential region of origin unless the $\delta^{13}C$ values are significantly elevated relative to currently available reference data from the United States. However, oxygen and strontium isotope data along with carbon isotoperatios provide a better argument to exclude possible regions of origin from consideration. Consideration of other lines of scientific evidence and cultural context are critical for careful evaluations of these types of cases.

Future research will involve a more focused effort toward the development of reference data, both organically through the identification process (as seen here with DPAA and UBC data sets) and through focused model-building studies of modern systems with careful consideration of sociocultural, political, economic, and environmental contexts. Development of these kinds of reference data sets and models will help provide more accurate predictions of possible region of origin of unidentified decedents given the context of the case. For example, given the increase in migration from Central America (via Mexico) into the United States, isotopic reference data from these populations would be invaluable in the mission to identify those who perish crossing the US/Mexico border. Additionally, understanding how different temporal sociopolitical factors embedded in both local and global networks interact to influence dietary patterns, water resources, and human migration for these communities will also likely help improve applications of isoscape models. Ethnographic representation, using participant observation and fieldwork to become familiar with factors important in shaping people's day-to-day lives, has the potential to allow for a more nuanced understanding of the variables shaping diet and migration patterns. Participant observation can also reveal hidden inequalities that are not necessarily calculable in a tangible form; thus, this can aid researchers from over-generalizing or treating populations as static through space and time (Albahari, 2016; Asad, 1994; Desrosières, 1991; Perry, 2003). Furthermore, it recognizes the fact that the human experience variable, complex, and often subjective, which will not be captured perfectly on statistical sampling procedures (Asad, 1994; Abu-Lughod, 1991; Haraway, 1988). Statistical methods are excellent, but ethnographic awareness provides routes to a more nuanced understanding of systems and, therefore, models for identification.

Although in its infancy, forensic SIA has been demonstrated to be an extremely valuable application in the toolkit of forensic anthropologists and other identification specialists. There is great potential for future collaborative work as identifications are made for creating reference databases. The further development of reference data sets will only serve to increase the efficacy and applicability of this method to future forensic identifications.

References

Abu-Lughod, L., 1991. Writing against culture. In: Recapturing Anthropology: Working in the Present. School of American Research Advanced Seminar Series. School of American Research Press, Santa Fe, pp. 137–162.

Albahari, M., 2016. Mediterranean carnage: heretical scholarship and public citizenship in an age of eloquence. Anthropol. Q. 89, 889–916.

Ambrose, S.H., Norr, L., 1993. Experimental evidence for the relationship of the carbon isotopes ratios of whole diet and dietary protein to those of bone collagen and carbonate. In: Lambert, J.B., Grupe, G. (Eds.), Prehistoric Human Bone: Archaeology at the Molecular Level. Springer-Verlag, Berlin, pp. 1–37.

Asad, T., 1994. Ethnographic representation, statistics and modern power. Soc. Res. 61, 55–88.

Baker, L.E., 2014. Identification of deceased unauthorized border crossers in the United States. In: Berg, G.E., Ta'ala, S.C. (Eds.), Biological Affinity in Forensic Identification of Human Skeletal Remains: Beyond Black and White. CRC Press, Boca Raton, pp. 271–285.

Bartelink, E.J., Berg, G.E., Beasley, M.M., Chesson, L.A., 2014a. Application of stable isotope forensics for predicting region of origin of human remains from past wars and conflicts. Ann. Anthropol. Pract. 38, 124–136.

Bartelink, E.J., Berry, R., Chesson, L.A., 2014b. Stable isotopes and human provenancing. In: Mallett, X., Blythe, T., Berry, R. (Eds.), Advances in Forensic Human Identification. Taylor and Francis, Boca Raton, pp. 157–184.

Bartelink, E.J., MacKinnon, A.T., Prince-Buitenhuys, Tipple, B.J., Chesson, L.A., 2016. Stable isotope forensics as an investigative tool in missing persons investigations. In: Morewitz, S.J., Sturdy Colls, C. (Eds.), Handbook of Missing Persons. Springer International Publishing, New York, pp. 443–462.

Bartelink, E.J., 2007. Identifying difference: Forensic methods and the uneven playing field of repatriation. In: Latham, K.A., O'Daniel, A. (Eds.), Sociopolitics of Migrant Death and Repatriation: Perspectives from Forensic Science. Springer, New York.

Beard, B.L., Johnson, C.M., 2000. Strontium isotope composition of skeletal material can determine the birth place and geographic mobility of humans and animals. J. Forensic Sci. 45, 1049–1061.

Bentley, R.A., 2006. Strontium isotopes from the earth to the archaeological skeleton: a review. J. Archaeol. Method Theory 13, 135–187.

Berg, G., Bartelink, E.J., Suhwan, L., Beasley, M., Chesson, L., 2016. Application of stable isotope analysis for provenancing human remains recovered from Asia and the Pacific. Paper Presented at the 23rd Symposium of the Australian and New Zealand Forensic Science Society. 18–22 September 2016, Auckland, New Zealand.

Bowen, G.J., West, J.B., Vaughn, B.H., Dawson, T.E., Ehleringer, J.R., Fogel, M.L., Hobson, K.A., Hoogewerff, J., Kendall, C., Lai, C.-T., Miller, C.C., Noone, D., Schwarcz, H., Still, C.J., 2009. Isoscapes to address large-scale earth science challenges. Eos Trans. Am. Geophys. Union 90, 109–110.

Cerling, T.E., Harris, J.M., MacFadden, B.J.Leakey, M.G., Quade, J., Eisenmann, V., Ehleringer, J.R., 1997. Global vegetation change through the Miocene/Pliocene boundary. Nature 389, 153–158.

Cerling, T.E., Barnette, J.E., Bowen, G.J., Chesson, L.A., Ehleringer, J.R., Remien, C.H., Shea, P., Tipple, B.J., West, J.B., 2016. Forensic stable isotope biogeochemistry. Annu. Rev. Earth Planet. Sci. 44, 175–206.

Chesson, L., Tipple, B., Youmans, L., O'Brien, M., Harmon, M., 2017. Forensic identification of human skeletal remains using isotopes: a brief history of applications from archaeological dig sites to modern crime scenes. In: Latham, K.E., Bartelink, E.J., Finnegan, M. (Eds.), New Perspectives in Forensic Human Skeletal Identification. Elsevier, New York, pp. 157–174.

Chesson, L.A., Tipple, B.J., Howa, J.D., Bowen, G.J., Barnette, J.E., Cerling, T.E., Ehleringer, J.R., 2014. Stable isotopes in forensics applications. In: Cerling, T.E. (Ed.), Treatise on Geochemistry, second ed. Elsevier, New York, pp. 285–317.

Craig, H., 1961. Isotopic variations in meteoric waters. Science 133, 1702–1703.

Dansgaard, W., 1964. Stable isotopes in precipitation. Tellus 16, 436–468.

Defense Prisoner of War Missing Personnel Office Website, 2017. http://www.dpaa.mil/.

De León, J., 2015. The Land of Open Graves: Living and Dying on the Migrant Trail. University of California Press, Berkeley.

Desrosières, A., 1991. The part in relation to the whole: how to generalize? The prehistory of representative sampling. In: The Social Survey in Historical Perspective 1880–1940. Cambridge University Press, Cambridge, pp. 217–244.

Ehleringer, J.R., Cerling, T.E., West, J.B., 2007. Forensic science applications of stable isotope ratios. In: Blackledge, R.D. (Ed.), Forensic Analysis on the Cutting Edge: New Methods for Trace Evidence Analysis. Wiley, San Diego, pp. 399–422.

Ehleringer, J.R., Thompson, A.H., Podlesak, D., Bowen, G.J., Chesson, L.A., Cerling, T.E., Park, T., Dostie, P., Schwarcz, H., 2010. A framework for the incorporation of isotopes and isoscapes in geospatial forensic investigations. In: West, J.B., Bowen, G.J., Dawson, T.E., Tu, K.P. (Eds.), Isoscapes: Understanding Movement, Pattern, and Process on Earth through Isotope Mapping. Springer, Dordrecht, pp. 357–387.

Froehle, A.W., Kellner, C.M., Schoeninger, M.J., 2010. Effect of diet and protein source on carbon stable isotope ratios in collagen: follow up to Warinner and Tuross (2009). J. Archaeol. Sci. 37, 2662–2670.

Fry, B., 2006. Stable Isotope Ecology. Springer Science, New York.

Haraway, D., 1988. Situated knowledges: the science question in feminism and the privilege of partial perspective. Fem. Stud. 14, 575–599.

Hodell, D.A., Quinn, R.L., Brenner, M., Kamenov, G., 2004. Spatial variation of strontium isotopes ($^{87}Sr/^{86}Sr$) in the Maya region: a tool for tracking ancient human migration. J. Archaeol. Sci. 31, 585–601.

Holland, T., Byrd, J., Sava, V., 2008. Joint POW/MIA accounting command's central identification laboratory. In: Warren, M.W., Walsh-Haney, H.A., Freas, L.E. (Eds.), The Forensic Anthropology Laboratory. CRC Press, Boca Raton, pp. 47–63.

Holland, T.D., Berg, G.E., Regan, L.A., 2012. Identification of a United States airman using stable isotopes. In: Proceedings of the 64th Annual Meeting of American Academy of Forensic Sciences, 20–25 February 2012, Atlanta, Georgia, USA, pp. 420–421.

Hülsemann, F., Lehn, C., Schneiders, S., Jackson, G., Hill, S., Rossmann, A., Scheid, N., Dunn, P.J.H., Flenker, U., Schänzer, W., 2015. Global spatial distributions of nitrogen and carbon stable isotope ratios of modern human hair. Rapid Commun. Mass Spectrom. 29, 2111–2121.

Juarez, C.A., 2008. Strontium and geolocation, the pathway to identification for deceased undocumented Mexican border-crossers: a preliminary report. J. Forensic Sci. 53, 46–49.

Jimenez, M., 2009. Humanitarian Crisis: Migrant Deaths at the US-Mexico Border. ACLU of San Diego and Imperial Counties and Mexico's National Commission of Human Rights, San Diego.

Kellner, C.M., Schoeninger, M.J., 2007. A simple carbon isotope model for reconstructing prehistoric human diet. Am. J. Phys. Anthropol. 133, 1112–1127.

Kennedy, C.D., Bowen, G.J., Ehleringer, J.R., 2011. Temporal variation of oxygen isotope ratios ($\delta^{18}O$) in drinking water: implications for specifying location of origin with human scalp hair. Forensic Sci. Int. 208, 156–166.

Kovic, C., 2013. Searching for the Living, the Dead, and the New Disappeared on the Migrant Trail in Texas. Preliminary report on migrant deaths in south Texas. In collaboration with the Prevention of Migrant Deaths Working Group of Houston United.

Laffoon, J.E., Sonnemann, T.F., Shafie, T., Hofman, C.L., Brandes, U., Davies, G.R., 2017. Investigating human geographic origins using dual-isotope ($^{87}Sr/^{86}Sr$, $\delta^{18}O$) assignment approaches. PLoS One 12, e0172562.

Martínez, D.E., Reineke, R.C., Rubio-Goldsmith, R., Parks, B.O., 2014. Structural violence and migrant deaths in Southern Arizona: data from the Pima County office of the medical examiner, 1990–2013. J. Migr. Hum. Secur. 2, 257–286.

Meier-Augenstein, W., 2007. Stable isotope fingerprinting – chemical element "DNA". In: Thompson, T., Black, S. (Eds.), Forensic Human Identification: An Introduction. Taylor and Francis Group, Boca Raton, pp. 29–53.

Meier-Augenstein, W., 2010. Stable Isotope Forensics: An Introduction to the Forensic Applications of Stable Isotope Analysis. Wiley, Chichester.

Meier-Augenstein, W., Fraser, I., 2008. Forensic isotope analysis leads to identification of a mutilated murder victim. Sci. Justice 48, 153–159.

Minagawa, M., Wada, E., 1984. Stepwise enrichment of ^{15}N along food chains: further evidence and the relation between $\delta^{15}N$ and animal age. Geochim. Cosmochim. Acta 48, 1135–1140.

Mützel Rauch, E., Lehn, C., Peschel, O., Hölzl, S., Roßmann, A., 2009. Assignment of unknown persons to their geographical origin by determination of stable isotopes in hair samples. Int. J. Leg. Med. 123, 35–40.

Nardoto, G., Silva, S., Kendall, C., Ehleringer, J.R., Chesson, L.A., Ferraz, E., Moreira, M., Ometto, J., Martinelli, L.A., 2006. Geographical patterns of human diet derived from stable-isotope analysis of fingernails. Am. J. Phys. Anthropol. 131, 137–146.

Perry, R.J., 2003. Five Key Concepts in Anthropological Thinking, first ed. Prentice Hall, Upper Saddle River.

Petzke, K.J., Boeing, H., Metges, C.C., 2005. Choice of dietary protein of vegetarians and omnivores is reflected in their hair protein ^{13}C and ^{15}N abundance. Rapid Commun. Mass Spectrom. 19, 1392–1400.

Rauch, E., Rummel, S., Lehn, C., Büttner, A., 2007. Origin assignment of unidentified corpses by use of stable isotope ratios of light (bio-) and heavy (geo-) elements: a case report. Forensic Sci. Int. 168, 215–218.

Regan, L.A., 2006. Isotopic Determination of Region of Origin in Modern Peoples: Applications for Identification of US. War-dead from the Vietnam Conflict (Ph.D.). University of Florida, Gainesville, FL.

Reineke, R., Martínez, D.E., 2014. Migrant deaths in the Americas (United States and Mexico). In: Brian, T., Laczko, F. (Eds.), Fatal Journeys: Tracking Lives Lost during Migration. International Organization for Migration, Geneva, pp. 45–83.

Rose, A., 2012. Showdown in the Sonoran Desert: Religion, Law, and the Immigration Controversy. Oxford University Press, Oxford.

Schoeninger, M.J., Deniro, M.J., Tauber, H., 1983. Stable nitrogen isotope ratios of bone-collagen reflect marine and terrestrial components of prehistoric human diet. Science 220, 1381–1383.

Someda, H., Gakuhari, T., Akai, J., Araki, Y., Kodera, T., Tsumatori, G., Kobayashi, Y., Matsunaga, S., Abe, S., Hashimoto, M., Saito, M., Yoneda, M., Ishida, H., 2016. Trial application of oxygen and carbon isotope analysis in tooth enamel for identification of past-war victims for discriminating between Japanese and US soldiers. Forensic Sci. Int. 261, 166.e1–166.e5.

Thompson, A.H., Chesson, L.A., Podlesak, D.W., Bowen, G.J., Cerling, T.E., Ehleringer, J.R., 2010. Stable isotope analysis of modern human hair collected from Asia (China, India, Mongolia and Pakistan). Am. J. Phys. Anthropol. 141, 440–451.

Tieszen, L.L., Fagre, T., 1993. Effect of diet quality and composition on the isotopic composition of respiratory CO_2, bone collagen, bioapatite, and soft tissues. In: Lambert, J.B., Grupe, G. (Eds.), Prehistoric Human Bone. Springer Berlin Heidelberg, Berlin, Heidelberg, pp. 121–155.

Valenzuela, L.O., Chesson, L.A., O'Grady, S.P., Cerling, T.E., Ehleringer, J.R., 2011. Spatial distributions of carbon, nitrogen and sulfur isotope ratios in human hair across the central United States. Rapid Commun. Mass Spectrom. 25, 861–868.

Valenzuela, L.O., Chesson, L.A., Bowen, G.J., Cerling, T.E., Ehleringer, J.R., 2012. Dietary heterogeneity among Western industrialized countries reflected in the stable isotope ratios of human hair. PLoS One 7, e34234.

Wright, L.E., 2005. Identifying immigrants to Tikal, Guatemala: defining local variability in strontium isotope ratios of human tooth enamel. J. Archaeol. Sci. 32, 555–566.

CHAPTER 16

Bomb Pulse Radiocarbon Dating of Skeletal Tissues

Bruce A. Buchholz[1] | Kanar Alkass[2] | Henrik Druid[2] | Kirsty L. Spalding[2,3]

[1]Lawrence Livermore National Laboratory, Livermore, CA, United States,
[2]Karolinska Institute, Stockholm, Sweden,
[3]Karolinska Institute, Huddinge, Sweden

Chapter Outline

■ INTRODUCTION

Radiocarbon dating is a well-established technique for determining the age of archaeological artifacts that were once alive. Radiocarbon or carbon-14 (^{14}C) is naturally produced in the upper atmosphere by nuclear reactions between neutrons generated by cosmic rays and nitrogen atoms in the atmosphere. Solitary carbon atoms in the atmosphere are chemically reactive and are quickly oxidized to carbon dioxide (CO_2). The atmospheric concentration of natural ^{14}C, with respect to all carbon, changes slightly with variations in cosmic ray flux and the Earth's magnetic field but has remained relatively stable throughout recorded human history. With a radioactive half-life of 5730 years, the radioactive decay of ^{14}C is minimal within the time periods of interest in medical forensic cases and rather applies to traditional radiocarbon dating of samples over 300 years of age. The Nobel Prize in Chemistry was awarded to Willard Libby in 1960 for the development of radiocarbon dating (Libby et al., 1949).

Above-ground testing of nuclear weapons during the 1950s and early 1960s nearly doubled the natural concentration of $^{14}C/C$ in the atmosphere. The rapid rise and gradual fall of elevated atmospheric radiocarbon has been captured in organic material worldwide and consequently offers an opportunity to determine a date of production for specific biomolecules. Since radiocarbon is incorporated into all living things, this pulse is an isotopic chronometer since 1955.

Carbon enters the food chain from the atmosphere. The isotopic carbon content of new plant growth reflects the isotopic carbon content of atmospheric CO_2, with small differences due to isotopic fractionation during molecular synthesis (O'Leary, 1988; Schoeller et al., 1986). New leaves and small fruits are produced in a matter of weeks, while larger fruits and vegetables form over the period of months. The isotopic signature of herbivores lags the atmosphere slightly because their primary carbon source is on the order of weeks to months old. The isotopic signatures of omnivores and carnivores lag the atmosphere further because their carbon sources are one or more steps removed from the atmosphere. Most humans are omnivores with the majority of their food produced regionally during regular growing seasons and stored as needed until the following harvest.

Tissues and specific molecules within cells or in the extracellular matrix turnover or remodel at different rates. Most soft tissues experience a relatively rapid carbon turnover of 1–2 years, providing an average isotopic signature of the past 2 years (Harkness and Walton, 1969, 1972; Libby et al., 1964; Nydal et al., 1971; Spalding et al., 2005a). Soft tissues also tend to decay rapidly in the environment after death and are often not amenable to forensic dating. Skeletal tissues can survive tens of thousands of years and provide an integrated lifetime carbon isotopic history. The structural protein collagen is the preferred molecule used for traditional radiocarbon dating of bone because the protein is less subject to diagenesis as is the mineral component of bone when buried for long periods of time (Brock et al., 2010a,b; Harvey et al., 2016; Sealy et al., 2014; Simpson et al., 2016). Collagen dating of bone is less helpful in recent forensic cases with bomb pulse dating due to the continuous but variable remodeling of bone throughout life and its net loss in age-related diseases (Babraj et al., 2005; Hedges et al., 2007; Jackson and Heininger, 1975; Manolagas and Jilka, 1995; Parfitt, 2002; Shin et al., 2004; Stenhouse and Baxter, 1977; Ubelaker and Parra, 2011; Ubelaker et al., 2006; Wild et al., 2000). Analyses of bone collagen can often only determine whether a subject has bomb pulse carbon or not. Dental enamel has been shown to be an exceptionally useful tissue for accurate year of birth estimation using the bomb pulse, often within 1–2 years, since permanent teeth are formed within relatively narrow age windows among people (Alkass et al., 2011, 2013; Buchholz and Spalding, 2010; Spalding et al., 2005b).

■ TRADITIONAL RADIOCARBON DATING

Traditional radiocarbon dating relates the $^{14}C/^{12}C$ ratio in a sample to an extensive historical record to determine the age of a sample (Hogg et al., 2013; Reimer et al., 2004a, 2006, 2009, 2013; Stuiver et al., 1998a). The natural production of ^{14}C in the upper atmosphere varies over time due to changes in the Earth's magnetic field and variations in the cosmic ray flux and is captured in the historical record. All living things renew their carbon inventories throughout their lives, with the rates of renewal varying among different biological molecules. The rate of radioactive decay of ^{14}C (radioactive half-life = 5730 years) is slow and predictable, so the concentration of $^{14}C/C$ changes slowly and reliably over time once a biological material dies and stops incorporating new carbon into its structure. The decrease in $^{14}C/C$ concentration due to radioactive decay from the contemporary value is used to determine the age of the sample. Extensive geological and archaeological records from around the world are used to account for the variations in atmospheric ^{14}C concentration over the chronological range of radiocarbon dating (300–50,000 years before present) (Hogg et al., 2013; Reimer et al., 2004a, 2006, 2009, 2013; Stuiver et al., 1998a). Any sample greater than 50,000 years old (approximately 9 half-lives) has too little ^{14}C remaining to measure accurately. Coal- or petroleum-derived carbon, often described as fossil or dead carbon, are older than 60,000 years and free of ^{14}C.

Bone Dating

Bone is the preferred sample matrix for traditional radiocarbon dating of archaeological human remains (Taylor et al., 1989; Ubelaker, 2014). The ability of bone to resist decay over hundreds to thousands of years in appropriate depositional environments while containing a relatively high concentration of carbon makes it a desirable material for traditional dating (Brock et al., 2010b; Harvey et al., 2016; Sealy et al., 2014; Simpson et al., 2016). The carbon in the structural protein collagen does turnover slowly while a person is alive, so the $^{14}C/C$ of collagen content is really an integrated lifetime average rather than a snapshot in time. Collagen extracted from bone is used in conventional bone dating to avoid potential complications with mineral exchange of carbonates (diagenesis) in bone buried for centuries. Collagen is the primary structural protein of bone and is not susceptible to environmental carbonate exchange such as the mineral component.

Specific procedures for collagen extraction and purification vary slightly among radiocarbon laboratories. In general, the mineral component of bone is dissolved in acid to free the collagen into solution. A variety of washing, rinsing, and filtering techniques are then applied to purify the collagen. The procedures are generally based on the Longin method (Longin, 1971) and are often described as modified Longin or ultrafiltration Longin methods (Brock et al., 2010a,b; Bronk Ramsey et al., 2004; Brown et al., 1988; Fuller et al., 2014; Sealy et al., 2014; Tuross, 2012). The major benefit of ultrafiltration is the removal of smaller peptide fragments (e.g., under 30 kDa) that may be residue from sources other than collagen. When bone is in poor condition due to weathering, the collagen can degrade into smaller than usual fragments and ultrafiltration can result in a poor yield. Once purified, collagen can be prepared for radiocarbon measurement like any organic sample.

If human remains are found without any other evidence, radiocarbon analysis of bone collagen or hair (if available) can determine whether authorities have an archaeological site or a crime scene. If the ^{14}C content of the collagen is elevated above the level in 1950, the person died sometime after 1955. The decrease in ^{14}C concentration due to decay can be measured over 100 years, but the small differences in natural production between 1650 and 1955, anthropogenic addition of ^{14}C-free CO_2 from burning fossil fuels known as the Suess Effect (Tans et al., 1979), and the radioactive decay combine to make it very difficult to separate samples chronologically over this time. Collagen from before 1650 can be clearly distinguished.

In the United States a ^{14}C date of remains can determine ownership or precipitate a court battle over ownership, such as the case of 8500-year-old remains of Kennewick Man found in 1996 along the Columbia River in Washington State (Bruning, 2006; Chatters, 2000; Musselman, 2005; Rasmussen et al., 2015; Taylor et al., 1998). The Native American Graves Protection and Repatriation Act (NAGPRA) enacted in 1990 requires institutions that receive US federal funding to return human remains and sacred artifacts to lineal descendants when they are available. After two decades of dispute over ownership of Kennewick Man, the US Army Corps of Engineers who have been holding his remains officially announced on April 27, 2016, that the Kennewick Man is related to modern Native American tribes, based on skeletal and DNA evidence (Rasmussen et al., 2015). DNA extracted from a metacarpal of the Kennewick Man was compared to DNA from ethnic groups from around the world and was found to be close to the Colville Native American population in Washington.

Radiocarbon Analyses

For the past 20 years nearly all ^{14}C-dating analyses have been conducted using accelerator mass spectrometry (AMS), although there are still labs that use decay counting. AMS is much faster and generally more precise than decay counting since the technique counts ^{14}C atoms and measures a stable ^{13}C or ^{12}C current rather than waiting for ^{14}C decay events to be counted. AMS uses smaller samples than decay counting (submilligram vs. gram), an important issue when analyzing rare and small specimens of forensic evidence.

The details of sample preparation and measurement vary among AMS facilities, depending on the type of sample to be analyzed and the spectrometer design. At most AMS labs, routine radiocarbon sample preparation and analyses are performed on samples containing 0.3–2 mg of carbon. Samples as small as 20 μg carbon can be analyzed at some labs, but special handling is usually needed and measurement uncertainties are larger. AMS facilities that perform high precision dating of organic samples follow general procedures to minimize contamination from outside sources of carbon and reduce measurement backgrounds. Samples are dried completely and then combusted with excess oxygen to produce CO_2. The CO_2 is purified cryogenically to remove water vapor, nitrogen, oxides of nitrogen, and oxides of sulfur. The carbon is then reduced to elemental carbon (graphite) on metal catalyst, cobalt, or iron powder.

Primary certified isotopic standards, secondary standards, and backgrounds are processed similarly to samples to produce graphite, which is the form of carbon analyzed by the majority of AMS systems. Graphite is the preferred form of carbon because it can be made easily at high purity and it produces intense negative ion currents while suppressing the isobaric interference from ^{14}N. It is important to have consistent sample source material (e.g., all carbon graphite) because different molecules ionize with different efficiencies. Some AMS facilities have gas-accepting ion sources that take direct feed of CO_2, but they are not typically used for high precision ^{14}C analyses.

The precision of radiocarbon dating depends on the ability to measure the ^{14}C concentration in a sample, the sample size, and the shape of the calibration curve. It is relatively easy to achieve a 0.5%–0.8% measurement precision when analyzing relatively young samples greater than 0.3 mg carbon. This measurement precision translates to a chronological uncertainty of ±30–50 years in most samples that are less than 5000 years old. Samples greater than 25,000 years old can still be measured to 1% precision, but uncertainty propagation from backgrounds and the calibration curve typically yields uncertainties greater than ±100 years (Brown and Southon, 1997). The conventions for reporting radiocarbon dates are described by Stuiver and Polach (1977).

■ RADIOCARBON BOMB PULSE

Atmospheric testing of nuclear weapons before the Nuclear Test Ban Treaty of 1963 significantly increased global atmospheric $^{14}CO_2$ between 1955 and the mid-1960s. The production of bomb-induced ^{14}C was noticed quickly and quantified in the environment and people (Broecker et al., 1959; Rafter and Fergusson, 1957). The radiocarbon bomb curves for higher latitude northern hemisphere (NH) and southern hemisphere (SH) annual growing season averages are shown in Fig. 16.1. The curves are constructed from multiple data sets in the literature that used tree rings, recent plant growth, and direct atmospheric sampling to provide carbon samples. Atmospheric detonations occurred at relatively few sites (Arms Control Association, 2016); therefore, the upswing in ^{14}C and the peak values of the curves vary with geographic location, with the southern hemisphere lagging the northern hemisphere and reaching a lower peak value due to most bomb-testing locations being in the north. However, since CO_2 is a gas and did not fall out of the atmosphere, the bomb pulse of $^{14}CO_2$ mixed with all other CO_2 to produce a relatively homogeneous distribution of atmospheric $^{14}CO_2$ by the late 1960s (Hua and Barbetti, 2004; Hua et al., 2013; Ubelaker and Buchholz, 2006). Since the peaks in the mid-1960s, the level of atmospheric $^{14}CO_2$ has decreased with a mean life of about 16 years globally. The decrease is not due to radioactive decay, but mostly due to mixing with large marine and land carbon reservoirs. The excess ^{14}C has not disappeared or decayed; it has simply moved out of the atmosphere.

The date of formation of a tissue or specific biomolecule can be estimated from the bomb curve by considering the lags in incorporation as carbon moves up the food chain and relating the ^{14}C/C concentration of specific biomolecules with the appropriate bomb pulse curve (Spalding et al., 2005a,b). Using an average of the carbon intake over annual growing seasons can account for much food chain lag and produce curves representative of the food supply of humans by integrating small oscillations in $^{14}CO_2$ seen in the atmospheric record. Caution must be exercised when dating an elevated sample since the bomb pulse curve is double valued. Placing a sample on the ascending or descending side of the pulse can often be accomplished if other information is available. In rare cases, a local source of elevated or depressed $^{14}CO_2$ can skew local plant growth high or low in ^{14}C/C (Milton et al., 1995; Rakowski et al., 2004; Stenstrom et al., 2010; Swanston et al., 2005). There is no evidence in the literature, however, that any local contaminating source produced a measurable shift in ^{14}C/^{12}C in human skeletal tissue.

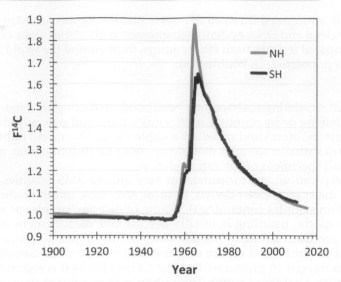

Figure 16.1 Growing season average of atmospheric $^{14}C/C$ in CO_2 for upper latitude northern hemisphere (NH) and southern hemisphere (SH). The NH for 1900–2015 curve is constructed from annual tree rings, recent plant growth, and atmospheric sampling records (Graven et al., 2012; Levin and Kromer, 2004; Levin et al., 2013; Stuiver et al., 1998b). The SH curve for 1900–2012 is constructed from annual tree rings, recent plant growth, and atmospheric sampling records (Hogg et al., 2013; Hua and Barbetti, 2004; Hua et al., 2013; Santos et al., 2015). The vertical axis uses the $F^{14}C$ nomenclature defined by Reimer et al. (2004b) specifically for bomb pulse applications.

The precision of bomb pulse dating depends on the ability to measure the $^{14}C/C$ in a sample and the slope of the bomb pulse curve. It is relatively easy to achieve 0.5%–0.8% precision of the isotope measurement by AMS when analyzing recent samples containing more than 0.3 mg carbon. As the slope of the bomb pulse curve becomes shallow, the same uncertainty in $^{14}C/C$ analysis translates into a larger chronological uncertainty. When the slope was steep, the uncertainty was typically ±1 year. Since 2000, that same measurement precision yields a chronological uncertainty of ±2–4 years. Although the curve has flattened considerably in the past decade, in 2016 it is still elevated above prebomb levels by about 4%.

■ TOOTH DATING

Although dental enamel is the hardest tissue in the body, teeth are not routinely used in traditional radiocarbon dating due to fear of carbonate mineral exchange during long periods of burial (Hedges et al., 1995). After enamel is completely formed, there is no turnover since it is not alive like bone, and the $F^{14}C$ of enamel reflects the level in the food supply at the time of enamel formation. Since teeth are formed at distinct, well-documented ages during childhood (Bolanos et al., 2000; Moorrees et al., 1963a,b; Nolla, 1960; Saunders et al., 1993), the $^{14}C/C$ of dental enamel can be used to determine an approximate date of birth (DOB) (Alkass et al., 2010, 2011, 2013; Cook et al., 2006; Kondo-Nakamura et al., 2011; Spalding et al., 2005b). The double-valued nature of the bomb pulse requires a means to place a $^{14}C/C$ measurement on the rising or falling side of the bomb pulse. This is accomplished by utilizing other information in a case or by measuring samples with different formation times. The investigator can analyze multiple teeth with different formation times or dissect a single tooth to isolate regions with different formation times, either different parts of the enamel crown or separate enamel crown from the later forming root. This technique yields an accurate estimation of birth year from teeth of known age with a precision of ±1.5 years (Alkass et al., 2010, 2011, 2013; Cook et al., 2006; Spalding et al., 2005b), a significant improvement over previous techniques (Cunha et al., 2009; Franklin, 2010; Ritz-Timme et al., 2000).

Procedures

Enamel Processing

Enamel samples are different than soft tissues or bone collagen because the carbon resides as carbonate within the hydroxyapatite mineral matrix. In collagen preparation of bone, the mineral phase is dissolved in acid and discarded while the protein is retained for analysis. For enamel analyses, the live part of the tooth is removed so that only the mineral phase is measured. The enamel is then dissolved in acid and the liberated CO_2 is trapped for analysis. The tooth root is formed after the crown and contains mineral hydroxyapatite and significant amounts of collagen in the dentin. When analyzing teeth, it is convenient to cut the root from the crown at the cervical line and analyze them separately.

The organic residue in the crown is generally dissolved in a strong base to leave the enamel intact. The crown is immersed in 10N NaOH and placed in a water-bath sonicator overnight. The water in the bath and the base solution starts at room temperature and gradually warms to about 70°C. After about 24 h, soft nonenamel structures (dentin and pulp) are scraped away by blunt dissection and the NaOH solution is replaced. The process is repeated until all nonenamel is removed, usually 2–5 days. The enamel is rinsed with DDH_2O to remove residual base, dried at 65°C overnight, weighed, and placed in sealed glass tube (Spalding et al., 2005b).

Enamel is ~0.5% carbon by weight so 100–150 mg aliquots are typically used to produce full-sized samples for ^{14}C analysis and splits for high precision $\delta^{13}C$ quantitation. Normal enamel samples are immersed in 1.0 N HCl at room temperature for 1 h, rinsed 3 times with DDH_2O, and placed on a heating block at 90°C overnight to dry. The acid treatment is designed to etch the outer surface of the enamel that was exposed to the earlier harsh base treatment while dissolving minimal mass. The rationale for the etching step is to remove any carbonate on the surface of the enamel that may have exchanged in the NaOH bath. Alkali solutions remove CO_2 from the ambient air to produce carbonate and bicarbonate in solution and base always contains some carbonate. The hardness of enamel varies among people, probably due to diet and water fluoridation, so if the reaction in the HCl is more rigorous than slow evolution of small bubbles on the surface, this etching step needs to be shortened (Buchholz and Spalding, 2010). Deciduous teeth tend to be softer than permanent teeth and are generally etched sufficiently in only 5–10 min (Speller et al., 2012). The acid etching procedure removes ~2%–5% of the surface enamel from a sample.

A cryo-crushing technique has also been used as an alternative to the strong base process (Alkass et al., 2010). The entire crown was separated from the root, washed with DDH_2O, and crushed with a liquid nitrogen–filled impact grinder. A fine powder is produced in about 15 min that was then processed similarly to the enamel described further. The small amount of dentin in the crown forms concurrently with the enamel and does not alter results. The cryo-crushing process is faster than NaOH method for individual teeth with similar precision and accuracy, as long as the mill is thoroughly cleaned between samples (Alkass et al., 2010).

Whole enamel crowns are often larger than 200 mg, so an aliquot is taken. A dried enamel sample is broken into 5–20 pieces, placed in individual single-use glass reaction tubes and weighed to the nearest 0.1 mg. Tubes are sealed and evacuated in preparation for the addition of concentrated orthophosphoric acid. Tubes are then placed on a 90°C heating block overnight to hydrolyze the enamel to CO_2. The evolved CO_2 is purified, trapped, and reduced to graphite in the presence of metal catalyst in individual reactors as described earlier for collagen. A CO_2 split can be taken from nearly all samples and $\delta^{13}C$ measured by stable isotope ratio mass spectrometry for isotope fractionation correction. If an enamel sample is too small to obtain a $\delta^{13}C$ measurement split, an average value for the geographical area can be used (Alkass et al., 2011, 2013).

Root Processing

Either the mineral or organic fraction of the root can be analyzed to provide a second younger date to place the tooth on the ascending or descending side of the bomb pulse. Cook et al. (2006) pursued the collagen approach as it utilizes the well-developed collagen extraction methods, levels of collagen are high in the dentin, collagen turnover is known to be extremely low in dentin (Ritz et al., 1990), and other stable isotope signatures available from the analysis of the collagen yield clues to diet and geographical origin of the subject. Using a collagen extraction approach similar to that described earlier for bone, collagen was slightly younger than enamel from the same tooth as expected from tooth formation guides. This approach enabled correct selection of the rising or falling side of the bomb pulse for the teeth examined.

The mineral portion of the root can also be analyzed as a means of obtaining a younger component of a single tooth (Alkass et al., 2013). A pretreatment procedure used for stable isotope ratio mass spectrometry (IRMS) followed by a mild acid etch to remove surface contamination was employed. Roots were soaked in 2% NaOCl solution at room temperature for 24 h and rinsed 10 times with deionized (DI) water. Roots were then immersed in 0.1N HCl for 30 min, rinsed 10 times with DI water, and dried on a heating block overnight. Approximately 120 mg of root was crushed and 1–2 mg of powder root was taken for IRMS analysis of ^{13}C and ^{18}O. The remainder of each powdered root was used for ^{14}C-AMS analysis and was processed similarly with orthophosphoric acid as the enamel described earlier to produce graphite. The aliquots of powdered root for IRMS analysis were reacted with supersaturated orthophosphoric acid at 90°C in an Isocarb common acid bath autocarbonate device attached to a Fisons Optima IRMS. The preparation methods of both IRMS and AMS liberated carbonate as CO_2 from the mineral fraction and did not sample the organic residue.

Radiocarbon Measurement

A major strength of AMS analysis is that once samples are reduced to graphitic carbon, all samples, standards, and backgrounds are measured identically. The same primary certified isotope standards are used for all sample normalization. Processing secondary standards and backgrounds are prepared with each sample set. Calcite devoid of ^{14}C serves as the background material for enamel and mineral root fractions. Measurement precision of 0.3%–0.8% is routinely obtainable for these young full-sized samples at most AMS facilities. Details on routine operation of the AMS system at Lawrence Livermore National Laboratory for enamel dating are available (Alkass et al., 2013; Buchholz and Spalding, 2010).

Determining Date of Birth

The papers outlining the development of permanent teeth are based on radiographic images (dental X-rays) of children in the 1940s and 1950s and were published more than 50 years ago (Moorrees et al., 1963b; Nolla, 1960). These guides assigned numerical values to stages of crown and root development of each tooth and examined developmental differences in ages between the sexes, the time to progress through the stages of development, and variation in age for the different stages of development. Nolla (1960) followed a population of 25 boys and 25 girls over the length of the study. Moorrees et al. (1963b) examined hundreds of radiographs from multiple sources and did not follow specific subjects. Both studies grouped similar teeth (e.g., right and left central maxillary incisors, right and left mandibular first bicuspids) as they found no differences in development between them.

The median of the stage of crown development corresponding to the completion of the crown, stage 4.5 (Nolla, 1960), was selected as the average age offset between the measured ^{14}C date and the DOB since a significant mass of enamel was deposited during the interval (Alkass et al., 2010, 2011; Spalding et al., 2005b). After measuring many teeth from subjects of known DOB, an average of the offset based on ^{14}C incorporation of each tooth was calculated (Alkass et al., 2013). In most, but not all cases, the average ^{14}C incorporation offset was smaller than the Nolla offset. The relationship between the radiographic visualization of mineralization and incorporation of carbonate in hydroxyapatite measured by AMS is not known, but the precision in calculating DOB was improved by using the average ^{14}C incorporation age, and reference data on this for each type of tooth are now available (Alkass et al., 2013). Fig. 16.2 illustrates how the tooth development offset is used to relate the measured $F^{14}C$ and DOB.

Placing a tooth on the ascending or descending side of the bomb pulse requires a second measurement of a related sample with a different formation time. This can be done by measuring the enamel of multiple teeth that develop at different ages, measuring the corresponding root of a crown (as described earlier) or by subdividing the enamel of the crown into early and late mineralization stages. Separating the occlusal and cervical sections of the enamel crown on a single tooth yields samples that are very close in time, has only been published for 2 teeth, and can be challenging to distinguish (Kondo-Nakamura et al., 2011). Since the root is always formed after the crown, analysis of both of these can place the more tightly constrained age of the enamel on the ascending or descending side of the bomb pulse (Fig. 16.2). Analysis of enamel and collagen extracted from the root has been utilized to discern which side of the pulse an enamel sample resides (Cook et al., 2006, 2015). The mineral fraction of the root can also be used, with the advantage that sample preparation is much simpler than collagen extraction (Alkass et al., 2013). We prefer analyzing the enamel of two teeth with different formation ages, when available. Independent enamel analyses provide multiple DOB determinations with relatively good accuracy and precision. Root formation times tend to be much longer than the crowns (Nolla, 1960) and carbon does turn over in the roots (Alkass et al., 2013). The absence of bomb pulse radiocarbon in enamel from all teeth places DOB in the 1940s or earlier. Bomb carbon has been found to be in the roots of all teeth measured, including a subject born in 1918 whose teeth had completely formed prior to the bomb pulse (Alkass et al., 2013). This indicates there is some turnover of mineral carbon in dentin and cementum into adulthood and probably throughout life (Gustafson, 1950; Meinl et al., 2007).

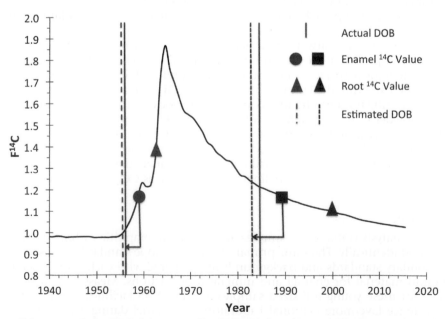

Figure 16.2 Illustration of the approach for determining date of birth (DOB) from ^{14}C in teeth. The enamel and root measurements of two teeth with similar enamel $F^{14}C$ are plotted on the northern hemisphere bomb curve. The *red circle* is tooth number 23 from a male from Texas. The corresponding root has a higher $F^{14}C$ placing the tooth on the ascending side of bomb pulse. The angled *red arrow* accounts for the offset due to the average ^{14}C incorporation time for tooth 23. The *blue square* is tooth 17 from a male in Montana. The corresponding root has a lower $F^{14}C$ placing the tooth on the descending side of the bomb pulse. The angled *blue arrow* accounts for the offset due to the average ^{14}C incorporation time for tooth 17 (Alkass et al., 2013).

Combining Bomb Pulse Dating With Other Techniques

Aspartic Acid Racemization

Racemization is the conversion of the naturally produced pure L-amino acids into a racemic mixture of D- and L-forms. The rates of conversion are slow and temperature dependent, so measuring the ratio of D/L gives the age of a protein. Aspartic acid is used most frequently since its conversion rate is relatively fast (approximately 8% conversion to D-form in 60 years). It was first applied to human dental enamel by Helfman and Bada (1975) and soon after extended to dentin with an improvement in precision due to much higher protein content (Helfman and Bada, 1976). The technique has been used around the world, reporting high correlations between aspartic acid racemization and age in most cases. Reported inaccuracies are generally ±3–7 years, with variations in temperature being an important driver (Alkass et al., 2010; Elfawal et al., 2015; Ohtani, 1997; Ohtani and Yamamoto, 2005, 2010; Ohtani et al., 2003, 2005a,b, 2004; Ritz et al., 1990; Ritz-Timme et al., 2000; Waite et al., 1999; Yekkala et al., 2006; Zapico and Ubelaker, 2013).

Racemization analyses require construction of a standard regression line from teeth of various known ages exposed to similar environments to determine the racemization rate and convert a D/L measurement into a chronological age. The analyses require pulverizing the dentin to powder followed by hydrolysis and derivatization prior to separation and quantitation by gas chromatography (Alkass et al., 2010; Ohtani and Yamamoto, 2010). Subtle differences of temperature among teeth in an individual's mouth alter the degree of racemization. Enamel from teeth at the front of the mouth experience lower temperatures over decades and possess less racemization than molars formed later in adolescence (Ohtani et al., 2005b). The dentin from roots under the gum line are more consistent than tooth enamel, probably due to a higher, more uniform temperature and greater protein content (Ohtani, 1997; Ohtani et al., 2005b). Furthermore, single-rooted teeth, such as mandibular incisors or mandibular premolars, where all the dentin can easily be collected, have yielded more accurate age estimates than teeth where only part of the dentin is used for racemization analyses (Ohtani, 1997; Ohtani et al., 2003; Ohtani and Yamamoto, 2010). In most climates, the ambient environmental temperature is significantly lower than the normal body temperature of 37°C. Hence, the racemization process nearly stops at death and the measured aspartic acid D/L in dentin can be used to estimate the age at death. The analysis is independent of the calendar years in which the person lived and cannot per se tell the date of death or the postmortem interval.

Combining aspartic acid racemization to estimate age at death and enamel bomb pulse dating to estimate DOB provides a means of estimating date of death, if it is unknown. This approach is a powerful tool for forensic pathologists and police investigators to limit possible matches and establish identity in the case of unidentified remains cases.

Case Report

Hunters in Sweden found a human skeleton covered by a tarp in the summer of 2006. The skeleton was almost complete with forensic evidence that the person had been shot in the back of the head. The skeleton was identified as male and estimated to be 30–40 years old at the time of death. The forensic anthropologist also estimated the body had been in the forest for less than 15 years before it was discovered. Four teeth were extracted and subjected to aspartic acid racemization and ^{14}C analysis. Three of the teeth formed at relatively young ages did not possess bomb pulse radiocarbon. Tooth numbers 11, 17, and 41 (FDI numbering system) possess enamel laydown times of 2.5–6.5 years (Nolla, 1960), placing the DOB before 1948.4. The upper third molar (tooth 48) had a small amount of bomb radiocarbon. Using the Nolla (1960) offset of 13 years at the time of analysis, the DOB was approximately early 1942. Using the same four teeth for aspartic acid racemization analyses, the estimated age at death was 46.8 ± 1.7 years. The date of death was then estimated to be 1988.8 ± 2.1 years. Although the person was not positively identified, despite Interpol contacts, local police suspected the person was a foreigner in his 40s that set fire to a business in 1988 and subsequently disappeared (Alkass et al., 2010). The data gathered from the bomb pulse analyses and racemization studies support this notion.

Geographical Differences in δ^{13}C and δ^{18}O

The geographical variations in stable isotope concentrations in tissues can be used to determine where an individual has resided prior to sampling (hair) or during childhood and adolescence (teeth) (Meier-Augenstein, 2010). Variations in water intake are reflected in ^{2}H and ^{18}O, while diet is reflected in ^{13}C, ^{15}N, and ^{34}S. Maps of the isotopic variations of H and O in surface water and precipitation, the main sources of drinking water, are available for regions worldwide (Bowen et al., 2007; Ehleringer et al., 2008; Katsuyama et al., 2015; Mant et al., 2016; Van der Veer et al., 2009). The differences in dietary ^{13}C are driven most strongly by regional grains, consumed directly in processed foods, or as feed grains for livestock and less strongly by consumption of seafood (Meier-Augenstein, 2010; O'Brien, 2015). Teeth record the ^{13}C and ^{18}O during development and can be easily analyzed in parallel to ^{14}C through the use of stable IRMS (Alkass et al., 2011, 2013; Cook et al., 2015).

If only ^{13}C analysis is desired, it is easiest to split the CO_2 evolved during the hydrolysis of the enamel as described earlier and analyze by IRMS (Alkass et al., 2010, 2011; Buchholz and Spalding, 2010). When both ^{13}C and ^{18}O are desired, it is better to use the tooth root with its much higher carbon content. Roots are cleaned by soaking in 2% NaOCl for 24 h, rinsed 10 times with DI water, etched with 0.1N HCl for 30 min, rinsed 10 times with DI water, and dried overnight on a 90°C heat block. About 120 mg of root is crushed to powder and a 1–2 mg aliquot is removed for ^{13}C and ^{18}O analysis. The remainder of the powder root can be hydrolyzed to CO_2 for ^{14}C analysis as described earlier to place the tooth on the ascending or descending side of the bomb pulse (Alkass et al., 2013).

Enamel from Scandinavians had the lightest (lowest concentration) average $\delta^{13}C$ (−14.8‰) of the populations measured, followed by subjects raised in Japan (−13.5‰), Middle East and North Africa (−12.7‰), South America (−10.9‰), and North America (−9.0‰) (Alkass et al., 2011, 2013). The variation in $\delta^{13}C$ of enamel from North America was significantly greater than other regions, ranging from the Pacific Northwest (−10.8‰) to Texas (−9.1‰) and Mexico (−4.8‰), indicating strong dietary differences in the intake of food based on C4 plants (corn, sugar cane) and C3 plants (wheat, potato, sugar beet) (Alkass et al., 2013). The $\delta^{13}C$ of the root was usually, but not always, lighter than the enamel. The variation in $\delta^{13}C$ among the roots collected in North America was smaller than the enamel, perhaps reflective of less variation in diet once children reach adolescence when the roots are formed (Alkass et al., 2013).

Among the roots sampled, the $\delta^{18}O$ levels were lightest in the Pacific Northwest (British Columbia, Washington) as expected based on maps of tap water (Bowen et al., 2007). Levels of $\delta^{18}O$ from teeth formed in Mexico were consistent; however, levels in the remainder of North America seemed more variable. The water contained in foods or beverages from outside the immediate region consumed in adolescence may be responsible for the variation in $\delta^{18}O$ observed (Alkass et al., 2013).

DNA

DNA can easily be extracted from roots using techniques developed for bone (Winskog et al., 2010). After a brief soak with 96% ethanol and a rinse with 0.5% NaOCl, roots are dried overnight at 56°C in open tubes on a heat block. Roots are ground to a fine powder and DNA is extracted using a phenol-chloroform/chloroform extraction method (Rainio et al., 2001) as described in Alkass et al. (2013). Approximately 1 ng of DNA is amplified by polymerase chain reaction (Winskog et al., 2010), and DNA profiles are analyzed by capillary electrophoresis. DNA profiles include amelogenin, the marker for determining biological sex (Nakahori et al., 1991). The results of the amelogenin gene analysis can be confirmed further by analysis of Y-chromosome–specific short tandem repeats (STR) markers in a subset of cases (Alkass et al., 2013).

In all 29 teeth analyzed, sex could be determined from the amelogenin gene used as a marker (Alkass et al., 2013). A full DNA profile was obtained from 22 of the teeth and the four cases in which multiple teeth were analyzed from the same person, the results were identical (Alkass et al., 2013). The Y-chromosome–specific STR markers confirmed the results of the amelogenin gene analysis.

Case Report

In 1968 a hunter found a partial cranium of a child on the banks of a northern Canadian river. Initially the cranium was linked to a 4-year-old boy who disappeared and was presumed drowned in the river in 1965. The anthropological assessment in 1969 misidentified an erupted second deciduous molar as a first permanent molar and estimated the age-at-death to be 7–9 years. Based on the error, the anthropologist concluded the remains were not those of the missing child.

The remains were held in a trust in a local museum for more than 35 years and remained a cold case. The remains were submitted to the Ancient DNA Laboratory in the Department of Archeology at Simon Fraser University in 2005 for a new attempt at identifying the child using current forensic techniques. Analyses were conducted blind to the case. The anthropological assessment of the hard tissues was repeated, associated botanical materials were analyzed, mtDNA was extracted and analyzed, and bomb pulse dating of enamel was conducted to establish a DOB (Speller et al., 2012).

The skeletonized cranium had a single erupted tooth (55, FDI nomenclature) and several nonerupted partially formed permanent teeth in the upper right maxilla. No soft tissue or grease remained and the cranium was discolored from extended contact with soil, in addition to having been gnawed by rodents. A rough estimate of the time elapsed from death to discovery was 5–10 years based on the taphonomy of the remains (Speller et al., 2012). The botanical remains found within the cranium were from plants that grow widely along the river. The plants did not provide any specific geographic information but indicated that buds had been deposited in the spring.

New radiographs of developing dentition, skeletal ossification observations, and cranial circumference were completed to estimate age at death. Since the child was immature at death, ancestry or sex could not be determined by common anthropological traits. The four partially formed right maxillary permanent teeth were evaluated with radiography and compared dental formation times of children of both sexes. The range for age-at-death based on the formation of permanent teeth was 3.19–5.45 years, with the estimate averaged at 4.0 years. When the lone deciduous molar was later removed for radiocarbon analysis, its incomplete root apices were noted, indicating an age-at-death of 3.5–3.9 years (Speller et al., 2012). Partial fusion of the basioccipital component of the occipital bone indicated an age less than 6 years, while its size suggested an age over 4.6 years (Speller et al., 2012). The measured cranial circumference (49.5 cm) was estimated to be 52.0 cm with soft tissue added, placing it in the 90–95th percentile for children 36 months old (World Health Organization, 2007). The dental and skeletal metrics available centered on an age-at-death of 4.4 ± 1.0 years (Speller et al., 2012).

Enamel samples from two teeth were analyzed for ^{14}C to determine a DOB. The deciduous upper second molar (tooth 55) possessed a $F^{14}C = 1.206 \pm 0.005$ fraction modern, placing the average enamel formation on the shoulder on the ascending side of the bomb pulse between 1959 and 1961.7. The formation age of tooth 55 was between 11 weeks prenatal and 11 months postnatal (Lunt and Law, 1974), so an average crown formation span would be 2–6 months with the birth year corresponding to the date range 1958–62. The intercept on the descending slope of the bomb pulse corresponds to 1984–85 and could be eliminated since the remains were found in 1968. The enamel from the permanent upper second premolar (tooth 15) possessed a $F^{14}C = 1.553 \pm 0.006$ fraction modern, placing it on the rapid rise of the ascending side of the pulse in 1963. At the time of death, tooth 15 was incomplete, indicating death occurred in, or shortly after, 1963. The stage of enamel formation and measured $F^{14}C$ of tooth 15 suggested a DOB between 1958 and 1960 (Speller et al., 2012). Combining the techniques described earlier suggested that the child was born between 1958 and 1962 and died between 1963 and 1968 (Speller et al., 2012).

Initial mtDNA sequencing focused on regions that could be used to establish geographic origin, and amelogenin analysis to identify biological sex. The mtDNA profile corresponded to that commonly found in Caucasian populations of European origin. Additionally, the Y-chromosome amelogenin fragment was amplified indicating the child was male (Speller et al., 2012).

The analyses that were performed blind to the case produced a biological profile from the partial cranium. A male of probable European ancestry was born between 1958 and 1962 and died at age 4.4 ± 1.0 between 1963 and 1968. After contacting the authorities it was revealed that a boy aged 4.6 years of European ancestry disappeared (presumed drowned) in the area in early 1965. On the basis of similarities of the missing boy and the cranium, a maternal relative was contacted to provide an mtDNA sample for comparison. The maternal relative of the missing boy provided two samples that were identical and matched the mtDNA profile of the cranium. The maternal reference displayed a mutation at a position that could not be amplified from the cranium, but the profiles matched at all other polymorphic locations (Speller et al., 2012). A paternal DNA reference was also investigated to increase evidence of the child's identity by mini-STR analysis. The paternal reference produced good DNA yields for STR profiling and produced full profiles for comparison. The tooth roots yielded negligible nuclear DNA, however, and the occipital bone had a very low yield of nuclear DNA with a very high drop out. The child could be identified as male based on the presence of the Y allele, but only moderate support for identification could be made based on nuclear DNA (Speller et al., 2012).

The radiocarbon analyses, anthropological evaluation, and match of the mtDNA profile from a maternal relative provided sufficient evidence to identify the remains 41 years after discovery of the cranium. Forty-four years after his disappearance, the identity of the missing boy was officially confirmed, a death certificate was issued, and his remains were released to his family.

■ CARTILAGE, BONE, AND HAIR

After death, most soft tissues decay quickly in the environment and are unsuitable for forensic dating. Hair tends to resist rapid decay and is sometimes found with skeletal remains (Geyh, 2001). Hair grows about 1 cm per month, records stable isotope intake of food and water and has been used to reconstruct the migration of humans and animals (Ehleringer et al., 2008). Hair can also provide an estimate of the date of death when using the bomb pulse (Wild et al., 2000) and record exposure to toxins and drugs, helping to determine a cause of death, especially as analytical techniques improve in sensitivity (Gerace et al., 2014; Moller et al., 2010; Porta et al., 2011). Although individual strands of hair have little mass, the carbon content of hair is high and milligram-sized samples are relatively easy to attain. While not widely used to determine a date of death, bomb pulse dating of hair has been used in several cases to establish a date of death (Wild et al., 2000; Nakamura et al., 2007). We have found that some personal care products, such as dyes, shampoos, or conditioners, can contaminate hair with petroleum-derived carbon that cannot be readily removed. Hence, caution must be exercised when interpreting $F^{14}C$ measurements of hair to estimate date of death.

As discussed earlier, attempts to use bone and cartilage for bomb pulse dating have had limited success. Bone and cartilage do not lock carbon in an inert structure like enamel or hair. Like bone, cartilage contains large amounts of collagen in the extracellular matrix. It is alive and exhibits low but variable turnover, depending on activity, location, and disease state (Akkiraju and Nohe, 2015; Bank et al., 1998; Catterall et al., 2016; Maroudas et al., 1998; Martel-Pelletier et al., 2008; Ohtani et al., 2002). Cartilage has many of the same limitations as bone but is less stable in the environment. Aspartic acid racemization indicates collagen in osteoarthritic cartilage varies widely among joints, with knee osteoarthritic cartilage 30 years younger and hip osteoarthritic cartilage 10 years older than nonosteoarthritic cartilage (Catterall et al., 2016). In 1964, an autopsy study of the cartilage collagen of 70-year-old adults showed little increase of artificial radiocarbon despite living throughout the entire rise of the bomb pulse from 1955 to 1964 (Libby et al., 1964). Bomb pulse dating of collagen from Achilles tendon and human articular cartilage indicates turnover or growth through adolescence but virtually no turnover during adulthood (Heinemeier et al., 2014, 2016).

■ CONCLUSIONS AND PROSPECTS

Radiocarbon bomb pulse dating of enamel is the most precise and accurate technique for determining year of birth for people born in the past 70 years. As in most forensic techniques, combining bomb pulse dating with other analytical techniques is more powerful than single analyses, narrowing possible matches in cases of unidentified decedents. A single tooth can be used to determine year of birth (^{14}C analyses of enamel and root), age at death (aspartic acid racemization), geographical origin ($\delta^{13}C$ and $\delta^{18}O$ in root), and sex (DNA extracted from root).

Approximately 100 AMS facilities are scattered around the globe with more than half residing in North America, Europe, or Japan. Most AMS labs can measure bomb pulse skeletal samples with good precision and accuracy since samples are large and well above instrumental background. The initial sample preparation can be performed in any laboratory free of tracer ^{14}C (Zermeño et al., 2004) and requires only standard laboratory equipment. Final AMS sample preparation of graphitic carbon is generally best done at the AMS facility shortly before analysis to take advantage of batch processing of samples, standards, and backgrounds utilizing customized graphitization apparatus. Interpretation of measurements needs to utilize appropriate data sets, incorporate carbon source integration, and account for realistic skeletal formation times when estimating date ranges. As is the case with all analytical forensic techniques, it is best to work with established labs possessing proven track records in the analyses of interest.

The atmosphere will likely return to prebomb ^{14}C level in the next 20 years; however, the bomb pulse dating technique will remain relevant for decades to come. Many of the thousands of the unidentified remains currently residing as cold cases in the United States are amenable to bomb pulse dating and the associated analyses described earlier. The techniques are also valuable in homicide investigations or identifying victims of mass disasters where limiting the possible leads is an important step in finding a match by DNA analysis.

Acknowledgments

This work performed in part under the auspices of the US Department of Energy by Lawrence Livermore National Laboratory under Contract DE-AC52-07NA27344. Document reviewed and released as LLNL-BOOK-693000. Support was provided by NIH/NIGMS P41GM103483, the Swedish Research Council, and the Swedish Foundation for Strategic Research. This document was prepared as an account of work sponsored by an agency of the US government. Neither the US government nor Lawrence Livermore National Security, LLC, nor any of their employees makes any warranty, expressed or implied, or assumes any legal liability or responsibility for the accuracy, completeness, or usefulness of any information, apparatus, product, or process disclosed, or represents that its use would not infringe privately owned rights. Reference to any specific commercial product, process, or service by trade name, trademark, manufacturer, or otherwise does not necessarily constitute or imply its endorsement, recommendation, or favoring by the US government or Lawrence Livermore National Security, LLC. The views and opinions of authors expressed herein do not necessarily state or reflect those of the US government or Lawrence Livermore National Security, LLC, and shall not be used for advertising or product endorsement purposes.

Disclaimer

This document was prepared as an account of work sponsored by an agency of the US government. Neither the US government nor Lawrence Livermore National Security, LLC, nor any of their employees makes any warranty, expressed or implied, or assumes any legal liability or responsibility for the accuracy, completeness, or usefulness of any information, apparatus, product, or process disclosed, or represents that its use would not infringe privately owned rights. Reference herein to any specific commercial product, process, or service by trade name, trademark, manufacturer, or otherwise does not necessarily constitute or imply its endorsement, recommendation, or favoring by the US government or Lawrence Livermore National Security, LLC. The views and opinions of authors expressed herein do not necessarily state or reflect those of the US government or Lawrence Livermore National Security, LLC, and shall not be used for advertising or product endorsement purposes.

References

Akkiraju, H., Nohe, A., 2015. Role of chondrocytes in cartilage formation, progression of osteoarthritis and cartilage regeneration. J. Dev. Biol. 3, 177–192.

Alkass, K., Buchholz, B.A., Ohtani, S., Yamamoto, T., Druid, H., Spalding, K.L., 2010. Age estimation in forensic sciences: application of combined aspartic acid racemization and radiocarbon analysis. Mol. Cell. Proteom. 9, 1022–1030.

Alkass, K., Buchholz, B.A., Druid, H., Spalding, K.L., 2011. Analysis of C-14 and C-13 in teeth provides precise birth dating and clues to geographical origin. Forensic Sci. Int. 209, 34.

Alkass, K., Saitoh, H., Buchholz, B.A., Bernard, S., Holmlund, G., Senn, D.R., Spalding, K.L., Druid, H., 2013. Analysis of radiocarbon, stable isotopes and DNA in teeth to facilitate identification of unknown decedents. PLoS One 8, e69597.

Arms Control Association, The Nuclear Testing Tally. Updated: January 2016 https://www.armscontrol.org/factsheets/nucleartesttally.

Babraj, J.A., Smith, K., Cuthbertson, D.J., Rickhuss, P., Dorling, J.S., Rennie, M.J., 2005. Human bone collagen synthesis is a rapid, nutritionally modulated process. J. Bone Miner. Res. 20, 930–937.

Bank, R.A., Bayliss, M.T., Lafeber, P.J.G., Maroudas, A., Tekoppele, J.M., 1998. Ageing and zonal variation in post-translational modification of collagen in normal human articular cartilage. The age-related increase in non-enzymatic glycation affects biomechanical properties of cartilage. Biochem. J. 330, 345–351.

Bolanos, M.V., Manrique, M.C., Bolanos, M.J., Briones, M.T., 2000. Approaches to chronological age assessment based on dental calcification. Forensic Sci. Int. 110, 97–106.

Bowen, G.J., Ehrleringer, J.R., Chesson, L.A., Stange, E., Cerling, T.E., 2007. Stable isotope ratios of tap water in the contiguous United States. Water Resour. Res. 43, W03419.

Brock, F., Higham, T., Ditchfield, P., Bronk Ramsey, C., 2010a. Current pretreatment methods for AMS radiocarbon dating at the Oxford Radiocarbon Accelerator Unit (ORAU). Radiocarbon 52, 103–112.

Brock, F., Higham, T., Bronk Ramsey, C., 2010b. Prescreening techniques for identification of samples suitable for radiocarbon dating of poorly preserved bones. J. Archaeol. Sci. 37, 855–865.

Broecker, W.S., Schulert, A., Olson, E.A., 1959. Bomb carbon-14 in human beings. Science 130, 331–332.

Bronk Ramsey, C., Higham, T., Bowles, A., Hedges, R., 2004. Improvements to the pretreatment of bone at Oxford. Radiocarbon 46, 155–163.

Brown, T.A., Nelson, D.E., Vogel, J.S., Southon, J.R., 1988. Improved collagen extraction by modified longin method. Radiocarbon 30, 171–177.

Brown, T.A., Southon, J.R., 1997. Corrections for contamination background in AMS ^{14}C measurements. Nucl. Instrum. Methods Phys. Res. Sect. B 123, 208–213.

Bruning, S.B., 2006. Complex legal legacies: the native American graves protection and repatriation act, scientific study, and Kennewick Man. Am. Antiq. 71, 501–521.

Buchholz, B.A., Spalding, K.L., 2010. Year of birth determination using radiocarbon dating of dental enamel. Surf. Interface Anal. 42, 398–401.

Catterall, J.B., Zura, R.D., Bolognesi, M.P., Kraus, V.B., 2016. Aspartic acid racemization reveals a high turnover state in knee compared with hip osteoarthritic cartilage. Osteoarthr. Cartil. 24, 374–381.

Chatters, J.C., 2000. The recovery and first analysis of an early Holocene human skeleton from Kennewick, Washington. Am. Antiq. 65, 291–316.

Cook, G.T., Dunbar, E., Black, S.M., Xu, S., 2006. A preliminary assessment of age at death determination using the nuclear weapons testing C-14 activity of dentine and enamel. Radiocarbon 48, 305–313.

Cook, G.T., Ainscough, L.A.N., Dunbar, E., 2015. Radiocarbon analysis of modern skeletal remains to determine year of birth and death—a case study. Radiocarbon 57, 327–336.

Cunha, E., Baccino, E., Martrille, L., Ramsthaler, F., Prieto, J., Schuliar, Y., Lynnerup, N., Cattaneo, C., 2009. The problem of aging human remains and living individuals: a review. Forensic Sci. Int. 193, 1–13.

Ehleringer, J.R., Bowen, G.J., Chesson, L.A., West, A.G., Podlesak, D.W., Cerling, T.E., 2008. Hydrogen and oxygen isotope ratios in human hair are related to geography. Proc. Natl. Acad. Sci. U.S.A. 105, 2788–2793.

Elfawal, M.A., Alqattan, S.I., Ghallab, N.A., 2015. Racemization of aspartic acid in root dentin as a tool for age estimation in a Kuwaiti population. Med. Sci. Law 55, 22–29.

Franklin, D., 2010. Forensic age estimation in human skeletal remains: current concepts and future directions. Leg. Med. 12, 1–7.

Fuller, B.T., Fahrni, S.M., Harris, J.M., Farrel, A.B., Coltrain, J.B., Gerhart, L.M., Ward, J.K., Taylor, R.E., Southon, J.R., 2014. Ultrafiltration for asphalt removal from bone collagen for radiocarbon dating and isotopic analysis of Pleistocene fauna at the tar pits of Rancho La Brea, Los Angeles, California. Quat. Geochronol. 22, 85–98.

Gerace, E., Petrarulo, M., Bison, F., Salomone, A., Vincenti, M., 2014. Toxicological findings in a fatal multidrug intoxication involving mephedrone. Forensic Sci. Int. 243, 68–73.

Geyh, M.A., 2001. Bomb radiocarbon dating of animal tissues and hair. Radiocarbon 43, 723–730.

Graven, H.D., Guilderson, T.P., Keeling, R.F., 2012. Observations of radiocarbon in CO_2 at La Jolla, California, USA 1992–2007: analysis of the long-term trend. J. Geophys. Res. 117, D02303.

Gustafson, G., 1950. Age determination on teeth. J. Am. Dent. Assoc. 41, 45–54.

Harkness, D.D., Walton, A., 1969. Carbon-14 in the biosphere and humans. Nature 223, 1216–1218.

Harkness, D.D., Walton, A., 1972. Further investigations of the transfer of bomb ^{14}C to man. Nature 240, 302–303.

Harvey, V.L., Egerton, V.M., Chamberlain, A.T., Manning, P.L., Buckley, M., 2016. Collagen fingerprinting: a new screening technique for radiocarbon dating ancient bone. PLoS One 11, e0150650.

Hedges, R.E.M., Lee-Thorp, J.A., Tuross, N.C., 1995. Is tooth enamel carbonate a suitable material for radiocarbon dating? Radiocarbon 37, 285–290.

Hedges, R.E.M., Clement, J.G., Thomas, C.D.L., O'Connell, T.C., 2007. Collagen turnover in the femoral mid-shaft: modeled from anthropogenic radiocarbon tracer measurements. Am. J. Phys. Anthropol. 133, 808–816.

Heinemeier, K.M., Schjerling, P., Heinemeier, J., Magnusson, S.P., Kjaer, M., 2014. Lack of tissue renewal in human adult achilles tendon is revealed by nuclear bomb C-14. FASEB J. 27, 2074–2075.

Heinemeier, K.M., Schjerling, P., Heinemeier, J., Møller, M.B., Krogsgaard, M., Grum-Schwensen, T., Petersen, M.M., Kjaer, M., 2016. Radiocarbon dating reveals minimal collagen turnover in both healthy and osteoarthritic human cartilage. Sci. Transl. Med. 8, 346ra90.

Helfman, P.M., Bada, J.L., 1975. Aspartic acid racemization in tooth enamel from living humans. Proc. Natl. Acad. Sci. U.S.A. 72, 2891–2894.

Helfman, P.M., Bada, J.L., 1976. Aspartic acid racemization in dentine as a measure of aging. Nature 262, 279–281.

Hogg, A.G., Hua, Q., Blackwell, P.G., Buck, C.E., Guilderson, T.P., Heaton, T.J., Niu, M., Palmer, J.G., Reimer, P.J., Reimer, R.W., Turney, C.S.M., Zimmerman, S.R.H., 2013. SHCal13 southern hemisphere calibration, 0–50,000 years cal BP. Radiocarbon 55, 1889–1903.

Hua, Q., Barbetti, M., 2004. Review of tropospheric bomb ^{14}C data for carbon cycle modeling and age calibration purposes. Radiocarbon 46, 1273–1298.

Hua, Q., Barbetti, M., Rakowski, A.Z., 2013. Atmospheric radiocarbon for the period 1950–2010. Radiocarbon 55, 2059–2072.

Jackson, S.H., Heininger, J.A., 1975. Proline recycling during collagen metabolism as determined by concurrent $^{18}O_2$- and ^{3}H-labeling. Biochim. Biophys. Acta 381, 359–367.

Katsuyama, M., Yoshioka, T., Konohira, E., 2015. Spatial distribution of oxygen-18 and deuterium in stream waters across the Japanese archipelago. Hydrol. Earth Syst. Sci. 19, 1577–1588.

Kondo-Nakamura, M., Fukui, K., Matsu'ura, S., Kondo, M., Iwadate, K., 2011. Single tooth tells us the date of birth. Int. J. Leg. Med. 125, 873–877.

Levin, I., Kromer, B., 2004. The tropospheric $^{14}CO_2$ level in mid latitudes of the northern hemisphere (1959–2003). Radiocarbon 46, 1261–1272.

Levin, I., Kromer, B., Hammer, S., 2013. Atmospheric Δ^{14}C trend in Western European background air from 2000 to 2012. Tellus B 65, 20092.

Libby, W.F., Anderson, E.C., Arnold, J.R., 1949. Age determination by radiocarbon content – world-wide assay of natural radiocarbon. Science 109, 227–228.

Libby, W.F., Berger, R., Mead, J.F., Alexander, G.V., Ross, J.F., 1964. Replacement rates for human tissue from atmospheric radiocarbon. Science 146, 1170–1172.

Longin, R., 1971. New method of collagen extraction for radiocarbon dating. Nature 230, 241–242.

Lunt, R.C., Law, D.B., 1974. A review of the chronology of calcification of deciduous teeth. J. Am. Dent. Assoc. 89, 599–606.

Meier-Augenstein, W., 2010. Provenancing people. In: Stable Isotope Forensics: An Introduction to the Forensic Application of Stable Isotope Analysis. John Wiley & Sons, Ltd., Oxford, UK, pp. 190–213.

Manolagas, S.C., Jilka, R.L., 1995. Bone marrow, cytokines and bone remodeling. N. Engl. J. Med. 332, 305–311.

Mant, M., Nagel, A., Prowse, T., 2016. Investigating residential history using stable hydrogen and oxygen isotopes of human hair and drinking water. J. Forensic Sci. 61, 884–891.

Maroudas, A., Bayliss, M.T., Uchitel-Kaushansky, N., Schneiderman, R., Gilav, E., 1998. Aggrecan turnover in human articular cartilage: use of aspartic acid racemization as a marker of molecular age. Arch. Biochem. Biophys. 350, 61–71.

Martel-Pelletier, J., Boileau, C., Pelletier, J.P., Roughley, P.J., 2008. Cartilage in normal and osteoarthritis conditions. Best. Pract. Res. Clin. Rheumatol. 22, 351–384.

Meinl, A., Tangl, S., Pernicka, E., Fenes, C., Watzek, G., 2007. On the applicability of secondary dentin formation to radiological age estimation in young adults. J. Forensic Sci. 52, 438–441.

Milton, G.M., Kramer, S.J., Brown, R.M., Repta, C.J.W., King, K.J., Rao, R.R., 1995. Radiocarbon dispersion around Canadian nuclear facilities. Radiocarbon 37, 485–496.

Moller, M., Aleksa, K., Walasek, P., Karaskov, T., Koren, G., 2010. Solid-phase microextraction for the detection of codeine, morphine and 6-monoacetylmorphine in human hair by gas chromatography mass spectrometry. Forensic Sci. Int. 196, 64–69.

Moorrees, C.F.A., Fanning, E.A., Hunt Jr., E.E., 1963a. Formation and resorption of three deciduous teeth in children. Am. J. Phys. Anthropol. 21, 205–213.

Moorrees, C.F.A., Fanning, E.A., Hunt, E.A., 1963b. Age variation of formation stages for ten permanent teeth. J. Dent. Res. 42, 1490–1502.

Musselman, J., 2005. Ninth circuit limits NAGPRA to remains linked with presently existing tribes. Ecol. Law Q. 32, 707–713.

Nakahori, Y., Takenaka, O., Nakagome, Y., 1991. A human X-Y homologous region encodes "amelogenin". Genomics 9, 264–269.

Nakamura, T., Kojima, S., Ohta, T., Nishida, M., Rakowski, A., Ikeda, A., Oda, H., Niu, E., 2007. Application of AMS C-14 measurements to criminal investigations. J. Radioanal. Nucl. Chem. 272, 327–332.

Nolla, C.M., 1960. The development of permanent teeth. J. Dent. Child. 27, 254–266.

Nydal, R., Lövseth, K., Syrstad, O., 1971. Bomb ^{14}C in the human population. Nature 232, 418–421.

O'Brien, D.M., 2015. Stable isotope ratios as biomarkers of diet for health research. Annu. Rev. Nutr. 35, 565–594.

Ohtani, S., 1997. Different racemization ratios in dentin from different locations within a tooth. Growth Dev. Aging 61, 93–99.

Ohtani, S., Masushima, Y., Kobayashi, Y., Yamamoto, T., 2002. Age estimation by measuring the racemization of aspartic acid from total amino acid content of several types of bone and rib cartilage: a preliminary account. J. Forensic Sci. 47, 32–36.

Ohtani, S., Ito, R., Yamamoto, T., 2003. Differences in the D/L aspartic acid ratios in dentin among different types of teeth from the same individual and estimated age. Int. J. Leg. Med. 117, 149–152.

Ohtani, S., Yamada, Y., Yamamoto, T., Arany, S., Gonmori, K., Yoshioka, N., 2004. Comparison of age estimated from degree of racemization of aspartic acid, glutamic acid and alanine in the femur. J. Forensic Sci. 49, 441–445.

Ohtani, S., Abe, I., Yamamoto, T., 2005a. An application of D- and L-aspartic acid mixtures as standard specimens for the chronological age estimation. J. Forensic Sci. 50, 1298–1302.

Ohtani, S., Yamamoto, T., 2005. Strategy for the estimation of chronological age using the aspartic acid racemization method with special reference to coefficient of correlation between D/L ratios and ages. J. Forensic Sci. 50, 1020–1027.

Ohtani, S., Ito, R., Arany, S., Yamamoto, T., 2005b. Racemization in enamel among different types of teeth from the same individual. Int. J. Leg. Med. 119, 66–69.

Ohtani, S., Yamamoto, T., 2010. Age estimation by amino acid racemization in human teeth. J. Forensic Sci. 55, 1630–1633.

O'Leary, M.H., 1988. Carbon isotopes in photosynthesis. BioScience 38, 328–336.

Parfitt, A.M., 2002. Misconceptions (2): turnover is always higher in cancellous than in cortical bone. Bone 30, 807–809.

Porta, T., Grivet, C., Kraemer, T., Varesio, E., Hopfgartner, G., 2011. Single hair cocaine consumption monitoring by mass spectrometric imaging. Anal. Chem. 83, 4266–4272.

Rafter, T.A., Fergusson, G.J., 1957. The atom bomb effect – recent increase of carbon-14 content of the atmosphere and biosphere. Science 126, 557–558.

Rainio, J., Karkola, K., Lalu, K., Ranta, H., Takamaa, K., Penttilä, A., 2001. Forensic investigations in Kosovo: experiences of the European Union Forensic Expert Team. J. Clin. Forensic Med. 8, 218–221.

Rakowski, A., Kuc, T., Nakamura, T., Pazdur, A., 2004. Radiocarbon concentration in the atmosphere and modern tree rings in the Kraków area, southern Poland. Radiocarbon 46, 911–916.

Rasmussen, M., Sikora, M., Albrechtsen, A., Korneliussen, T.S., Moreno-Mayar, J.V., Poznik, G.D., Zollikofer, C.P.E., Ponce de León, M.S., Allentoft, M.E., Moltke, I., Jónsson, H., Valdiosera, C., Malhi, R.S., Orlando, L., Bustamante, C.D., Stafford Jr., T.W., Meltzer, D.J., Nielsen, R., Willerslev, E., 2015. The ancestry and affiliations of Kennewick Man. Nature 523, 455–458.

Reimer, P.J., Baillie, M.G.L., Bard, E., Bayliss, A., Beck, J.W., Bertrand, C.J.H., Blackwell, P.G., Buck, C.E., Burr, G.S., Cutler, K.B., Damon, P.E., Edwards, R.L., Fairbanks, R.G., Friedrich, M., Guilderson, T.P., Hogg, A.G., Hughen, K.A., Kromer, B., McCormac, G., Manning, S., Ramsey, C.B., Reimer, R.W., Remmele, S., Southon, J.R., Stuiver, M., Talamo, S., Taylor, F.W., van der Plicht, J., Weyhenmeyer, C.E., 2004a. IntCal04 terrestrial radiocarbon age calibration, 0–26 cal kyr BP. Radiocarbon 46, 1029–1058.

Reimer, P.J., Brown, T.A., Reimer, R.W., 2004b. Discussion: reporting and calibration of post-bomb ^{14}C data. Radiocarbon 46, 1299–1304.

Reimer, P.J., Baillie, M.G.L., McCormac, G., Reimer, R.W., Bard, E., Beck, J.W., Blackwell, P.G., Buck, C.E., Burr, G.S., Edwards, R.L., Friedrich, M., Guilderson, T.P., Manning, S., Southon, J.R., Hogg, A.G., Stuiver, M., Hughen, K.A., van der Plicht, J., Kromer, B., van der Plicht, J., Manning, S., Weyhenmeyer, C.E., 2006. Comment on "Radiocarbon calibration curve spanning 0 to 50,000 years BP based on paired Th-230/U-234/U-238 and C-14 dates on pristine corals" by R.G. Fairbanks et al. (Quaternary Science Reviews 24 (2005) 1781–1796) and "Extending the radiocarbon calibration beyond 26,000 years before present using fossil corals" by T.-C. Chiu et al. (Quaternary Science Reviews 24 (2005) 1797–1808). Quat. Sci. Rev. 25, 855–862.

Reimer, P.J., Baillie, M.G.L., Bard, E., Bayliss, A., Beck, J.W., Blakwell, P.G., Bronk Ramsey, C., Buck, C.E., Burr, G.S., Edwards, R.L., Friedrich, M., Grootes, P.M., Guilderson, T.P., Hajdas, I., Heaton, T.J., Hogg, A.G., Hughen, K.A., Kaiser, K.F., Kromer, B., McCormac, F.G., Manning, S.W., Reimer, R.W., Richards, D.A., Southon, J.R., Talamo, S., Turney, C.S.M., vander Plicht, J., Weyhenmeyer, C.E., 2009. IntCal09 and marine09 radiocarbon age calibration curves, 0–50,000 years cal BP. Radiocarbon 51, 1111–1150.

Reimer, P.J., Bard, E., Bayliss, A., Beck, J.W., Blackwell, P.G., Ramsey, C.B., Buck, C.E., Cheng, H., Edwards, R.L., Friedrich, M., Grootes, P.M., Guilderson, T.P., Haflidason, H., Hajdas, I., Hatté, C., Heaton, T.J., Hoffmann, D.L., Hogg, A.G., Hughen, K.A., Kaiser, K.F., Kromer, B., Manning, S.W., Niu, M., Reimer, R.W., Richards, D.A., Scott, E.M., Southon, J.R., Staff, R.A., Turney, C.S.M., van der Plicht, J., 2013. IntCal13 and marine13 radiocarbon age calibration curves 0–50,000 years cal BP. Radiocarbon 55, 1869–1887.

Ritz, S., Schütz, H.W., Schwarzer, B., 1990. The extent of aspartic acid racemization in dentin: a possible method for a more accurate determination of age at death. Z. Rechtsmed. 103, 457–462.

Ritz-Timme, S., Cattaneo, C., Collins, M.J., Waite, E.R., Schutz, H.W., Kaatsch, H.J., Borman, H.I., 2000. Age estimation: the state of the art in relation to the specific demands of forensic practise. Int. J. Leg. Med. 113, 129–136.

Santos, G.M., Linares, R., Lisi, C.S., Filho, M.T., 2015. Annual growth rings in a sample of parana pine (*Araucaria angustifolia*): toward improving the ^{14}C calibration curve for the southern hemisphere. Quat. Geochronol. 25, 96–103.

Saunders, S., DeVito, C., Herring, A., Southern, R., Hoppa, R., 1993. Accuracy tests of tooth formation age estimations for human skeletal remains. Am. J. Phys. Anthropol. 92, 173–188.

Schoeller, D.A., Minigawa, M., Slater, R., Kaplan, I.R., 1986. Stable isotopes of carbon, nitrogen and hydrogen in the contemporary North American human food web. Ecol. Food Nutr. 18, 159–170.

Sealy, J., Johnson, M., Richards, M., Nehlich, O., 2014. Comparison of two methods of extracting bone collagen for stable carbon and nitrogen isotope analysis: comparing whole bone demineralization with gelatinization and ultrafiltration. J. Archaeol. Sci. 47, 64–69.

Shin, J.Y., O'Connell, T., Black, S., Hedges, R., 2004. Differentiating bone osteonal turnover rates by density fractionation; validation using the bomb ^{14}C atmospheric pulse. Radiocarbon 46, 853–861.

Simpson, J.P., Penkman, K.E.H., Demarchi, B., Koon, H., Collins, M.J., Thomas-Oates, J., Shapiro, B., Start, M., Wilson, J., 2016. The effects of demineralization and sampling point variability on the measurement of glutamine deamidation in type I collagen extracted from bone. J. Archaeol. Sci. 69, 29–38.

Spalding, K.L., Bhardwaj, R.D., Buchholz, B.A., Druid, H., Frisen, J., 2005a. Retrospective birth dating of cells in humans. Cell 122, 133–143.

Spalding, K.L., Buchholz, B.A., Druid, H., Bergman, L.E., Frisén, J., 2005b. Forensic medicine: age written in teeth by nuclear bomb tests. Nature 437, 333–334.

Speller, C.F., Spalding, K.L., Buchholz, B.A., Hildebrand, D., Moore, J., Mathewes, R., Skinner, M.F., Yang, D.Y., 2012. Personal identification of cold case remains through combined contribution from anthropological, mtDNA, and bomb-pulse dating analyses. J. Forensic Sci. 57 (5), 1354–1360.

Stenhouse, M.J., Baxter, M.S., 1977. Bomb ^{14}C as a biological tracer. Nature 267, 828–832.

Stenstrom, K., Skog, G., Nilsson, C.M., Hellborg, R., Svegborn, S.L., Georgiadou, E., Mattsson, S., 2010. Local variations in ^{14}C – how is bomb-pulse dating of human tissues and cells affected? Nucl. Instrum. Methods Phys. Res. Sect. B 268, 1299–1302.

Stuiver, M., Polach, H.A., 1977. Discussion: reporting of ^{14}C data. Radiocarbon 19, 355–363.

Stuiver, M., Reimer, P.J., Bard, E., Beck, J.W., Burr, G.S., Hughen, K.A., Kromer, B., McCormac, G., Van der Plicht, J., Spurk, M., 1998a. INTCAL98 radiocarbon age calibration, 24000-0 cal BP. Radiocarbon 40, 1041–1083.

Stuiver, M., Reimer, P.J., Baziunas, T.F., 1998b. High-precision radiocarbon age calibration for terrestrial and marine samples. Radiocarbon 40, 1127–1151.

Swanston, C.W., Torn, M.S., Hanson, P.J., Southon, J.R., Garten, C.T., Hanlon, E.M., Ganio, L., 2005. Initial characterization of processes of soil carbon stabilization using forest stand-level radiocarbon enrichment. Geoderma 128, 52–62.

Tans, P.P., de Jong, A.F.M., Mook, W.G., 1979. Natural atmospheric ^{14}C variation and the Suess effect. Nature 280, 826–828.

Taylor, R.E., Suchey, J.M., Payen, L.A., Slota, P.J., 1989. The use of radiocarbon (^{14}C) to identify human skeletal materials of forensic science interest,. J. Forensic Sci. 34, 1196–1205.

Taylor, R.E., Kirner, D.L., Southon, J.R., Chatters, J.C., 1998. Radiocarbon dates of Kennewick Man. Science 280, 1171.

Tuross, N., 2012. Comparative decalcification methods, radiocarbon dates and stable isotopes of the VIRI bones. Radiocarbon 54, 837–844.

Ubelaker, D.H., Buchholz, B.A., Stewart, J., 2006. Analysis of artificial radiocarbon in different skeletal and dental tissue types to evaluate date of death. J. Forensic Sci. 51, 484–488.

Ubelaker, D.H., Buchholz, B.A., 2006. Complexities in the use of bomb-curve radiocarbon to determine time since death of human skeletal remains. Forensic Sci. Commun. 8. Online Journal http://www2.fbi.gov/hq/lab/fsc/backissu/jan2006/research/2006_01_research01.htm.

Ubelaker, D.H., Parra, R.C., 2011. Radiocarbon analysis of dental enamel and bone to evaluate date of birth and death: perspective from the southern hemisphere. Forensic Sci. Int. 208, 103–107.

Ubelaker, D.E., 2014. Radiocarbon analysis of human remains: a review of forensic applications. J. Forensic Sci. 59 (6), 1466–1472.

Van der Veer, G., Voerkelius, S., Lorentz, G., Heiss, G., Hoogewerff, J.A., 2009. Spatial interpolation of the deuterium and oxygen-18 composition of global precipitation using temperature as ancillary variable. J. Geochem. Explor. 101, 175–184.

Waite, E.R., Collins, M.J., Ritz-Timme, S., Schutz, H.W., Cattaneo, C., Borrman, H.I.M., 1999. A review of the methodological aspects of aspartic acid racemization analysis for use in forensic science. Forensic Sci. Int. 103, 113–124.

Wild, E.M., Arlamovsky, K.A., Golser, R., Kutschera, W., Priller, A., Puchegger, S., Rom, W., Steier, P., Vycudilik, W., 2000. ^{14}C dating with the bomb peak: an application to forensic medicine. Nucl. Instrum. Methods Phys. Res. B 172, 944–950.

Winskog, C., Nilsson, H., Montelius, K., Lindblom, B., 2010. The use of commercial alcohol products to sterilize bones prior to DNA sampling. Forensic Sci. Med. Pathol. 6, 127–129.

World Health Organization, 2007. WHO Child Growth Standards Head: Circumference-for-Age, Arm Circumference-for-Age, Triceps Skinfold-for-Age and Subscapular Skinfold-for-Age. WHO Press, Geneva, Switzerland. http://www.who.int/childgrowth/standards/second_set/technical_report_2.pdf.

Yekkala, R., Meers, C., Van Schepdael, A., Hoogmartens, J., Lambrichts, I., Willems, G., 2006. Racemization of aspartic acid from human dentin in the estimation of chronological age. Forensic Sci. Int. 159 (Suppl. 1), S89–S94.

Zapico, S.C., Ubelaker, D.H., 2013. Applications of physiological bases of ageing to forensic sciences. Estimation of age-at-death. Ageing Res. Rev. 12, 605–617.

Zermeño, P., Kurdyla, D.K., Buchholz, B.A., Heller, S.J., Kashgarian, M., Frantz, B.R., 2004. Prevention and removal of elevated radiocarbon contamination in the LLNL/CAMS natural radiocarbon preparation laboratory. Nucl. Instrum. Methods Phys. Res. Sect. B 223–4, 293–297.

Further Reading

Cook, G.T., MacKenzie, A.B., 2014. Radioactive isotope analyses of skeletal materials in forensic science: a review of uses and potential uses. Int. J. Leg. Med. 128, 685–698.

Levin, I., Naegler, T., Kromer, B., Diehl, M., Francey, R.J., Gomez-Pelaez, A.J., Steele, L.P., Wagenbach, D., Weller, R., Worthy, D.E., 2010. Observations and modelling of the global distribution and long-term trend of atmospheric $^{14}CO_2$. Tellus 62B, 26–46.

CHAPTER 17

Species Determination From Fragmentary Evidence

Douglas H. Ubelaker

Smithsonian Institution, Washington, DC, United States

In the practice of forensic anthropology, species recognition represents a common and important goal. If remains are reasonably complete, forensic anthropologists are highly skilled and proficient in determining species from morphological characteristics. In cases involving isolated, incomplete remains and those altered by disease or taphonomic factors, comparative collections, coupled with the scientific literature (France, 2009; Gilbert, 1973; Mulhern, 2009; Olsen, 1964; Ubelaker, 1999), can prove helpful in clarifying if they are of human origin. Even incomplete, fragmentary bones and teeth present characteristics that facilitate definition of human status to the trained eye (Mulhern, 2009).

Unfortunately, many cases submitted for forensic anthropology analysis involve extreme fragmentation, usually associated with considerable taphonomic alteration. Such fragmentary evidence can prove challenging for even the most experienced anthropologists. In current practice, fragments are frequently submitted with the hope that human status can be determined, setting up molecular analysis aimed at identification. A variety of situations can produce fragmentation, including blast trauma, gunshot injury, and postmortem factors (Loe, 2009; Nawrocki, 2009).

Usually such evidence is recovered from contexts including many other small materials that might be confused with bone or tooth fragments. Sites of recovery can include fire debris, areas associated with residences or automobiles, trash deposits, and isolated, wooded areas. Such scenes present a variety of taphonomic factors that can alter the condition and appearance of evidence. These locations also usually contain many other materials that can resemble bones or teeth.

Following traditional morphological examination, microscopic analysis may be useful to determine if bone or tooth is present. Use of a quality dissecting microscope may reveal structural details on the surfaces that can prove diagnostic. Microscopic examination of thin sections may reveal histological features that also offer proof, but of course such an approach is time consuming and destructive (Crowder, 2009; Mulhern, 2009).

If after application of the methods described previously, it still is not clear if the materials present represent bone or tooth, then consideration should be given to analysis using scanning electron microscopy/energy dispersive spectroscopy (SEM/EDS). Analysis of a specimen using this approach involves production of a spectrum that reveals the elemental composition. An image of the material can also be generated, which can provide useful information. Comparison of the resulting spectra and thus elemental composition with existing databases representing known material can clarify the nature of the material present. Both bones and teeth have particular ratios of calcium and phosphorus that are shared with few other materials. Analysis using SEM\EDS will allow bone and tooth fragments to be distinguished from nearly all other materials commonly found at scenes (Ubelaker et al., 2002). Recent modifications include use of handheld (portable) X-ray fluorescence spectrometry (Zimmerman et al., 2015) offering mobility of applications.

While SEM/EDS analysis will successfully recognize materials representing bone or tooth, it will not differentiate human from nonhuman. Bones and teeth from all animals share similar patterns of elemental construction. Thus, to determine the species status of bone or tooth evidence, other techniques must be employed.

Histological examination can reveal some species information. Cortical bone cross-sections examined microscopically may reveal a banding osteon pattern or the presence of plexiform bone that can be diagnostic of nonhuman species (Mulhern, 2009; Mulhern and Ubelaker, 2001, 2003). Unfortunately, the human pattern is shared with some nonhuman animals. In addition, the technique is destructive and may limit the availability of additional sample for further analysis.

Protein radioimmunoassay (pRIA) represents one very useful technique available to make such determinations with certainty. As noted as early as 1980 by Lowenstein, the proteins albumin and collagen are species specific. As such, they can be identified by species through radioimmunoassay, even in ancient fossil material. Due to its

New Perspectives in Forensic Human Skeletal Identification. http://dx.doi.org/10.1016/B978-0-12-805429-1.00017-X

usefulness in species determination in ancient material, it has been utilized to explore mammalian evolutionary relationships (Lowenstein and Scheuenstuhl, 1991; Lowenstein et al., 1981).

In 2004, Ubelaker et al. published an improved pRIA technique aimed at species identification of small fragments recovered from forensic contexts. This modification calls for removal of 1–2 g of material from the forensically submitted specimen. A clean stainless steel Dremel drill bit is then employed to remove and discard the outer 1–2 mm of the sample. This reduction is done to reduce the probability of external protein contamination. The remaining sample is then reduced to powder and small particles using a different clean drill bit. This resulting material is then placed into solution within a 10-mL vacutainer with 1 M EDTA added. Following the creation of a partial vacuum within the capped vacutainer, it is gently shaken and rotated between 2 and 5 days to dissolve the bone material.

The resulting solution of 25 mL is then placed within the wells of a microtiter plate. After 2 h at room temperature, some of the protein within the solution becomes bound to the plate. All remaining liquids are then washed away using a soy protein solution, leaving behind the "solid-phase" protein of the specimen.

In the next step, 25 mL of species-specific antisera raised in rabbits are added to each of the wells of the plate. These antisera samples were produced by injecting rabbits with albumins or sera from a variety of species of animals, including humans. Following overnight exposure at room temperature, each species-specific antibody in each of the wells binds to the antigen of the unknown specimen. The most extensive binding occurs with the species antibody closest to the species of the unknown specimen.

To evaluate and quantify the magnitude of the binding described previously, a second phase of analysis is required. Once the plate is washed out, antirabbit gamma globulin raised in donkeys is applied to the wells of the plate. This material is marked with radioactive iodine-125, so that the extent of the binding can be measured. Using a scintillation counter, the extent of the binding can be measured. The species with the highest count represents the one closest to the species of the unknown forensic specimen.

Ubelaker et al. (2004) demonstrated how this technique can be used to identify species from small bone fragments. Small bone fragments, each weighing between one and two grams were collected from skeletal remains of known species. These samples consisted of (A) 1.3 g of bone from the sternal end of a left lower rib of an adult modern human, (B) 1.1 g of cortical bone from a nonhuman large ungulate, (C) 1.8 g of cortical bone representing an apparent dog, (D) 1.5 g of cortical bone from the distal diaphysis of the left femur of a prehistoric skeleton from Ecuador, (E) 1.7 g of cortical bone from a left fibula of a modern human, and (F) 1.1 g from the horizontal ramus of a left mandible from a deer. The fragments were sufficiently small that they were not diagnostic of species or human status from morphological characteristics.

Analysis of pRIA was conducted generally following the procedures outlined above. Results are presented in Table 17.1. The upper portion of the table reveals the quantification scores (% uptake of I-125) in testing the known antisera standards. This information verifies the accuracy of the standards and demonstrates how the variation in scores indicates species.

The lower portion of Table 17.1 (Test 1: Species of Submitted Samples) indicates how pRIA analysis correctly identified the species status of each of the six test samples. The comparative scores for samples A, D, and E all reveal their human status. Human/nonhuman scores were very distinct in the specimens A and E taken from modern humans.

The comparative scores for sample E from ancient Ecuador presented less separation but still revealed the human status. Due to taphonomic processes associated with the considerable antiquity of this archaeological sample, differences were minimal but still apparent. Elemental analysis revealed low phosphorous content in this sample. In addition, analysis revealed depletion of the amino acid concentration in specimen E. These factors likely combined to produce the reduced species separation apparent in the values reported in Table 17.1 (Ubelaker et al., 2004).

■ CONCLUSION

In summary, species identification of small fragments can prove difficult using conventional morphological criteria, especially with evidence that has been environmentally compromised. The technique of analysis solid-phase double-antibody radioimmunoassay can provide reliable results, even with specimens exhibiting considerable taphonomic alteration. Since such a small portion of the sample is needed for analysis, enough usually remains to allow follow-up molecular analysis or other procedures. Additional details regarding this procedure are available within the publications cited.

This technique should be considered when species determination is critically needed in investigation and more conventional techniques cannot be employed. Although the costs of analysis are significant, the method offers a means for species determination with very minimal specimen destruction. The specialized nature of the tests and the use of the radioactive tracer (iodine-125) limit the number of laboratories that can conduct the analysis and properly interpret results. The following laboratory has extensive experience in the analysis of forensic-related samples: MicroAnalytica, LLC, 7050 SW 86th Ave, Miami, Florida 33,143.

Table 17.1 pRIA Analysis of Standards and Six Submitted Samples

Applied Antisera Used	Known Origins of Antisera Used								
	Human	Bison	Bear	Rat	Elephant	Elk	Goat	Pig	Dog
	% Uptake I-125								
Human	22	3	3	6	1	0			
Bison	2	16	1	0	1	1			
Bear	8	3	23	3	5	2			
Rat	9	4	6	22	3				
Elephant	8	3	8	1	20				
Elk	6	6	8			20			
Goat		10				8	39	9	13
Pig		7				8	20	33	23
Dog		8				3	12	4	35

Lab No.	Test Species of Submitted Samples								
Submitter No.	Human	Bison	Bear	Rat	Elephant	Elk	Goat	Pig	Dog
MA-1506 A	10	4	1	0	0	0			
MA-1507 B	3	10	1	0	0	4		2	
MA-1508 C	11	3	17	2	2		7		2
MA-1509 D	3	2	0	0	0	2			
MA-1510 E	23	4	7	5	7				
MA-1511 F	5	6	6		6	17	13	6	10

Modified from Ubelaker, D.H., Lowenstein, J.M., Hood, D.G., 2004. Use of solid-phase double-antibody radioimmunoassay to identify species from small skeletal fragments. J. Forensic Sci. 49 (5), 924–929.

References

Crowder, C.M., 2009. Histological age estimation. In: Blau, S., Ubelaker, D.H. (Eds.), Handbook of Forensic Anthropology and Archaeology. Left Coast Press, Walnut Creek, California, pp. 222–235.

France, D.L., 2009. Human and Nonhuman Bone Identification: A Color Atlas. CRC Press, Boca Raton, Florida.

Gilbert, B.M., 1973. Mammalian Osteo-archaeology: North America. Missouri Archaeological Society Inc., Columbia, Missouri.

Loe, L., 2009. Perimortem trauma. In: Blau, S., Ubelaker, D.H. (Eds.), Handbook of Forensic Anthropology and Archaeology. Left Coast Press, Walnut Creek, California, pp. 263–283.

Lowenstein, J.M., 1980. Species-specific proteins in fossils. Naturwissenschaften 67, 343–346.

Lowenstein, J.M., Scheuenstuhl, G., 1991. Immunological methods in molecular palaeontology. Philos. Trans. R. Soc. Lond. Ser. B 333, 375–380.

Lowenstein, J.M., Sarich, V.M., Richardson, B.J., 1981. Albumin systematics of the extinct mammoth and Tasmanian wolf. Nature 291, 409–411.

Mulhern, D.M., 2009. Differentiating human from nonhuman skeletal remains. In: Blau, S., Ubelaker, D.H. (Eds.), Handbook of Forensic Anthropology and Archaeology. Left Coast Press, Walnut Creek, California, pp. 153–163.

Mulhern, D.M., Ubelaker, D.H., 2001. Differences in osteon banding between human and nonhuman bone. J. Forensic Sci. 46 (2), 220–222.

Mulhern, D.M., Ubelaker, D.H., 2003. Histologic examination of bone development in juvenile chimpanzees. Am. J. Phys. Anthropol. 122, 127–133.

Nawrocki, S.P., 2009. Forensic taphonomy. In: Blau, S., Ubelaker, D.H. (Eds.), Handbook of Forensic Anthropology and Archaeology. Left Coast Press, Walnut Creek, California, pp. 284–294.

Olsen, S.J., 1964. Mammal Remains from Archaeological Sites, Part 1, Southeastern and Southwestern United States. United States Papers of the Peabody Museum of Archaeology and Ethnology, vol. 56(1). Harvard University.

Ubelaker, D.H., 1999. Human Skeletal Remains: Excavation, Analysis, Interpretation, third ed. Taraxacum, Washington, District of Columbia.

Ubelaker, D.H., Lowenstein, J.M., Hood, D.G., 2004. Use of solid-phase double-antibody radioimmunoassay to identify species from small skeletal fragments. J. Forensic Sci. 49 (5), 924–929.

Ubelaker, D.H., Ward, D.C., Braz, V.S., Stewart, J., 2002. The use of SEM/EDS analysis to distinguish dental and osseus tissue from other materials. J. Forensic Sci. 47 (5), 940–943.

Zimmerman, H.A., Schultz, J.J., Sigman, M.E., 2015. Preliminary validation of handheld X-ray fluorescence spectrometry: distinguishing osseous and dental tissue from nonbone material of similar chemical composition. J. Forensic Sci. 60, 382–390.

CHAPTER 18

Bone Histology as an Integrated Tool in the Process of Human Identification

Christian M. Crowder[1] | Janna M. Andronowski[2] |
Victoria M. Dominguez[3]

[1]Harris County Institute of Forensic Sciences, Houston, TX, United States
[2]University of Saskatchewan, Saskatoon, SK, Canada
[3]The Ohio State University, Columbus, OH, United States

Chapter Outline

■ INTRODUCTION

The anthropological analyses of unknown skeletal remains should ideally employ a multilevel and multimodal approach. Determining which methods to use or what techniques will be required to assist with the identification process, however, is typically a case by case assessment involving the evaluation of the context in which the remains enter into the medicolegal process and the a priori knowledge that is guiding any antemortem record comparison. Generally, the role of the anthropologist in identification involves two primary analyses: (1) developing the biological profile (i.e., age, sex, ancestry, stature) of unknown remains to provide contributory data that will help with the process of including or excluding individuals from a missing persons search or decedent manifest (such as that constructed following a mass fatality incident) and (2) comparing antemortem medical records (e.g., dental charts, radiographs) to postmortem records to provide a recommendation to the pathologist regarding positive identification. In this light it may appear that bone histology plays a limited role. However, when considering the challenges presented to the anthropologist in the medicolegal setting regarding the condition of remains, which includes intact fleshed decedents to highly fragmented burned remains, the path to identification does not always begin with the question "who is this individual?". Under this framework, the inclusion of microscopic methods can strengthen analytical results and more importantly provide information that cannot be obtained from other methods used to construct the biological profile.

This chapter is divided into sections discussing approaches using bone histology that guide the anthropologist in decision making during the evaluation of unknown skeletal material. The first section discusses general topics regarding bone biology, histomorphology, and histomorphometry, which provide the background and tools needed to interpret the structure and organization of bone at the histological level. The next section discusses the histological approach to differentiating nonhuman bone from human bone. The following section discusses current research using bone histology to guide the sampling of human bone for nuclear DNA analysis. This research explores why certain bone samples may provide better DNA yields and provides guidelines for making sample selections during the identification process. The final section will explore the use of histological methods for estimating age-at-death, which is frequently discussed in the anthropological literature. This chapter will not discuss, in detail, technical

New Perspectives in Forensic Human Skeletal Identification. http://dx.doi.org/10.1016/B978-0-12-805429-1.00018-1

procedures to prepare and analyze bone at the histological level; however, the authors will guide the reader to important references that cover these aspects.

■ BONE BIOLOGY, HISTOMORPHOLOGY, AND HISTOMORPHOMETRY

The basis of all histological analyses of bone lies in the understanding and interpretation of bone biology, which guides the creation of histological structures. Understanding the processes that govern bone growth, development, and maintenance allow the analyst to interpret histological results and reliably evaluate bone at the histological level. The histological analysis of bone typically involves the examination of thin sections of cortical bone under the microscope to qualify and quantify the structures observed. Bone histomorphology refers to the form of tissues and cells, and involves a qualitative approach to examining the shape and structure of bone at the histological level. Bone histomorphometry is the quantification of microstructures or their characteristics in skeletal tissue. It is through the analysis of bone histomorphology and histomorphometry that anthropologists are able to develop and test hypotheses for interpreting bone biology. Because the information provided in this chapter provides only a brief summary of bone biology as it relates to histological analysis in anthropology, the authors recommend the following literature to provide a stronger background in this area of research: de Ricqlés (1993), Carter and Beaupre (2001), Hillier and Bell (2007), Crowder and Stout (2012), and Burr and Allen (2013).

Bone can be differentiated into two main structural types: cortical and cancellous. Generally speaking, long bones possess a diaphysis and two or more epiphyses, composed of an outer cortex of cortical bone surrounding cancellous bone within the medullary cavity. The outer surface of the cortex is covered by periosteum, with an outer soft tissue layer composed of a highly vascularized fibrous membrane and an inner layer containing osteogenic cells. The inner surface of the bone's cortex is the endosteum, which forms the boundary of the medullary canal.

Cortical, or compact, bone is dense and comprises the external surface of bones. It accounts for the majority of bone mass (~80%) and is composed of highly organized primary lamellar and secondary osteonal bone tissues (Carter and Beaupré, 2001). Primary lamellar bone tissue is formed during appositional growth or endochondral ossification, and is vascularized by primary vascular canals. Secondary osteonal bone tissue, or Haversian bone, refers to lamellar bone tissue that has replaced older bone tissue through bone remodeling. Concentric lamellar rings bordered by a cement, or a reversal, line characterize secondary osteonal bone tissue. Reversal lines are composed of a highly mineralized collagen matrix and separate secondary lamellar tissue from previously existing bone tissue (Stout and Crowder, 2012).

Cancellous bone is composed of thin plate-like structures called trabeculae and has a spongy appearance. It is typically found at the metaphyseal ends of bones and within the medullary cavities that house red and yellow bone marrow during life. For the most part, lamellae are arranged parallel to the trabecular surface forming half osteons called hemiosteons. One surface of the hemiosteon borders the bone marrow cavity, rather than a Haversian canal as seen in cortical bone (Burr and Allen, 2013). As such, cancellous bone's microstructure is comparable to that of cortical bone, with the exception that the latter includes Haversian systems. Both bone types contain specialized bone cells that are responsible for the resorption, formation, and maintenance of skeletal tissue: osteoclasts, osteoblasts, and osteocytes. These cells are histologically distinct and are differentiated by their origins, form, function, and locations within the bone matrix.

Osteoclasts are bone cells of hematopoietic origin that are responsible for the resorption of both inorganic and organic bone material. These are the largest of the three bone cells and are multinucleated. Osteoclasts remove excess bone tissues and microdamage, releasing minerals stored in mature bone tissue to assist with maintenance of mineral homeostasis (Robling et al., 2006). The activity and control of these cells play a large role in maintaining the balance between bone resorption and deposition that is required for healthy bone tissue. Osteoclasts and their precursors undergo a series of transformations during bone modeling and remodeling that include identified stages of activation, mobilization, resorption, and cessation.

The osteoblast is a uninucleated, mesenchymal-derived cell involved in the synthesis of bone proteins and the deposition of new bone material (Parfitt, 1983). Osteoblasts form cell layers over existing bony material and collectively act as a barrier to control the passage of ions in and out of bone. These cells are involved in the secretion of cytokines that regulate the formation of bone (Ortner and Turner-Walker, 2003). Osteoblasts are considerably smaller than osteoclasts, thus requiring 100–150 cells to form the amount of bone that can be broken down by the activity of a single osteoclast. As such, maintaining the balance between resorbed and new bone tissue is an ongoing process in which disruption of the normal activity of either osteoclastic or osteoblastic activity could be detrimental to bone health.

Osteocytes are often cited as the most ubiquitous bone cells in mature bone, amounting to approximately 90% of all cells in cortical bone tissue (Martin et al., 2015). Encased in the mineralized bone matrix, they reside in lacunae and are well distributed throughout. Communication is efficient with other osteocytes and with osteoblasts via canaliculi, which also aid in exchanging substances via an interconnected system. Due to their small size, they only compose about 1% of total bone volume (Martin et al., 2015). Despite this fact, they have vast surface area. Although the complete nature of osteocytes remains uncertain, they are considered essential to maintaining normal bone homeostasis and in the initiation of bone repair (Martin et al., 2015; Turner and Forwood, 1995). As such, osteocytes play an important role as sensors and represent a key element in the mechanosensory system. Some remain in direct contact with osteoblasts and with the internal surface of bone, forming a network of mechanosensing. A full understanding of the lacuno-canalicular system, however, remains elusive.

Knowledge of cellular activity and bone metabolism, whether related to growth and development, adaptation, homeostasis, disease, or the healing process, provides the basis for understanding bone histomorphology. Normal bone metabolism is the complex sequence of bone formation (modeling) and bone turnover (remodeling). Modeling is an adaptive mechanism, whereby the skeleton can alter and adjust its overall shape to meet the shifting mechanical demands on the skeleton throughout an animal's life. Remodeling serves two primary purposes; first, it serves as a maintenance mechanism, by which damaged bone is removed and replaced, keeping the integrity of the bone intact, and second, it is a response to metabolic demands, releasing calcium and other elements from skeletal reserves into the bloodstream when needed. While modeling alters the physical dimensions of the bone, removing bone in one place and replacing it elsewhere, remodeling removes and replaces bone in the same location. The end result of each remodeling event is a circular structure, created by concentric rings of lamellae and bounded by a hypomineralized reversal line (i.e., the point where bone resorption ceases and infilling of the created hollow commences), which is known either as a secondary osteon or a Haversian system.

Bone's unique properties make it an ideal tissue for histological investigations since it maintains a dynamic structure throughout an individual's lifespan, providing a temporal record of remodeling events. This continuous response allows for the maintenance of bone's microstructural organization when exposed to various physiological, mechanical, and metabolic demands. Because of the remodeling process, microscopic features accumulate in bone tissues that are believed to aid in understanding circumstances encountered during life. Histological studies have focused on the influences of physical activity, metabolism, nutrition, and age-related change (Agarwal, 2008; Kerley, 1965; Ruff, 2008).

Animals who develop an internal bony skeleton demonstrate organizational and structural differences at the histological level determined by genetics, growth rate, size, weight, hormones, activity, etc. Bone modeling and remodeling occurs in all animals with a skeleton, but the appearance of bone cells and overall organization is not universal and provides much of the basis for differentiating human from nonhuman bone. Evaluating the histomorphology of bone typically involves assessing the type of bone tissue and cells present and their organization. Bone populated by secondary osteons is often referred to as Haversian bone, indicative of its history of remodeling. In contrast, primary bone types, such as woven bone or primary lamellar, show no evidence of remodeling.

Histomorphometric analysis of bone provides quantitative data, such as bone turnover rates (a measure of remodeling) and microarchitecture information, which cannot be obtained from a histomorphological approach. The quantification of bone turnover, microarchitecture, and static and dynamic cell activity is performed through measuring and counting of structures to characterize changes in bone histomorphology. The evaluation of bone histomorphometry may be performed using manual methods, semiautomated methods, or fully automated methods to measure the size and shape of structures or their spatial relationship within the matrix. As technology improves, the collection of histomorphometric data is becoming less time-consuming and more accurate. Histomorphometrics are used in all aspects of bone histological analysis, particularly in methods for estimating age-at-death and increasingly in methods for identifying the species of origin for unknown fragments. Examples of such methods are described in greater detail in subsequent sections.

One final important note regarding histological analysis is the use of proper and consistent nomenclature. Anthropologists should follow the standardization of nomenclature, symbols, and units reported by Dempster et al. (2013), which is an update of the 1987 report by the ASBMR histomorphometry nomenclature committee. Following standard nomenclature assists in a universal understanding of bone histomorphometry and helps eliminates ambiguity in the reporting of data.

■ OSSEOUS VERSUS NONOSSEOUS MATERIAL AND HUMAN VERSUS NONHUMAN BONE

When confronted with fragmented and/or commingled remains, the anthropologist often begins their analysis by determining first if the fragments are bone and if so, whether they are human. Such determinations are usually accomplished by observation of gross morphology; however, when macroscopic analysis proves insufficient, histological approaches can be applied (Hillier and Bell, 2007). Histology offers a cost-effective, faster alternative to DNA analysis or other methods (e.g., chemical, elemental, and molecular), which though popular and often able to conclusively identify fragments, are also time-consuming, destructive, costly, or not readily available for some jurisdictions.

Determining whether materials are osseous or nonosseous depends on a familiarity with bone microstructure. Oftentimes, sectioning materials to prepare slides is enough to determine whether they are osseous or not. However, in cases where this distinction remains unclear, much like determinations made on the gross level, anthropologists with training in histology and knowledge of bone biology can readily identify the common components of bone microanatomy when viewed under magnification (i.e., lamellar or woven structure, vascular channels, remodeling events). Therefore, to make the determination of osseous versus nonosseous for unknown material one must be well versed in the various types of bone and how the bone matrix changes over the organism's lifetime.

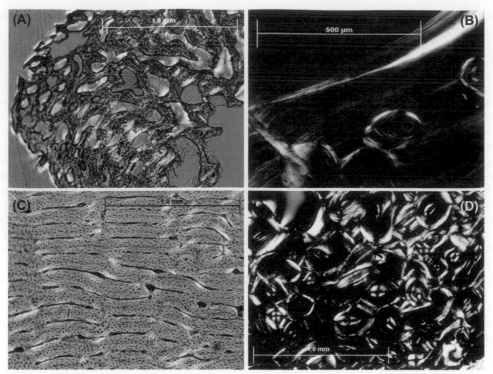

Figure 18.1 Different bone types by structure. (A) Woven bone, (B) primary lamellar bone with incipient remodeling, (C) fibrolamellar plexiform bone, and (D) Haversian bone, completely populated by secondary remodeling events.

Bone composition is often classified according to its tissue structure, overall organization, and its vascular presentation. Depending on the species, mammalian species in particular, their bone tissue may display woven, lamellar, fibrolamellar, or Haversian bone types (Mulhern and Ubelaker, 2012) (see Fig. 18.1). Woven bone is poorly organized primary bone. It is rapidly laid down, producing collagen fibrils and hydroxyapatite crystals that appear randomly arranged (Currey, 2002), resulting in numerous unmineralized regions and increased porosity. In humans, woven bone is replaced during skeletal maturity by highly organized primary lamellar and secondary osteonal bone tissues (Carter and Beaupré, 2001). Primary lamellar bone tissue forms during appositional growth or endochondral ossification and is vascularized by primary vascular canals. Lamellar bone is more organized and typically laid down in "sheets," with collagen fibrils appearing oriented in one direction within each layer.

Fibrolamellar bone, a combination of woven and lamellar bone, is most commonly observed in fast growing, large animals (Martin and Burr, 1989). The demand for bone matrix that is both strong and quickly produced results in alternating layers of the stronger lamellar bone with the rapidly deposited, but much weaker, woven bone. As such, it is often asserted that fibrolamellar bone does not occur in humans and may be used to differentiate human and nonhuman bone. Furthermore, vascular canals in fibrolamellar bone are further described by their orientation, which may be related to growth and mechanical stressors (Mulhern and Ubelaker, 2012). Radially oriented vascular canals, for example, achieve rapid growth due to the continuous and efficient creation of bony struts (Currey, 2002). In addition, laminar fibrolamellar bone may be distinguished by circumferential lamellar layers. A brick-like patterning of fibrolamellar bone is commonly identified as *plexiform bone* when the vascular channels separate layers of nonlamellar bone (Martin and Burr, 1989). However, it is essential to distinguish this structural type as *plexiform bone*, as it is often conflated with *fibrolamellar bone* or *laminar bone*. Thus, the term plexiform bone is often used to mean any type of nonhuman fibrolamellar bone.

Secondary osteonal bone, also known as Haversian bone, refers to lamellar bone tissue that replaces older bone via remodeling. Concentric lamellar rings bordered by a cement line, or a reversal line, characterize secondary osteonal bone tissue. Lamellar bone consisting of Haversian systems is observed in many species of mammals, including humans. As such, the simple presence of Haversian systems in bone is not diagnostic of human remains. Because differences in bone microstructure manifests as the result of extrinsic and intrinsic factors such as growth rates, biomechanical loading, and nutritional demands (to name a few), both qualitative and quantitative approaches should be applied to distinguish human from nonhuman bone.

Qualitative assessment of cortical bone principally relies on identifying the type and organization of bone tissue, as discussed earlier. We know that the plexiform-type of fibrolamellar bone commonly occurs in large bodied, fast-growing species, such as cows and horses (Martin et al., 2015). The presence of this bone type conclusively indicates a nonhuman origin, as this kind of bone is not observed in humans. As fibrolamellar bone transitions to Haversian bone, in some nonhuman species the osteons may form in bands, described as distinct rows of five or

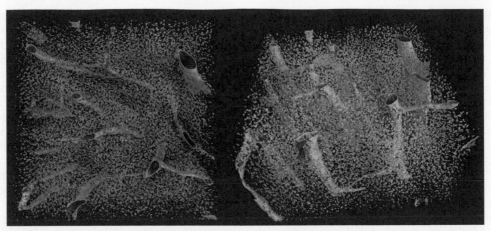

Figure 18.2 Three-dimensional renders of a human femur displaying osteocyte lacunae and Haversian canals. Superior view (left), oblique view (right). *Credit: JM. Andronowski.*

more osteons alternating with bands of lamellar bone (Mulhern and Ubelaker, 2001). Osteon bands are another strong indicator of nonhuman origins. Though harder to recognize and somewhat less definitive than the presence of plexiform bone, osteon banding, when taken together with other aspects of cortical microarchitecture, generally indicates a nonhuman species origin. It is important to note that osteon banding is not well defined in the literature. Furthermore, the authors have observed areas of linear-oriented osteons occurring in human cortical bone that could be identified as banding under the current definition. Therefore, an isolated band may not be diagnostic, and the analyst should look for a more significant pattern of banding.

In some cases, differences in micromorphology are too subtle to detect qualitatively. Most mammalian species, including humans, repair and renew their skeletal tissue via similar mechanisms, namely the process of remodeling. As such, the end product of remodeling, Haversian bone, is common throughout the animal kingdom; however, researchers and practicing anthropologists have long suggested the possibility of quantitatively distinguishing human from nonhuman Haversian bone. Nonhuman Haversian systems have been described as smaller and more circular in shape than those found in humans. However, these assertions, while not necessarily false, are confounded by the influences of age and loading environment, among other variables that are known to affect Haversian system formation. Presently, methods that rely on differences in Haversian canal size and osteon size and shape have been proposed, all with varying degrees of success. Use of these methods should be undertaken with caution, however, as most are still preliminary and in need of validation.

■ DNA SAMPLE SELECTION

Researchers continue to greatly benefit from two-dimensional (2D) histological techniques that often yield fine microstructural details, and cellular and/or functional information from sophisticated staining techniques. However, applications of three-dimensional (3D) imaging modalities to cortical and cancellous bone microstructure have recently provided a more comprehensive understanding of bone histology than was possible using traditional 2D methodologies (Andronowski, 2016; Andronowski et al., 2017; Carter et al., 2013; Cooper et al., 2003, 2006, 2011; Maggiano et al., 2016). Synchrotron radiation-based micro-computed tomography (SR micro-CT) technology has allowed for the quantitative analysis of minute microscopic features, including osteocyte lacunae (Fig. 18.2), in 3D. As soft tissue structures, osteocytes cannot be visualized using currently available X-ray imaging techniques (Carter et al., 2013). As such, their associated cellular spaces (lacunae) are used as substitutes.

Recent research by Andronowski (2016) and Andronowski et al. (2017) ascertained whether differences in 3D bone microstructure may be used to explain differential nuclear DNA yield among bone tissue types (cortical and cancellous bone), with a focus on osteocytes and the 3D quantification of their associated lacunae. Osteocytes and other bone cells are recognized to house nuclear DNA in bone tissue, thus examining the density of their lacunae may explain why DNA yield rates differ among bone tissue types. Identifying which bone tissue type(s) and/or bone envelope(s) (i.e., periosteal, intracortical, and endosteal) provide the highest nuclear DNA yields will further inform current bone-sampling protocols for human identification and limit the amount of bone tissue necessary for DNA analysis.

Andronowski (2016) and Andronowski et al's. (2017) expanded on results from a recent comparison of modern skeletal elements demonstrating that bones with high quantities of cancellous bone, including hand phalanges, tarsals, and patellae, yielded nuclear DNA at the highest rates, suggesting that preferentially sampling cortical bone is suboptimal (Mundorff and Davoren, 2014). This finding is significant, as molecular human identification has primarily focused on extracting nuclear DNA from sampling sites containing dense cortical bone, such as areas in the femur or tibia. Though Mundorff and Davoren (2014) indicated that bones with high cancellous quantity yielded DNA at higher rates, the reason remains unknown. Evidence from bone microarchitecture may help explain this variation and enrich our understanding of the density and morphology of bone microstructural features.

Andronowski (2016) and Andronowski et al. (2017) investigated the potential correlation of osteocyte lacunar density and recoverable nuclear DNA using SR micro-CT, thus offering promise in refining DNA bone sample-selection protocols for human identification. As SR micro-CT analysis is limited by a small specimen size since the camera field of view cannot exceed 2 mm, rectilinear bone blocks with dimensions of approximately $2 \times 2 \times 10$ mm were procured. This minimally destructive sampling protocol is beneficial, as the bone is not completely consumed and does not result in a minute sample that would hinder the ability to submit the specimen for future DNA analysis.

Volumes of interests (VOIs) from cortical (Figs. 18.3 and 18.4) and cancellous bone (Figs. 18.5 and 18.6) were comparatively analyzed from the three skeletons sampled for Mundorff and Davoren's (2014) study. The study skeletons are male donors who (1) died in the same calendar year (2009); (2) decomposed on a designated plot of land and in the same position (prone on the ground surface) at the Anthropology Research Facility (ARF) at the University of Tennessee, Knoxville; (3) were between the ages of 40 and 69 years at the time of death; and (4) had no known bone-affecting conditions at the time of death (Mundorff et al., 2012). Confounding taphonomic variables were limited by studying donated individuals who were exposed to the same gross environmental conditions, and decomposed in the same geographic location (Mundorff and Davoren, 2014).

Osteocyte lacunae were separated from the high-density bone using global thresholding and segmentation. These processes designate the air-filled spaces from the surrounding higher-density bone. Despeckling (denoising) was conducted to remove noise (structures less than $10 \mu m^3$). Elements above $2000 \mu m^3$ were assumed to be canals and remaining structures were designated as lacunae. The above volume limits are based on previous confocal

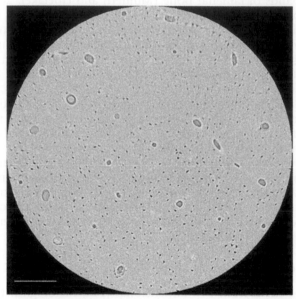

Figure 18.3 Synchrotron radiation micro-computed tomography single slice of a cortical bone cylindrical VOI from a human mandible. Scale = 100 μm. *Reprinted from Andronowski, J.M., Mundorff, A.Z., Pratt, I.V., Davoren, J.M., Cooper, D.M.L., 2017. Evaluating differential nuclear DNA yield rates and osteocyte numbers among human bone tissue types: a synchrotron radiation micro-CT approach. Forensic Sci. Int. Genet. 28, 211–218, with permission from Elsevier.*

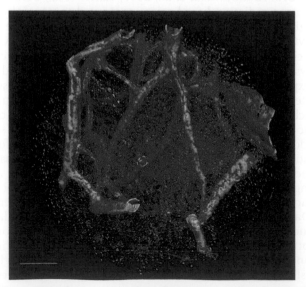

Figure 18.4 Synchrotron radiation micro-computed tomography three-dimensional render of a cortical bone cylindrical VOI from a human mandible. Scale = 100 μm. *Credit: JM. Andronowski.*

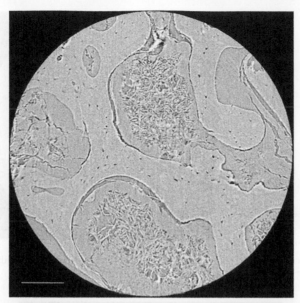

Figure 18.5 Synchrotron radiation micro-computed tomography single slice of a cancellous bone cylindrical VOI from a second cuneiform. Scale = 100 μm. *Reprinted from Andronowski, J.M., Mundorff, A.Z., Pratt, I.V., Davoren, J.M., Cooper, D.M.L., 2017. Evaluating differential nuclear DNA yield rates and osteocyte numbers among human bone tissue types: a synchrotron radiation micro-CT approach. Forensic Sci. Int. Genet. 28, 211–218, with permission from Elsevier.*

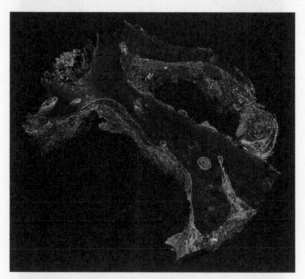

Figure 18.6 Synchrotron radiation micro-computed tomography three-dimensional render of a cancellous bone cylindrical VOI from a second cuneiform. *Reprinted from Andronowski, J.M., Mundorff, A.Z., Pratt, I.V., Davoren, J.M., Cooper, D.M.L., 2017. Evaluating differential nuclear DNA yield rates and osteocyte numbers among human bone tissue types: a synchrotron radiation micro-CT approach. Forensic Sci. Int. Genet. 28, 211–218, with permission from Elsevier.*

microscopy measurements, which determined human osteocyte volumes range from 28 to 1713 μm^3 (Carter et al., 2013; McCreadie et al., 2004). Subsequently, 3D renders of bone microarchitecture were created using AMIRA (Visage Imaging, Berlin, Germany) imaging software. Analyses tested the primary hypothesis that the abundance and density of bone's cellular spaces vary between cortical and cancellous bone tissue types.

Results demonstrated that osteocyte lacunar abundance and density vary between cortical and cancellous bone tissue types, with cortical bone VOIs containing a higher lacunar abundance and density. The osteocyte lacunar density values are independent of nuclear DNA yield, suggesting an alternative explanation for the higher nuclear DNA yields from predominantly cancellous bones. A plausible explanation focuses on remnants of potential soft tissue between trabeculae observed using SR micro-CT. Though soft tissue was not present on the surface of the bones, 3D scans consistently revealed soft tissues within the medullary cavities of skeletal elements with high cancellous content (Figs. 18.7 and 18.8). It is hypothesized that these residual soft tissues, which likely include endosteum and osteological lining cells, contributed to the higher nuclear DNA yields from cancellous bone.

Though the presence of soft tissue remnants in bones with higher cancellous content was consistent for all individuals in Andronowski (2016) and Andronowski et al's (2017) work, skeletal elements from individuals of increased postmortem intervals (PMIs) were not assessed for the presence of similar amounts of soft tissue. In a follow-up to the primary study (Phase 2), Mundorff and Davoren (2014) examined a subset of skeletal elements ($n = 120$) from 12 additional skeletons of increasing PMIs. Phase 2 comprised the eight highest DNA yielding skeletal elements from the

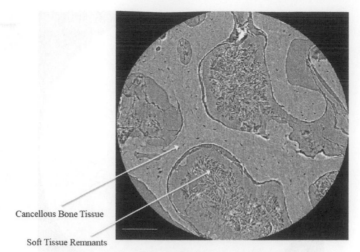

Cancellous Bone Tissue

Soft Tissue Remnants

Figure 18.7 Synchrotron radiation micro-computed tomography single slice of a cancellous bone cylindrical VOI from a second cuneiform. Soft tissue remnants are evident between the trabecular struts. Scale bar = 100 μm. *Credit: JM. Andronowski.*

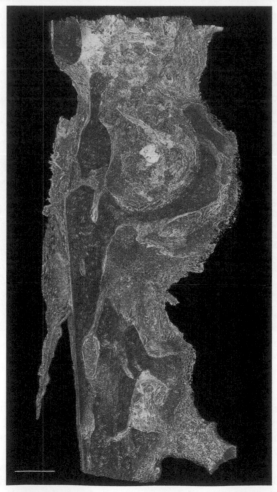

Figure 18.8 Synchrotron radiation micro-computed tomography 3D render of a cancellous bone VOI left second cuneiform. Soft tissue remnants (gray) are evident between the trabecular struts (black). Scale bar = 300 μm. *Reprinted from Andronowski, J.M., Mundorff, A.Z., Pratt, I.V., Davoren, J.M., Cooper, D.M.L., 2017. Evaluating differential nuclear DNA yield rates and osteocyte numbers among human bone tissue types: a synchrotron radiation micro-CT approach. Forensic Sci. Int. Genet. 28, 211–218, with permission from Elsevier.*

primary study plus the femur and tibia, which did not rank highly but are typically sampled for DNA by practitioners. Four predetermined PMIs (0–3 years, 4–10 years, 11–20 years, and >20 years) were identified and three skeletons were selected to represent each interval ($n = 12$). Skeletons with similar demographics to those examined in the current study were selected. This second phase was designed to determine if the same rank order of skeletal elements by DNA yield would maintain over increased PMIs, and to give an indication of how nuclear DNA degradation occurs over time.

The nuclear DNA results revealed that as PMI increased, the skeletal elements generally maintained a comparable rank order as the first phase, though certain bones did not conform to this pattern. Consistent with Phase 1 of Mundorff and Davoren's (2014) study, the first distal hand phalanx maintained relatively high yields of DNA while the femur and tibia possessed the lowest. The first distal hand phalanx had the highest yields of DNA from six individuals at three different PMI ranges. The fourth metacarpal was the highest yielding sample from three individuals, the talus was the highest yielding sample from two individuals, and the first cuneiform was the highest yielding sample for one individual (Mundorff et al., 2012). Overall, skeletal elements predominantly comprised of cortical bone were generally low yielding, with the femur possessing the lowest yields from three individuals at three varying PMI ranges, while the tibia had the lowest yields for four individuals at three different PMI ranges (Mundorff et al., 2012).

To further the argument that soft tissue between trabeculae of cancellous bone tissue is driving higher nuclear DNA yields in the Mundorff and Davoren (2014) sample, all skeletal elements from Phase 2 will be evaluated using 3D imaging modalities including clinical CT and SR micro-CT. If remaining soft tissue is revealed within medullary cavities of bone with differing PMIs, this could aid in explaining why the DNA yields observed by Mundorff and Davoren (2014) remained generally consistent over time and strengthen the argument that soft tissue remnants may be driving this trend.

As demonstrated by Mundorff and Davoren (2014), small bones with high cancellous content were shown to yield sufficient DNA profiles. Though the work of Andronowski (2016) and Andronowski et al. (2017) did not discover a higher density of osteocyte lacunae in cancellous bone, an alternative explanation suggests that remnants of soft tissue found in between trabeculae likely contributed to the higher nuclear DNA yields found by Mundorff and Davoren (2014). Thus, procuring small elements with higher cancellous content would allow for straightforward sample removal since small bones can be easily sampled whole in a field or lab setting with the use of a disposable scalpel blade. In turn, this recommended protocol would minimize contamination effects from sampling a wedge of cortical bone, safety hazards due to the use of an electric saw, and the time spent recovering samples by forensic personnel (Andronowski, 2016; Andronowski et al., 2017; Mundorff and Davoren, 2014).

As this sampling recommendation is currently context dependent, and relies on the preservation of remaining soft tissues within the medullary cavities of bones from skeletal elements recovered from the ground surface, it is likely that this hypothesis will not hold true for archaeological samples, though further investigation is warranted for confirmation. Over time, diagenetic alterations such as microbial degradation and infiltration of soil into medullary cavities and cancellous bone tissues may cause deterioration of remaining soft tissues and eventually the bone histology.

By employing SR micro-CT, Andronowski's (2016) and Andronowski et al. (2017) work was able to explore osteocyte lacunar density in cortical and cancellous bone tissue types within a single individual, and among multiple individuals, for the first time. This research highlights the variance in osteocyte lacunar populations within human cortical and cancellous bone tissues, which is an area of growing interest due to emerging high-resolution imaging techniques. It also provides evidence for preferentially sampling bones with primarily cancellous content with associated soft tissue remnants in forensic contexts. Although the 3D analysis of bone microstructure did not result in a concrete explanation for differential nuclear DNA yields among bone tissues types, the results encourage further exploration.

■ AGE ESTIMATION

The use of bone histology to estimate age is well established in the anthropological literature, and numerous publications have been devoted to the physiological basis for and the detailed description of histological age estimation methods (Crowder, 2009; Crowder et al., 2012; Crowder and Stout, 2012; Robling and Stout, 2008; Stout, 1989; Stout and Paine, 1992; to name several). Histological methods may differ in technique and application; however, they all follow the premise that as bone remodels over time (chronological age), the cortex becomes crowded with intact and fragmentary osteons. Although histological age estimation has been depicted, at times, as the answer to the problem of subjectivity associated with evaluating gross indicators of adult age estimation, it is not free from similar criticisms. The quantitative nature of histological age estimation does not alleviate it from the variability observed in the aging process, nor does it remove the nonage-related factors that govern bone remodeling. When possible, histological methods should be used in tandem with other methods of age estimation, forming a holistic approach to age estimation through the evaluation of bone at the gross and micro levels. A definite advantage of histological methods lies in the ability to estimate age when no gross age indicators are available due to fragmentation.

As mentioned previously, bone turnover occurs over the lifetime of an organism and, therefore, the length of time during which remodeling occurs will be the primary influence on how many secondary osteon creations (intact and fragmentary osteons) accumulate per unit of area (Kerley, 1965; Stout and Teitelbaum, 1976; Wu et al., 1967, 1970). In theory, age-related bone turnover will occur at a predictable rate over an individual's lifetime. While often suggested that these age-related changes are universal, differences in reported accuracy of methods when tested on samples outside of the reference population suggest that intrinsic and extrinsic factors have varying effects on bone microstructure (Crowder and Pfeiffer, 2010).

The approaches to histological age estimation, for the most part, are separated into methods that either count structures (intact osteons, fragmentary osteons, primary canals, etc.) or determine the percentage of osteonal or unremodeled bone area within an ROI. Often, methods require a combination of counting structures and calculating spatial relationships. Currently, the midshaft of the femur and the sixth rib are the preferred skeletal elements for histological analysis. The more frequently used methods for the femur include the Kerley (1965) and the Thompson (1979)

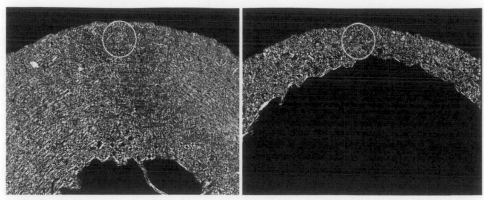

Figure 18.9 Two individuals demonstrating variation in cortical thickness with a standard field size represented by the *yellow circles*. The field on the left image evaluates structures located within the periosteal envelope, while the field on the right evaluates the periosteal, intracortical, and endosteal envelopes.

methods, or variations of these techniques. Methods involving the sixth rib include Stout and Paine (1992) and Cho et al. (2002), which build upon the original Stout (1986) method.

Kerley's (1965) age regression formulas for data collected from the midshaft of the femur, tibia, and fibula were based on four predicting variables including intact osteons, osteon fragments, non-Haversian canals, and percentage of circumferential lamellar bone. The variables were observed using four circular fields within the outer third of the cortex adjacent to the periosteal surface of the bone. The individual variables were counted within each field, including those partly obscured by periphery of the field, and then totaled to create a composite value. The percentage of circumferential lamellar bone was averaged for all four fields. These raw counts were then used to develop four different regression models to use when estimating age from a single bone slide.

Kerley and Ubelaker (1978) revised the original Kerley (1965) paper, warning investigators that the variability in field diameters of different microscopes would contribute to "apparent errors" and "unreasonable [age] estimates." Kerley and Ubelaker (1978) realized that using a smaller field size, as opposed to the original field size, would underestimate age since the sum of recorded structures is always less than that recorded when the regression models were created. During this revision, it became apparent that the original microscopes were not available for inspection and a survey of available microscopes suggested that the original field diameter used by Kerley was most likely 1.62 mm at 100× magnification, rather than the previously reported 1.25 mm diameter. A 1.62 mm field diameter results in an area 2.06 mm^2, indicating the method required a field correction factor. Stout and Gehlert (1982) suggest that the use of the correction factor may be of limited value due to the spatial variation of microstructures within the cortex. Thus, correcting the field size would likely result in inaccurate age estimations due to the somewhat stochastic nature of Haversian bone organization.

Other issues associated with, but not limited to, the Kerley method include subjective and variable definitions and the inability to incorporate remodeling events from the periosteal envelope to the endosteal envelope. The former point is a main factor in controlling the level of observer error associated with how researchers classify osteonal structures or, in other words, how intact and fragmentary osteons are differentiated. For example, Kerley (1965) classified intact osteons as being 80% intact with a complete Haversian canal present, while other methods may define an intact osteon as having a Haversian canal that is 90% intact. Similarly, the selection of observation fields in specific locations rather than sampling from the periosteal cortical envelope to the endosteal cortical envelope produces observation bias (Fig. 18.8). Using a standard field size (indicated by the circle), the amount of remodeling variation captured between the two individuals is not equal. In Fig. 18.9, the image on the left represents a young individual with a large cortex and the image on the right represents the cortex of an elderly individual that demonstrates age-related endosteal resorption. In the young individual, histological features associated with the periosteal envelope would be evaluated, while in the older individual a single field represents the histological variability from the periosteal to the endosteal surfaces.

In 1979, Thompson published a method designed to minimize the amount of destructive sampling, reduce observer error, and explore the utility of both the lower and the upper extremities for age estimation (Crowder, 2009). Thompson extracted 0.4 cm diameter bone cores from the femora, tibiae, humeri, and ulnae of known age cadavers. Nineteen variables were collected, including a number of gross measurements (e.g., core weight, cortical thickness, and cortical density). Various histomorphometric measurements were recorded through a method referred to as point counting using a 10 × 10 grid eyepiece reticule in four contiguous microscopic fields along the core's anterior periosteal surface. Percentage of osteonal bone area was noted as being the single best variable to estimate age.

While the Thompson method reduced subjectivity by developing more objective definitions and employing stereological techniques to evaluate histological structures, significant methodological issues are still prevalent. Thompson measured only a small amount of cortex (4 mm^2), which does not capture enough of the spatial variance known to occur within the cortex (Frost, 1969). The evaluation of the periosteal aspect limits the utility of the method

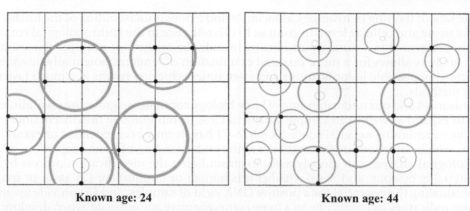

Known age: 24   **Known age: 44**

Figure 18.10 Illustration depicting the point count method to determine percentage of osteonal bone using the same level of magnification. The circles represent osteons with Haversian canals and the small dark circles indicate the number of grid "hits" over osteonal bone. Both fields have a point count of 14 "hits" and would result in identical age estimates with the Thompson (1979) method although there is a 20-year difference between known ages in this hypothetical example.

considering that younger individuals will likely not demonstrate significant remodeling in this area. Furthermore, the method does not provide an accurate assessment of remodeling events within the grid. Instead, it evaluates the percentage of osteonal area, meaning that a field of view containing fewer osteons with larger osteonal areas could provide similar results as a field of view with a higher osteon density but smaller osteonal areas (Fig. 18.10). Lastly, the method records point count "hits" over osteons with an intact or partially visible Haversian canal. This means that osteon fragments lacking a Haversian canal are not included, thus decreasing the amount of observed remodeling events and the correlation strength between bone turnover and skeletal age. Calculating the osteon population density (OPD) via counting intact and fragmentary osteon numbers per cortical area would likely provide a stronger correlation to skeletal age, which is the basis for the methods developed for the midshaft of the sixth rib.

In 1986, Dr. Sam D. Stout introduced a method for estimating age using the midshaft of the sixth rib. The entire cortical area was evaluated and the OPD was determined, which was calculated by adding intact and fragmentary osteons and dividing by the cortical area. The method was largely based on clinical research performed by Dr. Harold Frost and colleagues at the Henry Ford Hospital during the 1960s and 1970s, and sought to eliminate issues such as sampling error due to field location and the influence of biomechanical factors observed in weight-bearing bones. The method was further developed by Stout and Paine (1992) by increasing the sample size and using a checkerboard pattern (evaluating alternating ROIs) to reduce the amount of area evaluated while still capturing the intracortical variation.

The most recent improvement by Cho et al. (2002) provides for a more robust and versatile method by increasing the sample size and demographics (European American and African American samples) and using osteonal area as a variable to increase the accuracy of the age estimate. The method also provided a regression equation for fragmentary rib cross-sections. Associated with the issue of fragmentary rib cross-sections is the inability to seriate ribs, which could be problematic considering that the method was developed from a specific rib. In a pilot study by Crowder and Rosella (2007), ribs 4 through 7 were shown to provide similar OPD values compared to those of the sixth ribs, which is beneficial when there is uncertainty in rib seriation resulting in the inability to positively identify the sixth rib.

It is apparent that the accuracy and reliability of histological methods are debatable and exhibit significant levels of sampling error and observer error associated with the technique and variables employed. Current research has demonstrated that the amount of bone sampled/analyzed in histological age assessment can have a profound impact on the ability to accurately estimate age (Ingvoldstad, 2014; Gocha et al., 2016). As with any method of age estimation, histological methods with vague descriptions of samples, procedures, variables, or potential error rates should not be considered for use in skeletal analysis. Thus, new methods are needed to improve scientific standards within the field. Furthermore, methods that provide accurate age estimates for adult individuals, especially those over 50 years of age, are desperately needed. Research introduced by Crowder and Dominguez (2012) sought to develop a new method for the estimation of age using the anterior femur midshaft that reduces the methodological issues previously discussed and improves adult age estimation. This research, which is in its final stages of analysis, will offer variable definitions that reduce the subjectivity associated with collecting histological variables and provide a higher level of surety in age estimates, which unfortunately are wide, resulting in intervals similar to gross methods such as the pubic symphysis.

■ CONCLUSIONS

Histological analysis is an important tool that is infrequently used by anthropologists to assist with the identification process. Its greatest advantage lies in the ability to evaluate fragmentary skeletal remains that otherwise might only be submitted for DNA or other molecular analyses. Aversion to a histological approach to the skeletal survey is typically due to the lack of training in histological methods and a poor understanding of the broader implications of bone biology at the tissue and cellular level. In contrast to this reticence in the anthropological community, standard autopsy procedures performed by forensic pathologists include the analysis of multiple tissues at the histological level. Microscopic analysis allows for a more nuanced examination of remains, potentially providing new evidence that can aid in narrowing possible identifications and often times achieving results at a much faster pace than DNA analysis or similar methods.

As technology advances and our understanding of bone biology continues to grow, the possibilities for histological analysis continue to expand as well. For example, SR micro-CT is revolutionizing the current understanding of bone structural biology by contributing novel 3D data. SR micro-CT has recently been extended to examining human bone at the cellular level, which will continue to contribute to the understanding of bone adaptation, disease, and aging.

At present, histological analysis can already assist in streamlining the identification process by (1) determining if fragmentary material is osseous, and if so, whether it is human or nonhuman; (2) assist in triaging remains for DNA analysis by evaluating the potential for a positive DNA yield of samples; and (3) provide an age estimate in the absence of other age indicators, or contribute to a more comprehensive age estimate, when developing the biological profile to assist in narrowing the list of potential matches.

References

Agarwal, S.C., 2008. Light and broken bones: examining and interpreting bone loss and osteoporosis in past populations. In: Katzenberg, M.A., Saunders, S.R. (Eds.), Biological Anthropology of the Human Skeleton, second ed. Wiley-Liss, New York, pp. 387–410.

Andronowski, J.M., 2016. Evaluating Differential Nuclear DNA Yield Rates Among Human Bone Tissue Types: A Synchrotron Micro-CT Approach (Ph.D. Dissertation). University of Tennessee, Knoxville. Department of Anthropology.

Andronowski, J.M., Mundorff, A.Z., Pratt, I.V., Davoren, J.M., Cooper, D.M.L., 2017. Evaluating differential nuclear DNA yield rates and osteocyte numbers among human bone tissue types: a synchrotron radiation micro-CT approach. Forensic Sci. Int. Genet. 28, 211–218.

Burr, D.B., Allen, M.R. (Eds.), 2013. Basic and Applied Bone Biology. Academic Press, London, UK.

Carter, Y., Thomas, C.D.L., Clement, J.G., Peele, A.G., Hannah, K., Cooper, D.M.L., 2013. Variation in osteocyte lacunar morphology and density in the human femur – a synchrotron radiation micro-CT study. Bone 52, 126–132.

Carter, D.R., Beaupré, G.S., 2001. Skeletal Function and Form: Mechanobiology of Skeletal Development, Aging, and Regeneration. Cambridge University Press, Cambridge.

Cho, H., Stout, S.D., Madsen, R.W., Streeter, M.A., 2002. Population-specific histological age-estimating method: a model for known African-American and European-American skeletal remains. J. Forensic Sci. 47, 12–18.

Cooper, D.M.L., Thomas, C.D., Clement, J.G., Hallgrimsson, B., 2006. Three-dimensional microcomputed tomography imaging of basic multicellular unit-related resorption spaces in human cortical bone. Anat. Rec. A 288 (7), 806–816.

Cooper, D.M.L., Turinsky, A.L., Sensen, C.W., Hallgrimsson, B., 2003. Quantitative 3D analysis of the canal network in cortical bone by micro-computed tomography. Anat. Rec. B 274 (1), 169–179.

Cooper, D.M.L., Erickson, B., Peele, A., Hannah, K., Thomas, C.D.L., Clement, J.G., 2011. Visualization of 3D osteon morphology by synchrotron radiation micro-CT. J. Anat. 219 (4), 481–489.

Crowder, C., Stout, S. (Eds.), 2012. Bone Histology: An Anthropological Perspective. CRC Press, Boca Raton, FL.

Crowder, C.M., Heinrich, J., Stout, S., 2012. Rib histomorphometry for adult age estimation. In: Bell, L. (Ed.), Forensic Microscopy for Skeletal Tissue: Methods and Protocols. Springer.

Crowder, C.M., Dominguez, V.M., 2012. A new method for histological age estimation of the femur. In: Proceedings of the American Academy of Forensic Sciences, vol. 18. American Academy of Forensic Sciences, Atlanta, GA, pp. 374–375.

Crowder, C.M., Pfeiffer, S., 2010. The application of cortical bone histomorphometry to estimate age at death. In: Latham, K.E., Finnegan, M. (Eds.), Age Estimation of the Human Skeleton. CC Thomas, Springfield, IL, pp. 193–215.

Crowder, C.M., 2009. Histological age estimation. In: Blau, S., Ubelaker, D. (Eds.), Digging Deeper: Current Trends and Future Directions in Forensic Anthropology and Archaeology. World Archaeological Congress Handbook. Left Coast Press, pp. 222–235.

Crowder, C.M., Rosella, L., 2007. Assessment of intra- and intercostal variation in rib histomorphometry: its impact on evidentiary examination. J. Forensic Sci. 52 (2), 271–276.

Currey, J.D., 2002. Bones: Structure and Mechanics. Princeton University Press, Princeton, NJ.

Dempster, D.W., Compston, J.E., Drezner, M.K., Glorieux, F.H., Kanis, J.A., Malluche, H., Meunier, P.J., Ott, S.M., Recker, R.R., Parfitte, A.M., 2013. Standardized nomenclature, symbols, and units for bone histomorphometry: a 2012 update of the report of the ASBMR histomorphometry nomenclature committee. J. Bone Miner. Res. 28 (1), 2–17.

de Ricqlés, A.J., 1993. Some remarks on paleohistology from a comparative evolutionary point of view. In: Grupe, G., Garland, A.N. (Eds.), Histology of Ancient Human Bone: Methods and Diagnosis. Springer-Verlag, New York, pp. 37–77.

Frost, H.M., 1969. Tetracycline-based histological analysis of bone remodeling. Calcif. Tissue Res. 3, 211–237.

Gocha, T.P., Stout, S.D., Agnew, A.M., 2016. Examining the accuracy of age estimates from new histological sampling strategies at the femoral midshaft. In: Proceedings of the American Academy of Forensic Sciences., vol. 22. American Academy of Forensic Sciences, Las Vegas, NV, p. 135.

Hillier, M.L., Bell, L.S., 2007. Differentiating human bone from animal bone: a review of histological methods. J. Forensic Sci. 52 (2), 249–263.

Ingvoldstad, M.E., 2014. Femoral midshaft histomorphometric patterning: improving microscopic age-at-death estimates from adult human skeletal remains. In: Proceedings of the American Academy of Forensic Sciences, vol. 20. American Academy of Forenisc Sciences, Seattle, WA, pp. 297–298.

Kerley, E.R., 1965. The microscopic determination of age in human bone. Am. J. Phys. Anthropol. 23, 149–164.

Kerley, E.R., Ubelaker, D.H., 1978. Revisions in the microscopic method of estimating age at death in human cortical bone. Am. J. Phys. Anthropol. 49, 545–546.

Maggiano, I.S., Maggiano, C.M., Clement, J.G., Thomas, C.D.L., Carter, Y., Cooper, D.M.L., 2016. Three-dimensional reconstruction of Haversian systems in human cortical bone using synchrotron radiation-based micro-CT: morphology and quantification of branching and transverse connections across age. J. Anat. http://dx.doi.org/10.111/joa.12430.

Martin, R.B., Burr, D.B., 1989. Structure, Function, and Adaptation of Compact Bone. Raven Press, NY.

Martin, R.B., Burr, D.B., Sharkey, N.A., Fyhrie, D.P., 2015. In: Skeletal Tissue Mechanics. Springer Verlag, New York.

McCreadie, B.R., Hollister, S.J., Schaffler, M.B., Goldstein, S.A., 2004. Osteocyte lacuna size and shape in women with and without osteoporotic fracture. J. Biomech. 37, 563–572.

Mundorff, A.Z., Davoren, J.M., Huffine, E., Frank, E., Bettinger, S., Weitz, S., Jeanguenat, A., 2012. Developing an Empirically Based Ranking Order for Bone Sampling: Examining Differential Yield Rates Between Human Skeletal Elements – Final Results. U.S. Department of Justice, OJP, NIJ. The NIJ Conference June 2012, Arlington, Virginia.

Mundorff, A.Z., Davoren, J.M., 2014. Examination of DNA yield rates for different skeletal elements at increasing post mortem intervals. Forensic Sci. Int. Genet. 8, 55–63.

Mulhern, D.M., Ubelaker, D.H., 2001. Differences in osteon banding between human and nonhuman bone. J. Forensic Sci. 46 (2), 220–222.

Mulhern, D.M., Ubelaker, D.H., 2012. Differentiating human from nonhuman bone microstructure. In: Crowder, C.M., Stout, S.D. (Eds.), Bone Histology: An Anthropological Perspective. CRC Press, Boca Ranton, FL.

Ortner, D.J., Turner-Walker, G., 2003. The biology of skeletal tissues. In: Ortner, D.J. (Ed.), Identification of Pathological Conditions in Human Skeletal Remains, second ed. Academic Press, Amsterdam.

Parfitt, A.M., 1983. Calcium homeostasis. In: Mundy, G.R., Martin, T.J. (Eds.), Handbook of Experimental Pharmacology. Physiology and Pharmacology of Bone, vol. 107. Springer, Heidelberg, pp. 1–65.

Robling, A.G., Castillo, A.B., Turner, C.H., 2006. Biomechanical and molecular regulation of bone remodeling. Annu. Rev. Biomed. Eng. 8, 455–498.

Robling, A.G., Stout, S.D., 2008. Histomorphometry of human cortical bone: applications to age estimation. In: Katzenberg, M.A., Saunders, S.R. (Eds.), Biological Anthropology of the Human Skeleton, second ed. Wiley-Liss, New York, pp. 149–171.

Ruff, C.B., 2008. Biomechanical analyses of archaeological human skeletons. In: Katzenberg, M.A., Saunders, S.R. (Eds.), Biological Anthropology of the Human Skeleton, second ed. Wiley-Liss, New York, pp. 183–206.

Stout, S.D., Crowder, C.M., 2012. Bone remodeling, histomorphology, and histomorphometry. In: Crowder, C.M., Stout, S.D. (Eds.), Bone Histology: An Anthropological Perspective. CRC Press, Boca Ranton, FL.

Stout, S.D., Teitelbaum, S.L., 1976. Histological analysis of undecalcified thin-sections of archeological bone. Am. J. Phys. Anthropol. 44 (2), 263–269.

Stout, S.D., Gehlert, S.J., 1982. Effects of field size when using Kerley's histological method for determination of age at death. Am. J. Phys. Anthropol. 58, 123–125.

Stout, S.D., Paine, R., 1992. Brief communication: histological age estimation using rib and clavicle. Am. J. Phys. Anthropol. 87, 111–115.

Stout, S.D., 1986. The use of bone histomorphometry in skeletal identification: the case of Francisco Pizarro. J. Forensic Sci. 31 (1), 296–300.

Stout, S.D., 1989. The use of cortical bone histology to estimate age at death. In: Iscan, M.Y. (Ed.), Age Markers in the Human Skeleton. Charles C. Thomas, Springfield, pp. 195–210.

Thompson, D.D., 1979. The core technique in the determination of age at death in skeletons. J. Forensic Sci. 24, 902–915.

Turner, C.H., Forwood, M.R., 1995. What role does the osteocyte network play in bone adaptation? Bone 16 (3), 283–285.

Wu, K., Jett, S., Frost, H., 1967. Bone resorption rates in physiological, senile and postmenopausal osteoporosis. J. Lab. Clin. Med. 69, 810–818.

Wu, K., Schubeck, K., Frost, H., Villanueva, A., 1970. Haversian bone formation rates determined by a new method in a mastodon and in human diabetes mellitus and osteoporosis. Calcif. Tissue Res. 6, 204–209.

Advances in Radiographic and Superimposition Methods of Identification

CHAPTER 19

Overview of Advances in Forensic Radiological Methods of Human Identification

Mark Viner[1,2]
[1]Queen Mary University of London, London, United Kingdom
[2]Cranfield University, Shrivenham, United Kingdom

Chapter Outline

■ INTRODUCTION AND BACKGROUND

The announcement of the discovery of X-rays by Wilhelm Röntgen in December 1895 heralded a new era in scientific investigation. The ability of these invisible rays to penetrate objects and reveal their structure by casting "shadows" on photographic film was instantly recognized as having enormous potential. X-ray techniques were quickly developed in many fields including medicine, veterinary science, engineering, archaeology, law enforcement, and forensic science (Brogdon and Lichtenstein, 2011).

Since that time, radiological methods have been widely used to assist in the analysis and identification of human remains, and the applications of the use of X-rays first suggested by Levinsohn, Angerer, and Bordas (Brogdon and Lichtenstein, 2011; Levinsohn, 1899; Goodman, 1995) are the main methods by which radiology contributes to the identification and investigative process. In our modern era when the invasive nature of some forensic medical procedures are increasingly at odds with the acceptable norms of society (Clarke, 2001), medical imaging techniques enable the noninvasive examination of remains in a variety of states of decomposition from fully fleshed to completely skeletonized and afford the opportunity to obtain a considerable amount of data without the need to clean and completely deflesh the remains.

■ RADIOLOGICAL IMAGING METHODS

Until relatively recently, radiological images were acquired using the same basic techniques of radiography and fluoroscopy that Röntgen himself employed. While these techniques still form a major part of radiological investigation, they have been supplemented by newer techniques employing sophisticated computer technology, some of which rely on X-rays and others employ radioactive materials, sound waves, and magnetic fields. The majority of methods now in use permit images to be acquired and stored digitally. The main medical radiological imaging techniques used for forensic examination of skeletonized or partially decomposed remains are summarized in Radiography section.

Radiography

The term radiography is generally used to describe a static or "still" image produced by means of a single exposure to X-rays. Such images are now usually recorded and stored digitally but were previously recorded on X-ray sensitive photographic film. Digital imaging methods such as direct digital radiography (DR) and computed radiography have greatly increased the portability and accessibility of radiography which was previously dependent on complex and time-consuming photographic processing. Recent advances in battery and wireless technology have led to a new generation of highly portable digital X-ray systems that can be rapidly and easily deployed for forensic investigation in the laboratory or field environment (Fig. 19.1).

The advantages of digital X-ray detectors and computing power have also been applied to the previously obsolete techniques of scanography and single plane tomography. Digital scanography machines such as the Lodox provide the facility for rapid digital scanning of an entire body giving a high-resolution image at a very low radiation dose. Such machines, originally designed for the imaging of major trauma are now in widespread use in forensic centers in South Africa and increasingly in the United States, Europe, and Asia (Fig. 19.2; Benningfield et al., 2003).

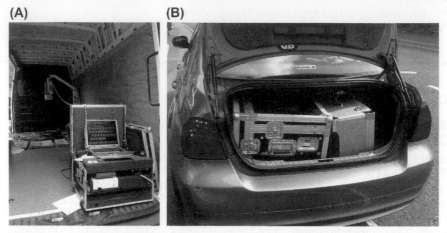

(A) **(B)**

Figure 19.1 (A) Direct digital X-ray unit in use in field conditions in the back of a van using a portable generator. (B) The same unit packed for transportation.

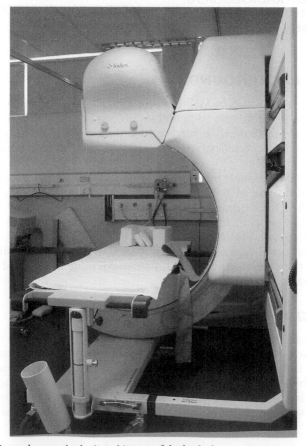

Figure 19.2 The Lodox Statscan which produces a single digital image of the body from a 16 s scan.

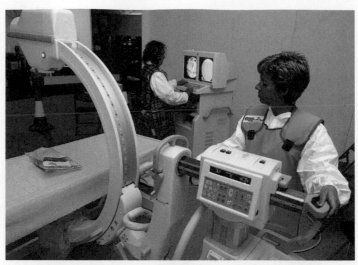

Figure 19.3 C-arm fluoroscopy unit in use in an emergency mortuary. *Photo with kind permission of the Metropolitan Police.*

Tomosynthesis (Dobbins and McAdams, 2009) is an updated version of multislice linear tomography with clinical radiological applications in the examination of chest and breast lesions. Research in the field of musculoskeletal radiography has demonstrated its ability to enable detection of more fractures than radiography while simultaneously providing lower metal artifact (Ha et al., 2015). Its forensic applications have yet to be fully investigated.

Fluoroscopy

The term fluoroscopy is used to describe an image directly visualized in real-time motion produced by a continuous exposure to X-rays. Such images are now produced using flat plate solid state detectors but were previously produced by viewing an image formed by fluorescence caused by radiation falling on a phosphor screen. In the early days these images were viewed directly, but this was later superseded by use of CCTV cameras capturing the output from a photomultiplier "image intensifier" system. Such systems are in widespread use in forensic facilities for the location and removal of ballistic material and other foreign bodies from cadavers (Fig. 19.3). Equipment, although mobile, is generally heavy and somewhat unwieldy and stringent procedures for radiation safety have to be in place. Modern dynamic flat plate detectors are bringing a decrease in the size of such equipment but the use of such units is still limited to the larger forensic medical facility.

Computed Axial Tomography

Computed axial tomography (CAT) or CT scanning was developed by Godfrey Hounsfield and the EMI Company in the 1970s and employs a computerized X-ray machine that uses an array of photoreceptors to detect minute differences in attenuation of X-rays emitted by an X-ray tube as it rotates around the body or body part. A computer generates an image of the body part in the axial or cross-sectional plane and modern multidetector CT (MDCT) scanners permit multiplanar, multidirectional sectional images to be displayed and/or reconstructed as three-dimensional (3D) images. Because the data are taken from multiple measurements throughout a full 360 degree rotation of the unit, measurements of attenuated radiation (and thus density) and dimension are highly accurate. Rapid computer processing power enables the generation of 3D rendered images and the facility to "isolate" and visualize individual bones, organs, or systems. The use of MDCT in forensic facilities is increasing rapidly. However, it comes at considerable cost and as yet is only available in a small number of well resource centers mainly in Europe, Australasia, and the Far East (Fig. 19.4). A rapid and lower radiation dose method of CT scanning that has been developed for dental applications uses a 3D "cone" beam of X-radiation in place of a slit fan beam and is able to rapidly acquire CT scans of the dentition and facial bones [cone beam computed tomography(CBCT)] (Fig. 19.5).

Magnetic Resonance Imaging

Magnetic resonance imaging (MRI) scanning employs static and electromagnetic fields to effect movement of the hydrogen nuclei in body tissue and the resultant signal emitted by the resonating nuclei is measured, recorded, and plotted to create a computer-generated image of the tissue. The hydrogen nuclei must be free to move, and for this reason the signal strength is higher in body tissue with a high water content (the soft tissues) and considerably lower or nonexistent in the hard tissues. MRI is being increasingly used in the postmortem examination of head injury—particularly in children—however, its application for examination of the soft tissues is currently limited and for this reason forensic imaging of human remains of interest to anthropologists does not usually include MRI. However, researchers at the University of Oxford have recently developed new MRI sequences for imaging bone, and it is possible that such methods will prove useful in postmortem imaging and craniofacial identification (Eley et al., 2012).

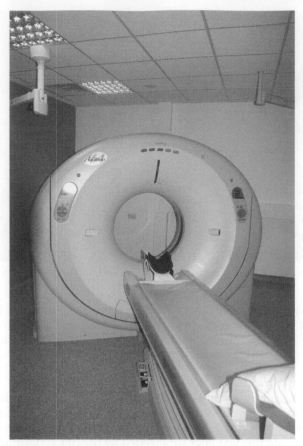

Figure 19.4 Modern multidetector computed tomography unit.

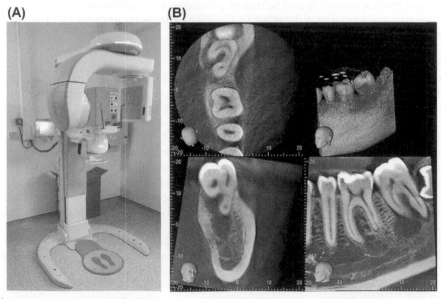

Figure 19.5 (A) Cone beam computed tomography. (B) Cone beam computed tomography Images.

Ultrasound

Ultrasound measures reflected sound waves using the same principle as sonar. To be effective the material being examined needs to be capable of transmitting sound and for this reason it has mainly been used in the examination of the soft tissues, particularly in the abdomen and the pelvis. It has seen limited forensic use for examination of the hard tissues, although some recent studies have demonstrated its effectiveness as an application for determination of bone age in the wrists of juveniles (Mentzel et al., 2005; Shimura et al., 2005).

Forensic radiology of the deceased has, until very recently, been limited to the use of still-image radiography and occasionally fluoroscopy (Brogdon and Lichtenstein, 2011). Increasingly, however, some of the more complex imaging techniques, such as MDCT and CBCT scanning, are being employed for postmortem imaging. In the years between 2005 and 2011, these methods showed an exponential increase in research in this area (Baglivo et al., 2013).

Complex imaging equipment comes at considerable financial cost both in terms of initial outlay and maintenance. Furthermore, the interpretation of cross-sectional imaging examinations requires specialist knowledge and skill that are not currently possessed by the majority of forensic medical investigators. For these reasons, the widespread adoption of such technologies in forensic investigation is likely take some considerable time.

■ APPLICATION OF RADIOLOGICAL METHODS TO HUMAN IDENTIFICATION

Radiology is now widely used to assist in the analysis and identification of human remains and provides the investigative team with a rapid method of triage and classification by answering a number of fundamental questions:

1. Establishing context
   a. Determination of human versus nonhuman remains
   b. Detecting commingling
   c. Locating and retrieving artifacts and personal effects
2. Identification
   a. Evaluation of the biological profile (age, sex, stature, and ancestry)
   b. Positive identification of individuals by comparison of antemortem and postmortem radiological data.

Establishing Context

Human Versus Nonhuman

In the majority of cases involving animal bones, a visual examination is all that is required for the forensic anthropologist to determine nonhuman characteristics. In some cases the articular surfaces or other distinctive bony elements may be missing due to fragmentation, decomposition, or animal activity, and in such cases, a radiographic examination of the bone structure and trabecular pattern can be useful to distinguish human from nonhuman remains (Brogdon, 2011a; Chilvarquer et al., 1987).

Detecting Commingling

In cases involving fragmentation, remains may be commingled and mixed with debris and artifacts. Physical examination of such remains, particularly in cases of fire damage or following exhumation where the discoloration of all material retrieved is uniform, is both difficult and time-consuming. In these circumstances, radiological examination can prove useful both in determining the presence of one or more individuals and also in identifying and locating small body parts, especially teeth, which may otherwise be overlooked, even in the absence of a thorough and time-consuming fingertip search (Goodman and Edelson, 2002; Kahana et al., 1997; Viner et al., 1998).

Locating and Retrieving Artifacts and Personal Effects

Radiological imaging can also be utilized to detect and retrieve hazardous objects, personal effects, projectiles and other artifacts, and forensic evidence that have been retrieved together with the remains during body recovery or exhumation. This can be especially useful in circumstances where fragmentation is extensive and has proved particularly useful in mass fatality incidents resulting from air disasters (Alexander and Foote, 1998; Mulligan et al., 1988), explosions, fires, and terrorist incidents (Harcke et al., 2002; O'Donnell et al., 2011; Nye et al., 1996), or following exhumation. In the latter case, it may also be useful to use X-ray techniques on-site to examine the associated soil and debris excavated with the body to detect small items such as jewelry or other personal effects which may have become disassociated from the body during decomposition (Gould, 2003; Tonello, 1998; Viner, 2014; Wessling and Loe, 2011) (Fig. 19.6). A practical application of this technique is further described in Wessling (Chapter 28).

Human Identification

Establishing the Biological Profile

Age Estimation

In the same way that a physical examination of the defleshed skeleton can determine age at the time of death, radiological examination of the skeleton radiography can deliver the same information in the case of less decomposed remains. There are a number of radiological standards for determination of bone age throughout the first two decades of life, based on the appearance and fusion of primary and secondary ossification centers within the developing skeleton. The final epiphysis to fuse is the medial end of the clavicle, normally occurring during mid to late 1920s.

Assessment of dental development in juveniles relies to a great extent on radiographic methods (AlQahtani et al., 2010), and in addition to dental assessment, one of the most useful examinations in determining the age of children is radiography of the hand and wrist (Fig. 19.2), although examination of the knee, foot, and ankle can also be helpful (Greulich and Pyle, 1959; Hansman, 1962; Hoerr et al., 1962; Pyle and Hoerr, 1955; Scheuer and Black, 2004).

(A)   **(B)**

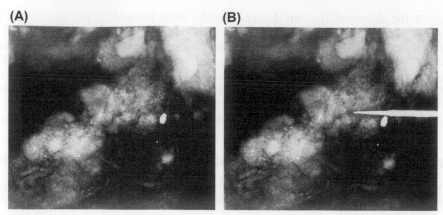

Figure 19.6 (A) X-ray of soil and loose clothing exhumed from a clandestine grave showing a bullet. (B) Forceps are used to localize the bullet under X-ray control prior to retrieval.

In the mature skeleton, it is the degenerative changes that begin to appear at the margins of the articular surfaces of major joints at around age 40 that will allow radiological estimation of adult age within the range ±5 to 10 years (Brogdon, 2011a). Calcification of the costal cartilage associated with the ribs and sternum may be readily visualized in people over 50, although it is sometimes observed in younger subjects (Mora et al., 2001). Although chest radiography demonstrates this calcification, its specificity as an aging method is reduced due to similar amounts of mineralization throughout adulthood (McCormick, 1980). It is, however, a quick, inexpensive method to obtain a general age estimate which can be used along with other anthropological examinations (e.g., pubic symphysis morphology). In the case of partially skeletonized remains, radiological examination using an MDCT may be particularly useful for aging from the pubic symphysis (Dedouit et al., 2011).

Sex Estimation

Differentiation of sexes by skeletal radiology is unreliable until after puberty, as the features that distinguish male from female are not sufficiently developed until this point (Krogman and Iscan, 1986). On examination the appearance of the male skeleton is more substantial than the female, being generally heavier and the long bones of greater length. However, it is the examination of certain bones that is most useful in estimating the sex of an individual. In particular, the shape, size, and geometry of the pelvis (Kurihara et al., 1996; Rogers and Saunders, 1994; Sutherland and Suchey, 1991); cranium; and mandible (Bass, 1990; Kurihara et al., 1996; Edwards et al., 2013). In addition, patterns of calcification of the costal (Navani et al., 1970), tracheobronchial, thyroid, and aretenoid cartilages (Kurihara et al., 1996) can be used to estimate sex from skeletal remains by radiological means (Brogdon, 2011a).

Stature Estimation

Stature is often estimated by direct measurement from unfleshed human remains. The length of the femur is most often used, as this has been shown to be reliable (Trotter and Gleser, 1952, 1958). In the case of fleshed remains, these measurements can be made radiographically, provided that a correction for magnification is made. This can either be achieved by means of an adapted radiographic technique, applying a simple correction factor or utilizing modern imaging techniques such as CT scanning and DR.

CT scanners and digital X-ray systems can be calibrated to undertake correction calculations automatically, thus allowing measurements to be made directly from the image. In the case of CT scanning, a scanogram is performed using the scanner to undertake an automated version of the manual process described earlier (Aitken et al., 1985). Digital X-ray machines using a slit beam can also be used to take direct measurements, and many other direct digital X-ray machines can be calibrated so as to render accurate anatomical measurements from the resultant images (Beningfield et al., 2003).

Ancestry Estimation

Estimation of ancestry is challenging, especially when the remains are badly decomposed or skeletonized. The methods used by physical anthropologists to determine ancestry from skeletal remains can be applied radiographically with fleshed remains. In particular, examination of the cranium and mandible (Bass, 1990; Fischman, 1985), the distal end of the femur (Craig, 1995), and the ratio of long bone length can be useful in determination of population ancestry (Krogman and Iscan, 1986).

Positive Identification of Individuals by Comparison of Antemortem and Postmortem Radiological Data

In cases involving skeletonization, fragmentation, decomposition, incineration, mutilation, or other disfigurement, identification by means of the hard tissues assumes a greater importance. Such incidents are often characterized by damage to the soft tissues caused by fire, water, or severe disarticulation due to explosion or rapid deceleration injury. In such circumstances, radiological methods of identification play a significant role.

Medical imaging has long been used for the identification of human remains and is well documented (Buchner, 1985; Craig, 1995; Jensen, 1991; Kahana and Hiss, 1997; Murphy et al., 1980; Sanders et al., 1972; Schwartz and Woolridge, 1977). Radiology is used extensively in anthropological and odontological assessment of postmortem and antemortem radiographs, records, or other images for concordance as they represent an excellent source of data for comparison of anatomical features (Fig. 19.3). Many specific cases have been reported in which radiology has played the leading role in the identification of human remains (Goodman and Edelson, 2002; Greulich and Pyle, 1959; Kahana et al., 1997; Viner and Lichtenstein, 2011).

Radiological identification of human remains requires specific and unique findings on postmortem images to be matched exactly with antemortem images of the individual. In some cases, identification can be made from a series of relatively common or nonspecific pathological anatomical changes that appear in identical locations in ante- and postmortem images. In other cases, a single unique feature is sufficient (Brogdon, 2011b). In 1927, Culbert and Law made the first identification of human remains by comparison of antemortem and postmortem radiographs of the frontal sinuses. The degree of human variation in sinus patterns, based on size, asymmetry, outline, partial septia, and supraorbital cells, makes effective comparison for identification possible (Kirk et al., 2002; Marlin et al., 1991; Nambiar et al., 1999).

Radiographs taken for medical purposes are often required by statute to be retained for long periods of time. In the United Kingdom, for example, the Department of Health requires that film or digitally recorded radiological images are retained for 8 years, and longer in the case of children (until the patient reaches their 25th year), and 3 years following death (Dimond, 2002; Information Governance Alliance, 2016). In many privately run clinics, radiographs or imaging data on CDR or DVD are routinely given to the patient for safe keeping, and thus they may be in existence for much longer than the statutory period. Records are thus, on the whole, fairly accessible.

Despite the advent of more modern techniques, radiography still remains a widely used method. In the UK National Health Service, for example, radiographs account for over half of the medical and dental X-ray examinations undertaken (NHS England, 2012/2013). Of these the majority are X-rays of the teeth, chest, and limbs. This position echoes Brogdon's (2011b) evaluation of the distribution of radiologic examinations by body part and modality in the United States. As Brogdon asserts, examinations of the chest demonstrate consistency of bony structures over time and extremities may contain useful radiographic identifiers due to previous injury, degenerative change, or malformation. All of the above points to a wealth of useful antemortem data being available to the investigator, with the possibility of obtaining a clear and decisive identification if postmortem and antemortem data can be matched (Brogdon, 2011b). A standardized approach to skeletal identification by radiographic comparison of the cardiothoracic region on chest radiographs is discussed in Stephan et al. (Chapter 24).

Comparison of antemortem and postmortem radiographs for the purposes of human identification is an exacting and time-consuming process. Current practice and validation of comparative radiography within the United States is discussed further in Streetman and Fenton (Chapter 22). Postmortem radiographs should be obtained using identical projections to those of the antemortem radiographs. For this reason it is recommended that postmortem radiography must be undertaken using standard hospital protocols with AP and lateral views for the spine and all long bones and AP, lateral, and occipitofrontal views of the skull (Blyth et al., 2011). In some cases it may be necessary to undertake additional postmortem radiographs to replicate exactly the antemortem projection—particularly if these are substandard. In all cases an appropriately trained and experienced operator should be considered essential. As Brogdon points out "However obtained, however trained, and however compensated, the person who actually positions and exposes the roentgenograms is absolutely critical to the success of the entire endeavor. The educated, experienced, and sophisticated eye of the radiologist or other professional observer may be required to detect and interpret the subtle nuances recorded on the film, but without adequate technical support that eye will be blinded" (Brogdon, 2011c).

Evaluation of the radiographs also requires a trained experienced eye and can be time-consuming if large numbers of images are involved in the mass casualty situation. In recent years computer-aided diagnosis has been introduced within some areas of radiology to address similar volume issues. An application of this technology for computer-assisted postmortem human identification is discussed in Derrick et al. (Chapter 23).

Examination by CT scan has increased dramatically in recent years due to advances in multidetector CT techniques. As a result, some radiography examinations have been almost completely replaced by CT. An example is that of radiographic examinations of the skull which have declined dramatically since the advent of CT scanning due to the vastly superior ability of CT to provide diagnostic images of the brain. As a result, antemortem radiographic data are less likely to be available. However, the multiplanar reconstruction capabilities of MDCT allow 2D images to be constructed and positive identification can be established either by comparison with postmortem CT scans or conventional radiographs (Brogdon, 2011b; Reichs and Dorion, 1992). Recent advances in the use of frontal sinuses for human identification using CT scan data are discussed in Christensen and Hatch (Chapter 20).

■ MASS FATALITY INCIDENTS

Radiological methods have been effectively employed in the investigation of mass fatality incidents and the identification of casualties (Viner and Lichtenstein, 2011). A systematic application is essential and is best described along the lines discussed below (IAFR, 2004).

- *Primary survey*—Initial triage and assessment to establish context; recognize comingling and locate and retrieve fragmented remains, artifacts, and personal effects
- *Secondary survey*—Standard examination of specific body parts (e.g., dentition) to produce a standard series of images which can then be compared with antemortem records to establish a positive identification.
- *Tertiary examinations*—Specific examinations performed in response to findings during primary or secondary surveys or during pathology, odontology, or anthropology assessment.

The manner in which these requirements are met will depend greatly on the imaging methodologies employed. In the majority of cases where radiography or fluoroscopy is used, separate imaging examinations will need to be conducted at each stage to acquire the radiological data necessary (Viner et al., 2015).

There are as yet very few mass fatality incidents in which MDCT has been employed, and the volume of data documenting its use in cases involving fragmentation and commingling is small. However, in two well-documented cases it is clear that MDCT has proved its effectiveness as a tool that in certain circumstances can combine the primary and secondary surveys, and with appropriate scanning protocols, offers the opportunity for the data acquired during this examination to be reexamined to provide additional information in place of a separate tertiary imaging examination (Rutty et al., 2007; O'Donnell et al., 2011).

The advantage of MDCT is that it has the potential to replace all three of the stages outlined earlier in this chapter. The digital nature of the technology enables accurate discrimination between hard and soft tissues and artifacts made from a range of different materials. Triangulation from a continuous sequence of X-ray transmissions through 360 degree provides for accurate location and measurement of anatomical structures, artifacts, ballistic material, etc. The vast data sets acquired can permit reconstruction in any plane, thus negating the need for accurately positioned comparison views, and the data can be shared, transmitted, displayed, and read remotely.

If MDCT is used, it may thus be possible simply to conduct one imaging examination at the start of the mass fatality DVI process and to review and evaluate the same data set at each stage of the process to gather the required information (Morgan et al., 2014; Rutty et al., 2007; O'Donnell et al., 2011).

While the initial scan may negate further radiological examination in most cases, intraoral radiography for dental identification and the use of either fluoroscopy or DR for rapid location and removal of ballistic material cannot currently be entirely ruled out.

It is perhaps for these logistical reasons that CT scanning has not yet been more widely used in mass fatality response. Mass fatality plans either need to incorporate the use of existing CT scanning facilities into the disaster mortuary (predisposing the use of static locations) or make use of mobile technology. Mobile (trailer mounted or containerized) CT scanners offer a possible one-stop solution for the emergency mortuary and have been adopted by national DVI teams including Denmark and the United Kingdom (Leth, 2007). Geography and/or cost may preclude others from adopting the same approach and there will thus be a continued reliance upon more conventional imaging methods.

This is recognized by the Disaster Victim Identification Working Group of the International Society of Forensic Radiology and Imaging (ISFRI) in their position statement on the use of radiology in disaster victim identification: "The modality used will be dependent upon the equipment available at the time and the question to be answered as part of the DVI process. It can include the use, either singularly or in combination or radiographs (plain film, computed or digital radiography), fluoroscopy, computed tomography or dental radiography. Currently magnetic resonance imaging (MR) is not considered a modality for use in DVI unless the only antemortem imaging available for comparison is MR" (Rutty et al., 2013).

■ SUMMARY

Radiology has a wide range of applications in the identification and analysis of human remains and associated artifacts and personal effects. It is an invaluable aid in the initial examination of suspected remains and related debris, enabling context to be established and facilitating the rapid identification and retrieval of small body parts, personal items, and forensic evidence. Its applications for human identification and analysis of trauma are especially valuable in situations involving partial decomposed remains or those which have been subjected to fire or fragmented by explosion. From assisting in the determination of biological profile to determination of positive identification through comparison of antemortem and postmortem images, radiology is an essential tool in the analysis of human remains and its application and deployment should be readily accessible.

Recent advances in technology have made simple radiography far more accessible and deployable, and radiography as a tool of forensic human identification should thus be of far more practical use than it has previously been. Coupled with the advantages of digital imaging and the ability to store, share, and analyze images using today's high-powered computers, "simpler" and more cost-effective techniques such as radiography, fluoroscopy, scanography, and linear tomography/tomosynthesis may see further development of applications in human identification.

Access to cross-sectional radiological techniques such as MDCT and MRI scanning for forensic and postmortem investigation is steadily improving as the technology becomes both more economical and widely available. Greater levels of accuracy and the ability to examine subjects and display images in three dimensions offer an increasingly wide range of applications to the forensic investigator.

References

Aitken, A.G., Flodmark, O., Newman, D.E., Kilcoyne, R.F., Shuman, W.P., Mack, L.A., 1985. Leg length determination by CT digital radiography. AJR Am. J. Roentgenoogyl. 144 (3), 613–615.

Alexander, C.J., Foote, G.A., 1998. Radiology in forensic identification: the Mt Erebus disaster. Australas. Radiol. 42 (4), 321–326.

AlQahtani, S.J., Hector, M.P., Liversidge, H.M., 2010. Brief communication: the London atlas of human tooth development and eruption. Am. J. Phys. Anthropol. 142, 481–490.

Bass, W.M., 1990. Forensic anthropology. In: Fierro, M.F. (Ed.), CAP Handbook for Postmortem Examination of Unidentified Remain; Developing Identification of Well Preserved, Decomposed, Burned, and Skeletonised Remains. College of American Pathologists, Stokie, IL.

Baglivo, M., Winklhofer, M., Hatch, G., Ampanozi, G., Thali, M.J., Ruder, T.D., 2013. The rise of forensic and post-mortem radiology—analysis of the literature between the year 2000 and 2011. J. Forensic Radiol. Imaging 1 (1), 3–9.

Beningfield, S., Potgieter, H., Nicol, A., van As, S., Bowie, G., Hering, E., Latti, E., 2003. Report on a new type of trauma full-body digital X-ray machine. Emerg. Radiol. 10 (1), 23–29.

Blyth, T., Faircloth, E., Conlogue, G., Viner, M., 2011. Imaging in the medical examiner's facility. In: Thali, M.J., Viner, M.D., Brogdon, B.G. (Eds.), Brogdon's Forensic Radiology, second ed. CRC Press, Boca Raton, FL, pp. 524–525.

Brogdon, B.G., 2011a. Radiological identification: anthropological parameters. In: Thali, M.J., Viner, M.D., Brogdon, B.G. (Eds.), Brogdon's Forensic Radiology, second ed. CRC Press, Boca Raton, FL, pp. 85–106.

Brogdon, B.G., 2011b. Radiological identification of individual remains. In: Thali, M.J., Viner, M.D., Brogdon, B.G. (Eds.), Brogdon's Forensic Radiology, second ed. CRC Press, Boca Raton, FL, pp. 153–176.

Brogdon, B.G., 2011c. Radiological identification of individual remains. In: Thali, M.J., Viner, M.D., Brogdon, B.G. (Eds.), Brogdon's Forensic Radiology, second ed. CRC Press, Boca Raton, FL, p. 160.

Brogdon, B.G., Lichtenstein, J.E., 2011. Forensic radiology in historical perspective. In: Thali, M.J., Viner, M.D., Brogdon, B.G. (Eds.), Brogdon's Forensic Radiology, second ed. CRC Press, Boca Raton, FL, pp. 9–23.

Buchner, A., 1985. The identification of human remains. Int. Dent. J. 35 (4), 307–311.

Chilvarquer, I., Katz, J.O., Glassman, D.M., Prihoda, T.J., Cottone, J.A., 1987. Comparative radiographic study of human and animal long bone patterns. J. Forensic Sci. 32 (6), 1645–1654.

Craig, E.A., 1995. Intercondylar shelf angle: a new method to determine race from the distal femur. J. Forensic Sci. 40 (5), 777–782.

Culbert, W.L., Law, F.M., 1927. Identification by comparison of roentgenograms of nasal accessory sinuses and mastoid processes. JAMA 88, 1632–1636.

Clarke, L.J., 2001. Marchioness/Bowbelle Formal Investigation under the Merchant Shipping Act 1995. Her Majesty's Stationary Office, London.

Dedouit, F., Telmon, N., Rousseau, H., Crubezy, E., Joffre, F., Rouge, D., 2011. Modern cross-sectional imaging in anthropology. In: Thali, M.J., Viner, M.D., Brogdon, B.G. (Eds.), Brogdon's Forensic Radiology, second ed. CRC Press, Boca Raton, FL, pp. 107–126.

Dimond, B., 2002. Legal Aspects of Radiography and Radiology. Blackwell Science, Oxford.

Dobbins, J., McAdams, H., 2009. Chest tomosynthesis: technical principles and clinical update. Eur. J. Radiol. 72 (2), 244–251.

Eley, K.A., McIntyre, A.G., Watt-Smith, S.R., Golding, S.J., March 2012. "Black bone" MRI: a partial flip angle technique for radiation reduction in craniofacial imaging. Br. J. Radiol. 85 (1011), 272–278.

Edwards, K., Viner, M.D., Schweitzer, W., Thali, M.J., 2013. Sex determination from the Foramen Magnum. J. Forensic Radiol. Imaging 1 (4), 186–192.

Fischman, S.L., 1985. The use of medical and dental radiographs in identification. Int. Dent. J. 35 (4), 301–306.

Greulich, W.W., Pyle, S.I., 1959. Radiographic Atlas of Skeletal Development of the Hand and Wrist. Stanford University Press, Stanford.

Goodman, P.C., 1995. The new light: discovery and introduction of the X-ray. Am. J. Roentgenol. 165 (5), 1041–1045.

Goodman, N.R., Edelson, L.B., 2002. The efficiency of an X-ray screening system at a mass disaster. J. Forensic Sci. 47 (1), 127–130. .

Gould, P., 2003. X-ray detectives turn images into evidence. Diagn. Imaging (Special Edition) http://www.diagnosticimaging.com/dimag/legacy/specialedition2003/forensics.html.

Ha, A., Lee, A., Hippe, D., Chou, S., Chew, F., 2015. Digital tomosynthesis to evaluate fracture healing: prospective comparison with radiography and CT. Am. J. Roentgenol. 205, 136–141.

Hansman, C.F., 1962. Appearance and fusion of ossification centers in the human skeleton. Am. J. Roentgenol. 88, 476–482.

Harcke, H.T., Bifano, J.A., Koeller, K.K., 2002. Forensic radiology: response to the Pentagon Attack on September 11, 2001. Radiology 223 (1), 7–8.

Hoerr, N.L., Pyle, S.I., Francis, C.C., 1962. Radiological Atlas of the Foot and Ankle. Charles C Thomas, Springfield IL.

Information Governance Alliance, 2016. Records Management Code of Practice for Health and Social Care. Department of Health, London.

International Association of Forensic Radiographers, 2004. Radiography Facilities for Temporary Emergency Mortuaries in the Event of a Mass Fatality Incident. London. www.iafr.org.uk/.

Jensen, S., 1991. Identification of human remains lacking skull and teeth. A case report with some methodological considerations. Am. J. Forensic Med. Pathol. 12 (2), 93–97.

Kahana, T., Hiss, J., 1997. Identification of human remains: forensic radiology. J. Clin. Forensic Med. 4 (1), 7–15.

Kahana, T., Ravioli, J.A., Urroz, C.L., Hiss, J., 1997. Radiographic identification of fragmentary human remains from a mass disaster. Am. J. Forensic Med. Pathol. 18 (1), 40–44.

Kirk, N.J., Wood, R.E., Goldstein, M., 2002. Skeletal identification using the frontal sinus region: a retrospective study of 39 cases. J. Forensic Sci. 47 (2), 318–323.

Krogman, W.M., Iscan, M.Y., 1986. The Human Skeleton in Forensic Medicine, second ed. Charles C Thomas, Springfield.

Kurihara, Y., Kurihara, Y., Ohashi, K., Kitagawa, A., Miyasaka, M., Okamoto, E., Ishikawa, T., 1996. Radiologic evidence of sex differences: is the patient a woman or a man? Am. J. Roentgenol. 167 (4), 1037–1040.

Leth, P., 2007. The use of CT scanning in forensic autopsy. Forensic Sci. Med. Pathol. 3 (1), 65. http://dx.doi.org/10.1385/FSMP.

Levinsohn, 1899. Beitraz zur feststellung der identitat. Arch. Krim. Anthr. 2, 221.

McCormick, W.F., 1980. Mineralization of the costal cartilages as an indicator of age: preliminary observations. J. Forensic Sci. 25 (4), 736–741.

Marlin, D.C., Clark, M.A., Standish, S.M., 1991. Identification of human remains by comparison of frontal sinus radiographs: a series of four cases. J. Forensic Sci. 36 (6), 1765–1772.

Mentzel, H.-J., Vilser, C., Eulenstein, M., Schwartz, T., Vogt, S., Bottcher, J., et al., 2005. Assessment of skeletal age at the wrist in children with a new ultrasound device. Pediatr. Radiol. 35 (4), 429–433.

Mora, S., et al., 2001. Applicability of the Greulich and Pyle standards. Pediatr. Res. 50, 624–812.

Morgan, B., Alminyah, A., Cala, A., O'Donnell, C., Elliott, D., Gorincour, G., Hofman, P., Iino, M., Makino, Y., Moskata, A., Robinson, C., Rutty, G.N., Sajantila, A., Vallis, J., Woodford, N., Woźniak, K., Viner, M.D., May 2014. Use of post-mortem computed tomography in disaster victim identification. Positional statement of the members of the disaster victim identification working group of the International Society of Forensic Radiology and Imaging. J. Forensic Radiol. Imaging 2 (3), 114–116.

Mulligan, M.E., McCarthy, M.J., Wippold, F.J., Lichtenstein, J.E., Wagner, G.N., 1988. Radiologic evaluation of mass casualty victims: lessons from the Gander, Newfoundland, accident. Radiology 168 (1), 229–233.

Murphy, W.A., Spruill, F.G., Gantner, G.E., 1980. Radiologic identification of unknown human remains. J. Forensic Sci. 25 (4), 727–735.

Nambiar, P., Naidu, M.D., Subramaniam, K., 1999. Anatomical variability of the frontal sinuses and their application in forensic identification. Clin. Anat. 12 (1), 16–19.

Navani, S., Shah, J.R., Levy, P.S., 1970. Determination of sex by costal cartilage calcification. Am. J. Roentgenol. 108 (4), 771–774.

NHS England, 2012/2013. NHS Imaging and Radiodiagnostic Activity in England. Department of Health, Leeds, UK.

Nye, P.J., Tytle, T.L., Jarman, R.N., Eaton, B.G., 1996. The role of radiology in the Oklahoma City bombing. Radiology 200 (2), 541–543.

O'Donnell, C., Iino, M., Mansharan, K., Leditscke, J., Woodford, N., 2011. Contribution of postmortem multidetector CT scanning for identification of the deceased in a mass disaster: experience gained from the 2009 Victorian bushfires. Forensic Sci. Int. 205, 15–28.

Pyle, S.I., Hoerr, N.L., 1955. Atlas of Skeletal Development of the Knee. Charles C Thomas, Springfield, IL.

Reichs, K., Dorion, R.B.J., 1992. The use of computed tomography (CT) scans in the analysis of frontal sinus configuration. Can. Soc. Forensic Sci. J. 25, 1.

Rutty, G.N., Robinson, C.E., BouHaidar, R., Jeffery, A.J., Morgan, B., 2007. The role of mobile computed tomography in mass fatality incidents. J. Forensic Sci. 52, 1343–1349.

Rutty, G.N., et al., 2013. Use of radiology in disaster victim identification: positional statement of the members of the disaster victim identification working group of the International Society of Forensic Radiology and Imaging. J. Forensic Radiol. Imaging 1 (4), 218.

Rogers, T., Saunders, S., 1994. Accuracy of sex determination using morphological traits of the human pelvis. J. Forensic Sci. 39 (4), 1047–1056.

Sanders, I., Woesner, M.E., Ferguson, R.A., Noguchi, T.T., 1972. A new application of forensic radiology: identification of deceased from a single clavicle. Am. J. Roentgenol. 115 (3), 619–622.

Scheuer, L., Black, S., 2004. The Juvenile Skeleton. Academic Press, London.

Shimura, N., Koyama, S., Arisaka, O., Imataka, M., Sato, K., Matsuura, M., 2005. Assessment of measurement of children's bone age ultrasonically with Sunlight BonAge. Clin. Pediatr. Endocrinol. 14 (Suppl. 24), 24.

Sutherland, L.D., Suchey, J.M., 1991. Use of the ventral arc in pubic sex determination. J. Forensic Sci. 36 (2), 501–511.

Schwartz, S., Woolridge, E.D., 1977. The use of panoramic radiographs for comparisons in cases of identification. J. Forensic Sci. 22 (1), 145–146.

Tonello, B., 1998. Mass Grave Investigations. Paper Presented at the Imaging Science & Oncology. British Institute of Radiology.

Trotter, M., Gleser, G.C., 1952. Estimation of stature from long bones of American whites and Negroes. Am. J. Phys. Anthropol. 10, 463–514.

Trotter, M., Gleser, G.C., 1958. A re-evaluation of estimation of stature based on measurements of stature taken during life and of ling bones after death. Am. J. Phys. Anthropol. 16, 79–123.

Viner, M.D., Cassidy, M., Treu, V., 1998. The Role of Radiography in a Disaster Investigation. Paper Presented at the Imaging Science and Oncology. British Institute of Radiology.

Viner, M.D., Alminyah, A., Apostol, M., Brough, A., Develter, W., O'Donnell, C., Elliott, D., Heinze, S., Hofman, P., Gorincour, G., Kaur, M., Singh, C., Iino, M., Makino, Y., Moskała, A., Morgan, B., Rutty, G.N., Vallis, J., Villa, C., Woźniak, K., 2015. Use of radiography and fluoroscopy in disaster victim identification – positional statement of the members of the disaster victim identification working group of the International Society of Forensic Radiology and Imaging. J. Forensic Radiol. Imaging 3 (2), 141–145.

Viner, M.D., 2014. The Use of radiology. In: Adams, B., Byrd, J. (Eds.), Mass Fatality Incidents, in Commingled Human Remains: Methods in Recovery, Analysis, and Identification. Academic Press, pp. 87–122.

Viner, M.D., Lichtenstein, J.E., 2011. Radiology in mass casualty situations. In: Thali, M.J., Viner, M.D., Brogdon, B.G. (Eds.), Brogdon's Forensic Radiology, second ed. CRC Press, Boca Raton, FL, pp. 177–198.

Wessling, R., Loe, L., 2011. The fromelles project: organizational and operational structures of a large scale mass grave excavation and on-site anthropological analysis. Paper Presented at the American Academy of Forensic Sciences 63rd Scientific Meeting, Chicago, IL.

CHAPTER 20

Advances in the Use of Frontal Sinuses for Human Identification

Angi M. Christensen[1] | Gary M. Hatch[2]

[1]Federal Bureau of Investigation Laboratory, Quantico, VA, United States
[2]University of New Mexico School of Medicine, Albuquerque, NM, United States

Chapter Outline

■ INTRODUCTION

Development, Anatomy, and Variation of Frontal Sinuses

Formation of the frontal sinuses begins around the fourth or fifth fetal month, with pneumatization reaching the frontal bone by around the second year (Fig. 20.1). The frontal sinuses become more conspicuous in size by the second or third year when their apex often extends above nasion. Further expansion into the vertical portion of the frontal bone begins around the fifth year, with most children over the age of six demonstrating vertical projection radiographically (Brown et al., 1984; Dolan, 1982; Donald et al., 1994; Libersa and Faber, 1958; Maresh, 1940; Prossinger and Bookstein, 2003; Szilvassy, 1973). The main enlargement of the sinuses occurs during puberty with a small additional increase in height several years after this growth spurt in some individuals, and frontal sinus growth is generally completed by the 20th year (Brown et al., 1984; Prossinger and Bookstein, 2003).

In adults, the frontal sinus usually appears as two irregularly shaped and asymmetric cavities extending backward and laterally for a variable distance between the tables of the frontal bone, often separated from each other by a thin bony septum that is usually deflected to one side of the median plane (Fig. 20.2). It is not uncommon for frontal sinuses to extend into the orbital margin of the frontal bone (sometimes called "supraorbital sinuses"), and in some cases, this is the only region where they are present, with no projection into the vertical portion (Cryer, 1907; Schaeffer, 1916; Shapiro and Janzen, 1960). Along the roof and the anterior wall there may be numerous septae of varying lengths, producing recesses and giving the sinuses their scallop-like outlines (Fig. 20.3). With exception of modifications due to injury, disease, and age-related bone thinning, the frontal sinus morphology does not change in adulthood.

Variation is well documented in the size and configuration of frontal sinuses (often measured as dimensions, volume, or cross-sectional area) ranging from absence to extending well into the frontal region or beyond. Two sinus cavities separated by a bony septum (most often located near the midsagittal plane) is the usual configuration, but variations have been reported on the number of sinus cavities present. A small percentage of individuals have been noted to have an unpartitioned central sinus (Quatrehomme et al., 1996). The presence of three or more sinus lobes is considered by some to be quite rare (Phrabhakaran et al., 1999), but others suggest that duplicate and triplicate (Schaeffer, 1916) or even four and five sinus cavities (Cryer, 1907) are quite common.

Since the left and right frontal sinus lobes develop independently, it is not surprising that they display a high degree of asymmetry (Zuckerkandl, 1895), generally attributed to a more rapid development on one side at the expense of the other (Turner, 1902). Occasionally, there is a complete absence or agenesis of one or both of the

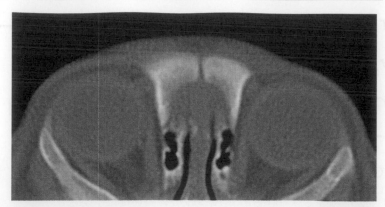

Figure 20.1 Oblique axial postmortem computed tomography image of an 8-week-old infant, demonstrating the lack of pneumatization in the areas of the frontal bone that normally contain the frontal sinuses.

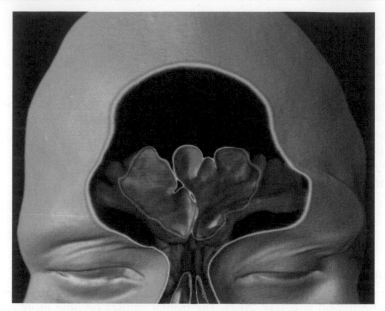

Figure 20.2 Slab volume rendering with opacity and color levels set to display air/tissue interfaces. The "slab" refers to the selection of a portion of the data that is several centimeters thick and, in this case, encompasses the majority of the frontal sinus, but not the anterior sinus or overlying bone and soft tissue (allowing the viewer to "look inside"). This is a view looking at the subject from the front, displaying the relationships of the internal sinus anatomy to recognizable external landmarks.

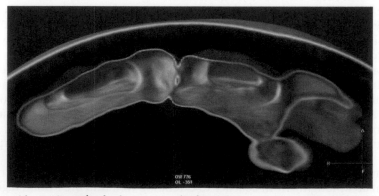

Figure 20.3 Volume rendering with opacity and color levels set to display air/tissue interfaces. This view is looking up into the frontal sinus, displaying the incomplete septae and scalloped superior margins.

frontal sinus lobes. Studies report varying findings but indicate that complete agenesis of the frontal sinus occurs in around 5%–15% of adults and the rate may vary in different geographic groups (Harris et al., 1987b). Estimates of the frequency of unilateral agenesis also vary but suggest that failure of development of one of the frontal sinuses occurs in 1%–15% of adults (Donald et al., 1994).

Variation has been noted in frontal sinus morphology related to sex (Buckland-Wright, 1970; Hanson and Owsley, 1980; Harris et al., 1987b; Schuller, 1943), climate (Koertvelyessy, 1972; Kondrat, 1995), extent of the supraorbital ridges (Hajek, 1926; Samuel and Lloyd, 1978), presence of a metopic suture (Hodgson, 1957; Montiero et al., 1957; Samuel, 1952; Samuel and Lloyd, 1978; Schuller, 1943; Torgersen, 1950; Van Alyea, 1951), acromegaly or cretinism (Schuller, 1943; Shapiro and Janzen, 1960), cranial indices (Gulisano et al., 1987; Strek, 1992; Turner and Porter, 1922), and ancestry (Brothwell et al., 1968; Ikeda, 1980; Turner, 1902).

Examination of Frontal Sinuses

Before the discovery of X-rays and the development of X-ray diagnostic methods, observations of frontal sinuses were limited to those made on cadavers by anatomists. It has now, of course, become possible (and indeed routine) to observe the anatomy of the frontal sinuses using radiologic methods for both the living and deceased. Sinuses may be examined radiologically for either diagnostic purposes or forensic identification applications. The earliest report of the use of radiographs in determining the presence or extent of paranasal sinuses was by Scheuer in 1896 (Maresh, 1940). For radiographs, the occipitofrontal or Caldwell position (Fig. 20.4) was a common clinically utilized position for imaging studies of the frontal sinus and is named for the first person to extensively investigate and report on studying the paranasal sinuses using radiography (Caldwell, 1918). The Water's view, also named for its creator, was another commonly used projection for evaluating the frontal sinus (Fig. 20.4), easily remembered as the resulting image looks as if the patient is treading "water," attempting to keep the nose above the water line.

For quite some time, computed tomography (CT) has been considered the first-line modality of choice for evaluating paranasal sinus disease, particularly when complications are suspected or the patient is refractory to standard medical therapy (Fig. 20.5). It offers the advantages of cross-sectional technique, direct visualization of the mucosa, and excellent visualization of all sinuses and the narrow passageways that drain the individual sinus cavities. The shift in imaging recommendations from radiography of the sinuses to CT means that fewer antemortem images for comparison will be two-dimensional (2D) radiographs. In fact, with the exception of a few outlying clinics and physicians who are practicing decades-old medicine, radiographs of the skull are now only routinely obtained as a part of safety screening prior to magnetic resonance imaging (MRI), to rule out metallic foreign bodies in the orbits. The paucity of antemortem radiograph studies might be an impediment to those practitioners who only have access to or experience with radiography. As explained later in this chapter, methods exist to create radiograph-like images from CT data. Depending on the antemortem scanning protocol used, it may be possible to render suitable images for comparison to postmortem radiographs. Ultrasound has limited utility in this setting and is not indicated or routinely used for the clinical evaluation of the sinuses. While MRI demonstrates excellent detail of the sinonasal mucosa and intrasinus masses, it does not depict the osseous anatomy with the level of detail obtained by CT (Fig. 20.6).

Frontal Sinuses in Identification

It has long been suggested that, due to the known variation in frontal sinus morphology, these structures could be used in personal identification similarly to a fingerprint. In fact, monozygotic twins are even noted to differ in their frontal

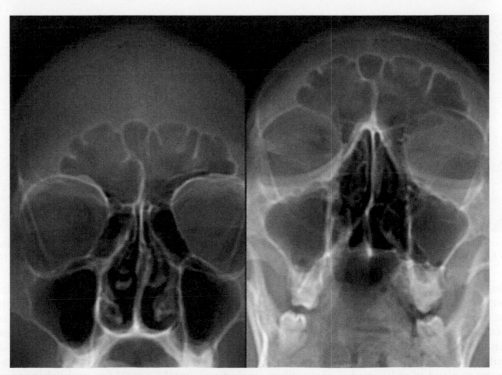

Figure 20.4 Thick slab multiplanar reformatted renderings of the frontal sinuses, oriented to match typical clinical views. The left image approximates the Caldwell view and the right image approximates the Water's view.

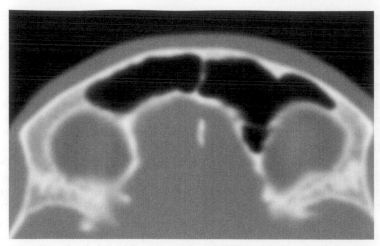

Figure 20.5 Axial postmortem computed tomography view of the frontal sinus, demonstrating a slightly bowed, midline septum.

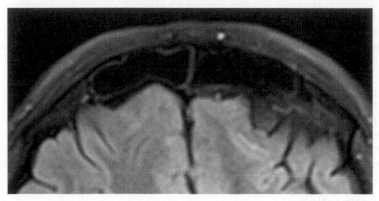

Figure 20.6 Axial magnetic resonance image of the frontal sinus. Although soft tissue, such as the sinonasal mucosa (the thin *gray line* along the inner margin of the frontal sinus) is easily observed, the osseous landmarks are less well depicted than by computed tomography. This is due to the fact that the tightly bound protons in cortical bone do not generate a large amount of signal, relative to the soft tissues.

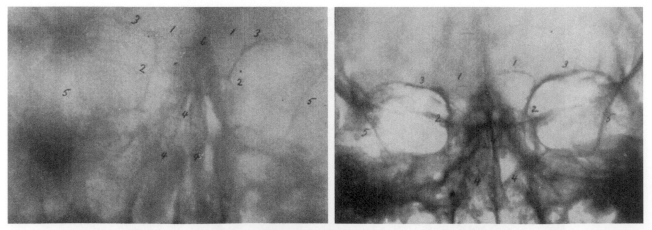

Figure 20.7 Antemortem radiograph (left) and postmortem radiograph (right) from first radiologic identification comparison in 1926. *From Culbert, W.L., Law F.L., 1927. Identification by comparison of roentgenograms of nasal accessory sinuses and mastoid processes. JAMA (88), 1634–1636.*

sinus morphology (Asherson, 1965; Schuller, 1921). The earliest suggestion of the use of radiology in the identification of unknown remains involved the observation that frontal sinus variability could be used for this purpose (Schuller, 1921). The first use of frontal sinus radiographs in identification of human remains dates to 1925 (Culbert and Law, 1927) when frontal sinus radiographs (along with other radiographic details) were compared in the positive identification of an American who was discovered in a river in India and whose body had been disfigured by decomposition, precluding identification by other means (Fig. 20.7). It was the first of its kind to be accepted in American court, setting a precedent for the method of radiographic comparison (including frontal sinuses) for establishing identity.

When the authenticity of postmortem radiographs taken during the autopsy of President John F. Kennedy was questioned by conspiracy theorists, two anthropology consultants, Drs. Ellis Kerley and Clyde Snow, were asked to examine the materials and, if scientifically possible, determine whether or not they were those of the late President. Based on comparisons of frontal skull views, they found that "the outlines of the frontal sinuses of the autopsy X-rays were virtually superimposable on those shown in the clinical X-rays" (Kerley and Snow, 1979).

In addition to these historically significant cases, there have been a number of publications in the forensic and radiological literature describing numerous cases in which identification was established based on frontal sinus comparison (see, for example, Anguyal and Derczy, 1998; Atkins and Potsaid, 1978; Camps, 1969; Cheevers and Ascencio, 1977; Haglund and Fligner, 1993; Harris et al., 1987a; Joblanski and Shum, 1989; Kirk et al., 2002; Marek et al., 1983; Marlin et al., 1991; Murphy and Gantner, 1982; Owsley, 1993; Phrabhakaran et al., 1999; Quatrehomme et al., 1996; Reichs, 1993; Reichs and Dorion, 1992; Stewart, 1979; Ubelaker, 1984; Yoshino et al., 1987; Wood, 2006). Traditionally, these identifications have been made by side-by-side or superimposed 2D radiographic records by a qualified expert (usually a forensic anthropologist, radiologist, or pathologist) who makes a visual assessment as to the agreement (or lack thereof), making a largely subjective judgment as to whether the two radiographs originated from the same individual. These assessments have received wide approval, have been published extensively, and the resulting opinions have been accepted in courts of law (see, for example, State of Tennessee v. David William Cosgrif, III, 2010). It has been demonstrated through the publication of numerous research studies and case reviews that this structure is highly variable and useful in personal identification (see, for example, Xavier et al., 2015).

In some cases, frontal sinus comparisons have been made by superimposing antemortem and postmortem images rather than side-by-side comparison (for example, Cheevers and Ascencio, 1977; Iino et al., 2013), the idea being that two images that can be superimposed must "match" and belong to the same person. Hashim et al. (2015), however, highlight problems in the superimposition approach, specifically that two 2D images obtained at different times are not superimposable even if they are derived from the same 2D source, and moreover that superimposition generates a mixed image that can lead to the illusion of a match.

Many studies note improved performance of visual comparison methods by observers with more training and experience in radiology, radiographic analysis, etc. Other studies have noted that mismatches are rare, even among untrained observers (Kullman et al., 1990). Many do support the need for trained interpreters in identification cases (including Hogge et al., 1993; Koot, 2003; Messmer, 1986; Murphy et al., 1980). It has been suggested, however, the technique would be enhanced by a methodology that did not depend solely on the expertise of the user, but which was standardized and repeatable by other forensic scientists (Wang et al., 2012; Christensen and Crowder, 2009; Cox et al., 2009). To date, however, there are no objective, reproducible comparison methods that are well accepted within forensic radiology or anthropology.

Frontal Sinuses in Sex and Ancestry Estimation

In addition to radiologic comparisons, frontal sinuses can potentially be used in the identification process as part of the biological profile used to narrow the pool of potential matches since variation in frontal sinus size and configuration has been noted for males and females as well as different ancestral groups. Earlier studies reported mixed results in regard to male and female dimensions and features such as scalloping, with some reporting greater dimensions and scalloping in males, and others in females (e.g., Buckland-Wright, 1970; Hajek, 1926; Harris et al., 1987b; Yoshino et al., 1987; Krogman and Iscan, 1986; Schuller, 1943; Hanson and Owsley, 1980). More recent studies seem to confirm that males have significantly greater frontal sinus dimensions in most groups examined. Hamed et al. (2014) found significant differences in frontal sinus dimensions between males and females as measured from axial and coronal CT scans in an Egyptian population. Kim et al. (2013) found significant differences between men and women in a variety of metric (total volume, width, height, depth, angle) and nonmetric (bilateral asymmetry, sinus shape) traits of three-dimensional (3D) frontal sinus images in a Korean sample. In a French sample using frontal volume from CT scans, Michel et al. (2015) found significant sex differences in male and female frontal sinus volume and achieved a 72.5% correct sex classification. Sai kiran et al. (2014) found significant sex differences in an Indian population utilizing lateral radiographs of the frontal sinus from which an index was developed based on maximum height and maximum width, developing a discriminant function equation that predicted sex with about 68% overall accuracy. Uthman et al. (2010) using frontal sinus measurements (width, height, and anterior-posterior length) achieved a sex discrimination accuracy of 76.9% in an Iraqi sample, which increased to 85.9% when skull measurements (maximum length, prosthio-bregmatic height, and maximum width) were used. One study (Michel et al., 2015) examined frontal sinus volume and age and found no correlation.

Although there are currently no established methods for reliably assessing ancestry from frontal sinuses, intergroup variability has been noted for many features of the frontal sinuses, with some studies suggesting an environmental or climatic factor contributing to their configuration or size (Koertvelyessy, 1972; Kondrat, 1995). For example, frontal sinuses are reported to be frequently absent in Australian Aborigines (Turner, 1902), while Africans often have well-developed sinuses (Brothwell et al., 1968). Alaskan Eskimos are reported to have relatively small sinus surface areas with a high frequency of bilateral absence while West Hudson Bay Eskimos are reported to have sinus surface areas smaller than Alaskans (Hanson and Owsley, 1980).

■ RECENT ADVANCES IN IDENTIFICATION USING FRONTAL SINUSES

Recent developments in the use of frontal sinuses in human identification are generally related to advances in imaging techniques and the use of quantified (versus strictly visual) methods of comparison. In addition, frontal sinuses records were admitted into evidence after a challenge on appeal by opposing counsel in a case of identification in a state court, highlighting the reliability and validity of this approach. These developments are reviewed in the next section.

Quantitative Comparisons

Although visual comparisons of frontal sinus morphology were traditionally (and by many still are) considered valid, various changes in the scientific, political, and legal landscapes including the *Daubert* ruling (Daubert, 1993), the National Academy of Sciences Report (National Academy of Sciences, 2009), and the recent formation of the National Institute of Standards and Technology's (NIST's) Organization of Scientific Area Committees (OSAC) (NIST, n.d.) are prompting a shift in the approach to identification sciences. Specifically, methods of personal identification should be objective, standardized, and repeatable by other experts. Some have argued that perhaps it is unnecessary or even detrimental to try to quantify pattern comparisons such as radiologic images. Jayaprakash (2013), for example, argues that since visual methods are successful in achieving correct pattern matches, it may be unnecessary to force qualitative techniques into quantifiable categories, and it may inadvertently lessen the effectiveness of conclusions. The human brain can likely process and distinguish far more detail in a radiologic image than could ever be potentially quantified. The trend toward standardization and quantification in identification sciences, however, seems to be gaining momentum and is certainly useful for identifying minimum levels of confidence.

Standardized comparison methods, however, have not traditionally been used in frontal sinus comparisons. Many claims of the individualized nature of frontal sinus morphology stem from observations of numerous radiographs and failing to find two that were identical, at least in the opinion of the observer [Asherson, 1965; Cryer, 1907; Culbert and Law, 1927; Poole (from Mayer, 1935); Schuller, 1921]. Although it has been shown that the probability of misidentification based on visual or superimposed comparisons is very low (e.g., Smith et al., 2010; Besana and Rogers, 2010), the final identification decision in visual comparisons is subjective and based largely on the knowledge, experience, and ability of the examiner. Moreover, such assessments do not permit the statistical assessment of the probability of two individuals possessing indistinguishable frontal sinus morphologies or to estimate the probability of misidentification.

Early attempts at standardized comparison methods involved quantification of sinus morphology using code systems for various attributes (e.g., Yoshino et al., 1987; Reichs and Dorion, 1992). Most proposed systems were based on a number of basic characteristic features of the frontal sinuses including the presence or absence of one or both lobes, size (codified by height, breadth, or cross-sectional area), symmetry/asymmetry, and position/number of septa (Marek et al., 1983; Reichs and Dorion, 1992; Ribeiro, 2000; Schuller, 1943; Yoshino et al., 1987). These methods were novel in their standardized approach to describing frontal sinuses but had a number of limitations.

Yoshino et al. (1987), for example, developed a coding system in which a frontal sinus pattern could be divided into a formula code based on area size, bilateral asymmetry, superiority of side, outline of upper border (left and right), partial septa, and supraorbital cells. The coding system resulted in more than 20,000 possible combinations for describing a frontal sinus. Because the code does not address morphology per se, however, differently shaped frontal sinuses could result in the same code. Tang et al. (2009) applied the Yoshino coding system to a Chinese sample and found 3 of 165 individuals shared the same code (Tang et al., 2009). Moreover, certain frontal sinus characteristics may covary. A 2010 study (Besana and Rogers, 2010) confirmed that many sinus traits are linked, and it is therefore problematic to use trait combinations in probability assessments.

Performance of coding systems are somewhat improved if specific frontal sinus measurements are considered. Tatlisumak et al. (2007) developed a coding system based on just three general features of frontal sinuses features (presence/absence, septum, scalloping) as seen in CT scans of a Turkish population. Based on these features alone, 93% of matches in their sample could be excluded. When three measurements were also considered (frontal sinus width, height, and anterior-posterior length), successful exclusions increased to 98%. Uthman et al. (2010) found good inter- and intraobserver reliability of the Tatlisumak method. Cameriere et al. (2008) further confirmed that using a coding system, few false positives were made, even among related individuals.

It has been stated that the greater the number of shared peculiarities between the antemortem and postmortem records, the greater the probability that the identification is correct (Dutra, 1944; Fischman, 1985). This "number of concordant points" approach, however, has been shown to lack validity (Acharya and Taylor, 2003) and has since been largely abandoned. More important in forensic identification sciences is how common or rare the shared trait is or its population frequency (Christensen and Hatch, 2016). An identification can confidently be based on even a single bony feature if that feature is sufficiently rare (Brogdon, 1998; Messmer, 1986). Note that it is not necessary to show that a trait is "unique," and it has been argued that this would be mathematically and philosophically impossible to achieve (Page et al., 2011). The task of comparing frontal sinus morphology, thus, is not to answer whether an outline is unique or whether two frontal sinus outlines are identical, but whether there is sufficient evidence to suggest that they originated from the same individual. Also important in forensic identification sciences is that the comparison methods are objective and repeatable (Christensen and Crowder, 2009). This can often be facilitated through the use of quantitative approaches, which can also be used to estimate the probability of misidentification.

One of the first methods to statistically assess variation in frontal sinus outline shape and to estimate the probability of correctly matching frontal sinuses used elliptic Fourier analysis (EFA) of more than 500 frontal sinus outlines to characterize shape and calculate likelihood ratios (Christensen, 2004, 2005). The approach used simulated "antemortem" and postmortem radiographs which were taken using the same protocols but at different times which introduced some positional variation which would be expected in a forensic context. Frontal sinus outlines, with an arbitrary inferior delineation, were digitized, with x- and y-coordinates assigned to each pixel along the outline (Fig. 20.8).

EFA is a procedure that can fit a closed curve to an ordered set of data points and with a desired degree of precision using an orthogonal decomposition of a curve into a sum of harmonically related ellipses (Kuhl and Giardina, 1982). The algorithm does not require the points to be equally spaced, and the ellipses can be combined to approximate practically any closed plan curve arbitrarily well given enough harmonics (Ferson et al., 1985). For these reasons, EFA (vs., for example, Procrustes) is well suited to structures such as frontal sinuses which do not share homologous landmarks. EFA generates four coefficients that are treated as a set of shape descriptors that can be used for variables in discriminatory or other multivariate analyses (Bookstein et al., 1982). In the Christensen (2004, 2005) study, EFA coefficients were computed using EFAWin (Isaev, 1995), and the coefficients were used to calculate likelihood ratios that represent the probability of the hypotheses is true (i.e., that the frontal sinus outlines belong to the same individual) versus the probability supposing the evidence is false (i.e., that the frontal sinus outlines belong to different individuals). In this study, the odds of a match given the correct identification were significantly greater than the odds of a match from the population at large (Fig. 20.9).

This approach, however, also has limitations to its application. Most notable is the fact that the method is statistically complex, and therefore cumbersome to apply. A reference data set of frontal sinus outlines for comparison is also needed. Cox et al. (2009) attempted to improve upon this approach by simplifying the software and calculations involved. Using archaeological, contemporary, and clinical samples, traced frontal sinus outlines were scanned and imported into Adobe Photoshop. Corresponding origin-to-border measurements of each frontal sinus outline were taken from an established fixed origin, and differences between two outlines were assessed as the sum of the differences of these corresponding measurements. Results were very favorable with an error rate of 0% achieved using the

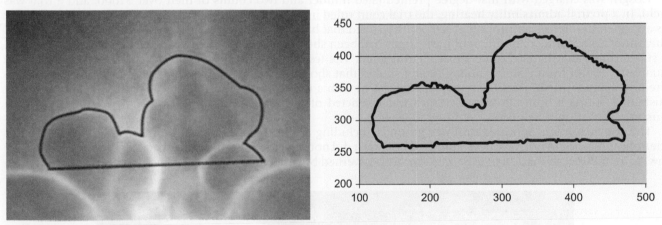

Figure 20.8 Frontal sinus outlined (left) and digitized (right). *From Christensen, A.M., 2003. An Empirical Examination of Frontal Sinus Outline Variability Using Elliptic Fourier Analysis: Implications for Identification, Standardization, and Legal Admissibility (Doctoral Dissertation). The University of Tennessee, Knoxville, TN.*

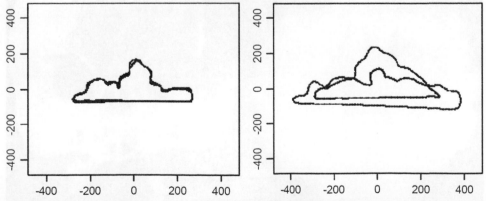

Figure 20.9 Simulated antemortem and postmortem outlines from the same individual (left) and outlines from two different individuals (right). *From Christensen, A.M., 2003. An Empirical Examination of Frontal Sinus Outline Variability Using Elliptic Fourier Analysis: Implications for Identification, Standardization, and Legal Admissibility (Doctoral Dissertation). The University of Tennessee, Knoxville, TN.*

study sample. A major criticism of this study, however (Arora et al., 2012), is that the simulated antemortem and postmortem radiographs were not from different radiographs, but were duplicate tracings. This approach would likely result in inflated match success rates.

Another recent study (Atit et al., 2015) used Euclidian distances and log-likelihood ratio values using a sample of 40 crania and found good discrimination between matched and nonmatched individuals. As with the approach by Christensen, however, these methods rely on a specific reference data set and no method is offered for the comparison of antemortem and postmortem images in an isolated comparison case. Moreover, all of the above studies use 2D images of a 3D structure. Wang et al. (2012) developed a quantification comparison approach involving 16 univariate functions obtained from CT scans, 12 of which were found to be significant for identity determination ($P < .001$), resulting in 65%–90% identification accuracy based on single measurements. Using four variables, a formula was developed for identity determination that resulted in an error rate of 0% on their sample.

Admissibility Challenges to Frontal Sinus Identification

Although routinely accepted as valid by forensic practitioners and within the medicolegal system, frontal sinus identification recently experienced a legal challenge in a state court and indeed appears to be the only instance of a radiologic/anthropological identification comparison being the subject of an admissibility hearing (Lesciotto, 2015). A 76-year-old woman, Kathleen Taylor, mysteriously disappeared from her Tennessee home in 2001. David William Cosgrif III, who was a friend of Taylor's grandson who lived with Taylor, aroused police suspicion by staying in the house after Taylor disappeared, using her debit card, driving her vehicle, forging checks on her bank account, and offering various accounts for his presence on Taylor's property and her whereabouts. In 2003, a hunter discovered skeletal remains and notified the police. The remains were turned over to Dr. Lee Meadows Jantz of the University of Tennessee's Forensic Anthropology Center for analysis. Dr. Jantz determined that the remains were from a human female of European ancestry who was at least 60 years of age. She further noted the presence of healed nasal bone fractures, unhealed perimortem blunt trauma to the left side of the face and skull, and estimated that the remains had been at the site for 1–5 years. No dental records for Taylor were available for comparison, but a clinical frontal sinus X-ray was available. Dr. Jantz concluded that the remains belonged to Taylor based on comparison of the antemortem and postmortem images of the frontal sinus (Fig. 20.10).

Cosgrif was charged with first-degree premeditated murder and two counts of theft over $1000, and a trial was held. In a pretrial admissibility hearing, the trial court ruled in favor of admitting Dr. Jantz's findings and testimony as an expert in forensic anthropology. Dr. Jantz testified that based on numerous published studies in peer-reviewed literature, frontal sinuses of different individuals had been shown to vary at a highly significant level, making them a statistically valid method of personal identification. The testimony relied heavily on recent developments in the quantification of frontal sinus variability and studies that show a low probability of misidentification. In addition, the noted antemortem nasal fractures were consistent with a radiologist's report on fractures that Taylor previously sustained during a home invasion. Cosgrif was convicted of second-degree murder and sentenced to 20 years in prison.

The conviction was appealed on three grounds, including a challenge Dr. Jantz's testimony on the frontal sinus identification should not have been admitted because it did not meet reliability indicia for admission under Tennessee law. In Tennessee, admission of expert testimony is governed by the Tennessee Rules of Evidence 702 and 703, which

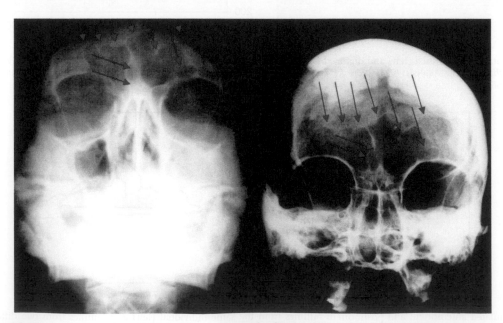

Figure 20.10 Comparison of antemortem clinical radiograph of Taylor (left) and postmortem image of remains (right).

are based to large extent on the Federal Rules of Evidence, and factors largely taken from the Daubert ruling apply. It was concluded by the court that Dr. Jantz's testimony was admissible, and the conviction was held on appeal though the sentence was reduced to 15 years. The fact that recent studies on frontal sinus variability have employed objective, statistically based approaches likely facilitated the admissibility of this evidence; subjective visual methods may have been viewed more skeptically.

Imaging and Software Advances

As mentioned, CT is the modern workhorse for clinically evaluating the paranasal sinuses. Adjustment of antemortem and postmortem CT for identification comparisons is generally not problematic. Wang et al. (2012), for example, achieved alignment of antemortem and postmortem CT scans using Amira to translate, rotate, and adjust images based on defined landmarks. Gross matching was performed by "fit to points" and then fine-tuned using minute adjustment commands. Continued maturation of the scanning technology and the software that supports it has probably been one of the most significant developments in radiologic identification, including the use of frontal sinus CTs (for example, see Hatch et al., 2014) (Fig. 20.11).

Although the use of CT is increasing, the antemortem data used in many identification comparisons are often-times still standard 2D radiographs, less recent CT technology, or different imaging protocols (especially for forensic anthropologists involved in many older or "cold cases"). It has been demonstrated, however, that differences in imaging modalities and orientations can be rather easily overcome. For example, there are many techniques for approximating antemortem radiographs using postmortem CT (Pfaeffli et al., 2007). In one early approach, Riepert et al. (1995, 2001) used CT data of frontal sinuses to approximate conventional X-rays for comparison using the Forensic X-ray Simulation and Identification System, which calculates conventional X-ray summation images using CT data records. 3D volume renderings can also be used to create images that closely match the appearance of radiographs, enabling comparison of antemortem radiographs to postmortem CT data (Kim et al., 2013). Slab multiplanar reformatted (MPR) CTs can also be made to approximate a "pseudoradiograph" (Fig. 20.12).

Cross-sectional 3D imaging allows for complete visualization of the entire volume of the frontal sinuses and can be manually adjusted, using a rendering technique called MPR, to match the orientation and slice thickness of antemortem imaging, which can vary depending on the patient positioning, modality, and the imaging protocol used (Hatch et al., 2014) (Fig. 20.13). Importantly, sinus CT clearly depicts additional structures such as the sphenoid and ethmoid sinuses and mastoid air cells that are more difficult to adequately visualize radiographically, making considerably larger numbers of anatomic sites available for comparison.

Other CT technologies have also been shown to be useful in visualizing and assessing features of frontal sinuses. One review (Sarment and Christensen, 2014) highlighted the potential of cone beam computed tomography (CBCT) in forensic applications. CBCT is a variant of conventional medical CT that utilizes a rotating X-ray source and opposing detectors and is most commonly used in maxillofacial applications. While conventional CT utilizes small detectors to construct an image in the long axis of the patent, CBCT images are obtained with one rotation on high-quality panels. CBCT offers several technical and practical advantages including portability, smaller size, lower cost, high spatial resolution for skeletal imaging, rapid results, low radiation, and minimal training for operation. Because it is most often used in cranial imaging, the likelihood is high that the frontal sinuses might be captured in the course of routine maxillofacial or otolaryngology investigation and may later be useful for forensic identification purposes (Fig. 20.14). It is also possible to extract from CBCT data cephalometric or frontal views for comparison to conventional X-rays.

Industrial and other forms of alternative CT represent other imaging technologies that can be useful in assessing frontal sinus morphology. Although most people associate CT with medical and dental applications, these are not

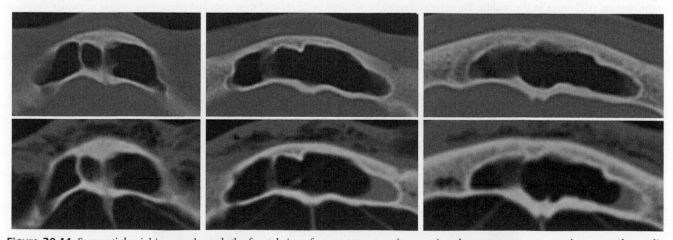

Figure 20.11 Sequential axial images through the frontal sinus from antemortem (top row) and postmortem computed tomography studies used to perform an identification in a case of a badly decomposed body discovered in a secured home. The postmortem computed tomography images were carefully adjusted to match the orientation of the antemortem scan using multiplanar reformatting. The morphology of the frontal sinuses match perfectly. Additionally, the remaining paranasal sinuses (maxillary, ethmoid, and sphenoid) were matched.

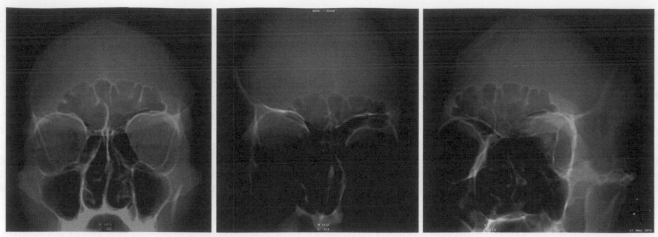

Figure 20.12 Slab multiplanar reformatting of the frontal sinus rendered to appear like a radiograph (the "pseudoradiograph"). The left image depicts a frontal view. This view can be adjusted at will using the rotate tool present in 3D visualization software. The middle image depicts slight rotation to the subject's left (image right). The right image depicts a more significant rotation to the subject's right (image left). In this manner, and with relative ease, postmortem computed tomography images can be adjusted to precisely match the orientation of antemortem radiographs.

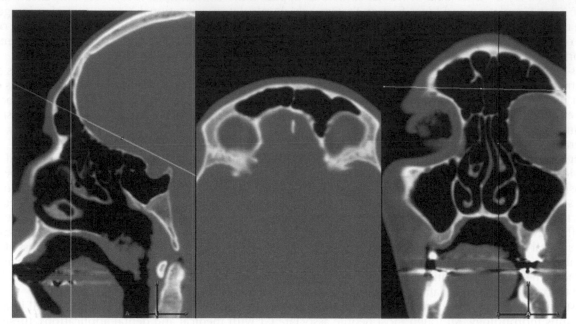

Figure 20.13 Multiplanar reformatted images of the frontal sinuses. The colored lines in the left-hand and right-hand images show the plane of the oblique axial image in the middle. These localizers can be adjusted by "grabbing" their ends and moving the mouse to change the plane of the cut as desired.

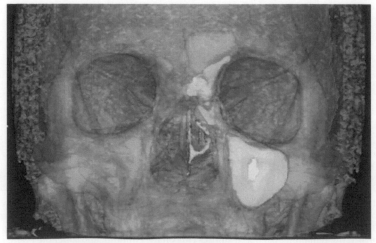

Figure 20.14 Frontal and maxillary sinus captured in cone beam computed tomography, with sinus volume extracted using associated software. *From Sarment, D.P., Christensen, A.M., 2014. The use of cone beam computed tomography in forensic radiology. J. Forensic Radiol. Imaging (2), 173–181.*

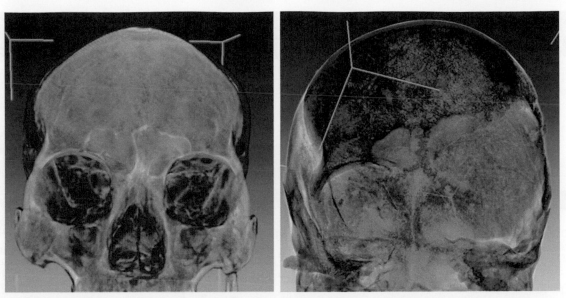

Figure 20.15 The frontal sinuses are easily visualized in this cranium (left) and partial cranium (right) using industrial computed tomography.

the only markets for CT. CT is used to examine internal structures and components in a wide variety of industries including security, aerospace, automotive, metrology, reverse engineering, electronics, food, manufacturing, explosives, military and defense, and forensic science. Virtually all of the devices used in these industries, some of which are capable of penetrating and examining extremely dense materials, can be adjusted to parameters suitable for examining bone (a comparatively light material). Medical CTs are commonly limited to certain dosages or tailored to specific diagnostic applications. Given that health concerns (e.g., radiation) of the subject are not a concern in postmortem computed tomography, alternative CT technologies permit longer scan times and allow for greater versatility in terms of the analytical parameters used. For example, the use of high intensity, microfocus X-ray sources on industrial CTs permit improved resolution and greater penetration of dense objects such as dental fillings, and frontal sinus imaging can be quite detailed (Fig. 20.15). Some scanners are capable of resolving much finer details than a typical medical CT scanner, including units with resolutions of less than 500 nm. As with other types of CT, the operator also has substantial control of the resulting image's brightness, contrast, and opacity.

Advanced Quantification/Automation

Although generally considered reliable structures for forensic identification, frontal sinus comparison has historically been (and most often is still) performed as a subjective visual assessment of image similarity. It is clear that quantified approaches are preferable from both a scientific and legal standpoint, and that population frequencies could form the basis for robust (even if lower threshold) confidence limits on the evidentiary value of a match. A major limitation of the implementation of population frequency data, however, is the need for documented population frequency data that are often either unavailable for certain radiologic traits or difficult to locate in others. In an effort to resolve this problem, a population frequency data repository, "the RADid Resource," was recently developed and made publicly available (Christensen and Hatch, 2016). The repository consists of a compilation of published population frequencies of various radiologic traits to which practitioners can refer to access currently available frequency data. Data are organized by body region, and information includes (where available) the original research/citation details, specific anatomy assessed, details of the study population, and the frequency of the trait examined (Fig. 20.16).

For the most part, the repository consist of data on traits that are either present or absent in the study population (for example, a dorsal patellar defect). An analysis of frontal sinus absence rates in various population groups is currently underway and will be added to the repository upon completion. For traits such as frontal sinuses where the configuration of the structure may be more informative than its presence or absence, additional study is needed on how to best assess the population frequency of a particular configuration. Future databases or repositories may need to include a large collection of reference structures for comparison, to which individual cases can be compared.

Advances in quantifying frontal sinus comparisons have significantly improved the value of frontal sinus identification comparisons, but automated comparison methods would even further facilitate and bolster the evidentiary strength of these analyses. Although not (yet) applied to frontal sinus, one computer-assisted approach to identification was tested by Derrick et al. (2015, 2017) and found excellent results for matching vertebral body shape while also calculating error rates. Part to part analysis, used routinely for quality control in industry, may also be applicable (Decker, 2016). This technology involves automated, quantifiable comparison of two 3D models created from CT data sets, aligned using a best fit method or predefined landmarks. Results are displayed in a color-coded model showing deviations between the models. Such approaches could conceivably be utilized to compare frontal sinuses as well.

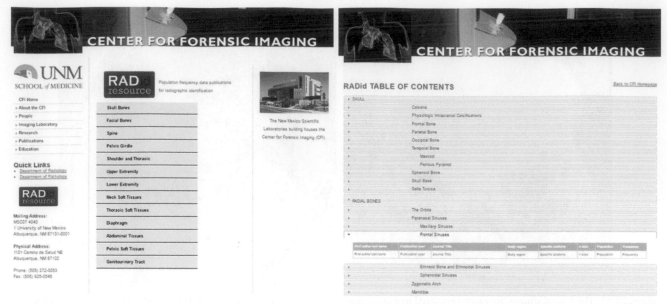

Figure 20.16 Screen captures from the RADid Resource. The user will be able to select their structure of interest from the anatomic regions listed in the left image. The right image displays a more detailed outline where individual studies are summarized for reference. This work in progress will enable practitioners to easily access population frequency data from disparate literature sources and across multiple disciplines.

The use of any identification method is dependent on the condition of the body. For example, a badly crushed skull may distort the frontal sinuses to such a degree that identification is impossible or at minimum would require either physical or digital skull reconstruction prior to comparison. Additionally, the availability of antemortem information about the supposed deceased for comparison may limit identification possibilities, regardless of the postmortem techniques employed.

■ CONCLUSION

The use of frontal sinuses in personal identification has a long history, dating back to the 1920s. Since that time, it has been the subject of numerous research analyses and case studies and is now widely recognized as a useful and reliable method of identification. Advances in imaging as well as quantified approaches have further verified and enhanced its application, and frontal sinuses will continue to be a valid approach in forensic identification.

Disclaimer

The views expressed are those of the authors and do not necessarily reflect the official policy or position of the FBI. Names of commercial manufacturers are provided for identification purposes only, and inclusion does not imply endorsement of the manufacturer or its products or services by the FBI.

References

Acharya, A.B., Taylor, J.A., 2003. Are a minimum number of concordant matches needed to establish identify in forensic odontology? J. Forensic Odontostomatol. 21 (1), 6–13.

Angyal, M., Derczy, K., 1998. Personal identification on the basis of antemortem and postmortem radiographs. J. Forensic Sci. 43, 1089–1093.

Arora, V., Gaunkar, R.B., Fareed, W.M., Nath, D.K., Gupta, N.K., Gupta, W., 2012. Commentary on Cox et al. 2009. J. Forensic Sci. 57 (6), 1679.

Asherson, N., 1965. Identification by Frontal Sinus Prints. H.K. Lewis, London.

Atit, P., Zambrano, C.J., Pampush, J.D., 2015. Quantification of frontal sinus morphology from radiographs for positive identification. In: Proceedings of the 67th Annual Meeting of the American Academy of Forensic Sciences.

Atkins, L., Potsaid, M.S., 1978. Roentgenographic identification of human remains. JAMA 240, 2307–2308.

Besana, J.L., Rogers, T.L., 2010. Personal identification using the frontal sinus. J. Forensic Sci. 55 (3), 584–589.

Bookstein, F.L., Strauss, R.E., Humphries, J.M., Chernoff, B., Elder, R.L., Smith, G.R., 1982. A comment upon the uses of Fourier methods in systematics. Syst. Zool. 31, 85–92.

Brogdon, B.G., 1998. Forensic Radiology. CRC Press, New York, NY.

Brothwell, D.R., Molleson, T., Metreweli, C., 1968. Radiological aspects of normal variation in earlier skeletons: an exploratory study. In: Brothwell, D.R. (Ed.), The Skeletal Biology of Earlier Human Populations. Pergamon Press, New York, pp. 149–172.

Brown, W.A.B., Molleson, T.I., Chinn, S., 1984. Enlargement of the frontal sinus. Ann. Hum. Biol. 11, 221–226.

Buckland-Wright, J.C., 1970. A radiographic examination of frontal sinuses in early British populations. Man 5, 512–517.

Caldwell, E.W., 1918. Skiagraphy of the accessory sinuses of the nose. Am. J. Radiol. 5, 569–574.

Cameriere, R., Ferrante, L., Molleson, T., Brown, B., 2008. Frontal sinus accuracy in identification as measured by false positives in kin groups. J. Forensic Sci. 53 (6), 1280–1282.

Camps, F.E., 1969. Radiology and its forensic application. In: Camps, F.E. (Ed.), Recent Advances in Forensic Pathology. J. & A. Churchill, London, pp. 149–160.

Cheevers, L.S., Ascencio, R., 1977. Identification by skull superimposition. Int. J. Forensic Dent. 13, 14–16.

Christensen, A.M., Hatch, G.M., 2016. Quantification of radiologic identification: development of a population frequency data repository. In: 68th Annual Meeting of the American Academy of Forensic Sciences, Las Vegas.

Christensen, A.M., 2004. The impact of Daubert: implications for testimony and research in forensic anthropology (and the use of frontal sinuses in personal identification). J. Forensic Sci. 49 (3), 1–4.

Christensen, A.M., 2005. Testing the reliability of frontal sinuses in positive identification. J. Forensic Sci. 50 (1), 1–5.

Christensen, A.M., Crowder, C.M., 2009. Evidentiary standards for forensic anthropology. J. Forensic Sci. 54 (6), 1211–1216.

Cox, M., Malcolm, M., Faigrieve, S.I., 2009. A new digital method for the objective comparison of frontal sinuses for identification. J. Forensic Sci. 54 (4), 761–772.

Cryer, M.H., 1907. Some variations in the frontal sinuses. JAMA 48, 284–289.

Culbert, W.L., Law, F.L., 1927. Identification by comparison of roentgenograms of nasal accessory sinuses and mastoid processes. JAMA 88, 1634–1636.

Daubert V. Merrell Dow Pharmaceuticals, Inc., 509 U.S. 579, 1993.

Derrick, S.M., Raxter, M.H., Hipp, J.A., Goel, P., Chan, E.F., Love, J.C., Wiersema, J.M., Akella, N.S., 2015. Development of a computer-assisted forensic radiographic identification method using the lateral cervical and lumbar spine. J. Forensic Sci. 60 (1), 5–12.

Derrick, S.M., Hipp, J.A., Goel, P., 2017. The computer-assisted decedent identification method of computer-assisted radiographic identification. In: Latham, K.A., Bartelink, E., Finnegan, M. (Eds.), New Perspectives in Forensic Human Skeletal Identification, Elsevier/Academic Press (in this volume).

Decker, S.J., 2016. Part-to-part comparison of computed tomographic (CT) three-dimensional (3D) reconstructions for forensic identification. In: Presented at the 5th Annual Meeting of the International Society of Forensic Radiology and Imaging, Amsterdam, Netherlands.

Dolan, K.D., 1982. Paranasal sinus radiology part 1A: Introduction and the frontal sinuses. Head Neck Surg 4, 301–311.

Donald, P.J., Gluckman, J.L., Rice, D.H., 1994. The Sinuses. Raven Press, New York.

Dutra, F.T., 1944. Identification of person and determination of cause of death from skeletal remains. Arch. Path. 38, 339–349.

Ferson, S.F., Rohlf, F.J., Koehn, R.K., 1985. Measuring shape variation of two-dimensional outlines. Syst. Zool. 34, 59–68.

Fischman, S.L., 1985. The use of medical and dental radiographs in identification. Int. Dent. J. 35, 301–306.

Gulisano, M., Pacini, P., Orlandini, G.E., Colosi, G., 1987. Anatomico-radiological findings on the frontal sinus: statistical study of 520 human cases. Arch. Ital. Anat. Embriol. 83, 9–32.

Haglund, W.D., Fligner, C.L., 1993. Confirmation of human identification using computerized tomography (CT). J. Forensic Sci. 38, 708–712.

Hajek, M., 1926. Normal anatomy of the frontal sinuses. In: Hajek, M., Heitger, J.D. (Eds.), Pathology and Treatment of the Inflammatory Diseases of the Nasal Accessory Sinuses, fifth ed. The C.V. Mosby Company, St. Louis, pp. 35–43.

Hamed, S.S., El-Badrawy, A.M., Fattah, S.A., 2014. Gender identification from frontal sinus using multi-detector computed tomography. J. Forensic Radiol. Imaging 2, 117–120.

Hanson, C.L., Owsley, D.W., 1980. Frontal sinus size in Eskimo populations. Am. J. Phys. Anthr. 53, 251–255.

Harris, A.M., Wood, R.E., Nortje, C.J., Thomas, C.J., 1987a. The frontal sinus: a forensic fingerprint? A pilot study. J. Forensic Odontostomatol. 5, 9–15.

Harris, A.M., Wood, R.E., Nortje, C.J., Thomas, C.J., 1987b. Gender and ethnic differences of the radiographic image of the frontal region. J. Forensic Odontostomatol. 5, 51–57.

Hashim, N., Hemalatha, N., Thangaraj, K., Kareem, A., Ahmed, A., Hasan, N.F., Jayaprakash, P.T., 2015. Practical relevance of prescribing superimposition for determining a frontal sinus pattern match. Forensic Sci. Int. 253 137-e1–137-e7.

Hatch, G.M., Dedouit, F., Christensen, A.M., Thali, M.J., Ruder, T.D., 2014. RADid: a pictorial review of radiologic identification using postmortem CT. J. Forensic Radiol. Imaging 2, 52–59.

Hodgson, G., 1957. third ed. A Text-book of X-ray Diagnosis, vol. 1. H.K. Lewis, London.

Hogge, J.P., Messmer, J.M., Doan, Q.N., 1993. Radiographic identification of unknown human remains and interpreter experience level. J. Forensic Sci. 39, 373–377.

Ikeda, J., 1980. Interpopulation variations of the frontal sinus measurements: comparison between the Jamon and recent Japanese population. J. Anthr. Soc. Nippon. 90 (Suppl).

Iino, M., Fujimoto, H., Yoshida, M., Matsumoto, H., Matoba, R., 2013. Identification of a jawless skull by superimposing AM and PM CT images. J. Forensic Radiol. Imaging 1, 83–84.

EFAWin Isaev, M., 1995. Morphometrics at SUNY Stony Brook. http://life.bio.sunysb.edu/morph/.

Jablonski, N.G., Shum, B.S., 1989. Identification of unknown human remains by comparison of antemortem and postmortem radiographs. Forensic Sci. Int. 42, 221–230.

Jayaprakash, P.T., 2013. Practical relevance of pattern uniqueness in forensic science. Forensic Sci. Int. 231 403-e1–403-e16.

Kerley, E.R., Snow, C.C., 1979. Authentication of John F. Kennedy autopsy radiographs and photographs. In: Final Report to the Select Committee on Assassinations, U.S. House of Representatives March 9.

Kim, D.-I., Lee, U.-Y., Park, S.-O., Kwak, D.-S., Han, S.-H., 2013. Identification using frontal sinus by three-dimensional reconstruction from computed tomography. J. Forensic Sci. 58 (1), 5–12.

Kirk, N.J., Wood, R.E., Goldstein, M., 2002. Skeletal identification using the frontal sinus region: a retrospective study of 39 cases. J. Forensic Sci. 47 (2), 318–323.

Koertvelyessy, T., 1972. Relationships between the frontal sinus and climatic conditions: a skeletal approach to cold adaptation. Am. J. Phys. Anthr. 37, 161–172.

Kondrat, J.W., 1995. Frontal Sinus Morphology: An Analysis of Craniometric and Environmental Variables on the Morphology of Modern Human Frontal Sinus Patterns (thesis). Northern Illinois University, Dekalb (IL).

Koot, M.G., 2003. Radiographic human identification using the bones of the hand: a validation study. In: Proceedings of the 55th Annual Meeting of the American Academy of Forensic Sciences February 17-22, Chicago.

Krogman, W.M., Iscan, M.Y., 1986. The Human Skeleton in Forensic Medicine, second ed. C.C. Thomas, Springfield.

Kuhl, F.P., Giardina, C.R., 1982. Elliptic Fourier features of a closed contour. Comput. Graph. Image Process. 18, 236–258.

Kullman, L., Eklund, B., Grundin, R., 1990. The value of the frontal sinus in identification of unknown persons. J. Forensic Odontostomatol. 8, 3–10.

Lesciotto, K.M., 2015. The impact of Daubert on the admissibility of forensic anthropology expert testimony. J. Forensic Sci. 60 (3), 549–555.

Libersa, C., Faber, M., 1958. Etude Anatomo-radiologique du Sinus Frontal Chez L'enfant. Lille Med. 3, 453.

Maresh, M.M., 1940. Paranasal sinuses from birth to late adolescence. Am. J. Dis. Child. 60, 55–78.

Marek, Z., Kusmiderski, J., Lisowski, Z., 1983. Radiograms of the paranasal sinuses as a principle of identifying catastrophe victims and unknown skeletons. Arch. Kriminol. 172 (1–2), 1–6.

Marlin, D.C., Clark, M.A., Standish, S.M., 1991. Identification of human remains by comparison of frontal sinus radiographs: a series of four cases. J. Forensic Sci. 36, 1765–1772.

Mayer, J., 1935. Identification by sinus prints. Va. Med. Mon. 62, 517–519.

Messmer, J.M., 1986. Radiographic identification. In: Fierro, M.F. (Ed.), CAP Handbook for Postmortem Examination of Unidentified Remains. College of American Pathologists, Skokie, pp. 68–75.

Michel, J., Paganelli, A., Varoquaux, A., Piercecchi-Marti, M.D., Adalian, P., Leonetti, G., Dessi, P., 2015. Determination of sex: interest in frontal sinus 3D reconstructions. J. Forensic Sci. 60 (2), 269–273.

Montiero, H., Pinto, S., Ramos, A., Taveres, A.S., 1957. Aspects morphologiques des sinus para-nasaux. Acta Anat. 30, 508–522.

Murphy, W.A., Gantner, G.E., 1982. Radiologic examination of anatomic parts and skeletonized remains. J. Forensic Sci. 27, 9–18.

Murphy, W.A., Spruill, F.G., Gantner, G.E., 1980. Radiologic identification of unknown human remains. J. Forensic Sci. 25, 727–735.

National Academy of Sciences Committee on Identifying the Needs of the Forensic Sciences Community, National Research Council, 2009. Strengthening Forensic Science in the United States: A Path Forward. National Academies Press.

National Institute of Standards and Technology. Organization of Scientific Area Committees. http://www.nist.gov/forensics/osac.cfm.

Owsley, D.W., 1993. Identification of the fragmentary, burned remains of two U.S. journalists seven years after their disappearance in Guatemala. J. Forensic Sci. 38 (6), 1372–1382.

Page, M., Taylor, J., Blenkin, M., 2011. Uniqueness in the forensic identification sciences – fact or fiction? Forensic Sci. Int. 206, 12–18.

Pfaeffli, M., Vock, P., Dirnhofer, R., Braun, M., Bolliger, S.A., Thali, M.J., 2007. Post-mortem radiological CT identification based on classical ante-mortem x-ray examinations. Forensic Sci. Int. 171, 111–117.

Prossinger, H., Bookstein, F.L., 2003. Statistical estimators of frontal sinus cross-section ontogeny from very noisy data. J. Morphol. 257, 1–8.

Phrabhakaran, N., Naidu, M.D.K., Subramaniam, K., 1999. Anatomical variability of the frontal sinuses and their application in forensic identification. Clin. Anat. 12, 16–19.

Quatrehomme, G., Fronty, P., Sapanet, M., Grevin, G., Bailet, P., 1996. Identification by frontal sinus pattern in forensic anthropology. Forensic Sci. Int. 83 (2), 147–153.

RADid Resource. http://cfi.unm.edu/rad-id-index.html.

Reichs, K.J., 1993. Quantified comparison of frontal sinus patterns by means of computed tomography. Forensic Sci. Int. 61, 141–168.

Reichs, K.J., Dorion, R.B.J., 1992. The use of computerized axial tomography (CAT) scans in the comparison of frontal sinus configurations. Can. Soc. Forensic Sci. J. 25, 1–16.

Ribeiro, F.A., 2000. Standardized measurements of radiographic films of the frontal sinuses: an aid to identifying unknown persons. Ear Nose Throat J. 79, 26–33.

Riepert, T., Ulmcke, D., Jandrysiak, U., Rittner, C., 1995. Computer-assisted simulation of conventional roentgenograms from three-dimensional computed tomography (CT) data – an aid in the identification of unknown corpses (FoXSIS). Forensic Sci. Int. 71, 199–204.

Riepert, T., Ulmcke, D., Schweden, F., Nafe, B., 2001. Identification of unknown dead bodies by x-ray image comparison of the skull using the x-ray simulation program FoXSIS. Forensic Sci. Int. 117, 89–98.

Sai kiran, Ch, Ramaswamy, P., Khaitan, T., 2014. Frontal sinus index – a new tool for sex determination. J. Forensic Radiol. Imaging 2, 77–79.

Samuel, E., 1952. Clinical Radiology of the Ear, Nose and Throat. H.K. Lewis, London.

Samuel, E., Lloyd, G.A.S., 1978. Clinical Radiology of the Ear, Nose and Throat, second ed. W.B. Saunders Company, Philadelphia.

Sarment, D.P., Christensen, A.M., 2014. The use of cone beam computed tomography in forensic radiology. J. Forensic Radiol. Imaging 2, 173–181.

Schuller, A., 1921. Das Rontgenogram der Stirnhohle: ein Hilfsmittel fur die Identitatsbestimmung von Schadeln. Monatsschrift feur Ohrenheilkunde und Laryngo-Rhinologie 5, 1617–1620.

Schuller, A., 1943. A note on the identification of skulls by x-ray pictures of the frontal sinuses. Med. J. Aust. 1, 554–556.

Schaeffer, J.P., 1916. Further observation of the anatomy of the sinus frontalis in man. Ann. Surg. 665–671.

Shapiro, R., Janzen, A.H., 1960. The Normal Skull: A Roentgen Study. Paul B. Hoeber, Inc, New York.

Smith, V.A., Christensen, A.M., Myers, S.W., 2010. The reliability of visually comparing small frontal sinuses. J. Forensic Sci. 55 (6), 1413–1415.

Stewart, T.D., 1979. Essentials of Forensic Anthropology. Thomas, Springfield.

State of Tennessee v. David William Cosgrif, III, No. E2009-02547-CCA-R3-CD, 2010.

Strek, P., Kaczanowski, K., Skawina, A., Pitynski, K., Kitlinski, Z., Mrowka, D., Naklicka, B., 1992. The morphological evaluation of frontal sinuses in Human Skulls. Folia Morphol. (Warsz.) 51, 319–328.

Szilvassy, J., 1973. Stirhohlenvariatoinen in Ostosterreich (Wein, Nienderosterreich und Bergenland). Mitt Anthr. Ges. Wein 102, 48–59.

Tang, J.-P., Hu, D.-Y., Jiang, F.-H., Yu, X.-J., 2009. Assessing forensic applications of the frontal sinus in a Chinese Han population. Forensic Sci. Int. 183 104-e1–104-e3.

Tatlisumak, E., Ovali, G.Y., Aslan, A., Asirdizer, M., Zeyfeoglu, Y., Tarhan, S., 2007. Identification of unknown bodies by using CT images of frontal sinus. Forensic Sci. Int. 166, 42–48.

Torgersen, J., 1950. A roentgenological study of the metopic suture. Acta. Radiol. 33 (1).

Turner, A.L., 1902. The Accessory Sinuses of the Nose. Longmans, Green & Co, New York.

Turner, A.L., Porter, W.G., 1922. The structural type of mastoid process, based upon the skiagraphic examination of one thousand crania of various races of mankind. J. Laryng. Otol. 37, 115–121 161–175.

Ubelaker, D.H., 1984. Positive identification from the radiographic comparison of frontal sinus patterns. In: Rathbun, T.A., Buikstra, J. (Eds.), Human Identification: Case Studies in Forensic Anthropology. Charles C. Thomas, Springfield, IL, pp. 399–411.

Uthman, A.T., Al-Rawi, N.H., Al-Naaimi, A.S., Tawfeeq, A.S., Suhail, E.H., 2010. Evaluation of frontal sinuses and skull measurements using spiral CT scanning: an aid in unknown person identification. Forensic Sci. Int. 197 124-e1–124-e7.

Van Alyea, O.E., 1951. Nasal Sinuses: An Anatomic and Clinical Consideration, second ed. The Williams & Walkins Company, Baltimore.

Wang, J.-J., Wang, J.-L., Chen, Y.-L., Li, W.-S., 2012. A post-processing technique for cranial CT image identification. Forensic Sci. Int. 221, 23–28.

Wood, R.E., 2006. Forensic aspects of maxillofacial radiology. Forensic Sci. Int. 159S, s47–S55.

Xavier, T.A., Terada, A.S.S.D., da Silva, R.H.A., 2015. Forensic application of the frontal and maxillary sinus: a literature review. J. Forensic Radiol. Imaging 3, 105–110.

Yoshino, M., Miuasaka, S., Sato, H., Tsuzuki, Y., Seta, S., 1987. Classification system of frontal sinus patterns. Can. Soc. Forensic Sci. J. 22 (2), 135–146.

Zuckerkandl, E., 1895. Anatomie des sinus frontaux. In: Anatomie Normale et Pathologique des Fosses Nasales et de Leurs Annexes Pneumatiques. G. Masson, Paris, pp. 349–361.

CHAPTER 21

Advances in the Use of Craniofacial Superimposition for Human Identification

Colleen F. Milligan[1] | Janet E. Finlayson[2] | Colleen M. Cheverko[3] | Kristina M. Zarenko[4]

[1]California State University, Chico, Chico, CA, United States
[2]University of Florida, Gainesville, FL, United States
[3]The Ohio State University, Columbus, OH, United States
[4]University of South Carolina, Columbia, SC, United States

Chapter Outline

■ INTRODUCTION

A wide variety of disciplines utilize superimposition, defined as the practice of placing one object over another to make comparisons between objects. Superimposition techniques may include a variety of object types as their media of comparison, including two-dimensional (2D) and three-dimensional (3D) images, videography, 3D objects, and audio formats. Historically, the use of superimposition techniques traces back to at least the late 1800s when researchers tried to identify individuals from death masks and portraits; photographs and other antemortem images are now used in forensic cases to aid in establishing personal identification of unknown decedents.

To assist in personal identification efforts, forensic anthropologists may employ photographic or video superimposition methods. This practice is typically done by performing comparisons of a decedent's skull or cranium to an antemortem photograph (skull–photo superimposition) or by superimposing both images via the use of video devices (skull–video superimposition). Such craniofacial comparisons evaluate the concordance between the soft tissue features of the available antemortem image and the skeletal features of an unknown decedent. More recently, medical images such as those from diagnostic radiographic imaging [e.g., conventional X-ray radiography and computed tomography (CT) scans] have been introduced as comparative images.

This chapter aims to provide an overview of craniofacial superimposition techniques and their utility in personal identification. It reviews the historical development of superimposition techniques and discusses both the recent developments and limitations of this identification method. The chapter concludes with a skull–video superimposition case study highlighting the application of craniofacial superimposition in the identification of unknown skeletal remains, particularly when combined with multiple approaches to establishing an identity.

■ USES IN PERSONAL IDENTIFICATION

The perceived value of superimposition techniques as evidence for personal identification varies internationally. Radiographic superimposition can be used as a method of positive identification in countries such as Hungary (Angyal and Dérczy, 1998), while photographic superimposition has been used for positive identification in South Africa (Gordon and Steyn, 2012). The countries that use superimposition for positive identification often do so because other more reliable comparison methods such as DNA or odontology are not widely available (Gordon and Steyn, 2012). In contrast, superimposition techniques are not considered a reliable means of establishing positive identification within the United States (Austin-Smith and Maples, 1994; Damas et al., 2015; Gordon and Steyn, 2012; Gaudio et al., 2016; Ibáñez et al., 2015), and some research suggests that more countries should assume this position (Gordon and Steyn, 2012). Superposition currently fails to meet *Daubert* criteria (for more information see Daubert v. Merrill Dow Pharmaceuticals, Inc., 1993; Komar and Buikstra, 2008; Kritzer and Beckstrom, 2007) as a method of identification and is therefore considered inadmissible in the United States legal system as a means for positive identification. Specifically, superimposition does not meet the *Daubert* criteria because it lacks the rigorous scientific testing required of evidence, known or potential error rates, and general acceptance as a method of identification in the field of forensic anthropology (Komar and Buikstra, 2008). A later section in this chapter reviews validation studies that address some of these concerns.

In light of these concerns, superimposition is valuable to identification efforts as an exclusionary technique, rather than to establish positive identifications (Komar and Buikstra, 2008). Forensic anthropologists are able to use superimposition to help exclude potential matches between antemortem and postmortem images (SWGANTH, 2010). Through comparison of soft tissue features and corresponding bony landmarks, the technique examines whether or not differences exist between the features in the images (Komar and Buikstra, 2008). The conclusion drawn from the comparison of images is either a failure to exclude or exclusion of an individual from consideration. An exclusionary conclusion arises from unexplainable differences between images, such as inconsistencies between images that cannot be explained by time, application of the method, or image quality. The person in question is then removed from the potential identification list. When forensic anthropologists fail to exclude an individual, the remains and the individual pictured in the photograph are considered potential matches, but further validation is required before identity is confirmed.

Superimposition techniques have limitations even when they are only used as exclusionary criteria. These limitations stem from trying to merge a 2D image with a 3D skull. The quality and angle of available photographs also poses challenges. Poor-quality photographs may obscure landmarks or make determining an exclusion difficult. Multiple photographs showing different angles of the face raise the probability of coming to an accurate conclusion (Gordon and Steyn, 2012, 2016). Camera distortion and positioning must also be taken into account when practicing craniofacial superimposition. Eliášová and Krsek (2007) designed a mathematical model that overcomes differences in camera angles and positions. However, this model is complicated and requires an in-depth understanding of mathematics and photography, so it is not a simple solution (Gordon and Steyn, 2012). Forensic anthropologists should be aware of these limitations so that they can take steps to reduce their impact on this method.

Stephan (2009) highlights the importance of recent antemortem photographs to diminish the impact of age-related changes between the remains and the antemortem image. In some cases, growth, development, or degeneration may explain differences between antemortem and postmortem images of the same individual; in other instances, they may be explained by occurrences of trauma or pathological conditions. Shorter intervals of time between the age at which an individual's antemortem photograph was taken and the individual's time of death minimize the effects that aging processes, trauma, or pathological conditions incur on soft and hard tissues. Despite limitations, craniofacial superimposition is a valuable exclusionary technique that has a long history in the forensic sciences (Stephan, 2017).

■ HISTORICAL DEVELOPMENT OF CRANIOFACIAL SUPERIMPOSITION

Several trends in the development of superimposition techniques have been identified in the literature (e.g., Austin-Smith and Maples, 1994; Damas et al., 2015; Shahrom et al., 1996; Ubelaker, 2015). Photographs have been used since the mid-19th century to aid in individual identification (Gordon and Steyn, 2012). Methods associated with this beginning phase relied on manual techniques such as using tracing paper for overlaying antemortem facial photographs with postmortem photographs of the skull (Austin-Smith and Maples, 1994). In addition, Reddy (1973) describes the use of bromide paper and photographic negatives for superimposing images. These techniques utilized abnormal variation in anatomical features in their comparisons and, when available, focused on objects of known size to appropriately scale the two images (Ubelaker, 2015).

The next phase, involving video superimposition, utilized a video image of an antemortem photograph and a video image of the skull (Damas et al., 2015; Komar and Buikstra, 2008; Shahrom et al., 1996; Ubelaker, 2015). Fig. 21.1 depicts a traditional setup involving two digital video cameras, a digital audiovisual video switcher mixing board, a screen and recording device.

The orientation of the skull is manipulated until it aligns with the size and orientation of anthropometric landmarks in the photograph, a process labeled the dynamic orientation process by Fenton et al. (2008). Various studies advanced the need for standardizing the methodology associated with superimposition (Seto and Yoshino, 1993) and focused on new technology that could assist in quantifying the similarities and differences between features (Ubelaker et al., 1992). The methods used in superimposition techniques have utilized digital technologies in both 2D and 3D images (Fenton et al., 2008). The use of these techniques allows researchers to quantitatively assess landmark distances and proportionality, as well as overall shape characteristics. Researchers have noted that definitions of anatomical landmarks, estimations of soft tissue depths, the correlation between soft tissue features and bony landmarks, and orientation between a 2D photo or video image and a 3D skull are central issues in craniofacial superimposition.

There have been several methodological approaches used to establish the proper orientation of superimposed images and the evaluation of agreement between features. Generally, these approaches use either morphological

Figure 21.1 Skull–video superimposition setup.

Table 21.1 Morphological Feature Considerations for Skull–Photograph Superimposition

Morphological Considerations for a Frontal View of the Skull and Face

1. The bregma–menton length on the skull fits within the face.
2. The skull's cranial width fills the face's forehead.
3. If the temporal line can be observed on the photograph, it should coincide with the line on the skull.
4. The eyebrow and upper edge of the orbit generally follow each other especially on the medial and central one-third of each feature. The two features diverge at the lateral superior one-third.
5. The orbit completely encircles the eye and its medial and lateral folds. The folds usually align with the medial and lateral palpebral ligament attachment sites.
6. If the lacrimal groove can be distinguished in the photograph, it aligns with the groove in bone.
7. The nasal bridge breadth on the cranium is similar to that of the face.
8. The external auditory meatus opening is medial to the tragus of the ear.
9. The nasal aperture width and length falls within the borders of the nose.
10. The anterior nasal spine sits superior to the lower border of the medial nose crus.
11. If the oblique line of the mandible is observable in the face, it corresponds to the line of the mandible.
12. The curve of the jaw on the face mirrors the curve of the mandible.

Reproduced from Austin-Smith, D., Maples, W.R., 1994. The reliability of skull/photograph superimposition in individual identification. J. Forensic Sci. 39 (2), 446–455.

features, anatomical landmarks in bone and soft tissue, or a combination of both. The morphological approach, as suggested by Austin-Smith and Maples (1994), looks at the agreement of shape and proportionality in certain facial features between images. In contrast, the landmark approach looks for anatomical alignment between known bony landmarks and corresponding soft tissue landmarks. The technique outlined by Gordon and Steyn (2012) uses three easily identifiable landmarks for orientation, three primary landmarks with a high degree of overlap between bone and soft tissue, and four secondary landmarks that show proximity between the landmarks on each image. Table 21.1 outlines the morphological features established by Austin-Smith and Maples (1994); Table 21.2 outlines the landmark-based technique developed by Gordon and Steyn (2012) and Gaudio et al. (2016). Gordon and Steyn (2012) and Ubelaker (2015) provide a concise and thorough overview of the historical roots of craniofacial superimposition.

Recent trends center around computer technology for superimposing images for identification purposes, particularly utilizing techniques that focus on digital 3D images or scans. Establishing the corresponding orientations between digital images can be done manually or automatically with the assistance of software programs (Damas et al., 2015). Traditionally, laser scanners are used to create a digital 3D image of the skull. They represent a commonly available and cost-effective method for digitizing images, although most have limitations on how well they can capture the surfaces of curved objects. While not cost-effective for most researchers, the utility of 3D multislice computed tomography scans, or more recently cone-beam computed tomography, has allowed a more precise rendering of an object. Medical imaging such as CT scans and digital radiographs have also been introduced as alternative antemortem comparative images, especially as a CT scan has the ability to see cross-sectional slices of an object.

Radiographic images have also been shown to be useful as both antemortem and postmortem comparative images. Common types of antemortem radiographic imaging that may be available for comparison include conventional X-ray radiography, angiography, fluoroscopy, and CT. In the United States, full body postmortem conventional X-ray radiographs are commonly taken prior to autopsy, allowing for a noninvasive preliminary investigation of a

Table 21.2 Descriptions of Important Landmarks for Skull–Photograph Superimposition

Landmark	Landmark on the Skull[a]	Soft Tissue Landmark[b]	Bilateral
Orientation			
Ectocanthion (ec)	Palpebral ligament attachment point on lateral orbital margin at frontozygomatic suture	Point where the upper and lower eyelids meet at the lateral bony orbital margin	Yes
Subnasal point (ns)	The point where the nasal spine is formed by the meeting of the right and left nasal bones	The point where the skin of the upper lip meets the nasal septum in the midsagittal plane of the face	No
Nasion (n)	The convergence point of the nasofrontal suture with the internasal suture in the midsagittal plane	The most superior point of the nasal bridge in the midsagittal plane where the nasal bridge meets the skin of the forehead	No
Primary Landmarks			
Glabella (g)	The most forward-projecting point of the forehead in the midsagittal plane at the level of the supraorbital ridges superior to the nasofrontal suture	The mildly protruding area between the supraciliary arches, slightly above the nasal bridge	No
Dacryon (d)	The point of junction of the lacrimomaxillary suture and the frontal bone on the medial orbital wall	The point where the upper and lower eyelids meet medially, just below nasion	Yes
Frontotemporale (ft)	The most medial and anterior point on the incurve of the temporal ridge on the frontal bone	The narrowest point on the temple when viewing the face from an anterior perspective	Yes
Secondary Landmarks			
Gonial angle (go)	The midpoint of the angle of the mandible where the body meets the ramus. The angle of the mandible should match between the photograph and skull	The posterior area where the bony protuberance of the angle of the mandible is visible	Yes
Gnathion (gn)	The lowest midline point of the lower border of the mandible	The lowest midline point on the chin	No
Zygion (zy)	The point on the most lateral area of the zygomatic arch	The lateral most point on the ridge of the cheekbone	Yes
Alare (al)	The most lateral point on the margin of the nasal apertures	The lateral points where each ala of the nose meets the skin of the cheek and philtrum	Yes
Superior incisal (is)[c]	The most inferior midpoint on the lower border of the superior central incisors	The midpoint on the inferior border of the superior central incisors	No

[a]Descriptions of landmarks on the skull (bony landmarks) are based on Gordon and Steyn (2012), originally derived from Martin (1957), Knussman (1980), Moore-Jansen et al. (1994),and Farkas (1994).
[b]Descriptions of soft tissue landmarks are based on Gordon and Steyn (2012), originally derived from Farkas (1994).
[c]Landmark added by Gaudio et al. (2016), not included in Gordon and Steyn (2012).
Reproduced from Gaudio, D., Olivieri, L., De Angelis, D., Poppa, P., Galassi, A., Cattaneo, C., 2016. Reliability of craniofacial superimposition using three-dimensional skull model. J. Forensic Sci. 61 (1), 5–11.

decedent's remains. Increasingly, CT technology is also being incorporated into death investigations. This practice has utility in regions such as Japan where cremation is common practice and the identification of an individual may not occur prior to the cremation process (Ishii et al., 2011).

In these scenarios, CT technology is used to capture craniofacial data before deposition of the body and then is used as the comparative postmortem image. Estimated soft tissue thickness, morphological consistency, and digitally recorded craniofacial measurements are used to orient the two images and are the basis upon which a determination of exclusion or failure to exclude is made (Ischii et al., 2011). To assess the accuracy of CT imaging as a 3D representation of the decedent, Sakuma et al. (2010) looked at the correspondence between measurements taken from an actual skull following autopsy and measurements taken from a 3D CT reconstruction of the skull. Their research results showed a mean difference of 0.9 mm between the two sets of measurements, suggesting that the CT image accurately reflected the actual skull (Sakuma et al., 2010).

Craniofacial superimposition methods have also grown with the study of facial approximation. While facial approximation is used to estimate the antemortem appearance, it utilizes closely aligned techniques with that of superimposition, such as evaluation of soft tissue depths and alignment of soft and hard tissue features. Several recent studies have focused on the automation of superimposition and facial approximation techniques (Guyomarc'h et al., 2014). In particular, data extracted from CT scans can be analyzed with various software programs for computer-assisted orientation rather than manual orientation. Bailey et al. (2014) utilized Microsoft PowerPoint software and JASC graphics software to orient, superimpose, and compare a known antemortem photograph and a CT scan of the purported skull of the historical figure Clelland "Clell" Miller, a member of the 19th century James–Younger gang, who was believed to have been killed during a 1876 bank robbery in North Dakota. This comparison failed to exclude Clelland "Clell" Miller from consideration as a potential match.

In addition, the use of geometric morphometric techniques to help orient and analyze images based on anatomical landmarks and the shape of facial organs has been increasingly discussed in craniofacial identification studies (Kustár et al., 2013; Guyomarc'h et al., 2014). For instance, Procrustes analysis is a statistical method commonly used in morphometric analyses to transform images by scaling them to the same size, rotating them to the same orientation, and superimposing them over each other for a uniform comparison of shape (Zelditch et al., 2004). Use of Procrustes analysis may provide a more reliable method of comparison between antemortem and postmortem images and can be performed in various software programs.

■ RELIABILITY OF SUPERIMPOSITION: VALIDATION STUDIES

Some experimental studies have evaluated the accuracy and reliability of craniofacial superimposition as an identification technique, revealing a mixed consensus about its performance within the anthropological community. These studies typically support the assertion that superimposition should be considered an exclusionary technique (i.e., it has poor performance as a positive identification method). In an assessment of false identification rates using video superimposition, Austin-Smith and Maples (1994) compared 97 lateral view and 98 anterior view photographs of individuals to three identified human skulls known to not represent any of the individuals in the photographs. This study found that there was a false identification rate of 9.6% from lateral comparisons and 8.5% from frontal comparisons, which reduced to 0.6% when frontal and lateral views of the same individual were both compared to one skull. A validation study by Yoshino et al. (1995) supports the importance of comparing multiple facial photographs of an individual from varying perspectives and angles to skulls, and found the outline from semilandmarks trichion to gnathion in the lateral or oblique view particularly useful in comparisons.

A more recent publication by Ibáñez et al. (2015) evaluated the performance of craniofacial superimposition methods. Ibáñez et al. (2015) conducted a study of superimposition approaches by issuing a prepared set of comparative material to participants from 17 different institutions to independently perform craniofacial superimposition, using their personally preferred techniques. This study found that evaluation of landmark consistency between comparative material—either with landmarks as the sole criteria or in conjunction with craniofacial morphology as methods of evaluation—negatively affects the evaluation process of anatomical consistency. Participants who employed fewer craniofacial landmarks relative to morphological features to assess anatomical consistency between comparative material performed best, selecting the correct identification outcome (i.e., negative or positive matches) more often. Sole evaluation of landmark consistency was reported to have the poorest performance, resulting in selection of the correct identification outcome at a rate close to chance. When the fit of morphology between comparative material is considered in addition to the location of craniofacial landmarks, performance is improved (Ibáñez et al., 2015).

While the poor performance of craniofacial landmarks is surprising, a publication by Damas et al. (2015), which furthers the Ibáñez et al. (2015) study, notes that each participant applied different landmark criteria including selection of landmarks they perceived as most informative, as well as selection of studies that inform soft tissue depths at these locations. Further confounding these observations may be the individual participant's level of experience with craniofacial superimposition and personal criteria of decision-making (Damas et al., 2015).

The Ibáñez et al. (2015) study also identified two approaches found to have higher relative accuracy than other methods: computer-assisted manual superimposition of 3D digital models to photographs and computer-aided manual video superimposition of a 3D printed model to photographs. Computer assisted manual superimposition techniques included in this study utilized a computer program or accessory computer hardware equipment to facilitate either the process of overlaying images and/or assist in assessment of consistency between images. Common computer software programs used by several of the participants included versions of Adobe Photoshop, 3D Rugle software, and Geomagic Studio. Accessory equipment utilized by some participants included a Geomagic Freeform Plus Phantom Desktop Haptic Device and a Wacom tablet; the haptic devices were used to assist in proper orientation of a 3D model, and the tablet assisted in tracing morphological outlines to facilitate shape comparisons. Computer-aided manual video superimposition techniques either utilized a computer software or monitor system to aid in the video image–3D model overlay process, but were not used for evaluation for the images (Ibáñez et al., 2015).

A 2012 study by Gordon and Steyn also evaluated the performance of morphology and craniofacial landmarks in superimposition comparisons. In this study, they produced 3D scans of 10 skulls from cadavers for morphological and landmark comparison to 2D scans of 40 facial photographs. All 10 skulls were represented within the photographic sample. Their experiment found that assessments based solely on morphological or landmark comparisons performed similarly (85% and 80% correct skull listed as a potential match, respectively), but did not perform as well in listing the correct skull as a potential match to a particular photograph as combining the two methods (97.5% correct skull listed as a potential match). Additionally, the rates of false identification were high for each method of comparison. Due to the rates of high false positive and low false negative identifications, the authors suggest that superimposition may perform best as initial screening of potential matches rather than for identification purposes, making it most useful as an exclusionary technique.

Gaudio et al. (2016) investigated the reliability of craniofacial superimposition in comparisons that exclusively utilize craniofacial landmarks or morphology and also a combination of the two methods; this study also evaluated whether the presence of the mandible affected the superimposition process and outcome. Gaudio et al. (2016) employed 3D scans of five skulls to compare landmarks and morphology to 10 2D facial photographs. From the results of this study, they argue that the mandible is valuable in efforts to correctly scale and orient the skull. The authors also found that evaluation of landmarks of the entire skull produced the highest rate of correct identifications (100%; i.e., the five skulls were correctly matched to photographs), although this also resulted in a high rate of false positive associations (i.e., other photographs were incorrectly identified as a match with the skulls). These high rates of false positive identification persist through all methods of comparison investigated by this study, which precludes the use of craniofacial superimposition as a means of positive identification.

■ LIMITATIONS OF SUPERIMPOSITION

Despite these evaluations of craniofacial superimposition in the published literature, the use of craniofacial superimposition lacks standardized protocols. Scientific assessment of facial exclusivity is difficult given the abundance of variables available to consider, including use of technology and quality of comparative materials. Most proposed techniques of craniofacial superimposition highlight different suites of facial features, cranial landmarks, and methods of comparison. While a variety of methods can be beneficial for forensic contexts where some cranial landmarks may be absent or altered due to taphonomic damage or trauma, leaving only select landmarks available for assessment, the probative value of cranial landmarks relative to others as reliable comparison points requires further scrutiny.

Several additional sources of error must be taken into consideration when performing skull–photo superimposition. First, the orientation of the skull must match the orientation of the face in the photograph. Failing to keep the orientations consistent will distort key areas of the skull that would be most informative for comparison. When using skull–photo superimposition as a supplemental line of inquiry during a forensic investigation, it may be difficult to obtain high-quality photographs of the individual. Often, the use of poor-quality photographs makes the implementation of this technique more challenging. Using better-quality photographs will increase the likelihood that the match is a true match and not a false positive result (Bastiaan et al., 1986).

Since the primary sources of antemortem images are often photographs, the techniques used for superimposition must also account for optical effects associated with the photographs before the anatomical comparison of features can be conducted (Stephan, 2017). In particular, the subject-to-camera distance (SCD) is noted as problematic. Stephan (2017) outlines a technique for calculating SCD using the following variables: focal length of the lens (mm); real-life object size (mm); object size measured on the photograph (pixel units); and manufacturer's specifications of image receptor pixel size (mm). An overview of the technique and online links to a useable computer script, *PerspectiveX*, developed for *R*, can be found in Stephan (2015, 2017).

In addition, several studies have addressed the correlation of soft and hard tissues of the head to provide information about the average soft tissue depths associated with various points of the face. However, much of these existing data are complex, and the collection and application of these data are unstandardized (Stephan and Simpson, 2008). Several variables factor into soft tissue depth, including age, sex, ancestry, and body composition. Additionally, some variation may be confounded by the parameters of soft tissue depth studies, such as the use of cadaveric or in vivo measurements. For example, Stephan and Simpson (2008) synthesized mean adult soft tissue depth data from over 60 publications, finding differences between subcategories of data (e.g., publication year of the original study, measurement methodology, "race," and sex) are significant, but minimal. Nonetheless, consideration of measurement error and variation in methodology diminish certainty that these differences hold practical meaning for adults (Stephan and Simpson, 2008). A follow-up study by Stephan (2014) added more than 2500 individuals to the pooled data of adult facial soft tissue depths, concluding that the combined data sufficiently reflected population means.

There is a dearth of data in the anthropological literature investigating and validating the probabilities of multiple faces sharing similar skull morphology, inhibiting the acceptance of photographic superimposition as a method of positive identification. Among the few studies in support of facial exclusivity, Dong-Sheng et al. (1989) demonstrated the individuality of faces based on the analysis of 52 facial indices in 224 Chinese individuals. The results suggest that identification is possible through detailed assessments of the relationship of facial landmarks; however, further evaluation of facial exclusivity in other populations is necessary.

The addition of validation studies to the literature regarding comparison techniques, equipment, perspective, and the probative value of points of comparison can assist in method standardization. Damas et al. (2015) interprets the results of the 2015 study by Ibáñez et al. (briefly discussed in Reliability of Superimposition: Validation Studies section) to recommend best practices for craniofacial superimposition. These best practices outline the following: it is best to utilize the real cranium/skull as one of the comparative materials; if it is necessary to create a 3D facsimile, marking the location of relevant landmarks on the skull before scanning; it is important to consider postmortem positioning of the mandible relative to the cranium to match the antemortem image; if available, use multiple, original/unaltered, high-quality, unobscured, most recent, and most informative antemortem images; if possible, infer conditions of photograph (focal length, distance from subject, etc.); describe the morphology, the dimensions, and the individualizing characteristics of all comparative material before superimposition comparison and sort all comparative antemortem images by likelihood of matching the decedent; and to use as many criteria as is possible to evaluate comparisons, while carefully considering the power of each criterion in its discriminative ability.

■ CASE EXAMPLE

In September 2011, a partial cranium was recovered in a heavily forested area in Butte County, California. Officers with the Butte County Sheriff-Coroner's Office and the California State University, Chico Human Identification Laboratory (CSUC-HIL) recovery team performed a subsequent search of the surrounding area. Items of clothing were found during this search, but no additional remains. The CSUC-HIL was asked to conduct an anthropological analysis and help with the identification of the recovered remains.

The partial cranium consisted of part of the neurocranium, representing most of the calotte (Fig. 21.2). Due to this, there was a paucity of features typically used to establish aspects of the biological profile, limiting the possible analyses. However, there was evidence of a craniotomy to the right parietal/temporal region with two nonserialized surgical screws and two nonserialized surgical plates affixed to the remains.

The investigating agency was able to link the recovered remains to a possible 2006 missing person's report of an 81-year-old woman. In 2007, a year after she was reported missing, her vehicle was located in the same vicinity as the remains recovered in 2011. At the time of the vehicle recovery, no human remains were found. The missing woman's medical records showed evidence of a craniotomy to the right parietal/temporal region. The CSUC-HIL received printed images from a CT scan taken after the surgical procedure to compare to the calotte and assist in the identification process (Fig. 21.3).

Skull–video superimposition was used to compare the morphology of the surgery evident on the cranium to that of the antemortem CT scan. Two Canon FS300 video cameras, purchased together and likely of similar manufacturing date, were each mounted on a copy stand equipped with lamps, making the position of the cameras adjustable to account for scale differences between the skull and medical image. The video cameras were oriented such that the lens was facing the copy stand base. Each camera was connected to a Panasonic video mixing console to control image overlay, which was viewed on a monitor. A DVD recording device was used to record the analysis. The setup for superimposition was calibrated using a printed checkerboard image prior to the analysis to reduce possible skewness and lens distortion (Fig. 21.4).

The calotte was repositioned and scaled to find the correct angle for comparison with the CT scan. Once the calotte was correctly oriented, superimposition comparisons were made from inferior to superior (Fig. 21.5) and posterior to anterior. A third superimposition, that in which the skull fades into the CT image, was also performed (Fig. 21.6).

The shape and orientation of the surgical cut and several bony landmarks were consistent between the two images. The locations of the surgical screws were also consistent between the cranium and CT scan. Slight differences in the shape of the skull along the posterior and inferior edge were observed between the two images, which was explained by postmortem taphonomic damage to the skull caused by animal scavenging. Based on morphological similarities between the antemortem medical image and the postmortem cranial fragment, as well as the consistency of the surgical hardware between the two images, anthropologists at the CSUC-HIL failed to exclude the individual from consideration.

In addition to the superimposition, both a neurological surgeon and a representative from Stryker, a surgical implement company, were consulted. Surgical records for the missing woman indicated that the surgical hardware was manufactured by Stryker, so the surgical hardware associated with the cranium was examined by the Stryker

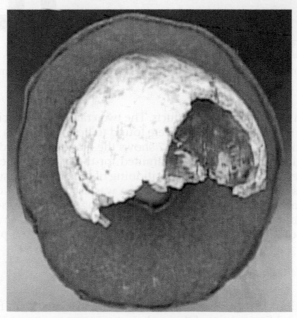

Figure 21.2 Partial cranium (right side shown) with evidence of a craniotomy. The surgical screws and surgical plates can be observed along the superior and posterior border of the craniotomy.

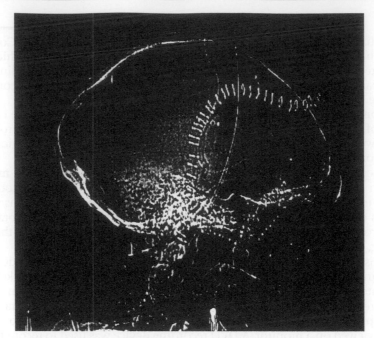

Figure 21.3 Printed computed tomography image (right lateral view shown) taken postcraniotomy.

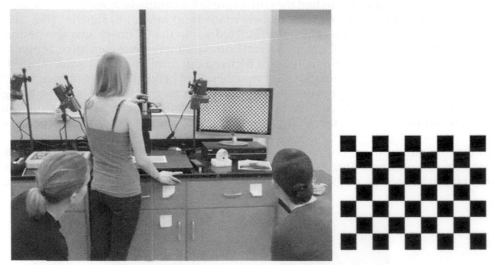

Figure 21.4 Calibration of video cameras measuring possible lens distortion, shown (left image) using a checkerboard target (right image).

representative for consistency with their surgical products. The two craniomaxillofacial titanium straight plates (each with four holes) attached to the skull with one screw were found to be consistent in style and date of manufacturing to the hardware used with the missing woman. Fig. 21.7 shows the manufacturer's drawing of the plates.

In addition, the features of the craniotomy were examined for their fit with the surgical records of the missing individual. Both the shape of the surgical cut and the positioning of the observable surgical hardware were consistent with the antemortem CT images. In this case, superimposition was used alongside other evidence to assist with the identification of the cranial remains. The consistencies observed using skull–photo superimposition, combined with the location of the car in proximity to where the remains were recovered and the likely manufacturing age of the surgical hardware, led law enforcement investigators to narrow their identification process associated with a missing person case.

■ CONCLUSION

While craniofacial superimposition does not currently satisfy the *Daubert* standard for positive identification, evaluation of the reliability, validity, and limitations of this technique are necessary to work toward methodological standardization and admissibility. Despite these issues, superimposition is still valuable as an aide to the identification

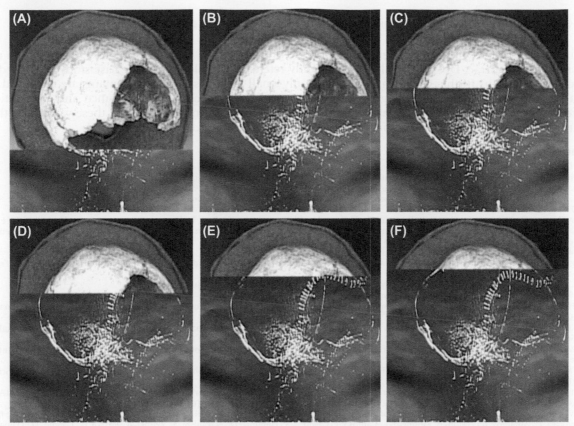

Figure 21.5 Sequential superimposition starting from inferior to superior. (A) The alignment of the base of the skull with the computed tomography image. (B) The beginning of the alignment of the posterior/inferior edge of the craniotomy. (C) The alignment directly below the posteriorly positioned surgical plate with misalignment due to postmortem damage visible along the occipital. (D) Overlap with the posteriorly positioned surgical plate. (E) Alignment directly below the superiorly positioned surgical plate. (F) Overlap with the superiorly positioned surgical plate.

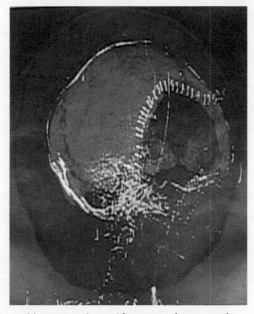

Figure 21.6 Superimposition comparison with computed tomography scan using a fade mode.

Straight Plates

4 holes, regular

Figure 21.7 Drawing from the Stryker Craniomaxillofacial Universal 2 Reference Guide (2011) depicting a four-hole straight titanium plate, similar to the ones used for the decedent.

process in circumstances precluding other methods of identification (e.g., lack of comparative antemortem medical records, inability to extract DNA, unavailability of family reference samples, etc.). The case study presented in this chapter demonstrates its further utility in cases where only small amounts of skeletal remains are recovered. Recent modifications such as the use of 3D imaging, geometric morphometrics, computer assistance, and automation processes are more recent techniques facilitating craniofacial superimposition. The utility of these various methodologies requires further scrutiny, although they may prove useful toward standardization.

References

Angyal, M., Dérczy, K., 1998. Personal identification on the basis of antemortem and postmortem radiographs. J. Forensic Sci. 43 (5), 1089–1093.
Austin-Smith, D., Maples, W.R., 1994. The reliability of skull/photograph superimposition in individual identification. J. Forensic Sci. 39 (2), 446–455.
Bailey, J., Brogdon, G., Nichols, B., 2014. Use of craniofacial superimposition in historic investigation. J. Forensic Sci. 59 (1), 260–263.
Bastiaan, R., Dalitz, G., Woodward, C., 1986. Video superimposition of skulls and photographic portraits – a new aid to identification. J. Forensic Sci. 31 (4), 1373–1379.
Damas, S., Wilkinson, C., Khana, T., Veselovskaya, E., Abramov, A., Janauskas, R., Jayaprakash, P.T., Ruiz, E., Navarro, F., Huete, M.I., Cunha, E., Cavalli, F., Clement, J., Lestón, P., Molinero, F., Briers, T., Viegas, F., Imaizumi, K., Humpire, D., Ibáñez, O., 2015. Study on the performance of different craniofacial superimposition approaches (II): best practices proposal. Forensic Sci. Int. 257, 504–508.
Daubert v. Merrell Dow Pharmaceuticals, Inc., 1993. 509 U.S. 579.
Dong-Sheng, C., Yu-Wen, L., Cheng, T., Run-Ji, G., Yong-Chuan, M., Jian-Hai, F., 1989. A study on the standard for forensic anthropologic identification of skull-image superimposition. J. Forensic Sci. 34 (6), 1343–1356.
Eliášová, H., Krsek, P., 2007. Superimposition and projective transformation of 3D object. Forensic Sci. Int. 167, 146–153.
Farkas, L., 1994. Anthropometry of the Head and Face. Raven Press, New York.
Fenton, T., Heard, A., Sauer, N., 2008. Skull-photo superimposition and border deaths: identification through exclusion and the failure to exclude. J. Forensic Sci. 53 (1), 34–40.
Gaudio, D., Olivieri, L., De Angelis, D., Poppa, P., Galassi, A., Cattaneo, C., 2016. Reliability of craniofacial superimposition using three-dimensional skull model. J. Forensic Sci. 61 (1), 5–11.
Gordon, G.M., Steyn, M., 2012. An investigation into the accuracy and reliability of skull-photo superimposition in a South African sample. Forensic Sci. Int. 216, 198. e1–198.e6.
Gordon, G.M., Steyn, M., 2016. A discussion of current issues and concepts in the practice of skull-photo/craniofacial superimposition. Forensic Sci. Int. 262, 287.e1–287.e4.
Guyomarc'h, P., Dutailly, B., Charton, J., Santos, F., Desbarats, P., Coqueugniot, H., 2014. Anthropological facial approximation in three dimensions (AFA3D): computer-assisted estimation of the facial morphology using geometric morphometrics. J. Forensic Sci. 59 (6), 1502–1516.
Ibáñez, O., Vincente, R., Navega, D.S., Wilkinson, C., Jayaprakash, P.T., Huete, M.I., Briers, T., Hardiman, R., Navarro, F., Ruiz, E., Cavalli, F., Imaizumi, K., Jankauskas, R., Veselovskaya, E., Abramov, A., Lestón, P., Molinero, F., Cardoso, J., Çağdir, A.S., Humpire, D., Nakanishi, Y., Zeuner, A., Ross, A.H., Gaudio, D., Damas, S., 2015. Study on the performance of different craniofacial superimposition approaches (I). Forensic Sci. Int. 257, 496–503.
Ishii, M., Yayama, K., Motani, H., Sakuma, A., Yasjima, D., Hayakawa, M., Yamamoto, S., Iwase, H., 2011. Application of superimposition-based personal identification using skull computed tomography images. J. Forensic Sci. 56 (4), 960–966.
Knussman, R., 1980. Vergleichende Biologie es Menschen: Lehrbuch der Anthropolgie und Humangenetik. Fisher, Stuttgard.
Komar, D.A., Buikstra, J.E., 2008. Forensic Anthropology: Contemporary Theory and Practice. Oxford University Press, New York.
Kritzer, H.M., Beckstrom, D.C., 2007. Daubert in the States: diffusion of a new approach to expert evidence in the courts. J. Empir. Leg. Stud. 4 (4), 983–1006.
Kustár, A., Forró, L., Kalina, I., Fazekas, F., Honti, S., Makra, A., Friess, M., 2013. FACE-R – a 3D database of 400 living individuals' full head CT- and face scans and preliminary GMM analysis for craniofacial reconstruction. J. Forensic Sci. 58 (6), 1420–1428.
Martin, R., 1957. Lehrbuch der Anthropologie, Band 1, third ed. G. Fisher, Stuttgart.
Moore-Jansen, P., Ousley, S., Jantz, R., 1994. Data Collection Procedures for Forensic Skeletal Material Report No. 48. University of Tennessee Department of Anthropology, Knoxville.
Reddy, K.S.N., 1973. Identification of dismembered parts: the medicolegal aspects of the Nagaraju case. Forensic Sci. 2, 351–374.
Sakuma, A., Ischii, M., Yamamoto, S., Shimofusa, R., Kobayashi, K., Motani, H., Hayakawa, M., Yajima, D., Takeichi, H., Iwase, H., 2010. Application of postmortem 3D-CT facial reconstruction for personal identification. J. Forensic Sci. 55 (6), 1624–1629.
Seto, S., Yoshino, M.A., 1993. A combined apparatus for photographic and video superimposition. In: Iscan, M.Y., Helmer, R.P. (Eds.), Forensic Analysis of the Skull. Wiley-Liss, Wilmington, DE, pp. 161–190.
Shahrom, A.W., Vanezis, P., Chapman, R.C., Gonzales, A., Blenkinsop, C., Rossi, M.L., 1996. Techniques in facial identification: computer-aided facial reconstruction using a laser scanner and video superimposition. Int. J. Leg. Med. 108 (4), 194–200.
Stephan, C.N., 2009. Craniofacial identification: techniques of facial approximation and craniofacial superimposition. In: Blau, S., Ubelaker, D.H. (Eds.), Handbook of Forensic Anthropology and Archaeology. Left Coast Press, Walnut Creek, CA, pp. 304–321.
Stephan, C.N., 2014. The application of the central limit theorem and the law of large numbers to facial soft tissue depths: T-Table robustness and trends since 2008. J. Forensic Sci. 59 (2), 454–462.
Stephan, C.N., 2015. Perspective distortion in craniofacial superimposition: logarithmic decay curves mapped mathematically and by practical experiment. Forensic Sci. Int. 257, 520 e1-520.e8.
Stephan, C.N., January 18, 2017. Estimating the skull-to-camera distance from facial photographs for craniofacial superimposition. J. Forensic Sci. Early View. http://dx.doi.org/10.1111/1556-4029.13353.
Stephan, C.N., Simpson, E.K., 2008. Facial soft tissue depths in craniofacial identification (part I): an analytical review of the published adult data. J. Forensic Sci. 53 (6), 1257–1272.
Stryker Craniomaxillofacial Universal 2 Reference Guide, 2011. Stryker Corporation, Kalamazoo, MI.
SWGANTH, 2010. Scientific Working Group for Forensic Anthropology Personal Identification Draft.
Ubelaker, D.H., Bubniak, E., O'Donnell, G., 1992. Computer-assisted photographic superimposition. J. Forensic Sci. 37 (3), 750–762.
Ubelaker, D.H., 2015. Craniofacial superimposition: historical review and current issues. J. Forensic Sci. 60 (6), 1412–1419.
Yoshino, M., Imaizumi, K., Miyasaka, S., Seta, S., 1995. Evaluation of anatomical consistency in cranio-facial superimposition images. Forensic Sci. Int. 74, 125–134.
Zelditch, M., Swiderski, D., Sheets, H., 2004. Geometric Morphometrics for Biologists: A Primer. Academic Press, San Diego.

Further Reading

Yoshino, M., Matsuda, H., Kubota, S., Imaizumi, K., Miyasaka, S., Seta, S., 1997. Computer-assisted skull identification system using video superimposition. Forensic Sci. Int. 90 (3), 231–244.

CHAPTER 22

Comparative Medical Radiography: Practice and Validation

Emily Streetman | Todd W. Fenton

Michigan State University, East Lansing, MI, United States

Chapter Outline

■ INTRODUCTION

Comparative medical radiography is a method of scientific identification that can be performed by forensic anthropologists for medical examiner and coroner (ME/C) offices. According to the Scientific Working Group for Forensic Anthropology (SWGANTH, 2010) best practices document on personal identification, "comparative radiography is an identification technique involving the direct (side-by-side) comparison of antemortem radiographs of a missing person with those obtained from the remains." ME/C offices usually request scientific identifications, including comparative medical radiography, when a body is no longer visually identifiable due to decomposition, trauma, or thermal changes (Christensen and Anderson, 2013). Michigan Compiled Laws Section 52.205 states: "If visual identification of a decedent is impossible as a result of burns, decomposition, or other disfiguring injuries or if the county medical examiner is aware that the death is the result of an accident that involved 2 or more individuals who were approximately the same age, sex, height, weight, hair color, eye color, and race, then the county medical examiner shall verify the identity of the decedent through fingerprints, dental records, DNA, or other definitive identification procedures" (Michigan Compiled Laws, 2010, sec. 52.205). The regulations in other states may differ; note that in Michigan, the definition of "definitive identification procedures" is a flexible term that allows the medical examiner to use comparative medical radiography.

For comparative medical radiography to be performed, the medicolegal death investigator must have a presumptive identity for the deceased and provide the anthropologist with antemortem (AM) medical radiographs. The forensic anthropologists then take postmortem (PM) radiographic images with matching exposure and angle of the unknown remains. The report furnished by the forensic anthropologist to the ME/C makes a recommendation of identification, exclusion, or insufficient evidence. The ME/C then makes the personal identification legal via the death certificate.

Comparative medical radiography is a relatively fast and accurate method of scientific identification (Hurst et al., 2013). In Michigan, it allows the ME/C to release a body to the family quickly and at low cost to the ME/C office, although this is not the case in all states. While the technicalities of jurisdiction and the relationship of the forensic anthropologist to the medicolegal death investigation may differ across states, the process of scientific identification by means of comparative medical radiography outlined here should be applicable in many areas. Validation studies show that when performed by experienced practitioners, false positives (making an incorrect identification) are extremely rare as are false negatives (failing to make identification) (Stephan et al., 2011). Although this chapter is not the first to tackle scientific identification via comparative radiography (Brogdon, 2011; Hines et al., 2007; Hurst et al., 2013; Kahana and Hiss, 1997; Messman, 1986), our goal is to provide a review of comparative medical radiographic casework and validation researched carried out at a forensic anthropology laboratory in a university setting, followed by a comprehensive guide for practitioners with some experience to perform side-by-side comparative medical radiography successfully.

■ PRACTICE IN THE FORENSIC ANTHROPOLOGY LABORATORY

Comparative medical radiography has made up a large portion of the casework at the Michigan State University Forensic Anthropology Laboratory (MSUFAL) in this millennium. Dr. Norm Sauer (D-ABFA) was the MSUFAL director from 1971 to 2011. He spearheaded early modern research on the ability of normal osseous structures to provide individualizing information for the identification of unknown remains (Sauer and Brantley, 1989; Sauer et al., 1988) and trained his students in the application of comparative medical radiography. The current director, Dr. Todd Fenton (D-ABFA), was trained under Dr. Walter Birkby (D-ABFA). Dr. Birkby received early career training as a radiology technician, and he brought this expertise into his forensic anthropological practice, advocating as early as the 1980s that forensic anthropologists should be trained in comparative medical radiography for medicolegal identification cases (Birkby and Rhine, 1983). Throughout his career, Dr. Birkby worked on more than 2000 forensic anthropology cases, hundreds of which were comparative radiography. Additionally, Dr. Birkby trained his students in the practice of comparative medical radiography, a tradition continued at Michigan State University(MSU).

Training in comparative medical radiography at the MSUFAL consists of coursework and hands-on experience during the doctoral program. Graduate students are required to take two semester-long courses in forensic anthropology methods. In the first course, they focus on forensic radiography, learning how to shoot and develop standard radiographic images on dry skeletal material. In this course, students learn technical skills for radiographic imaging, as well as how to correctly identify anatomical features in radiographs. In the second course, students practice side-by-side comparative medical radiography using dozens of real cases. The example cases represent a cross section of the regions and angles used in MSU's forensic casework (detailed in the following). Students in this course gain the ability to visually identify the best matched pair of AM and PM images and to find and compare normal morphologies, anomalies, and pathologies in paired images. In addition, students learn the history of comparative radiography through readings completed in Advanced Osteology, a course that focuses on primary sources and peer-reviewed literature in forensic anthropology. Following coursework, graduate analysts participate in active cases, with guidance from the laboratory manager (who is also a graduate student) and faculty. When the laboratory director determines that a student has had sufficient experience shadowing cases, he will assign the graduate analyst to draft coauthored identification reports.

One of the reasons that we see a high volume of comparative medical radiographic identification cases is that the MSUFAL consults for several medical examiner offices that are housed in local hospitals and integrated with the hospitals' information systems. We believe that one outcome of this arrangement is that the medical examiner is more likely to search for (and find) medical radiographs within the hospital system, resulting in more scientific identifications being made with comparative medical radiography. Without immediate access to medical records, freestanding medical examiner offices may find it easier to ask the next of kin for the name of the decedent's dentist.

Between 2002 and 2015, the MSUFAL consulted on a total of 193 comparative medical radiography cases (Fig. 22.1). The details that follow were collected from final case reports. Comparative medical radiography cases were received as consults from five medical examiner offices across 22 of Michigan's 83 counties. The majority

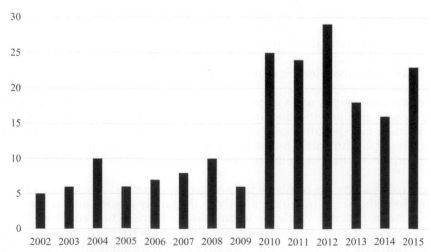

Figure 22.1 Number of comparative medical radiographic identifications done per year at the Michigan State University Forensic Anthropology laboratory, from 2002 to 2015 (n = 193).

of unidentified bodies in these cases were fully fleshed or still articulated at the time of assessment, whether decomposing (60.1%), burned (20.2%), or fresh (14.0%). Only 1.0% were recorded as skeletonized at the time of assessment (Table 22.1).

From 193 total comparative medical radiography cases, information was collected from 267 images used in final reports. The majority of cases used only one radiographic image (68.9%), but the use of two (25.9%), three (3.1%), and even four (2.1%) images was reported (Table 22.2). In cases where multiple images were used to make the identification, sometimes more than one projection of a single region were used and sometimes different regions were used.

The most common regions used were chest/thoracic (32.2%), abdominal/lumbar (18.0%), and ankle/foot (16.9%) (Table 22.3). The chest and abdomen represent many of the radiographs taken in life to visualize the viscera. However, a clinical focus on soft tissue structures sometimes makes visualization of skeletal structures difficult—this is especially true where the heart and aorta are superimposed over the thoracic spine in a chest radiograph. The frequency of the use of the ankle/foot, wrist/hand, and knee in casework is unsurprising. These areas are likely to provide high AM image quality because the target structures are skeletal. The skull is less commonly used in our practice than might be expected (3.7%), in part because head/skull radiographs are not particularly common in AM records, despite extensive research on individualizing characteristics of the frontal sinus (Christensen, 2005; Kirk et al., 2002; Quatrehomme et al., 1996; Smith et al., 2010; Ubelaker, 1984) and other cranial structures (Rogers and Allard, 2004; Rhine and Sperry, 1991). We have also noticed that the ME/C will often ask for a scientific identification in cases of self-inflicted gunshot wounds to the head. Whether or not AM head/skull radiographs are present, extensive damage to the skull excludes the use of this region for identification.

The most common projection was a posterior to anterior (PA) or anterior to posterior (AP) (77.2%), with lateral (19.9%) and oblique (3.0%) projections also represented (Table 22.4). PA/AP projections are relatively easy to

Table 22.1   State of Decomposition of the Remains in Michigan State University Forensic Anthropology Laboratory Comparative Medical Radiography Cases From 2002 to 2015

State of Remains	Cases	Percentage
Decomposing	116	60.1
Burned	39	20.2
Fresh	27	14.0
Skeletonized	2	1.0
Not reported	9	4.7
Total	193	100.0

Table 22.2   Number of Radiographic Images Noted in the Final Report for Each Michigan State University Forensic Anthropology Laboratory Comparative Medical Radiography Case From 2002 to 2015

Images Used	Cases	Percentage
1	133	68.9
2	50	25.9
3	6	3.1
4	4	2.1
Total	193	100.0

Table 22.3   Regions Used in All Images From Michigan State University Forensic Anthropology Laboratory Comparative Medical Radiography Cases From 2002 to 2015

Region	Cases	Percentage
Chest/thoracic	86	32.2
Abdominal/lumbar	48	18.0
Ankle/foot	45	16.9
Knee	27	10.1
Wrist/hand	20	7.5
Head	10	3.7
Hip/pelvis	11	4.1
Shoulder	9	3.4
Neck/cervical	5	1.9
Elbow	2	0.7
Tibia/fibula	2	0.7
Not reported	2	0.7
Total	267	100.0

Table 22.4 Radiographic Projection of All Images Used in Michigan State University Forensic Anthropology Laboratory Comparative Medical Radiography Cases From 2002 to 2015

Projection	Cases	Percentage
PA/AP	206	77.20
Lateral	53	19.90
Oblique	8	3.00
Total	267	100.00

AP, anterior to posterior; PA, posterior to anterior.

Table 22.5 The Presence and the Use of Surgical Therapy or Implants for Matching in Michigan State University Forensic Anthropology Laboratory Comparative Medical Radiography Cases From 2002 to 2015

Surgical Implants	Cases	Percentage
Yes–only surgical implant used	3	1.6
Yes—osseous traits also used	32	16.6
None present	158	81.9
Total	193	100.0

replicate on an unknown decedent and include some of the most common clinical views used in chest, abdomen, head, and wrist/hand radiographic imaging.

Only 35 of 193 cases included descriptions of surgical implants or other therapy in the details of image comparisons, including joint replacements and stabilizing plates and screws. However, surgical implants are rarely the only criterion reported in radiographic comparisons (1.6% of total cases) (Table 22.5). As discussed below, surgical implants are most commonly used in comparative medical radiography alongside osseous features visible in the radiographs.

■ RECENT RESEARCH IN COMPARATIVE MEDICAL RADIOGRAPHY

Before the *Daubert* ruling (Daubert v. Merrell Dow Pharmaceuticals, 1993), comparative medical radiography had been used by pathologists and radiologists for more than 60 years (Culbert and Law, 1927). However, publications on the topic were almost exclusively case studies or actualistic studies (retrospectives of casework) (Angyal and Derczy, 1998; Atkins and Potsaid, 1978; Jablonski and Shum, 1989; Kirk et al., 2002; Mundorff et al., 2006; Murphy et al., 1980; Owsley and Mann, 1992; Ubelaker, 1990). Since *Daubert*, a number of researchers at the MSUFAL have responded to the call for validation studies. The studies at the MSUFAL consist of region-specific validation studies, and the choice of region has always been case driven. They use surveys to test participant examiners' ability to match a PM radiograph to a pool of real or simulated AM radiographs. Participants are usually practicing forensic anthropologists and forensic anthropology graduate students with variable experience in reading radiographs.

An early validation study focused on a lateral projection of the hyoid, as seen in neck and cervical radiographs (Cornelison et al., 2002). The researchers surveyed six participants with experience in reading radiographs including forensic anthropologists, forensic anthropology graduate students, and forensic radiologists. These participants produced no false positives or false negatives when matching a series of 10 images to a pool of 50 possible matches, representing a 100% accuracy rate.

Koot et al. (2005) increased the participant sample size to 12 in their validation of PA wrist and hand radiographs. Participants included a forensic pathologist, forensic anthropologists, and forensic anthropology graduate students. Koot et al. (2005) tested similar image pool sizes to Cornelison et al. (2002), asking participants to match 10 images to 40 possibilities. Forensic anthropologists demonstrated a 100% accuracy rate, while the forensic pathologist performed at an 80% accuracy rate. Forensic anthropology graduate students overall performed well, with a 92% accuracy group rate. However, close examination of the results of Koot et al. shows that all but one graduate student performed with 100% accuracy, and the poor performer was a first-year graduate student.

In her validation study of the lumbar vertebrae, Wankmiller (2010) surveyed 25 participants, asking them to match 5 images to a pool of 20 possibilities. She included forensic anthropologists and forensic graduate students in her survey sample. Both subsamples achieved an accuracy of 91%, with false positives and false negatives occurring within each participant subsample. Many of the vertebral radiographic traits noted in Wankmiller's research also apply to the thoracic and cervical regions.

Due to the increasing use of panoramic radiographs by dentists, Soler (2011) performed a comparative radiographic validation study focusing on the skeletal features captured in such images. The dentition was removed from the images so that the maxillary sinuses, nasal aperture, nasal septum, and other skeletal features were used for matching. Forty-eight participants used an online survey to attempt to match 5 radiographs to a pool of 20 possibilities. The participant examiner group included forensic odontologists, forensic anthropologists, and forensic anthropology graduate students. As in previous studies, a high overall accuracy rate was found (89.8%), with more experienced participants achieving higher correct classification rates.

Niespodziewanski et al. (2016) took a combined quantitative and qualitative approach to assessment of the individualizing nature of the patella in lateral projection. The validation study (qualitative) portion of this research followed the MSU model, surveying 35 forensic anthropologists and forensic anthropology graduate students, with participants being asked to match 5 radiographs to a pool of 20 possibilities. The quantitative portion used methods similar to those found in Stephan et al. (2014) to compare 3D scans of each patella to the 2D radiographic outlines. The validation study produced a correct classification rate of 97.1%, with little discernible difference among experience cohorts.

Other participant examiner validation studies of comparative medical radiography have tested multiple regions (Hogge et al., 1994) or focused on a single region, such as AP chest radiographs (Kuehn et al., 2002; Stephan et al., 2011), pre- and postsurgical ankle and foot radiographs (Rich et al., 2002), and small frontal sinuses (Smith et al., 2010).

Additional research has focused specifically on methodological aspects of comparative medical radiography. For example, practitioner experience was determined to be an important factor in practitioner accuracy in matching radiographs (Hogge et al., 1994). These findings were confirmed by most of the later MSUFAL studies. Later, Bayesian statistics was applied to the question of probability of an individual demonstrating a suite of traits (Steadman et al., 2006). The results of Steadman et al. (2006) demonstrated that comparative medical radiography can produce likelihood ratios of a correct identification analogous to those produced by DNA matching. Although this "explicit probabilistic approach" has not been extensively utilized in forensic casework since its publication, it provides robust statistical support for the ability of radiographs to be individualizing.

In addition to the side-by-side visual assessment detailed in this chapter, recent studies have also used computerized methods to assess the quantitative differences among frontal sinuses (Christensen, 2005; Christensen and Hatch, 2017), clavicles (Stephan et al., 2014; Stephan and Guyomarc'h, 2014; Stephan et al., 2017), trabeculae (Ciaffi et al., 2010; Kahana et al., 1998), vertebrae (Derrick et al., 2015, 2017), and patellae (Niespodziewanski et al., 2016). Despite some practitioners anticipating a shift in preference toward advanced imaging techniques such as computed tomography (CT) and magnetic resonance imaging (MRI) (Hines et al., 2007), our laboratory has continued to find film and digital radiography to be an accessible and effective imaging modality for the identification of unknown remains.

■ PROCEDURE

Standards and Best Practices

The formation of the SWGANTH by the FBI and JPAC-CIL in 2008 represented an important step toward developing best practices and standards for the field. Through this body, a series of best practice documents and drafts were developed, including one for personal identification that highlights comparative medical radiography (SWGANTH, 2010). Personal identification lists comparative radiography and surgical implants as methods that establish identification. Most of the SWGANTH documents have been transitioned into a subcommittee on anthropology within the National Institute of Justice (NIJ) and National Institute of Standards and Technology's (NIST) Organization of Scientific Area Committees (OSAC) in 2014. The following procedure aligns with the spirit, intent, and best practices outlined in the SWGANTH document while expanding on the details of method application.

Producing Postmortem Radiographs

When the medical examiner office is presented with a case requiring scientific identification and medical radiographs are available for the presumed decedent, they will call the MSUFAL and request a consult. Typically, this consult occurs after the normal autopsy protocols have been completed. A PhD-D-ABFA will normally travel to the morgue with a graduate student analyst to examine the AM images, select an image to attempt to match, and assist in taking the PM images.

On arrival at the morgue, the forensic anthropology team will first evaluate the AM images available. The medicolegal death investigator may acquire digital images or hard copies of AM radiographs. A number of factors contribute to selecting which AM image to attempt to match. The image quality and visibility of osseous features in AM radiographs guide the decision-making process, while at the same time, the state of the remains may preclude certain images from being replicated. Almost all AM images are standard radiographs, but infrequently, the only AM radiographic image available will be a CT "scout." These are low-resolution AP or lateral skull radiographs that are used as a guiding image to the following CT.

The forensic anthropologist should either be trained to use an X-ray machine to take PM radiographs or instead should request a radiology technician to do so. In either case, analysts must be familiar with standard imaging techniques and positions (Ballinger and Frank, 2003; Bontrager, 1993; Thali et al., 2011). PM radiographs should replicate the projection, angle, and body position of the AM radiograph. This is often challenging, as differences in body position may result from PM changes including decomposition, mummification, and thermal trauma. For these reasons, it is recommended that PM radiographs be taken for the express purpose of identification; usually standard autopsy radiography will not sufficiently match AM images in angle and exposure by chance. Furthermore, the presence of metal, clothing, and internal organs obscures bony structures in PM images, especially in cases of decomposition. In the region-specific sections mentioned in the following, additional tips are provided for recreating or mimicking AM body position during PM image capture.

After the first series of PM X-rays are produced, they are compared side by side with the AM radiographs. It is often necessary to modify the brightness and contrast in the imaging software to improve visualization of the skeletal structures in digital images before comparison. If the radiographs are sufficiently well aligned, detailed note-taking and comparison may begin. However, if the alignment is poor, or good in some places but not in others, the anthropologist should take another set of radiographs. This process is potentially quite laborious and time-consuming. In fact, in some cases, many PM radiographs need to be generated before the correct angle is acquired. There is no predetermined number of radiographs that should be processed; instead, the cycle of image processing and comparison is repeated until a result is reached (see Outcomes of Comparison section).

AM and PM Radiograph Comparison

The analysis detailed here consists of side-by-side radiograph comparisons (for radiographic superimposition, see Milligan, 2017). We either print films and compare hard copies of AM and PM films side by side on light boxes or use multiple monitors to view the digital images. We visually assess the images, looking for matching osseous features and taking detailed notes on their type and location. Osseous features highlighted by SWGANTH (2010) on comparative radiography include: bone morphology including size and shape, trabecular patterns including radiopaque (white) or radiolucent (dark) regions of correspondence, skeletal anomalies, pathological conditions, trauma including healed fractures, and surgical interventions. Normal structures, morphologies, and trabecular patterns are reliable because they provide sufficient individualizing characteristics and are unlikely to change over time. In our experience, internal structures are at least as important as the margins of bones and bony features. Trabeculae have been demonstrated to be useful in image matching (Mann, 1998), consistent over time up to 23 years (Sauer et al., 1988), and quantitatively comparable (Kahana et al., 1998). Pathological conditions, anomalies, and surgical therapies are very useful points of comparison (Murphy et al., 1980; Rhode et al., 2012; Simpson et al., 2007), but they are not always present. There is no predetermined number of features required to establish a match (SWGANTH, 2010). When the PM image is sufficiently matched in angle to the AM image, dozens of osseous features of the types listed above should be available for comparison. The subsequent sections will highlight the specific procedures and osseous features used in MSUFAL identification casework in commonly used regions of the body: the chest and abdomen, the hands and feet, and the knees. Osseous features that are most useful in these regions are noted in the text and shown in figures.

Chest and Abdominal Radiographs

Radiographs of the chest and abdomen make up 50.2% of the images used in MSUFAL casework (Table 22.3). Of the images detailed in reports, the overwhelming majority are PA/AP views, with only a few lateral chest and abdomen images used in the last decade. When aligning PA/AP chest and abdominal radiographs, the structures that come into useful alignment are the vertebrae and the posterior ribs. Because the autopsy will have been performed, the chest plate and organs need to be removed from the thoracic cavity when producing PM radiographs. The anthropologist or the radiologist should take a series of images at slightly differing angles: first with the beam perpendicular to the table/body, a second with the beam tilted 5–10 degree caudally, and a third with the beam tilted 5–10 degree cranially. In our experience, a true AP only occasionally matches the AM image angle. We take this range of radiographic angles to account for PM changes in body position and find that we are more likely to identify a successful match this way. Brogdon (2011, p. 163) notes the difficulty of matching PM radiographs to the body position used to generate PA chest radiographs in the living, with the patient "standing with the shoulders thrust forward." Further adjustments may need to be made to attempt to match the body position captured by the AM image, such as placement of a block to move the head anteriorly, mimicking the spine's alignment in an erect position.

Some features of the vertebrae that are commonly used for comparison, of our preference for inclusion, are: the spinous processes, pedicles, osteophytic growths at the superior and inferior margins of the centra, overall shape of the centra, margins of the interlaminar space, and transverse processes (Fig. 22.2) (Mundorff et al., 2006; Wankmiller, 2010). In the thoracic region, margins of the costovertebral and costotransverse joints are also helpful. Because in our practice we focus on aligning the vertebrae in image matching, we find that the further structures are from the midline, the less likely the AM and the PM images are to align sufficiently for radiographic comparison. Although advanced research has been done on the usefulness of the clavicle in chest radiograph matching (Stephan et al., 2014), we find that in an articulated body, the clavicles are difficult to align. Nevertheless, other analysts do use the morphology of the clavicles, humeral heads, and scapular margins when comparing chest radiographs (Adams and Maves, 2002; Stephan et al., 2011; Telmon et al., 2001). In the abdominal region, the margins of the sacroiliac joint are often individualizing; Owsley and Mann (1992) use bony projections along the margins of the ilium and ischium and radiolucencies and radiodensities of the femoral head.

Hands and Feet

The extremities make up another 24.4% of images used in MSUFAL comparative medical radiography casework (Table 22.3). The wrist, hand, ankle, and foot contain many bones and are frequent locations of injury, making

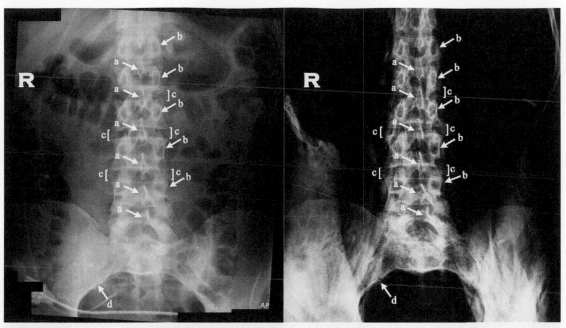

Figure 22.2 Antemortem (left) and postmortem (right) anterior to posterior abdominal radiographs. Where vertebral bodies are visualized in the postmortem image, they provide useful matching features. The (a) spinous processes of T12-L5 and (b) left pedicles of the T12-L4 vertebrae provide excellent matches in this pair of images. The (c) inferior and superior margins of the interlaminar spaces are also comparable. The (d) anterior margins of the right sacroiliac joint are consistent.

images of these regions common in AM records. The number of bones to analyze also makes hands and feet a preferred region for casework. Medical records are likely to contain a series of projections of the wrist or ankle, allowing us to choose the image to attempt to match. The wrist and hand are most frequently radiographed in PA/AP projection. In the ankles and feet, we use a PA/AP or oblique image to visualize the metatarsals and phalanges and a lateral image to visualize the tarsals.

Due to decompositional changes, the hand is often difficult to flatten, which is a necessary step in mimicking the AM body position. To overcome this, we will sometimes use the "hand-press" described by Koot et al. (2005): two pieces of radiolucent plexiglass between which the hand is placed and flattened by means of screws in each of the four corners of the device. We also note that it is extremely difficult to align the metatarsals and phalanges in a lateral ankle/foot radiograph. Therefore, we focus on alignment of the calcaneus.

There are numerous possible points of comparison in the phalanges, metatarsals, and metacarpals when PA/AP hand or foot radiographs are compared. Brogdon et al. (2009) identify seven points of concordance in a single distal hand phalanx. Features of the hands and feet that are commonly noted in radiographic comparison include the overall size and shape (morphology) of the bones, sesamoid bones, osteophytic growths, and radiopacities and radiolucencies in the trabeculae of metacarpals, metatarsals, and phalanges (Figs. 22.3–22.5). We do not typically rely on features of the carpals and tarsals to determine a match in the PA/AP view. This is because they are difficult to align when capturing PM images and poorly visualized due to overlapping structures. In lateral ankle/foot images, we look first at osseous features of the calcaneus and then at the margins of the talus and navicular (Fig. 22.6; see also Koot et al., 2005.)

Knee

Images of the knee make up 10.1% of the views used in our casework (Table 22.3). The appendicular skeleton usually provides high AM image quality due to an absence of overlapping structures, in contrast to radiographs of the axial skeleton. This does not make the appendicular skeleton "easier" to use. Rather, interpreter experience level becomes more important as less complex skeletal elements are compared (Hogge et al., 1994). Radiographic images of knees are increasingly found in AM records, as knee injuries and surgeries are more frequent in the general population. Knee images used in MSUFAL comparative medical radiographic casework included both lateral and PA/AP views, although PA/AP images are usually used as supplementary views. The lateral view is preferred for analysis because it has sufficient individualizing structures and has been validated as a radiographic view (Niespodziewanski et al., 2016). Ideal positioning for a lateral knee radiograph should use a 10- to 15-degree flexion of the knee joint and result in superimposed medial and lateral femoral condyles and a clear view of the patellofemoral joint space. However, matching to the *actual* AM radiograph is the goal, whether the AM image is aligned as described.

In a lateral view, commonly used features of the knee include the following: trabecule, bony spurs, overall shape, and anomalies of the patella; and morphology of the distal femur and proximal tibia (Fig. 22.7). In a PA/AP view, the patella is superimposed on the distal femur and is difficult to visualize for comparison, but the long bones may still provide enough detail to establish a match. However, if a dorsal defect is present on the patella, this feature

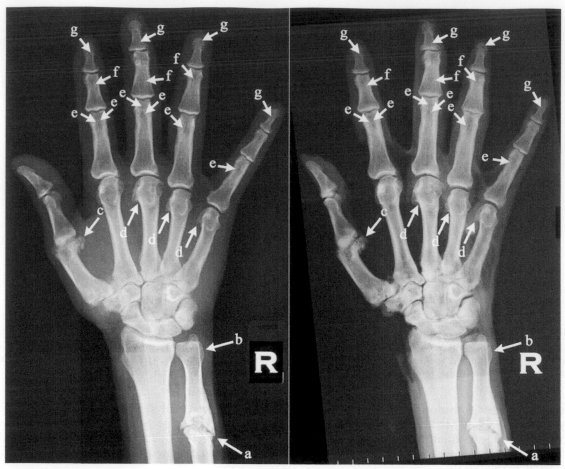

Figure 22.3 Antemortem (left) and postmortem (right) anterior to posterior wrist and hand radiographs. The normal morphologies of the meta-carpals and phalanges match well in this pair of images. The (a) pseudarthrosis in the distal ulna is also a helpful pathology. Matching features in this pair of images include: (b) morphology of the distal ulna including a radiolucent medial aspect; (c) presence and morphology of a sesamoid near the distal first metacarpal; (d) morphology of the heads of metacarpals 3–5; (e) trabecular patterns in proximal phalanges 2–5; (f) trabecular patterns in intermediate phalanges 2–4; and (G) morphologies of distal phalanges 2–5.

may contribute to identification in a PA/AP view (Riddick et al., 1983). The lateral view of the patella, however, is quite individualizing, especially as changes occur as a normal part of aging. Elsewhere, we note that anomalies and pathological conditions are uncommon, but this is untrue in the case of the patella. Small superiorly and inferiorly oriented bony projections and spurs along the anterior aspect in this sesamoid bone are normal and quite helpful in image matching. Furthermore, the margins of the articular surface demonstrate osteophytic lipping in some individuals, which can be seen in the posterosuperior and posteroinferior corners of the patella. Although Sauer et al. (1988) found trabecular patterns in radiographs to be consistent over decades, no study has yet examined how bony spurs or osteophytes change over a similar period. At present, the analyst must use his/her best judgment to determine whether differences in AM and PM images due to bony growths are explainable.

Surgical Implants

Surgical implants were noted in 18.2% of comparative medical radiography cases from 2002 to 2015 (Table 22.3). Surgical implants and therapies seen in MSUFAL casework have included hardware fusing adjacent vertebrae, joint replacements, and stabilizing plates and screws, especially in the lower leg and ankle. In most MSUFAL case reports, aspects of the surgical implants are detailed alongside osseous features (16.6% of total cases). Only rarely are details of surgical implants noted with no accompanying osseous traits (1.6% of total cases). When surgical implants are a factor in comparative medical radiography, the same principles of matching image angle and projection apply as when osseous structures are the focus.

When matching radiographs are acquired, a detailed comparison is undertaken, using the presence, number, and morphological details of implants, using the same level of detail and matching techniques as would be applied to bony comparisons (Simpson et al., 2007). Surgical therapies that are particularly useful are ones with high levels of detail, such as those seen in Fig. 22.8. Some useful features of surgical implants include the following: position and placement of plates and screws on the underlying skeletal structures; numbers of screw threads; relative angles of screws to each other and/or to the plate they pass through; and overall morphology of implant. We also recommend that analysts include region-appropriate osseous features in detailed comparisons. Research has demonstrated that surrounding osseous structures remain reliable following the installation of surgical implants (Rich et al., 2002).

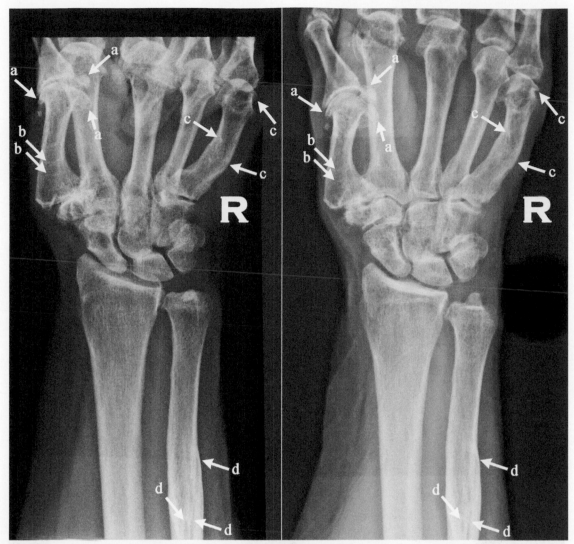

Figure 22.4 Antemortem (left) and postmortem (right) anterior to posterior wrist radiographs. The trabecular patterns, pathologies, and normal morphologies seen in this pair of images furnish an excellent match, despite the slightly different body positions (notice the metacarpals in the antemortem image appear foreshortened compared to the postmortem image). Matching morphologies include: (a) pathological conditions of the distal first metacarpal and correlated shape of the proximal end of the first proximal phalanx; (b) trabecular patterns appearing as transverse radiopaque lines in the proximal shaft of the first metacarpal; (c) overall morphology of the fifth metacarpal including evidence of a healed fracture; and (d) morphology of the ulnar midshaft.

In sum, surgical implants can be an important component when employing comparative medical radiography, if there is enough individualizing information to support a radiographic match. We remind analysts that some implants may *not* provide sufficient individualizing detail (we are cautious when comparing joint replacement hardware).

Outcomes of Comparison

The potential outcomes of comparative medical radiography are as follows: (1) identification, (2) exclusion, or (3) insufficient evidence (Hurst et al., 2013; SWGANTH, 2010). Identification occurs when detailed comparisons of the images agree in sufficient detail with no unexplained discrepancies. Fig. 22.8 shows an excellent example of an explainable change in a lateral right ankle image, where a surgical screw was removed between AM and PM image capture. This change is explainable, and the bony structures in the PM image still provide evidence of the bone growing around the now-absent screw. An exclusion occurs when significant disparities between AM and PM images preclude the possibility of the two images being from the same individual; and insufficient evidence is usually due to either poor AM image quality, which limits the number of comparable features, or due to extreme changes in the body preventing a matching PM image from being acquired (such as in cases of extensive thermal trauma).

Although legal responsibilities differ across states, here we use the term "identification" to indicate the scientific identification report provided by a forensic anthropologist to the ME/C. In Michigan, it is the legal responsibility of the medical examiner to accept or decline this report and finalize the personal identification of the human remains through creation of the death certificate.

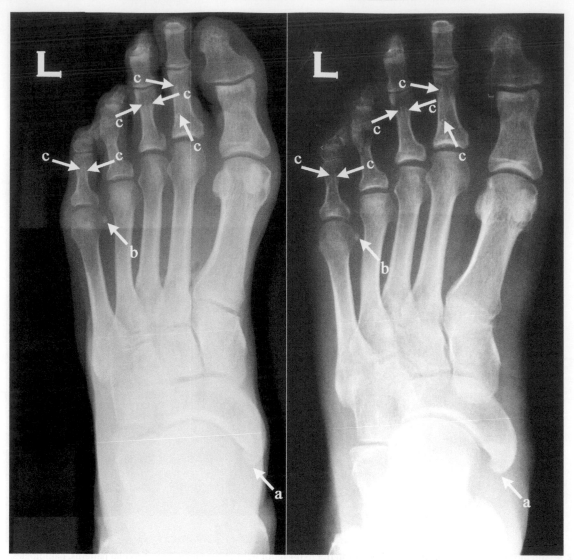

Figure 22.5 Antemortem (left) and postmortem (right) anterior to posterior foot radiographs. The different density of the tarsals in comparison to the phalanges prevents comparison of the entire foot in one radiograph. However, the (a) medial margin of the navicular provides an excellent point of concordance in this pair of images. Other matching features include: the overall morphology of metatarsals 1–5, proximal phalanges 2–5, and intermediate phalanges 2–5; (b) the morphology of a sesamoid bone near the head of the fifth metacarpal; (c) trabecular patterns in proximal phalanges 2, 3, and 5, and morphology of all distal phalanges.

Limitations and Cautions

Identification of remains is the ultimate goal of the medicolegal death investigation system, and scientific identification via comparative medical radiography is the most important service offered by MSUFAL. The consequences of an incorrect identification are grave. Not all practicing forensic anthropologists are trained in the use of comparative medical radiography as a method of scientific identification, and we urge forensic anthropologists not to perform comparative medical radiography unless they are properly trained to do so.

Analysts are cautioned to be very familiar with osseous structures as they are seen in standard radiographic views in addition to 3D view in the laboratory setting. This is recommended so that analysts can differentiate between radiographic features that represent universal skeletal features from individualizing details.

Writing the Case Report

The details discussed in this chapter are a good starting point for the information that should be included in a comparative medical radiography report to the ME/C office. The practice at the MSUFAL is to have a graduate student analyst write the draft case report, with analytical and administrative oversight from a faculty member. Additional information to incorporate may include:

- the agency case number;
- the forensic anthropology case number;
- the decedent's full name and date of birth;
- the date and time of initial examination;

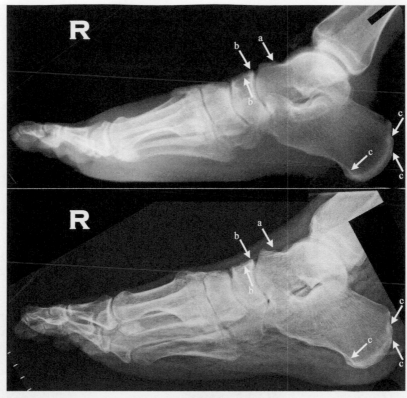

Figure 22.6 Antemortem (above) and postmortem (below) lateral foot radiographs. The morphologies of the tarsals provide evidence of a match in this pair of images. In particular, note the matching morphology of the dorsal margins of the (a) talus, (b) navicular, and (c) all visible margins of the calcaneus.

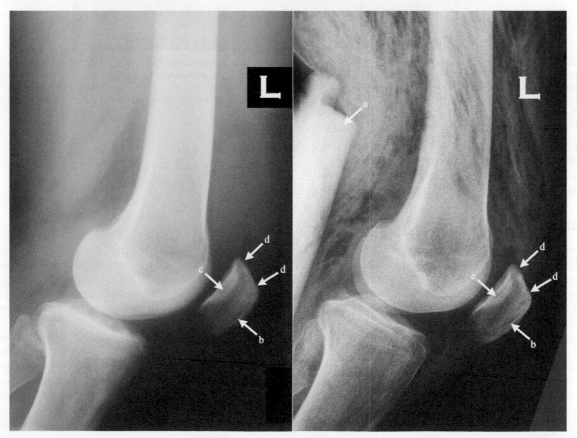

Figure 22.7 Antemortem (left) and postmortem (right) lateral views of a left knee. A (a) block, visible in the postmortem image, was used to maintain flexion of the knee during postmortem image capture. This radiographic comparison focuses solely on the patella. Although the alignment of the femoral condyles does not match exactly, the patella provides sufficient matching detail for identification. Specific patellar morphologies that match well include: the overall shape of the patella, the (b) elongated radiolucent region near the anterior margin, the (c) radiopacity (the articular surface) along the posterior margin, and the (d) morphology of the superior margin.

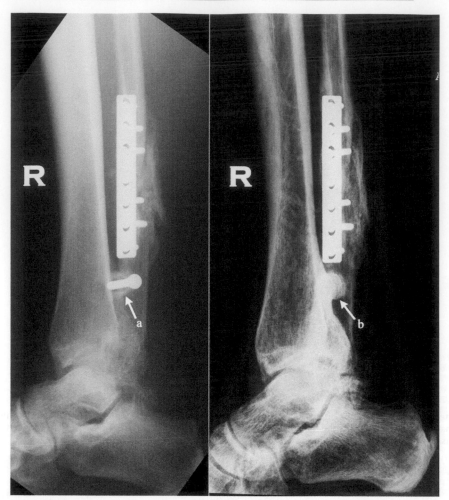

Figure 22.8 Antemortem (left) and postmortem (right) lateral view of a right ankle with surgical implants. In the antemortem views (left), a bar with seven screws and (a) one additional screw are visible on the fibula. In the postmortem images (right), the bar and screws are still visible, with the same angle and number of threads per screw. The additional screw is not present, but we can see (b) where the screw was by looking at the comparable osseous structures of the distal tibia. The "missing" screw was likely removed surgically in life after the antemortem radiographs were taken.

- the agency from which the AM radiographs were acquired;
- the date and name label on the AM radiographs;
- who took the PM radiographs; and
- a detailed list of radiographic features used in the comparison.

■ CASE STUDY

A 66-year-old man deceased in his residence was found by local police, 3 weeks after the last time he was seen alive by his daughter. Since the remains were found in a locked residence and matched the biological profile of the owner, the remains were assigned the presumptive identity of the 66-year-old resident at intake. Because the remains were in a state of advanced decomposition and visual identification was no longer possible, the medical examiner's office called the MSUFAL to perform comparative medical radiography. A faculty member and a graduate analyst visited the medical examiner's office.

Because the local morgue is housed in a hospital, the investigators had access to the imaging software used by the regional healthcare system. A search for the presumptive identity resulted in a variety of images ranging from 2 to 10 years before the time of death. Images included a flourograph of the ankle, a CT scan of the head including an AP "scout" shot, and a series of radiographs of the chest and abdomen. One AM PA abdominal radiograph, dated 4 years before death, was chosen by the forensic anthropologist for an attempted match with the unidentified remains. Autopsy technicians removed the organ bag and assisted the MSUFAL team with taking a series of PM radiographs. Before printing the films and performing the comparison of the AM and PM images, the brightness and contrast were adjusted in the imaging software to provide the best visibility of the bones.

The AM abdominal image was compared with each of the PM abdominal images. The best matching pair of images was chosen for the final comparison based on matching osseous features. In this case, we first considered the spinous processes,

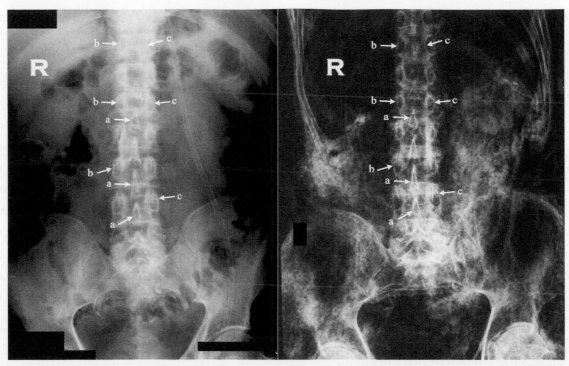

Figure 22.9 Antemortem (left) and postmortem (right) anterior to posterior abdominal radiographs used in the case study, with corresponding features indicated. These include: (a) the morphology of spinous processes L1, L3, and L4; (b) the right pedicles of T11, L1, and L3; and (c) the left pedicles of T11, L1, and L4.

finding a good match between L1, L3, and L4. We then looked at the pedicles and transverse processes, finding good correspondence between pedicles on T11, L1, L3, and L4 (Fig. 22.9). We also tried to examine vertebral margins—osteophytic lipping, when present, is usually a useful feature—but no margins were used in this case. The high contrast seen in the PM image obscured the margins of the centra. The inconsistent density of decomposing tissue, with its potential to obscure bony features, can be seen in the image on the right and explains the high contrast required to visualize bony features in the PM image. Furthermore, no unexplainable inconsistencies were seen between the AM and the PM radiographs.

While case notes listed about 20 matching features, the case report and Fig. 22.9 use only the 9 clearest features. The successful radiographic match resulted in a scientific identification of the remains by the anthropology team. This was communicated to the morgue staff while the forensic anthropology team was still on site, and a formal written report followed shortly. With their identification paperwork complete, the morgue was able to release the remains to a funeral home immediately. The final case report was written back at the MSUFAL. Following standard procedure, the graduate analyst provided a draft report to the forensic anthropologist, and the two signed the final report to the medical examiner as coauthors. Based on the findings detailed in the preceding paragraph, the MSUFAL team reported its professional opinion that the unidentified remains and the person represented by the AM radiographic films are the same individual.

■ CONCLUSIONS

Comparative medical radiography is a scientific identification service provided by the MSUFAL to medical examiners across the state of Michigan. It is a relatively fast and inexpensive method and has strong scientific support for its accuracy when used by trained practitioners. Over a 13-year period, 193 forensic case reports were completed under the supervision of three Diplomates of the American Board of Forensic Anthropology at the MSUFAL. The most commonly used regions in these comparisons were the chest and abdomen, followed by the extremities (hands and feet). Validation studies have tested the application of comparative medical radiography on these commonly used regions (lumbar vertebrae, wrist and hand, and knee), therefore meeting the *Daubert* criteria for scientific evidence. The existing best practice guidelines in the personal identification document were developed by the SWGANTH (2010), and the procedure detailed in this chapter is intended to conform to these best practices.

When AM radiographs can be acquired and matched in detail to PM radiographs taken of the decedent, normal osseous morphologies as well as anomalies and pathologies contribute to successfully matching a pair of radiographs. External features (margins and bony spurs) and internal features (trabecular patterns, radiolucencies, and radiopacities) provide points of correspondence between two radiographs. The case report should provide adequate detail on the circumstances of the consult, the images used, and the corresponding features found in the radiographs. Aspiring practitioners are cautioned not to attempt using this method in casework unless they are familiar with osseous structures as viewed radiographically and properly trained in radiographic comparisons. We hope that this chapter has clarified the research on and the use of comparative medical radiography.

References

Adams, B.J., Maves, R.C., 2002. Radiographic identification using the clavicle of an individual missing from the Vietnam conflict. J. Forensic Sci. 47, 369–373.

Angyal, M., Derczy, K., 1998. Personal identification on the basis of antemortem and postmortem radiographs. J. Forensic Sci. 43, 1089–1093.

Atkins, L., Potsaid, M.S., 1978. Roentgenographic identification of human remains. J. Am. Med. Assoc. 240, 2307.

Ballinger, P.W., Frank, E.D. (Eds.), 2003. Merrill's Atlas of Radiographic Positions and Radiographic Procedures. Mosby, St. Louis.

Birkby, W.H., Rhine, S., 1983. Radiographic comparisons of the axial skeleton for positive identifications. In: Paper Presented at the American Academy of Forensic Sciences. Cincinnati, OH.

Bontrager, K., 1993. Textbook of Radiographic Positioning and Related Anatomy, Expanded third ed. Mosby Year Book, St. Louis.

Brogdon, B.G., 2011. Radiological identification of individual remains. In: Thali, M.J., Viner, M.D., Brogdon, B.G. (Eds.), Brogdon's Forensic Radiology, second ed. CRC Press, Boca Raton, pp. 153–176.

Brogdon, B.G., Sorg, M.H., Marden, K., 2009. Fingering a murderer: a successful anthropological and radiological collaboration. J. Forensic Sci. 55 (1), 248–250.

Christensen, A.M., 2005. Testing the reliability of frontal sinuses in positive identification. J. Forensic Sci. 50, 18–22.

Christensen, A.M., Anderson, B.E., 2013. Methods of personal identification. In: Tersigni-Tarrant, M.A., Shirley, N.R. (Eds.), Forensic Anthropology: An Introduction. CRC Press, Boca Raton, pp. 397–420.

Christensen, A.M., Hatch, G.M., 2017. Advances in the use of frontal sinuses for human identification. In: Latham, K.A., Bartelink, E., Finnegan, M. (Eds.), New Perspectives in Forensic Human Skeletal Identification. Elsevier/Academic Press (in this volume).

Ciaffi, R., De Angelis, D., Gherardini, P.F., Arcudi, G., Nessi, R., Cornalba, G.P., Grandi, M., Cattaneo, C., 2010. Identification from chest x-rays: reliability of bone density patterns of the humerus. J. Forensic Sci. 55, 478–481.

Cornelison, J., Fenton, T.W., Sauer, N.J., 2002. Comparative radiograph of the lateral hyoid: a new method for human identification. In: Proceedings of the American Academy of Forensic Sciences. Atlanta, GA, p. 243.

Culbert, W.L., Law, F.M., 1927. Identification by comparison of roentgenograms of nasal accessory sinuses and mastoid processes. J. Am. Med. Assoc. 88, 1634–1636.

Daubert v. Merrell Dow Pharmaceuticals, 1993. Daubert v. Merrell Dow Pharmaceuticals, Inc. 1993. 113 S.Ct. 2786; U.S. LEXIS 4408., F. 3d.

Derrick, S.M., Raxter, M.H., Hipp, J.A., Goel, P., Chan, E.F., Love, J.C., Wiersema, J.M., Akella, N.S., 2015. Development of a computer-assisted forensic radiographic identification method using the lateral cervical and lumbar spine. J. Forensic Sci. 60, 5–12.

Derrick, S.M., Hipp, J.A., Goel, P., 2017. The computer-assisted decedent identification method of computer-assisted radiographic identification. In: Latham, K.A., Bartelink, E., Finnegan, M. (Eds.), New Perspectives in Forensic Human Skeletal Identification. Elsevier/Academic Press (in this volume).

Hines, E., Rock, C., Viner, M., 2007. Radiography. In: Thompson, T.J.U., Black, S.M. (Eds.), Forensic Human Identification: An Introduction. CRC Press, Boca Raton, pp. 221–228.

Hogge, J.P., Messmer, J.M., Doan, Q.N., 1994. Radiographic identification of unknown human remains and interpreter experience level. J. Forensic Sci. 39, 373–377.

Hurst, C.V., Soler, A., Fenton, T.W., 2013. Personal identification in forensic anthropology. In: Siegel, J.A., Saukko, P.J. (Eds.), Encyclopedia of Forensic Sciences. Academic Press, Waltham, pp. 68–75.

Jablonski, N.G., Shum, B.S.F., 1989. Identification of unknown human remains by comparison of antemortem and postmortem radiographs. Forensic Sci. Int. 42, 221–230. http://dx.doi.org/10.1016/0379-0738(89)90089-3.

Kahana, T., Hiss, J., 1997. Identification of human remains: forensic radiology. J. Clin. Forensic Med. 4, 7–15. http://dx.doi.org/10.1016/S1353-1131(97)90002-X.

Kahana, T., Hiss, J., Smith, P., 1998. Quantitative assessment of trabecular bone pattern identification. J. Forensic Sci. 43, 1144–1147.

Kirk, N., Wood, R., Goldstein, M., 2002. Skeletal identification using the frontal sinus region: a retrospective study of 39 cases. J. Forensic Sci. 47, 318–332.

Koot, M.G., Sauer, N.J., Fenton, T.W., 2005. Radiographic human identification using bones of the hand: a validation study. J. Forensic Sci. 50, 263–268.

Kuehn, C.M., Taylor, K.M., Mann, F., Wilson, A.J., Harruff, R.C., 2002. Validation of chest X-ray comparisons for unknown decedent identification. J. Forensic Sci. 47, 725–729.

Mann, R.W., 1998. Use of bone trabeculae to establish positive identification. Forensic Sci. Int. 98, 91–99. http://dx.doi.org/10.1016/S0379-0738(98)00138-8.

Messman, J., 1986. Radiographic identification. In: Fierro, M.F. (Ed.), CAP Handbook for Postmortem Examination of Unidentified Remains: Developing Identification of Well-preserved, Decomposed, Burned, and Skeletonized Remains. College of American Pathologists, Skokie, Ill.

Michigan Compiled Laws, 2010. County Medical Examiners (Excerpt). Act 181 of 1953 Section 52.205.

Milligan, C., 2017. Advances in radiographic superimposition. In: Latham, K.A., Bartelink, E., Finnegan, M. (Eds.), New Perspectives in Forensic Human Skeletal Identification. Elsevier/Academic Press (in this volume).

Mundorff, A.Z., Vidoli, G., Melinek, J., 2006. Anthropological and radiographic comparison of vertebrae for identification of decomposed human remains. J. Forensic Sci. 51, 1002–1004. http://dx.doi.org/10.1111/j.1556-4029.2006.00233.x.

Murphy, W.A., Spruill, F.G., Gantner, G.E., 1980. Radiologic identification of unknown human remains. J. Forensic Sci. 25, 727–735.

Niespodziewanski, E., Stephan, C.N., Guyomarc'h, P., Fenton, T.W., 2016. Human identification via lateral patella radiographs: a validation study. J. Forensic Sci. 61, 134–140.

Owsley, D.W., Mann, R.W., 1992. Positive personal identity of skeletonized remains using abdominal and pelvic radiographs. J. Forensic Sci. 37, 332–336.

Quatrehomme, G., Fronty, P., Sapanet, M., Grévin, G., Bailet, P., Ollier, A., 1996. Identification by frontal sinus pattern in forensic anthropology. Forensic Sci. Int. 83, 147–153.

Rhine, S., Sperry, K., 1991. Radiographic identification by mastoid sinus and arterial pattern. J. Forensic Sci. 36 (1), 272–279.

Rhode, M.P., Goodhue, W.W., Stephan, C.N., 2012. Radiographic comparison of a fractured clavicle exhibiting a pseudo-arthrosis. J. Forensic Sci. 57, 1094–1097.

Rich, J., Tatarek, N.E., Powers, R.H., Brogdon, B.G., Lewis, B.J., Dean, D.E., 2002. Using pre-and post-surgical foot and ankle radiographs for identification. J. Forensic Sci. 47, 1319–1322.

Riddick, L., Brogdon, B.G., Lasswell-Hoff, J., Delmas, B., 1983. Radiographic identification of charred human remains through use of the dorsal defect of the patella. J. Forensic Sci. 28 (1), 263–267.

Rogers, T.L., Allard, T.T., 2004. Expert testimony and positive identification of human remains through cranial suture patterns. J. Forensic Sci. 49, 1–5.

Sauer, N., Brantley, R., 1989. Effects of aging on antemortem–postmortem comparisons of the peripheral skeleton for positive identification. Can. Soc. Forensic Sci. 22, 8.

Sauer, N.J., Brantley, R.E., Barondess, D., 1988. The effects of aging on the comparability of antemortem and postmortem radiographs. J. Forensic Sci. 33, 1223–1230.

Scientific Working Group for Forensic Anthropology (SWGANTH), 2010. Personal Identification.

Simpson, E.K., James, R.A., Eitzen, D.A., Byard, R.W., 2007. Role of orthopedic implants and bone morphology in the identification of human remains. J. Forensic Sci. 52, 442–448.

Smith, V.A., Christensen, A.M., Myers, S.W., 2010. The reliability of visually comparing small frontal sinuses. J. Forensic Sci. 55, 1413–1415. http://dx.doi.org/10.1111/j.1556-4029.2010.01493.x.

Soler, A., 2011. Positive identification through comparative panoramic radiography of the maxillary sinuses: a validation study. In: Proceedings of the American Academy of Forensic Sciences. Chicago, IL, pp. 379–380.

Steadman, D.W., Adams, B.J., Konigsberg, L.W., 2006. Statistical basis for positive identification in forensic anthropology. Am. J. Phys. Anthropol. 131, 15–26. http://dx.doi.org/10.1002/ajpa.20393.

Stephan, C.N., Amidan, B., Trease, H., Guyomarc'h, P., Pulsipher, T., Byrd, J.E., 2014. Morphometric comparison of clavicle outlines from 3D bone scans and 2D chest radiographs: a shortlisting tool to assist radiographic identification of human skeletons. J. Forensic Sci. 59, 306–313. http://dx.doi.org/10.1111/1556-4029.12324.

Stephan, C.N., Guyomarc'h, P., 2014. Quantification of perspective-induced shape change of clavicles at radiography and 3D scanning to assist human identification. J. Forensic Sci. 59, 447–453.

Stephan, C., Guyomarc'h, P., D'Alonzo, S., 2017. Skeletal identification by radiographic comparison of the cervicothoracic region on chest radiographs. In: Latham, K.A., Bartelink, E., Finnegan, M. (Eds.), New Perspectives in Forensic Human Skeletal Identification. Elsevier/Academic Press (in this volume).

Stephan, C.N., Winburn, A.P., Christensen, A.F., Tyrrell, A.J., 2011. Skeletal identification by radiographic comparison: blind tests of a morphoscopic method using antemortem chest radiographs. J. Forensic Sci. 56, 320–332. http://dx.doi.org/10.1111/j.1556-4029.2010.01673.x.

Telmon, N., Allery, J.-P., Scolan, V., Rougé, D., 2001. A case report demonstrating the value of chest X-rays in comparative identification. J. Clin. Forensic Med. 8, 77–80. http://dx.doi.org/10.1054/jcfm.2001.0472.

Thali, M.J., Viner, M.D., Brogdon, B.G. (Eds.), 2011. Brogdon's Forensic Radiology, second ed. CRC Press, Boca Raton, FL.

Ubelaker, D.H., 1984. Positive identification from radiograph comparison of frontal sinus patterns. In: Rathbun, T.A., Buikstra, J. (Eds.), Human Identification. Charles C. Thomas, Springfield, IL.

Ubelaker, D.H., 1990. Positive Identification of American Indian skeletal remains from radiograph comparison. J. Forensic Sci. 35 (3), 466–472.

Wankmiller, J.C., 2010. Positive Identification Using Comparisons of Lumbar Spine Radiographs: A Validation Study (M.S. Thesis). Michigan State University, United States – Michigan.

CHAPTER **23**

The Computer-Assisted Decedent Identification Method of Computer-Assisted Radiographic Identification

Sharon M. Derrick[1] | John A. Hipp[2] | Priya Goel[2]

[1]Harris County Institute of Forensic Sciences, Houston, TX, United States
[2]Medical Metrics, Inc., Houston, TX, United States

Chapter Outline

■ INTRODUCTION

Computer-assisted decedent identification (CADI) is a semiautomated method developed to assist in personal identification of deceased individuals (decedents) under the jurisdiction of a medical examiner or coroner (ME/C). Through grant funding provided by the National Institute of Justice, Derrick et al. (2014) modified proprietary software for measuring motion from medical images (QMA, Medical Metrics, Inc., Houston, Texas; MMI) into a forensic version, dubbed CADI. The current version of CADI analyzes the radiographic shapes of targeted skeletal elements relative to an array of standard radiographs and quantifies whether a particular pair of radiographs is a better match than other pairs of radiographs in the array. The method has been validated for biometric comparison of antemortem and postmortem imaging of the lateral spine and has been specifically tailored to the ME/C setting. A mathematically derived match score is provided for each comparison that either increases or decreases support for ME/C decisions regarding personal identification of decedents.

Identification in the Medical Examiner/Coroner Setting

ME/Cs in the United States are responsible for the personal identification of decedents who fall under their jurisdiction. Each ME/C office determines standard procedures for identification of decedents based on the investigative evidence for each case, the reliability and accessibility of identification modalities, and the resources available to the office. The composition of each ME/C office decedent population is also somewhat different based on the geographic location and the demographic and cultural makeup of the local population. Despite these variations, one commonality for ME/C offices is that the majority of decedents are received with a presumed personal identification based on hospital records, visual identification by family or friends, or other types of documentary evidence.

New Perspectives in Forensic Human Skeletal Identification. http://dx.doi.org/10.1016/B978-0-12-805429-1.00023-5

In these cases, the identification is confirmed before or soon after the autopsy is completed. The remainder of the decedents, the number of which varies among offices, arrives either completely unknown or with only a tentatively associated name due to the circumstances of death, disfiguring trauma, or decomposition that renders the decedent unrecognizable. The methods used to identify unknown and tentatively identified decedents vary by the available options and by the standard operating procedures of the individual ME/C. The following description is based on the methods used at the Harris County Institute of Forensic Sciences but may be generalized to ME/C governed by similar regulatory statutes.

The first identification method typically attempted is fingerprinting, either through electronic means or, if the dermal gloves are in poor condition, using other methods of dermal ridge capture, such as rehydration for ink printing or silicone casting. The fingerprints are then sent electronically through multiple databases of fingerprint records for a computer-based match. If no association is made through this effort, there is another option for those decedents with a tentative name. A latent fingerprint examiner may attempt a manual fingerprint comparison of the postmortem prints with a fingerprint record listed under the tentative name that was not associated through the computerized search. Reviews of the current science of fingerprinting, including techniques, procedures, and submission policies, are available in the literature (National Institute of Justice, 2005; Neumann and Stern, 2016). When fingerprinting is unsuccessful or the prints do not associate with a fingerprint record through computerized search or latent comparison methods, the options for identification are significantly narrowed.

At this point, most ME/Cs move directly to submission of unknown decedent samples to an accredited DNA laboratory for analysis while continuing to work on gathering more evidence of identity and potential next of kin. However, DNA analysis can have a lengthy turnaround time for results (Hayes, 2010). In the cases of decedents with a tentative name, next of kin or other family members often have already been notified of the death and are preparing for funeral services. They may be confused and upset when the body cannot be released immediately postautopsy, leading to complaints and misunderstandings. Storage of the body is another important issue because long-term storage, even under low temperature refrigeration, results in continued decomposition with potential fungal growth that presents health safety issues for morgue workers. For those decedents with a tentative name, obtaining dental records and radiology for comparison with postmortem imaging is usually the next ME/C course of action.

A consultant forensic odontologist, if available, is contacted to perform the dental analysis (Pretty et al., 2012). Unfortunately, one problem associated with dental comparison is the lack of dental care accessed by many individuals who die unexpectedly and become ME/C cases (Eisen et al., 2015). Dental records are incomplete or absent for a certain proportion of the ME/C caseload depending on the community within jurisdictional boundaries of the office. However, medical imaging of other parts of the body, such as the standard chest radiograph or computerized axial tomography scan (CT) of the head, is relatively common, especially for elderly individuals and those who are without a primary care physician and regularly receive treatment in the hospital emergency department (Berdahl et al., 2013; Korley et al., 2010). When these records are obtained, comparison of antemortem radiological images with postmortem images may be performed at the ME/C by a forensic radiologist, forensic pathologist, or forensic anthropologist because of the specialized anatomical training of practitioners in these professions. The following are illustrations of two ME/C cases in which antemortem and postmortem imaging were available but could not be used to make the identification. These types of cases likely would have benefited from the application of CADI if it had been available to the ME/C at the time.

Medical Examiner/Coroner Case Study I—Tentatively Identified Adult Male

The death of a 74-year-old Asian–American male was reported to the ME/C office by law enforcement. The man lived alone in a rented home. His sister stopped by the house for a welfare check after she had not heard from him per usual and discovered him prone on the living room floor in a state of moderate decomposition. His face was unrecognizable. Forensic investigators from the ME/C traveled to the scene to gather information and documented a tentative name. The decedent was brought to the ME/C for autopsy. The dermal gloves did not provide fingerprints despite enhanced procedures. Although the man had been recovered from a residence reported to be his rental home, confirmation of identity could not be performed without additional evidence.

The forensic investigators requested information from the sister regarding dental or medical records. The family stated that they had no recollection of a dentist's name and did not know if the man was in the care of a dentist. Fortunately, the sister did remember that he had been treated for diabetes at a local hospital. A forensic investigator located chest radiographs (anterior to posterior and lateral views) in the hospital records. The digital images were submitted to a forensic anthropologist at the ME/C to compare with postmortem films for identification. The anterior to posterior view of the chest was overexposed and the organs clouded visualization of the spine and ribs. The shoulder girdle and articulated humeri were only partially represented in the view. In contrast, the lateral view of the spine was clear and the outlines of each vertebra could be easily visualized. During the comparison with the postmortem radiographs (Fig. 23.1), the anthropologist did not find any anatomical inconsistencies nor did she find well-defined consistencies to provide support for the personal identification. After discussion regarding possible DNA analysis, an identification based on contextual evidence was eventually accepted by the ME/C pathologist.

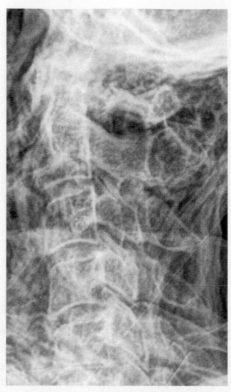

Figure 23.1 Postmortem radiograph of lateral cervical spine in a decomposed, fleshed individual.

Medical Examiner/Coroner Case Study II—Skeletal Remains Associated With a Missing Person Case

The partially skeletonized remains of an unknown adult were discovered in a campsite within a wooded area. The campsite was part of a large encampment of homeless people, many of whom visited each other and socialized. A bystander suggested a first and last name for a man who lived at the campsite, stating he had not seen him for "quite a while." However, no documentary evidence of identity was found, the face was completely skeletonized, and the remains were partially disarticulated. The decedent was transported to the ME/C, received preautopsy radiographic imaging for foreign objects, and was examined by a forensic pathologist. The remains were submitted to a staff forensic anthropologist for analysis. The anthropologist processed the remains and constructed a biological profile, estimating the decedent as a relatively tall male of European ancestry who was over the age of 50 years at death. As a part of the anthropological analysis, the skeletal elements were again imaged in standard radiographs. The vertebrae were articulated and scanned in anterior to posterior and lateral views. The pelvis was articulated and imaged in a position similar to that of a standard abdominal film.

Through investigative efforts, a missing person's name was soon associated with the remains. The name was similar but not identical to the name provided by the bystander at the homeless camp. Medical records that included radiographs were available for the missing person. The films, consisting of standard chest radiographs, were obtained and compared with the postmortem radiographs. The radiographs taken prior to the anthropological examination were not imaged in the correct plane for comparison with a clinical chest radiograph. The shapes of the thoracic and abdominal elements were poorly visualized and slightly distorted. Yet, the vertebral body shapes in the images of the rearticulated cervical spine taken by the anthropologist were easily compared with the cervical spine in the chest radiographs (Fig. 23.2). However, visual comparison of these few elements by an analyst was not deemed sufficient for an unknown partial skeleton with little supporting context. No additional antemortem radiographs were available to strengthen the comparison; therefore, bone specimens were submitted for DNA analysis to compare with a family reference sample.

■ FORENSIC RADIOLOGICAL COMPARISON FOR PERSONAL IDENTIFICATION

The history of radiological comparison is long and well reported in the forensic literature (for a historical sample, see Adams and Maves, 2002; Barondess et al., 1988; Bunch and Fielding, 2005; Cox et al., 2009; Dérczy and Angyal, 1998; Fahmy et al., 2004; Gantner and Murphy, 1982; Goldstein et al., 2002; Harris et al., 1987; Hogge et al., 1994; Kuehn et al., 2002; Kullman et al., 1990; Lichtenstein et al., 1988; Mann, 1998; Martel et al., 1977; Moser and Wagner, 1990; Owsley and Mann, 1992; Ribeiro, 2000; Riepert et al., 2001; Sanders et al., 1972; Spruill et al., 1980; Telmon et al., 2001). Radiological comparison for medicolegal identification is performed through a point-by-point

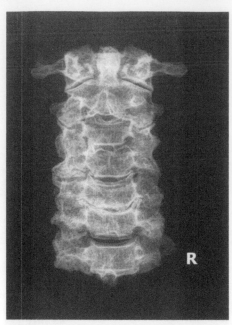

Figure 23.2 Postmortem anterior to posterior radiograph of cervical spine—rearticulated skeletal remains.

comparison of similar antemortem views of a missing person and postmortem views of a decedent. The forensic analyst compares the anatomy pictured in the images using his/her particular field of training (i.e., dental, radiology, pathology, anthropology), noting consistencies and inconsistencies in trabecular bone patterns, developmental variants, sequelae of previous injury or pathological conditions, or evidence of medical/dental treatment, such as fillings, crowns, wires, and orthopedic hardware. With some notable exceptions (Christensen, 2005; Christensen et al., 2014; Maxwell and Ross, 2014; Stephan, 2017; Stephan et al., 2014; Derrick et al., 2015; Ross et al., 2015; Fournier and Ross, 2016; Niespodziewanski et al., 2016), radiological comparison of skeletal anatomy has been qualitative. Similar to expert fingerprint and bite mark assessment, there was no accepted minimum number of matching points necessary to make a positive identification, nor a set of standard anatomical locations and features found at each location that could be used to form a decision tree or protocol for radiological comparison (Ross et al., 2015).

As early as 15 years ago, Riepert et al. (2001) called for additional research in digital radiograph comparison methods as well as quantification of those methods. Rogers and Allard opined in 2004, "A mathematical means of arriving at a positive identification ensures replicability, makes criteria explicit, and provides a method that can be debated and discussed" (Rogers and Allard, 2004). Taking heed of these comments and strong language provided in the National Research Council Report (National Research Council, 2009), advances in the forensic sciences over the past 15 years have focused on development of quantitative and empirically testable methods that increase the reliability of comparison results.

A number of forensic anthropologists, radiologists, and biometric researchers are currently working to provide standardized, quantifiable methods of radiological comparison. For example, Ross et al. (2015) reported results from the study of a large compilation of radiographs obtained from the records of an ME/C. The researchers developed standardized protocols for radiographic comparisons of the cranial vault, chest, and femur, based on visual assessment of points of concordance entered into classification decision trees. The results were quantitatively analyzed using receiver operating characteristic statistics and then recommendations for statistically supported minimum points of concordance were provided.

Several recent studies utilize elliptical Fourier analysis (EFA), a numerically based method used to characterize the shape of two dimensional forms. For example, Christensen (2005) quantitatively tested the reliability of frontal sinuses in positive identification and found using EFA coefficient comparison to estimate the probability of a correct identification to be a reliable technique. Thus, she recommended EFA comparison of frontal sinuses as a quantified form of substantiation in forensic identification. Her study obtained outlines for comparison by superimposing each original radiograph and assessing the result (Christensen, 2005). Continued investigation of the frontal sinuses by Christensen and other researchers (Christensen et al., 2014; Maxwell and Ross, 2014) has led to common application of the sinuses as a basis for personal identification.

Stephan et al. (2014, 2011, 2017) have used EFA in extensive, successful work with digitally enhanced antemortem chest radiographs compared with 3D bone scans of skeletonized clavicles from unaccounted for Korean War soldiers recovered from the National Memorial Cemetery of the Pacific. Importantly, assessment of the skeletonized clavicles requires careful anatomical positioning within the postmortem images to facilitate shape comparison.

Promising investigations of the outline shape of the lateral patella in 3D scans have also used EFA to quantify shape matching (Streetman and Fenton, 2017; Niespodziewanski et al., 2016). The knee is an area of particular interest for medicolegal radiological comparison. Due to advances in knee surgery procedures for injuries and natural orthopedic conditions resulting in improved surgical outcomes, patient access to knee surgery has increased, and medical records containing the associated radiological assessment films have increased as well. The use of the lateral patella is well chosen because the shape of the patella is easily visualized in lateral radiological views. Previously, Shamir et al. (2009) used 1275 radiographic images in 20 repeated experiments to show that individuals can be identified by comparison of knee joint radiographs. Although the recognition accuracy of the knee joint was statistically higher than random, it became less accurate as the number of individuals in the dataset increased. These results support the inclusion of more than one anatomic region in a radiographic comparison analysis.

All the methods mentioned earlier rely on visual comparison by analysts, which may be influenced by the quality of the films, the degree to which the postmortem image corresponds to the positioning of the antemortem image, the training and level of expertise of the analyst, and the perceived "rarity" of the anatomical characteristics under assessment (Steadman et al., 2006). CADI provides computer-assisted biometric matching that mitigates the radiological quality error and removes much of the unintentional error or cognitive bias introduced by the analyst.

■ COMPUTER-ASSISTED BIOMETRIC MATCHING OF RADIOLOGICAL IMAGING

The use of computer software programs for biometric analysis is the basis of DNA identification, fingerprint comparison, and facial recognition, among other major modalities used for personal identification in the forensic sciences. The challenge of determining whether an antemortem radiograph and a postmortem radiograph are from the same individual is analogous to the challenges of biometric facial recognition based on images of faces. Facial recognition has been extensively studied and three distinct methods have been defined: verification, identification, and recognition (Grother et al., 2010; Wayman, 2015). Verification occurs when the biometric system attempts to confirm an individual's claimed identity by comparing a submitted sample to one or more previously chosen templates. Identification occurs when the biometric system attempts to determine the identity of an individual. The submitted sample is compared with all the templates in a database (closed-set identification). The person of interest is not guaranteed to exist in the template database, and the system must determine if there is actually a match template present. Recognition is a generic term that does not imply verification or identification. All biometric systems perform recognition of previously compiled samples or templates.

In some applications of biometric facial recognition, radiographs were used in an attempt to verify an identity, while radiographs were used for decedent identification in other studies (De Greef and Willems, 2005). When used for either verification or identification of a medicolegal decedent's identity, a computer-assisted radiographic method would ideally account for the prior probability of finding a matching antemortem radiograph within the jurisdiction that they serve. Application of Bayes' theorem and related statistical analysis to the process based on objective specification of prior odds can dramatically improve the reliability of the test (Budowle et al., 2011; Dunson, 2007; Gelman, 2006; Lee and Song, 2004; Spiegelhalter and Freedman, 1988; Wijeysundera et al., 2009). However, care must be taken that contextual information is not provided to the analyst so as not to foster cognitive bias and introduce error that is not measured, quantified, and reported with the results (Dror et al., 2006).

Advances in biometric technology have also been explored in nonforensic fields. One such application is the use of radiological comparison to improve the efficiency of hospital medical record storage. Picture archiving and communication system (PACS) is widely used in major hospital networks (Morishita et al., 2001, 2004; Shimizu et al., 2016; Toge et al., 2013). PACS servers can hold a large quantity of digital images, but if a radiograph is misfiled, it is difficult to retrieve and may be lost indefinitely in the system, or worse, used in the treatment of a different patient. Radiologists and hospital administrators have published a number of articles reporting successful use of digital radiology patient matching to prevent these errors. Morishita et al. (2001, 2004), in their work with chest radiographs, described the method as a form of "biological fingerprint." The majority of the PACS work was based on edge detection and edge enhancement, with computer-assisted overlay of comparison images to match up the outlines. CADI is based on the theoretical concepts and practical applications of biometric system analysis and computer-assisted shape matching of object outlines.

■ THE COMPUTER-ASSISTED DECEDENT IDENTIFICATION METHOD

The CADI method utilizes a forensic version of QMA software, created and developed through collaboration between forensic anthropologists, biomedical engineers, software engineers, and software coding professionals. The original QMA has been validated (Reitman et al., 2004; Zhao et al., 2005) and used in multiple therapeutic studies and used in over 100 peer-reviewed studies of spinal biomechanics and spinal treatments. QMA is vertebral tracking software that matches the shapes of specific vertebrae in multiple images. It has most commonly been used to measure motion between vertebrae and changes in spatial relationships between vertebrae over time. The software tracks a specific object (e.g., a cervical vertebra) between radiographic images (Fig. 23.3). This is a fundamental feature of CADI that calculates the likelihood that a specific anatomical feature is a match as imaged in radiographs taken at different time periods.

Development of CADI has focused on lateral views of the spine for the following reasons. First, the QMA software had already been validated for tracking vertebrae in lateral view, simplifying the first phase of development by

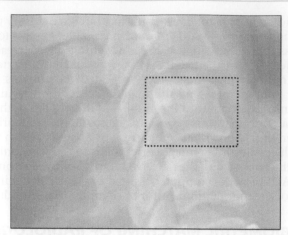

Figure 23.3 Computer-assisted decedent identification mask of the fourth cervical vertebra.

allowing the method to be built on that tested platform. Second, the relative stability of vertebral elements, with regard to locomotion, and the regular shapes of vertebral bodies were suitable for the software to select and analyze. Finally, in the experience of the forensic anthropologists working on the project, there is a high frequency of available antemortem chest radiographs in medicolegal cases, either as stand-alone diagnostic imaging or as "scout" imaging prior to a CT scan. Most of these films include both an anterior to posterior view and a lateral view of the spine. The cervical and lumbar regions (C1–7, L1–5) were selected for the initial phases of the project based on availability of sufficient lateral radiographs of these regions for comparison. Spine radiographs focusing on the cervical and lumbar regions were available in an MMI-archived database of images used in previous QMA testing. Additional spine radiographs were obtained from the second National Health and Nutrition Examination Survey (NHANES II), which is a nationwide sample of radiographic images from 27,801 people (National Health and Nutrition Examination Survey (NHANESII), 2014).

The first phase of CADI development was a time-consuming process to determine the optimal filters and match algorithms required by QMA to perform automated analysis of skeletal element shape in this novel forensic context. Custom codes were written to perform the image processing and generate similarity metrics (match scores) using MATLAB (Mathworks, Natick, MA). Five preprocessing filters (None, Histogram Equalization, Adaptive Histogram Equalization, North filter, Kalman Stack filter) and five image-match algorithms (Dice, Jaccard, Structural Similarity, Mutual Information, Matrix Correlation) were tested for their ability to delineate the shape characteristics of the vertebral body and generate a match score for a pair of radiographs representing a single individual when placed into an array of radiographs representing multiple individuals (Nomir and Abdel-Mottaleb, 2007, 2008; Wang et al., 2004). For the cervical region, the optimal filter and algorithm combination was a histogram equalization filter, which improves contrast when the pixel value distribution is similar across the image, followed by the Jaccard algorithm similarity coefficient, a statistical measure of the similarity between sample sets. For the lumbar region, the optimal filter and match score algorithm was adaptive histogram equalization filter, which improves contrast when the pixel value distribution is not uniform across the image, followed by the Jaccard algorithm similarity coefficient. These filters and match score algorithm combinations were used for subsequent testing of the software performance.

Once the optimal filters and algorithms were identified, the project moved forward with further coding revision of QMA into the CADI software prototype followed by validation testing for the cervical and lumbar vertebrae. Prior to analysis, the compiled radiographs were anonymized and reviewed for artifacts, excessive noise, poor contrast, obstruction, or out-of-plane artifacts that could confound the assessment and possibly eliminate the radiograph from use in an actual decedent identification case. Radiographs of subjects with visible surgical implants and/or severe osteophytic growth between scans that would introduce artificial error were also excluded for purposes of testing software performance.

CADI was used to spatially register each targeted vertebra in the preprocessed images using the chosen semiautomated pattern matching algorithm. The result of CADI spatial registration occurs when two radiographs are alternately displayed and the software holds a specific vertebra in a constant position on the computer display. When a human subjectively compares an anatomic feature between radiographs, they perform the equivalent of this spatial registration process in their mind before they decide if anatomic features match. As the first step in the match detection process, the individual feature of interest (e.g., C3) was spatially registered for all images in the test array, using the postmortem radiograph from the ID pair as the reference. The spatial registration process was completed by MMI analysts with extensive experience in performing spatial registration in clinical spine studies but who were blinded to the CADI study design. A close spatial registration was easily achieved with similarly shaped vertebral bodies, but an approximate overall registration had to be accepted for some of the vertebrae with highly inconsistent morphology. Differences in magnification between images were minimized by scaling all radiographs in each array so that the superior endplate of every vertebra in the array was the same apparent size. Although this step eliminates the possibility of using true differences in the size of vertebrae to aid in identification, it was deemed necessary to control for the variable and unknown magnification that can occur between radiographs in real-world scenarios. Finally, a polygon region of interest was manually defined around the vertebral body to mask out everything but the target vertebral body, excluding the posterior morphology of the vertebra. The posterior elements were excluded due to the variability in orientation of the central X-ray beam with the anatomy. This variability can result in large differences in the radiographic appearance of the posterior elements between radiographs. The effect of differences in X-ray beam orientation has less of an effect on the radiographic image of the vertebral body.

Multiple test scenarios were executed using lateral images of C1–5 and L1–5 vertebrae. Test arrays comprising "ID pair(s)" and comparison images were constructed. ID pairs included an early time point radiograph (simulating antemortem) and a radiograph taken 2–3 years later (simulating postmortem) from the same individual. Cases were randomly selected for each test array based on age and sex cohorts, using only cases that had two lateral radiographs of the cervical spine imaged in the same plane and taken at least 2 years apart. Population specific cohorts reflecting ancestry/race were not developed due to the lack of available information regarding specific differences in vertebral morphology attributed to ancestry. Multiple age and sex specific arrays containing 12–30 images and up to five ID pairs were assembled for the over 54,000 individual tests completed during the validation project. For each test array, a match score between the postmortem image of the ID pair(s), the antemortem image of the ID pair(s), and all comparison radiographs in the array was calculated. Match scores were statistically analyzed using Stata (StataCorp, College Station, TX). The match scores were normalized to the highest match score within the array and were represented as percentages, such that the highest match score was 100%. The normalized match scores were then listed in descending order with the highest match score representing the radiograph in the array that was objectively the most similar to the postmortem radiograph. To summarize the results of the validation testing, the individual cervical vertebrae results ranged from 95% to 100% of the ID pairs correctly matched. The lumbar results ranged from 92% to 99% of the ID pairs correctly matched (Derrick et al., 2015).

The ability of CADI to determine the correct match from an array using individual cervical and lumbar vertebral bodies was successfully validated in the initial testing phase (Derrick et al., 2015). However, the statistical confidence that a correct match has been identified can theoretically be improved by using multiple anatomic features visible in a single radiograph, for example, assessment of more than one vertebral body. Subsequent rounds of testing evaluated the function of CADI with specific reference to combining match scores for multiple skeletal elements identified in radiographs of the spine. To do this, CADI was used to assess different levels of lateral cervical and lateral lumbar vertebrae first individually, then subsequently combining the results of the individual tests.

Second-Phase Testing of CADI

Cervical and lumbar spine radiographs from males and females aged 40–69 years were selected from the compiled images used in the first CADI testing phases. The available age range was predetermined by the age distribution comprising the archived images. Based on the source of the test radiographs (NHANES II), the radiographs were deemed to be representative of typical clinical images that might be used as an antemortem radiograph for a medicolegal identification case. The selection criteria were as follows: each case radiograph had to have at least three clearly visualized cervical or lumbar vertebral levels that could be analyzed, and each case had to contain two lateral radiographs taken at least 2 years apart.

In the cervical spine, C2–C7 were often visualized in the sample radiographs but the C3–C5 vertebrae were the most clearly and consistently visible. These levels were generally free from overlap with other skeletal elements or the fleshed shoulders and were less likely to contain implants. For the lumbar spine, the L2–L4 vertebral levels were the most consistently visualized.

The radiographs were analyzed in arrays composed only of individuals of the same sex whose ages fell within the same 5-year range. Base arrays were created to simulate a closed-set identification trial in which the correct match was assumed to exist within the array. Each array consisted of an ID pair and comparison images comprised one radiograph each from 10 different subjects obtained from the NHANES II representing a pool of other antemortem radiographs from the same sex and age cohort. Thus, each test array consisted of a simulated postmortem radiograph, a correct match, and 10 incorrect matches. Multiple base arrays representing each vertebrae of interest were then created by duplicating the base radiograph arrays. From the cervical base arrays, an array was created for each of the vertebral bodies from C3 to C5. Additional test arrays were created if more than one ID pair was available in the image databases.

The histogram equalization filter was applied, followed by an edge-detection algorithm. The same filter and edge detection were applied to all images. The similarity between the features was calculated using the Jaccard similarity index. For each array, a match score between the postmortem image of the ID pair, the antemortem image of the ID pair, and all comparison antemortem radiographs within the array was calculated. The match scores within each array were normalized and then ranked in descending order. Each time an array was analyzed for a specific vertebra, the array was classified a success if the actual match to the representative postmortem radiograph had the highest match score and also if the match score was among the top three match scores for purposes of exploring statistical interpretation models.

Table 23.1 provides representative raw and normalized data for one array. Tables 23.2 and 23.3 present the percent of tested arrays where, for three different vertebrae, the test was a success if the match score within an array of

Table 23.1 Summary Results for a Representative Base Array (Male 50–54)

Antemortem (AM) Radiograph	L2			L3			L4		
	Match Score	Normalized Match Score	Rank	Match Score	Normalized Match Score	Rank	Normalized Match Score	Match Score	Rank
AM 1[a]	0.05407	100.00	1	0.05538	100.00	1	73.01	0.03751	3
AM 2	0.01193	22.06	8	0.02106	38.02	11	33.56	0.01724	9
AM 3	0.02678	49.54	5	0.03229	58.30	4	28.84	0.01481	10
AM 4	0.01615	29.87	7	0.03464	62.56	3	92.92	0.04774	2
AM 5	0.00671	12.42	11	0.02636	47.59	8	100.00	0.05137	1
AM 6	0.01034	19.12	10	0.02328	42.03	9	34.77	0.01786	8
AM 7	0.01133	20.96	9	0.02314	41.78	10	43.98	0.02259	6
AM 8	0.04073	75.34	3	0.03538	63.89	2	22.52	0.01157	11
AM 9	0.04158	76.91	2	0.02672	48.25	7	57.21	0.02939	5
AM 10	0.02948	54.52	4	0.02686	48.50	6	58.45	0.03003	4
AM 11	0.02140	39.58	6	0.03088	55.76	5	41.15	0.02114	7

[a]The AM 1 radiograph is the true match to the postmortem radiograph and is consistently ranked among the top three ranks for each lumbar vertebral level by computer-assisted decedent identification.

Table 23.2 Percent Correctly Classified by Computer-Assisted Decedent Identification for Multiple Vertebral Levels

Base Arrays	Number of Base Arrays Tested (Each Array Has a Unique ID Pair)	Percentage of the Arrays Where the ID Pair Had the Highest Match Score for All Three Vertebrae	Percentage of Arrays Where the ID Pair Had One of the Three Highest Match Scores for All Three Vertebrae
Male 40–44	3	100	100
Male 45–49	3	100	100
Male 50–54	3	100	100
Male 55–59	3	77.8	88.9
Male 60–64	2	100	100
Female 40–44	1	100	100
Female 45–49	3	100	100
Female 50–54	2	100	100
Female 55–59	3	100	100
Overall result with base arrays combined	23	97.1	98.55

Table 23.3 Lumbar Analysis: Percentage of the ID Pairs Ranked Among Top Three Scores

Base Arrays	Number of Base Arrays Tested (Each Array Has a Unique ID Pair)	Percentage of the Arrays Where the ID Pair Had the Highest Match Score for All Three Vertebrae	Percentage of Arrays Where the ID Pair Had One of the Three Highest Match Scores for All Three Vertebrae
Male 40–44	3	44.4	55.6
Male 45–49	4	58.3	75.0
Male 50–54	6	77.8	88.9
Male 55–59	6	50.0	72.2
Male 60–64	5	53.3	80.0
Male 65–69	2	83.3	83.3
Female 40–44	2	50.0	83.3
Female 45–49	2	33.3	83.3
Female 50–54	2	66.7	100
Female 55–59	3	55.6	88.9
Female 60–64	5	60.0	80.0
Female 65–69	5	40.0	60.0
Overall result with base arrays combined	45	56.3	77.8

radiographs was highest for the postmortem and antemortem images from the ID pair. Tables 23.2 and 23.3 also provide the percent of tested arrays where, for three different vertebrae from a base array, the test was a success if the match score for the postmortem and antemortem images from the ID pair was one of the three highest match scores. Of note, the lumbar results yielded lower percentages of successful tests. This may be partly due to lumbar vertebrae possessing more uniform vertebral shapes across individuals. Lumbar spinal radiographs also tended to exhibit bowel gas obstructions and greater X-ray scatter and noise from surrounding soft tissues. The challenge is to determine how to interpret these data in an actual identification case.

The basic probability of successfully determining the correct match by chance in a closed-set array of 12 radiographs with one ID pair is 1 in 11 for each individual vertebra tested (Fig. 23.4). When the tested array was a success for two individual vertebrae, the nominal probability of doing that by chance is $1/11 \times 1/11 = 1/121$. When the test could be repeated successfully for three individual vertebrae, the nominal probability of that happening by chance increases to $1/11 \times 1/11 \times 1/11 = 1/1331$.

When a single pair of antemortem and postmortem radiographs is qualitatively assessed for the purposes of decedent identification, the expert examines specific primary features that they determine to have a high degree of similarity between the two radiographs. They may also identify secondary features that appear similar, but to a lesser degree than with the primary features. Having both primary and secondary features that appear similar increases their confidence in the identification. In an analogous fashion, obtaining a match score that is one of the highest should increase, to an extent, overall confidence in the match. It is for this reason that match scores in the present study were analyzed both for being the best match and also for being one of the top three matches. However, there is as yet no consensus on how to handle these types of data statistically such that the overall test would yield a validated probability of a positive or negative identification.

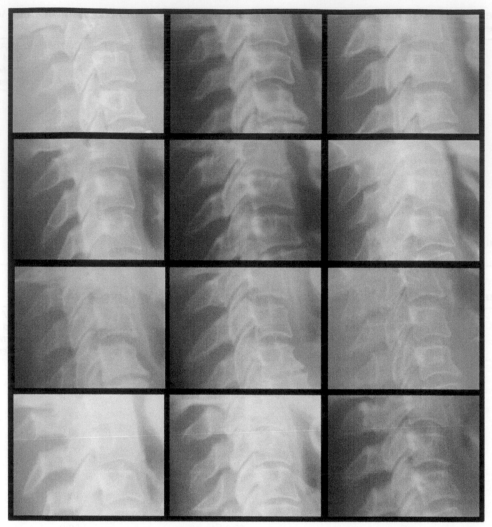

Figure 23.4 Radiographic array of 12 cervical radiographs used in validation.

Using multiple anatomic features and defining success as having one of the highest match scores (instead of the highest) allows for additional strategies to establish confidence that a correct (or incorrect) match was determined. It is reasonable to define success as having one of the highest match scores when analyzing radiographs for identification due to the many variables that can affect radiograph quality and the differences between the antemortem and postmortem radiographs. The central X-ray beam is not always oriented and positioned the same with respect to the anatomy, the source-to-image distance is not always the same (changing the amount of parallax), the soft tissues and gas in front of and behind the skeletal element can change, and the X-ray equipment and exposure settings can differ. Despite these variables, it may still be possible to observe that several features of a vertebra are similar in two radiographs. For these reasons, further assessment of images that yielded the top three match scores can help to provide confidence in the results.

The simplistic way to interpret these data would be to use simple probability statistics. However, by increasing the number of known incorrect radiographs in the array, or by increasing the number of anatomic features tested, the probabilities could be substantially improved. A correction for making repeated tests on the same set of radiographs within an array is likely necessary, but methodology for performing this correction has not been established. In addition, it is not clear how the probabilities would be downgraded if the match score for the antemortem and postmortem radiograph pair was one of the lowest. The integration of these objective match score data with the probability that the correctly matched antemortem radiograph could have been found by chance alone can substantially improve confidence in an identification.

■ IMPLEMENTING COMPUTER-ASSISTED DECEDENT IDENTIFICATION IN PRACTICE

The potential value of CADI to the ME/C is easily recognized. CADI could be used almost daily in larger offices for routine identification of tentatively identified decedents with accessible medical records. Although still expensive for local agencies, the availability of rapid whole body radiographic scanning instrumentation (e.g., Lodox) is increasing and more ME/Cs are purchasing these scanners. Utilization of rapid scanning technology reduces the time it takes to perform preautopsy radiographs, preventing imaging of artifacts produced during autopsy that may interfere with CADI matching.

The potential of CADI in a mass fatality scenario is also easily imagined. Mobile radiographic and CT instrumentation in the field could image charred and/or dismembered regions of bodies and send them electronically for real-time CADI assessment and time-sensitive personal identification. However, CADI must be developed further to ascertain the actual value of the method to the ME/C. To be used fully, CADI must be validated for multiple regions of the skeleton, such as the frontal sinuses, clavicle, knee, and pelvis. Once CADI is functional for additional regions, the method must be validated in quality assurance exercises using actual forensic images. Further, CADI is not currently stand-alone software. To solve this challenge, the software must be developed into a stand-alone version, a node system set up at participating ME/C for access to the program. Costs for each of these options have not yet been explored.

■ SUMMARY

The CADI method of radiographic comparison has the potential to simplify the personal identification process for the ME/C, not only for routine casework but also in mass fatality events where disaster victim identification can be extremely difficult and time-consuming. Although showing early promise as a statistically based method to assist in personal identification, CADI is still in the prototype stage. The developers must surmount a number of testing and funding hurdles, including a cost beneficial method of software access for ME/C use before CADI can be accepted as standard practice for personal identification.

Acknowledgments

The authors acknowledge and thank Michelle H. Raxter, PhD, Jim Zeigler, PhD, Elaine F. Chan, PhD, Jennifer C. Love, PhD, Jason M. Wiersema, PhD, and N. Shastry Akella, PhD, for their creative input, hard work, and support provided during the development of the CADI method.

References

Adams, B.J., Maves, R.C., 2002. Radiographic identification using the clavicle of an individual missing from the Vietnam conflict. J. Forensic Sci. 47, 369–373.

Baroudess, D.A., Sauer, N.J., Brantley, R.E., 1988. The effects of aging on the comparability of antemortem and postmortem radiographs. J. Forensic Sci. 33, 1223–1230.

Berdahl, C.T., Vermeulen, M.J., Larson, D.B., Schull, M.J., 2013. Emergency department computed tomography utilization in the United States and Canada. Ann. Emerg. Med. 62, 486–494.

Budowle, B., Ge, J., Chakraborty, R., Gill-King, H., 2011. Use of prior odds for missing persons identifications. Investig. Genet. 2, 1–6.

Bunch, A.W., Fielding, C.G., 2005. The use of World War II chest radiograph in the identification of a missing-in-action US Marine. Mil. Med. 170, 239–242.

Christensen, A.M., 2005. Testing the reliability of frontal sinuses in positive identification. J. Forensic Sci. 50 (1), 18–22.

Christensen, A.M., Hatch, G.M., Brogdon, B., 2014. A current perspective on forensic radiology. J. Forensic Radiol. Imaging 2, 111–113.

Cox, M., Malcolm, M., Fairgrieve, S.I., 2009. A new digital method for the objective comparison of frontal sinuses for identification. J. Forensic Sci. 54, 761–772.

De Greef, S., Willems, G., 2005. Three-dimensional cranio-facial reconstruction in forensic identification: latest progress and new tendencies in the 21st century. J. Forensic Sci. 50 (1), 12–17.

Dérczy, K., Angyal, M., 1998. Personal identification on the basis of antemortem and postmortem radiographs. J. Forensic Sci. 43, 1089–1093.

Derrick, S.M., Wiersema, J.M., Hipp, J.A., Akella, N.S., Zeigler, J., 2014. Novel Computer-Assisted Identification Method Using Radiograph Comparison (NIJ Final Technical Report).

Derrick, S.M., Raxter, M.H., Hipp, J.A., Goel, P., Chan, E.F., Love, J.C., Wiersema, J.M., Akella, N.S., 2015. Development of a computer-assisted forensic radiographic identification method using the lateral cervical and lumbar spine. J. Forensic Sci. 60, 5–12.

Dror, I.E., Charlton, D., Péron, A.E., 2006. Contextual information renders experts vulnerable to making erroneous identifications. Forensic Sci. Int. 156, 74–78.

Dunson, D.D., 2007. Bayesian methods for latent trait modelling of longitudinal data. Stat. Methods Med. Res. 16 (5) Biostatistics Branch, National Institute of Environmental Health Sciences, Research Triangle Park, NC.

Eisen, C.H., Bowie, J.V., Gaskin, D.J., LaVeist, T.A., Thorpe Jr., R.J., 2015. The contribution of social and environmental factors to race differences in dental services use. Bull. N.Y. Acad. Med. 92, 415–421.

Fahmy, G., Nassar, D., Haj-Said, E., Chen, H., Nomir, O., Zhou, J., Howell, R., Ammar, H.H., Abdel-Mottaleb, M., Jain, A.K., 2004. Towards an automated dental identification system (ADIS). In: Davide, M., Jain, A.K. (Eds.), Biometric Authentication. Springer, Berlin-Heidelberg, pp. 789–796.

Fournier, N.A., Ross, A.H., 2016. Sex, ancestral, and pattern type variation of fingerprint minutiae: a forensic perspective on anthropological dermatoglyphics. Am. J. Phys. Anthr. 160 (4), 625–632.

Gantner, G., Murphy, W.A., 1982. Radiologic examination of anatomic parts and skeletonized remains. J. Forensic Sci. 27, 9–18.

Gelman, A., 2006. Prior distributions for variance parameters in hierarchical models (comment on article by Browne and Draper). Bayesian Anal. 1, 515–534.

Goldstein, M., Kirk, N.J., Wood, R.E., 2002. Skeletal identification using the frontal sinus region: a retrospective study of 39 cases. J. Forensic Sci. 47, 318–323.

Grother, P.J., Quinn, G.W., Phillips, P.J., 2010. Report on the Evaluation of 2D Still-Image Face Recognition Algorithms. NIST Interagency Report 7709.

Harris, A., Wood, R., Nortje, C., Thomas, C., 1987. The frontal sinus: forensic fingerprint? A pilot study. J. Forensic Odonto-Stomatol. 5 (1), 9.

Hayes, J., 2010. Forensic Turnaround Time in 50 States. OLR Research Report https://www.cga.ct.gov/2010/rpt/2010-R-0086.htm.

Hogge, J.P., Messmer, J.M., Doan, Q.N., 1994. Radiographic identification of unknown human remains and interpreter experience level. J. Forensic Sci. 39, 373–377.

Korley, F.K., Pham, J.C., Kirsch, T.D., 2010. Use of advanced radiology during visits to US emergency departments for injury-related conditions, 1998–2007. JAMA 304, 1465–1471.

Kuehn, C.M., Taylor, K.M., Mann, F., Wilson, A.J., Harruff, R.C., 2002. Validation of chest X-ray comparisons for unknown decedent identification. J. Forensic Sci. 47, 1–5.

Kullman, L., Eklund, B., Grundin, R., 1990. Value of the frontal sinus in identification of unknown persons. J. Forensic Odonto-Stomatol. 8, 3–10.

Lee, S.-Y., Song, X.-Y., 2004. Evaluation of the Bayesian and maximum likelihood approaches in analyzing structural equation models with small sample sizes. Multivar. Behav. Res. 39, 653–686.

Lichtenstein, J., Fitzpatrick, J., Madewell, J., 1988. The role of radiology in fatality investigations. AJR 150, 751–755.

Mann, R.W., 1998. Use of bone trabeculae to establish positive identification. Forensic Sci. Int. 98, 91–99.

Martel, W., Wicks, J.D., Hendrix, R.C., 1977. The accuracy of radiologic identification of humans using skeletal landmarks: a contribution to forensic pathology. Radiology 124, 681–684.

Maxwell, A.B., Ross, A.H., 2014. A radiographic study on the utility of cranial vault outlines for positive identifications. J. Forensic Sci. 59, 314–318.

Morishita, J., Katsuragawa, S., Kondo, K., Doi, K., 2001. An automated patient recognition method based on an image-matching technique using previous chest radiographs in the picture archiving and communication system environment. Med. Phys. 28, 1093–1097.

Morishita, J., Katsuragawa, S., Sasaki, Y., Doi, K., 2004. Potential usefulness of biological fingerprints in chest radiographs for automated patient recognition and identification. Acad. Radiol. 11, 309–315.

SECTION III

Moser Jr., R.P., Wagner, G.N., 1990. Nutrient groove of the ilium, a subtle but important forensic radiographic marker in the identification of victims of severe trauma. Skelet. Radiol. 19, 15–19.

National Health and Nutrition Examination Survey (NHANESII), 2014. Centers for Disease Control. http://www.cdc.gov/nchs/nhanes/about_nhanes.htm.

National Institute of Justice, 2005. Mass Fatality Incidents: a Guide for Human Forensic Identification. Special Report, Technical Working Group for Mass Fatality Forensic Identification NCJ 199758. National Institute of Justice, US Department of Justice, Office of Justice Programs, United States of America.

National Research Council, 2009. Strengthening Forensic Science in the United States: a Path Forward. https://www.ncjrs.gov/pdffiles1/nij/grants/228091.pdf.

Neumann, C., Stern, H., 2016. Forensic examination of fingerprints: past, present, and future. Chance 29, 9–16.

Niespodziewanski, E., Stephan, C.N., Guyomarc'h, P., Fenton, T.W., 2016. Human identification via lateral patella radiographs: a validation study. J. Forensic Sci. 61, 134–140.

Nomir, O., Abdel-Mottaleb, M., 2007. Combining matching algorithms for human identification using dental X-ray radiographs. In: 2007 IEEE International Conference on Image ProcessingII, pp. 409–412.

Nomir, O., Abdel-Mottaleb, M., 2008. Fusion of matching algorithms for human identification using dental X-ray radiographs. IEEE Trans. Inf. Forensics Secur. 3, 223–233.

Owsley, D.W., Mann, R.W., 1992. Positive personal identity of skeletonized remains using abdominal and pelvic radiographs. J. Forensic Sci. 37, 332–336.

Pretty, I.A., Barsley, R., Bowers, C.M., Bush, M., Bush, P., Clement, J., Dorian, R., Freeman, A., Lewis, J., Senn, D., Wright, F., 2012. Odontology–dentistry's contribution to truth and justice. In: Ubelaker, D.H. (Ed.), Forensic Science: Current Issues, Future Directions. John Wiley & Sons, Ltd., Chichester, UK, pp. 179–210.

Reitman, C.A., Hipp, J.A., Nguyen, L., Esses, S.I., 2004. Changes in segmental intervertebral motion adjacent to cervical arthrodesis: a prospective study. Spine 29 (E), 221–226.

Ribeiro, F.d.A.Q., 2000. Standardized measurements of radiographic films of the frontal sinuses: an aid to identifying unknown persons. Ear, Nose Throat J. 79 (1), 26.

Riepert, T., Ulmcke, D., Schweden, F., Nafe, B., 2001. Identification of unknown dead bodies by X-ray image comparison of the skull using the X-ray simulation program FoXSIS. Forensic Sci. Int. 117, 89–98.

Rogers, T.L., Allard, T.T., 2004. Expert testimony and positive identification of human remains through cranial suture patterns. J. Forensic Sci. 49, 1–5.

Ross, A.H., Lanfear, A.K., Maxwell, A.B., 2015. Testing the Validity of Radiographic Comparisons in Positive Identifications. National Institute of Justice Final Technical Report.

Sanders, I., Woesner, M.E., Ferguson, R.A., Noguchi, T.T., 1972. A new application of forensic radiology: identification of deceased from a single clavicle. AJR 115, 619–622.

Shamir, L., Ling, S., Rahimi, S., Ferrucci, L., Goldberg, I.G., 2009. Biometric identification using knee X-rays. Int. J. Biom. 1, 365–370.

Shimizu, Y., Matsunobu, Y., Morishita, J., April 2016. Evaluation of the usefulness of modified biological fingerprints in chest radiographs for patient recognition and identification. Radiol. Phys. Technol. 30, 1–5.

Spiegelhalter, D., Freedman, L., 1988. Bayesian approaches to clinical trials. Bayesian Stat. 3, 453–477.

Spruill, F., Gantner, G., Murphy, W., 1980. Radiologic identification of unknown human remains. J. Forensic Sci. 25, 727–735.

Steadman, D.W., Adams, B.J., Konigsberg, L.W., 2006. Statistical basis for positive identification in forensic anthropology. AJPA 131, 15–26.

Stephan, C.N., 2017. Skeletal identification by radiographic comparison of the cervicothoracic region on chest radiographs. In: Latham, K.A., Bartelink, E., Finnegan, M. (Eds.), New Perspectives in Forensic Human Skeletal Identification, Elsevier/Academic Press (this volume).

Stephan, C.N., Amidan, B., Trease, H., Guyomarc'h, P., Pulsipher, T., Byrd, J.E., 2014. Morphometric comparison of clavicle outlines from 3D bone scans and 2D chest radiographs: a shortlisting tool to assist radiographic identification of human skeletons. J. Forensic Sci. 59, 306–313.

Stephan, C., Guyomarc'h, P., D'Alonzo, S., 2017. Morphometric identification methods. In: Latham, K.A., Bartelink, E., Finnegan, M. (Eds.), New Perspectives in Forensic Human Skeletal Identification, Elsevier/Academic Press (in this volume).

Stephan, C.N., Winburn, A.P., Christensen, A.F., Tyrrell, A.J., 2011. Skeletal identification by radiographic comparison: blind tests of a morphoscopic method using antemortem chest radiographs. J. Forensic Sci. 56, 320–332.

Streetman, E., Fenton, T.W., 2017. Comparative medical radiography: practice and validation. In: Latham, K.A., Bartelink, E., Finnegan, M. (Eds.), New Perspectives in Forensic Human Skeletal Identification, Elsevier/Academic Press (in this volume).

Telmon, N., Allery, J., Scolan, V., Rouge, D., 2001. A case report demonstrating the value of chest X-rays in comparative identification. J. Clin. Pathol. Forensic Med. 8, 77–80.

Toge, R., Morishita, J., Sasaki, Y., Doi, K., 2013. Computerized image-searching method for finding correct patients for misfiled chest radiographs in a PACS server by use of biological fingerprints. Radiol. Phys. Technol. 6, 437–443.

Wang, Z., Bovik, A.C., Sheikh, H.R., Simoncelli, E.P., 2004. Image quality assessment: from error visibility to structural similarity. IEEE Trans. Image Process. 13, 600–612.

Wayman, J.L., 2015. Biometric verification/identification/authentication/recognition: the terminology. In: Li, S.Z., Jain, A.K. (Eds.), Encyclopedia of Biometrics. Springer, Boston, pp. 263–268.

Wijeysundera, D.N., Austin, P.C., Hux, J.E., Beattie, W.S., Laupacis, A., 2009. Bayesian statistical inference enhances the interpretation of contemporary randomized controlled trials. J. Clin. Epidemiol. 62 (15), 13–21.

Zhao, K.D., Yang, C., Zhao, C., Stans, A.A., An, K.N., 2005. Assessment of noninvasive intervertebral motion measurements in the lumbar spine. J. Biomech. 38, 1943–1946.

CHAPTER 24

Skeletal Identification by Radiographic Comparison of the Cervicothoracic Region on Chest Radiographs[a,b]

Carl N. Stephan | Susan S. D'Alonzo | Emily K. Wilson |
Pierre Guyomarc'h | Gregory E. Berg | John E. Byrd

Defense POW/MIA Accounting Agency, Joint Base Pearl Harbor-Hickam, HI,
United States

Chapter Outline

■ INTRODUCTION

The comparison of antemortem (AM) and postmortem (PM) radiographs is widely accepted as a primary means of skeletal identification in the forensic science literature (Angyal and Derczy, 1998; Atkins and Potsaid, 1978; Brogdon, 1998; Evans et al., 1981; Greulich, 1960; Hogge et al., 1994; Kade et al., 1987; Kahana et al., 1997; Mundorff et al., 2006; Scott, 1946; Singleton, 1951; Thali et al., 2011; Ubelaker, 1984; Zanjad and Godbole, 2007). A combination of factors award the method high utility including resilience of bones to decomposition; good stability of bone morphology in adults over lengthy time frames; broad range in morphology between individuals as a result of genetic and environmental influences; and commonality of radiographic images taken during life for medical examinations (see e.g., D'Alonzo et al., 2017; Stephan et al., 2010, 2014).

While the outline shape and septa of the frontal sinuses serve as a flagship for capabilities of radiographic comparison methods (Asherson, 1965; Christensen, 2005a,b; Cox et al., 2009; Kirk et al., 2002; Kullman et al., 1990; Nambiar et al., 1999; Ubelaker, 1984), the principles of application are identical no matter what region of the body is concerned—a comparison of the details of the osteological morphology between the AM and PM image sets. To date almost every region of the body has been examined for its utility, and the region ranges from skull (Rhine and Sperry, 1991), to vertebrae (Mundorff et al., 2006), pelvis (Owsley and Mann, 1992), clavicles (Adams and Maves, 2002; Sanders et al., 1972; Stephan et al., 2011), hands (Greulich, 1960; Koot et al., 2005), knees (Niespodziewanski

---

[a]This work was conducted during several appointments to the Research Participation and Visiting Scientist Programs at the former Joint POW/MIA Accounting Command (JPAC), Central Identification Laboratory, now the Defense POW/MIA Accounting Agency (DPAA), administered by the Oak Ridge Institute for Science and Education (ORISE) through an interagency agreement between the US Department of Energy and the JPAC-CIL/DPAA. Writing by some participants has been conducted following program conclusion, but in most cases affiliations remain as ORISE Visiting Scientists and/or External Consultants.

[b]The views and opinions contained herein are solely those of the authors and are not to be construed as official, or as views of the US Department of Defense and/or any of the US Armed Forces.

New Perspectives in Forensic Human Skeletal Identification. http://dx.doi.org/10.1016/B978-0-12-805429-1.00024-7

et al., 2016; Riddick et al., 1983), and feet (Rich et al., 2002), to name just a few. High resolution and good image quality of both the AM and PM radiographs facilitate comparisons that may even include details of trabecular bone structure in addition to gross shape and form of the cortex in some cases (Mann, 1998; Quatrehomme et al., 2014). Short time frames between AM and PM radiography are preferred, so that windows for shape and density change with bone remodeling are reduced (Sauer, 1988; Sauer and Brantley, 1989). However, once adulthood has been reached, investigations indicate that bone morphology remains remarkably consistent (Sauer, 1988; Sauer and Brantley, 1989) alleviating some of the concern around remodeling across longer time intervals. As a matter of good practice the most recent AM radiographs (closest to the time of death) should always be sought and used when its image quality is suitable and does not preclude comparisons using these images.

Comparisons can of course only be conducted using the AM images that are available for the case at hand, which in the context of everyday medicolegal casework of a medical examiner's office, typically requires flexible (nonquantitative and visual) procedures to handle the variety of body regions encountered and image qualities presented. Quantitative methods are easier to formulate for radiographic sets that are more standardized and so have been derived for flagship methods of frontal sinus comparison (Christensen, 2005a,b; Cox et al., 2009) and chest radiograph comparison (D'Alonzo et al., 2017; Stephan et al., 2010, 2014). While they are not as flexible as subjective methods, quantitative approaches are useful for assigning numbers to degree of anatomical correspondence and conducting automated searches of large radiographic data sets, which in particular circumstances can be especially useful (D'Alonzo et al., 2017; Stephan et al., 2010, 2014), i.e., where large numbers of the same type of radiographs exist for multiple individuals. It should be noted, however, that quantitative methods are rarely fully automated; a human operator is required for segmenting structures and/or ultimately required for image examination to ensure the legitimacy of the computer results and to undertake detailed inspection of the short-listed candidates (D'Alonzo et al., 2017; Stephan and Guyomarc'h, 2014). This applies to radiographic comparisons in the same manner as it does to other biometric search functions such as fingerprints (Ulery et al., 2011). The human involvement is required because computer algorithms cannot currently match the performance of the highly evolved human visual system that can not only identify, differentiate, and interpret fine complexities embedded in biological images, but can perform under nonideal circumstances such as degraded image qualities.

The human visual system is widely known, for example, to possess complex edge enhancement functions readily demonstrated by Mach bands (Fig. 24.1). These enhancements can function in positive or negative favor depending on the context. The limits of current computerized approaches are exemplified by mean errors of 1.1 ± 1.6 mm for current clavicle segmentation algorithms when operating on similar images of high quality (Hogeweg et al., 2012), errors which are too high for radiographic comparison procedures or other diagnostic approaches and which have thereby inspired the Chest Radiograph Anatomical Structure Segmentation Grand Challenge that has been running since 2013 to derive medically suitable clavicle segmentation protocols (http://grand-challenge.org/all_challenges/). These limits have driven a preference for manual, rather than computer automated, segmentation of clavicle shape as the basis for computer automated searching of chest radiograph databases (D'Alonzo et al., 2017; Stephan et al., 2010, 2014). In the context of present day technology, this means that the radiographic comparison method, whether computer automated or not, hinges upon human operator expertise. It is thereby crucial that individuals conducting radiographic comparisons be skilled at analyzing radiographic images.

The interpretation of radiographic images is a complex and difficult skill to master drawing on the integration of several bodies of knowledge including anatomy, projective geometry, and radiography (Lesgold et al., 1988). Consequently the skill may take years to master (Lesgold et al., 1988) and analysts must be intimately familiar with the anatomy of the body region concerned, including the *soft* and *hard* tissues (which are both visible on AM

(A)   (B)   (C)   (D)

Figure 24.1 Diagrams illustrating high-performance edge detection in the human visual system. (A) Mach bands. The human visual system applies edge enhancement (spatial high-boost filtering) such that monotone gray bands appear darker near their lighter neighbors and lighter near their darker neighbors—enhancing the edges. This effect may be active during radiographic examinations and while beneficial in some instances it has also been known to result in false-positive calls of dental caries or root fracture in dentistry (Nielsen, 2001) and misdiagnosis of pneumothorax in clinical medicine (Parker et al., 2009). These edge enhancement features are an important phenomenon to be aware of for chest radiograph comparison. (B) Removal of intermediate gray tone bands removes the Mach effect. (C) A poor-quality chest radiograph, but one in which the inferior clavicle margins are visible at their lateral extent if examined closely. (D) Three-dimensional projection of pixel intensity values showing how similar the inferior clavicle edge values are to the background noise in (C) making it difficult for a computer program to recognize the clavicles from the pixel intensities alone without any a priori knowledge/input of basic anatomical form.

radiographs in superimposed fashion); they must understand the principles of radiographic image generation (fundamentals of equipment and image generation using a "point" source of X-rays); and they must be able to integrate this information to correctly extract anatomical data.

There exist vast differences in image interpretation approach between novices and experts (Lesgold et al., 1988), with novices using different image evaluation schema than experts (Lesgold et al., 1988). This makes novices less flexible in regard to adjusting their schema in response to new information and this may prevent novices from reaching correct diagnoses, for which experts can normally offer greater amounts of image-derived supporting information (Lesgold et al., 1988). For forensic casework then, it is important that analysts be experts in *interpreting* radiographic images. Passing familiarity with radiographs is not sufficient. A tertiary qualification in anthropology, pathology, or radiography does not guarantee these specialist skills. Physical anthropologists may, for example, be trained through social science or archaeology streams and/or pathologists and radiologists may rarely handle dry skeletons. In this context, targeted training, competency tests, and ongoing performance checks are crucial to any quality assurance program to ensure radiographic comparison skill (Stephan et al., 2011, 2014).

While the general principle of radiographic comparison for skeletal identification is invariant—assess the osteological morphology for degree of anatomical correspondence—there has been little general attempt to standardize the radiographic comparison procedure (see Ross et al., 2016; Stephan et al., 2011 for exceptions). The vast volume of case reports and validation tests in the literature (see abovementioned citations) each describe slightly different approaches or leave these approaches open for analysts to decide what exact method to use. Moreover, radiographic comparisons have most commonly been reported for soft tissue encased (not skeletonized) remains, where exact replication of bone orientations in the former context is difficult.

In this chapter, we (1) review a standardized approach for PM radiography of the cervicothoracic region as undertaken at the Defense POW/MIA Accounting Agency (DPAA), made possible by the analysis of dry skeletons such that bone positions on the AM radiograph can be exactly reproduced at PM radiography; (2) provide frequency statistics for morphological features contributing to 84 successful case resolutions using these methods; (3) provide graphic exemplars of some of the most common/useful anatomical morphologies for cervicothoracic region for comparison; and (4) illustrate how the methods can provide strong biological support for a name association with two exemplar cases. This information should be of particular value to new analysts entering the field.

■ STANDARDIZED POSTEROANTERIOR CHEST RADIOGRAPH COMPARISON FOR DRY SKELETAL ELEMENTS

Skeletonized remains are ideal candidates for radiographic comparisons because, with a little time and skill, single elements (clavicles and C3-T3 vertebrae) can be orientated in the exact same position for PM radiography as recorded on the AM radiograph (Stephan et al., 2011). Not only does this provide directly comparable images without any reservation for the effects of different orientations on bone morphology, but it enables image superimpositions to be conducted for the long bones (i.e., clavicles) that cross-validate the degree of anatomical correspondence initially identified at the triage stage (Stephan et al., 2011; see case examples below).

Chest radiographs are well suited to radiographic comparisons because AM images are generally taken in highly standardized positions. Posteroanterior (PA) radiographs are most common (subject facing away from the X-ray source and toward the image receptor or film) with the backs of the hands placed on or behind the hips, chin on top of the image receptor, and the shoulders rotated forward to touch the image receptor (Ballinger and Frank, 2003; Military Roentgenology: Technical Manual 8-275, 1942; Military Roentgenology: Technical Manual 8-280, 1944, 1967) (Fig. 24.2). This sets a characteristic pose that is easily recognizable on the radiograph to the trained eye: size of heart in good proportion (it is close to the image receptor), superior lung fields free of scapulae (shoulders rotated anteriorly), and clavicles sloping toward the midline (forming a V-like appearance) (Ballinger and Frank, 2003).

Furthermore, the cervicothoracic region of the chest radiograph lends itself especially well to radiographic comparison because there is little shielding of the osteological structures in this region compared to the remainder of the thorax (Stephan et al., 2011; Telmon et al., 2001). This is particularly the case for the cervical (C3-7) and upper thoracic (T1-3) vertebrae. While the cervical vertebrae offer uninhibited views of their lateral margins free from superimposition with any other osteological structures, the thoracic vertebrae retain value even with sometimes complex superimpositions, due to their large transverse processes (Fig. 24.2). Additionally, the clavicles are useful because they resist decomposition well, are commonly recovered from the field, possess a thick cortex so they are readily differentiated from other superimposed structures (on the radiograph), and are highly variable as a result of forming part of the pectoral girdle such that differences in limb use between individuals gives rise to large anatomical variations in clavicle shape (Stephan et al., 2011). While the strength of frontal sinuses comparison resides in a single large anatomical structure in a single (frontal) bone that portrays salient differences (easily recognized even by untrained practitioners), a major strength of chest radiograph comparison resides in the capture of multiple separate bone in a single view, which can be used in a multivariate fashion to strengthen opinions for a match or nonmatch result.

It is important to note here that the chest radiograph comparison analyst is not responsible for making the chief decision of the identity of the skeletal remains. That task usually falls to the medical examiner, a forensic pathologist, and is typically made in view of multiple lines of identity evidence of which the radiographic comparison is only one component (other lines of evidence include, for example, circumstantial factors, mitochondrial DNA, or written

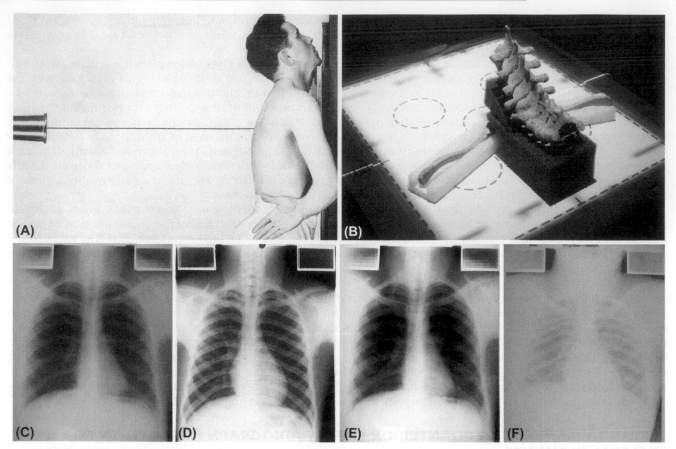

Figure 24.2 US military chest radiographs. (A) Subject position for posteroanterior capture as per Military Roentgenology: Technical Manual 8-280 (1944). (B) Positioning of the cervicothoracic region bones from the skeleton for triage radiography (Stephan et al., 2011). (C) Typical antemortem radiographic image quality (unenhanced). (D) Example of good contrast radiograph for osteological comparison (unenhanced). (E) Electronically enhanced version of (C) using the *Exposure Tool* in Adobe Photoshop CS3: exposure = 1.25, offset = 0.0163, gamma correction = 0.72. (F) Example of poor contrast radiograph (unenhanced image).

dental records). The result from a chest radiograph comparison should be a finding of the degree of anatomical correspondence that is arrived at by a documented list of items-of-concordance (IoCs), and analysts must be aware that correspondence findings may not be in the same direction for each osteological element included in the skeletal assemblage (there may be commingling in what are otherwise presumed to be uncommingled remains that the analyst must be potentially alert to in every instance). Depending on the organizational policy, radiographic comparisons may be conducted in strictly blind or selectively blinded environments. In the latter instance, analysts should be conscious of bias risks (as for example, might occur for cases that are thought ahead of time, not to be commingled).

The bone orientations used for PM radiography should be generic in the first instance (see e.g., Fig. 24.2), facilitating triage comparisons that allow for the exclusion of implausible candidates (Stephan et al., 2011). Small amounts of dental wax are used to hold the vertebrae in the desired orientations at the joint surfaces (Fig. 24.3), with the bones placed on foam supports (Fig. 24.2B). Both the dental wax and the foam supports are radiographically translucent (invisible on X-ray). Analysts should be aware of all perimortem trauma and PM taphonomic damage to the remains so that misinterpretations of bone morphology are not made (Fig. 24.3). In the event of a potential match, the position of the osseous elements should be fine-tuned to match the exact positions of the bones on the AM radiograph(s) that provide promising corresponding morphologies (multiple or strong IoCs, ideally across multiple bones) (Stephan et al., 2011).

Solid appreciation of anatomy and radiographic procedure provides the basis for interpreting the AM radiograph to compare the AM bone orientation in the PM condition. Some common examples of points of confusion by untrained analysts are the most readily opaque and visible bands that correspond to the C3-7 vertebrae on the radiographs that are formed principally by the neural arches, not the vertebral bodies (Figs. 24.2, 24.3, and 24.7–24.9); rib and/or vertebral margins may be confused for medial clavicle margins; the rhomboid fossa may not be recognized when they superimpose with the ribs; and double silhouettes produced by skin over the clavicles usually appear just above the superior clavicular margins. These mistakes are easily avoided with proper training and tests to demonstrate competency (see section on exemplar features for graphic depiction of abovementioned structures).

Once the near-exact position is reached for PM radiography, using the AM radiograph as the referent, a detailed comparison of the IoCs can be undertaken. Failure to replicate morphologies at this step is grounds for a nonmatch and should in turn be recorded in the bench notes. Near-identical positioning will enable superimpositions of the

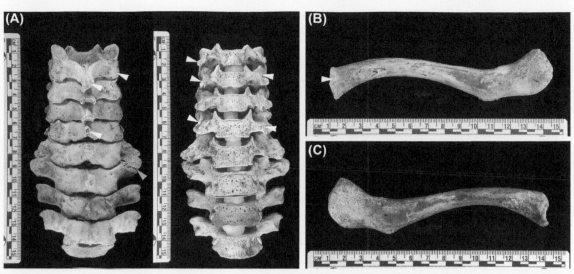

Figure 24.3 Skeletal elements pertaining to the cervicothoracic region on chest radiographs. (A) C3 T3 vertebrae in articulated sequence and showing utility wax at joints to hold vertebrae together in purpose-set position. (B) Inferior view of left clavicle. (C) Inferior view of right clavicle. Note rhomboid fossae in (B) and (C). *White arrows* indicate postmortem damage; *dark gray arrow* indicates perimortem trauma.

clavicles from the PM radiograph with those on the AM radiograph (see Examples of Two DPAA Chest Radiograph Comparison Cases section). Failure to obtain an exact superimposition again mandates exclusion.

IoCs are defined by the analyst and represent similarities in shape and/or densities at specific regions of the osteological elements. As morphological shapes and densities are highly variant and cannot be anticipated ahead of time for any particular case, the analyst is not restricted in DPAA methods to report only a prescribed set of features. There is also no requirement for a minimum number of IoCs since the weight carried by each IoC is not the same. There is, however, an upper limit of 25 IoCs set by the DPAA chest radiograph SOP, since this number is accepted to be overwhelmingly indicative of a match result and the addition of further IoCs likely adds little further value to the radiographic comparison findings.

■ WHICH ITEMS-OF-CONCORDANCE ARE MOST COMMONLY USED?

The numbers presented below are based on 84 cases so far conducted at the DPAA using the chest radiograph comparison method described earlier (as of and up to January 29, 2016). In interpreting these IoC frequencies it is important to note the following:

1. 33 of the 84 skeletons possessed all 10 osteological elements preferred for chest radiograph comparison (2 clavicles and 8 vertebrae) and so were complete skeletal sets, while 43 were incomplete (missing at least one element). In general, clavicles were more commonly present in the skeletal sets (c. 95%), while the vertebrae had higher rates of absence (any vertebrae present c. 60% of the time). Of the cases where a specific skeletal element was present, that element was also visible on the AM chest radiograph most frequently for the clavicles (96%) and the thoracic vertebrae (90%). Visibility of lower cervical vertebrae was also high (85%); however, the visibility of the C3 and C4 vertebrae was more variable (17%–64%) in part due to body positioning at the time of AM radiography. These elements fall at the periphery of the field-of-view, and deterioration of photoflurographs of 1930s to 1950s reduced their ability to be observed in some cases (Table 24.1).
2. The DPAA sample comprises radiographs taken in the 1930s to 1950s using photoflurograph technology, and so image quality is often reduced compared to modern-day radiographic images (Fig. 24.2). Moreover, the image size is typically 4 × 5″ and the age of the films has resulted in fading and deterioration in some cases. In most cases, image processing techniques can be used to overcome poor contrast and image fades to relatively good degrees (Fig. 24.2C and D).
3. Analysts performing DPAA chest radiograph comparison are subject to a stringent competency test procedure prior to being eligible for casework, whereby candidates examine nine radiographic arrays: five for training/practice and four pretest arrays where 100% accuracy must be attained in the latter to qualify for undertaking two competency test arrays. Correct answers to both of these competency test arrays must be provided to attain competency certification, after which two cases are completed in conjunction with an already qualified analyst, prior to the new analyst being able to undertake work independently. By the time the analysts are competency certified they have undertaken more than six arrays comprising AM radiographs of 20–40 individuals and a PM radiograph set and have attained a straight run of correct results in all six arrays. Some arrays may not include the correctly matching individual and so using conservative estimates, this roughly puts the odds of passing the competency test by chance at <1 in 160,000 ($0.05^4 = 1$ in 20 chance of a correct guess across four arrays and discounting any arrays excluding a match).

Table 24.1   Summary Data Concerning Numbers of Bones Present in the 84 Cases of Chest Radiograph Comparison Analyzed

	Of 84 Cases, Number of Cases With Element Present	%	Of Cases With Element Present, Number of Cases With This Element Visible on Radiograph	%
L_Clavicle	82	98	79	96
R_Clavicle	77	92	74	96
C3	42	50	7	17
C4	42	50	27	64
C5	43	51	37	86
C6	46	55	39	85
C7	50	60	43	86
T1	54	64	51	94
T2	51	61	46	90
T3	52	62	45	87

For the 33 complete skeletal cases all resulting in a "match" result (of the 84 total cases), the IoC data are min = 10, max = 25, mean = 20. For 43 incomplete skeletal cases all resulting in a "match" result, the IoC data are min = 6, max = 25, mean = 14. For the remaining eight incomplete skeletal cases resulting in a "cannot exclude" result, the IoC data are min = 2, max = 11, mean = 6. It is worth remembering at this point that a single nonconformity supports an exclusion and thus the same asymmetry exists here as for most other forensic tests, where it is easier to make a nonmatch than a match result.

As casework IoCs sometimes include features that cross multiple osseous elements (e.g., lateral cervical border margins; see later), from this point forward in this chapter we classify IoCs in a modified fashion (designated as mICs), by counting the number of IoCs pertaining to each osseous element from the case files. This means that while the ceiling of IoCs in casework is 25, the number of mICs can exceed 25. The frequency of mIC should be useful to novices who need to formulate an analytical schema to undertake radiographic comparisons with understanding about which features are typically awarded most attention and in what sequence.

Unfortunately, counts do not communicate intrinsically embedded weights. Therefore, while commonly reported mICs should be paid attention, it must also be noted that analysts cannot ignore other regions of the radiograph that might be important in any given circumstance/case. Each radiograph presents its own set of morphologies and circumstances surrounding the quality of the radiographic images and what parts of the skeleton are present in the skeletal recovery, and all regions must be assessed. Any one unexplainable difference between AM and PM morphology results in a nonmatch, at any stage of this process, highlighting the importance of a thorough radiographic examination.

The mIC trait frequencies reported here simply offer a starting guide to analysts as to which characteristics are often useful. Sometimes there will be features that fall outside of the cervicothoracic region that analysts must be alert to—examples include cervical ribs, bifid ribs, pseudoarthroses, healed fractures, scoliosis, developmental abnormalities etc.—as these should also be manifested on the skeleton, they are useful for informing and formulating identity decisions. It would be remiss of the chest radiograph analyst, as an expert in forensic identification, to ignore these other very important features even if they fall outside the primary region of interest. This again highlights the necessity for comprehensive examinations of the radiographic images by an expert analyst in every instance.

Table 24.2 presents the mIC trait frequencies for clavicles using nine broad classes. In terms of ceiling frequencies, the clavicle shaft holds the greatest number of mICs reported for any clavicle region: c. 150 concordances corresponding to c. 90% of skeletons with a clavicle receiving at least one mIC for this trait. This is followed by

- the lateral clavicle end—c. 130 concordances corresponding to c. 82% of skeletons with a clavicle receiving at least one mIC for this region.
- the medial clavicle end—c. 100 concordances corresponding to c. 73% of skeletons with a clavicle receiving at least one mIC for this region.

The conoid tubercle and medullary cavity hold the fewest reported concordances, but it is important to note here that both features may naturally be absent or invisible on the radiograph; some people do not possess rhomboid fossae and conoid tubercles may not be visible on radiographs due to positioning behind the shaft, so subsequent superimposition and/or radiographic quality may obscure these features. While rhomboid fossae were used for only 31% skeletons including a clavicle, it is important to note that when the feature was present on the skeleton and visible on the AM radiograph it was always used, awarding this trait 100% utility.

Table 24.3 presents the mIC trait frequencies for the vertebrae. Here notable traits are listed in sequence of most-to least-commonly used respective to each trait:

- Transverse processes for the T1 vertebra—64 concordances corresponding to c. 78% of skeletons with a T1 receiving at least one mIC for this region;
- Zygapophyseal joints (z-joints) for C6—c. 30 concordances corresponding to c. 50% of skeletons with a C6 receiving at least one mIC for this feature;

Table 24.2   mICs for Clavicles in 84 DPAA Chest Radiograph Comparison Cases

		L_Clavicle	R_Clavicle	Total
Concordance	Clav_Sup_End	33	34	67
	Clav_Med_Border	32	36	68
	Clav_InfMed_End	35	48	83
	Rhomboid_Fossa	25	26	51
	Clav_Shaft	154	145	299
	Conoid tubercle	19	18	37
	Clav_SupLat_End	72	75	147
	Clav_InfLat_End	58	54	112
	Medullary	16	14	30
	Other	4	2	6
	Total	448	452	900

DPAA, Defense POW/MIA Accounting Agency; *mICs*, items-of-concordance in a modified fashion.

Table 24.3   mICs for Vertebrae in 84 DPAA Chest Radiograph Comparison Cases

		C3	C4	C5	C6	C7	T1	T2	T3	Total
Concordances	Lateral margins	1	17	21	21	6	0	0	0	66
	Z-joints	4	19	34	30	23	11	2	0	123
	Spinous processes	0	3	6	10	21	38	27	27	132
	Neural arches	0	1	4	9	22	11	4	4	55
	Transverse processes	0	0	0	0	21	64	16	6	107
	Vertebral body outlines	0	2	0	1	0	0	1	0	4
	Other	1	1	3	5	2	5	3	0	20
	Total	6	43	68	76	95	129	53	37	507

DPAA, Defense POW/MIA Accounting Agency; *mICs*, items-of-concordance in a modified fashion.

- Spinous processes for C7-T3—c. 28 concordances corresponding to c. 54% of skeletons with a vertebrae present in the range of C7-T3 present receiving at least one mIC for this feature;
- Lateral cervical margins for the C5 and C6—21 concordances corresponding to 40% of skeletons with a vertebrae present in the C5/C6 range receiving at least one mIC for this feature;
- Neural arch features of the C7—22 concordances corresponding to c. 28% of skeletons with a C7 receiving at least one mIC for this region.

Overall, more mICs were reported for the clavicles (900) than the vertebrae (507), translating to roughly 6 mICs per clavicle when the clavicle was represented in the dry skeleton *and* visible on the AM radiograph, in contrast to approximately 2 mICs per vertebrae when the vertebra was represented in the skeleton *and* visible on the AM radiograph. The range in number of concordances for any comparison of complete skeletal sets (n = 33) resulting in a strong correspondence and subsequent recommendation of a name association was 11–33 mICs (mean = 22). For incomplete skeletal sets with strong correspondence and subsequent recommendation of a name association (n = 43) the range was only slightly less, 6–28 mICs (mean = 15). The range for weaker degrees of correspondence and a "fail to exclude" result was 3–10 mICs (mean = 6).

Fewer mICs thereby generally correlate to "cannot exclude" calls as should be expected. For incomplete skeletal sets, recommendations for a match draw upon an average of 15 mICs and were always above 6. In all cases mICs were documented for more than two osseous elements in any case. Multiple concordances (upwards of 15) across multiple bones provide powerful weight for assigning a match as recently quantified elsewhere by Ross et al. (2016) as being >98% probability for a correct identification. In our own large scale validation tests using 589 AM radiographic pairs, analysts with a talent for radiographic comparison perform with positive predictive values >95% and negative predictive values >90% (so slightly less than the numbers reported by Ross et al., 2016). In radiographic array tests we see similar performance by some analysts (Stephan et al., 2011). Novices rarely perform at these same high rates, but there are some exceptional individuals who appear to hold a natural talent for pattern recognition.

■ EXEMPLAR FEATURES OF THE CERVICOTHORACIC REGION USEFUL FOR RADIOGRAPHIC COMPARISON

In this section we illustrate classic skeletal variation in the cervicothoracic region as would be documented by an IoC table in the chest radiograph comparison report. It is important to reiterate that analysts should not feel restricted to a predefined suite of IoC since unusual anatomical morphologies cannot be anticipated ahead of casework analysis.

Instead, analysts should supplement the base features reported here with other (especially atypical) anatomical morphologies encountered on the radiographs as appropriate.

Overarching Clavicle Form

Clavicles are generically described as adhering to a thematic sigmoid shape, which is best observed in superior or inferior view (Fig. 24.3). However, the shape of the clavicle is considerably more complex than this upon closer inspection. Torsion may also be present to differing degrees, and clavicles may bend from superior to inferior as seen in frontal views. While the 2D nature of radiographic imaging precludes all shape information being recorded, it is extremely difficult to force any clavicle to match a different individual's radiographic image by simply modifying the orientation of the clavicle in relation to the image receptor.

In terms of their more complex anatomy, clavicles can be long and slender, thick and short, or any combination therein (Fig. 24.4). These are basic, but important features for the chest radiograph comparison analyst to assess and, in most cases, will enable nonmatching AM radiographs to be quickly and correctly excluded. In PA views, clavicles also take the form of the typical sigmoid shape, straight shaft, or arched shaft (Fig. 24.5). Rotation of a clavicle anteriorly along its long axis (decrease in pitch) will exaggerate the sigmoid shape of the clavicle if it adheres to the typical S-pattern. Posterior rotation of the clavicle along its long axis (increase in pitch) will provide a more arched structure. These positional movements rarely change the overarching bone morphology. That is, sigmoid-shaped clavicles will simply become more sigmoid shaped with decreased pitch and less sigmoid shaped with increased pitch, rather than changing from a "sigmoid" to an "arched" form (see Fig. 24.3).

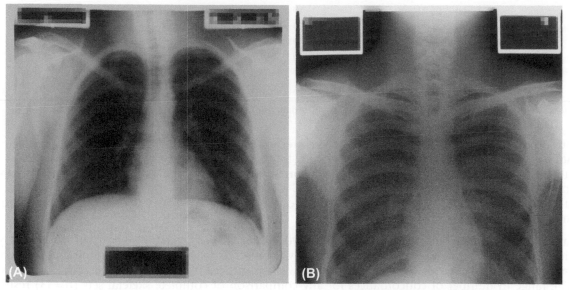

Figure 24.4 Clavicle morphology: (A) long and slender; and (B) short and thick.

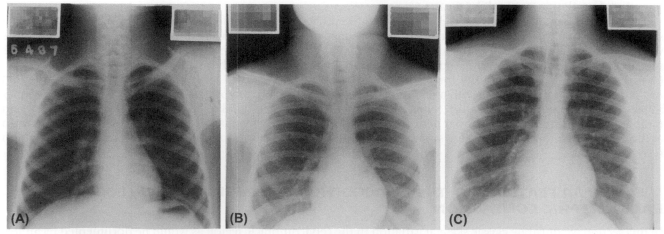

Figure 24.5 Clavicle morphology: (A) sigmoid-shaped clavicles; (B) straight clavicles; and (C) arched clavicles.

Medial Clavicle Edge Shape

The medial edge of the clavicle can be concave, straight, or convex (Fig. 24.6). In the written explanation of the IoC describing this feature, the opacities of the cortical margins should be noted. In some subjects the medial end of the clavicle is dramatically enlarged as easily referenced against relative height of the ribs (Fig. 24.6C).

Medial Clavicle Borders

As the clavicle shaft approaches the medial extreme the superior and inferior cortical margins may be fluted, flaring, or straight or exhibit an inferior or superior arch morphology (Fig. 24.7). Of course, different intensities of each trait, except for the straight class, may occur. Opacities at these borders may also be noted.

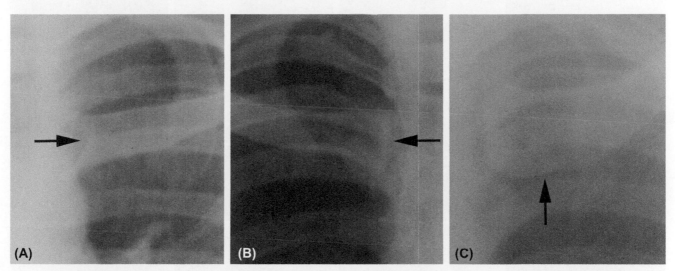

Figure 24.6 Medial end clavicle morphology: (A) concave medial edge; (B) straight medial edge; and (C) enlarged/bulbous.

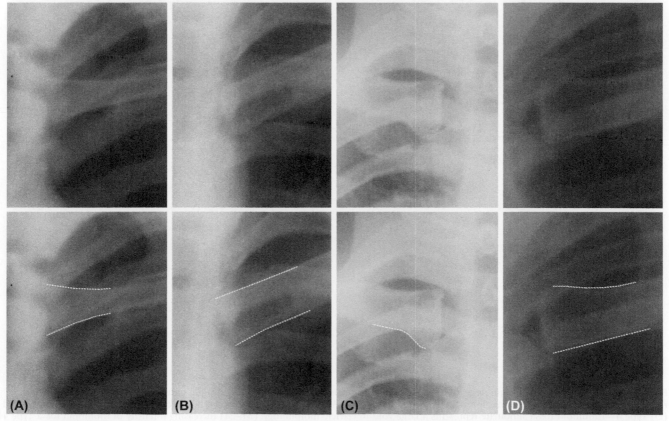

Figure 24.7 Medial end clavicle margin morphology: (A) fluted; (B) straight; (C) inferior arch; and (D) superior arch.

Rhomboid Fossa Morphology

When present (typically in 36% of right clavicles in males and 8% in females; Rogers et al., 2000) the rhomboid fossa can take a multitude of forms, but there are some common classes, which include the following:

- The roof of the fossa may be represented as a dense straight cortical line on the radiographs (Fig. 24.8A);
- A groove may be present where the inferior cortical edge meets the medial aspect of the fossa (Fig. 24.8B);
- The inferior clavicle edge remains visible with a superimposed shadow of the fossa (Fig. 24.8C);
- The inferior clavicle edge is broken (invisible) on the radiograph with the rhomboid fossa being most prominent (Fig. 24.8D).

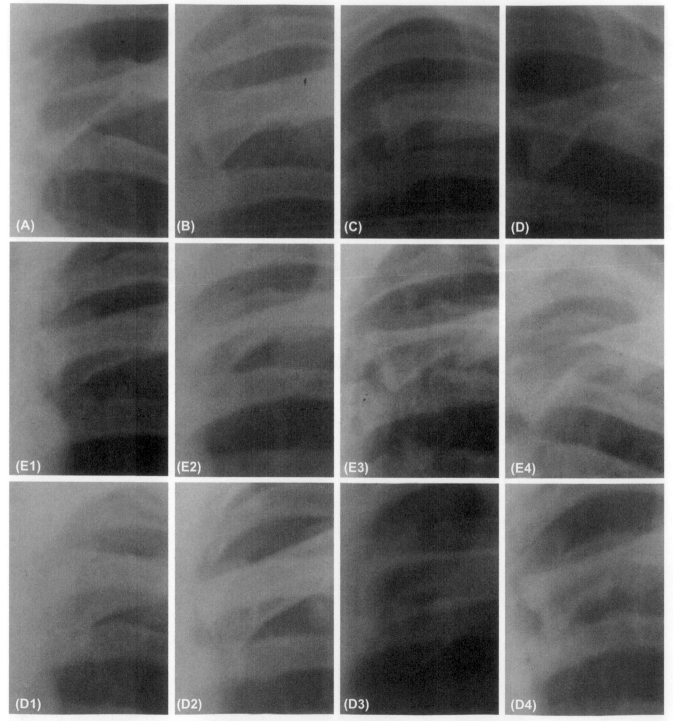

Figure 24.8 Rhomboid fossa morphology: (A) Type 1—marked superior fossa edge line with minimal transparency at fossa; (B) Type 2—superior fossa edge line with groove at inferior margin of clavicle; (C) Type 3—oval translucency at fossa but inferior clavicle margin still visible; and (D) Type 4—rhomboid fossa silhouette represents a large void in clavicle morphology. (E1–E4) Increasing intensity of rhomboid fossa Type 4 expression. (D1–D4) Increasing intensity of rhomboid fossa Type 3 expression.

Again, there are different sizes and degrees of manifestation of all of these traits, some of which are illustrated in Fig. 24.8, and each rhomboid fossa possesses its own subtleties in terms of shape and radiographic opacities that should be noted within the IoC description.

Lateral Clavicle

The superior lateral border can be curved or straight. The angle of lateral bend can be broad and rounded versus more angular. The length of lateral ends tends to be long and narrow or short and squat. The lateral end can be bulbous with differing degrees of cortical densities at the lateral end and also the thickness of the medullary cavity.

Cervical Vertebrae Morphology

As for clavicles, the cervical vertebrae represent variations on a generic pattern, each displaying idiosyncratic features between individuals. While subtleties of cortical opacities are numerous throughout the vertebrae, some of the larger features include the following:

- Short vertebrae that are narrow in height with z-joints separated by little vertical distance, in contrast to vertebrae that are tall (Fig. 24.9);
- The lateral vertebral column margins differ between individuals as a result of vertebrae heights and indentations along their lateral margins that are idiosyncratic and rarely symmetrical (Figs. 24.9 and 24.10);
- Outlines of the spinous processes differ from vertebra to vertebra, sometimes being small or large and of different shape such as round, triangular, square, elliptical, narrow ellipse with pointed ends, or teardrop-shaped (Figs. 24.9–24.11). The spinous processes can also fall at different levels on the neural arch—some will be high, some in the center, some low—and depending on the articulations and form of the vertebra the spinous process may not project directly posteriorly from the subject—instead it may project superiorly, contributing to an exaggerated inverted V-shape of the neural arch;
- Z-joint "spaces" may be seen directly if they happen to fall end-on to the X-ray beam such that the X-rays pass directly through the articular cartilage "on-edge." In other individuals superior and inferior articular facets and processes may be superimposed without any dark band representing the decreased cartilage density. If an articular process is dense enough, its superior border shape may dominate the superimposition, enabling it to be used as an IoC.

C7 Neural Arch Outline

In chest radiographs, the body is positioned such that the C7 neural arch, especially the lamina, faces directly into the X-ray beam often generating a very clear outline that represents the bulk of the cortical margin that has been shot end-on. This outline frequently takes the form of an inverted V and its shape differs in complex ways between individuals (Fig. 24.10). On occasion the ends of the V are rounded, in others they are pointed, and yet in other individuals they have a "pinched" appearance (Fig. 24.10). In some individuals the arch drops below the level of the superior border of the T1 lamina/transverse process, in other individuals it does not. This morphology should be described in detail as a key IoC feature.

T1 Transverse Process Morphology

Transverse process morphology of the thoracic vertebrae is another prime structure for consideration as one or more IoC. It is most easily observed at the T1 region where there is little other hard tissue superimposition and soft tissue shielding, but this feature can also be seen from C7 to T3 vertebrae. The major classes of T1 transverse processes

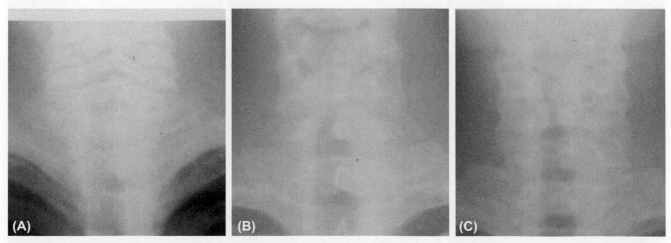

Figure 24.9 Cervical vertebra morphology: (A) narrow vertebrae; (B) tall vertebrae; and (C) intermediate vertebrae. Also note the different contours of the lateral vertebral margins across each image and difference in shape and intensity of spinous process outlines. Note: Height of vertebral bodies is in part due to angulation of the neck at the time of image capture, but this position is characteristic for this individual in the diagnostic antemortem position—i.e., it would be impossible to force image (B) into the same morphology as image (A) simply by anterior tilt on the vertebral column.

include long versus short (Fig. 24.11) and horizontal versus angled (Fig. 24.11). Morphology may also be symmetrical for the left and right sides or asymmetrical (Fig. 24.11).

Other Vertebral Opacities

Analysts should pay attention to the other cortical opacities that fall within the limits of the vertebral margins and are superimposed with other bone. These routinely differ from individual to individual and sometimes may even take the form of distinctive opaque swirls on the radiograph, separate to the oval outline opacities of the pedicles (see Fig. 24.13).

■ EXAMPLES OF TWO DPAA CHEST RADIOGRAPH COMPARISON CASES

These two cases are selected to provide examples of major classes of IoCs outlined earlier, but also to highlight briefly some of the widely divergent radiographic morphologies between individuals. These cases pertain to corporals who were listed as missing-in-action after their regiments pushed toward the outskirts of Seoul in 1951. Mitochondrial DNA analysis was attempted from at least three bone samples in both cases, however, no usable mtDNA sequence data were obtained. Subsequently, the chest radiograph comparisons that were undertaken highlight the utility of the methods in these contexts.

Case 1 concerns a skeleton possessing 9 of the 10 preferred osseous elements including a right clavicle with a marked rhomboid fossa and a left clavicle with only a very tiny (almost absent) fossa (Fig. 24.12). Case 2 concerns a different skeleton that also possesses 9 of the 10 preferred osseous elements, but with one clavicle exhibiting a large canal that penetrates the medial clavicle end and encircled by an actively fusing medial epiphysis (Fig. 24.12). The juxtaposition of AM and PM films in each case illustrates the IoC drawn by the case analyst (Fig. 24.13) and superimpositions reaffirm the match with precise superimposition of the PM clavicles with those depicted in the AM films (Fig. 24.14). The chest radiograph findings in combination with other lines of congruent identification evidence, including dental pattern, biological profile, and circumstantial data, resulted in the identification of these individuals.

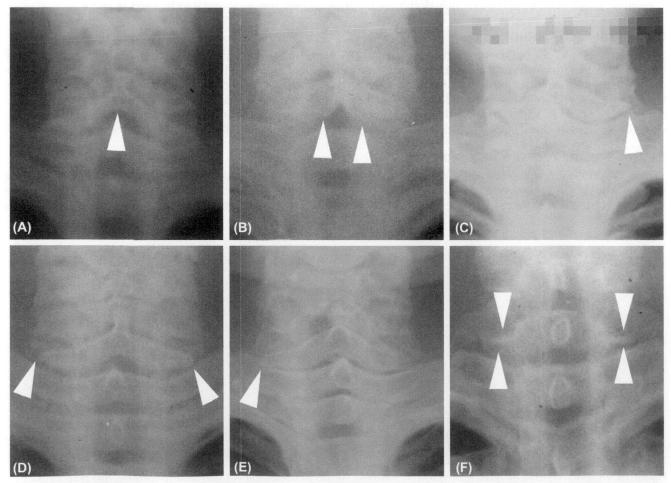

Figure 24.10 C7 neural arch morphology: (A) narrow inverted "V"; (B) broad neural arch, with void under spinous process; (C) irregular neural arch with pointed lateral margins and full visibility of inferior articular facets with T1 superior articular processes; (D) pointed lateral margin (*left arrow* to reader); rounded lateral margin (*right arrow* to reader); (E) right lateral extreme of C7 neural arch dips below, and is superimposed with, the T1 right transverse process (*white arrow*); and (F) "pinched" C7 neural arch morphology—note the intensely opaque horizontal *white lines*.

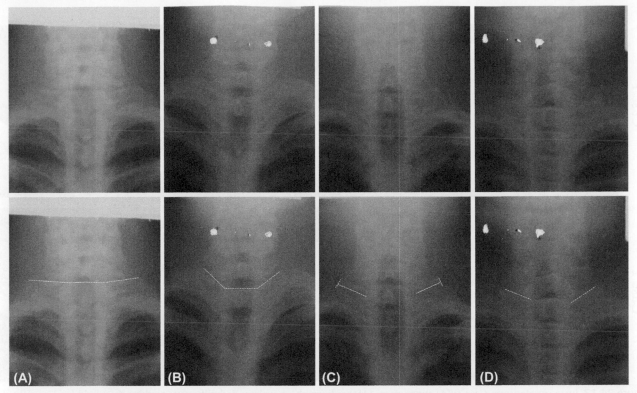

Figure 24.11 T1 transverse process morphology: (A) flat; (B) angled; (C) short; and (D) asymmetrical.

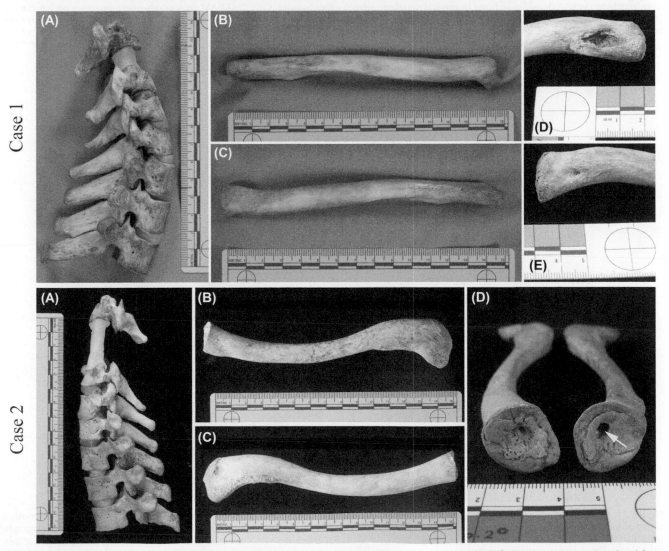

Figure 24.12 Skeletal elements of exemplar cases. Case 1: (A) vertebrae (C4 absent); (B) right clavicle; (C) left clavicle; (D) large rhomboid fossa of right clavicle (inferior view); and (E) small rhomboid fossa of left clavicle (inferior view). Case 2: (A) vertebrae (C4 absent); (B) left clavicle; (C) right clavicle; and (D) medial view of clavicles; *white arrow* marks canal on left clavicle.

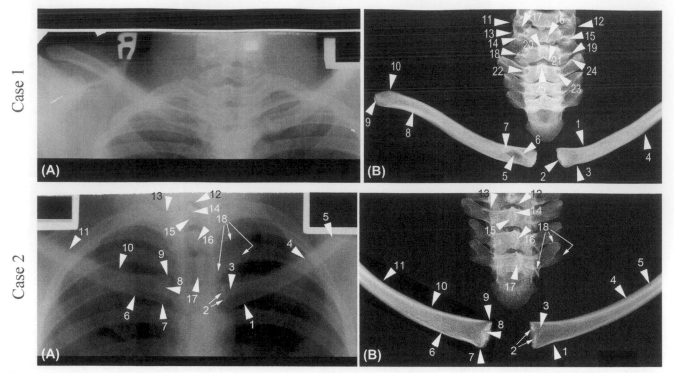

Figure 24.13 Juxta-comparisons. Case 1: (A) antemortem (AM) radiograph—note large dark silhouette marking rhomboid fossa on right clavicle (reader's left side); (B) postmortem (PM) radiograph—note rhomboid fossa morphology matching AM radiograph on right clavicle. Also note matching circular densities of bone in cervical vertebrae among other features. Case 2: (A) AM radiograph—note opacities on left clavicle (reader's right side) marking the medial clavicle epiphysis and entrance to the bony canal (canal walls also evident on the radiograph with close inspection); (B) PM radiograph—note matching canal outline and medial clavicle epiphysis morphology to AM radiograph.

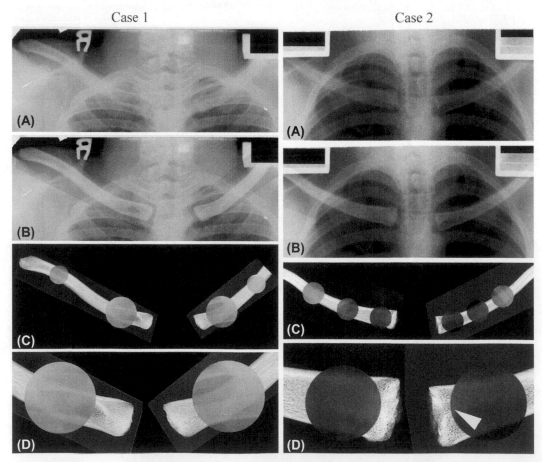

Figure 24.14 Clavicle superimpositions. Case 1: (A) raw antemortem (AM) radiograph; (B) AM with postmortem (PM) clavicle superimposition at partial transparency; (C) superimposition of PM radiograph at 100% opacity and with windows of complete transparency to view AM radiograph; (D) enlarged view of (C). Note in (C) and (D) correspondence of cortical margins and opacities of rhomboid fossa. Case 2: (A) raw AM radiograph; (B) AM with PM clavicle superimposition at partial transparency; (C) superimposition of PM radiograph at 100% opacity and with windows of complete transparency to view AM radiograph; (D) enlarged view of (C) illustrating alignment of bony canal on medial end of left clavicle (*white arrow*).

■ CONCLUSIONS

The use of skeletonized remains for radiographic comparison offers a means to standardize methods and increase their objectivity by precisely matching PM bone positions to AM bone orientations. When the parameters used for acquiring the AM radiographic images are known (as is commonly the case for diagnostic images), one-to-one comparisons via image juxtaposition and superimposition of long bones are possible, negating any ambiguity arising from positional discrepancy and adding increased weight to the test results. The cervicothoracic region of the chest radiographs provides an ideal region for examination with two long bones and multiple other irregular bones that display limited soft or hard tissue shielding (C3-T1 vertebrae) for a robust multivariate approach. In our analysis of DPAA cases reported here, morphological features of the clavicles were the most commonly reported IoCs for comparisons using the cervicothoracic region. For complete skeletal cases (all 10 elements of interest present), an average of 20 IoCs were used in support of a match result, and these were always further legitimized by clavicle superimpositions. By exceeding single digit criteria used for match associations reported elsewhere, these analyses provide comprehensive data toward identity and high levels of discrimination. Pictorial illustration of major classes of IoCs and exemplar cases should provide useful reference guides for analysts who are learning methods. These graphic exemplars also provide clear and convincing evidence of the methods utility in addition to validation tests (Stephan et al., 2011).

Acknowledgments

Special thanks go to Thomas Holland and Andrew Tyrrell for technical, administrative, and management support during research, testing, and establishment of the casework methods reported here. Thanks also go to Vince Sava for discussions and input on terminology that shaped the Chest Radiograph Comparison SOPs for DPAA and which have subsequently flowed through this manuscript.

References

Adams, B.J., Maves, R.C., 2002. Radiographic identification using the clavicle of an individual missing from the Vietnam conflict. J. Forensic Sci. 48, 369–373.

Angyal, M., Derczy, K., 1998. Personal identification on the basis of antemortem and postmortem radiographs. J. Forensic Sci. 43, 1089–1093.

Asherson, N., 1965. Identification by Frontal Sinus Prints. Lewis, HK, London.

Atkins, L., Potsaid, M.S., 1978. Roentgenographic identification of human remains. JAMA 240, 2307–2308.

Ballinger, P.W., Frank, E.D., 2003. Merrill's Atlas of Radiographic Positions and Radiographic Procedures. Mosby, St. Louis.

Brogdon, B.G., 1998. Radiographic identification of individual remains. In: Brogdon, B.G. (Ed.), Forensic Radiology. CRC Press, Boca Raton, pp. 149–187.

Christensen, A.M., 2005a. Assessing the variation of individual frontal sinus outlines. Am. J. Phys. Anthropol. 127, 291–295.

Christensen, A.M., 2005b. Testing the reliability of frontal sinuses in positive identification. J. Forensic Sci. 50, 18–22.

Cox, M., Malcom, M., Fairgrieve, S.I., 2009. A new digital method for the objective comparison of frontal sinuses for identification. J. Forensic Sci. 54, 761–772.

D'Alonzo, S., Guyomarc'h, P., Byrd, J.E., Stephan, C.N., 2017. A large-sample test of a semi-automated clavicle search engine to assist skeletal identification by radiograph comparison. J. Forensic Sci. 62, 181–186.

Evans, K.T., Knight, B., Whittaker, D.K., 1981. Forensic Radiology. Blackwell Scientific Publications, Oxford.

Greulich, W.W., 1960. Value of X-ray films of hand and wrist in human identification. Science 131, 155–156.

Hogeweg, L., Sánchez, C.I., de Jong, P.A., Maduskar, P., van Ginneken, B., 2012. Clavicle segmentation in chest radiographs. Med. Image Anal. 16, 1490–1502.

Hogge, J.P., Messmer, J.M., Doan, Q.N., 1994. Radiographic identification of unknown human remains and interpreter experience level. J. Forensic Sci. 39, 373–377.

Kade, H., Meyers, H., Wahlke, J.E., 1987. Identification of skeletonized remains by x-ray comparison. J. Crim. Law Criminol. Police Sci. 58, 261–264.

Kahana, T., Ravioli, J.A., Urroz, C.L., Hiss, J., 1997. Radiographic identification of fragmentary human remains from a mass disaster. Am. J. Forensic Med. Pathol. 18, 40–44.

Kirk, N.J., Wood, R.E., Goldstein, M., 2002. Skeletal identification using the frontal sinus region: a retrospective study of 39 cases. J. Forensic Sci. 47, 318–323.

Koot, M.G., Sauer, N.J., Fenton, T.W., 2005. Radiographic human identification using bones of the hand: a validation study. J. Forensic Sci. 50, 1–6.

Kullman, L., Eklund, B., Grundin, R., 1990. The value of the frontal sinus in identification of unknown persons. J. Forensic Odontostomatol. 8, 3–10.

Lesgold, A.M., Rubinson, H., Feltovich, P., Glaser, R., Klopfer, D., Wang, Y., 1988. Expertise in a complex skill: diagnosing x-ray pictures. In: Chi, M.T.H., Glaser, R., Farr, M.J. (Eds.), The Nature of Expertise. Psychology Press, New York, pp. 311–342.

Mann, R.W., 1998. Use of bone trabeculae to establish positive identification. Forensic Sci. Int. 98, 91–99.

Military Roentgenology: Technical Manual 8-275, 1942. War Department, Washington, DC.

Military Roentgenology: Technical Manual 8-280, 1944. War Department, Washington, DC.

Military Roentgenology: Technical Manual 8-280, 1967. Department of the Army, Washington, DC.

Mundorff, A.Z., Vidoli, G., Melinek, J., 2006. Anthropological and radiographic comparison of vertebrae for identification of decomposed human remains. J. Forensic Sci. 51, 1002–1004.

Nambiar, P., Naidu, M.D.K., Subramaniam, K., 1999. Anatomical variability of the frontal sinuses and their application in forensic identification. Clin. Anat. 12, 16–19.

Nielsen, C.J., 2001. Effect of scenario and experience on interpretation of mach bands. J. Endod. 27, 687–691.

Niespodziewanski, E., Stephan, C., Guyomarc'h, P., Fenton, T.W., 2016. Human identification via lateral patella radiographs: a validation study. J. Forensic Sci. 61, 134–140.

Owsley, D.W., Mann, R.W., 1992. Positive personal identity of skeletonized remains using abdominal and pelvic radiographs. J. Forensic Sci. 37, 332–336.

Parker, M.S., Chasen, M.H., Paul, N., 2009. Radiologic signs in thoracic imaging: case-based review and self-assessment module. Am. J. Roentgenol. 192, S34–S48.

Quatrehomme, G., Biglia, E., Padovani, B., Dujardin, P., Alunni, V., 2014. Positive identification by X-rays bone trabeculae comparison. Forensic Sci. Int. 245.

Rhine, S., Sperry, K., 1991. Radiographic identification by mastoid sinus and arterial pattern. J. Forensic Sci. 36, 272–279.

Rich, J., Tatarek, N.E., Powers, R.H., Brogdon, B.G., Lewis, B.J., Dean, D.E., 2002. Using pre- and post-surgical foot and ankle radiographs for identification. J. Forensic Sci. 47, 1319–1322.

Riddick, L., Brogdon, B.G., Lasswell-Hoff, J., Delmas, B., 1983. Radiographic identification of charred human remains through use of the dorsal defect of the patella. J. Forensic Sci. 28, 263–267.

Rogers, N.L., Flournoy, L.E., McCormick, W.F., 2000. The rhomboid fossa of the clavicle as a sex and age estimator. J. Forensic Sci. 45, 61–67.

Ross, A.H., Lanfear, A.K., Maxwell, A.B., 2016. Establishing standards for side-by-side radiographic comparisons. Am. J. Forensic Med. Pathol. 37, 86–94.

Sanders, I., Woesner, M.E., Ferguson, R.A., Noguchi, T.T., 1972. A new application of forensic radiology: identification of deceased from a single clavicle. Am. J. Roentgenol. Radium Ther. Nucl. Med. 115, 619–622.

Sauer, N.J., 1988. The effects of aging on the comparability of antemortem and postmortem radiographs. J. Forensic Sci. 33, 1223–1230.

Sauer, N.J., Brantley, R.E., 1989. The effects of aging on antemortem – postmortem comparisons of the peripheral skeleton for positive identification. Can. Soc. Forensic Sci. J. 22, 61–68.

Scott, C.C., 1946. X-ray pictures as evidence. Mich. Law Rev. 44, 773–796.

Singleton, A.C., 1951. The roentgenological identification of victims of the "Noronic" disaster. Am. J. Roentgenol. 66, 375–384.

Stephan, C., Amidan, B., Trease, H., Guyomarc'h, P., Pulsipher, T., Byrd, J., 2014. Morphometric comparison of clavicle outlines from 3D bone scans and 2D chest radiographs: a shortlisting tool to assist radiographic identification of human skeletons. J. Forensic Sci. 59, 306–313.

Stephan, C., Guyomarc'h, P., 2014. Quantification of perspective-induced shape change of clavicles at radiography and 3D scanning to assist human identification. J. Forensic Sci. 59, 447–453.

Stephan, C.N., Emanovsky, P.D., Tyrrell, A.J., 2010. The use of the clavicle boundary outlines to identify skeletal remains of US personnel recovered from past conflicts: results of initial tests. In: Lestrel, P.E. (Ed.), Biological Shape Analysis. World Scientific Manuscripts, Singapore, pp. 105–130.

Stephan, C.N., Winburn, A.P., Christensen, A.F., Tyrrell, A.J., 2011. Skeletal identification by radiographic comparison: blind tests of a morphoscopic method using antemortem chest radiographs. J. Forensic Sci. 56, 320–332.

Telmon, N., Allery, J.-P., Scolan, V., Rouge, D., 2001. A case report demonstrating the value of chest X-rays in comparative identification. J. Clin. Forensic Med. 8, 77–80.

Thali, M., Viner, M., Brogdon, B., 2011. Brogdon's Forensic Radiology. CRC Press, Boca Raton.

Ubelaker, D.H., 1984. Positive identification from radiographic comparison of frontal sinus patterns. In: Rathbun, T.A., Buikstra, J. (Eds.), Human Identification. Charles C. Thomas, Springfield, pp. 399–411.

Ulery, B.T., Hicklin, R.A., Buscaglia, J., Roberts, M.A., 2011. Accuracy and reliability of forensic latent fingerprint decisions. Proc. Natl. Acad. Sci. U.S.A. 108, 7733–7738.

Zanjad, N.P., Godbole, H.V., 2007. X-ray examination – a good tool for identification in decomposed body: a case report. JIAFM 29, 92–93.

INTERNATIONAL STUDIES AND MASS DISASTERS

CHAPTER 25

International Advances in Identification of Human Remains

Douglas H. Ubelaker

Smithsonian Institution, Washington, DC, United States

Chapter Outline

Positive identification of human remains represents a primary goal of the practice of forensic anthropology. Actual positive identification results when unique features are found on recovered remains and demonstrated to be shared with antemortem information provided about a particular missing person. Identification is thus a two-step process. First, shared features must be found between recovered remains and a missing person. Second, it must be demonstrated that the shared features are unique and could not be found in another missing person. If uniqueness cannot be demonstrated, the probabilities must be assessed in regard to the strength of the identification. This seemingly simple process can prove to be quite complex and challenging given the unpredictable nature of the identifying features and the paucity of experimental studies addressing many of the key issues. In addition, positive identification with its high level of uniqueness must be distinguished from possible and putative identifications that involve a lower degree of probability.

Much of the efforts within forensic anthropology are focused on gathering information that can contribute to positive identification. Assessment of species, age at death, sex, living stature, ancestry, time since death, and many other aspects of analysis provide information that narrows the search for identification of recovered remains. When anthropologists make positive identifications themselves, they usually utilize antemortem radiographs associated with a particular missing person. These radiographs can reveal unique skeletal details that can be compared with those observed on recovered remains. However, even when identifications are made by other forensic scientists, in particular odontologists or DNA specialists, anthropologists frequently are involved through determinations discussed above. Identification is a team process that can involve many disciplines within the forensic sciences.

The last 10 years have witnessed a surge of international professional activity and interest in anthropological contributions to identification. Although historically, much of the development of the field has centered in Europe and North America, today, progress is marked globally. Many factors have contributed to such international activity, but most importantly, accurate identification of recovered human remains represents a goal shared by all. Methodology, training and resources to effect positive identification are being addressed globally through a variety of means. This chapter presents discussion of many of the key factors embedded in this effort.

■ POPULATION VARIATION

Through research and casework, forensic anthropologists have recognized the impact of population variation on many aspects of methodology. Such factors have long been recognized in relation to formulae for stature estimation (Willey, 2009) and ancestry assessment (Sauer and Wankmiller, 2009). Increasingly, population factors have emerged regarding age and sex estimation, as well as other aspects of forensic anthropological analysis (Braz, 2009; Rogers, 2009). Many of the popular methods developed from the Terry collection curated at the Smithsonian Institution in Washington, D.C., or the Hamann–Todd collection in Cleveland, Ohio, are not ideally suited for applications in other parts of the world.

New Perspectives in Forensic Human Skeletal Identification. http://dx.doi.org/10.1016/B978-0-12-805429-1.00025-9

Research studies in other areas of biological anthropology have long demonstrated the complex relationship between skeletal morphology and underlying genetic, environmental, disease, and dietary factors (Bogin, 2001; Eveleth and Tanner, 1990). Thus it is predictable that much methodology within forensic anthropology needs to be as population specific as possible. Ideally such methodology should not only consider region but also socioeconomic status and other factors that contribute to growth and development.

Even within North America, such variation is apparent through secular change and regional variation. Methods developed from the traditional collections such as Terry and Hamann–Todd reflect the nature of samples within those collections. These methods are not ideal for applications to other regions or to individuals from contrasting socioeconomic status. Such concerns led to the formation of the forensic anthropology data bank, organized at the University of Tennessee. The data bank captured measurements and observations using a standard format from actual identified forensic cases. Since such data were derived from contemporary forensic cases, they were ideally suited for application to other such cases. In addition, the data bank has been supplemented with global perspective through inclusion of some non-North American samples and the W.W. Howells (1973, 1989) craniometrics database. FORDISC 3.1 offers a custom interactive discriminant function system based on the database to augment methodology within forensic anthropology. However, the authors caution that effectiveness may be reduced in applications to cases not well represented within the database. Such problems were illustrated in the experimental application of the system to a Spanish sample (Ubelaker et al., 2002). In this application, FORDISC 2.0 (the version available at the time) was applied to 95 crania dating from the 16th to 17th century from the Spanish site of Wamba near the towns of Villanubla and Valladolid in northwestern Spain. Since Spain was not well represented in the database utilized in the generation of FORDISC, the ancestry classifications produced in this test did not match well the known provenience of the Spanish sample.

Through global research, many publications have emerged that provide regional perspective to many aspects of forensic anthropology methodology (e.g., Terazawa et al., 1985, 1990). Recent examples include Savall et al. (2015) examining sexual dimorphism of the pelvis in a French sample, Jeelani et al.'s (2015) study of facial soft tissue thickness in Pakistani adults, Colarusso's (2016) test of a method of estimating age at death from sacrum using a Canadian sample, the Hens and Godde (2016) study of age changes in the auricular area of the pelvis in samples from Portugal, the United States, and Thailand, and an examination of postnatal ossification timing in an Australian sample (Lottering et al., 2016).

■ COLLECTIONS

The recent published literature in forensic anthropology presents new international methodology that addresses many of the issues discussed above. Recent global research on methodology is not only based on the clinical literature but also on new collections of documented human remains in different countries. At an impressive rate, collections of human remains are being assembled with known, documented information regarding the individuals represented. Such collections provide vital resources to develop population-specific methodology applicable to local forensic cases.

Ubelaker (2014) provides a listing and discussion of many of the primary global collections of documented human remains suitable for forensic research (Table 25.1). These examples include the following: Brest bone collection, Brest, France; British Museum of Natural History Collections, London, England; Cape Town documented skeletal collection, Cape Town, South Africa; Chiang Mai University skeletal collection, Chiang Mai, Thailand; Coimbra identified skeletal collection, Coimbra, Portugal; Coimbra international exchange skull collection, Coimbra, Portugal; Coimbra medical school skull collection, Coimbra, Portugal; Francis J. Ranier collection, Bucharest, Romania; George Huntington collection, Smithsonian Institution, Washington, D.C., USA; Grant collection, Toronto, Ontario, Canada; Hamann–Todd osteological collection, Cleveland, Ohio, USA; Institute of Normal Human Anatomy collection, Siena, Italy; Jikei collection, Tokyo, Japan; Johns Hopkins fetal collection, Cleveland, Ohio, USA; Luis Lopes collection, Lisbon, Portugal; Maxwell Museum's documented skeletal collection, Albuquerque, New Mexico, USA; Modern collection of Santiago, Santiago, Chile; Modern Japanese osteological collection, Tokyo, Japan; Museo Nazionale di Antropologia ed Etnologia de Firenze skull collection, Florence, Italy; National Museum of Health and Medicine skeletal collections, Washington, D.C., USA; Oloriz collection, Madrid, Spain; Pretoria Bone collection, Pretoria South Africa; Raymond Dart collection, Johannesburg, South Africa; Robert J. Terry collection, Smithsonian Institution, Washington, D.C., USA; San Nicolas Tolentino collection, Mexico City, Mexico; Sassari collection, Sardinia, Italy; Scheuer collection, Dundee, Scotland; Spitalfriedhof St. Johann known age collection, Basel, Switzerland; St. Bride's Church, London, England; St. Thomas Anglican Church, Belleville, Ontario, Universidad de Complutense collection, Madrid, Spain; Universidad Nacional Autónoma de México collection, Mexico City, Mexico; Universitat Autònoma de Barcelona collection of Identified Human skeletons, Barcelona, Spain; University of Athens Human Skeletal Reference Collection, Athens, Greece; University of Szeged Collection, Szeged, Hungary; W. Montague Cobb human skeletal collection, Howard University, Washington, D.C., USA; William F. McCormick clavicle collection, University of Tennessee, Knoxville, Tennessee, USA; William M. Bass donated skeletal collection, University of Tennessee, Knoxville Tennessee, USA. Consult Ubelaker, 2014 and references cited within that publication for additional details on these collections. Publications by Corsini et al. (2005), El-Najjar (1977), Quigley (2001), and Usher (2002) also provide discussion on available collections and aspects of their documentation.

Table 25.1 List of Primary Global Collections of Documented Human Remains Suitable for Forensic Research

Collection	Institution	Location
Brest Bone Collection	Centre Hospitalier Universitaire	Montpellier, France
British Museum of Natural History Collections	British Museum of Natural History	London, England
Cape Town Documented Skeletal Collection	University of Cape Town	Cape Town, South Africa
Chiang Mai University Skeletal Collection	Chiang Mai University	Chiang Mai, Thailand
Coimbra Identified Skeletal Collection	University of Coimbra	Coimbra, Portugal
Coimbra International Exchange Skull Collection	University of Coimbra	Coimbra, Portugal
Coimbra Medical School Skull Collection	University of Coimbra	Coimbra, Portugal
Francis J. Ranier Collection	Anthropology Institute of the Romanian Academy	Bucharest, Romania
George Huntington Collection	Smithsonian Institution	Washington, D.C., USA
Grant Collection	University of Toronto	Toronto, Ontario, Canada
Hamann–Todd Osteological Collection	Cleveland Museum of Natural History	Cleveland, Ohio, USA
Institute of Normal Human Anatomy Collection	University of Siena	Siena, Italy
Jikei Collection	Jikei University	Tokyo, Japan
Johns Hopkins Fetal Collection	Cleveland Museum of Natural History	Cleveland, Ohio, USA
Luis Lopes Collection	National Museum of Natural History in Portugal	Lisbon, Portugal
Maxwell Museum's Documented Skeletal Collection	University of New Mexico	Albuquerque, New Mexico, USA
Modern Collection of Santiago	University of Chile	Santiago, Chile
Modern Japanese Osteological Collection	University of Tokyo	Tokyo, Japan
Museo Nazionale di Antropologia ed Etnologia di Firenze Skull Collection	Museo di Storia Naturale	Florence, Italy
National Museum of Health and Medicine Skeletal Collections	National Museum of Health and Medicine	Washington, D.C., USA
Oloriz Collection	Complutense Universitaria	Madrid, Spain
Pretoria Bone Collection	University of Pretoria	Pretoria, South Africa
Raymond Dart Collection	University of Witwatersrand	Johannesburg, South Africa
Robert J. Terry Collection	Smithsonian Institution	Washington, D.C., USA
San Nicolas Tolentino Collection	Escuela Nacional de Antroplogía e Historia	Mexico City, Mexico
Sassari Collection	University of Bologna	Sardinia, Italy
Scheuer Collection	Centre for Anatomy and Human Identification at the University of Dundee	Dundee, Scotland
Spitalfriedhof St. Johann Known Age Collection	Natural History Museum of Basel	Basel, Switzerland
St. Bride's Church	St. Bride's Church	London, England
St. Thomas Anglican Church	St. Thomas Anglican Church	Belleville, Ontario, Canada
Universidad de Complutense Collection	Universidad de Complutense	Madrid, Spain
Universidad Nacional Autónoma de México Collection	National Autonomous University of Mexico	Mexico City, Mexico
Universitat Autònoma de Barcelona Collection of Identified Human Skeletons	Universitat Autònoma de Barcelona	Barcelona, Spain
University of Athens Human Skeletal Reference Collection	University of Athens	Athens, Greece
University of Szeged Collection	University of Szeged	Szeged, Hungary
W. Montague Cobb Human Skeletal Collection	Howard University	Washington, D.C., USA
William F. McCormick Clavicle Collection	University of Tennessee	Knoxville, Tennessee, USA
William M. Bass Donated Skeletal Collection	University of Tennessee	Knoxville, Tennessee, USA

■ HUMAN RIGHTS INVESTIGATIONS/HUMANITARIAN ACTION

Many international advances in human identification have been stimulated by augmented professional activity in the arena of human rights investigations and humanitarian action. Increasing numbers of forensic anthropologists have been incorporated into international teams seeking the recovery and identification of human remains in trouble spots throughout the world. Forensic archaeologists have proven their worth in many recovery efforts and maximized the retrieval of both information and materials. Colleagues working in laboratories have established biological profiles from recovered remains that greatly assist identification efforts. The growing long-term contributions of forensic anthropologists to these efforts have stimulated considerable new research unique to these applications. Such efforts also have led to augmented international cooperation and forged important new working relationships among colleagues. Such advances are particularly marked in the former Yugoslavia region as well as in Latin America.

REGIONAL DEVELOPMENT OF FACILITIES

The quality of international applications of forensic anthropology depends not only on the availability of qualified personnel but also on adequate facilities and equipment. Methodology of modern forensic anthropology requires not only the traditional sliding and spreading calipers and osteometric board but also facilities supporting radiographic, microscopic, and advanced computer analysis. Funds and/or facilities for analysis of chemical isotopes, radiocarbon, and DNA also are rapidly becoming standard necessities. While these advances can challenge local forensic budgets, they are increasingly addressed through capacity building and augmentation of broader forensic science facilities. Laboratory accreditation processes also strengthen anthropological facilities through enhanced security measures and equipment calibration.

In most areas of the world, efforts of forensic anthropology aimed at identification take place in a broader facility context of forensic science. Facilities and equipment of forensic anthropology are closely linked with those of forensic pathologists, forensic odontologists, and other specialists. Facilities are usually shared with these specialists and thus all benefit when general improvements are made. Improvements tend to be funded by central government agencies and frequently stimulated by major disclosed problems within existing forensic science (Ubelaker, 2015).

CERTIFICATION

Who is qualified to conduct anthropological analysis leading to identification? This question is of great importance in global identification efforts. Improper analysis and interpretation can lead to errors in identification with tremendous negative impact on affected families and forensic institutions. Horror stories of misidentification abound in the global forensic experience to remind all of the importance of reliance on qualified and thoroughly trained individuals (examples from various countries are available in Ubelaker, 2015). Certification of forensic anthropologists represents an important development to support quality of analysis.

The American Board of Forensic Anthropology (ABFA) in the United States pioneered this effort within North America. The ABFA is closely linked with the Anthropology section of the American Academy of Forensic Sciences (AAFS). Incorporated in 1977, the ABFA certified 111 diplomates by 2015 (www.theabfa.org, accessed March 22, 2016). Applicants for certification may originate from the United States or Canada; however, others can be considered by petition. Requirements include 3 years of experience after receipt of the PhD degree, examples of case reports, and successful completions of both multiple choice and practical examinations.

While the ABFA now also considers qualified international applicants, the global need for certification in forensic anthropology is being addressed by other organizations and certification programs.

In the United Knigdom, three levels of certification are offered through the Royal Anthropological Institute. Applicants must be Fellows of the Royal Anthropological Institute and meet requirements that vary depending on the level of certification applied for. The highest level (I) includes submission of relevant case reports and successful completion of an oral examination. As of March, 2016, nine forensic anthropologists had been certified at level I (www.therai.org.uk).

In Latin America, certification in forensic anthropology is available through the Asociación Latinoamericana de Antropología Forense alafforense.org. To date, 10 forensic anthropologists have been certified. Examinations to qualified applicants are administered in association with meetings of the organization.

Certification also is offered by the Forensic Anthropology Society of Europe (FASE), a section of the International Academy of Legal Medicine www.ialm.info. FASE offers two levels of certification, in addition to a Honoris Causa category. The level 2 category is offered to colleagues who work with supervision from a more senior forensic scientist. Level 2 applicants mostly hold a master's degree in a relevant field and pass both written and practical examinations. The higher level 1 category requires an MD and/or a PhD degree, evidence of significant casework experience, at least 5 years of experience after receipt of the highest degree, and successful completion of written, practical, and oral examinations. The Honoris Causa category is reserved for senior colleagues with at least 15 years of experience and recognized academic status. The FASE evaluation committee in 2016 consists of experienced colleagues and FASE members from the United Kingdom, Italy, Portugal, France, and the United States.

INTERNATIONAL SUPPORT IN FORENSIC ANTHROPOLOGY

Recognizing the importance of quality, global applications of forensic anthropology, several key organizations have offered direct support. Of course, many individual efforts have almost routinely stimulated quality international development and collegial cooperation. However, the institutional efforts are particularly noteworthy in signaling the importance and priority of international advances in forensic anthropology.

The Ellis R. Kerley Forensic Sciences Foundation www.Kerleyfoundation.org was established in 2000 in recognition of the pioneering accomplishments of forensic anthropologist Ellis R. Kerley, PhD (1924–98). In addition to other contributions to advancement of the field of forensic anthropology, the Foundation offers an international travel award for a deserving candidate to attend the annual meeting of the AAFS. The award includes a generous contribution toward travel expenses, complimentary registration at the AAFS meeting, and introduction to colleagues attending the Anthropology section reception. This award recognizes the global nature of progress in forensic anthropology and the importance of international collaboration and communication.

In 2015, the AAFS (aafs.org) inaugurated the Humanitarian and Human Rights Resource Center (HHRRC). The Center seeks to utilize the assets of the AAFS to promote the application of contemporary forensic science and forensic medicine principles to global human rights and/or humanitarian projects requiring special assistance. The HHRRC also encourages AAFS members to become engaged in such applications. Through grants and appropriations from AAFS, the Center provides support to projects deemed worthy by an International Advisory Council. Subcommittees of the HHRRC focus on education, equipment, laboratory and analysis protocols, and publications and relevant documents. The HHRRC also maintains a database of AAFS volunteers who have expressed a willingness to assist in projects. In its first year, the HHRRC has provided support to worthy projects in Cambodia, the Philippines, and Mexico, as well as research aimed at improving scientific methodology applicable to case investigation.

The International Commission on Missing Persons (ICMP) was established in 1996 at the G-7 summit in Lyon, France, as an initiative of then-US President Bill Clinton. The initial mandate of the ICMP involved accounting for the thousands of missing persons following the conflict in the former Yugoslavia from 1991 until 1995. The ICMP works with governments and other organizations to improve efforts of search, recovery, and identification of missing persons (www.icmp). Since their initial work in the former Yugoslavia, they have expanded efforts internationally. The ICMP emphasizes DNA-based identification, but their programs have utilized anthropologists extensively, especially in search and recovery efforts.

As part of its many activities, the International Committee of the Red Cross (ICRC) provides support for forensic science and humanitarian action. This effort involves training, advice, and other assistance for local authorities and others involved in many countries with issues in need of forensic guidance. Although the ICRC provides some direct support, they emphasize local capacity building in relation to forensic approaches to issues related to armed conflict, disasters, migration, and others. Anthropologists represent important contributors to ICRC initiatives.

Many other organizations include and even feature anthropologists in their approaches to global problems, especially in relation to attempts at search, recovery, and identification. Notable among these are the Argentine Forensic Anthropology Team www.eaaf.org, the Guatemalan Forensic Anthropology Foundation fafg.org, the Peruvian Forensic Anthropology Teamepafperu.org, the Committee on Missing Persons in Cyprus www.cmp-cyprus.org/, the Interpol Disaster Victim Identification initiative www.interpol.int/Interpol-expertise/Forensics and the United States Department of Defense POW/MIA Accounting Agency www.dpaa.mil.

■ CONCLUSION

Since positive identification represents a universal goal of forensic anthropological analysis, advances in methodology and procedures are international in nature. While some global variation exists in training, methodology, availability of facilities, and equipment and case applications, most of the concerns and issues are shared. In recognition of the need for local collections and population-specific methodology, forensic anthropologists in many world countries have led research-driven efforts to strengthen the science involved and improve accuracy of application. These global developments have greatly improved the dynamic field of forensic anthropology. New applications in the area of humanitarian action and human rights investigations have stimulated innovative methodology aimed at specialized problem resolution. Growing numbers of highly qualified students are attracted to this rapidly expanding field of science.

The formation of international organizations and certification programs has provided stimuli for growth and improvement of forensic anthropology. Notable among these developments are the Forensic Anthropological Society of Europe, the Asociación Latinoamericana de Antropología Forense, and the British Royal Anthropological Institute, with their certification programs.

The importance of international collaboration and development within forensic anthropology has been formally recognized by key organizations. Major examples include the association of FASE with the International Academy of Legal Medicine, the Kerley Foundation, AAFS HHRRC, ICMP, and the forensic component of the ICRC.

Advances in forensic anthropology contributions to human identification clearly are global in scope. Major achievements include formation of documented collections of human remains in many countries and population-specific research to improve methodology. This rapidly expanding and dynamic field continues to attract top students internationally, ensuring that progress will likely be sustained for many years to come.

References

Bogin, B., 2001. Patterns of Human Growth, second ed. Cambridge University Press, Cambridge.
Braz, V.S., 2009. Anthropological esimation of sex (Chapter 17). In: Blau, S., Ubelaker, D.H. (Eds.), Handbook of Forensic Archaeology and Anthropology. Left Coast Press, Walnut Creek, California, pp. 201–207.
Colarusso, T., 2016. A test of the Passalacqua age at death estimation method using the sacrum. J. Forensic Sci. 61 (S1), S22–S29.
Corsini, M., Schmitt, A., Bruzek, J., 2005. Aging process variability on the human skeleton: artificial network as an appropriate tool for age at death assessment. Forensic Sci. Int. 148, 163–167.
El-Najjar, M.Y., 1977. The distribution of human skeletal material in the continental United States. Am. J. Phys. Anthropol. 46, 507–512.
Eveleth, P.B., Tanner, J.M., 1990. Worldwide Variation in Human Growth. Cambridge University Press, Cambridge.
Hens, S.M., Godde, K., 2016. Auricular surface aging: comparing two methods that assess morphological change in the ilium with Bayesian analyses. J. Forensic Sci. 61 (S1), S30–S38.
Howells, W.W., 1973. Cranial Variation in Man. Papers of the Peabody Museum of Archaeology and Ethnology, vol. 67, pp. 1–259.
Howells, W.W., 1989. Skull Shapes and the Map: Craniometric Analysis in the Dispersion of Modern Homo. Papers of the Peabody Museum of Archaeology and Ethnology, vol. 79, pp. 1–189.
Jeelani, W., Fida, M., Shaikh, A., 2015. Facial soft tissue thickness among three skeletal classes in adult Pakistani subjects. J. Forensic Sci. 60 (6), 1420–1425.
Lottering, N., MacGregor, D.M., Alston, C.L., Watson, D., Gregory, L.S., 2016. Introducing computed tomography standards for age estimation of modern Australian subadults using postnatal ossification timings of select cranial and cervical sites. J. Forensic Sci. 61 (Suppl. 1), S39–S52.
Quigley, C., 2001. Skulls and Skeletons: Human Bone Collections and Accumulations. McFarland and Co., Jefferson, North Carolina.

Rogers, T.L., 2009. Skeletal age estimation (Chapter 18). In: Blau, S., Ubelaker, D.H. (Eds.), Handbook of Forensic Archaeology and Anthropology. Left Coast Press, Walnut Creek, California, pp. 208–221.

Savall, F., Faruch-Bilfeld, M.F., Dedouit, F., Sans, N., Rousseau, H., Rougé, D., Telmon, N., 2015. Metric sex determination of the human coxal bone on a virtual sample using decision trees. J. Forensic Sci. 60 (6), 1395–1400.

Sauer, N.J., Wankmiller, J.C., 2009. The assessment of ancestry and the concept of race (Chapter 16). In: Blau, S., Ubelaker, D.H. (Eds.), Handbook of Forensic Archaeology and Anthropology. Left Coast Press, Walnut Creek, California, pp. 187–200.

Terazawa, K., Akabane, H., Gotouda, H., Mizukami, K., Nagao, M., Takatori, T., 1990. Estimating stature from the length of the lumbar part of the spine in Japanese. Med. Sci. Law 30, 354–357.

Terazawa, K., Takatori, T., Mizukami, K., Tomil, S., 1985. Estimation of stature from somatometry of vertebral column in Japanese. Jpn. J. Leg. Med. 39, 35–40.

Ubelaker, D.H., 2014. Osteology reference collections. In: Smith, C. (Ed.), Encyclopedia of Global Archaeology, vol. 8. Springer Reference, New York, pp. 5632–5641.

Ubelaker, D.H. (Ed.), 2015. The Global Practice of Forensic Science. Wiley-Blackwell, Oxford.

Ubelaker, D.H., Ross, A.H., Graver, S.M., 2002. Application of forensic discriminant functions to a Spanish cranial sample. Forensic Sci. Commun. 4 (3), 1–6.

Usher, B.M., 2002. Reference samples: the first step in linking biology and age in the human skeleton. In: Hoppa, R.D., Vaupel, J.W. (Eds.), Paleodemography: Age Distributions from Skeletal Samples. Cambridge University Press, Cambridge, pp. 29–47.

Willey, P., 2009. Stature estimation (Chapter 20). In: Blau, S., Ubelaker, D.H. (Eds.), Handbook of Forensic Archaeology and Anthropology. Left Coast Press, Walnut Creek, California, pp. 236–245.

CHAPTER 26

Using Elliptical Fourier Analysis to Interpret Complex Morphological Features in Global Populations

Stephen P. Nawrocki[1] | Krista E. Latham[1] | Thomas Gore[2] | Rachel M. Hoffman[3] | Jessica N. Byram[4] | Justin Maiers[1]

[1]University of Indianapolis, Indianapolis, IN, United States
[2]Certified Prosthetist Orthotist (CPO), Fairfield, OH, United States
[3]Eli Lilly and Company, Indianapolis, IN, United States
[4]Indiana University School of Medicine, Indianapolis, IN, United States

Chapter Outline

The human skeleton is a complex three-dimensional armature comprised of tubes, cubes, plates, and projections all combined to create structures that support, protect, and move the soft tissues of the body. While some of the features of the skeleton can be analyzed in relatively straightforward fashion using linear measurement techniques, others seem to defy simple description, with shapes that vary across multiple dimensions. Traditionally, osteologists have used categorical (nonmetric, discrete) scoring strategies to describe these more complex traits. For example, variability in the size and shape of the brows, mastoid process, and chin is usually scored on three to five point scales, with extremes of expression (small vs. large, flat vs. projecting, round vs. square) being denoted by the extremes of the scale (Buikstra and Ubelaker, 1994; Hauser and DeStefano, 1989).

Inherent in the concept of discrete trait scoring is the idea that the overall form of the feature can be captured as a complex visual image, and training the eye to see the different forms of these images is a reliable strategy that can be passed on to other investigators with simple images and textual descriptions. In other words, the eye and brain work together as a camera that essentially takes the place of a pair of calipers, becoming the actual measuring tool. In this fashion, the researcher trades the precision and reliability of linear measurement for the greater subjectivity of visual assessment but gains the ability to assess the complex shape in ways that a few measurements cannot.

One drawback of categorical scoring is that the method is, in theory, less sensitive than linear measurement; with only a few possible "levels" of variability for each trait, differences between individuals must be relatively large to "trigger" a different score. Subtle differences in form, therefore, are lost. Compared to the much finer gradation of decimal values in a linear measurement scale, differences between samples in linearly measured traits may be easier to discover than in coarsely measured discrete traits. Furthermore, the statistical procedures available for linear measurements are generally more complex and elegant, allowing for more thorough hypothesis testing. However, even linear measurements can fail to capture the essential shapes of complex objects. Forms with curving outlines may require more measurements to describe than is practical, even if geometric morphometric techniques (Slice, 2005) can process that data effectively. In addition, it is sometimes difficult to manipulate the rigid caliper jaws to fit the shapes accurately or consistently enough to actually take those measurements, forcing the investigator to adopt other means of recording the object's properties. Digitizers that can take multilandmark data and 3D scanners are not yet standard equipment in all labs and are not as portable as cameras.

◼ ELLIPTICAL FOURIER ANALYSIS

Elliptical Fourier analysis (EFA) provides the means to analyze complex skeletal shapes without reducing sensitivity or requiring complex batteries of measurements (Kuhl and Giardina, 1982; Lestrel, 1988, 1997; Gore et al., 2011). The technique analyzes closed outlines that are either clearly present on the feature or that can be interpolated into the feature easily by the analyst. Because it uses the outlines of the feature, the method does not require the use of any predefined anatomical landmarks and is therefore known as a "landmark-free" method. EFA has proven to be an important tool in the study of an array of anatomical features in humans and other species (Schmittbuhl et al., 1999, 2007; Momtazi et al., 2008; Courtiol et al., 2010; Daegling and Jungers, 2000).

EFA creates a representation of the original contour of the object by using a chain code that breaks the shape down into vectors with standardized lengths. Each "link" in the chain code represents a change in direction around the contour of the shape. The chain code in turn serves as a guide for generating the elliptical Fourier harmonics, resulting in a series of ellipses that increasingly estimate the shape's contour and define the outline as a series of transitional shapes. More harmonics yield a better match between the recreated outline and its original form, but the exact number of harmonics needed depends on the irregularity of the shape being analyzed. The first harmonic describes the long axis of the shape and thus is responsible for noting the object's size and orientation, the second harmonic describes the ellipticity of the shape, the third harmonic describes the shape's triangularity, the fourth harmonic describes its quadrangularity, and so forth. Each subsequent harmonic originates from the previous harmonic's end point and generates progressively more information.

The software program "SHAPE" v.1.3 (Iwata and Ukai, 2002)[1] calculates elliptical Fourier coefficients of digital images from a chain code, traces the contour using the EFA harmonics, normalizes the image for shape comparison, and executes a principal component analysis (PCA) of the harmonic coefficients (Gore et al., 2011). PCA searches for patterns in the expression of the shape, essentially breaking it down to a few (usually three to seven) major elements ("effective PCs") by which the shape varies systematically from individual to individual in the sample. For example, if one were to analyze automobiles as photographed in side view, the program might identify a half-dozen ways by which the different makes and models vary: in overall proportion (van vs. sedan), in the shape of the tail (hatchback vs. trunk), in the slope of the hood and windshield, etc. Furthermore, the program ranks these components in decreasing order of importance: the first PC explains the largest portion of systematic variance in shape, whereas the second PC explains a lesser amount of the variance, and so forth. Each specimen in the sample is given a single numerical PC score for each of the effective PCs, describing that specimen's particular shape characteristics for the feature. These scores are saved and can be analyzed as continuous dependent variables.

The SHAPE software also generates an illustration of each effective PC, allowing the investigator to see how that aspect of shape varies between its extremes. The mean (typical) shape across all effective PCs is given as the central reference point, and the shapes lying at ±2 standard deviations from the mean are also provided. The diagrams for different effective PCs isolate the aspects of the variance that the viewer might identify when examining the actual objects but more clearly, in nonoverlapping form.

EFA uses a digitized two-dimensional image of the shape in question. These images may be obtained through any convenient means such as photography, drawing, tracing, or projecting a shadow of the object. In this way, despite its apparent complexity, EFA is intuitively similar to how the human eye and brain recognize and score complex shapes. When we look at, for example, the nasal aperture, we naturally seek its flattened outline and search for its consistent or defining features: the gentle horizontal arching of its inferior borders, its nearly vertical lateral walls, the constriction of its upper third, the notching at the tips of the nasals, etc. With training, we learn to recognize departures from the "typical" pattern: an aperture that is much wider or narrower relative to its height, a poorly defined ("guttered") inferior border or one that is interrupted in the midline by a strongly projecting nasal spine, or a widely arching rather than pinched upper third. EFA and the SHAPE software proceed in a similar fashion: they define the outline and look for variants, quantifying departures from the norm.

EFA has a number of benefits that are relevant to the analysis of complex skeletal traits:

1. EFA allows for the quantitative assessment of the shape of a feature independently of its size and initial orientation. Therefore, even if there are larger and smaller individuals in the sample, the procedure can ignore size variation that could potentially confuse the observer or otherwise obscure subtle changes in shape;

---

[1]The software package can be downloaded for free at http://lbm.ab.a.u-tokyo.ac.jp/~iwata/shape/.

2. The different subparts or elements that combine to make up the total shape are separated and unambiguously displayed, allowing the researcher to focus on specific aspects of the shape's morphology if desired. This feature also makes it easier to illustrate essential components of the shape to others and to teach strategies for recognizing variants on real specimens;

3. Metrics are produced for the shape that can be analyzed as if they were actual linear measurements taken on each specimen, allowing the analyst to test hypotheses in the search for subgroup differences;

4. The potential for intra- and interobserver error in the description or recognition of the shape and its varieties is greatly reduced.

While EFA and PCA are analytical (descriptive and comparative) procedures and thus do not produce predictive equations themselves, the information acquired can be used to develop or inform methods that are subsequently used to generate hypotheses about the characteristics of unknown individuals.

■ ACQUIRING AND PROCESSING THE DIGITAL IMAGES

Perhaps the most involved aspect of PCA is the acquisition of a clear image of the shape or skeletal feature so that the SHAPE software can analyze it. If the shape existed in only two dimensions, as a drawing on a piece of paper or a radiograph, the analyst could scan the image with a flatbed scanner. However, most skeletal features complex enough to require PCA instead of direct linear measurement are likely to vary across three dimensions. The most direct method for acquiring these images is digital photography. Digital single-lens reflex (DSLR) cameras provide the most flexibility because they allow for precise control of depth of field, focusing point, and exposure. Furthermore, DSLRs can be outfitted with a variety of changeable lenses with different potential focal lengths and fields of view, each of which will have a different effect on the perceived shape and proportions of the object. In general, the 55-mm lens most closely matches what the human eye tends to see with respect to proportion.

The analyst must employ a consistent photographic method for each specimen. Of utmost importance are (1) establishing a consistent angle of the object relative to the film (sensor) plane of the camera, (2) keeping the distance from the object to the lens the same, (3) using a consistent lens focal length, and (4) maximizing the clarity of the shape's outline. The easiest way to ensure that all four of these criteria are met is to establish a stable, consistent workstation into which each new specimen is inserted for photography. The camera should be secured on a tripod or camera stand and adjusted so that the lens face and camera body are either parallel with or perpendicular to the tabletop. A fixed focal length lens is easiest to use; if a variable focal length lens is employed (such as a 35–135 mm telephoto zoom), the analyst must take care to keep it fixed at a specific focal length throughout. In this case, the lens can be moved to its highest or lowest focal setting and left in that position, assuming that the resulting image of the object is adequate. The image should be large enough so that it can be seen easily and with sufficient detail, but not so large that the shape is cropped by the frame or loses sharpness at the periphery of the photo.

The distance from the lens to the object can be measured with a fixed length of string or a tape to ensure consistency; as specimens with different sizes are encountered, the tripod or camera stand can be adjusted to move the entire camera assembly closer to or further from the specimen as needed. It should be noted that while EFA and SHAPE exclude the effects of size, the effort taken by the analyst to use a consistent focal length and camera distance helps to reduce parallax error and ensures that the perceived shape of the object does change as a result of inconsistent methods.

Depending on its overall size and shape, the bone can be placed either flat on the table or supported by rings or soft foam. A solid (unpatterned) cloth backdrop of neutral color and moderate brightness can help with image processing later. The analyst should slowly rotate and adjust the bone so that the feature in question is presented to the camera lens in exactly the same plane and orientation each time, as the eye would see it. In this case it helps to develop a consistent sighting strategy; one or more landmarks or prominent features can be used to establish the correct angle. The outline of the feature can be enhanced by the strategic use of side (low-angle) lighting, although care should be taken to ensure that shadows do no cross the field of view. At close range, a flash may produce marked shadows and harsh contrast; natural background lighting is usually preferred over a flash. The focus selector should be placed on the same point of the feature each time. Color pictures tend to capture more image detail than black and white images, which helps in discerning the feature margins.

After photography, the images are further manipulated in a standard software package such as Adobe Photoshop. Each .jpg image is cropped and the outline of the feature is traced by hand using a brush tool (Fig. 26.1). This outline is then filled (Fig. 26.2), extracted from the background, and saved as a separate bitmap (24 bit .bmp) file. The subroutines of SHAPE then process this bitmap file and generate the output. Extracting the image outline from the original photo and processing it in SHAPE typically entail the greatest investment of time during the analysis. Specific photographic and image-processing strategies will vary depending on the bone and the nature of the feature being analyzed; for additional details and hints, see Gore (2008), Richardson (2011), and Byram (2015).

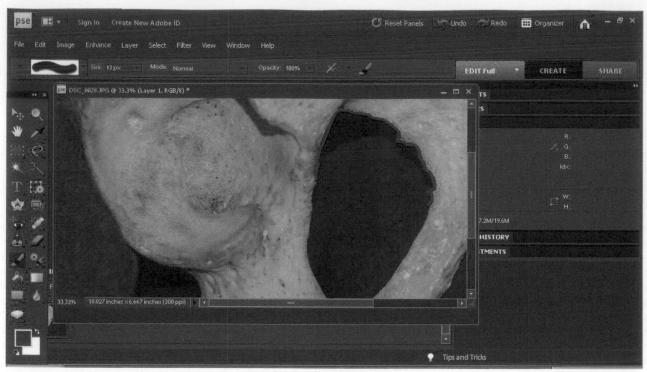

Figure 26.1 Tracing the obturator foramen in Adobe Photoshop Elements 8.0 in red. *Adapted from Richardson, R., 2011. Ecogeographic Variation in the Human Pelvis: A Quantitative Investigation of Obturator Foramen Shape Using Elliptical Fourier Analysis (M.S. thesis in Human Biology). University of Indianapolis, Fig. 3a; used with permission.*

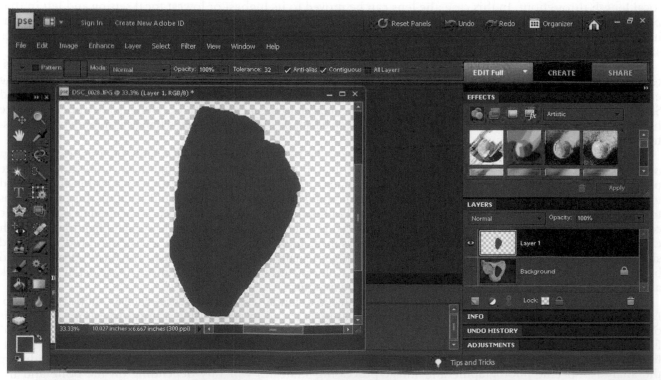

Figure 26.2 The extracted image of the obturator foramen filled in red. *Adapted from Richardson, R., 2011. Ecogeographic Variation in the Human Pelvis: A Quantitative Investigation of Obturator Foramen Shape Using Elliptical Fourier Analysis (M.S. thesis in Human Biology). University of Indianapolis, Fig. 3b; used with permission.*

■ APPLICATIONS OF ELLIPTICAL FOURIER ANALYSIS TO DISCRETE SKELETAL TRAITS

The authors have completed four studies of complex human skeletal features using EFA, focusing on the orbital rim and nasal aperture of the cranium and the obturator foramen and greater sciatic notch of the coxa. Generally, the goals of this body of research are as follows:

1. Quantify and elucidate the exact nature of the shape differences observed in each feature;
2. Determine the degree to which the variance in each feature is influenced by the sex, ancestry, age at death, and (in some cases) body size of the individual;
3. Explore the possible effects of environmental and genetic factors in the expression of each feature by using large, multiancestral, cross-continental samples.

To these ends, three of the four studies used a global sample consisting of specimens from South Africa and the Southeastern United States; one of the studies (Byram, 2015) used specimens from Chile and the United States. The University of Pretoria Bone Collection (L'Abbé et al., 2005) served as the source of the South African specimens. These skeletons were obtained from donated and unclaimed dissecting room cadavers, all decedents having died after 1950. The William M. Bass Donated Collection at the University of Tennessee at Knoxville provided specimens for all four studies. These individuals also died after 1950. For the US sample, Byram (2015) also added data from the Hamann-Todd Collection at the Cleveland Museum of Natural History. These skeletons were obtained from dissecting rooms prior to 1938 and therefore represent a somewhat different biological population than the more modern individuals in the Bass Collection. Finally, Byram also used native Chileans drawn from the Cementerio General Collection at the Universidad de Chile and the Servicio Medicolegal Collection, both in Santiago. These individuals died after 1950.

All individuals included in these studies had known demographic information including sex, ancestry, and age at death. Only adults were chosen, and pathological or broken specimens were excluded. Sex and ancestry distributions were manipulated where possible to create a balanced sample; specimens were chosen to include at least a few individuals in each half-decade age bracket in each sex/ancestry subgroup (Nawrocki, 1998). Total sample sizes are provided below for each study and ranged from a low of 162 to a high of 975 individuals.

Classifying the ancestral group of origin of the study samples is complicated by their global origin; terms used by anthropologists in any one of the locales may not universally apply. Individuals referred to here as "Euro-Africans" are native born (i.e., African born) "White" Africans of British, Portuguese, and Dutch descent. "Euro-Americans" in the Bass and Hamann-Todd collections also tend to have a Western European origin. The native "Black Africans" in the Pretoria Collection are drawn primarily from indigenous South African groups such as the Zulu, Xhosa, and Sotho (L'Abbé et al., 2005). Therefore, they may differ morphologically from the "Afro-Americans" in the Bass and Hamann-Todd collections, who are likely drawn from West African slave groups that experienced subsequent intermixture with Euro-American and Native American groups in North America (Curtin, 1969). The native Chileans from the Santiago area are likely the product of intermixture between native South American Indians and various Western European (Hispaniolan) groups.

The primary analytical technique applied to the principal component output was fully factorial analysis of covariance (ANCOVA), a powerful test that permits for the simultaneous assessment of all relevant independent variables (Sokal and Rohlf, 2012; Chapter 2). Although the exact model differed slightly according to the aims of the different analysts, the results presented here are based primarily on the following variance equation:

$$\text{Principal component score} = \text{sex} + \text{ancestry} + \text{continent} + \text{sex}^*\text{ancestry} + \text{sex}^*\text{continent} + \text{ancestry}^*\text{continent} + \text{sex}^*\text{ancestry}^*\text{continent} + \text{age} + \text{error}$$

where the specific principal component score for an effective PC for a particular skeletal shape is the dependent variable and all terms on the right side of the equation are independent variables: sex, ancestry, and continent are categorical main effects; age at death is a continuous covariate; the terms separated by asterisks (sex*ancestry, sex*-continent, ancestry*continent, and sex*ancestry*continent) are the two-way and three-way interactions between the categorical main effects; and "error" represents all variance in the dependent variable that cannot be explained by the variance in all independent variables combined. Continent of origin is presumed to be a proxy for environmental and cultural factors that affect both sexes and ancestral groups living together in one particular region of the globe.

■ VARIANCE IN THE SHAPE OF THE ORBITAL MARGINS

Gore (2008) photographed the orbital cavities of 162 crania from the Bass and Pretoria collections. Analysis in SHAPE produced five effective PCs that accounted for 94.9% of the observed shape variation while controlling for overall size; the first two of these (describing a combined 80.2% of the total variation in orbit shape) will be discussed here. PC1 measures differences in the height:breadth ratio of the orbital cavity, with most of that variation occurring in its height (Fig. 26.3). The −2SD extreme is wide and low, while the +2SD extreme is relatively taller. PC2 measures the angularity of the corners, ranging from squarish (−2SD) to rounded (+2SD). In particular, the −2SD extreme shows marked angularity of the superomedial and inferolateral corners, producing an asymmetry along an oblique line that gives the impression of a "drooping" eye that is similar to traditional nonmetric descriptors of "obliquity" or "angularity" of the orbital cavity (Wood-Jones, 1930/1931). While the effect of PC1 can be captured using traditional height and breadth measurements of the orbital cavity, PC2 cannot as there are no reliable landmarks located in the corners of the orbital margins. In this case, EFA analysis of photographic images helps to quantify a feature of orbital margin shape that would be largely invisible to standard morphometric analysis.

ANCOVA indicates that none of the main effects influence the variation in PC1, although the interaction of ancestry*continent is significant: Euro-Americans from Tennessee and Black Africans from Pretoria both display a lower (flatter) orbit shape, while Afro-Americans from Tennessee and Euro-Africans from Pretoria both display a higher orbit shape. In other words, select subgroups of *different* ancestries exhibit *similar* shapes. This finding contradicts the assumption that genetically related ancestral groups and their diaspora (e.g., African + American Blacks) can always be lumped together into one broadly defined biological subpopulation. These results also suggest that some combination of shared environment, geographic distance, and genetic drift complexly influences facial morphology (Smith et al., 2007; von Cramon-Taubadel and Lycett, 2008).

ANCOVA on PC2 indicates that both sex and continent of origin significantly affect orbit shape: males and the entire Tennessee sample tend to have an angular shape (−2SD), while females and the entire Pretoria sample tend to have a more rounded shape (+2SD). Interestingly, individuals of different ancestral groups but living in the *same geographic region* are more similar to each other than they are to distant relatives living on another continent. ANCOVA results for the remaining three effective PCs reveal additional significant influences for sex and continent of origin but not for ancestry, age at death, or the remaining interactions.

In summary, while EFA combined with PCA had no trouble describing and quantifying the ways that orbital cavity shape varies in humans, very little of the overall variance in shape was actually attributable to any of the independent variables used in the variance model. For example, in the ANCOVA for PC1, only 2.6% of the variance in the height:breadth ratio can be attributed to the ancestry*continent interaction variable (the only independent that was significant); *the remaining 97.4% of the observed variation in that shape cannot be explained by any variable examined by the anthropologist!* While the two significant variables in PC2 explained a combined 4.6% of the variance in orbit roundness, PC2 in turn explained less of the variance overall in orbital shape (19%) than PC1 (61%), and as such that 4.6% is proportionately much less important. Calculations by Richardson (2011) indicate that less than 3% of *all* variance in orbital shape is explainable, meaning that there is far more unexplained variance (error) in this skeletal feature.

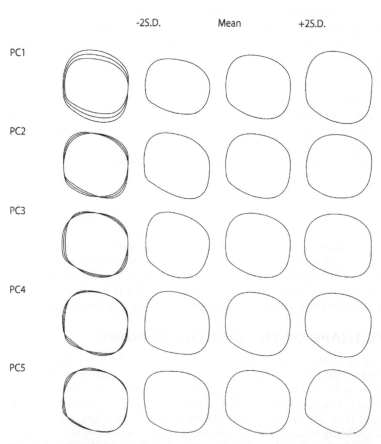

Figure 26.3 Shape variation of the right orbital cavity as reflected in PC1 and PC2. The left column shows the superimposed images, and the range of shapes are shown in the remaining three columns. *Adapted from Gore, T., 2008. The Use of Elliptical Fourier Analysis on Orbit Shape in Human Skeletal Remains (M.S. thesis in Human Biology). University of Indianapolis, Fig. 11; used with permission.*

■ VARIANCE IN THE SHAPE OF THE OBTURATOR FORAMEN

Richardson (2011) photographed the obturator foramen of 198 pelves from the Bass and Pretoria collections, using many of the same specimens employed by Gore (2008). Analysis in SHAPE produced five effective PCs that accounted for 92.5% of the observed shape variation while controlling for overall size; the first two of these (describing a combined 79.7% of the total variation in obturator shape) will be discussed here. PC1 measures differences in the height:breadth ratio of the obturator foramen, with most of that variation occurring in its height (Fig. 26.4). In addition, the angularity of the medial (pubic) border is reflected in PC1. The −2SD extreme is wide and low with a sharply angled medial border, giving it a triangular shape overall. The +2SD extreme is relatively taller with a more gently curving medial border, giving it a more oval shape overall. PC2 describes the degree to which the long (vertical) axis of the foramen is rotated anteriorly or posteriorly. The axis for the −2SD extreme is rotated slightly anteriorly (top toward the pubis), while the axis for the +2SD extreme is rotated posteriorly (top toward the acetabulum).

More of the independent variables appear to affect obturator shape than was observed for the orbital cavity, and those variables that are significant control a greater percentage of the variance. ANCOVA indicates that sex, continent of origin, and the three-way interaction (sex*ancestry*continent) all significantly influence the variation in PC1. Specifically, females and the entire Tennessee sample have shorter, more triangular foramina, whereas males and the entire Pretoria sample have taller, more oval foramina. ANCOVA on PC2 indicates that only continent of origin significantly affects obturator shape: the entire Tennessee sample tends to be rotated toward the pubis (−2SD), while the entire Pretoria sample

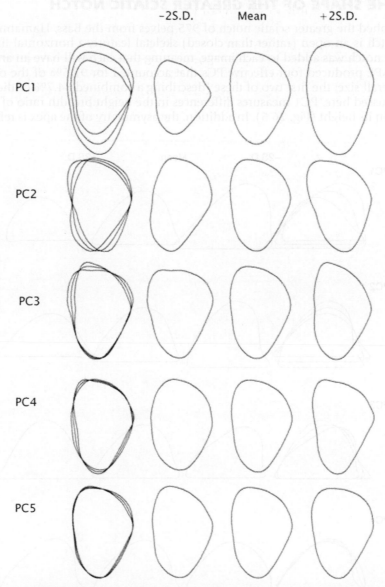

Figure 26.4 Shape variation of the right obturator foramen as reflected in PC1 and PC2. The left column shows the superimposed images, and the range of shapes are shown in the remaining three columns. *Adapted from Richardson, R., 2011. Ecogeographic Variation in the Human Pelvis: A Quantitative Investigation of Obturator Foramen Shape Using Elliptical Fourier Analysis (M.S. thesis in Human Biology). University of Indianapolis, Fig. 8; used with permission.*

tends to be rotated toward the acetabulum (+2SD). ANCOVA results for the remaining three effective PCs reveal additional significant influences for sex, continent of origin, ancestry, and for various two-way interactions, but not for age at death.

Not surprisingly for the pelvis, sex is the major determinant of the shape of the obturator foramen, being a significant factor in four of the five PCs and consistently scoring as the most important independent variable. EFA indicates that the traditional shape definitions based on simple visual assessment of the obturator foramen (Washburn, 1948) are largely correct but somewhat inadequate for describing its actual shape and transitional shapes are the norm. As was seen for the orbital cavity, the significant influence of continent of origin on three of the PCs indicates that individuals of different ancestral groups and different sexes but living in the same geographic region tend to display the same shape characteristics, suggesting that environmental conditions, altitude, and/or nutrition have a subtle influence on the morphology of the anterior pelvis. When controlling for sex and continent of origin, the effects of ancestry on the obturator foramen are significantly lower than prior research on the pelvis would seem to predict (Patriquin et al., 2002; Işcan, 1981).

Again, however, the vast majority of the variance in obturator foramen shape cannot be accounted for by the independent variables used in the study. For example, in the ANCOVA for PC1, only ~10% of the variance in the height:breadth ratio can be attributed to the combination of two significant main effects and a two-way interaction. Furthermore, when combining the effects of *all* significant independent variables across *all five* effective PCs, only ~11% of the total variation in obturator shape is attributable to the variables controlled for in the study.

■ VARIANCE IN THE SHAPE OF THE GREATER SCIATIC NOTCH

Byram (2015) photographed the greater sciatic notch of 975 pelves from the Bass, Hamann-Todd, and Chilean collections. Because the notch is an open (rather than closed) skeletal feature, a horizontal line bridging the anterior and posterior legs of the notch was added to each image, meaning that each will have an artificially straight inferior margin. Analysis in SHAPE produced four effective PCs that accounted for 97.5% of the observed shape variation while controlling for overall size; the first two of these (describing a combined 84.7% of the total variation in obturator shape) will be discussed here. PC1 measures differences in the height:breadth ratio of the notch, with most of that variation occurring in its height (Fig. 26.5). In addition, the asymmetry of the apex is reflected in PC1. The −2SD

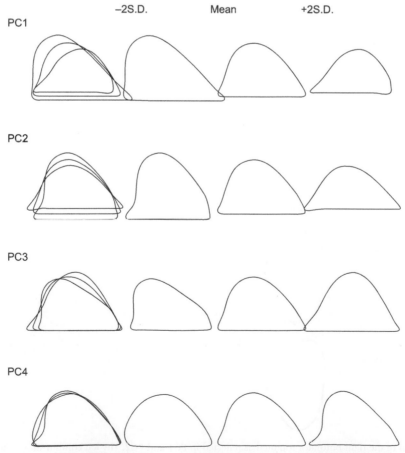

Figure 26.5 Shape variation of the internal aspect of the left greater sciatic notch as reflected in PC1 and PC2. The left column shows the superimposed images, and the range of shapes are shown in the remaining three columns. *Adapted from Byram, J., 2015. Quantifying the Shape of the Greater Sciatic Notch Using Elliptical Fourier Analysis (M.S. thesis in Human Biology). University of Indianapolis, Fig. 7; used with permission.*

extreme is taller (deeper), wider along its base, and the apex is displaced more posteriorly (toward the auricular surface), resulting in a notch that is more asymmetrical. The +2SD extreme is relatively shorter, narrower, and the apex is oriented more anteriorly (toward the pubis), producing a more symmetrical notch. More specifically, PC1 seems to be sensitive to the forward extension of the anterior leg of the notch, which accounts for the changing width of the base; in the −2SD diagram the anterior leg is more forward projecting. Furthermore, as the apex migrates posteriorly, the posterior wall of the notch becomes increasingly vertical.

PC2 also describes variation in height:breadth ratio but in a slightly different manner than in PC1. In addition, the degree of posterior convexity of the notch is reflected in PC2. The −2SD extreme is taller, narrower, and has a posterior indentation (bony convexity) near the posterior inferior iliac spine; this convexity is likely the origin tubercle for the piriformis muscle. The +2SD extreme is shorter, wider, and more symmetrical, with a less marked posterior indentation. The difference in widths between the shapes is less marked than for PC1; the increased width of the +2SD diagram relative to the other diagrams is accomplished by projecting the posterior leg of the notch backward *and* the anterior leg forward.

Because the South American sample is represented by only one ancestral group (Chileans), it could not be compared to the North American sample in the same way as Africans could be compared to North Americans; "continent of origin" and its associated interactions were therefore omitted from the variance equations. ANCOVA indicates that sex, ancestry, and age at death all significantly influence the variation in PC1. Specifically, males, Euro-Americans, and Chileans have taller, wider, asymmetrical notches, whereas females and Afro-Americans have short, narrow, symmetrical notches. Furthermore, a weak negative Pearson's correlation ($r = -0.12$, $P < .000$) between PC1 and age at death indicates that younger individuals tend to have more feminine notches whereas older individuals have more masculine notches.

ANCOVA on PC2 indicates that sex and ancestry significantly affect notch shape. Males, Afro-Americans, and Chileans tend to have notches that are taller and posteriorly concave, whereas females and Euro-Americans tend to have notches that are shorter and symmetrical. ANCOVA results for the remaining two effective PCs reveal additional significant influences for sex, ancestry, their interaction, and age at death.

As for the obturator foramen, sex is the major determinant of the shape of the greater sciatic notch, being the most significant factor in all four effective PCs and accounting for between ~9% and ~18% of the total variance in shape. EFA broadly supports the traditional anthropological interpretation of a symmetrical female notch and an asymmetrical male notch. However, whereas conventional wisdom suggests that females will have short and wide notches and males will have tall and narrow notches, our PCA found that when size is removed from the picture, females are more likely to have relatively short and *narrow* notches and males are more likely to have relatively tall and *wide* notches.

It may be difficult for the analyst to separate the effects of shape and size when examining the greater sciatic notch visually. Byram looked at whether variation in body size influences notch shape by including maximum femur length as an independent covariate in one of her variance equations for North Americans. She found that taller individuals tend to have more masculine notches (the −2SD extreme in PC1) and shorter individuals have more feminine notches (the +2SD extreme in PC1), and this effect exists independently of the actual effects of sex on the notch. Therefore, all else being equal, taller females should display more masculine notches and shorter males should display more feminine notches, irrespective of their actual sex. However, these body size effects are fairly weak (controlling less than ~1% of the total variance) and are always much less marked than the direct effects of sex on notch shape. Thus the inclusion of body size as an independent variable only slightly improved the amount of explained variance in the full model and did not change substantively the effects of the other variables.

Although continental ecogeographic effects could not be evaluated with this sample, some ancestral effects were noted, accounting for up to ~9% of the variance in notch shape. Furthermore, age at death becomes relevant for the first time but is less important than ancestry and sex. Additional exploration by Byram suggests that there are significant differences between the Bass and Hamann-Todd collections with respect to PC1: the more modern specimens from Tennessee display shorter, narrow, symmetrical (feminine) notches, whereas the less recent specimens from Cleveland are taller, wider, and asymmetrical (masculine).

Again, the majority of the variance in notch shape cannot be accounted for by the independent variables used in the study. For example, in the ANCOVA for PC1, only ~14% of the variance in the height:breadth ratio can be attributed to the combination of three main effects. Furthermore, when combining the effects of *all* significant independent variables across *all four* effective PCs, only ~15% of the total variation in notch shape is attributable to the variables controlled for in the study.

■ VARIANCE IN THE SHAPE OF THE NASAL APERTURE

Maiers (Maiers and Nawrocki, 2017) photographed the nasal aperture of 840 crania from the Bass and Pretoria collections using many of the same specimens employed by Gore (2008) and Richardson (2011). The variance equation therefore includes the "content of origin" independent variable and associated interactions. Analysis in SHAPE produced four effective PCs that accounted for 94.4% of the observed shape variation while controlling for overall size; the first and third of these (describing a combined 88.2% of the total variation in aperture shape) will be discussed here. PC1 describes 86% of that variance in aperture shape, more for a single PC than seen in any of the studies described here and suggesting that an anterior view of the midfacial skeleton can be distilled down to a single major shape element. PC1 measures differences in the height:breadth ratio of the aperture, with most of that variation occurring in its height (Fig. 26.6). In addition, superior projection of the inferior border in the midline is reflected in PC1. The −2SD extreme is wide and high with a concave inferior border. The +2SD extreme is relatively shorter and narrower with a projection of the inferior border that encroaches slightly on the aperture in the midline. PC3 describes the width of the upper third of the aperture: the −2SD extreme is tightly pinched at the nasals, producing an overall pear- or teardrop-shaped effect, while the +2SD extreme has broad and flat nasals, producing a more even, oval-shaped aperture.

ANCOVA indicates that ancestry very strongly influences the variation in PC1, accounting for nearly ~14% of the variance; sex, continent of origin, and the ancestry*continent interaction each have a significant but weak (~0.5%) influence. Specifically, "Blacks" from both Tennessee and Pretoria, and (to a far lesser extent) males overall and Africans overall, have relatively short and narrow apertures. "Whites" from both Tennessee and Pretoria, and (to a far lesser extent) females overall and North Americans overall, have relatively tall and wider apertures.

To determine whether facial size influences the shape of the aperture, nasion-prosthion height was measured directly on the specimens with sliding calipers and added as a continuous covariate to the ANCOVA model for PC1. The results indicate a low level (<1%) but significant effect for size: not surprisingly, individuals with taller faces have taller and wider nasal apertures (the −2SD extreme in PC1), and this effect exists independently of the effects of ancestry, sex, and continent of origin on the aperture. Therefore, larger individuals should have more "White-looking" faces regardless of their actual ancestry, although this trend is overpowered by the much stronger, direct effect of ancestry on aperture shape. The inclusion of facial height as an independent variable only slightly improved the amount of explained variance in the full model and did not change substantively the effects of the other variables, suggesting that facial morphology is less influenced by body size than it is by other factors.

ANCOVA on PC3 indicates that continent of origin and the ancestry*continent interaction significantly but weakly (<1%) affect superior aperture shape: all Africans are *more* pinched (the −2SD extreme), whereas all North Americans are *less pinched* (flattened; the +2SD extreme)—although the measure is much more variable in Africans. Afro-Americans in particular display extremely flattened superior nasal apertures and stand in significant contrast to the other three subgroups. In other words, the pinching of the upper nasal aperture should be a more effective indicator of ancestry in North America than it is in South Africa. However, these observations are still swamped by the massive percentage of unexplained variance, meaning that any systematic trends in upper nasal form can be used for prediction only imperfectly. ANCOVA results for the remaining two effective PCs reveal only a single additional significant influence on aperture shape (continent of origin, for PC4); age at death never reached significance in any of the effective PCs.

EFA indicates that most of the variation in the shape of the nasal aperture can be boiled down to a single phenomenon that is strikingly apparent from the diagram of PC1 (Fig. 26.6): encroachment of the upper and lower aperture boundaries toward the center (toward each other), resulting in a significant reduction of aperture height relative to width. Other aspects of nasal aperture shape are largely swamped by this central phenomenon. Furthermore, the vast majority of systematic (predictable) variation in aperture shape in the study sample is due to the effects of ancestry,

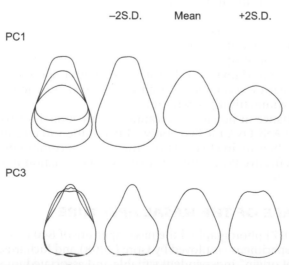

Figure 26.6 Shape variation of the nasal aperture as reflected in PC1 and PC3. The left column shows the superimposed images, and the range of shapes are shown in the remaining three columns. *Adapted from Maiers, J., Nawrocki, S., 2017. Elliptical Fourier analysis of the human nasal aperture. Paper Presented at the 69th American Academy of Forensic Sciences Conference, New Orleans; used with permission.*

with weaker but consistent contributions from sex and continent of origin (environment). However, the explained variance is still overshadowed by the unexplained variance: in the ANCOVA for PC1, only ~15% of the variance in the height/breadth ratio can be attributed to the combination of three significant main effects and a two-way interaction. Furthermore, when combining the effects of *all* significant independent variables across *all four* effective PCs, only ~13% of the total variation in aperture shape is attributable to the variables controlled for in the study.

■ CONCLUSIONS

EFA combined with principal components analysis has proven to be a powerful and effective strategy in the analysis of complex skeletal features, particularly for those that seem to defy simple categorization and measurement. While the compression of a feature down to a two-dimensional image does not necessarily substitute for three-dimensional landmark analysis (Gore, 2008, p. 45), the conversion does mimic some of the intuitive processing that anthropologists undertake when examining or distilling a complex skeletal feature down to its essential elements. Therefore, in some ways EFA should make the illustration and teaching of skeletal variation more effective.

The application of EFA in our studies of cranial and pelvic variation in global samples has led us to a few general conclusions. First, many of the traditional beliefs regarding the features of the cranium and pelvis are, in essence, correct: male obturator foramina are indeed tall and oval, and Afro-American upper nasals are indeed broadly curving. However, because it quantifies shapes more accurately, ignores the confounding influence of size, and reduces observer error, EFA was able to tease out important aspects of shape variation that have been missed in the past. For example, female greater sciatic notches are *not* relatively wide, but their symmetry may mislead the observer into scoring them as such. Also, focusing on the width of the nasal aperture to diagnose ancestry ignores the much more important phenomenon of encroachment of the upper and lower boundaries of the aperture on the center. These findings will alter the way we describe the systematic variability of these features and how we generate hypotheses for unidentified individuals with those features.

Second, powerful and thorough hypothesis testing procedures such as fully factorial ANCOVA can reveal or confirm important patterns of variation not previously recognized. A surprising outcome of the studies described here is the consistent effect of ecogeography or environment on the expression of these complex skeletal traits: individuals living in one part of the world are more likely to look alike, irrespective of their differing biological (presumably genetic and evolutionary) ancestries. The "continent of origin" variable may reflect climatic, altitudinal, nutritional, and/or socioeconomic forces that individuals living in one part of the globe tend to share, and these forces have measurable effects on skeletal variance. This finding underscores the potential plasticity of skeletal morphology and suggests that analysts must be careful neither to overdichotomize the ancestral groups living together in their particular region of the world nor take for granted the homogenizing effects such proximity can produce.

Third, despite using complex variance models with simultaneous control of an array of important independent variables and their interactions, *very little of the systematic variance in the shapes of these skeletal features could be explained!* While sex, ancestry, and continent of origin each had significant influences in particular circumstances for specific skeletal features, the vast majority of the variation in these features appears to be random. Even the best models could only explain a maximum of 10%–15% of the total variance in shape, and the inclusion of body size measures in some of the models did not produce any substantial improvements. Given these rather disappointing results, the real wonder is how forensic anthropologists manage to get *anything* right! With so much unsystematic variability, the shape trends that we identify in the skeleton can only be weakly linked to sex or ancestry, explaining why investigators often report considerable overlap between subgroups, high rates of intra- and interobserver error and misclassification, and seemingly random variability in discrete skeletal features. Taken together, these findings suggest that even after two centuries of investigating the human skeleton, considerable work still lies before us.

References

Buikstra, J., Ubelaker, D., 1994. Standards for Data Collection from Human Skeletal Remains. Arkansas Archaeological Survey Press, Fayetteville.

Byram, J., 2015. Quantifying the Shape of the Greater Sciatic Notch Using Elliptical Fourier Analysis (M.S. thesis in Human Biology). University of Indianapolis.

Courtiol, A., Ferdy, J., Godelle, B., Raymond, M., 2010. Height and body mass influence on human body outlines: a quantitative approach using an elliptic Fourier analysis. Am. J. Phys. Anthropol. 142, 22–29.

Curtin, P., 1969. The Atlantic Slave Trade. University of Wisconsin Press, Madison WI.

Daegling, D., Jungers, W., 2000. Elliptical Fourier analysis of symphyseal shape in great ape mandibles. J. Hum. Evol. 39, 107–122.

Gore, T., 2008. The Use of Elliptical Fourier Analysis on Orbit Shape in Human Skeletal Remains (M.S. thesis in Human Biology). University of Indianapolis.

Gore, T., Nawrocki, S., Langdon, J., Bouzar, N., 2011. The use of elliptical Fourier analysis on orbit shape in human skeletal remains. In: Lestrel, P. (Ed.), Biological Shape Analysis. World Scientific, Singapore, pp. 242–265.

Hauser, G., DeStefano, G., 1989. Epigenetic Variants of the Human Skull. E. Schweizerbart'sche Verlagsbuchhandlung, Stuttgart.

Işcan, M., 1981. Race determination from the pelvis. OSSA 8, 95–100.

Iwata, H., Ukai, Y., 2002. SHAPE: a computer program package for quantitative evaluation of biological shapes based on elliptic fourier descriptors. J. Hered. 93 (5), 384–385.

Kuhl, F., Giardina, C., 1982. Elliptic Fourier features of a closed contour. Comput. Graph. Image Process. 18, 236–258.

L'Abbé, E., Loots, M., Meiring, J., 2005. The Pretoria bone collection: a modern South African skeletal sample. J. Comp. Hum. Biol. 56 (2), 197–205.

Lestrel, P., 1988. Method for analyzing complex 2-D forms: elliptical Fourier functions. Am. J. Hum. Biol. 1, 149–164.

Lestrel, P., 1997. Fourier Descriptors and Their Applications in Biology. Cambridge University Press, Cambridge.

Maiers, J., Nawrocki, S., 2017. Elliptical Fourier analysis of the human nasal aperture. In: Paper Presented at the 69th American Academy of Forensic Sciences Conference, New Orleans.

Momtazi, F., Darvish, J., Ghassemzadeh, F., Moghimi, A., 2008. Elliptical Fourier analysis on the tympanic bullae in three meriones species (Rodentia, Mammalia): its application in biosystematics. Acta Zool. Crac. 51A (1–2), 49–58.

Nawrocki, S., 1998. Regression formulae for the estimation of age from cranial suture closure. In: Reichs, K. (Ed.), Forensic Osteology: Advances in the Identification of Human Remains, second ed. C.C. Thomas, Springfield IL, pp. 276–292.

Patriquin, M., Steyn, M., Loth, S., 2002. Metric assessment of race from the pelvis in South Africans. Forensic Sci. Int. 127, 104–113.

Richardson, R., 2011. Ecogeographic Variation in the Human Pelvis: A Quantitative Investigation of Obturator Foramen Shape Using Elliptical Fourier Analysis (M.S. thesis in Human Biology). University of Indianapolis.

Schmittbuhl, M., Le Minor, J., Allenbach, B., Schaaf, A., 1999. Shape of the orbital opening: individual characterization and analysis of variability in modern humans, *Gorilla gorilla*, and *Pan troglodytes*. Ann. Anat. 181, 299–307.

Schmittbuhl, M., Rieger, J., Le Minor, J., Schaaf, A., Guy, F., 2007. Variations of the mandibular shape in extant hominoids: generic, specific, and subspecific quantification using elliptical Fourier analysis in lateral view. Am. J. Phys. Anthropol. 132, 119–131.

Slice, D., 2005. Modern Morphometrics in Physical Anthropology. Kluwer Academics/Plenum Publishers, New York.

Smith, H., Terhune, C., Lockwood, C., 2007. Genetic, geographic, and environmental correlates of human temporal bone variation. Am. J. Phys. Anthropol. 134, 312–322.

Sokal, R., Rohlf, J., 2012. Biometry, fourth ed. Freeman, NY.

von Cramon-Taubadel, N., Lycett, S., 2008. Brief communication: human cranial variation fits iterative founder effect model with African origin. Am. J. Phys. Anthropol. 136, 108–113.

Washburn, S., 1948. Sex differences in the pubic bone. Am. J. Phys. Anthropol. 6 (2), 199–208.

Wood-Jones, F., 1930/1931. The non-metrical morphological characters of the skull as criteria for racial diagnoses: Part I. General discussion of the morphological characters employed in racial diagnosis. J. Anat. 65, 179–195.

CHAPTER 27

Forensic Anthropology and the Biological Profile in South Africa

Gabriele C. Krüger[1] | Leandi Liebenberg[1] | Jolandie Myburgh[1] | Anja Meyer[2] | Anna C. Oettlé[1,3] | Deona Botha[2] | Desiré M. Brits[2] | Michael W. Kenyhercz[1,4,5] | Kyra E. Stull[1,6] | Clarisa Sutherland[1] | Ericka N. L'Abbé[1]

[1]University of Pretoria, Pretoria, South Africa,
[2]University of the Witwatersrand, Johannesburg, South Africa
[3]Sefako Makgatho University, Pretoria, South Africa
[4]Department of Defense POW/MIA Accounting Agency, Honolulu, HI, United States
[5]University of Tennessee, Knoxville, TN, United States
[6]University of Nevada, Reno, NV, United States

Chapter Outline

To die nameless and be put away in some no man's land where the relics are as shadows. Bone orchard just beyond the outer limits of the city where sense peters away in vacancy and evening will have the feathers of ravens

Breytenbach (2008, p. 12)

■ INTRODUCTION

Poverty and lack of access to education and health care are commonly noted as the ugliest manifestations of social abuse in South Africa, but the social shortcoming of not being able to identify the deceased is rarely recognized. With a population of approximately 55 million, and close to 47,000 unnatural deaths per year, South Africa has one of the world's highest rates of fatal accidents (motor vehicles) and homicides (Statistics South Africa, 2015, 2014). While the South African police service (SAPS) and the forensic pathology services (FPS) are able to provide identifications for many decedents through standard methods (e.g., identification documents, fingerprints, DNA comparisons, etc.), a large number of skeletal remains are found annually, for which a more specialized approach is required.

Each year in the Gauteng province of South Africa, approximately 1300 bodies from morgues are incinerated without a known identity (Bloom, 2015), many of whom may be illegal immigrants and/or migrant laborers from other provinces in the country. Additionally, many poor South Africans do not have dental/hospital records or identification documents. When such a person dies and the case arrives for forensic anthropological analyses, there is often little to no context available about the unknown individual, except in the police district where the body was discovered. Therefore, other more creative methods, including facial reconstruction, have been implemented to assist in the identification of unknown persons from their skeletal remains. In collaboration with the Victim's Identification Unit (VIC) of the SAPS, identification of unknown skeletal remains has started to improve within the last few years. The increase in identification has been partially a product of ongoing research of modern human variation within

South Africa, continual testing of new methodologies on South African populations, and educating new and current forensic practitioners in advances within the field in South Africa.

This chapter explores the most recent developments and improvements for ancestry, sex, age at death, and stature estimations for South African groups.

■ ANCESTRY ESTIMATION

The presumptive identification of an unknown individual is based on the presence of biological features (human variation) on the skeleton and the relationship of these features to the sociocultural identity of the individuals. Because South Africa has such a heterogeneous population (Petersen et al., 2013), the estimation of ancestry is an important component of the biological profile.

Sociocultural identity in South Africa is based on the classifications assigned to people during the segregation era. For most of the 20th century—and legally from 1948 to 1990—South Africans were classified into strict social categories, namely "white," "black," "coloured," and "Indian," which also had implications for geographic location.

"White" individuals were mostly descendants from European settlers, specifically settlers from the Netherlands, France, Germany, and Britain (L'Abbé et al., 2011). "Black" individuals were the descendants of Nguni, Sotho, Venda, and Shangaan-Tsonga migrants who arrived in southern Africa due to the migration of the Bantu speakers from western and central Africa (Franklin et al., 2007; Liebenberg et al., 2015). "Indian" individuals were mostly the descendants of slaves and indentured laborers from Asia (Christopher, 1990). The "coloured" population, however, can be considered as an indigenous South African group. "Coloureds," often referred to as "Cape Coloureds" due to their large presence in the Western Cape, are an admixed population—the result of colonization, slavery, and the prolonged cohabitation of different groups (Stull et al., 2014a; Tishkoff et al., 2009).

In summary, people of different classifications were originally from different geographical backgrounds and already displayed a myriad of cultural and biological variation. The further legal segregation imposed by the Apartheid era separated different groups of people socially and geographically for another 100 years—a time within which the different groups developed and perpetuated their own cultures. Positive assortative mating within these groups strengthened the already notable biological variation between groups (Sutherland, 2016).

Yet, modern South Africans continue to socially self-identify according to the classifications imposed on themselves or their parents by Apartheid. Although racial classification is no longer legally imposed in South Africa, a need to self-identify as one of the previously prescribed groups is pervasive in all aspects of life and is an important part of a person's cultural place in the country's citizenship. Today the majority of the population in South Africa self-classifies as black (80.5%), coloured (8.8%), white (8.3%), and Indian/Asian (2.5%) South African (Statistics South Africa, 2015).

Ironically, past legal segregation contributed to the perpetuation of skeletal variation that makes it possible for forensic anthropologists to classify an unknown deceased individual as most similar to black, coloured, or white South African. However, while modern techniques have allowed for the estimation of ancestry for most South African groups, there is a paucity of South African Indian/Asian reference samples. Because no large collections of known Indian/Asian skeletal material exist in South Africa, Indians and Asians are often omitted from ancestry estimation studies which provide a unique problem when remains of possible Indian/Asian descent are brought in for forensic anthropological analysis.

Nonetheless, South African groups are morphologically distinct from their parental populations to other populations with a similar history on account of a long-term, and often legally imposed, endogamy (Sutherland, 2016). When evaluating the biohistory of modern South Africans with hierarchical clustering statistics, modern South African groups (black, coloured, and white) tend to cluster with one another, despite black and coloured South Africans showing greater affinity to historic African groups (Bahutu and Basuku) and indigenous Khoesan groups as opposed to white South Africans (Stull et al., 2016).

Using craniometric data, white and black South Africans showed roughly the same level of homogeneity that resulted in greater correct classifications, while coloureds were highly heterogeneous, which resulted in less optimistic correct classifications (Stull et al., 2016). The tendency to split groups into white and nonwhite clusters was also noted in observations on nasal aperture shapes (McDowell, 2012; McDowell et al., 2015).

A further advancement in ancestry research in South Africa is the addition of geometric morphometric analyses. When assessing cranial variation among modern black, coloured, and white South Africans cranial geometric morphometrics outperformed the traditional craniometrics, 89% versus 84% total cross-validated correct classification (Stull et al., 2014a). The coloureds are more commonly misclassified as white using craniometrics, and nearly equally as black and white in the morphometric analyses, indicating that coloureds are more similar to whites in size but more similar to blacks in shape. While geometric morphometrics may provide an advantage when analyzing highly admixed groups, such as the South African coloureds, the application of the method in a forensic context still needs to be refined.

However, for methods to be useful, they must be operationalized. Fordisc 3.1 (FD3.1) (Jantz and Ousley, 2005) is a commonly used computer program to estimate sex and ancestry within South Africa and much of the world. Traditionally, FD3.1 uses the Forensic Data Bank (FDB) reference database of skeletal measurements to compare an unknown skeleton with positively identified individuals within the FDB. Currently, the FDB is primarily populated with positively identified cases across North America. Ancestry and sex estimation within FD3.1 is based on linear discriminant function analysis (LDA), wherein group membership is considered mutually exclusive—individuals will be classified into a group based on the most similar morphology as expressed through osteometrics. As a result of LDA, FD3.1 will classify an unknown into the most similar reference group, even if an individual's actual group is not represented. The structure of the FDB is problematic when analyzing South African cases because the reference samples are simply not adequate. L'Abbé et al. (2013a) have shown that South African skeletons commonly misclassify when using the FDB within FD3.1. Taking into consideration the manner in which LDA forces an unknown individual into defined reference groups, it is necessary to have appropriate reference samples that adequately encapsulate the normal range of human variation.

In recent years, numerous studies have been conducted building upon foundational research by local and international researchers, leading to an advancement in ancestry research in South Africa: the creation of a South African, population-specific database of cranial measurements for use within statistical software programs, such as a custom database within FD3.1 (L'Abbé et al., 2013a). Multivariate analyses conducted on the cranial data collected from black, white, and coloured South Africans can now be used as a means to assess variation in the country (L'Abbé et al., 2013a).

Although not as commonly used as the skull, the postcranial skeleton has been shown to advance standards for South African sex and stature estimation as opposed to techniques developed on other populations (Small et al., 2012; Steyn and İşcan, 1999, 1997; Steyn and Smith, 2007). White South Africans (both males and females) are significantly taller than black and coloured South Africans, who are more similar in stature (Steyn and Smith, 2007); this between-group variation inherently indicates the potential of the postcranial skeleton specifically for the estimation of ancestry. Thus, indicating that although extrinsic factors—such as climate—may affect postcranial variation, it is likely not powerful enough to completely obscure the inherent genetic variation present among populations. Furthermore, multivariate postcranial studies have demonstrated the potential for ancestry estimation achieving accuracies ranging from 80% to 97% (Bidmos, 2006; Dibennardo and Taylor, 1983; İşcan, 1983; Patriquin et al., 2002; Uhl, 2014). Yet, the limited number of variables and small sample sizes constrain the potential of these studies for forensic purposes within South Africa.

Improving on previous work, postcranial variation among black, coloured, and white South Africans was recently assessed using standard linear measurements (Liebenberg, 2015). All postcranial elements included in the study were found to be significant with regard to ancestry but demonstrated limited success in distinguishing among the different population groups. As expected, a univariate approach, consisting of sectioning points created from the group means, performed poorly and could not sufficiently distinguish among the three population groups. Essentially, univariate techniques cannot capture the range of variation associated with ancestry. However, applying a multivariate approach and including only the most highly discriminatory variables, groups could be separated with accuracies of up to 85% (Liebenberg et al., 2015).

Group means demonstrated similarities between black and coloured South Africans in their fairly narrow long bone diaphyses and small pelves. Coloured South Africans also tend to have shorter limbs that distinguish them from black South Africans. Both of these groups can be distinguished from white South Africans who have a combination of long limbs, robust epiphyseal and diaphyseal dimensions, and large pelves. The postcranial variability observed among South African groups is largely related to differences in size, whereas whites typically demonstrated the largest dimensions and coloureds the smallest dimensions. As a result of the study, postcranial data for the estimation of ancestry were added to the South African custom database for use with FD3.1.

Because of the rich cultural and biological makeup of the South African population, forensic anthropologists in the country have the unique opportunity to rapidly advance methods for ancestry estimation from skeletal remains. The development of population-specific databases, of metric and nonmetric nature, and the advancements in technology and statistical analyses, provides an exciting glimpse into the future of ancestry estimations, not only in South Africa but also across the globe.

Research planned for the near future includes the expansion of the population-specific databases to include Indian and Chinese South Africans and other common migrant groups, such as Zimbabweans and Somalians, especially in reference to parental populations.

■ SEX ESTIMATION

Adult Sex Estimation

Sex estimation is a fairly common research area in physical anthropology, and most skeletal elements have been assessed in the last century for their potential in distinguishing between males and females. The sheer number of sex estimation studies is expected, and paramount, as correct sex estimates in a biological profile have the potential to divide the number of possible matches in half. Because so many studies have assessed the skeleton for differences between males and females (Asala, 2001; Barrier and L'Abbé, 2008; Bidmos and Asala, 2003; Dayal et al., 2008; Kenyhercz, 2012; Klales et al., 2012; Krüger et al., 2015; Spradley and Jantz, 2011; Steyn and İşcan, 1999, 1997; Walker, 2008), it is well known that sexual dimorphism is highly population-specific. Although much research has been conducted in this field, the fact that population-specific standards are necessary to accurately estimate sex has provided many new avenues for research, as new data need to be collected and assessed to create modern standards for all populations worldwide.

To demonstrate the need for modern, population-specific sex estimation methods, black and white South Africans were compared with their North American counterparts (Krüger et al., 2015; L'Abbé et al., 2013a). Findings suggested that sexual dimorphism was lower for both South African groups. The decreased sexual dimorphism observed in black and white South Africans may be associated with increased levels of admixture, older mean ages in skeletal collections, and lower socioeconomic status present in the South African population (Krüger, 2015; Krüger et al., 2015).

Further limitations associated with previous studies on sexual dimorphism in South Africans include a lack of standards for population groups, apart from black and white South Africans, as well as a focus on only individual measurements or one or two bones, at a time (Asala, 2001; Barrier and L'Abbé, 2008; Bidmos and Asala, 2003; Dayal et al., 2008; Steyn and İşcan, 1999, 1998, 1997). Recently, to improve on previous studies, more multivariate approaches have been applied to morphoscopic (Krüger et al., 2015), craniometric (L'Abbé et al., 2013a), and post-craniometric data (Krüger, 2015).

Morphoscopic analyses were applied to the pelvis (Klales et al., 2012) and the skull (Walker, 2008), as both skeletal elements exhibited features that could be described and scored. The pelvis has long been recognized as the best sex estimator in the skeleton due to the requirements of human reproduction. Three morphological traits on the pubis, as described by Phenice (1969), illustrated as line diagrams and scored on a five-point ordinal scale, could be used to produce sex estimates with correct classification rates up to 95% (Klales et al., 2012). Recently, the Klales et al. (2012) method was tested on a modern South African sample and resulted in total correct classifications ranging between 90% and 99%, depending on the statistical methods applied (Kenyhercz, 2012). While standards for black and white South Africans now exist, further population groups need to be assessed and the resulting standards to be incorporated into the method.

Although very high correct classification accuracies were obtained when using the pelvis, this particular skeletal element is not always well preserved. Alternatively, the skull is commonly located in forensic contexts, is generally well preserved, and has been shown to exhibit differences between males and females (Dayal et al., 2008; Novotný et al., 1993; Steyn and İşcan, 1998; Walker, 2008). Therefore, a similar, morphoscopic approach, as previously defined by Buikstra and Ubelaker (1994) and Walker (2008), was tested on a modern South African sample and the resulting equations were recalibrated to maximize correct classifications with South African population groups (Krüger et al., 2015).

Five morphoscopic traits on the cranium and mandible were assessed using line diagrams and a five-point ordinal scale (Walker, 2008). Validation of the method for use in South Africans demonstrated a need for not only population-specific standards but also standards specific to black, white, and coloured South Africans, on account of vastly different degrees of sexual dimorphism among the three population groups. When trait score frequencies were compared for black, white, and coloured South Africans, white males were the most robust, followed by coloured and black males, respectively. The South African females followed a similar pattern where white females were the most robust, followed by coloured and black females, respectively (Krüger et al., 2015).

Recalibration of the ordinal logistic regression equations, to be able to assess sex in black, white, and coloured South Africans, resulted in a method that was able to produce sex estimates with cross-validated correct classifications up to 93% (Krüger et al., 2015; Walker, 2008).

While sex estimation from the skull using morphoscopic traits performed quite well, a craniometric approach is not able to obtain equally high correct classification rates in South Africa and may need to be combined with other methods to improve accuracies.

While osteometric sex differences have previously been explored in the postcranial skeleton (Asala, 2001; Barrier and L'Abbé, 2008; Bidmos and Asala, 2003; Patriquin et al., 2005; Steyn and İşcan, 1999, 1997; Steyn and Patriquin, 2009), disadvantages of the studies included limited samples and the applications of univariate statistics or bone-by-bone approaches (multiple measurements from individual bones), which did not necessarily incorporate the most sexually dimorphic variables in the skeleton.

In a recent postcraniometric sex estimation study by Krüger et al., (2017), long bones were shown to reliably distinguish between males and females (correct classification rates up to 98%) among black, coloured, and white South Africans. Differences were also noted among all sex and ancestry groups (six groups), with an accuracy of 80%. Breadth measurements outperformed length measurements, with coloured South Africans demonstrating the greatest degree of sexual dimorphism followed by black and white South Africans, respectively (Krüger, 2015).

Among South African groups, postcranial bones achieved comparable classification accuracies to morphoscopic analysis of the pelvis and higher accuracies than metric or morphological techniques using the cranium in South Africa (Klales et al., 2012; Krüger et al., 2015; Phenice, 1969; Walker, 2008). Multivariate subsets of postcranial measurements captured more information on sexually dimorphic variation and also produced higher correct classification rates (up to 98%) than both the bone-by-bone approach (up to 90%) and univariate methods (up to 82%) (Krüger, 2015; Krüger et al., 2017).

As with ancestry estimation, craniometric and postcraniometric custom databases for the estimation of sex in South Africans were created and are available for use with FD3.1 (Krüger, 2015; L'Abbé et al., 2013b). Similarly, South African logistic regression formulae for sex estimation using morphoscopic cranial and pelvic traits are available to conduct routine forensic anthropological analyses (Kenyhercz, 2012; Krüger et al., 2015).

While the techniques mentioned earlier are able to distinguish between males and females with high correct classification accuracies, research in physical anthropology is never ending. Methods and skeletal elements are constantly reassessed as populations undergo temporal or secular changes, or as new statistical techniques or study limitations come to light.

The mandible has previously been assessed as a means of sex estimation, although generally as part of the skull and not on its own, and often to explore differences between juvenile males and females (Loth and Henneberg, 2001). A recent study, using a South African sample, has highlighted that while linear dimensions of the mandible seem to be valuable in estimating both sex and ancestry in adults; some of the dimensions were sensitive to tooth loss and advancing age, which could affect the outcome of the estimates (Oettlé, 2014; Oettlé et al., 2009). For example, the mandibular angle demonstrated clear sex differences among South Africans only when tooth loss was disregarded; however, an absence of sexual dimorphism was noted in groups where molars were retained (Oettlé, 2014). When assessing different linear measurements in the mandible related to the degree of prognathism, black and white South Africans yielded 90.4% correct classification rates and even higher when tooth loss patterns were taken into account (Oettlé, 2014). Therefore, if the age of the individual and any antemortem tooth loss are taken into account, mandibular dimensions may be useful in estimating sex and ancestry. However, the inclusion of more population groups also needs to be addressed in future research.

Juvenile Sex Estimation

While substantial research has been dedicated to improving sex estimation among adult South Africans, little research has been dedicated to improving subadult sex estimation. The lack of research is reasonable, considering the overall acceptance that subadult age estimation is the most informative and accurate biological parameter in children. Because subadult sex estimation has consistently provided inapplicable results, such as low classification accuracies and poor reliability, less emphasis has been placed on its research.

Stull (2014) addressed the obstacle of subadult sex estimation with the assessment of sexual dimorphism in long bone dimensions and the subsequent creation of a graphical user interface, KidStats (KidStats: Subadult age and sex estimations based on long bone measurements, 2015), that operates through R (R Core Team, 2013), to perform robust statistics using South African subadult data.

Although numerous studies have demonstrated sexually dimorphic differences in long bone dimensions (Gindhart, 1973; Humphrey, 1998; Johnston and Malina, 1966; Malina and Johnston, 1967; Maresh, 1970; Smith and Buschang, 2004; Smithgall et al., 1966), many studies around the world mainly focused on the pelvis and the mandible (Blake, 2014; Loth and Henneberg, 2001; Schutkowski, 1993, 1987; Weaver, 1980). The long bones were consistently labeled as impractical in estimating sex in subadults, as the lower levels of sex hormones present before puberty were believed to limit the quantification of sexual dimorphism in subadults.

In the large cross-sectional study by Stull, 2014, long bone lengths and breadths of 1380 demographically diverse South African male and female children from birth to 12 years were assessed and the degree of sexual dimorphism expressed in long bone dimensions was explored. Sex differences were shown in sympercents in an attempt to mitigate the asymmetry in percent differences. On average from birth to nine years, males have larger proximal breadths, distal breadths, and midshaft breadths than females. However, in contrast to the breadths, males and females generally displayed very small differences for the majority of the growth period (Stull, 2014).

Following the expression of sexual dimorphism, Stull (2014) used long bone dimensions in numerous classification statistics in an attempt to estimate sex (Stull, 2014; Stull et al., 2017). Using a multiple predictor model, classification methods achieved high accuracies ranging between 72% and 94%. Proximal and distal breadth measurements were consistently recognized as the most important measurements in model creation, similar to the measurements that produce the highest classification accuracies in adult sex estimation (Krüger et al., 2017; Spradley and Jantz, 2011).

■ AGE-AT-DEATH ESTIMATION

Juvenile Age Estimation

Close to 5000 children, under the age of 14 years, die annually of unnatural deaths in South Africa. These deaths include motor vehicle accidents, drowning, homicide, or any other deaths that cannot be attributed to natural causes and are required to be investigated by medicolegal professionals (Statistics South Africa, 2014). In the case of unknown subadults, particularly when advanced decomposition has limited the usual methods of identification, age estimation is still the most reliable factor of the biological profile, followed by sex estimation.

Subadult age estimation is based on morphological and metric evaluation of indicators associated with growth and development (Franklin, 2010; Stull et al., 2014b). Primarily, long bone dimensions, dental formation, and epiphyseal fusion rates have been utilized in age-at-death studies for South African children.

Using the same South African sample of juveniles used to estimate sex, Stull (2014) noted a strong correlation between chronological age and long bone dimensions, but the relationship is nonlinear and this heteroscedasticity needs to be accounted for in model creation for age estimation. To address this nonlinear variation, multivariate adaptive regression splines were employed and yielded 95% prediction intervals (PIs) that could fluctuate as the variance increased with age (Stull et al., 2014b).

Instead of only providing single variable models for application, Stull and colleagues also evaluated the potential of a multivariable model. Results proved that multivariate models yield the smallest PIs in older children, whereas single variable models result in the smallest PIs in younger children (Stull et al., 2014b). The multiple predictor models succeeded in estimating age, but the vast number of tables required to present all combinations of variables necessitated a program that allowed the assessment of all possible combinations based on available skeletal elements. KidStats was developed to calculate PIs using multiple predictor models and is able to estimate age at death and sex from subadult remains. Although the models lose some precision in older age categories, the 95% PIs adjust and as a result the accuracies of chronological ages falling within the PIs range from 94% to 100% (Stull, 2014; Stull et al., 2014b). Additional information regarding KidStats can be found at https://github.com/geanes/kidstats.

As age progresses, dental formation and epiphyseal fusion become more informative age indicators for subadults. Methods that are often used in forensic and clinical settings include the use of hand-wrist radiographs and the scoring of the stage of fusion for the secondary ossification centers (i.e., proximal and distal long bone epiphyses). Recently, fusion of the long bones was scored from radiographic images on a large South African sample ($n = 1891$; ages ranging from 6 to 24 years) (Lakha, 2015). While the pattern of fusion was consistent between the sexes (e.g., the elbow, hip, ankle, knee, wrist, and shoulder), females were two years ahead of males. All joints exhibited complete union in females at 21 years and in males at 24 years. The iliac crest was the last epiphysis to fuse in both males and females (Lakha, 2015).

Population differences and socioeconomic status are consistently recognized as intrinsic and extrinsic factors, respectively, which affect the rate of growth and development (Cardoso, 2007). However, in the South African sample, no difference among ethnic groups or individuals from different socioeconomic statuses and epiphyseal fusion was observed (Lakha, 2015).

As for advances in dental formation, most research has focused on testing the Moorrees et al. (1963) and Demirjian et al. (1973) methods. On a sample between the ages of 7 and 16 years old, Phillips and van Wyk Kotze (2009a) demonstrated that the other methods overestimated or underestimated ages of South African children (Demirjian et al., 1973; Moorrees et al., 1963; Phillips and van Wyk Kotze, 2009a). On completion of testing the accuracy of the methods, correction factors for dental age estimation methods were created, based on multiple South African population groups (e.g., white, Indian, and black [Xhosa and Zulu]), which resulted in more accurate age estimations (Phillips and van Wyk Kotze, 2009b).

Although several studies exist, the application of these studies to an unknown person is difficult on account of differences and lack of standardization in statistical methods and analyses. Additional validation studies and novel statistical analyses for dental age estimation are needed in South African subadults.

Adult Age Estimation

Age-related changes in the adult human skeletal remains are challenging to quantify within a forensic context in South Africa. Biological age, representative of the physiological status of the skeletal remains, is correlated with chronological age, which constitutes the actual number of years lived (Acsádi and Nemeskéri, 1970; Garvin et al., 2012; Kemkes-Grottenthaler, 2002). However, this correlation decreases drastically with the advancement of age (Buikstra et al., 1994; Garvin et al., 2012; Schaefer et al., 2009; Scheuer et al., 2000). Factors leading to decreased accuracy in age-at-death assessment include population differences and interpersonal and intrapersonal variability, incompleteness and poor skeletal preservation, and interobserver bias (Baccino and Schmitt, 2006; Brickley et al., 2015; Falys and Lewis, 2011; İşcan, 1989; Jackes, 2000; Kemkes-Grottenthaler, 2002; Schmitt et al., 2002; Spirduso et al., 1995; Ubelaker, 1999; Waldron, 1987; Walker et al., 1988). Variation between individuals is largely based on genes, secular changes, environmental conditions, bone pathology, and physical activity (Jackes, 2000; Kemkes-Grottenthaler, 2002).

Currently, South African forensic laboratories mainly assess skeletal remains using four morphological methods: symphyseal face of the pubis (Brooks and Suchey, 1990), auricular surface (Buckberry and Chamberlain, 2002; Lovejoy et al., 1985), cranial suture closure (Meindl and Lovejoy, 1985), and the sternal end of the fourth rib (Oettlé and Steyn, 2000). However, the first three methods are generally used in combination through the transition analysis program ADBOU 2.1 (Boldsen et al., 2002; Milner and Boldsen, 2012). The application of transition analysis has been widely accepted as it addresses the problem of age mimicry of the reference sample by creating a maximum likelihood age estimate based on the accuracy and reliability of the age indicators (Boldsen et al., 2002; Milner and Boldsen, 2012).

While transition analysis using ADBOU 2.1 is currently the most comprehensive age estimation method employed in analyses, population specificity and the reliability of the methods to estimate adult age have recently been questioned (Jooste, 2015; Jooste et al., 2016).

Numerous other methods, based on South African standards, have also been published. These include linear regression formulae for histomorphometric variables from the anterior midshaft of the femur (Keough, 2007), the Lamendin technique using the canine (Ackermann and Steyn, 2014), and morphological changes observed in the acetabulum (Botha et al., 2015). Although these methods often require specialized equipment for analysis, they may prove useful alternatives to the commonly used transition analysis. Additional methods are currently being validated for use on South African individuals and include an endocranial suture closure method and a further histological approach to age-at-death estimation that may also assist in forensic anthropological analyses.

■ STATURE ESTIMATION

An individual's stature, regardless if tall, medium, or short, is commonly relayed during statements to police officials. Therefore, it is a feature that needs to be estimated and included in biological profiles, as it can assist in the identification of an unknown individual from skeletal remains.

The two main approaches to stature estimation from unknown individuals in South Africa include the anatomical and mathematical methods, which are based on a well-defined relationship between stature and long bone length (Himes, 1989; Meadows and Jantz, 1995; Meadows-Jantz and Jantz, 1999; Villanueva-Cañadas and Castilla-Gonzalo, 1991). If a complete skeleton is available, the anatomical method, commonly referred to as Fully's method

(Fully, 1956), is preferred. However, recent studies have questioned the accuracy of this method as it has been found to underestimate stature (Bidmos, 2005; Bidmos and Manger, 2012; King, 2004; Maijanen, 2009; Raxter et al., 2006). This underestimation has been linked to the use of soft tissue correction factors that have been found to be specific to sex, age, and population and tend to underestimate stature between 14.8 and 15.8 cm (Bidmos, 2005; Bidmos and Manger, 2012; King, 2004; Raxter et al., 2006).

While the inaccuracies reported lead to the creation of population-specific standards for South African black males, the application thereof to black females resulted in stature overestimations, indicating sex specificity (Bidmos and Manger, 2012). As a result of the overestimations in black females, new soft tissue correction factors were created based on MRI measurements to approximate skeletal measurements (Brits, 2016). However, the use of MRI measurements has been previously criticized (Ruff et al., 2012) and thus warrants further research into novel approaches to create sex- and population-specific soft tissue correction factors for South African populations when using the total skeletal height.

The second approach to stature estimation includes the use of regression formulae (mathematical approach). Recent research has revealed that applying standards developed in North America to South African populations can lead to over- or underestimations of stature in white and black South African groups, as distinct differences were observed in the limb proportions between Northern American and South African sex and ancestry groups (Myburgh, 2016).

Although specific regression formulae have been developed using mathematical methods to estimate stature in black (Lundy and Feldesman, 1987) and white South African groups (Dayal et al., 2008), secular changes in limb proportions also lead to over- or underestimation of stature (Myburgh, 2016).

South Africans exhibit secular trends in the upper and lower limbs, making the use of outdated regression formulae inappropriate. For example, the distal limb lengths, which exhibit a negative secular trend, may result in an underestimation of stature, while using the proximal limb lengths, which show a positive secular trend, may lead to an overestimation of stature (Myburgh, 2016). Thus, the regression formulae need to be frequently updated, and further research is warranted.

Until more reliable methods become available, caution should be exercised when making use of existing soft tissue correction factors and regression formulae, especially from single long bones, as this may lead to inaccurate stature estimates. Currently, research is being conducted to address these problems and new correction factors, and regression formulae will be developed to improve stature estimates in South Africa.

■ CONCLUSION

The unique composition of the South African population, its history of immigration and migration, and a high rate of crime and accidents provide a mandate for South African forensic anthropologists to validate and improve methods used to establish biological profiles (L'Abbé and Steyn, 2012). With the historical circumstances of the country, as well as modern migrations of various African population groups from either war-torn areas or destabilized governments into South Africa, a need exists to evaluate and reevaluate methods used to develop biological profiles from an unknown person. An outcome of this is the establishment of modern cranial and postcranial databases for evaluating sex, ancestry, and subadult age at death.

In light of the Daubert decision (Daubert v. Merrell Dow Pharmaceuticals, Inc., 1993), scientific conclusions need to follow certain guidelines, using reliable techniques and methods for which estimated error rates have been calculated and which are generally accepted by the peer community (Klales et al., 2012). While the Daubert standards are not yet required by the legal system in South Africa, the Daubert decision simply reinforces the value of good science. The practice of good science has been demonstrated in all areas of the biological profile, with several more advances taking place in data acquisition, application, and methods. Overall, the practice of good science has already contributed to the increased number of presumptive and positive identifications in South African Forensic Anthropology.

As most methods are in need of validation and increased sample sizes, alternate data sources need to be explored. Modern radiographic images, such as Lodox Statscan and computed tomographic (CT) scans, are instrumental to our research as we no longer need to solely rely on skeletal collections to collect modern data for the biological profile, particularly with regard to children. Ongoing research addresses obtaining Lodox and CT scans from various provinces in South Africa, so as to validate our current published results on age estimation in children and to possibly further validate many of our current methods with modern skeletal data.

Other technological advances leading to improved research include the micro-CT scanning of bone to gauge internal and microstructure, and density. Two micro-CT scanning facilities that have been used for this purpose include the MIXRAD facility at the South African Nuclear Energy Corporation SOC Limited (NECSA) and the micro-CT scanning facility at the University of the Witwatersrand. Through close collaborations with these institutions, large numbers of ambitious, national, and international researchers are already embracing the new direction of physical anthropological research, with the hopes of improving the biological profile and increasing the number of positive identifications from skeletal remains in South Africa.

Acknowledgments

We would like to thank all the members of the Forensic Anthropology Research Center and the Victim Identification Center for their hard work in attempting to find identities for the nameless. Most of the research presented in this chapter was funded by the National Research Foundation (NRF). Any opinions, findings, and conclusions or recommendations expressed in the material are those of the authors, and therefore, the NRF does not accept any liability in regard thereto.

References

Ackermann, A., Steyn, M., 2014. A test of the Lamendin method of age estimation in South African canines. Forensic Sci. Int. 236, 192.e1–192.e6.

Acsádi, G., Nemeskéri, J., 1970. History of Human Life Span and Mortality. Akadémiai Kiadó, Budapest, Hungary.

Asala, S.A., 2001. Sex determination from the head of the femur of South African whites and blacks. Forensic Sci. Int. 117, 15–22.

Baccino, E., Schmitt, A., 2006. Determination of adult age at death in the forensic context. In: Schmitt, A., Cunha, E., Pinheiro, J. (Eds.), Forensic Anthropology and Medicine. Humana Press Inc., pp. 259–280.

Barrier, I.L.O., L'Abbé, E.N., 2008. Sex determination from the radius and ulna in a modern South African sample. Forensic Sci. Int. 179, 85.e1–85.e7.

Bidmos, M.A., 2006. Metrical and non-metrical assessment of population affinity from the calcaneus. Forensic Sci. Int. 159, 6–13.

Bidmos, M.A., 2005. On the non-equivalence of documented cadaver lengths to living stature estimates based on Fully's method on bones in the Raymond A. Dart Collection. J. Forensic Sci. 50, 1–6.

Bidmos, M.A., Manger, P.R., 2012. New soft tissue correction factors for stature estimation: results from magnetic resonance imaging. Forensic Sci. Int. 214, 212.e1–212.e7.

Bidmos, M., Asala, S.A., 2003. Discriminant function sexing of the calcaneus of the South African whites. J. Forensic Sci. 48, 1–6.

Blake, K., 2014. Analysis of non-metric subadult sex determination traits in four samples of known age and sex: sex determinants or population variants? In: American Academy of Forensic Sciences 66th Annual Scientific Meeting. Presented at the American Academy of Forensic Sciences 66th Annual Scientific Meeting (AAFS). American Academy of Forensic Sciences, Seattle, WA.

Bloom, J., 2015. 1272 Unidentified Bodies in Gauteng Mortuaries in 2014/2015. [WWW Document]. Politicsweb. URL: http://www.politicsweb.co.za/politics/1272-unidentified-bodies-in-gauteng-mortuaries-in-.

Boldsen, J.L., Milner, G.R., Hylleberg, R., 2002. ADBOU Age Estimation Software.

Botha, D., Pretorius, S., Myburgh, J., Steyn, M., 2015. Age estimation from the acetabulum in South African black males. Int. J. Leg. Med. 1–9.

Breytenbach, B., 2008. A Veil of Footsteps. Human & Rousseau, Cape Town, South Africa.

Brickley, M., Dragomir, A.-M., Lockau, L., 2015. Age-at-death estimates from a disarticulated, fragmented and commingled archaeological battlefield assemblage. Int. J. Osteoarchaeol.

Brits, D.M., 2016. Stature Estimation in South African Juveniles and Adult Females (Ph.D.). University of the Witwatersrand, Johannesburg, South Africa.

Brooks, S., Suchey, J.M., 1990. Skeletal age determination based on the os pubis: a comparison of the Acsádi-Nemeskéri and Suchey-Brooks methods. Hum. Evol. 5, 227–238.

Buckberry, J.L., Chamberlain, A.T., 2002. Age estimation from the auricular surface of the ilium: a revised method. Am. J. Phys. Anthropol. 119, 231–239.

Buikstra, J.E., Ubelaker, D.H., Aftandilian, D., 1994. Standards for Data Collection from Human Skeletal Remains. Arkansas Archeological Survey, Fayetville, AR.

Cardoso, H.F.V., 2007. Environmental effects on skeletal versus dental development: using a documented subadult skeletal sample to test a basic assumption in human osteological research. Am. J. Phys. Anthropol. 132, 223–233.

Christopher, A.J., 1990. Apartheid and urban segregation levels in South Africa. Urban Stud. 27, 421–440.

Daubert v. Merrell Dow Pharmaceuticals, Inc., 1993. US Supreme Court 509 U.S. 579,113S.Ct.2786, 125L. Ed.2d 469.

Dayal, M.R., Spocter, M.A., Bidmos, M.A., 2008. An assessment of sex using the skull of black South Africans by discriminant function analysis. HOMO 59, 209–221.

Demirjian, A., Goldstein, H., Tanner, J.M., 1973. A new system of dental age assessment. Hum. Biol. 211–227.

Dibennardo, R., Taylor, J.V., 1983. Multiple discriminant function analysis of sex and race in the postcranial skeleton. Am. J. Phys. Anthropol. 61, 305–314.

Falys, C.G., Lewis, M.E., 2011. Proposing a way forward: a review of standardisation in the use of age categories and ageing techniques in osteological analysis (2004–2009). Int. J. Osteoarchaeol. 21, 704–716.

Franklin, D., 2010. Forensic age estimation in human skeletal remains: current concepts and future directions. Leg. Med. 12, 1–7.

Franklin, D., Freedman, L., Milne, N., Oxnard, C.E., 2007. Geometric morphometric study of population variation in indigenous southern African crania. Am. J. Hum. Biol. 19, 20–33.

Fully, G., 1956. Une nouvelle méthode de détermination de la taille. Ann. Med. Leg. 35, 266–273.

Garvin, H.M., Passalacqua, N.V., Uhl, N., Gipson, D.R., Overbury, R.S., Cabo, L.L., 2012. Developments in forensic anthropology: age-at-death estimation. In: Dirkmaat, D.C. (Ed.), A Companion to Forensic Anthropology. Wiley-Blackwell, UK, pp. 202–223.

Gindhart, P.S., 1973. Growth standards for the tibia and radius in children aged one month through eighteen years. Am. J. Phys. Anthropol. 39, 41–48.

Himes, J.H., 1989. Reliability of anthropometric methods and replicate measurements. Am. J. Phys. Anthropol. 79, 77–80.

Humphrey, L.T., 1998. Growth patterns in the modern human skeleton. Am. J. Phys. Anthropol. 105, 57–72. http://dx.doi.org/10.1002/(SICI)1096-8644(199801)105:1<57::AID-AJPA6>3.0.CO;2-A.

İşcan, M.Y. (Ed.), 1989. Age Markers in the Human Skeleton. Charles C. Thomas, Springfield, IL.

İşcan, M.Y., 1983. Assessment of race from the pelvis. Am. J. Phys. Anthropol. 62, 205–208.

Jackes, M., 2000. Building the bases for paleodemographic analysis: adult age determination. In: Biological Anthropology of the Human Skeleton. Wiley-Liss, New York, NY, pp. 417–466.

Jantz, R.L., Ousley, S.D., 2005. Fordisc 3: Computerized Forensic Discriminant Functions. University of Tennessee, Knoxville, TN.

Johnston, F.E., Malina, R.M., 1966. Age changes in the composition of the upper arm in Philadelphia children. Hum. Biol. 38, 1–21.

Jooste, N., 2015. Validating the Accuracy and Repeatability of Transition Analysis for Age Estimation in South Africa (M.Sc.). University of Pretoria, Pretoria, South Africa.

Jooste, N., L'Abbé, E.N., Pretorius, S., Steyn, M., 2016. Validation of transition analysis as a method of adult age estimation in a modern sample. Forensic Sci. Int. 266, 580e1–580e7.

JKemkes-Grottenthaler, A., 2002. Historical perspectives on age indicator methods. In: Hoppa, R.D., Vaupel, J.W. (Eds.), Paleodemography: Age Distributions from Skeletal Samples. Cambridge University Press, Cambridge, UK, pp. 48–72.

Kenyhercz, M.W., 2012. Sex estimation using pubic bone morphology in a modern South African sample: a test of the Klales et al. method. In: Proceedings of the American Association of Physical Anthropology. Presented at the 81st Annual Meeting of the American Association of Physical Anthropology, American Association of Physical Anthropology, Portland, OR.

Keough, N., 2007. Estimation of Age at Death from the Microscopic Structure of the Femur (M.Sc.). University of Pretoria, Pretoria, South Africa.

KidStats: Subadult age and sex estimations based on long bone measurements, 2015.

King, K.A., 2004. A test of the fully anatomical method of stature estimation. Am. J. Phys. Anthropol. Wiley-Blackwell, 125.

Klales, A.R., Ousley, S.D., Vollner, J.M., 2012. A revised method of sexing the human innominate using Phenice's nonmetric traits and statistical methods. Am. J. Phys. Anthropol. 149, 104–114.

Krüger, G.C., 2015. Comparison of Sexually Dimorphic Patterns in the Postcrania of South Africans and North Americans (M.Sc.). University of Pretoria, Pretoria, South Africa.

Krüger, G.C., L'Abbé, E.N., Stull, K.E., 2017. Sex estimation from the long bones of modern South Africans. Int. J. Leg. Med. 131, 275–285.

Krüger, G.C., L'Abbé, E.N., Stull, K.E., Kenyhercz, M.W., 2015. Sexual dimorphism in cranial morphology among modern South Africans. Int. J. Leg. Med. 129, 869–875.

L'Abbé, E.N., Kenyhercz, M.W., Stull, K.E., Keough, N., Nawrocki, S., 2013a. Application of Fordisc 3.0 to explore differences among crania of North American and South African blacks and whites. J. Forensic Sci. 58, 1579–1583.

L'Abbé, E.N., Kenyhercz, M.W., Stull, K.E., Ousley, S.D., 2013b. Craniometric assessment of modern 20th-century black, white, and "colored" South Africans. In: Proceedings of the American Academy of Forensic Sciences. Presented at the Annual Meeting of the American Academy of Forensic Sciences, American Academy of Forensic Sciences, Washington, DC, p. 444.

L'Abbé, E.N., Steyn, M., 2012. The establishment and advancement of forensic anthropology in South Africa. In: Dirkmaat, D.C. (Ed.), A Companion to Forensic Anthropology. Wiley-Blackwell, UK, pp. 626–638.

L'Abbé, E.N., Van Rooyen, C., Nawrocki, S.P., Becker, P.J., 2011. An evaluation of non-metric cranial traits used to estimate ancestry in a South African sample. Forensic Sci. Int. 209, 195.e1–195.e7.

Lakha, K., 2015. Standards for Epiphyseal Union in South African Children between the Ages of 6 to 24 years Using Low Dose X-ray (Lodox) (dissertation). University of Cape Town, Cape Town, SA.

Liebenberg, L., 2015. Postcraniometric Assessment of Ancestry in among Modern South Africans (M.Sc.). University of Pretoria, Pretoria, South Africa.

Liebenberg, L., L'Abbé, E.N., Stull, K.E., 2015. Population differences in the postcrania of modern South Africans and the implications for ancestry estimation. Forensic Sci. Int. 257, 522–529.

Loth, S.R., Henneberg, M., 2001. Sexually dimorphic mandibular morphology in the first few years of life. Am. J. Phys. Anthropol. 115, 179–186.

Lovejoy, C.O., Meindl, R.S., Pryzbeck, T.R., Mensforth, R.P., 1985. Chronological metamorphosis of the auricular surface of the ilium: a new method for the determination of adult skeletal age at death. Am. J. Phys. Anthropol. 68, 15–28.

Lundy, J.K., Feldesman, M.R., 1987. Revised equations for estimating living stature from the long bones of the South-African Negro. South Afr. J. Sci. 83, 54–55.

Maijanen, H., 2009. Testing anatomical methods for stature estimation on individuals from the WM Bass Donated Skeletal Collection. J. Forensic Sci. 54, 746–752.

Malina, R., Johnston, F., 1967. Relations between bone, muscle, and fat widths in the upper arms and calves of boys and girls studied cross-sectionally at ages 6 to 16 years. Hum. Biol. 39, 211–223. http://dx.doi.org/10.2307/41448847.

Maresh, M., 1970. Measurements from roentgenograms. In: McCammon, R. (Ed.), Human Growth and Development. CC. Thomas, Springfield, IL, pp. 157–200.

McDowell, J.L., 2012. Nasal Aperture Shape and its Application for Estimating Ancestry in Modern South Africans (M.Sc.). University of Pretoria, Pretoria, South Africa.

McDowell, J.L., Kenyhercz, M.W., L'Abbé, E.N., 2015. An evaluation of nasal bone and aperture shape among three South African populations. Forensic Sci. Int. 252, 189.e1–189.e7.

Meadows, L., Jantz, R.L., 1995. Allometric secular change in the long bones from the 1800s to the present. J. Forensic Sci. 40, 762–767.

Meadows-Jantz, L., Jantz, R.L., 1999. Secular change in long bone length and proportion in the United States, 1800–1970. Am. J. Phys. Anthropol. 110, 57–67.

Meindl, R.S., Lovejoy, C.O., 1985. Ectocranial suture closure: a revised method for the determination of skeletal age at death based on the lateral-anterior sutures. Am. J. Phys. Anthropol. 68, 57–66.

Milner, G.R., Boldsen, J.L., 2012. Transition analysis: a validation study with known-age modern American skeletons. Am. J. Phys. Anthropol. 148, 98–110.

Moorrees, C.F.A., Fanning, E.A., Hunt Jr., E.E., 1963. Age variation of formation stages for ten permanent teeth. J. Dent. Res. 42, 1490–1502.

Myburgh, J., 2016. Limb Proportions in South Africans: Secular Changes, Population Differences and Implications for Stature Estimation (Ph.D.). University of Pretoria, Pretoria, South Africa.

Novotný, V., İşcan, M.Y., Loth, S.R., 1993. Morphologic and osteometric assessment of age, sex and race from the skull. In: İşcan, M.Y., Helmer, R.P. (Eds.), Forensic Analysis of the Skull: Craniofacial Analysis, Reconstruction, and Identification. Wiley-Liss, New York, NY, pp. 71–88.

Oettlé, A.C., 2014. Effects of Dental Loss and Senescence on Aspects of Adult Mandibular Morphology in South Africans (Ph.D.). University of Pretoria, Pretoria, South Africa.

Oettlé, A.C., Becker, P.J., de Villiers, E., Steyn, M., 2009. The influence of age, sex, population group, and dentition on the mandibular angle as measured on a South African sample. Am. J. Phys. Anthropol. 139, 505–511.

Oettlé, A.C., Steyn, M., 2000. Age estimation from sternal ends of ribs by phase analysis in South African blacks. J. Forensic Sci. 45, 1071–1079.

Patriquin, M.L., Steyn, M., Loth, S.R., 2005. Metric analysis of sex differences in South African black and white pelves. Forensic Sci. Int. 147, 119–127.

Patriquin, M.L., Steyn, M., Loth, S.R., 2002. Metric assessment of race from the pelvis in South Africans. Forensic Sci. Int. 127, 104–113.

Petersen, D.C., Libiger, O., Tindall, E.A., Hardie, R., Hannick, L.I., Glashoff, R.H., Mukerji, M., Fernandez, P., Haacke, W., Schork, N.J., Hayes, V.M., 2013. Complex patterns of genomic admixture within southern Africa. PLoS Genet. 9, e1003309.

Phenice, T.W., 1969. A newly developed visual method of sexing the os pubis. Am. J. Phys. Anthropol. 30, 297–301.

Phillips, V.M., van Wyk Kotze, T.J., 2009a. Testing standard methods of dental age estimation by Moorrees, Fanning and Hunt and Demirjian, Goldstein and Tanner on three South African children samples. J. Forensic Odontostomatol. 27, 20–28.

Phillips, V.M., van Wyk Kotze, T.J., 2009b. Dental age related tables for children of various ethnic groups in South Africa. J. Forensic Odontostomatol. 27, 29–44.

R Core Team, 2013. R: A Language and Environment for Statistical Computing. [WWW Document] R Found. Stat. Comput., Vienna, Austria. URL: http://www.R-project.org/.

Raxter, M.H., Auerbach, B.M., Ruff, C.B., 2006. Revision of the Fully technique for estimating statures. Am. J. Phys. Anthropol. 130, 374–384.

Ruff, C.B., Holt, B.M., Niskanen, M., Sladék, V., Berner, M., Garofalo, E., Garvin, H.M., Hora, M., Maijanen, H., Niinimaki, S., Salo, K., Schuplerová, E., Tompkins, D., 2012. Stature and body mass estimation from skeletal remains in the European Holocene. Am. J. Phys. Anthropol. 148, 601–617.

Schaefer, M., Black, S.M., Scheuer, L., 2009. Juvenile Osteology: A Laboratory and Field Manual. Academic Press.

Scheuer, L., Black, S.M., Cunningham, C., 2000. Developmental Juvenile Osteology. Academic Press.

Schmitt, A., Rougé, D., Cunha, E., Murail, P., 2002. Variability of the pattern of aging on the human skeleton: evidence from bone indicators and implications on age at death estimation. J. Forensic Sci. 47, 1203–1209.

Schutkowski, H., 1993. Sex determination of infant and juvenile skeletons: I. morphognostic features. Am. J. Phys. Anthropol. 90, 199–205.

Schutkowski, H., 1987. Sex determination of fetal and neonatal skeletons by means of discriminant analysis. Int. J. Anthropol. 2, 347–352.

Small, C., Brits, D.M., Hemingway, J., 2012. Quantification of the subpubic angle in South Africans. Forensic Sci. Int. 222, 395.e1–395.e6.

Smith, S., Buschang, P., 2004. Variation in longitudinal diaphyseal long bone growth in children three to ten years of age. Am. J. Hum. Biol. 16, 648–657.

Smithgall, E., Johnston, F., Malina, R., Galbraith, M., 1966. Developmental changes in compact bone relationships in the second metacarpal. Hum. Biol. 38, 141–151. http://dx.doi.org/10.2307/41448776.

Spirduso, W.W., Francis, K.L., MacRae, P.G., 1995. Physical Dimensions of Aging.

Spradley, M.K., Jantz, R.L., 2011. Sex estimation in forensic anthropology: skull versus postcranial elements. J. Forensic Sci. 56, 289–296.

Statistics South Africa, 2015. Mid-year Population Estimates (Census No. P0302). South Africa.

Statistics South Africa, 2014. Mortality and Causes of Death in South Africa, 2013: Findings from Death Notification (Statistical Release No. P0309.3). South Africa.

Steyn, M., İşcan, M.Y., 1999. Osteometric variation in the humerus: sexual dimorphism in South Africans. Forensic Sci. Int. 106, 77–85.

Steyn, M., İşcan, M.Y., 1998. Sexual dimorphism in the crania and mandibles of South African whites. Forensic Sci. Int. 98, 9–16.

Steyn, M., İşcan, M.Y., 1997. Sex determination from the femur and tibia in South African whites. Forensic Sci. Int. 90, 111–119.

Steyn, M., Patriquin, M.L., 2009. Osteometric sex determination from the pelvis—does population specificity matter? Forensic Sci. Int. 191, 113.e1–113.e5.

Steyn, M., Smith, J.R., 2007. Interpretation of ante-mortem stature estimates in South Africans. Forensic Sci. Int. 171, 97–102.

Stull, K.E., 2014. An Osteometric Evaluation of Age and Sex Differences in the Long Bones of South African Children from the Western Cape (Ph.D. dissertation). University of Pretoria, Pretoria, South Africa.

Stull, K.E., Kenyhercz, M.W., L'Abbé, E.N., 2014a. Ancestry estimation in South Africa using craniometrics and geometric morphometrics. Forensic Sci. Int. 245, 206. e1–206.e7.

Stull, K.E., Kenyhercz, M.W., Tise, M.L., L'Abbé, E.N., Tuamsuk, P., 2016. The craniometric implications of a complex population history in South Africa craniometric. In: Pilloud, M.A., Hefner, J.T. (Eds.), Biological Distance Analysis: Forensic and Bioarchaeological Perspectives. Academic Press, USA.

Stull, K.E., L'Abbé, E.N., Ousley, S.D., 2014b. Using multivariate adaptive regression splines to estimate subadult age from diaphyseal dimensions: subadult Age Estimation from Diaphyses. Am. J. Phys. Anthropol. 154, 376–386.

Stull, K.E., L'Abbé, E.N., Ousley, S.D., 2017. Subadult sex estimation from diaphyseal dimensions in subadult up to 12 years old. Am. J. Phys. Anthropol (in print).

Sutherland, C., 2016. Biological Distance Among Modern and Parental South African Groups Using Discrete Traits of the Skull (M.Sc.). University of Pretoria, Pretoria, South Africa.

Tishkoff, S.A., Reed, F.A., Friedlaender, F.R., Ehret, C., Ranciaro, A., Froment, A., Hirbo, J.B., Awomoyi, A.A., Bodo, J., Doumbo, O., 2009. The genetic structure and history of Africans and African Americans. Science 324, 1035–1044.

Ubelaker, D.H., 1999. Human Skeletal Remains: Excavation, Analysis and Interpretation, third ed. Taraxacum, Washington, DC.

Uhl, N., 2014. Using Multivariate Calibration to Evaluate Hominin Brain/body Size Relationships (Ph.D.). University of Illinois, Urbana-Champaign, Illinois, USA.

Villanueva-Cañadas, E., Castilla-Gonzalo, J., 1991. Identificación del cadàver. In: Gisbert Calabuig, J.A. (Ed.), Medicina Legal Y Toxicología. Masson, Barcelona, Spain, pp. 1011–1020.

Waldron, T., 1987. The relative survival of the human skeleton: implications for palaeopathology. In: Death, Decay and Reconstruction: Approaches to Archaeology and Forensic Science. Manchester University Press, Manchester, UK, pp. 55–64.

Walker, P.L., 2008. Sexing skulls using discriminant function analysis of visually assessed traits. Am. J. Phys. Anthropol. 136, 39–50.

Walker, P.L., Johnson, J.R., Lambert, P.M., 1988. Age and sex biases in the preservation of human skeletal remains. Am. J. Phys. Anthropol. 76, 183–188.

Weaver, D., 1980. Sex differences in the ilia of a known sex and age sample of fetal and infant skeletons. Am. J. Phys. Anthropol. 52, 191–195.

CHAPTER 28

The Influence of Operational Workflow and Mortuary Environment on Identification: A Case Study From the WWI Battle of Fromelles

Roland Wessling
Cranfield University, Shrivenham, United Kingdom

Chapter Outline

The aim of this chapter is to address two factors that enable the anthropologist to do at their work: the physical environment they work in and the workflow of information from other aspects of an excavation, such as archaeology, personnel effects finds, radiography, or surveying. Superficially, it is not difficult to argue that an anthropologist needs a good environment to work in (Cox et al., 2008). The best food cannot be served without a plate and it could not even be cooked without a kitchen. Equally, an adequate workflow is essential, since the best chef cannot cook a meal if the butcher, greengrocer, or fish monger have no produce to supply.

However, while the argument of needing a good working environment and efficient workflow processes is relatively obvious, operational, financial, political, and security reasons are often recognized as limiting factors in the development of ideal environments and workflows. Many international mass fatality identification operations are fragmented with excavations occurring in different places within a certain geographical boundary, mortuaries being either centrally or regionally located, DNA laboratories being located in other cities or even countries, and with repatriation operations occurring yet somewhere else. Often multiple organizations are involved in the different aspects of an overall operation.

The various operational efforts after the Balkan Wars in the 1990s provide good examples. While overall very successful operations, many aspects of the processes involved were very fragmented. The organizations involved in forensic and humanitarian investigations included the International Committee of the Red Cross (ICRC),

New Perspectives in Forensic Human Skeletal Identification. http://dx.doi.org/10.1016/B978-0-12-805429-1.00028-4

the International Criminal Tribunal for the former Yugoslavia (ICTY), the United Nations Mission in Kosovo (UNMIK), the International Commission on Missing Persons (ICMP), as well as various national and international nongovernmental organizations (Djuric et al., 2007). The involvement of these different organizations inevitably led to fragmented working environments and workflows, which occurred in any one of these organizations. For example, the ICTY established a very well-equipped central mortuary in Visoko, near Sarajevo, where most remains were transported to, and still almost 300 individuals were examined at an ad hoc mortuary facility in Sanski Most, in the north of the country (Baraybar and Gasior, 2006). During an earlier investigation, over 60 individuals were transported to Croatia for examination (Primorac et al., 1996). Each fragmented aspect of an overall operation raises the risk of noncompatible protocols, SOPs, methods, reporting, etc. Thus, this chapter concentrates on the importance of well-planned and coordinated working environments and workflows, and uses the WWI Fromelles investigations as an example.

■ BACKGROUND

The Battle of Fromelles occurred on July 19–20, 1916. Fromelles is a small village near Lille, France, and is 11 km away from the French/Belgium border. The action was directed toward a German stronghold called the Sugar Loaf and was intended partly as a diversion to the Battle of the Somme that was taking place about 80 km (50 mi) to the south. Fromelles was a combined operation between British troops and the Australian Imperial Force (AIF). It would be the first occasion that the AIF saw action on the Western Front (Corfield, 2009; Lindsay, 2008).

A combination of factors, including poor planning and insufficient ammunition supplies, led to substantial losses and no strategic gains (Loe et al., 2014). After a night and a day of fighting, 1500 British and 5533 Australian soldiers were killed, wounded or taken prisoner, while the German troops suffered fewer than 1500 casualties (Lindsay, 2008). The Australian War Memorial describes the battle as the worst 24 h in the Australia's history. The 5533 casualties were equivalent to the combined total Australian losses in the Boer War, Korean War, and Vietnam War combined.

While some of the Allied casualties were recovered by their own side, many were buried by German soldiers, which included the eight mass graves at Pheasant Woods, Fromelles. They apparently began burying the corpses on July 22, 1916, and ended later that month (Loe et al., 2014). Details on the battle, its context within WWI, and the ongoing forensic investigations can be found in a series of publications (see Loe et al., 2014; Lindsay, 2008; Wilkinson, 2011; Pollard and Barton, 2013; Lee, 2017; Corfield, 2009).

Historians have long speculated that up to 400 of the missing dead were recovered by the Germans in the days following the attack and buried behind their lines. Between 2002 and 2008, amateur historian Lambis Englezos and a few supporters gathered evidence, such as aerial photos sourced from the Imperial War Museum and documents from German archives, all pointing toward graves behind German lines in 1916 at Pheasant Wood (Loe et al., 2014).

After initial noninvasive surveys in 2007 by GUARD Archaeology Ltd, commissioned by the Australian Department of Defense, the Australian Government asked the Commonwealth War Grave Commission (CWGC) to oversee site confirmation project at Pheasant Woods to establish whether or not the pits contained remains. The 3-week project began in May 2008 and was carried out by GUARD; they found conclusive evidence that substantial numbers of Allied soldiers had been buried in five of the eight pits identified. In November 2008, the CWGC invited a number of organizations to declare their interest in an excavation of the eight pits at Pheasant Woods and for postmortem examinations of all soldiers recovered. Oxford Archaeology Ltd was contracted to carry out the excavations in 2010. A group of permanent Oxford Archaeology staff and international experts in mass grave investigations began their work in May 2010.

■ SITE ORGANIZATION

The overall site was separated into three distinct areas: (1) public relations and offices by the Commonwealth War Graves Commission; (2) the excavation area; and (3) the temporary mortuary area (Fig. 28.1). Having all three areas in such close proximity is unusual. Most operations, such as ICTY's excavations in Bosnia, have a central mortuary facility, and casualties from excavations anywhere in the country are transported to that central facility, while public relations may be handled from an entirely different office or even country. Being able to create your own setup of excavation and mortuary right next to each other was a unique and very valuable experience.

The CWGC area played no part in the scientific operation and needs no further mention in this context. The temporary mortuary will be explained in great detail in the next section. The excavation area, although entirely separate from the temporary mortuary will also be covered in the next section because it is the foundation of the operation onto which the anthropological processes were developed. It is therefore essential to examine that aspect in great detail too.

The site was not accessible to the public and was secured through fencing and security guards and a CCTV system day and night throughout the project. There were specific groups of visitors invited to view the operation but only under close supervision. This was mostly to prevent potential DNA contamination of remains.

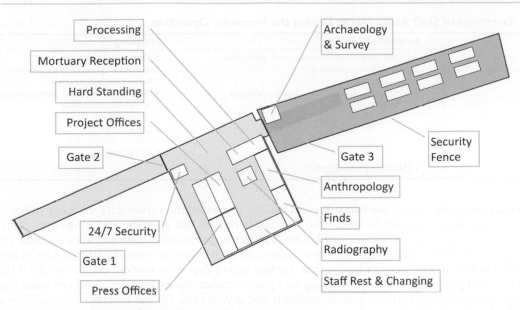

Figure 28.1 Layout of the mortuary and field sections. *Drawing by Roland Wessling.*

■ OVERALL IDENTIFICATION PROCESS

There were several elements to the overall identification process, including (1) the archaeological context from the excavation; (2) the detailed anthropological analysis, including biological profiles, dental analysis, unique personal identifying features, antemortem and perimortem trauma, and pathological conditions; and (3) the DNA profile matching between the casualties and living relatives. All evidence was presented to the Identification Commission, which met annually for 5 years, in case further historic information or additional relatives with DNA consistencies came forward.

The excavation and anthropological analysis comprised one of the three elements in the identification process. The others were the DNA analysis and the Identification Commission that would assess all results and conclusions from the anthropological analysis, the finds analysis, and the DNA analysis to decide on the level of identification achieved.

Two further aspects that were entirely remote from the onsite work were the gathering of DNA samples from relatives of the presumed missing and historical investigations of casualty records. These aspects, while enormously important, will not be discussed in this chapter because it falls outside of the author's area of expertise.

■ TEAM COMPOSITION

During the next two sections on environment and workflow, there will be frequent references to the team members involved in the operation. Depending on demand, there were slight variations in staff numbers but most of the time, the three sections consisted of staff categories and numbers as indicated in Table 28.1.

The site contained eight pits that had been dug presumably for up to 400 casualties. Two of them contained no human remains, five graves had between 44 and 52 casualties and one grave had only three sets of remains. Two graves were excavated parallel at any time under the supervision of the two senior forensic archaeologists. Both graves were served by the team of two surveyors. Typically one surveyed the remains and evidence and the other processed the data.

The role of the photographer will be addressed in detail in both the environment and workflow sections. The photographer took all photos on the excavation and all detail images in the temporary mortuary for the anthropologists. Overview images of the bodies were technically taken by the anthropologists but with cameras fixed to the ceiling, which had been installed and tested by the photographer. The finds analysts took their own images.

■ ENVIRONMENT

In the context of this chapter, the working environment, which the team was able to create from scratch, includes the office containers/rooms that formed the mortuary as well as the tents that covered the graves. Next, it included the equipment used in the mortuary and field, such as having cameras at each mortuary table. Furthermore, it included how the equipment was used, e.g., installing cameras on the ceiling by a professional photographer and having them directly connected to computers, which in turn were networked.

■ THE EXCAVATION SITE

Obviously, the excavation site layout was largely dictated by the positioning of the mass graves. However, there were two aspects that are relevant to the overall identification process: (1) a site office container with a networked computer workstation for the surveyors; and (2) a change in logistical approach for covering the graves during excavation.

Table 28.1 Overview of Staff Assignments During the Fromelles Operation

Operations	Excavation	Mortuary
1 Project director 1 Assistant/translator	2 Grave supervisors/forensic archaeologists 10–12 Osteoarchaeologists 1 Site manager 2 Temporary mechanical digger operators 1–2 Surveyors	1 Mortuary manager 2–6 Remains/artifacts processors 1 Senior anthropologist 3–5 Physical/forensic anthropologists 1 Senior finds analyst 1–2 finds analysts 1 Data clerk 1 CSI 1 Radiographer
	1 (Shared) photographer	

As mentioned previously, one of the two surveyors usually processed the survey data. In most archaeological operations, surveyors would concentrate on gathering data while on site and after the end of an operation, process the data and produce site maps, representations of bodies within the graves, and distribution of artifacts. However, with two surveyors assisting on the project, the data processing and results were processed within 2 days of being gathered.

It was decided before the excavation began that the two graves that were worked on at any given time would be covered. This was partly to ensure that even during very poor weather, the excavation could continue but also to protect the human remains from exposure to both sunlight and prying eyes. For the first two graves, blow-up tents were used. The site had main electricity and electric blowers were used to permanently keep the tents erect during the day. Since power outages were a very real danger, the tents had to be deflated each night and reinflated each morning. To prevent disturbance of the remains, the entire excavation pit was covered by 7-m-long wooden beams with wooden planks across them as well as fencing panels on top of them. This took the entire excavation team around 75 min per day to complete. As soon as that data became available, a secondary plan was assessed in which one large (30 × 40 m) tent would be placed over the remaining four graves. Although its hire and installation was costly, it was still considerably more cost-effective than paying up to 15 archaeologists to inflate and deflate tents.

The use of the tent had more of an impact than just time and cost savings. A number of improvements could be seen:

- The whole team could simply walk into the tent each morning and get straight to excavating rather than getting side-tracked by logistics;
- The area surrounding the graves was available for tables, equipment, etc.;
- The white tent canvas produced diffused light, which benefited both the archaeologists and the photographer (on very cloudy days some artificial light was used to improve visibility within the site);
- A special visitor's platform could be erected easily and cordoned off to prevent DNA contamination;
- The work environment of the excavation was more like that of an operating room than an archaeological excavation. Considering that the soil was almost pure clay and under normal, archaeological conditions would quickly turn into mud, the tent protected the whole surrounding area from excessive moisture.

While most of these changes were unintentional, they were nevertheless very welcomed. It undoubtedly improved the quality of excavation, which in turn, improved the anthropological and finds analysis. The more accurately the archaeologist can excavate and record their work, the better anthropologists can analyze the remains and the better the finds experts can put patterns of buttons into the context of a particular uniform, indicating a particular regiment or unit.

■ THE TEMPORARY MORTUARY

The temporary mortuary consisted of a series of connected office containers. A foundation of compacted gravel had been laid by a local contractor prior to the team's arrival to ensure a stable and level surface for the containers. The senior representative of the project, i.e., project and team leaders, were there 2 weeks ahead of the official operations start date to design the layout and finalize the workflow. The individual office containers were placed according to the team leader's instructions.

The temporary mortuary was structured according to a one-way traffic following the workflow, which will be discussed in detail in the next section. Here, another aspect will be discussed that made a considerable difference in the results of the anthropological examinations and with it to the identification process: the setup of each workstation and connection to the rest of the network (Fig. 28.2).

Anthropology Workstations

Up to five separate anthropology tables were available for analysis. The locations of the tables were marked permanently on the floor, since their exact position was key to proper photography. Each table had a DSLR camera attached to the ceiling, which was connected to a computer workstation via USB cables and could be controlled remotely. Focus and focal length were set up by the photographer and fixed. This ensured that extremely consistent, high-quality images could be taken efficiently. The mortuary was prepared for up to 400 casualties and considering that each case

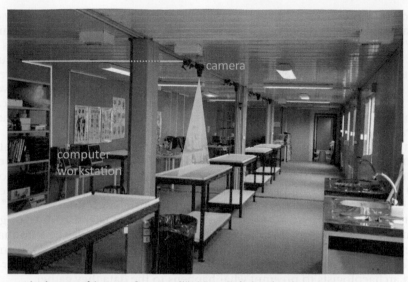

Figure 28.2 Mortuary layout with photographic setup. *Image modified from Oxford Archaeology.*

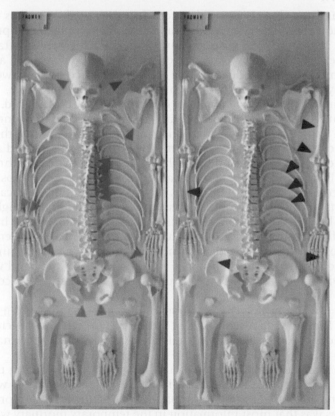

Figure 28.3 Demonstration of the photographic recording system for antemortem and perimortem trauma, postmortem damage, taphonomic alterations, taphonomy, and other pathological conditions. *Images modified from Oxford Archaeology.*

usually had four overview images taken. This means that up to 1600 images could be produced for which anthropologists did not have to climb on a step ladder, holding cameras overhead, hoping to catch the entire table in the right light, etc. When comparing the time saved for which an anthropologist would have to be paid, the setup quickly pays for itself, even in a temporary operation, let alone in a permanent one. However, the true improvement and argument for such a setup is the quality and guaranteed consistency of the images. They can be cropped in large batches automatically to remove unnecessary floor space and will no longer feature the anthropologist's feet.

The anthropologists agreed on a system of visually recording skeletal inventory, epiphyseal fusion states, antemortem and perimortem injuries, postmortem damage, and pathological conditions. The first image was taken of the skeletal remains laid out in a standardized anatomical position with only a label including the case number, date, etc. Then followed a series of images with colored triangles that indicated the abovementioned anatomical features (Fig. 28.3). This meant that when the senior anthropologist later worked on the case reports and final project report, she or he could easily detect patterns in any of the anomalies because she or he could quickly compare, for example, perimortem injury images for all 250 casualties, because they had all been taken in such a standardized manner.

In the context of WWI, historians have conducted decades of research that show patterns of injuries to soldiers who were in particular functions, e.g., front-line infantry, sniper units, supply units, medical support, etc. Some individuals would be more likely to sustain grenade blast injuries whereas others would be more likely to die of bullet wounds. This is by no means an accurate science and on the list of identification evidence would probably rank as tertiary; however, this information can still help considerably in narrowing down missing casualties lists and can enable DNA experts to check specific samples of relatives rather than comparing all injury characteristics against all reported missing information.

Perimortem trauma and postmortem damage have often been ignored entirely in operations that were purely aimed at identification and which would not result in criminal court proceedings. Such operations, often labeled "humanitarian" (distinguishing them from "forensic"), would only document healed, antemortem trauma that may have been recorded in the individual's lifetime. The Fromelles team's project proposal had clearly stated that they would not, as a matter of principle, make a distinction between "forensic" and "humanitarian" approaches. The team members consider every operation "forensic" regardless of whether a court later uses the data gathered. In bioarchaeology and physical anthropology, all possible information should be gathered. The information and conclusions may then be used to revise historical accounts, a truth and reconciliation program, or an international tribunal. This would depend on the circumstances of the conflict, region, nation, population, among other factors. It is not up to the anthropologist and archaeologists to preempt what happens to the data they gather.

The Information Network

One of the reasons why the anthropologists were able to conduct their work as well as they did was that they had a massive amount of information about each case easily available to them on their computer workstation. These were networked to the computers of the archaeologists and surveyors, allowing two-way traffic of information, such as position of the casualty, context of casualty in relation to other casualties and artifacts, and photographs of the excavated casualty. At the same time, the data produced by the anthropologist could be viewed by all other sections, such as archaeology or radiography, as well as being backed up immediately for data safety.

Most archaeological exhumations see large amounts of documentation produced. Photographs, forms, drawings, and survey maps are only some of the types of data accumulated. While some of this data may reach an anthropologist working on a particular set of remains, it is unlikely that all of it is at their fingertips. The Fromelles operation was designed to do specifically that. By the time the remains were X-rayed and cleaned, all photos and survey data had been uploaded to the system and the anthropologist could access it through a database specifically designed for this operation. They could also see the casualties who may have been positioned next to or below the one they worked on, which could quickly address issues, such as commingling or localized taphonomic phenomena. If, despite the best efforts of the archaeologists, a phalanx from individual A's right hand had been recovered with individual B's left hand by mistake, this could quickly and easily be addressed. The anthropologist would first look at the survey data and discover that the two hands had been on top of each other. They could then see which colleague is working on the other individual and ask if they have an extra hand phalanx associated with their case. If so, that phalanx could be compared in its appearance with the others of the hand where it may be from and if it fits, it could be reunited with the correct individual (although it would still be recorded as "reunited" and not used for DNA analysis).

One luxury the Fromelles operation had was the presence of a radiographer and a direct digital X-ray unit. All remains and most finds were X-rayed. The casualties went through an initial primary screening prior to cleaning and later the anthropologists could request further, more detailed X-rays to assist with the analysis of trauma or biological profile estimations.

The level of dataflow had many advantages throughout the operation and during the report and identification phase. Information could be queried from the database instantly. Bottlenecks in the workflow and within specific processes could be detected and addressed through a simple analysis of the times each process was started and ended. One of the greatest advantages was that most information in the temporary mortuary was directly entered electronically and did not have to be transcribed from paper forms. This meant a considerable time saving and increased data quality, since no poor handwriting had to be interpreted.

■ WORKFLOW

The workflow (Fig. 28.4) for both the excavation and the mortuary will be quite familiar for many practitioners who have worked on mass grave investigations or disaster victim identification operations. One aspect that is not reflected in the diagram is the fact that recovery site and mortuary site were right next to each other. Normally, mass fatality operations find these two sites far away from each other and both have to operate quite independently. Sadly, this often leads to information from the field being ignored in the mortuary. In theory, the Fromelles networking solution could have easily been achieved over any distance. It was almost ironic that an operation where all information could have been exchanged by simply taking some paper forms and walking over from the grave to the mortuary decided to completely network the system.

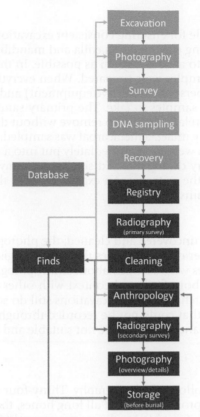

Figure 28.4 Workflow diagram for the Fromelles operation. *By Roland Wessling.*

When it was clear that excavation and mortuary would be next to each other, all standard forms were reviewed. The forms for Fromelles were adapted versions of the Inforce Foundation forms first published in 2008 (Cox et al., 2008). They had since been developed further considerably but had always been designed to serve two largely separate operations. With that came a number of necessary duplications in logs and forms to ensure quality control. All forms and logs were reviewed and several could be combined, simplified, or removed altogether. Only information essential should be recorded and it is well worth reviewing forms for every operation.

■ THE EXCAVATION

The overall excavation team was split into two groups of five or six osteologists or forensic archaeologists with considerable experience in human remains recovery. Each team was led by an experienced forensic archaeologist to oversee and coordinate the efforts. The senior archaeologists also oversaw the DNA sampling following the agreed upon protocol that was developed in collaboration with a neutral DNA expert advisor, and the company that had been awarded the contract to analyze the DNA samples in the United Kingdom.

Grave Preparation

Initially, a mechanical digger (360 degrees, 5 tons) was used to remove the overburden. From the detailed test excavation the previous year, the depth of the graves was well known. One experienced archaeologist closely watched the digger bucket and would alert the operator to stop digging at the first sign of disturbance, remains, or artifacts. The sides of the graves were then sloped and covered with thick plastic sheeting to avoid erosion. To one of the long sides of the grave, an area level with the top of remains was excavated to allow easy access into the grave. The grave cuts were destroyed in the process after being recorded. Considering that the "excavation mode" had been known (Bavarian soldiers had received an order to dig it), the grave cut was not important to goals of the project.

Excavation

The excavation team was spread throughout the grave to start removing fill. The very heavy clay could neither be dry or wet sieved realistically but had to be checked for small items of evidence or personal effects. This was achieved by carefully squeezing the soil between the fingers (with surgical gloves), a time-consuming effort but was the most efficient, given time constraints. When a set of human remains was initially located, one archaeologist would start an excavation form after being allocated an evidence number. The entire operation worked with one, single evidence number system that was used for everything, from remains and artifacts to DNA samples and even nonmaterial types of evidence, such as a grave cut. This prevented the accidental duplication of numbers during the excavation.

DNA Sampling

The senior archaeologists were responsible for ensuring consistent excavation of all remains as well as the documentation. The remains were excavated, leaving clay on the maxilla and mandible and on both hands and feet. This was done to minimize exposure of the DNA to as little oxygen as possible. In the meantime, the paperwork and sample pods, and evidence bags for the DNA samples were prepared. When everything was ready for sampling, the senior archaeologists would change their PPE (personal protective equipment) and after the last soil was removed from the covered areas quickly decide what DNA samples to take. The primary samples targeted were canine teeth because they are single rooted and still large and relatively easy to remove without damaging the root, and a second or third metatarsal, however, if not present or fully intact, a metacarpal was sampled. This entire process could be conducted, on average, in less than 30 s. The samples were then immediately put into a cool box on site and moved to the DNA storage facility in the temporary mortuary during the next site break. Many have questioned whether this measure and/or the PPE made any difference to the outcome. An exact answer to this will never be known but the overall success in the identification process remains.

Photography

When an individual's remains were fully uncovered and cleaned, the photographer was asked to take overview photographs and would then ask what further detailed images the archaeologist wanted. This would vary considerably between causalities. These detailed images were as much about anthropological issues, such as trauma, missing skeletal elements, or taphonomy, as it was about finds and context with other casualties. No plan or section drawings were done during this operation. Many archaeological excavations still do so and therefore the team discussed what could be recorded through these means that could not be recorded through forms, survey, and photographs. It was concluded that for this excavation, plans and sections were not suitable and that the other recording means were the most appropriate and efficient.

Surveying

Surveying was conducted immediately following photography. Thirty-four survey points were recorded that represented the extent of the head, distal and proximal ends of all long bones, the extent of hands and feet, as well as the spine. In addition, all finds were surveyed. Considering there were around 6500 finds on the 250 casualties (and 200 rounds of ammunition on a casualty would count as one single find), a group of buttons would be surveyed as one item and detailed photos and quick sketches would be made available to military historians.

Lifting and Handover

When all data were recorded, the senior archaeologists double checked the forms, and then the remains were transferred into open plastic boxes for transport. The boxes were packed following a strict order that was displayed as a laminated poster on the grave wall. After the remains and the associated artifacts were lifted and packed, the soil below the head, neck, chest/arm, pelvis, and leg areas was collected in plastic bags. Each bag was labeled and sealed, never containing more than a third of its potential volume (see Radiography section for reason). Under the supervision of the CSI, the remains, artifacts, and the soil were brought to the mortuary reception and signed over from the archaeologist to the mortuary manager using a continuity form.

■ THE TEMPORARY MORTUARY PROCESS

Reception

The mortuary manager was responsible for the remains while they were going through the various processes in the mortuary. Considering that multiple sets of remains would be present in each stage of the process, there could be around 10 sets of remains open at any given time. The risk of accidental commingling was considerable, thus an experienced mortuary manager was essential to oversee the process. The manager also ensured that potential bottlenecks were addressed and quickly resolved.

Radiography

The presence of a full-time radiographer on site was based on previous experience of various mass fatality operations, where it has always added considerable value to both safety and scientific investigations. It took some convincing that such a role was even required on this operation but it proved itself more than worth it in the end. Before the remains and artifacts were excavated, the soil from underneath the remains was X-rayed. It was a relatively expedient, primary survey to highlight potential issues to the processing team. For example, sharp grenade shrapnel may be stuck in a bone covered in soil or a delicate, eroded metal item present in the soil sample. Without knowing this, it was more than likely that someone in the processing team would have sooner or later cut themselves on the shrapnel and the delicate artifact could be lost. X-raying relatively dry bones is not much of a challenge to any radiographer. A bag of wet soil, especially clay, however, is. Through some test screenings, it was decided that each bag was only filled to a third of its capacity so that the radiographer could spread the soil in the bag without opening it. This way, the soil matrix became thin enough to detect items within. The number of finds made this way were very numerous (to the dismay of the archaeologists but the soil conditions were rather unforgiving). This soil X-raying has now been acknowledged as "the fourth way of sieving" and will be published in detail in future work.

Processing

The processing was carried out by experienced archaeologists who oversaw a permanent core team. Toward the end of each single grave, access to casualties would get more difficult and it was prudent for anyone who was not needed to assist the processing team, including the senior archaeologists. The two main tasks were the separation of human remains from artifacts and the cleaning of both. Those tasks are undoubtedly monotonous but nevertheless have to be done to very high standards. The remains and artifacts were then allowed to dry naturally. The room was well ventilated and had a dehumidifier but no artificial heat source was used.

Anthropology

The anthropologists used methods widely accepted in the field of physical anthropology. The team reviewed recent articles and textbooks to see which biological profile methods should be used and how trauma, pathological conditions, and nonmetric traits should be interpreted, etc. The overview images taken for the various types of trauma and pathology were already covered in the previous section. Another recording aspect is the type of form used. Generally, there are two main types of forms: (1) "free writing" forms that give the user broad headings, such as trauma or condition and (2) option forms, where the user is asked to mostly tick boxes, such as trauma presence or absence.

The first type usually has few but large boxes allowing the user to record what they feel is important to the level deemed appropriate. While this allows the user to ignore what is unimportant and concentrate on what it is crucial in each case, it leaves an operation open to considerable inconsistencies. Different anthropologists may consider certain aspects to be more important than others. One may be particularly interested in nonmetric traits while another considers them as unreliable. The time the senior anthropologist would have had to spend to achieve consistency through reviewing would be far too great. Therefore, a very detailed form that lists every aspect of the recording was used, again based on the forms developed by the Inforce Foundation. It had a minimum of 17 pages but could have many more pages depending on the circumstances. It would, for example, contain an overview page to record antemortem observations and then each one would get a separate page to record it in detail by linking an observation number to the overview page and to the detailed page. Much of the form allows the anthropologist to simply tick boxes. When using such a process, it is crucial to enable the anthropologist to record not just "presence" or "absence," for example, but also why something may not be present, e.g., something like Schmorl's nodes can be absent because the vertebrae bodies are all perfectly fine and show no trace or because all vertebrae bodies are so eroded that it cannot be recorded. This needs to be reflected in the option boxes on the form.

Photography

Detailed photographs were all taken by the photographer. The photographer had to balance considerable demands from the field team and the mortuary. Due to the ease of digital photography, some have argued that photographs can be taken by nonexperts. While they may well be sufficient to some, the images taken by a professional photographer at Fromelles show what can be achieved in this area. There is more to a photograph than pressing a button. Framing, lighting, and depth of field are just some of the variables that are second nature to a photographer and mean little to most anthropologists and archaeologists. Furthermore, when a photographer takes every image during an operation, he or she can act as a quality control measure. A photographer does not just look but they observe. For example, they can tell an archaeologist that a set of remains need more cleaning to fit in with everyone else's efforts. A good photographer adds considerable value to an operation.

One further process needs to be addressed here, which was developed by the Fromelles photographer. Superimposition is one of the methods used to aid in the identification process. The challenge is that no one can predict from which angle an individual may have been photographed during his or her lifetime. Therefore, it is difficult to decide from what angle to photograph the skull. A surprisingly simply solution was used at Fromelles. The skull (including mandible) was mounted upside down on a rotating disk and at a steady speed videoed using a standard DSLR camera. The video was then digitally rotated to appear the right way up. If a photograph of an individual was found, a still image could be taken by advancing the video to the same angle as was taken on the antemortem photograph. This process only covered two dimensions but more portraits are taken with the camera being more or less at eye level. Thus, this solution was efficient in regard to time and was inexpensive to implement.

Finds

The finds were recorded and treated for short-term conservation where necessary. It had been decided that most of the possessions would be buried with the casualties unless a casualty was positively identified, and it was deemed appropriate that the relatives would receive an item. Such decisions were not taken by the Fromelles team but by the British and Australian authorities. The finds curators simply executed the policy given. However, all finds, except ammunition, were cleaned and recorded in great detail. Many items were X-rayed to ensure that the maximum amount of information could be extracted. Ammunition was recorded in the field and then handed over to the French police for safe and secure destruction.

Data Management

A full-time data management clerk was present throughout the operation. Considering the amount of data produced throughout the operation, this was justifiable. The onsite server was used as a primary storage device and provided the working copy for all involved. The server was then backed up to a fully encrypted second server in the United Kingdom to ensure complete data security. Some processes, at the time, had to be done manually because dataflow capacities were not sufficient. The digital X-rays, for example, were burned on DVDs and then added to the server. Although they could be accessed through the server, the amount of data (around 2 GB) per case was too much to flow through network cables. Undoubtedly, this would now be possible. Paper forms from the excavation were scanned and their information transcribed into the operations database to be accessible in both forms (searchable and in the original).

■ CONCLUSIONS

The more nonanthropological tasks can be taken off an anthropologist, the more they can concentrate on what they do best. Knowing that the necessary photography will be done by a photographer or was set up by a photographer will first enable the anthropologist to concentrate on their own work and second will give them the confidence that this aspect of the operation will yield good quality results. Both aspects improve efficiency and anthropological end results.

Information flow improves the anthropological results in many ways. It enables the anthropologist to solve problems, such as commingling or understanding taphonomic microenvironments quickly and conclusively. The networking of data enables all involved to see "the bigger picture" and will lead to new perspectives being developed and new data to be recorded, which in turn leads to new conclusions to be drawn.

The approach taken at Fromelles may appear to be very complex and very cost intensive. However, many methods, processes, and workflows developed during the operation ended up being cost efficient by saving considerable time, and time usually accounts for around 85% of the costs of such a project. Furthermore, many, if not all, of the methods, processes, and workflows can be adapted or adopted with less investment. It is not always about funds but more about creativity and the attitude to want to work to the highest forensic standards with the resources available. The reason why the Fromelles operation was such a success and why the methods, processes, and workflow worked so well, was that a group of experienced, senior scientists were given a chance to apply their knowledge and expertise gathered in various deployments to set up their operation from scratch. The best ideas from various previous operations were adapted to work together. Collectively, the team developed their ideal environment and ideal workflow to function within that environment. The result of the operation with more than half of the casualties positively identified after they had been buried in mass graves for 93 years speaks for itself.

References

Baraybar, J.P., Gasior, M., 2006. Forensic anthropology and the most probable cause of death in cases of violations against international humanitarian law: an example from Bosnia and Herzegovina. J. Forensic Sci. 51 (1), 103–108 Office on Missing Persons and Forensics (OMPF), Department of Justice, United Nations Mission in Kosovo (UNMIK).

Corfield, R.S., 2009. Don't Forget Me, Cobber: The Battle of Fromelles. MUP.

Cox, M., Flavel, A., Hanson, I., Laver, J., Wessling, R. (Eds.), 2008. The Scientific Investigation of Mass Graves. Towards Protocols and Standard Operating Procedures. Cambridge University Press, Cambridge.

Djuric, M., Dunjic, D., Djonic, D., Skinner, M., 2007. Identification of victims from two mass-graves in Serbia: a critical evaluation of classical markers of identity. Forensic Sci. Int. 172 (2–3), 125–129 Elsevier.

Lee, R., 2017. The Battle of Fromelles: 1916. Big Sky Publishing Pty, Limited.

Lindsay, P., 2008. Fromelles Australia's Darkest Day and the Dramatic Discovery of our Fallen World War I Diggers. Hardie Grant Books. 940.4272 LIN.

Loe, L., Barker, C., Brady, K., Cox, M., Webb, H., 2014. "Remember Me to All": The Archaeological Recovery and Identification of Soldiers Who Fought and Died in the Battle of Fromelles 1916. Oxford Archaeological.

Pollard, T., Barton, P., 2013. The use of first world war aerial photographs by archaeologists: a case study from Fromelles, Northern France. In: Archaeology from Historical Aerial and Satellite Archives, pp. 87–103. http://dx.doi.org/10.1007/978-1-4614-4505-0_6. ISBN: 9781461445.

Primorac, D., Definis-Gojanovic, M., Drmic, I., Rezic, B., Baden, M.M., Kennedy, M.A., Schanfield, M.S., Skakel, S.B., Lee, H.C., Andelinovic, S., 1996. Identification of war victims from mass graves in Croatia, Bosnia, and Herzegovina by the use of standard forensic methods and DNA typing. J. Forensic Sci. 41 (5), 891–894 DNA Laboratory, Zagreb University School of Medicine, Clinical Hospital.

Wilkinson, C., 2011. Fromelles: Australia's Bloodiest Day at War. Black Dog Books.

CHAPTER 29

Advances in Disaster Victim Identification

Benjamin J. Figura
West Tennessee Regional Forensic Center, Memphis, TN, United States

Chapter Outline

■ INTRODUCTION

The identification and return of victim remains is one of the most important aspects of disaster response. Culturally, identification of a victim's remains makes his or her death real in the eyes of his or her family and the local community and allows for certain cultural and religious practices to proceed (Eyre, 2002; Keough and Samuels, 2004; Keough et al., 2004; Robben, 2004; Stover and Ryan, 2001). From a practical and legal standpoint, identification allows for the issuance of the death certificate that documents that the individual in question is indeed dead. This documentation is required for the handling of the deceased's estate and will, for transport of the body, and for the dispersal of insurance monies. Investigators may also glean important clues to incident causation by studying injury patterns in victims and correlating them with the individual's location at the time of the incident (National Transportation Safety Board, 2000). This type of analysis is only feasible if remains of the victims are identified.

Identification becomes more difficult as mass fatality incidents (MFIs) become more complex (e.g., fragmentation, commingling, degradation, etc.). Various taphonomic insults have the effect of limiting the amount of postmortem information available for identification purposes (Kontanis and Sledzik, 2008; Sledzik and Rodriguez, 2002). In extreme cases, such as the September 11, 2001 World Trade Center (WTC) disaster, the identification process can extend for years and rely on DNA for the overwhelming majority of identifications. As of 2016, 15 years after the event, only 60% of the WTC victims have had remains identified to them and only 65% of the recovered remains have been identified (New York City Office of Chief Medical Examiner WTC Operations Stats June 2, 2016).

Disaster Victim Identification

The identification process following a disaster typically utilizes a standard set of identification modalities or methods. Comparisons of fingerprints, DNA, and dental or medical radiographs are the primary modalities (Beauthier and Lefèvre, 2008; Blau and Briggs, 2011; Byard and Winskog, 2010; Lessig and Rothschild, 2012; Morgan et al., 2006). In this context, disaster victim identification (DVI) operations are often cited as being "multidisciplinary" in nature (Byard and Winskog, 2010; Mundorff et al., 2008; Valenzuela et al., 1999). This is only true in which multiple disciplines were involved in the response. However, as typically practiced, identifications by individual modalities stand on their own; subsequent inputs from other modalities for the same remains generally serve only to confirm the initial identification. It is true that in some instances the entity overseeing the DVI operations may require confirmation of the identification (or at least input) from each discipline before making the outcomes official, but this is merely an operational decision that has more to do with reducing the chance of error than actually making the identification (Interpol, 2013; Morgan et al., 2006).

At first glance, it is easy to assume that the lack of identifications in a complex incident is a result of a lack of identifying information. This is not necessarily true. All recovered remains in any disaster will possess information of one form or another. While not every set of remains will possess sufficient information for identification using the standard identification modalities (DNA, dental, fingerprints, etc.), even data deemed "insufficient" for identification are still data. Furthermore, multitudes of data exist outside the standard identification modalities. The question then is how do we optimize the identification effort by utilizing insufficient data or data that fall outside the standard identification modalities?

■ A HOLISTIC APPROACH TO DISASTER VICTIM IDENTIFICATION

The merit of forensic anthropology in mass fatality situations has been increasingly documented in recent years (Anđelinović et al., 2005; Komar, 2003; Kontanis and Sledzik, 2008; Mundorff et al., 2008; Sledzik et al., 2009; Ubelaker et al., 1995). The detailed knowledge of skeletal anatomy makes anthropologists ideally suited for work involving human remains that are fragmented or otherwise difficult to analyze. The traditional roles for the forensic anthropologist are in field recovery (Sledzik et al., 2009), morgue triage (Mundorff et al., 2008), and in the construction of biological profiles. This work indirectly helps the identification process by providing information to narrow down the list of potential victims. This information includes determining whether the remains are human or nonhuman, sorting commingled remains, and constructing a biological profile of the deceased including age, sex, stature, ancestry, and possible pathological conditions.

In the United States, anthropology is traditionally taught with an emphasis on holism, where the entire human experience is available for study (evolutionarily, biologically, psychologically, and socioculturally) (see Shore, 1999). Furthermore, forensic anthropology is one of the only disciplines where the identification of remains is a core purpose. The holistic view that anthropologists are trained with makes them ideal candidates to play a significant role in DVI, particularly in the reconciliation phase where antemortem and postmortem data are compared and identifications are made (Interpol, 2013). It is here that a truly multidisciplinary or holistic identification process can take place.

A holistic approach to DVI considers any available evidence that might be quantified for a set of remains, whether for or against a potential identification. This can be accomplished in a probabilistic framework using Bayes' theorem. Data on age, sex, dentition, recovery location, and fingerprints may be incorporated in the form of likelihood ratios as a singular measure of the strength of the evidence (Brenner, 2006).

■ BAYESIAN STATISTICS

Bayesian statistics is a school of statistical thought based on a mathematical statement developed by Bayes (1764), commonly known as Bayes' theorem. Bayes' theorem describes the way in which one's prior beliefs about a particular event are informed or updated based on the consideration of additional evidence. A Bayesian approach to statistics allows the researcher to assign probabilities to a particular event or observation based on any additional knowledge that might be available. Bayes' theorem can be written generally as follows:

$$P(A|B) = \frac{P(B|A)\,P(A)}{P(B)} \tag{29.1}$$

where $P(A)$ and $P(B)$ are the probabilities of each observation independent of one another, $P(A|B)$ is the conditional probability of observing A given that B has occurred, and $P(B|A)$ is the conditional probability of observing B given that A has occurred. In forensic science, Bayes' theorem is more frequently presented in the odds form as follows:

$$\text{Posterior odds} = \text{Likelihood Ratio} \times \text{Prior Odds (Lucy, 2013)} \tag{29.2}$$

The prior odds are the odds of an event prior to the consideration of other information. The likelihood ratio is a comparison of the probabilities of two competing hypotheses. The numerator is the probability of making a particular observation under one hypothesis, whereas the denominator is the probability of making the same observation under the null hypothesis. The posterior odds are a revision of the prior odds after consideration of any additional evidence (in the form of a likelihood ratio).

The utility of Bayesian statistics has been demonstrated in both anthropology (Konigsberg and Frankenberg, 2013) and forensic science (Brenner, 2006; Brenner and Weir, 2003; Lucy, 2013). The approach has been the standard method for presenting professional opinions for DNA identifications for many years (Evett and Weir, 1998; National Research Council, 1996) and was integral to the WTC DNA identification efforts (National Institute of Justice, 2006). More recently the Bayesian approach has been applied in other disciplines involved in identification work such as forensic anthropology (Konigsberg et al., 2008; Steadman et al., 2006).

■ BAYESIAN STATISTICS AND IDENTIFICATION

For the forensic identification of human remains, the use of Bayesian statistics centers on the development of a likelihood ratio comparing two alternative hypotheses (Lucy, 2013):

1. H_1 = The remains in question belong to individual X.
2. H_0 = The remains in question do not belong to individual X.

Before considering additional evidence beyond a possible match between individual X and a set of remains, there is a prior probability that H_1 is correct. In a conservative application, the prior odds are considered to be even between the two hypotheses, meaning the probability in favor of H_1 is the same as in favor of H_0. This is known variously as uniform, uninformative, or equal prior odds, as they are indifferent between the two hypotheses and do not favor one outcome over the other (Biedermann et al., 2007). As Biedermann et al. (2007) explain, it is standard for forensic scientists to avoid consideration of prior odds as this is considered outside their role as the "objective scientist." However, in the context of both an MFI and medicolegal death investigations as typically practiced in the United States, the consideration of prior odds is not only appropriate, but it is absolutely essential for the application of Bayesian statistics to be useful. As Thompson et al. (2013, p. 2) note:

> If forensic scientists will make the ultimate determination, for legal purposes, with regard to a particular proposition of interest, then they should, and indeed must, consider their prior probabilities that the hypotheses are true.

As the medical examiner or coroner is the likely authority who establishes the identity of a decedent by completing the death certificate, it is appropriate for a "full Bayes approach" (Biedermann et al., 2007, p. 85) to be applied. The consideration of prior odds is not only appropriate, but in a mass fatality context with a generally defined victim population, it is also highly advantageous as it likely involves a much smaller pool of potential identifications than the "population at large." Furthermore, the smaller prior odds allow for the establishment of a threshold for identification decisions that is obtainable with DNA and other evidence. Informed prior odds can be defined as ones that are based on known information. For an MFI, with a defined victim population, informed prior odds are as follows:

$$\text{Prior odds} = \frac{1}{(v-1)} \tag{29.3}$$

where v is the known or estimated number of victims (Brenner and Weir, 2003, p. 174). With intact remains, the prior odds may be adjusted down with each identification, essentially making each subsequent identification easier as there are fewer possibilities to consider. However, with fragmented or commingled remains, the prior odds would be kept static over the course of the DVI process, as there is an equal probability of the remains belonging to any of the victims, even ones who have already been identified. From this point any quantifiable evidence of identification may be considered in light of the prior probability in the form of the likelihood ratio (lr). The likelihood ratio may be written as follows:

$$\text{lr} = \frac{P(E|H_1)}{P(E|H_0)} \tag{29.4}$$

where E is the evidence under consideration (Brenner and Weir, 2003, p. 175; Lucy, 2013, pp. 112–114). This equation compares the probability of observing a particular piece of evidence if the identification is correct with the probability of observing the same evidence if the identification is not correct.

This is the approach that was taken for DNA identifications in New York City following the September 11, 2001 World Trade Center disaster. A group called the Kinship and Data Analysis Panel (KADAP) was formed to provide the New York City Office of Chief Medical Examiner with guidance on appropriate steps to take for DNA identification work (National Institute of Justice, 2006). The KADAP recommended setting a posterior probability of 99.9% over 1000 victims as a target for all identifications. With prior odds of 1:3000, any DNA evidence for a particular identification would need to reach a likelihood ratio of 4×10^9 to maintain the overall posterior probability of 99.9% (see Brenner and Weir, 2003 for a more detailed explanation). By establishing a predetermined statistical threshold for identification, the need for interpretation of DNA results has been removed. Analysts simply report out the results that meet or exceed the threshold.

■ WHAT WOULD A HOLISTIC APPROACH TO DISASTER VICTIM IDENTIFICATION LOOK LIKE?

Applying Bayesian statistics beyond the realm of DNA to incorporate data from other modalities is dependent on the availability of relevant quantitative information. This may seem as overly burdensome, too complex, or dependent on research in other disciplines that may not yet exist. The good news is relevant research already exists in a number of disciplines, including anthropology, and useful datasets are sometimes publicly available. The primary criteria for data are that they come from an appropriate population, that the possible outcomes are unambiguous (mutually exclusive, can only fit one category), that they provide expected frequencies in a population, and that the observations can be safely assumed to be independent from all other considered variables. Ideally, the frequency of observed items comes from the victim population itself (i.e., the number of victims with tattoos); however, antemortem datasets are rarely complete and may have varying degrees of accuracy as they often rely on recollections from family or friends who may be psychologically traumatized at the time of interview or may not share the same knowledge of a particular person. The data may also not be available for the victim population due to the nature of the variable in question (e.g., pubic symphyseal stages). If enough antemortem data exist, it would be possible to model the expected frequencies for the population as a whole. Alternatively, these data can come from a relevant reference population.

Outside anthropological estimates relating to the biological profile, the establishment of a likelihood ratio for a particular observation may be directly obtained as the inverse of the frequency of the observation in an applicable reference sample (Konigsberg and Frankenberg, 2013; Steadman et al., 2006).[1]

■ ANTHROPOLOGY

The most complex category of data is the anthropological assessments of the biological profile. The development of a likelihood ratio for most anthropological factors (age, sex, race, stature) is not as straightforward as making a simple observation as there is a level of imprecision inherent to the techniques that must be accounted for. Observations made for continuous variables such as age or stature indicate a range of values, and those values have an implicit amount of error in them. The larger the range of suggested values, the less powerful the anthropological evidence. Categorical values, such as sex or ancestry, must also accommodate the imprecision inherent to the techniques. Because of the more complex statistical approaches, this section will be limited to anthropological assessments of age and trauma.

Some work already exists in the anthropological literature for assessing the weight of identification evidence in a Bayesian framework, most notably Steadman et al. (2006). The researchers demonstrated statistical methods for assigning likelihood ratios for a number of features of the biological profile including age, sex, and stature estimates in the context of a single forensic case.

Age

The development of likelihood ratios for estimates of age is statistically complex. The basic approach is to determine two different probabilities: the probability for a person of a particular age to display a particular age indicator of an anthropological technique (phase, stage, etc.) and the probability of a person of any other age from the victim population to display the same age indicator. To accomplish this, it is necessary to know or to be able to model the age distribution for the victim population as well as to have a suitable reference dataset for establishing the probability of obtaining a particular age phase/stage given age. A good demonstration of this approach is detailed in Steadman et al. (2006). They determined likelihood ratios of approximately 1.61 for stage/phase given age. The contributory power of the likelihood ratio will be mostly dependent on the age distribution of the victim population. Age estimates will be less powerful in an incident with a fairly homogenous population.

Trauma

The presence or absence of antemortem trauma is more readily applicable as it only requires a suitable reference sample. Steadman et al. (2006) demonstrate this approach using a dataset of modern military personnel. Adjusting their approach based on the method in which the sample data were recorded (i.e., less versus more detail), they establish a likelihood ratio for the presence of an antemortem fracture in the leg (tibia) at 31.6 (the inverse of 258 leg fractures in a sample of 8147 males) (2006, p. 24).

Komar and Lathrop (2006) published a more forensically appropriate sample. Their sample consisted of 482 individuals from the University of New Mexico and the Bass Collection at the University of Tennessee (2006, p. 975). The published data include fracture observations in 30 skeletal regions (e.g., left tibia), 8 pathological conditions (e.g., spina bifida), and 14 surgical interventions (e.g., right knee replacement). Using the same information presented in Steadman et al. (2006) of a fracture to the tibia, the Komar and Lathrop data show 17 observations out of 482 individuals (combined dataset), resulting in a likelihood ratio of 28.4 (inverse of 17 tibial fractures in 482 individuals), a similar result to what Steadman et al. (2006) found.

An alternative sample was published by Steyn et al. (2010). In this study the authors studied three modern skeletal populations from Greece and South Africa and documented healed trauma on most of the skeletal elements (the sternum and bones of the hand and foot were not recorded). Whereas Komar and Lathrop (2006) observed just healed fractures, Steyn et al. documented additional trauma such as sharp force or pathological conditions (on some elements). As a result, the frequencies from Steyn et al. are less specific than Komar and Lathrop. Whereas Komar and Lathrop demonstrate the frequencies of antemortem fractures, Steyn et al. present frequencies for more general antemortem trauma. This resource may be useful based on case circumstances; however, the more general nature of the data will likely decrease any resulting likelihood ratios.

Caution must be made if attempting to combine likelihood ratios for multiple pathological conditions as this may violate the product rule requirement of independence (Steadman et al., 2006). It is very likely that observed trauma or other pathologies in different regions of the skeleton may originate from the same incident.

---

[1]See Brenner (2014) for a different approach.

FORENSIC PATHOLOGY

One of the most informative components of postmortem examination is the observations of identifying features made during examination by a forensic pathologist. Observations of the sex of the individual and the presence or absence of features such as scars, marks, tattoos, or evidence of prior surgeries help to narrow down the pool of potential identifications.

As opposed to the anthropological assessments of sex based on observations of skeletal features, assessments based on observations of external genitalia can be assumed to be highly accurate, to the point that the incorporation of a measure of the potential error of an observation is not necessary (transgendered and intersex individuals will certainly complicate this approach, but these issues are beyond the scope of this chapter). In this simple scenario, the likelihood ratio for the evidentiary strength towards identification is the inverse of the proportion of one sex to the other. This may also be considered in the form of alternative or informed prior odds based on matching a subset of the victim population. In an open population where the exact number of males or females is unknown, the proportion may be cautiously estimated, or a relevant reference sample based on local census data or other sources may be used instead (Steadman et al., 2006). It should be noted here that the potential evidentiary strength for a binary observation such as sex (male vs. female) is dependent on the ratio of males to females in the victim population. If the victim population were equally distributed between males and females (50% males vs. 50% females), the maximum likelihood ratio that could be obtained for a match on sex is 2. If the victim population is uniformly male or female, then the evidentiary value of the observation becomes 1, meaning the consideration of sex in that circumstance does not provide any probative value. The more informative the consideration of sex in an MFI, the more there is a bias towards one sex over the other, for the sex with the smaller percentage.

Tattoos

Assessing the frequency of tattoos or prior surgeries is more complicated. Even in a closed population, antemortem information from the victim population may not be complete. In this case, it is necessary to find appropriate reference samples. Perhaps the simplest source for data on tattoo frequencies is from survey or polling data. For example, a simple Internet search for tattoo frequencies returned a poll that indicated 71% of the respondents did not have any tattoos, whereas 29% had one or more (http://www.theharrispoll.com/health-and-life/Tattoo_Takeover.html). The binary nature of the data (presence or absence) limits the strength of the resulting likelihood ratios. Based on the poll data, the likelihood ratio for the presence of a tattoo would be 3.4 (inverse of 645 people with tattoos out of 2225 respondents).

More precise data based on tattoo location have the potential to return much higher evidentiary strength. A 2006 article in the *Journal of the American Academy of Dermatology* performed telephone surveys of 500 individuals and documented both the presence or absence of tattoos and general location on the body (Laumann and Derick, 2006). For example, tattoos on the arm were reported in 52 of the 500 respondents, which translates to a likelihood ratio of 9.61.

In 2008, Komar and Lathrop published a much larger study involving data on 3430 individuals from the New Mexico Office of the Medical Investigator. They did not report on tattoo location, but they did demonstrate significant differences in tattoo frequencies between two ethnic groups (white Hispanics and white non-Hispanics) and between males and females. Their data suggest overall tattoo frequencies similar to the polling data, with slightly lower resulting likelihood ratios for the presence of tattoos of 2.47.

Surgery

Data on the frequency of surgical procedures are difficult to find. The National Center for Health Statistics at the Centers for Disease Control tracks the number and type of surgical procedures performed each year; however, as pointed out by Steadman et al. (2006), the data are reported as incidence rates (number of people who have had various surgeries in a particular period). The data only tell you how many people had a surgery in a particular period, and they do not tell you how many people had the procedure performed before this period, nor do they tell you how many people did not have a procedure performed. As a result, it is difficult to determine the number of people in the general population who have skeletal evidence of prior surgical intervention.

The 2008 study by Komar and Lathrop is the only relevant data available on the frequency of prior surgeries in a modern population. Their data are somewhat generalized based on location and are limited only to those procedures that are detectable on the skeleton (e.g., the presence of orthopedic hardware). Surgical procedures involving soft tissues only would not be accounted for. Even with these restrictions, the presence of evidence of a matching surgical procedure provides more weight toward an identification than the other factors. Based on their data, the presence of a surgical repair of the femur would result in a likelihood ratio of 28.3 (inverse of 18 observations out of 482 individuals).

DENTAL

Consideration of dental evidence has the potential to be highly informative in an MFI. While dental identifications are generally made based on comparison of X-rays, dental records may be incomplete or insufficient for identification on their own. Dental information may also come from nontraditional sources, such as family interviews describing the condition of the victim's dentition (e.g., "wore dentures," "missing two front teeth"). While this type of information does not fit the traditional paradigm for dental identifications it still provides value.

Adams (2003a,b) established a large sample population to study the diversity of dental patterns in the United States in a manner similar to mtDNA. This research led to the creation of the Odontosearch (www.odontosearch.com) program, which allows investigators to estimate how frequently a pattern of missing, restored, or unrestored teeth would be seen in the general population. The current Odontosearch database contains records of 57,980 individuals, which means the likelihood ratio for a particular match has the potential to be as high as 57,981 (for a pattern unobserved in the database).

As demonstrated by Steadman et al. (2006), the resulting likelihood ratio is calculated as the inverse of the pattern frequency, or

$$\text{lr (Dental)} = \left(\frac{N+1}{X+1} \right) \tag{29.5}$$

where N is the total number of samples (57,980) and X is the number of observed matches in the database. Both the numerator and denominator are increased by one to account for fact that the pattern is known to occur in at least one individual (the remains in question).

If we take an example where the only available dental information is from an interview with a family member who states that the victim was missing his or her two front teeth (tooth numbers 8 and 9), a search of the Odontosearch database shows that this pattern has been observed in 7255 of 57,980 individuals. Using the formula mentioned earlier results in a likelihood ratio of 7.99.

■ FINGERPRINTS

Fingerprints have been used for identification for more than 100 years; however, the results of comparisons are not typically reported out in a statistical manner. A match between 10 fingerprints based on ridge minutiae, or the characteristics of the ridges themselves (i.e., ridge endings, bifurcations, islands), is considered sufficient for identification. Recent research has suggested potential ways to report fingerprint matches in a probabilistic fashion (Neumann et al., 2006, 2007). However, in a mass fatality scenario, particularly one involving fragmentation and degradation of soft tissues, it may be difficult to obtain fingerprints of sufficient quality for a full 10-print examination. The overall flow of the ridges, or what is called the first level of detail, may be the only observation to be made. At this level, individuating a fingerprint to a single person would not be possible as these characteristics are not unique to the individual. However, it would be possible to assign a likelihood ratio to a first-level match if the frequency of that feature on a particular finger were known in the general population.

Anthropologists have a long history of research in fingerprint variation across populations, and there are numerous publications indicating the frequency of fingerprint classes for different fingers (Fournier and Ross, 2016; Meier, 1980). Unfortunately, nearly all research studies on pattern frequencies present results for each digit independent of its relationship with other digits. These data would be insufficient for inclusion in a probabilistic identification framework because they ignore the potential dependence between fingers.

Only a handful of papers list frequencies of patterns across all five digits (see Lu, 1968; Nanakorn et al., 2013). Lu (1968) treated both hands as a single unit and documented the sequence of fingerprint patterns across all 10 fingers. He then used these data to compare overall pattern frequencies across different populations. The manner in which the data were captured is useful to demonstrate how a frequency for a particular pattern may be determined. For example, of one sample out of 158 individuals in this research, a pattern of all ulnar loops on the right hand and four ulnar loops on the left hand with an arch on the last digit (pinky finger) is observed only one time. Based on these data, a match of this pattern between a body and a potential identification would result in a likelihood ratio of 158. Of course these data are only relevant in the current form for an entire hand. More comprehensive data that would allow for establishing frequencies of fingerprint patterns with any combination of available fingers would make this approach much more applicable for a disaster involving a high degree of fragmentation.

■ RECOVERY LOCATION

The consideration of recovery location is an overlooked tool toward identification. Although the previous examples stressed simple features where the likelihood ratios may be obtained directly from the observed frequency in a reference population, recovery location requires a more complex framework. There is little in the way of published literature on the quantification of recovery locations for incorporation into a statistical identification framework. Brenner (2006) theorized on the use of recovery location for victims of the Boxing Day tsunami in Thailand. Given the geography of the hardest hit areas (numerous beaches geographically isolated from one another), Brenner presented a method for factoring in the recovery of a body at a particular beach given the missing person having been at that beach. He did so by modifying the prior odds for the identification. Instead of considering all victims in Thailand, he reduced the prior odds for a potential identification to only those missing persons known to have been at the beach, adding a small factor to account for error.

Another example can be drawn from the September 11, 2001 WTC disaster. During the recovery process the location of remains was documented based on the use of a grid system overlaid on a map of the site. If a set

Table 29.1   Distribution of Identified Remains From the World Trade Center by Location and Victim Group

	L = Footprint	L ≠ Footprint	Row Sum
$G = WTC_N$	295	811	1106
$G \neq WTC_N$	129	801	930
Column sum	424	1612	2036

WTC_N, north World Trade Center tower.

Table 29.2   Estimated Probability of Location Given Victim Group

$P(L|G)$	L = Footprint	L ≠ Footprint
$G = WTC\ 1$	0.27	0.73
$G \neq WTC\ 1$	0.21	0.86

WTC, World Trade Center.

of remains were found in a particular grid location, for example, in the footprint of the North Tower, and are believed to belong to a victim who was known to be in the North Tower, we can ask the question of how likely it is that remains found in that grid location are from a victim in that tower versus a victim from another location. To do this we first need to divide the victim population into mutually exclusive groups based on their known locations at the time of the event. The WTC disaster can be viewed as multiple separate events: two building collapses and two airplane crashes. From this perspective we can simply divide the victim population by their locations in either the North or South Tower or either of the two airplanes (United Airlines 175 and American Airlines 11). Two other groups are established for members of the Fire Department of New York, who were in general proximity to one another at the base of the two towers, and one simply labeled "Other" for victims in the general plaza area.

As stated earlier, the likelihood ratio compares the probability of an event under one hypothesis with the probability of the same event under the null hypothesis. To determine the numerator for recovery locations at the WTC, or the probability of remains being found in a particular location if they came from a victim in a particular group (i.e., if the identification is correct or H_1), we need to first know the number of remains from each group recovered in that location. We can base this on a reference sample of already identified remains with known recovery locations. These data provide an estimate of the number of victims from each subgroup whose remains were recovered from that location. So if remains from 100 victims were recovered in grid B, and 50 of them have been identified to victims from group A, the probability of another set of remains also found in grid B also belonging to a victim in the same group would be 51/101, or about 50%. The denominator in this likelihood ratio needs to represent the probability of remains being recovered from a grid location if they do not belong to the same group as the victim in question, or the null hypothesis.

As a simplified example, let us say a set of remains are tentatively associated by a partial DNA profile to a victim who was in the North WTC tower (WTC_N). We also know that the remains were recovered from within the footprint of WTC_N. Given that the remains were recovered from the footprint of WTC_N, how much weight does this recovery location information add to the tentative DNA identification? To determine this, we need to compare the probability of the remains being recovered in the footprint of WTC_N if they belong to a victim from that same building $P(L = \text{footprint}|G = WTC_N)$ to the probability of the remains being found in the same location if they came from a victim of one of the other groups $P(L = \text{footprint}|G \neq WTC_N)$. This is the likelihood ratio.

Table 29.1 shows the total number of remains recovered within and outside the footprint of WTC_N for victims who were in WTC_N and victims who were not. To determine $P(L = \text{footprint}|G = WTC_N)$ we simply take the proportion of WTC_N victims recovered within the footprint and divide that by the total number of recovered WTC_N victims or 295/1106 = 0.27 = 27% (Table 29.2). Conversely, to determine $P(L = \text{footprint}|G \neq WTC_N)$ we divide the number of victims recovered in the footprint of WTC 1 who were not from that group by the total number of recovered non-WTC_N victims, or 129/930 = 0.21 = 21% (see Table 29.2). Dividing 0.27 by 0.21 gives a likelihood ratio of 1.23.

■ DISCUSSION

The premise of this chapter is to outline the potential use of likelihood ratios in a Bayesian framework for disaster victim identification purposes beyond DNA. The reason for this approach is because it allows the analyst to consider much more information about an identification than that of the main identification modalities. The potential is to synthesize identifications based on all available evidence, no matter how seemingly insufficient it is for a standard modality. The typical training of forensic anthropologists makes them ideally suited for this role.

While the use of Bayesian statistics to assess the "strength" of an identification is not new (see Steadman et al., 2006), the application for disaster victim identification has not been adequately explored. The benefit of this approach for DVI is because the more restricted size of the pool of potential identifications (i.e., the victim pool or the prior odds) makes targeted statistical thresholds much easier to reach as opposed to the "population at large."

Using the examples given earlier, we can see how an approach such as this may be useful. Assuming we have a potential victim identification with the following consistencies: fracture of leg ($lr = 31.6$), sex ($lr = 2$, assuming 50/50 sex ratio in victim population), tattoo on arm ($lr = 9.61$), surgery of femur ($lr = 28.3$), missing teeth 8 and 9 ($lr = 7.94$), consistent arrangement of fingerprint patterns ($lr = 158$), and recovery location ($lr = 1.23$), the resulting likelihood ratio for the identification is larger that 2.6×10^7 ($31.6 \times 2 \times 9.61 \times 28.3 \times 7.94 \times 158 \times 1.23$). As stated earlier, one of the requirements for considering multiple lines of evidence is that each line must be assumed to be independent, to prevent counting the same observation more than once. In the above example we would be remiss if we did not consider a "fracture of the leg" and "surgery of the femur" to be from a related event. We may even want to limit the use of dental if there is any evidence the missing teeth are related to a traumatic event. These are all considerations that the analyst would need to assess prior to moving forward with an identification.

■ CONCLUSION

The identification of remains following an MFI involving high levels of fragmentation, commingling, or degradation is exceedingly more difficult than less complex incidents due to the fragmentation and degradation of associated identifying information. The process is made even more difficult when dealing with incidents with open victim populations. The response is to overwhelmingly rely on DNA for the identification process (Brenner and Weir, 2003; Mundorff et al., 2008). Forensic anthropologists can play a critical role in these types of incidents based on their expertise in both skeletal anatomy and identification processes.

This chapter discusses an alternative approach to complex MFIs and highlights an expanded role for forensic anthropologists. This statistical approach enables analysts to utilize identifying information that was previously deemed insufficient for identification purposes. Using a probabilistic framework to incorporate multiple lines of evidence to assess identification will create a truly multidisciplinary disaster victim identification effort and potentially allow for additional identifications be made when the standard modalities have maximized their efforts.

References

Adams, B.J., 2003a. The diversity of adult dental patterns in the United States and the implications for personal identification. J. Forensic Sci. 48, 497–503.

Adams, B.J., 2003b. Establishing personal identification based on specific patterns of missing, filled, and unrestored teeth. J. Forensic Sci. 48, 487–496.

Andelinović, Š., Sutlović, D., Erceg, I.I., Škaro, V., Ivkošić, A., Paić, F., et al., 2005. Twelve-year experience in identification of skeletal remains from mass graves. Croat. Med. J. 46, 530–539.

Bayes, T., 1764. An essay towards solving a problem in the doctrine of chances. Philos. Trans. R. Soc. Lond. 53, 370–418.

Beauthier, J.-P., Lefèvre, P., 2008. Roles of forensic pathologists, anthropologists and odontologists during Belgian DVI team activities. A review of the organization and the management of these situations with the aim of an optimal victims' identification. Biométrie Humaine et Anthropologie 26, 45–55.

Biedermann, A., Taroni, F., Garbolino, P., 2007. Equal prior probabilities: can one do any better? Forensic Sci. Int. 172, 85–93.

Blau, S., Briggs, C.A., 2011. The role of forensic anthropology in disaster victim identification (DVI). Forensic Sci. Int. 205, 29–35.

Brenner, C.H., 2006. Some mathematical problems in the DNA identification of victims in the 2004 tsunami and similar mass fatalities. Forensic Sci. Int. 157, 172–180.

Brenner, C.H., 2014. Understanding Y haplotype matching probability. Forensic Sci. Int. Genet. 8, 233–243.

Brenner, C.H., Weir, B., 2003. Issues and strategies in the DNA identification of World trade center victims. Theor. Popul. Biol. 63, 173–178.

Byard, R.W., Winskog, C., 2010. Potential problems arising during international disaster victim identification (DVI) exercises. Forensic Sci. Med. Pathol. 6, 1–2.

Evett, I., Weir, B., 1998. Interpreting DNA Evidence. Sinauer Associates, Inc., Sunderland, MA.

Eyre, A., 2002. Improving procedures and minimising distress: issues in the identification of victims following disasters. Aust. J. Emerg. Manag. 17, 9.

Fournier, N.A., Ross, A.H., 2016. Sex, ancestral, and pattern type variation of fingerprint minutiae: a forensic perspective on anthropological dermatoglyphics. Am. J. Phys. Anthropol. 160, 625–632.

Interpol, 2013. Disaster Victim Identification Guide.

Keough, M.E., Samuels, M.F., 2004. The Kosovo family support project: offering psychosocial support for families with missing persons. Soc. Work 49, 587–594.

Keough, M.E., Simmons, T., Samuels, M., 2004. Missing persons in post-conflict settings: best practices for integrating psychosocial and scientific approaches. J. R. Soc. Promot. Health 124, 271–275.

Komar, D., 2003. Lessons from Srebrenica: the contributions and limitations of physical anthropology in identifying victims of war crimes. J. Forensic Sci. 48, 713–716.

Komar, D., Lathrop, S., 2006. Frequencies of morphological characteristics in two contemporary forensic collections: implications for identification. J. Forensic Sci. 51, 974–978.

Komar, D., Lathrop, S., 2008. Tattoo types and frequencies in New Mexican white Hispanics and white non-Hspanics: autopsy data from homicidal and accidental deaths, 2002–2005. Am. J. Forensic Med. Pathol. 29, 285–289.

Konigsberg, L.W., Frankenberg, S.R., 2013. Bayes in biological anthropology. Am. J. Phys. Anthropol. 152, 153–184.

Konigsberg, L.W., Herrmann, N.P., Wescott, D.J., Kimmerle, E.H., 2008. Estimation and evidence in forensic anthropology: age-at-death. J. Forensic Sci. 53, 541–557.

Kontanis, E.J., Sledzik, P.S., 2008. Resolving Commingling Issues During the Medicolegal Investigation of Mass Fatality Incidents. Recovery, analysis, and identification of commingled human remains. Springer, pp. 317–336.

Laumann, A.E., Derick, A.J., 2006. Tattoos and body piercings in the United States: a national data set. J. Am. Acad. Dermatol. 55, 413–421.

Lessig, R., Rothschild, M., 2012. International standards in cases of mass disaster victim identification (DVI). Forensic Sci. Med. Pathol. 8, 197–199.

Lu, K., 1968. An information and discriminant analysis of fingerprint patterns pertaining to identification of mongolism and mental retardation. Am. J. Hum. Genet. 20, 24.

Lucy, D., 2013. Introduction to Statistics for Forensic Scientists. John Wiley and Sons.

Meier, R.J., 1980. Anthropological dermatoglyphics: a review. Am. J. Phys. Anthropol. 23, 147–178.

Morgan, O., Tidball-Binz, M., Alphen, D.V., 2006. Management of Dead Bodies after Disasters: A Field Manual for First Responders. Pan American Health Organization.

Mundorff, A.Z., Shaler, R., Bieschke, E., Mar-Cash, E., 2008. Marrying Anthropology and DNA: Essential for Solving Complex Commingling Problems in Cases of Extreme Fragmentation. Recovery, analysis, and identification of commingled human remains. Springer, pp. 285–299.

Nanakorn, S., Kutanan, W., Chusilp, K., 2013. An exploration of fingerprint patterns and their concordance amongst Thai adolescents. Chiang Mai J. Sci. 40, 332Ā343.

National Institute of Justice, 2006. Lessons Learned from 9/11 : DNA Identification in Mass Fatality Incidents. Department of Justice, Washington, D.C., U.S.

National Research Council, 1996. The Evaluation of Forensic DNA Evidence. National Academies Press, US.

National Transportation Safety Board, 2000. In-Flight Breakup Over the Atlantic Ocean, Trans World Airlines Flight 800, Boeing 747-131, N93119, Near East Moriches, New York, July 17, 1996. Aircraft Accident Report NTSB/AAR-00/03. National Transportation Safety Board, Washington, D.C.

Neumann, C., Champod, C., Puch-Solis, R., Egli, N., Anthonioz, A., Bromage-Griffiths, A., 2007. Computation of likelihood ratios in fingerprint identification for configurations of any number of minutiae. J. Forensic Sci. 52, 54–64.

Neumann, C., Champod, C., Puch-Solis, R., Egli, N., Anthonioz, A., Meuwly, D., et al., 2006. Computation of likelihood ratios in fingerprint identification for configurations of three minutiae. J. Forensic Sci. 51, 1255–1266.

Robben, A.C.G.M., 2004. Death, Mourning, and Burial: A Cross-Cultural Reader. Blackwell Pub, Malden, MA.

Shore, B., 1999. Strange fate of holism. Anthropol. News 40, 5–6.

Sledzik, P., Dirkmaat, D., Mann, R., Holland, T., Mundorff, A.Z., Adams, B., et al., 2009. Disaster Victim Recovery and Identification: Forensic Anthropology in the Aftermath of September 11th. Prentice Hall, Upper Saddle River.

Sledzik, P.S., Rodriguez, W.C., 2002. Damnum fatale: the taphonomic fate of human remains in mass disasters. In: Advances in Forensic Taphonomy: Method, Theory, and Archaeological Perspectives, pp. 321–330.

Steadman, D.W., Adams, B.J., Konigsberg, L.W., 2006. Statistical basis for positive identification in forensic anthropology. Am. J. Phys. Anthropol. 131, 15–26.

Steyn, M., İşcan, M., De Kock, M., Kranioti, E., Michalodimitrakis, M., L'Abbé, E.N., 2010. Analysis of ante mortem trauma in three modern skeletal populations. Int. J. Osteoarchaeol. 20, 561–571.

Stover, E., Ryan, M., 2001. Breaking bread with the dead. Hist. Archaeol. 35, 7–25.

Thompson, W.C., Vuille, J., Biedermann, A., Taroni, F., 2013. The role of prior probability in forensic assessments. Front. Genet. 4, 220.

Ubelaker, D., Owsley, D., Sandness, K., Houck, M., Peerwani, N., Woltanski, T., et al., 1995. The role of forensic anthropology in the recovery and analysis of branch davidian compound victims: techniques of analysis. J. Forensic Sci. 40, 341–348.

Valenzuela, A., Villanueva, E., Bohoyo, J.M., Exposito, N., Martin-de las Heras, S., Marques, T., 1999. Methods for identification of 28 burn victims following a 1996 bus accident in Spain. J. Forensic Sci. 44, 428–431.

CHAPTER 30

Summary: The Future of Forensic Identification Methods From the Human Skeleton

Eric J. Bartelink[1] | Krista E. Latham[2] | Michael Finnegan[3]

[1]California State University, Chico, Chico, CA, United States
[2]University of Indianapolis, Indianapolis, IN, United States
[3]Kansas State University, Manhattan, KS, United States

Over the past 30 years, forensic anthropology has emerged as both a multidisciplinary and interdisciplinary field of study. One of the defining features of the growth of modern forensic anthropology is the ability to incorporate new technologies and methods into the practitioner's toolkit. The current volume highlights several new developments within the field, which demonstrate the expanding role of forensic anthropology in personal identification. The increasing involvement of forensic anthropologists in the personal identification of human remains from mass disasters, past wars and conflicts, undocumented border crossings, and mass fatality incidents reflects the growth of the field and the relevance of forensic anthropology to society. These large-scale identification challenges have resulted in technological and methodological advancements in personal identification, including the use of more advanced statistical approaches, the use of advanced software and databases, improvements in biological profile estimations, the use of sophisticated radiography and 3D scanning technology, the use of isotopes for estimating year of birth and for provenancing unidentified human remains, and advances in DNA-based identifications. The majority of topics discussed in the current volume were not available in 1970 when T. Dale Stewart's seminal volume *Personal Identification in Mass Disasters* was published. In fact, the 1970 volume focused primarily on constructing biological profiles, with only some discussion of the use of radiography and molecular methods of identification. Clearly, forensic anthropology has emerged as a healthy and growing field that continues to expand its reach well beyond its original boundaries.

The 30 chapters in this volume provide a snapshot of current advanced personal identification methods in forensic anthropology. The editors of this volume sought out the lead authors for each chapter based on their high level of involvement in developing forensic anthropology methods within their own specialized areas of research. Although we were not able to convince everyone we invited to contribute to this volume, we were pleasantly surprised to get such a positive and enthusiastic response from those who did. We believe this volume showcases the core state-of-the-art forensic identification methods based on the human skeleton.

The 10 chapters comprising Section I (Advances in Biological Profile Construction) focus on advances in the study of human biological variation, which forms the foundation of different aspects of biological profile construction, as well as the development of the National Missing and Unidentified Persons System (NamUs). Chapter 2 by Nawrocki and colleagues addresses theoretical and methodological approaches in forensic anthropology and emphasizes the need to look at the interaction between variables when estimating parameters, to understand human skeletal variation from a broader perspective, to carefully apply statistical models, and to understand the limitations of reference samples (among others).

Chapters 3 and 4 focus on advances in sex and ancestry determination from the skeleton. Spradley and Stull's Chapter 3 addresses current perspectives for evaluating sexual dimorphism and ancestry in human skeletal samples and emphasizes the need for diverse data collection methods and the use of diverse samples. Chapter 4 by Pilloud and colleagues focuses on recent applications of macromorphoscopic and dental traits for ancestry determination. Using appropriate statistical frameworks, they demonstrate how these traits of the skull and dentition can be used to predict ancestry with a reasonable degree of confidence. This research is of tremendous value for personal identification as it provides new ways for approaching ancestry outside of traditional craniometrics, morphometrics, or the presence versus absence of nonmetric traits (i.e., "trait list" approach).

Chapter 5 by Kenyhercz and Berg focuses on new statistical approaches as well as a graphical user interface (GUI) software program based on morphological traits and measurements of the mandible to predict ancestry. This program provides a novel application that is both flexible and statistically robust.

New Perspectives in Forensic Human Skeletal Identification. http://dx.doi.org/10.1016/B978-0-12-805429-1.00030-2

Chapters 6–8 focus on recent developments in age estimation from immature and adult skeletal remains. Schaefer and colleagues (Chapter 6) provide a critical summary of different methods used for estimating age at death from juvenile remains, including epiphyseal union timing, diaphyseal length, and the application of new imaging technology (e.g., MRI, CT, MDCT, and ultrasound). They highlight these applications for age estimation of the dead as well as the living. They emphasize the population-specific nature of skeletal aging and the fact that standards are often based on unrepresentative samples. The use of advanced imaging technology provides the means to acquire osteological data without having to only rely on dry skeletal remains. This will potentially revolutionize the future development of age estimation standards for juvenile remains since there are very few skeletal collections with enough subadults to draw meaningful conclusions. Chapter 7 by Ubelaker provides a historical perspective on dental aging of juveniles, as well as more recently developed population-specific standards that address variation in skeletal aging. Although dental formation provides the best estimates of chronological age in the juvenile skeleton, Ubelaker emphasizes the need to perform a comprehensive analysis of age using information gleaned from the entire skeleton. Chapter 8 by Hartnett and colleagues emphasizes the need for population-specific aging standards for age at death estimation of adult remains. They provide a historical review of the age estimation literature and focus on newly developed standards that help reduce certain biases identified in previous age estimation studies, such as those including larger, more representative samples. While the population-specific nature of aging has received significant attention, transition analysis age estimation may overcome this bias as it is further developed into a tool for use in forensic anthropology and paleodemography. The importance of using multiple skeletal indicators is emphasized as its focus is on using methods with statistically known error rates.

Chapters 9 and 10 focus on advances in stature estimation. Chapter 9 by Konigsberg and Jantz provides a critique of regression-based stature estimation methods and instead recommends the use of an informative prior for stature estimation from a relevant population to serve as a population-specific method. This approach is mathematically complex but provides new and exciting directions for future applications to stature estimation in forensic anthropology and bioarchaeology. Chapter 10 by Raxter and Ruff instead focuses on refining the full skeleton stature estimation method and provides recommendations for various correction factors related to measuring cadaveric stature and age-related decline in stature. This represents the most up-to-date application of the full skeleton method.

Chapter 11 by Murray and colleagues provides the history and development of the NamUs. This key chapter discusses how the NamUs software program works, as well as how it has developed over time to expand its utility as an identification tool. As the first national database on missing persons, NamUs represents an integrative system that can be used by members of the medicolegal community as well as by the public. The authors have extensive experience in the development and use of NamUs and provide an up-to-date perspective on the use of the system as well as some of its current limitations.

The seven chapters comprising Section II (Advances in Molecular and Microscopic Methods of Identification) focus on advances in the use of DNA, stable isotopes, radioisotopes, scanning electron microscopy/energy dispersive spectroscopy (SEM-EDS), solid-phase double-antibody radioimmunoassay (pRIA), and histology. Chapter 12 by Osborn-Gustavson and colleagues provides a history of the use of DNA technology for human identification, recommendations for current practice, and insight regarding the need to develop robust DNA databases for DNA-based identifications (e.g., CODIS). Chapter 13 by Edson and colleagues focuses more specifically on the development of methods for extracting DNA from taphonomically compromised samples. They recommend that DNA experts attempt a variety of methods for DNA extraction and amplification when working with challenging samples. Their experience working on samples from a wide range of contexts has promoted their view of the context-specific nature of DNA degradation, and hence the need to apply diverse approaches.

Chapters 14–16 focus on novel applications of stable isotope forensics to the identification of human remains. Chapter 14 by Chesson and Tipple provides a detailed overview of the use of stable isotopes as an investigative tool for predicting the region of origin of unidentified human remains. They recommend the use of multiple isotopes on several tissues (e.g., hair, nails, teeth, and bone) to provide various snapshots of an unidentified person's life history, all of which can provide clues to their identity. They further discuss the assumptions and limitations of the use of isotopes for narrowing down a region of origin for an unidentified person. In Chapter 15, Bartelink and colleagues demonstrate novel applications of stable isotope forensics to issues of personal identification for deceased undocumented border crossers found in south Texas and military remains recovered by the Defense POW/MIA Accounting Agency. This chapter emphasizes the use of stable isotopes to aid in provenancing unidentified human remains from these larger-scale contexts. Chapter 16 by Buchholz and colleagues focuses on the use of the bomb-pulse curve to determine the age of materials (including human remains) if they postdate the mid-1950s. Bomb-pulse radiocarbon dating has been successfully used to estimate an unidentified person's date of birth (using M1) as well as determine whether an individual was born before or after the increase in artificial radiocarbon. These novel methods have provided a useful tool for forensic identification.

Chapters 17 and 18 provide an overview of developments for determining whether unknown remains are human versus other animal species. Chapter 17 by Ubelaker discusses applications for the identification of small and fragmented remains that lack morphological detail. These challenging fragments can be analyzed using SEM-EDS to determine if suspected remains are actually osseous or dental materials, whereas pRIA and histology can especially aid in differentiating human from nonhuman remains as well as narrowing down a possible nonhuman animal species. Chapter 18 by Crowder and colleagues provides an overview of the use of histology for determining whether remains are osseous versus nonosseous and human versus nonhuman. They also address the importance of histological analysis in aiding the selection of DNA samples and as an age estimation tool. They orient histological analysis as a tool to guide the workflow of an unidentified sample from the most general assessment (osseous versus nonosseous) to the most specific (DNA-based identification).

The six chapters comprising Section III (Advances in Radiographic and Superimposition Methods of Identification) focus on advances in the use of various imaging methods for the noninvasive identification of human skeletal remains. Viner's chapter provides an overview of various imaging technologies and discusses multiple applications of imaging methods utilized during the course of an investigation.

Chapters 20 and 21 discuss the use of imaging methods for identification purposes. Chapter 20 by Christensen and Hatch focuses specifically on utilizing the frontal sinuses for identification purposes and the admissibility of this particular forensic tool in the US court system. Chapter 21 by Milligan and colleagues discusses various craniofacial superimposition techniques, as well as the advantages and limitations of this identification tool. Streetman and Fenton's chapter reviews research and validation studies employing comparative medical radiography and offers advice on conducting the procedure and constructing the case report. These chapters reflect common types of cases for forensic anthropologists, especially those who work in a medical examiner's office.

Chapter 23 by Derrick and colleagues introduces computer-assisted decedent identification (CADI), which is a program that analyzes the shapes of cervical or lumbar vertebral bodies in a lateral radiographic view. The program then determines potential matches and, when released, will be utilized for personal identification in routine forensic casework and during mass fatality events.

Chapter 24 by Stephan and colleagues reviews the radiographic comparison of the cervicothoracic region using posteroanterior chest radiographs as implemented at the Defense POW/MIA Accounting Agency (DPAA) to assist identification of unknown soldiers. They discuss this identification tool in detail and find that the clavicles are most frequently utilized for identification purposes at the DPAA. The methods discussed in this section of the book provide the opportunity for personal identification using nondestructive imaging techniques and can be applied to multiple bony elements of the skeleton.

The final section of the book (International Studies and Mass Disasters) includes five chapters aimed at discussing advances in forensic anthropology internationally, as well as advances in victim identification during mass disaster events. Chapter 25 by Ubelaker provides an introduction to the section by discussing the need for forensic anthropology internationally, the collections available to begin investigating human variation and creating population-specific analytical tools, and the creation of new facilities, organizations, and certification programs worldwide. Chapter 26 by Nawrocki and colleagues describes the benefits of using elliptical Fourier analysis to describe complex skeletal features and to better understand geographical variation in human skeletal anatomy. They also stress the importance of environment and geography in human skeletal variation and the overwhelming preponderance of unexplained variability that is usually underestimated by osteologists. Chapter 27 by Krüger and colleagues introduces readers to recent developments in utilizing forensic anthropology as a personal identification tool in South Africa. Chapter 28 by Wessling describes how various aspects of the work environment can impact forensic anthropological analyses. He discusses these points using the investigation of World War I mass graves at Pheasant Woods, Fromelles, as an example. Lastly, Chapter 29 by Figura discusses the potential for a disaster victim identification process based on Bayesian statistics. Such a tool would be utilized during mass fatality incidents where remains are highly fragmented and degraded, thus limiting the utility of traditional identification methods.

This robust collection of forensic tools aimed at the identification of human skeletal remains emphasizes the rapidly growing nature of the field of forensic anthropology. Broad training in anthropology allows forensic anthropologists to develop, utilize, and understand a wide variety of approaches for documenting human skeletal variation and subsequently applying that information to specific identification hypotheses. From gross macroscopic to microscopic approaches to identification of the human body, it provides the medicolegal community with an assortment of tools appropriate for use in multiple domestic and international contexts.

Index

Note: Page numbers followed by "f" indicate figures, "t" indicate tables.

Printed and bound by CPI Group (UK) Ltd, Croydon, CR0 4YY

03/10/2024

01040328-0017